N COMPUTER SYSTEMS AND TELECOMMUNICATIONS

Video training courses are available on the subjects of these books
in the James Martin ADVANCED TECHNOLOGY LIBRARY from
Deltak Inc., East/West Technological Center, 1751 West Diehl Road,
Naperville, Ill. 60566 (Tel: 312-369-3000).

EMS MANIFESTO

		PRINCIPLES OF DATA COMMUNICATION (second edition)	SECURITY, ACCURACY, AND PRIVACY IN COMPUTER SYSTEMS
AN END USER'S GUIDE TO DATABASE			
			A BREAKTHROUGH IN MAKING COMPUTERS FRIENDLY: THE MACINTOSH COMPUTER
PRINCIPLES OF DATABASE MANAGEMENT (second edition)	COMPUTER NETWORKS AND DISTRIBUTED PROCESSING	TELEPROCESSING NETWORK ORGANIZATION	DESIGN OF MAN-COMPUTER DIALOGUES
COMPUTER DATABASE ORGANIZATION (third edition)	DESIGN AND STRATEGY FOR DISTRIBUTED DATA PROCESSING	SYSTEMS ANALYSIS FOR DATA TRANSMISSION	DESIGN OF REAL-TIME COMPUTER SYSTEMS
MANAGING THE DATABASE ENVIRONMENT (second edition)	Books On Distributed Processing	DATA COMMUNICATION TECHNOLOGY	STRATEGIC DATA-PLANNING METHODOLOGIES (second edition)
DATABASE ANALYSIS AND DESIGN	TELECOMMUNICATIONS AND THE COMPUTER (third edition)	DATA COMMUNICATION DESIGN TECHNIQUES	INFORMATION ENGINEERING (Volume I: Introduction and Strategy)
VSAM: ACCESS METHOD SERVICES AND PROGRAMMING TECHNIQUES	FUTURE DEVELOPMENTS IN TELECOMMUNICATIONS (third edition)	SNA: IBM's NETWORKING SOLUTION	INFORMATION ENGINEERING (Volume II: Analysis, Design, and Construction)
DB2: CONCEPTS, DESIGN, AND PROGRAMMING	COMMUNICATIONS SATELLITE SYSTEMS	LOCAL AREA NETWORKS	WORLD INFORMATION ECONOMY
IDMS/R: CONCEPTS, DESIGN, AND PROGRAMMING	ISDN	OFFICE AUTOMATION STANDARDS	
STRATEGIC DATA-PLANNING METHODOLOGIES (second edition)	WORLD INFORMATION ECONOMY	CORPORATE COMMUNICATIONS NETWORKS	
		NETWORK STANDARDS	
Books On Data Base	**Books On Telecommunications**	**Books On Teleprocessing**	**Books On Systems In General**

DATA COMMUNICATION
TECHNOLOGY

A *James Martin* **BOOK**

THE JAMES MARTIN BOOKS

- Application Development Without Programmers
- Communications Satellite Systems
- Computer Data-Base Organization, Second Edition
- Computer Networks and Distributed Processing: Software, Techniques, and Architecture
- Design and Strategy of Distributed Data Processing
- Design of Man-Computer Dialogues
- Design of Real Time Computer Systems
- An End User's Guide to Data Base
- Fourth-Generation Languages, Volume I: Principles
- Future Developments in Telecommunications, Second Edition
- Information Engineering
- An Information Systems Manifesto
- Introduction to Teleprocessing
- Managing the Data-Base Environment
- Principles of Data-Base Management
- Programming Real-Time Computer Systems
- Recommended Diagramming Standards for Analysts and Programmers
- Security, Accuracy, and Privacy in Computer Systems
- Strategic Data Planning Methodologies
- Systems Analysis for Data Transmission
- System Design from Provably Correct Constructs
- Technology's Crucible
- Telecommunications and the Computer, Second Edition
- Telematic Society: A Challenge for Tomorrow
- Teleprocessing Network Organization
- Viewdata and the Information Society

with Carma McClure

- Action Diagrams: Clearly Structured Program Design
- Diagramming Techniques for Analysts and Programmers
- Software Maintenance: The Problem and Its Solutions
- Structured Techniques: The Basis for CASE, Revised Edition

with The ARBEN Group, Inc.

- A Breakthrough in Making Computers Friendly: The Macintosh Computer
- Data Communication Technology
- Fourth-Generation Languages, Volume II: Representative Fourth-Generation Languages
- Fourth-Generation Languages, Volume III: 4GLs from IBM
- Principles of Data Communication
- SNA: IBM's Networking Solution
- VSAM: Access Method Services and Programming Techniques

with Adrian Norman

- The Computerized Society

DATA COMMUNICATION TECHNOLOGY

JAMES MARTIN

with

Joe Leben
The ARBEN Group, Inc.

PRENTICE HALL, Englewood Cliffs, New Jersey 07632

Library of Congress Cataloging-in-Publication Data

Martin, James (date)
    Data communication technology.

    Includes index.
    1. Data transmission systems.   2. Information networks.
I. Leben, Joe.   II. Title.
TK5105.M3558 1988   004.6   87-17582
ISBN 0-13-196643-X

Editorial/production supervision: *Kathryn Gollin Marshak*
Jacket: *Bruce Kenselaar*
Jacket photograph: *Courtesy of Megatek Corp.*
Manufacturing buyer: *S. Gordon Osbourne*

Printed in the United States of America

10   9   8   7   6   5   4   3   2

ISBN 0-13-196643-X   025

PRENTICE-HALL INTERNATIONAL (UK) LIMITED, *London*
PRENTICE-HALL OF AUSTRALIA PTY. LIMITED, *Sydney*
PRENTICE-HALL CANADA INC., *Toronto*
PRENTICE-HALL HISPANOAMERICANA, S.A., *Mexico*
PRENTICE-HALL OF INDIA PRIVATE LIMITED, *New Delhi*
PRENTICE-HALL OF JAPAN, INC., *Tokyo*
SIMON & SCHUSTER ASIA PTE. LTD., *Singapore*
EDITORA PRENTICE-HALL DO BRASIL, LTDA., *Rio de Janeiro*

**FOR
CAROL**

**AND
CORINTHIA**

ABOUT THIS BOOK

Data Communication Technology

Data Communication Technology is for data processing and telecommunications administration technical staff members who require an in-depth understanding of the complex technology surrounding data communication networks. This book uses examples and case studies to show how data communication technology supports modern data processing applications. It will enable the reader to select appropriate communication lines, equipment, and software in constructing data communication systems. A general background in data processing fundamentals is assumed, but no programming background or knowledge of data communication techniques is required. *Data Communication Technology* could be used as the text in an in-depth course on data communication.

ABOUT RELATED BOOKS

Principles of Data Communication

Principles of Data Communication was first published in 1972 under the title *Introduction to Teleprocessing*. This second edition has been completely rewritten. The technical content of this book has been derived from the more detailed books entitled *Data Communication Technology* and *Data Communication Design Techniques*, and has been edited to form an introduction to data communication. This book can be read by programmers, analysts, managers, and telecommunications technical staff members who require an introduction to data communication facilities. Technical terms are used, but all are clearly defined. This book has no prerequisites other than a general understanding of data processing fundamentals, and no programming background is required. *Principles of Data Communication* could be used as the text for an introductory course on data communication.

Data Communication Design Techniques

Data Communication Design Techniques was first published in 1972 under the title *Systems Analysis for Data Transmission*. This second edition has been completely rewritten. This book is for data processing and telecommunications administration technical staff members. It has a how-to-do-it orientation and shows the technical staff member how to perform the systems analysis and design tasks that are required in designing data communication systems and telecommunications networks. The book includes the source code for a series of programs, written in BASIC for an IBM or IBM-compatible personal computer, that can be used in performing many of the tasks necessary in designing minimum-cost networks. This book assumes a basic knowledge of data communication, which can be gained by reading either *Principles of Data Communication* or *Data Communication Technology*. *Data Communication Design Techniques* could be used as the text for an in-depth course on designing data communication systems.

CONTENTS

18   Data Codes   255

19   Contention and Polling   267

20   Error Detection and Correction   275

21   Asynchronous Protocols   287

35   The Open Systems Interconnect Model   *511*

36   Public Data Networks and Information Utilities   *535*

37   Packet Switching and X.25   *557*

PREFACE

One of the most exciting technological developments in this century is the marriage of telecommunications and the computer. Both of these fields are developing at a fast pace. Either the computer industry or the telecommunications industry, alone, is capable of bringing about changes that will change ways of life throughout the world. But in combination, they add power to each other. Few major information systems today do not use some form of data communication facilities. For this reason, it is particularly important in today's information systems environment for technical staff to be well acquainted with the technology involved in transmitting computer data from one place to another.

This book is meant to be read by data processing and telecommunications administration technical staff members who require a thorough understanding of the complex technology surrounding data communication networks. Its purpose is to provide an in-depth look at the technology that surrounds the marriage of telecommunications facilities and computing that has occurred in recent years. After completing this book, the reader will be better able to select appropriate communication lines, equipment, and software in constructing data communication systems. A general background in data processing fundamentals is assumed, but no programming background or knowledge of data communication techniques is required. Page vii of this book presents a comparison of the three major James Martin books on data communication and shows how they relate to one another.

James Martin
Joe Leben

PART **I** INTRODUCTION

1 THE DATA COMMUNICATION ENVIRONMENT

In eighteenth-century England, the spinning jenny and a variety of weaving inventions portended a revolution in clothmaking. In this same period, the steam engine was invented. While these two inventions complemented each other, either, by itself, would have caused major changes. But in combination, they brought about an upheaval that was to alter drastically people's way of life. The attractive villages with their cottage industry gave way to the dark satanic mills of the early industrial revolution. The pounding new machines dominated people's lives.

Today, as then, new technologies sweep across our society too fast for the sociologists and politicians to plan the type of world they want to build or to comprehend the new potentials. Today there are large numbers of new technologies that in combination promise to change the world more drastically than did the spinning jenny and the steam engine.

Microelectronics makes it possible to produce ultraminiaturized computer circuitry so inexpensively that it now costs less to buy a complete computer on a chip than it does to fill the tank with gasoline. The communications satellite can provide high-capacity communication links with the potential of providing channels whose cost is independent of distance. The helical waveguide is an empty pipe that can carry a quarter of a million or more telephone calls, or equivalent information, in digital form. Waveguide technology has already been superseded by the optical fiber and the semiconductor laser. They form communication links, now under the streets in many cities, that have the potential of carrying millions of simultaneous telephone calls, or their equivalent. Public data networks allow computers and computer terminals to communicate with one another as economically, and with the same flexibility, as using the telephone for voice communication.

These revolutionary technologies exist today. The future lies in their widespread availability and in the new applications that will use them. Any one of them has enormous potential. Taken in combination, they will change the entire fabric of society. The last years of the twentieth century will be remembered as the era when people acquired new communication channels to other people, to libraries of film and data, and to the prodigious machines.

IMPORTANT TERMINOLOGY   When discussing computer systems that use communication facilities, the terms *telecommunications, data communication,* and *teleprocessing* are often misused. Consequently, we will begin this book by defining these important terms.

- **Telecommunications.** *Telecommunications* refers to the electronic transmission of any type of electronic information. So it is really an all-inclusive term that encompasses telephone communication, the transmission of television signals, data communication of all forms, electronic mail, facsimile transmission, telemetry from spacecraft, and so on. *Data communication,* the form of telecommunications that is discussed in this book, is only one use of telecommunications facilities.

- **Data Communication.** The term *data communication* refers to the electronic transmission of *data.* The term *data transmission* is synonymous with data communication. These terms are usually used in reference to data that is manipulated by computers. However, in the true sense of the term, data communication also encompasses telegraph, telemetry, and similar forms of electronic data transmission as well. In this book we will generally use the terms *data communication* and *data transmission* to mean the transmission of computerized data.

- **Teleprocessing.** The term *teleprocessing* is a more recent term than either telecommunications or data communication. Originally coined by IBM, it has now become a generally accepted term throughout the computer industry. *Teleprocessing* refers to the accessing of computing power and computerized data files from a distance, generally using terminals and telecommunications facilities.

Note from the definitions that *teleprocessing* is a more inclusive term than *data communication.* Generally, when we examine the *data communication* aspects of a system, we are referring only to those parts of the system that are involved in the transmission of data from one point to another. However, when we discuss a *teleprocessing* system, we are referring to the total system, including computers, terminals, telecommunications lines, and all associated hardware and software used to implement a complete data processing application.

COMPUTERS AND COMMUNICATIONS   At the very lowest level of implementation, all computer systems use data transmission techniques. A modern computer consists of a number of devices wired together with cables. Generally, the cables are out of sight under the computer room floor. These cables are actually data transmission lines that operate at high bit rates—into the millions of bits per second (bps) for those cables that connect tape and disk drives to the I/O channels. Figure 1.1 shows how an I/O device is typically attached to a mainframe computer. One or more devices, a disk drive in our example, is connected to a control unit. The control unit provides control functions for the disk drive and provides a standard interface to the mainframe's I/O channel.

As we discuss later, if we had long-distance communication lines with characteristics similar to machine-room cables, we could connect devices at remote locations directly to the CPU's I/O channels using a device similar to the disk drive's control unit, and data communication would not be a topic of interest. But, of course, such channels do not exist—at least not in so simple a form as a machine-room cable. So a system that connects a computer with devices at remote locations has characteristics different from those of systems that connect local devices only.

A DATA COMMUNICATION SYSTEM   We continue this chapter by examining the various components that make up a data communication system and showing how those components relate to the organization of this book. In Part I we discuss the general characteristics of systems that use data transmission, discuss the design of data communication systems, and introduce network architectures.

Figure 1.2 shows the physical structure of a simple data communication system implemented using a simple personal computer. Notice that its configuration is similar to the configuration used to connect a set of local devices to the main computer. The disk drive is replaced with a *terminal;* the disk control unit is replaced by a specialized device, sometimes called a *communications adapter;* and the cable connecting the disk drive to the control unit is replaced by a *telecommunications channel.*

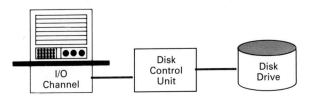

Figure 1.1   Conventional I/O device connection

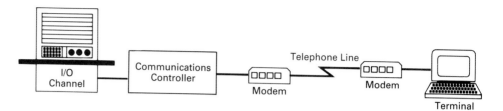

Figure 1.2 Simple data communication system

COMMUNICATION CHANNELS

A major portion of this book is concerned with the channels that are used to transmit information from one place to another. In Part II we discuss the characteristics of the various types of channels that are used for data communication. In the chapters in Part III we examine the physical media that are used to construct communication channels. In Part IV we present the methods that are used for controlling the transmission of data over a communication channel.

DATA COMMUNICATION HARDWARE

Part V is concerned with the hardware that is used to implement data transmission systems. In addition to the terminals and the communications controller, which we have already introduced, devices called *modems* (short for *modulator-demodulator*) are generally used at either end of the communication line to create a *data link* between the terminal and the communications controller.

The computer and the terminal in Fig. 1.2 work with digital bit streams. When an in-house cable is used, these digital bit streams can be transmitted directly from one device to another. A communication line, on the other hand, often consists of an ordinary telephone circuit that works with continuously varying analog signals. Modems are used to convert digital data to and from the analog signals that can be carried over an ordinary telecommunication line.

DATA COMMUNICATION SOFTWARE

Part VI is concerned with the software that is used in implementing data communication systems. In the earliest systems, the application programs together with specialized control programs performed all communication functions. This is shown in Fig. 1.3. After experience with data transmission systems was gained, computer manufacturers developed general-purpose *telecommunications access methods,* such as IBM's BTAM (Basic Telecommunications Access Method). As shown in Fig. 1.4, these telecommunications access methods effectively place a layer of software between the application program and the communication equipment. With these specialized ac-

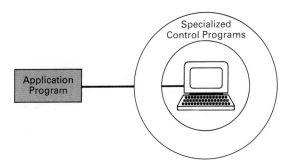

Figure 1.3   Early data communication software environment

cess methods, much of the programmer's interface with the communication channels is simplified, but application programming is still rather complex and is often done in assembler language. Additional software systems, called *teleprocessing monitors* (TP monitors), were later developed to make the job of application programming easier. Examples of these are IBM's CICS (Customer Information Control System) and IMS/DC (Information Management System/ Data Communication), the TP monitor software component of IMS (see Fig. 1.5). These systems place a layer of software between the application program and the telecommunications access method. Most of today's data transmission systems use all three software entities: the application program, the teleprocessing monitor, and the telecommunications access method.

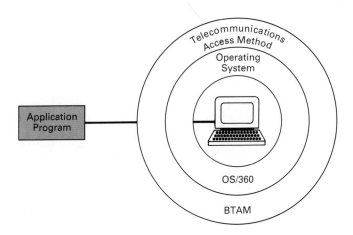

Figure 1.4   Telecommunications access method

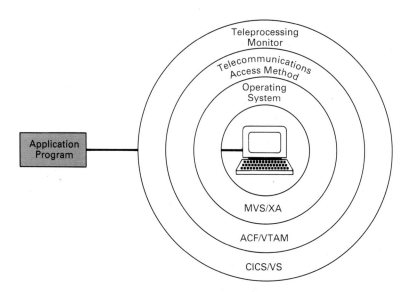

Figure 1.5 Teleprocessing monitor

DISTRIBUTED PROCESSING AND NETWORK ARCHITECTURES

Until about 1975, most data transmission systems were similar in configuration to the simple one we have been examining here. Today, many systems that use data communication are much more complex.

One of the things that has drastically changed the way we use data transmission has been the rapid shift toward the use of distributed processing techniques. More and more we are seeing data transmission being used to connect computers to one another, rather than being used to connect simple terminals to a central computer. These more complex systems are the subject of the chapters in Part VII, the final part of this book.

Figure 1.6 shows an example of a typical distributed processing application. Mainframe computers located in computer rooms in different parts of the country each use specialized processors called *communications controllers* to take over the job of controlling communication functions. The communications controllers are connected to each other and to other specialized processors called *cluster controllers* located in end-user locations. Each cluster controller is connected to a group of terminals or personal computers.

Specialized software is required not only in the mainframes, but in the communications controllers, cluster controllers, and often the terminals as well. If the hardware and software components are properly integrated, it is possible for a terminal in any end-user location to communicate with an application program running in any of the mainframes. The end user need not even be aware of where the mainframe is located. Such systems are complex and require a degree of hardware and software integration that is not possible using the simple

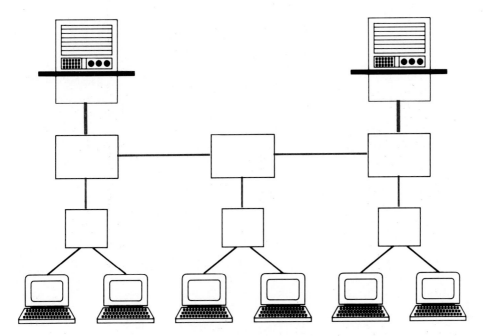

Figure 1.6   Interconnected computers

methods of the past. Today, *communication network architectures,* such as IBM's SNA, are required to achieve close cooperation between the various hardware and software components of the system.

Also discussed in Part VII are advanced data communication services that are now offered by common carriers. (We use the term *common carrier* to refer to a company that offers telecommunications services of any type to the public. Examples of common carriers are Bell System operating companies, companies that provide long-distance telephone service, and companies that operate public data transmission networks.) Although advanced facilities, such as digital networks and data transmission services, have been in operation for many years, they remain quite specialized. In the future, the providers of telecommunications facilities will provide communication services through *integrated services digital networks* (ISDNs) in which a user will be able to plug any type of device (telephone, data terminal, computer, facsimile machine, video camera, etc.) into the network and be able to request a connection to any compatible device on the network. The network itself, which will eventually be worldwide, will be able to determine the characteristics of the two communicating devices and automatically allocate the proper type of channel that is required and then make the connection. ISDN technology is discussed in detail in Chapter 41.

There are many ways to categorize computer systems that use data communication facilities. In Chapter 2 we classify data communication systems using a number of criteria and discuss the general characteristics of such systems.

2 DATA COMMUNICATION SYSTEMS

Systems that use data transmission facilities are built for a variety of purposes and perform different functions. Today, the most common data transmission system takes the form of people at terminals communicating with a distant computer. The computer usually responds quickly, with a dialog taking place between each terminal user and the remote computer. In the future, systems that connect multiple computers will become more common. In this chapter we categorize data communication systems according to the following criteria:

- Whether the system is online or offline
- Whether the system is interactive or noninteractive
- Quantity of data transmitted
- Response-time requirements
- Degree of independence of the system's users
- Degree to which communication facilities are shared

Figure 2.1 shows how these six criteria can be used to separate data transmission systems into various categories.

ONLINE AND OFFLINE SYSTEMS

Many data communication systems are required merely to move data from one point to another. The communication links in such systems can be either online or offline to a computer. In an offline system, the data is collected by a device that simply stores the data on an intermediate storage device, such as a diskette. The data on the diskette is then processed at a later time, possibly on some other system. In an online system, the input data enters the computer

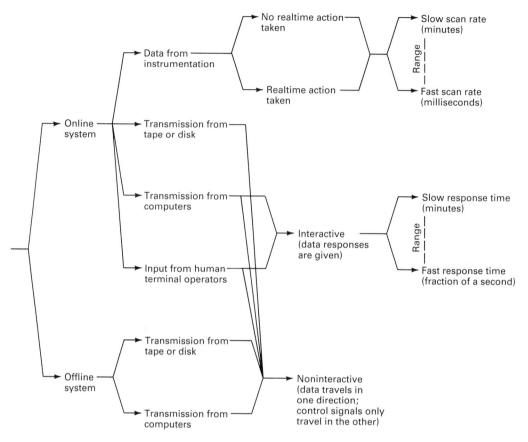

Figure 2.1   Categories of data transmission system

directly from its point of origination and/or output data is transmitted directly to where it is used. The intermediate stages of data storage are avoided.

**INTERACTIVE AND
NONINTERACTIVE
SYSTEMS**

An offline system is of necessity also *noninteractive*. Because a computer is not connected directly to the communication line at the location to which the data is sent, no data response will be received from that location. Simple control signals, however, might be received to control the mechanical functioning of the devices and to indicate whether the transmission has been found free of errors. An online system may also be noninteractive. The computer might receive a batch transmission and might not need to respond to it. Sometimes it takes a hash total at the end of a batch transmission to ensure that no data has been garbled. Here the only interactive response is confirmation of correct receipt of the transmission.

Most systems that support transmission from terminal operators at terminals are *interactive*. It is poor user-interface design not to give responses to operators, leaving them wondering whether their input has reached the computer. With some inexpensive terminal devices, however, there is no mechanism for responding. Such is the case with some factory data collection terminals into which a worker might insert a machine-readable badge or set some keys or dials. The system might respond with a light or mechanical action, indicating simply that it has received the message.

For noninteractive systems, or systems that give very rudimentary responses, the data might flow in only one direction. The data transmission system might not be designed to be entirely one-way, because it is useful for a small trickle of control signals to flow in the other direction. Occasionally, in applications such as telemetry, the use of radio makes two-way transmission difficult, and a purely one-way link is used. An interactive system, on the other hand, has a high flow of data in both directions. These factors will sometimes affect the data transmission techniques used.

QUANTITY OF DATA TRANSMITTED

The quantity of data required to be transmitted varies enormously from one system to another. At one extreme, entire files are transmitted. At the other, one bit will suffice to indicate a "yes" or "no" condition. Sometimes a single transaction is transmitted, and sometimes a batch of many transactions is sent at once. When immediate action is unnecessary when a batch of data is received, the information can be collected at its source and then transmitted in a batch to its destination. This can be less expensive than sending the data one transaction at a time. Sometimes the contents of entire magnetic tapes or disks must be sent. Payroll data or machine-shop schedules, for example, could be transmitted from one location to another. In many systems a *dialog* takes place between a terminal user and a computer, with the sizes and contents of the messages exchanged depending on the design of the user interface. The input to the computer could be one statement by the user, and the output might be the computer's response. The response may range from a one-character confirmation to a screen full of data or a printed listing.

RESPONSE-TIME REQUIREMENTS

It is sometimes necessary to transmit data quickly. The required speed depends on the system. A system for relaying one-way messages, such as telegrams, can be required to deliver the message in an hour. It would be convenient to have it done more quickly, but no major economic need may exist to do so.

The time available for transmission is generally referred to as the *response time*. When batches of data are sent for batch processing on a distant computer, a response time longer than 1 hour is sometimes acceptable. However, when a dialog is taking place between a person and the computer, the quicker the response, the less chance of impeding the operator's train of thought. A response time of 1 or 2 seconds is typical in today's interactive systems, although there are many instances where subsecond response times are necessary or desirable for many types of interactions. In realtime systems, in which a machine or process is being controlled, response times can vary from a few milliseconds to many minutes.

Response time can be defined as the time interval from the operator's pressing the last key of the input to the terminal's displaying the first character of the response. Response time can be defined in a more general way as the interval between an event and the system's response to that event. Systems differ widely in their response-time requirements, and the response time needed can, in turn, have a major effect on the design of the data transmission network.

Systems that are not interactive might have a *delivery time* specified. Here the data is flowing in one direction. Delivery time is defined as the time interval from the start of transmission at the transmitting terminal to the completion of reception at the receiving terminal.

The required response time or delivery time will affect the cost of the data communication subsystem. When designing a computer system that requires operators to maintain a continuing train of thought, responses within 2 seconds are usually needed, although, as we mentioned earlier, subsecond response times are sometimes required. When the input is a simple inquiry, a request for a listing, or a request for a program to be run, the response time can be longer. When machinery is being controlled, a faster response time is sometimes necessary, and when one computer is requesting data from another computer, it might be needed very quickly so that the requesting computer itself can provide a user with a specified response time.

Figure 2.2 shows some of the common requirements for delivery time, response time, and for quantity of data transmitted. There are three major categories of response-time requirements: terminal dialog systems, terminal inquiry systems, and message delivery systems.

Terminal Dialog Systems

The block labeled "terminal dialog systems" indicates a response-time requirement from 1 to 10 seconds and a message size from 1 character (usually 7 to 8 bits) to about 4000 characters (around 30,000 bits). A few exceptional cases will extend beyond the blocks shown (as with the blocks on the diagram). In many terminal dialog systems, subsecond response times are required for certain types of interactions. For example, with a system designed for word processing, the terminal must respond instantly to requests for certain types of editing functions. It would be unbearable for a writer to have to wait for 2 seconds for a character to be deleted from the screen. Systems that have requirements for very fast responses have two alternatives. One alternative is to provide for extremely

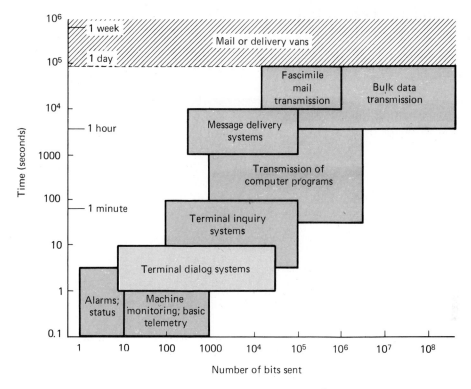

Figure 2.2   Response time and data volume

fast transmission of messages between the computer and the terminal. The second alternative is to build intelligence into the terminal so that interactions requiring extremely fast responses are handled by the terminal itself and do not require that data be transmitted back and forth between the terminal and the central computer. In today's environment, it is generally cheaper to use an intelligent terminal, such as a terminal with editing capabilities or a personal computer, in conjunction with data transmission facilities that provide responses in the 1- or 2-second category. Those interactions that require subsecond response times are handled by the terminal itself; all other interactions are handled by the distant computer using data transmission.

Terminal Inquiry Systems

The block labeled *terminal inquiry systems* extends on the time scale to 100 seconds. A wait of this duration is unacceptable in a dialog, but if a storekeeper or factory worker is making a request for an entire listing, a wait of 1 minute might not cause inconvenience. In all such cases, the cost of providing different response times should be related to the requirements of the user.

Message-Delivery Systems

Systems for delivering messages, commonly called *message switching* or *electronic mail* systems, are referred to with the block labeled *message delivery systems*. Electronic mail services are increasing in popularity—they have already become the fastest way of delivering mail. Delivery times of up to 1 day are often acceptable for the bulk transmission of data. Bulk transmission of data extends to the extreme right of the diagram, because sometimes very large quantities are sent.

Data transmission over communication facilities with a delivery time of more than 24 hours is not ordinarily appropriate. In these cases, the use of ordinary mail or an overnight delivery service is often more economical than the use of data transmission.

Future Response-Time Requirements

In the future it is probable that data transmission will be used in areas outside the blocks shown in the diagram. To some extent, the areas in which it has been used have been determined by the speeds of available transmission lines. For most of the applications shown in the figure, the speed of teletype and telephone lines—speeds up to, say, 9600 bps, usually suffice unless a huge bulk of data must be sent. Most of today's systems are designed around low-speed links that operate at 300, 1200, and 2400 bps over ordinary dial-up telephone circuits.

The computer industry changes quickly. In many systems in use today, a computer responds to a machine or another computer, rather than to a person, and different types of transmission facilities are required. One computer can request a program or a portion of a file from another distant machine. One computer might pass jobs on to another because it does not have the capacity to handle them itself or possibly for the purpose of load sharing. The requirement for access time in obtaining data from disks—the time taken to seek and read a record—might, in the future, become the time requirement for obtaining data from a distant computer over telecommunications links. Sometimes, small local computers will pass their compiling work to larger, distant machines with better facilities. The initial program loading of small local computers is often done by a large remote computer. The computers and file units connected by cabling in the machine room today might be connected by telecommunications links tomorrow if channels of suitable speed become available at low-enough cost.

Systems such as those described above require data transmission speeds of 56,000 or 64,000 bps, or even higher. Today such communication links are available, but they are typically expensive. When ISDN technology becomes widely available, 64,000-bps links will be available to the user at no higher cost than that of today's slow-speed links. Much higher speeds, such as the 1.544-million-bps rate that is handled by many common carrier facilities, will also be available economically (see Chapters 13 and 41). Systems will change drastically in the coming years to take advantage of this increase in transmission speed.

USER INDEPENDENCE

Most systems with manually operated terminals are *time shared,* meaning that more than one user is using them at the same time. When the machine pauses in the processing of one user's item, it switches its attention to another user. The term *time sharing* is commonly used to refer to a system in which the users are *independent* of one another. Each user feels as though he or she is the only person using the system. The processing requested by one terminal user is quite unrelated to the processing requested by other users.

However, in many systems the users are not independent. They are each using the same application system to perform related functions. For example, they could be insurance or railroad clerks, possibly using the same programs and the same database. In time-shared systems, however, the computing facility is being divided between separate users who can invoke whatever application they wish, independently of one another. Four different types of online systems, differing by the degree of user independence, are commonly used:

- Systems that carry out a carefully specified and limited function: for example, banking systems or airline reservation systems in which all terminal users access and update the same files or databases

- Systems for a specific limited function in which the users have personal, independent files or in which shared files can be read but not updated by general terminal users

- Systems in which users employ terminals to perform a variety of tasks, but where those tasks are limited to a narrow range of functions supported by the machine and its software; typically, all the users have access to the same type of terminal

- General-purpose systems in which the users employ various types of terminals for a wide range of purposes

The last two types of systems are, in effect, dividing up the computing facility timewise and giving the pieces to different users, who decide what will be done with their time slots. The files and databases are also divided according to use. It cannot be known beforehand how much space the various users will occupy in the files. This is quite different from the first category, in which the file size and organization are planned in detail.

When many online systems exist for functions such as banking and ticket reservations, the next logical step is for separate systems to be interlinked. An airline agent should be able to interrogate the reservation systems of other airlines so that multiairline journeys can be planned and booked. A travel agent should have access to systems that book hotels, cars, theater tickets, boats, trains, and airline seats. An electronic funds transfer system should interlink with the computers of many banks. Computerized terminals in supermarkets and stores are now commonly connected to bank computers by telecommunications links. A society is evolving that will employ vast networks of machines connected by data transmission facilities.

COMMUNICATION LINE SHARING

The reason that time sharing is important is that the human keying rate and reading speed are much slower than computer speeds. Furthermore, human beings require lengthy pauses to think between transactions. As we have seen above, the key to using the computer efficiently for realtime dialog operations is to make it divide its time among many users. The same is true with telecommunications. A voice line can transmit many more bits than a terminal operator employs in an alphanumeric dialog with a computer. The key to efficient computer use is to share telecommunications facilities among many users. The sharing of communication facilities is discussed in detail in Chapters 9 and 27, but we introduce this important topic here.

The sharing of telecommunications facilities will become more popular in the future as more facilities capable of transmitting higher bit rates are employed. Today's telephone lines commonly are made to carry data rates of 300 to 9600 bps. However, on AT&T's digital long-distance circuits, of which many millions of miles are already installed, each telephone channel can carry a data rate of 56,000 bps. As mentioned earlier, when ISDNs become commonplace, channels with a capacity of 64,000 bps will be available to all users of the network.

Degree of Independence

The degree of independence of users on a shared communication line varies. On some shared lines, all users must employ the same terminal type with the same line control procedure. On others, the terminals can be different but must use the same character code. With some systems, they can be entirely independent, each using different codes. The users can be of one type, in one organization, such as reservations agents linked to an airline system. On the other hand, they might be different types of users that might share communication facilities installed within one organization. Finally, they could be entirely independent users sharing public data transmission facilities. It is in the latter case that the largest savings will result, and eventually public data networks will play a very important part in a nation's data processing.

Resource Sharing

An even greater level of sharing exists in systems in which the user's terminal might be attached, not to one computer, but to a data transmission network that links many diverse resources. The network can provide the user with rapid access to distant computers, programs, libraries, information-retrieval systems, databases, message delivery facilities, mail-printing facilities, and so on. The cost of personal computers has already dropped to the point where the primary reason for using data communication is not to gain access to a computer, but to gain access to these other resources.

One of the best known resource-sharing networks is *Arpanet*, a network that gives its users fast access to a wide variety of resources. It was constructed with Department of Defense funds by the Advanced Research Projects Agency [now the Defense Advanced Research Projects Agency (DARPA)]. The network was initially used to interlink major university and other computer centers, and most researchers at those universities had access to the network. Today, for security reasons, access to the network is more limited than it was during the first few years of its use. The techniques that were pioneered in implementing Arpanet helped pave the way for public data networks, such as Telenet and Tymenet, which are used extensively today (see Chapter 36). An early configuration of Arpanet is illustrated in Fig. 2.3.

The users of Arpanet share both the telecommunications facilities and the distant resources to which the communication lines are connected. A user sitting at a terminal anywhere can gain access to any of the diverse collection of computers shown in the diagram and their diverse library of programs. The transmission time on the network is fast enough for most interactive users, so that it does not significantly degrade the response time. Users who live with Arpanet become accustomed to employing its remote facilities and sending messages to one another. They feel isolated when they are at a location where the terminals are not connected to their network.

In today's environment, many individual personal computer users are enjoying access to similar types of networks. Examples of these are *The Source* and *Compuserve*. These services provide, for very reasonable fees, access to vast databases that contain information on a wide range of consumer-oriented subjects, such as business reports, securities prices, and airline travel schedules.

THE EVOLUTION OF COMPUTING

Computing might evolve such that expensive or important data processing resources, such as large computers, databases, and program libraries, will be locked away in fireproof, theftproof, sabotageproof, operatorproof vaults. Except for maintenance, they will be accessible only by telecommunications cables

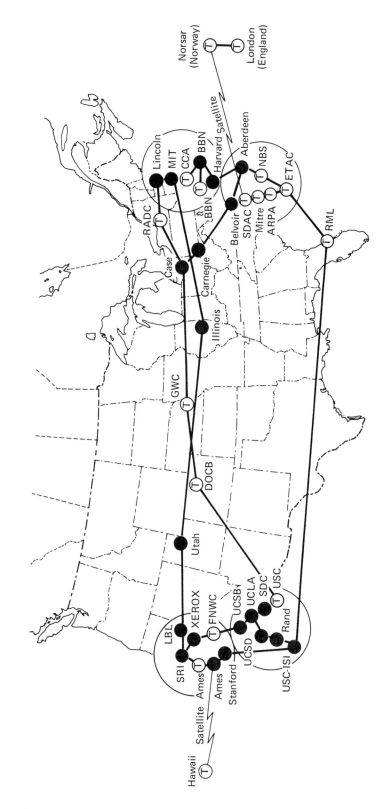

Figure 2.3 Arpanet geographical map

that pass through the walls of the vaults. But the users will have access to the libraries of the world and to the world's most powerful data processing facilities.

MILITARY
SYSTEMS

To a large extent, the pioneering work for systems combining telecommunications facilities and computers was done in the military. We conclude this chapter by examining some of these early military systems.

THE SAGE
SYSTEM

One of the first, and still one of the most spectacular, military data communication systems is SAGE, the U.S. Air Force's *Semi-Automatic Ground Environment* system. SAGE, which was designed in the early 1950s to protect the United States from surprise air attack, is no longer in operation. SAGE was designed to maintain a constant watch on the air space over North America, to provide early warning of airborne attack, and to give its Air Force operators the information needed to conduct an air battle. Its input came over data transmission links from a variety of radars that swept the skies of the continent. These included the *Canadian Integration North* (CADIN) line and many other land-based radars.

Input also came from observation aircraft, ground observer corps stations, and picket ships. The computers digested this constant stream of data and prepared displays for their output screens. In addition, the system contained aircraft flight plans, weapons and base status reports, weather data, and other information.

The United States was divided into a number of SAGE sectors, each served by a variety of radar sites and computer centers. These locations were all connected to the computer, and the computers were interlinked by telegraph and telephone lines carrying digital data.

Air Force personnel sat in front of screens on console units designed for their various responsibilities. They communicated with the computer by using light pens—forerunners of the light pens used on today's commercial systems. They could request displays of particular situations and could command the machines to compile special displays for their own use. The computer, on its own initiative, would flash displays of particular urgency on the screen. If an unidentified aircraft approached, the system notified command personnel, who would then use the screen to investigate and, if necessary, dispatch interceptor aircraft.

Since SAGE, many command and control sytems, and other systems using telecommunications, have been installed and planned.

SYSTEMS RELATED TO SAGE

The U.S. Marine Corps built the *Marine Tactical Data System* (MTDS), which is, in effect, a mobile SAGE, transportable by helicopter to an operational theater.

The U.S. Navy built the *Naval Tactical Data System* (NTDS), which had computers and display screens on board ships linked together on a worldwide basis to form a mobile command and control system. The Pentagon could obtain on its screens the positions and status of ships anywhere, and could display data being used by the Navy on the other side of the world.

The U.S. Army planned an immensely complex command and control system to be used by every level of command and for handling intelligence and logistics information. Information on tactical operations, fire support, personnel, and other administrative matters was kept up to date in the system, and the output was available either on individual consoles or on large group displays.

THE BMEWS SYSTEM

The *Ballistic Missile Early Warning System* (BMEWS) uses giant radar units for the detection of potentially hostile missiles aimed at the West. Its duplexed computers in the United States and England ceaselessly scan the radar signals they receive and notify appropriate military personnel if they conclude that an attack might have been launched. It is these computers that would give us 20 minutes of grace prior to nuclear devastation, in which time the United States could launch its counterattack and do whatever else was needed.

THE ABM SYSTEM

The *Anti Ballistic Missile* (ABM) system is even more spectacular in its technology, in which computers attempt to shoot down missiles as they scatter multiple warheads toward their targets at speeds close to 20,000 miles per hour. The ABM is deployed in only one or two locations. The missiles attempt to deceive the ABM by sending out many decoys to draw attention from the real warhead, and the ABM tries to compute which are real and which are decoys.

The Pentagon wishes to be online to these and many other military systems so that the President and the Joint Chiefs of Staff can display details of all actions. The task of linking all the systems to a central information system is one of herculean magnitude because of the incompatibilities among the various techniques, record formats, and means of display.

THE AUTOVON AND AUTODIN NETWORKS

The telecommunications networks used by the military are gigantic. They employ many more communications satellites than do the civilian authorities. In addition to the communication links connecting the various military systems, the U.S. Defense Communications Agency has two vast telecommunications networks: Autovon for voice and Autodin for data. These were first installed only within the United States but then became part of a rapidly developing global system.

The networks provide for prioritized traffic. For example, a general's telephone call can preempt lower-priority calls. The system is designed to handle the high traffic volumes that occur during an emergency. It presents no unusually attractive target to potential attack, and its facilities are highly distributed. Above all, it has widespread alternative routings to survive massive nuclear attack. A configuration of trunk groups, in the form of multiple overlapping hexagons and diagonals, links the numerous switching centers with many alternative paths.

Other countries also make spectacular use of communicating computer systems. A confrontation—a life-and-death struggle with satellite jamming, decoys, software bugs, and attacks on computer centers—is always possible and is hardly a welcome prospect.

Now that we have examined the general characteristics of systems that use data communication facilities, in Chapter 3 we introduce the design techniques that are employed to create these systems.

3 DATA COMMUNICATION SYSTEM DESIGN

The main purpose of this chapter is to introduce the steps that are involved in designing application software for data transmission systems and to put into perspective the various tasks that are involved in the design process. Box 3.1 lists the major steps that are involved in the design of a computer system that uses data transmission. In this chapter we examine these steps and discuss some of the factors that affect the designer's choices.

THE USER INTERFACE

A first and major factor in the design of a data transmission system is whether the system is designed for human terminal operators. If it is for batch transmission, telemetry, intercomputer communication, or other interlinking of mechanical devices, the design decisions that must be made all depend on technical issues. On the other hand, where human operators generate the input or carry on a dialog with the system, the psychology and needs of these users will have a major effect on design decisions. The starting point in the design of such a system should be concern for the design of the user interface.

Users come in a variety of types. Some can program; some cannot. Some may be highly trained; some are casual users. Some are highly intelligent; some are less so. Some have a natural ability to communicate with computers; some have only to sit at a terminal for a form of paralysis to set in. (Worse, some seem magically to cause paralysis in the system itself!)

There is a big difference between a factory worker entering data into a shop-floor terminal and a statistician entering data into a spreadsheet using a personal computer. There is also a difference between an airline ticketing agent sorting out changes in a passenger's itinerary and a high-level manager trying to sort out changes in a customer's order. Airline agents spend the entire day

BOX 3.1   Steps in data communication system design

1. Determine the needs of the users.
2. Determine types of messages that will be transmitted.
3. Determine traffic volumes.
4. Establish response-time criteria.
5. Plan the terminal considerations.
   a. Determine terminal locations.
   b. Establish desirable terminal characteristics.
   c. Determine the number of terminals per location.
   d. Determine whether dial-up procedures are required.
   d. Design the user interface.
   e. Determine the number of characters to be transmitted.
6. Plan the network considerations.
   a. Determine the locations of intelligent machines.
   b. Determine network structures.
   c. Determine networking software requirements.
   d. Choose the network equipment.
7. Build models of a single communication path.
8. Establish a traffic rate table.
9. Establish a minimum-cost geographical layout of lines.
10. Make refinements to the network.

operating terminals; managers, if they operate terminals at all, only do so occasionally in the midst of harassing schedules. These differences will lead to differences in the structure of the user interface. The structures of various types of user interfaces differ *very* widely from system to system. Furthermore, in the future, when more varied communication facilities are available, they will differ still more widely.

The type of user interface that is designed has, in turn, a major influence on the design of the data transmission facilities. If the communication lines are long, and perhaps expensive, this factor may be a constraining one on the permissible user-interface structures. Conversely, some effective but seemingly expensive user-interface structures can be employed by restructuring the communication network to make use of intelligent communications controllers, cluster controllers, and concentrators. The considerations of user psychology, then, can permeate all aspects of the network design.

**OPERATOR
ERRORS**
All terminal operators make errors occasionally. The errors may be particularly serious if the operator is *entering* data that is then used for further processing or that resides in the system's files or databases. The percentage of errors that are made can be affected to a major degree by the structure of the user interface. Once again there is an important relationship between psychological factors and system design.

Where the operators enter data, it is particularly important that facilities for correcting their errors be well thought out. If possible, the system should be designed to catch an error at the time it is made. An error message can then be sent immediately to the operator. In those cases where the operator does not have an interactive terminal (e.g., many factory data-collection terminals), the errors may be referred later to a special operator or staff with facilities to correct them. Sometimes the errors will be detected long after they are made, by continuing or periodic checks. In this case a mechanism must be constructed for sending an unsolicited message about the errors either to the operator who originated them or to a special operator or group charged with the responsibility for correcting errors.

**THIRD-PARTY
OPERATORS**
Where a system is designed to provide information, the persons needing the information need not necessarily operate the terminal. There are a variety of circumstances in which it would be better if they did not. These circumstances are not always recognized by the systems analyst. First, giving everyone terminals may be too expensive. Second, the job of obtaining adequate results from the terminal may be too difficult for the people in question. Systems analysts often tend to overestimate the ability of untrained people to operate terminals. Young people learn to operate them easily, but people set in their ways usually do not, particularly when, as is the case with many managers, they cannot afford the time and may not have the patience needed to learn. Third, it may be desirable, for security reasons, to allow only certain authorized individuals to operate the terminals.

Where a system is designed to *gather* information, as well as to *provide* it, the same arguments apply. Sometimes it is even more necessary that the data residing in the files for commercial use be entered by a person trained to be accurate rather than by someone who uses the terminal infrequently.

The people, then, who do not operate a terminal may gain access to a computer either by having assistants who do operate one or by contacting specialist terminal operators. They may obtain information in this way, or they may cause information to be entered into the system. This is exactly what you do when you telephone an airline to make a reservation. You speak to a specialist terminal operator who obtains details of flights and seat availability for you;

then when you decide on your trip, you give that operator details which are then recorded in the computer files. You need not have access to a terminal yourself to make a reservation (although airline schedules can be consulted and seats can be booked by anyone with access to one of the major information utilities, such as The Source or Compuserve). The same reasoning can apply to management and other persons in an organization who will interact with an information system.

SECURITY

A subject related to the users of the system that will be of increasing concern in data processing is security. Many files and databases contain data that organizations wish to keep confidential. Files and databases also store a wide variety of personal information about private individuals. Keeping such information out of the reach of unauthorized personnel is extremely important. Still more important is the need to prevent unauthorized persons from changing data in the files; otherwise, a rich variety of new forms of embezzlement and sabotage would be possible. Many techniques are available for maintaining security. An interlinking set of measures that cover many aspects of the design is required. For the data transmission network, these can include positive identification of the terminal being used; means to prevent wiretapping; a positive identification of the individual using the terminal by means of identification cards, passwords, and other measures; locks on the terminals; authorization tables; security logs; surveillance techniques; and the use of cryptography. In some cases, one of the procedures will be to notify a security officer immediately of any suspected breach in security. Security officers may be used at terminal locations, or, as with the control of errors, a specially trained person or group may be employed in a central location.

TERMINAL CONSIDERATIONS

After analyzing the types of messages that will be transmitted, determining the traffic volumes, and establishing response-time criteria, a very important aspect of the design involves the terminals that will be used. As you can see in Box 3.1, the first terminal-oriented task in the design is to determine where the terminals are to be located.

LOCATION OF TERMINALS

When the terminals are not in the office of the person originating or requiring information, the question arises: Where should they best be positioned? If the user has a telephone link to the person with the terminal, that person could be almost anywhere. It is up to the systems analyst who is designing the system to decide where to put the terminals. You can group them together in such a way as to minimize the probability of the user not receiving immediate service, or to minimize queuing delays. You can gather together in one room different types of terminals connected to different types of systems, thus combining, perhaps, different types of expertise in the operators. You can build ''information rooms'' having a variety of functions. Given the constraints imposed by these factors, you will generally locate the terminals so as to minimize the overall system cost.

Where a user community is provided with a terminal room, in a laboratory, for example, each person may not have a separate terminal but may instead go to a communal group of terminals. What is the probability that a user will not find a terminal free when one is needed? Again the systems analyst must determine the grade of service that must be achieved and on this basis do a probability calculation to determine the number of terminals that must be installed.

NUMBER OF CHARACTERS TRANSMITTED

The last terminal-related factor on the list in Box 3.1 is an important one. Both the quantity of data in a single transmission and the time available to deliver it vary enormously. These two factors together determine the transmission speed that is necessary.

LINE SPEED SUMMARY

Figure 3.1 summarizes some of the available line speeds. Four line speeds are shown: a teletype line of 150 bps, a voice-grade line used at 4800 bps, a wideband line of 64,000 bps, and the bit rate of commonly used long-distance transmission lines of North American common carriers: 1,544,000 bps.

Most of the blocks representing today's uses of data transmission do not intersect the line speed of 64,000 bps. This fact is perhaps not surprising because speeds in the 64,000-bps range have not been generally available at acceptable prices until only recently. If a ubiquitous switched network at this speed had been widely available at appropriate cost when data transmission systems were first being extensively deployed in the 1960s, the utilization of data transmission would probably have developed very differently. It is a chicken-and-egg argument: Which comes first, the communication facility or the market demand for it?

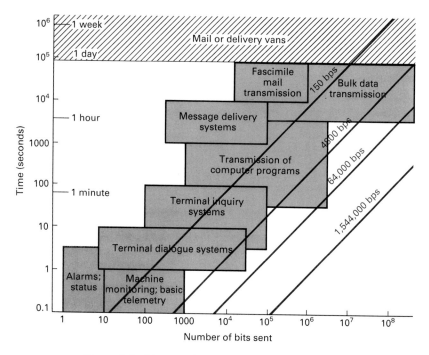

Figure 3.1 Line speeds and data communication uses

NETWORK CONSIDERATIONS

The choice of communication line types, network structures, and equipment to be used in supporting the application software depends mainly on the following three factors:

- **Space:** the distance between the transmitting and receiving devices, or if there are many of them, their geographical distribution
- **Time:** the time within which the transmission or message should be sent, or within which a response should be received
- **Quantity:** the number of bits to be sent in a single transmission or message

In some cases an examination of these three factors may lead a systems analyst to conclude that data transmission should not be used at all. (Sending diskettes through the mail or by messenger can still be the most cost-effective method for transporting data in many situations.) In addition to these points, there are a number of secondary but still important considerations, such as accuracy of transmission, line-failure probability, probability of obtaining a busy signal, whether a device should be connectable to one, or many, other devices, and how many times the transmission reverses direction (as when many terminals used for terminal dialogs are connected to the same line).

LOCATION OF INTELLIGENT MACHINES

The computers and other intelligent nodes of the network should normally be positioned so as to minimize the overall cost of the total system. If a system covering a large geographical area is to have one central computer center, this computer center should be positioned, if possible, in such a way as to minimize the cost of the other parts of the network. Another factor is whether a single computer should be used with lines linking distant terminals to it or whether several computers with shorter-distance lines should be used. If several computers are decided on, how many should there be, and where should they be located? What is the optimum balance between computer cost and network cost?

To provide a nationwide time-sharing or information service, a computer in each city may be used, or a computer covering a group of cities. On the other hand, groups of computers in the same building may serve many locations, the grouping being designed to minimize the probability of a user not having access to a machine when access is needed. Again, a load-sharing network may be designed; and when one computer is fully loaded, jobs may be switched to a different machine. The balance in cost between having many local machines with short-distance transmission or fewer machines with long-distance transmission needs to be evaluated. This cost balance will steadily change in the future as both long-distance transmission costs and computer costs drop and transmission efficiency increases.

DUPLICATING FILES AND DATABASES

Just as we may have a choice between many localized computers and one centralized one, so there is a choice on some systems between localized databases with duplicate data and one centralized database. Sometimes a single database is desirable because of the need for simultaneous updating from many sources. On other systems, however, the updating may be done at preplanned intervals, which makes it possible to have multiple identical databases in different places, thus reducing transmission cost. The systems analyst should evaluate which is lower in cost, as well as where to position the databases.

DETERMINING THE NETWORK STRUCTURES

Once the basic decisions have been made regarding the location of intelligent devices and files, the structure of the network that is required to tie these together becomes of primary importance. Some data transmission links simply interconnect two points, as in link 1 in Fig. 3.2. More commonly, more than two places have to be linked. They may be linked with a permanent connection that may be leased on a monthly basis from a common carrier, or ordinary dial-up telephone circuits can be used (see Chapter 16). A

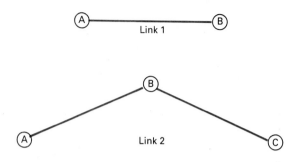

Figure 3.2   Network structures

leased line is generally less expensive than a dial-up connection if the line is used a high-enough proportion of the time. Link 2 in Fig. 3.2 connects three links, and there may be some form of switch at point B to enable A to be connected to B, B to C, or A to C.

When more than a few terminals are used, some form of logic is needed to automatically establish interconnections between them. One possible way to connect seven terminals is shown in Fig. 3.3. Here a single communication line interconnecting all seven terminals is used. This line can be designed so that when a message is transmitted by terminal A, the electrical impulses that travel on the line are received by all of the other six. However, only one of the six takes any notice of them, for it has been informed that the message is meant for it. The others, not so informed, ignore the signals.

As we will see in the chapters in Part IV, this process can be achieved by sending an addressing message before the data message or, alternatively, by tagging an address onto the front of the data message itself. Each terminal then has a logic circuit that searches for its own address. In such a scheme, only one terminal may be permitted to transmit at once, so it is normal for one of the

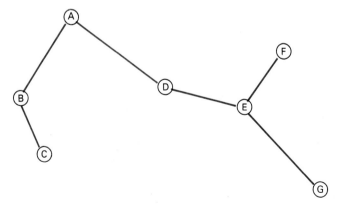

Figure 3.3   Multipoint link

locations to have a controlling device, which, like a traffic policeman, instructs the terminals when they may transmit.

Another way of interconnecting the same seven terminals is illustrated in Fig. 3.4. Here all the terminals are connected to a switch, which operates in the same manner as a telephone exchange. Any terminal user can dial any other terminal. The total line distance in Fig. 3.4 is greater than that in Fig. 3.3, which may not matter if the lines are short. If they are long, it will mean that the configuration shown in Fig. 3.4 is substantially more expensive than that of Fig. 3.3. However, the exchange at D might have more than one path through it, so that more than one pair of terminals can be interconnected at once. For example, terminal A can transmit to terminal F, while terminal E transmits to terminal C.

When large numbers of terminals are connected by leased communication lines, the network configuration can become complex. Figure 3.5 shows terminals in more than 100 cities on the eastern side of the United States, connected to a computer center in Chicago. In designing such a network, it is desirable to achieve the minimum line cost within the constraints of other requirements, such as response time. A wide variety of network configurations can be used in designing complex networks. For example, Fig. 3.6 shows the same terminals connected to intermediary locations with individual point-to-point lines.

IN-PLANT AND OUT-PLANT LINES   Communication lines that run exclusively within a user's premises can be laid down by the user rather than leased from a common carrier. These lines are referred to as *in-plant* lines, and those going outside the premises are called *out-plant* lines. The designer thus has three choices: in-plant lines, which have been privately installed; private out-plant lines, which are leased from a common carrier; and public lines, such as those of the public telephone network.

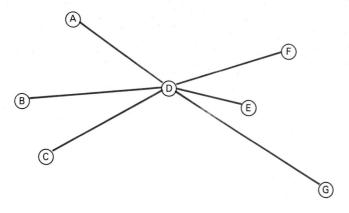

Figure 3.4   Star configuration

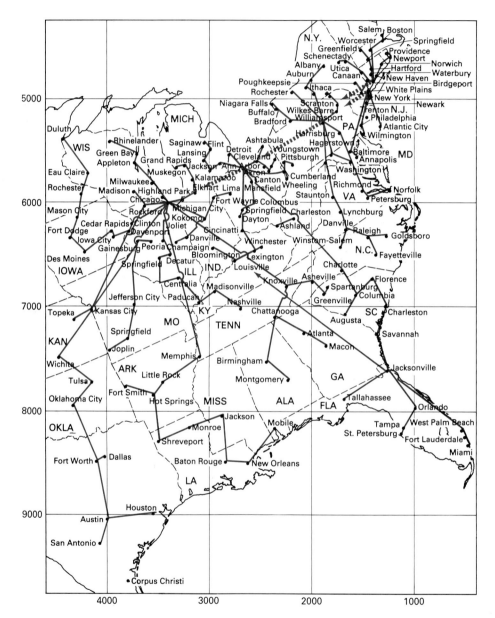

Figure 3.5 Complex network

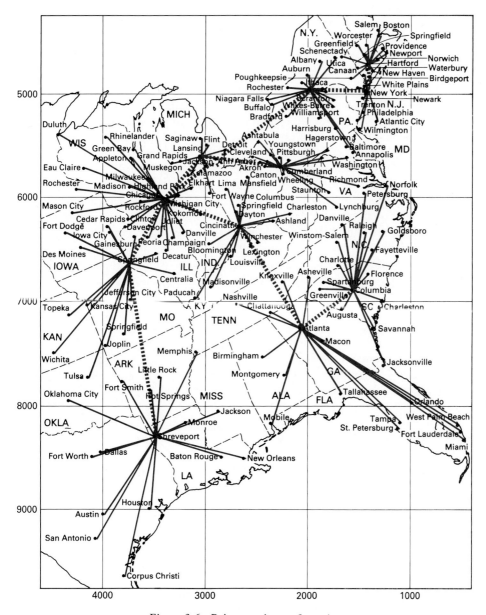

Figure 3.6 Point-to-point configuration

An organization, or perhaps a group of organizations, that frequently needs to transmit over long distances will often use private leased lines, for such lines can be cheaper than dial-up public lines. On the other hand, if the lines are short (i.e., within one city), or their usage is low, it may be cheaper to use the public network.

SWITCHING REQUIREMENTS

In many systems a terminal is installed for one purpose only; it will communicate with only one application running in one computer. This is the case with many terminals for special commercial functions, such as those in banks, airlines, stockbrokerages, and those forming parts of specialized information systems. Sometimes terminals on general-purpose, time-sharing systems are installed to communicate with many applications, but all running in the same computer. In other cases, however, a terminal can be linked to many different computers. If such is the case, there must be some means of switching the connection between the different machines. The most common way of doing so today is to use the public telephone network. The operator dials the telephone number of the desired computer, and the terminal is then connected to it. A terminal used by one person for programming in APL on one computer may be used by another for accessing a database on a different computer.

Although the public telephone network is useful for switching the connection, because of the ubiquitousness of the telephone connections, other switching means may be used to give access to machines within a building complex or within an organization. The latter are often constructed from leased or privately installed communication facilities. The need for communication with more than one computer center is a parameter that will affect the design.

BUSY SIGNALS

In a switched network there will be a certain probability of receiving a busy signal. The busy signal may occur because the computer dialed has no more free ports or because there are no free trunks or paths through an exchange. The systems analyst must determine what probability of being denied access to the computer is acceptable and must then design the trunks, exchanges, and computer facilities so as to achieve this condition.

LINE CONTENTION AND QUEUING

Where several terminals are attached to one line, not all of them can transmit at the same time. When the line is in use and another terminal wants it, there will be no busy signal. Instead, there will be a waiting time. The terminal wanting the line waits until it becomes free. If the messages are short and the line speed is high, the waiting times will be short. The organization of the line will affect the terminal response times. The systems analyst should evaluate the probabilities of obtaining different response times and should adjust the line configuration so that it is in keeping with the users' time requirements.

ERROR RATES

A certain number of errors will occur in data transmitted over telecommunications lines. For most types of lines, statistics are available giving the distributions of error rates that can be expected. On some systems the numbers of errors that can be expected from the terminal operators far exceed those caused by line errors, and the same checking means may be used for dealing with both operator errors and line errors. When the data originates from a machine, however, we generally expect its transmission to be correct. Error-detecting or error-correcting codes are normally employed in data transmission systems. Error-detecting codes give the higher measure of safety. When they are used and an error is detected, the message containing it is ordinarily retransmitted. If a large number of errors occur, a large amount of time will be spent in retransmission. This situation can be controlled by adjusting the block size that is transmitted and by selecting transmission means with appropriate speed and error characteristics. Such factors may also be under the control of the system designer.

NETWORK AVAILABILITY

In some systems it is necessary to have a high degree of certainty of obtaining access to the computer. This is true in military systems and is important on some commercial systems as well. To achieve a high system availability, the computers, and sometimes the data on the files, are sometimes duplicated. It is also necessary to design a communication network that will not fail to establish the necessary connection. In such cases, leased lines that do not pass through switching equipment are normally used. Several terminals are often connected to one leased line. Every such line will enter the computer so that there is no possibility of blocking. In this way, the possibility of receiving busy signals is eliminated.

A further problem remains—that of line failure. If the probability of leased-line failure is deemed unacceptably high, alternative routing must be planned. The public telephone network can be used to provide backup for a leased-line system.

MULTIPLE USAGE

Leased communication lines and equipment are used for many systems. Many different types of computer system are in use in some organizations, and it is becoming increasingly desirable that they should *share* the leased communication facilities. Sharing is a key to cost reduction. There is a variety of ways in which a leased network can be constructed such that it can be shared by different systems. Techniques for sharing data transmission facilities are discussed in Chapters 9 and 27.

THE REMAINING STEPS

After the initial design work is done regarding the terminals and the network configuration, the remaining steps consist of highly technical tasks (see Box 3.1). These often involve the use of the computer in running mathematical models or computer simulations of various parts of the design.

THE MASTER PLAN

An organization making extensive use of·data transmission today is likely to have a wide diversity of needs. It will use many different types of both real-time systems and batch data transmission. Different realtime systems may have fundamentally different modes of operation. In addition to the data transmission, organizations spend enormous amounts of money on ordinary voice communication.

Ideally and theoretically, it would be best to have one integrated network that handles all the organization's information transmission. This is the goal of ISDN technology. However, in today's environment, many large organizations today have a proliferation of separate networks. The proliferation has grown up over a period of years with a variety of reasons for installing new facilities.

Typically, a new computer system is installed with its own particular requirements. It is economical for it to use new transmission facilities rather than an extension of the old ones. But the old ones are still in use for a different purpose and are not dismantled. There are also *current* reasons for using separate networks, and these are based on the cost of contemporary technology.

In particular, the choice of the services used in various networks is dependent on facilities that are available and their costs. Some computer systems need the speed of high-speed lines. Others can operate at the maximum speed of voice lines. Many require only teletype speeds. Some data transmission devices need the communication line continuously or very frequently, and it is economical for them to have a private leased line. Others need the connection only occasionally, so that the lowest-cost answer is a dial-up line. Where an organization has many calls, data or voice, that are placed between certain locations, it may use a mechanism for switching separate calls onto leased lines connecting these points. Many organizations make a substantial use of leased voice lines (often called *tie lines*). In this case, the ability to use the leased-line network may become a major factor in designing the data transmission facilities. Often, however, the data transmission network is set up independently using separate facilities.

Probably, however, the most important reason for the growth of separate transmission networks concerns the difficulty of implementing complex computer systems. A data processing team does not implement all the systems required by a large organization in one gigantic integrated step. Doing so would be far too complex. Instead, the organization's data processing facilities evolve step by step, each step being concerned with the installation of a new system or a change to an existing system, which can be implemented by the available staff. If the staff members attempt to bite off more than they can chew at any one step, grave difficulties lie ahead. On the other hand, in a large organization, several steps may be proceeding simultaneously. The result is a patchwork of different computer systems interlinked in a variety of different ways. In Chapter 38 we show an example of how a number of unrelated data transmission networks were installed in one large corporation.

Although different systems may evolve separately, it is desirable that, as far as possible, the data processing designers have a *master plan* for the future evolution of data transmission facilities in their organization. Only in this way can there be an adequate measure of compatibility between the systems. This is particularly important in systems for performing commercial or administrative operations. Without such advanced planning, the systems become more difficult to link together, often more difficult for the terminal operators to use, more cumbersome in the database planning, and more expensive in application of resources and in telecommunications costs.

Adherence to a neatly conceived master plan has rarely been achieved in reality. The state of the art is moved by unpredictable tides and their pressures are strong enough to distort the best-laid plans. A certain machine or software package suddenly becomes available. One approach works and another fails. Natural selection takes over, and we have a process of evolution dominated by the survival of whatever is most practical.

The master plan, then, must not be too rigid. It must be permissible for different systems to evolve in their own ways. The master plan may call for defined interfaces between separately evolving systems. The separate systems should each be of a level of complexity that is currently practicable. Components of the plan should be designed, as far as possible, with proliferation in mind. A master plan for the communication network may exist separately from a master plan for the evolution of computer systems. Its purpose would be to lower the overall cost of the data transmission and other telecommunications links.

Designers of new systems should be expected to use the planned communication facilities where it is reasonable for them to do so. The saving can be worthwhile, especially in large nationwide corporations, which often spend many millions of dollars per month on telecommunications. There is a variety of ways in which a data network can be constructed to meet the needs of different types of users.

ADVANCED SYSTEMS

When networks were simple and each terminal was dedicated to only one application, few options were available to the system designer, and designers typically depended entirely upon the equipment manufacturer and the common carriers to provide data communication facilities. The increasing complexity of today's data communication environment has led to a requirement for networking software that provides many advanced functions, over and above transmitting a stream of bits from one location to another. An overall plan into which a set of data communication hardware and software components fits is called a *network architecture*. Network architectures are introduced in Chapter 4.

4 NETWORK ARCHITECTURES

In the early days of data communication, individual computer manufacturers produced communication products that worked only on their equipment, and data communication connections between the equipment of different manufacturers was difficult. Today, networks have evolved and have increased in capability and complexity. In modern data communication systems, the functions relating to data transmission for each station connected to a communication line or to a network are performed by software or firmware installed in the communicating stations. The functions performed by that software or firmware are divided into independent *layers*, much like the skins of an onion. Each layer isolates the layers above it from the complexities below.

The need is now apparent for a high degree of standardization in the functions performed by each of these software layers. This is the role of a *network architecture*. A network architecture is an overall plan that governs the design of the hardware and software components that make up a data communication system. Several such network architectures are in existence today, and we introduce two important ones in this chapter. Before we discuss these two specific architectures, we examine the functions that are performed in a data communication system and see how those functions are performed by independent software layers.

HUMAN COMMUNICATION ANALOGY

An analogy can be made between the functions that are performed in a data communication system and the functions that are performed when ordinary human communication takes place. Figure 4.1 shows how the functions performed during human communication might be divided into three layers: an *ideas* layer, a *language* layer, and a *physical* layer.

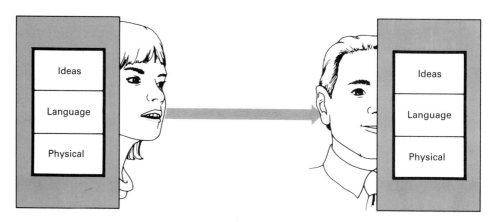

Figure 4.1 Levels of human communication

THE PHYSICAL LAYER

In the physical layer, the two parties must agree to and use a common communication medium. Typical communication media used in human communication are sound waves in air or letters by mail. For example, Fig. 4.2 shows the physical medium used when two parties are involved in a face-to-face conversation. In human communication, it is important that both parties agree to and use the same communication medium. For example, if one party is speaking, but the other party is waiting for a letter to arrive, no communication takes place.

THE LANGUAGE LAYER

Once a common physical medium has been chosen, each party involved in a conversation must use a language understood by the other. If one party speaks

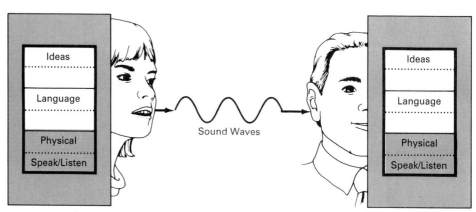

Figure 4.2 Physical level: human speech

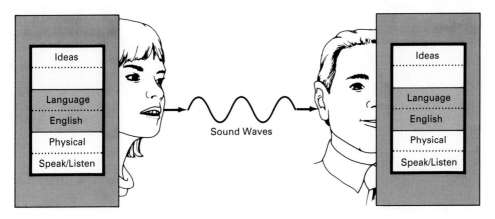

Figure 4.3   Language level: English

only French and the other understands only English, little communication will take place. Figure 4.3 shows the language layer when two parties are conducting a conversation. With no common language, there is no successful dialog, even though both parties may have agreed to use the same communication medium. If I call a Tokyo hotel and get a clerk who does not speak English, I will not be able to make a reservation, even though I might have an excellent telephone connection.

THE IDEAS LAYER   We might think of the highest layer in human communication as the *ideas* layer. In this layer, each person involved in a conversation must have some idea of what the conversation is about and must understand the concepts being discussed. Figure 4.4 shows the ideas layer when two parties are discussing fiber optics. If an English-speaking engineer establishes a good telephone connection with another English-speaking person and begins a technical discussion on fiber optics, little real communication is likely to take place if the second party is a 3-year-old.

PROTOCOLS   In each layer in any communication system, a set of *rules* must be agreed to and followed by both parties in order for communication to be successful. The rules that govern communication are called *protocols*. Each set of protocols can be thought of as a rule book that governs communication at a given layer.

HUMAN COMMUNICATION PROTOCOLS   The protocols involved in the *physical* layer of human communication are simple. When two parties agree to use a common communication medium, they

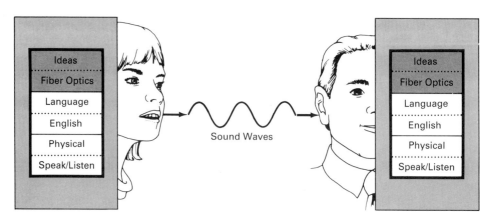

Figure 4.4   Ideas level: fiber optics

must both observe the same rules in using that medium. For example, on many long-distance telephone circuits, both people are not able to talk at the same time; only one party at a time is allowed to speak. If both people speak at once, no communication takes place.

For the *language* layer, the protocols are more complex and are governed by a larger rule book. These protocols involve the rules of grammar and syntax for the common language. When two parties agree to use English, they agree to abide by the rules of grammar and syntax that govern the English language.

For the *ideas* layer, the protocols are even more complex. The rules for this layer involve the body of knowledge concerning the subject being discussed. If two parties are discussing fiber optics, the rule book might consist of descriptions of the technical details concerning semiconductor lasers and the optical characteristics of glass fibers.

CHANGING PROTOCOLS   When people communicate, they can change the protocol for a given layer as long as both parties agree and change to the same new protocol. In effect, they agree to change the rule book for one of the layers. The rule book can be changed for one layer without requiring the rule books to be changed for the other layers. This makes each layer independent of the others.

For example, in business, people often begin by exchanging letters and then mutually decide that a telephone conversation is needed. They may then decide that a face-to-face meeting is required to continue the discussion. The rules, or protocols, that govern the ideas and language layers remain the same each time the discussion is resumed, even though the protocol that governs the physical layer has changed three times. Multilingual people who are conversing might shift to a second language when appropriate. As long as both parties agree to do this, the change in protocol for the language layer does not necessitate changes in the physical or ideas layers. In a typical phone call, two parties might discuss several topics. The protocol involved in the ideas layer may change several times, but protocols for the language and physical layers remain fixed throughout the conversation.

MESSAGE TRANSMISSION

To draw a further analogy between human communication and data communication, a dialog can be viewed as taking place via *messages* that are transmitted back and forth over a *channel* between the two parties (see Fig. 4.5). For each message, there must be a *sender* and a *receiver*. On the sending end, an idea originates a message, which is transmitted to the second party via the agreed-upon physical medium (the channel). At the receiving end, the message is received and converted (hopefully) back into the original idea.

SOFTWARE LAYERS

Messages that are sent from a sender to a receiver in a human dialog can be viewed as passing through *layers of software*. Messages are processed by *hardware* and *software* residing in, or controlled by, the two communicating parties. For example, in a face-to-face conversation, the hardware consists of the nervous systems, mouths, and ears of the two people. The software consists of the thought processes, both conscious and unconscious, that are used to conduct the conversation. A message passes down through layers of software on the sending end, across the channel using hardware in the physical layer, and up through corresponding layers of software on the receiving end.

As shown in Fig. 4.6, the sender uses a high-level, conscious software layer operating at the ideas level to formulate a message. A largely unconscious software layer, operating at the language level, is used to place that message

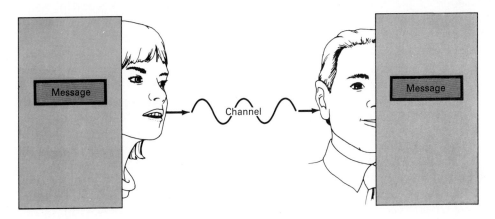

Figure 4.5 Message transmission

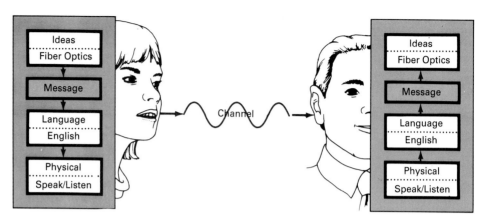

Figure 4.6 Layers of software

into words. Another unconscious software layer operating at the physical level controls the mouth and tongue in sending the message orally over the communication channel, which consists of sound waves in air.

The ear of the receiver is controlled by a low-level software layer, operating at the physical level, that detects the sound waves that are carrying the message. A software layer operating at the language level translates those sounds into words. A conscious software layer operating at the ideas level reconstructs the meaning of the original message from those words.

TRANSPARENT AND VIRTUAL

In discussing complex systems that use layered software, it is important to have a clear understanding of the meaning of the terms *transparent* and *virtual*. A *transparent* facility is one that actually exists but appears not to exist. A *virtual* facility is one that appears to exist but in fact does not. The concept of transparent and virtual facilities make it easier to understand the principles involved in data communication. The ordinary human dialog examined above provides an illustration of transparent and virtual facilities.

TRANSPARENT FACILITIES

Much of the complexity involved in an ordinary two-way dialog is *transparent* to the communicating parties because many aspects of the complex chain of events that implements the two-way conversation are handled automatically. In conducting a conversation, the two parties are ordinarily conscious only of the thought processes operating in the ideas layer. The thought processes operating in the language and physical layers are transparent (see Fig. 4.7). For example, you are not ordinarily consciously aware that you are translating between sounds

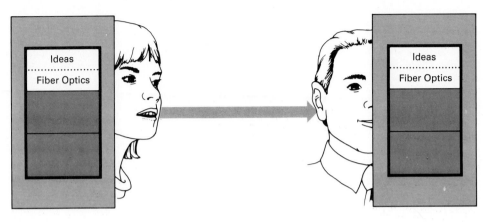

Figure 4.7   Transparent processes

and words when you speak. Nor are you aware that you are creating sounds and listening for them. These lower-level thought processes actually do exist, but *appear* to your ideas software layer as if they do not. In other words, they are transparent.

The idea of transparent facilities is important because transparent facilities isolate higher-level layers from the complexities of the lower-level layers. Two parties converse with one another effortlessly because the complexities involved in conducting a conversation are isolated from high-level thought processes. If two parties had to consciously think about forming each word that makes up an exchange in a conversation, not much mental energy would be left for carrying on the conversation.

In a similar manner, transparent facilities are used in modern computer systems to isolate higher-level software layers, and ultimately the end user, from the complexities of the lower software layers and the network itself. A modern, sophisticated data communication system might use a number of independent software layers that are all quite complex. All but the topmost layer are transparent to the user. The total system can be made to *appear* quite simple. The user might see only a simple set of commands for requesting easy-to-use network services.

VIRTUAL FACILITIES

A virtual facility is a seemingly simple facility that may actually be implemented by something quite complex. For example, in our human communication example, a message moves down through layers of software on the sending side, across the channel, and up through the layers on the receiving side. Since the lower layers are transparent to the ideas layer, the dialog can be viewed as if it were being conducted purely in the ideas layer. When two people are engaged in a dialog, a ''meeting of the minds'' can take place in which the two parties communicate their thoughts to one another. The thought processes in the ideas layer operate as if there existed a simple communication channel between the ideas layer in the sender and the ideas layer in the receiver.

This connection is called a *virtual* channel because it does not actually exist, but only appears to. The virtual channel is implemented by a transparent, but quite complex, system of software and hardware components operating at lower-level layers (see Fig. 4.8). A virtual channel can also be said to exist between the language layer in the sender and the language layer in the receiver (see Fig. 4.9). At the language layer, the physical layer is transparent. It appears to the language layer as if a virtual channel connects the sender and the receiver at this level. Virtual facilities are also quite important in modern data communication systems.

HIDING COMPLEXITY

Virtual facilities provide a simple way of viewing a complex system. A given network might actually look like that shown in Fig. 4.10. However, a network user needs a simpler way to view the part of the network being used. A given user who needs to use a terminal to access one of the computers might perceive the network as if it appeared as shown in Fig. 4.11. The user views the network as if a simple point-to-point connection (a *virtual channel*) exists between the terminal and the computer. The user can ignore the complexities of the hardware and software facilities that implement the virtual channel—they are transparent to the user.

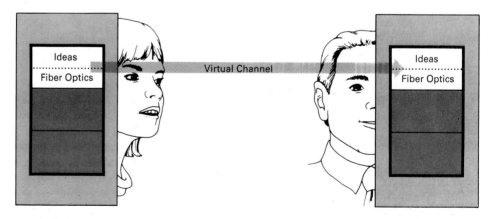

Figure 4.8   Virtual channel: ideas layer

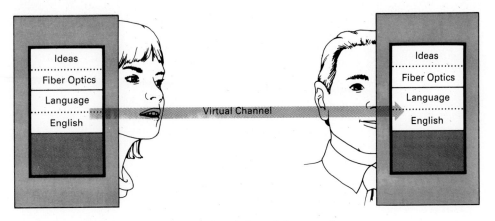

Figure 4.9   Virtual channel: language layer

**COMMUNICATION
SYSTEM
SOFTWARE
LAYERS**

A data communication system can be viewed on a number of different levels, just as can human communication. At each level, a layer of software works together with hardware to provide a useful set of functions. As with the model of human communication discussed earlier, each software layer is independent of all the others. In-

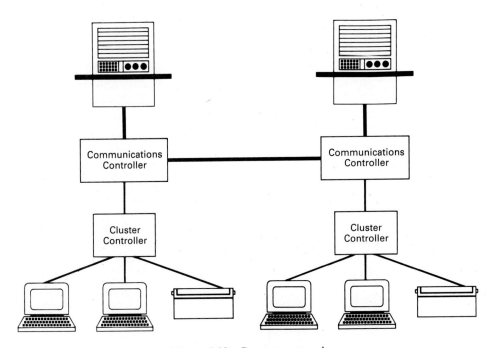

Figure 4.10   Computer network

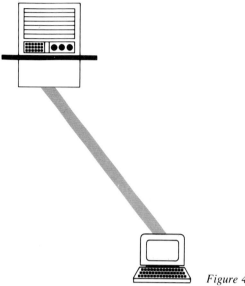

Figure 4.11   Virtual channel

dependence of the layers gives a modern data communication system great flexibility. All data communication systems have at least two layers in common.

THE PHYSICAL LAYER

The lowest layer of any data communication system implements a physical connection between two devices that allows electrical signals to be exchanged between them. Figure 4.12 shows a simple point-to-point data link that connects a terminal to a small computer. The hardware consists of a cable, appropriate connectors, and the two communicating devices, each of which is capable of both generating and detecting voltages on the connecting cable. This lowest-level layer is analogous to the *physical layer* of human communication. The physical layer, shown in Fig. 4.13, is simple and consists of firmware permanently installed in both the computer and the terminal. This firmware controls the generation and detection of voltages on the cable that represent zero bits and one bits.

The physical layer does not assign any significance to the bits. For example, this layer is not concerned with how many bits make up each unit of data, nor is it concerned with the meaning of the data being transmitted. For example, in the physical layer, the sender transmits a string of bits, and the receiver

Figure 4.12   Simple data link

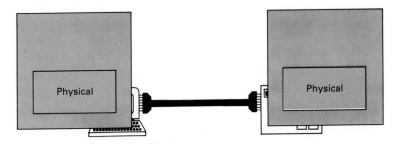

Figure 4.13   The physical layer

detects them. The chapters in Parts II and III are concerned mainly with the physical layer in a data communication system and discuss the general characteristics of communication channels.

DATA LINK LAYER   The second layer of software or firmware in any data communication system is generally called the *data link* layer (see Fig. 4.14). Software in this layer implements a logical connection between the two communicating devices that can be used to transmit meaningful data between them. In the chapters in Part IV we discuss the functions performed by the data link layer in modern data communication systems.

The data link layer is normally implemented by firmware permanently installed in the communicating machines. This firmware is concerned with how bits are grouped into collections called *frames*. There are any number of ways that bits can be grouped to form meaningful data, so standards are as important for the data link layer as they are for the physical layer. A number of standards, called *data link protocols,* have been published that describe how bits should be grouped for various purposes. In the chapters in Part IV we discuss the most commonly used data link protocols.

As an example of what happens at the data link layer, suppose that a terminal is connected to a computer via a simple point-to-point connection. The process that occurs is illustrated in Fig. 4.15. The terminal user presses the A

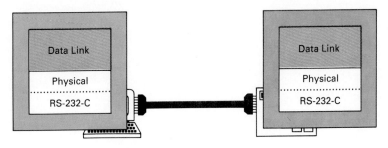

Figure 4.14   The data link layer

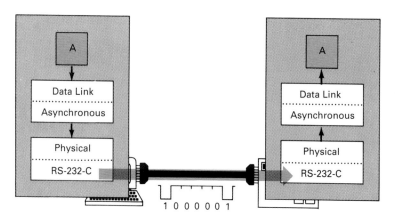

Figure 4.15 Message transmission

key on the keyboard, and the keyboard sends the bits that make up the letter A to the firmware operating in the data link layer. The data link firmware interprets these bits and causes the firmware operating in the physical layer to send the appropriate electrical signals out on the physical connection. Firmware operating in the physical layer in the computer detects the signals and passes them up to the firmware operating in its data link layer. The data link layer firmware in the computer then interprets the signals as the bit configuration for the letter A.

HIGHER-LEVEL LAYERS

Figure 4.16 shows that there are functions above the levels of the data link layer that must operate in both the sender and the receiver. In the simplest case, these functions may be performed by the human terminal operator. For example, some functions must be performed by the sender in deciding that an appropriate

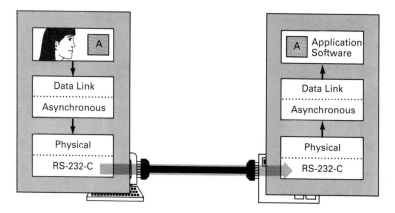

Figure 4.16 Higher-level layers

action is to press the A key on the keyboard. And on the receiving end, some higher-level function, either in higher-level data communication software or in an application program, must attach some significance to receiving the letter A. In the chapters in Part VII we discuss the functions that are performed in these higher-level layers.

LAYER INDEPENDENCE

Earlier in this chapter we introduced the principle of *layer independence*. The protocol, or rule book, can be changed for one layer without affecting the functions of the other layers. The same layer independence applies for the two software layers in our simple data communication system.

The physical layer can be changed by installing a new cable with different connectors, or by changing the signals that are used for transmitting bits. The same techniques could still be used at the data link layer over the new physical connection. At the data link layer, many data link protocols exist. In the chapters in Part IV we examine *asynchronous* protocols, the *binary-synchronous* protocol, and bit-oriented protocols, such as *high-level data link control* (HDLC) and *synchronous data link control* (SDLC). The data link protocol can be changed without affecting the software layers that operate above the data link layer.

The principle of layering allows the functions that are performed by lower layers in a data communication system to be transparent to the upper layers. At the level of the user at the terminal and the application program in the computer, the functions performed by the data link layer and by the physical layer are transparent. The system can be viewed as if there existed a virtual channel between the user at the keyboard and the high-level software in the computer (see Fig. 4.17). The user knows that pressing the A key will cause the high-level software to receive the letter A.

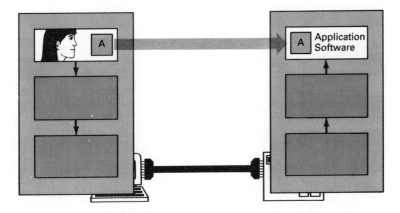

Figure 4.17   Virtual channel

In the same manner, the functions performed by the physical layer are transparent to the firmware in the data link layer. At this level, the system can be viewed as if there existed a virtual connection between the data link layer in the terminal and the data link layer in the computer (see Fig. 4.18). It is the principle of transparency that allows systems of great complexity to be built, while isolating the user from those complexities.

NETWORK ARCHITECTURES   A network architecture defines the way in which communication functions are divided into the layers we have been discussing. These architectures also define the protocols, standards, and message formats to which different machines and software modules must conform in order to achieve given goals. When new products are created that conform to an architecture, they will then be compatible, and they can be interlinked to share data, resources, and programs that already exist.

The goals and standards of a network architecture are important to both the users of data communication systems and the companies that provide data communication equipment and services. The architecture must provide users with a variety of choices in the configuration of data communication systems, and it must allow them to change a configuration with relative ease as their systems evolve. Architectures permit the mass production of hardware and software building blocks that can be used in a variety of different systems. They also provide standards and definitions that allow development laboratories to create new machines and software that will be compatible with existing machines. The new products can then be integrated into existing data communication systems without the need for costly interfaces and program modifications.

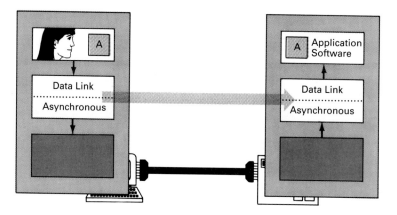

Figure 4.18   Data link layer

THE NATURE OF ARCHITECTURE

Although network architectures provide rules for the development of new products, these rules can change. This is because the term *architecture* in the computer industry often implies an overall scheme or plan that has not necessarily yet been fully implemented. The architecture represents the goal toward which its implementors strive. Thus architectures are bound to evolve and change as new hardware, software, and techniques are developed.

The term *architecture* is often used to describe database management systems, operating systems, and other highly complex software/hardware mechanisms. Architecture is a particularly important concept in describing data communication and computer network systems because in these systems so many potentially incompatible hardware devices and software packages must fit together to form an easily used and easily modified whole.

With much complex software there is an *architectural definition* stating the eventual requirements. For database systems, for example, CODASYL (the committee that developed COBOL) has defined a long-range database architecture and has specified in great detail some of the protocols involved in database management. As with network architectures, individual implementations often provide only some of the functions defined in the complete architecture.

A good architecture ought to relate primarily to the needs of the end users rather than to enthusiasms for particular techniques. A well architected house, for example, is one that reflects the desired life-style of its owners rather than one that is designed to exploit a building technique that is currently in vogue. Fred Brooks, author of *The Mythical Man-Month* (Reading, Mass: Addison-Wesley, 1975. Reprinted with corrections January 1982.), defined architecture in a way that makes a clear distinction between architecture and engineering: "Computer architecture, like other architecture, is the art of determining the needs of the user of a structure and then designing to meet those needs as effectively as possible within economic and technological constraints. Architecture must include engineering considerations, so that the design will be economical and feasible; but the emphasis in architecture is upon the needs of the user, whereas in engineering the emphasis is upon the needs of the fabricator."

DEVELOPERS OF ARCHITECTURES

Because of the importance of network architectures, several different types of organizations have gotten involved in standards and architecture development. These organizations can be categorized into three classes: *standards organizations, common carriers* (or the teleprocessing administrations that are their international counterparts), and *computer manufacturers*. Architectures designed by these groups have many characteristics in common. They all define the rules of a network and define how the components of a network can interact. But there are also major differences among these three types of architecture developers.

Standards Organizations

The following organizations in the United States and Europe are actively involved in developing standards for data communication and computer networking:

- American National Standards Institute (ANSI)
- Electronics Industry Association (EIA)
- European Computer Manufacturers' Association (ECMA)
- *Comité Consultatif International Télégraphique et Téléphonique* (CCITT) (generally translated as International Telegraph and Telephone Consultative Committee)
- International Organization for Standardization (ISO)

Box 4.1 describes the primary organizations that are involved in developing data communication standards and indicates how copies of their respective standards can be obtained. Figure 4.19 illustrates the close working relationships

BOX 4.1   Standards organizations

- **American National Standards Institute (ANSI).** The ANSI is a group of about 200 organizations representing various interest groups and is the foremost standards organization in the United States. ANSI technical committees are responsible for drafting recommended standards. ANSI standards can be obtained by writing to ANSI, Inc., 1430 Broadway, New York, NY 10018.

- **Electronics Industry Association (EIA).** The EIA is an organization whose members come primarily from companies that produce a broad range of electronics products. The standards developed by the EIA are concerned primarily with communication interfaces. The best known EIA standard is RS-232-C, which documents the way a terminal or computer is attached to a modem (see Chapter 10). EIA standards can be obtained from the EIA Engineering Department, Standards Sales, 2001 Eye Street, N.W., Washington, DC 20006.

- **European Computer Manufacturers' Association (ECMA).** ECMA represents the interests of computer manufacturers in Europe and works closely with many of the committees of both the ISO and the CCITT. Many U.S. corporations are represented in ECMA via their European branches. ECMA standards can be obtained by writing to ECMA, 114 Rue du Rhone, 1204 Geneva, Switzerland.

BOX 4.1　*(Continued)*

- **International Telegraph and Telephone Consultative Committee (CCITT).** The CCITT is an international standards organization based in Geneva, Switzerland. The CCITT is one of three technical divisions of the *International Telecommunications Union* (ITU), whose authority derives from a United Nations treaty. The CCITT has developed a complex and sophisticated set of standards for computer networks that is described in a series of recommendations with names such as *X.3, X.25, X.28,* and *X.29.* Many of these recommendations are discussed in this book. CCITT recommendations can be obtained from the U.S. Department of Commerce, National Technical Information Service, 5285 Port Royal Road, Springfield, VA 22161. The following organization also stocks copies of CCITT recommendations: OMNICOM, 501 Church Street, N.E., Vienna, VA 22180; telephone: (703) 281–1135.

- **International Organization for Standardization (ISO).** Each member country of ISO sends representatives from that country's most important standards organization. ANSI is the ISO representative for the United States. ISO has published the description of a particularly important architecture for computer networks called the *Open Systems Interconnect (OSI) Reference Model.* The OSI model is introduced later in this chapter and is the subject of Chapter 35. ISO standards are available through the American National Standards Institute.

- **Institute of Electrical and Electronic Engineers (IEEE).** The Computer Society of the IEEE is also active in standards development. Of particular interest to users of data communication services are the standards that the IEEE has developed for local area networks (see Chapter 40). IEEE standards can be obtained by writing to IEEE Computer Society, 10662 Los Vaqueros Circle, Los Alamitos, CA 90720; telephone: (800) 272–6657.

that exist among the various standards organizations. Another source of information about standards is *McGraw-Hill's Compilation of Data Communication Standards,* edited by Harold C. Folts (New York: McGraw-Hill Book Company, 1982). This book contains reprints of the most commonly used standards from a variety of standards organizations. Be warned, however, that this publication is over 2000 pages in length and is 3 inches thick, even though printed on thin paper. Standards documents should not as a rule be read late at night, unless used as a cure for insomnia.

It is important to note that standards organizations are empowered only to document or recommend the use of the standards and recommendations they develop. They cannot implement the standards, nor can they build the machines

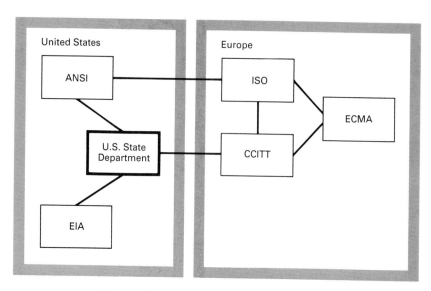

Figure 4.19 International standards organizations

they describe. These functions must be handled either by common carriers and telecommunications administrations or by computer manufacturers.

CCITT Red Book

The CCITT publishes a comprehensive set of recommendations that are widely used throughout the telecommunications industry. Various working groups in the CCITT develop these recommendations, which are then published at 4-year intervals. The CCITT changes the color of the covers of its documents when each new set of recommendations is published. The color of the covers was yellow for the set of documents that covered recommendations developed during the period 1976–1980. The set of CCITT recommendations for that period was referred to as the *Yellow Book;* the Yellow Book was in common use until 1985. The color of the cover of the current set of CCITT recommendations is red; thus the CCITT recommendations are currently called the *Red Book*. The Red Book contains the most current set of CCITT recommendations and will be useful through about 1989, when a new series of recommendations will replace it.

The Red Book is published in the form of a series of volumes, each of which is divided into separately bound *fascicles*. Each fascicle can be ordered separately and can be obtained in the United States from either of the two sources listed with the description of the CCITT in Box 4.1. Box 4.2 lists the various volumes and fascicles in the CCITT Red Book.

BOX 4.2   The CCITT Red Book

Volume I

- Minutes and reports of the plenary assembly
- Opinions and resolutions
- Recommendations on:
  —The organization and working procedures of the CCITT
  —Means of expression
  —General telecommunications statistics
- List of study groups and questions under study

Volume II (five fascicles, sold separately)

- **Fascicle II.1:** General tariff principles—charging and accounting in international telecommunications services. Series D Recommendations (Study Group III)
- **Fascicle II.2:** International telephone service—operation. Recommendations E.100-E.323 (Study Group II)
- **Fascicle II.3:** International telephone service—network management traffic engineering. Recommendations E.401-E.600 (Study Group II)
- **Fascicle II.4:** Telegraph services—operations and quality of service. Recommendations F.1-F.150 (Study Group I)
- **Fascicle II.5:** Telematic services—operations and quality of service. Recommendations F.160-F.350 (Study Group I)

Volume III (five fascicles, sold separately)

- **Fascicle III.1:** General characteristics of international telephone connections and circuits. Recommendations G.101-G.181 (Study Groups XV, XVI, and CMBD)
- **Fascicle III.2:** International analog carrier systems: transmission media—characteristics. Recommendations G.211-G.652 (Study Groups XV and CMBD)
- **Fascicle III.3:** Digital networks—transmission systems and multiplexing equipment. Recommendations G.700-G.956 (Study Group XV and XVIII)
- **Fascicle III.4:** Line transmission of nontelephone signals: transmission of sound-program and television signals. Series H, J Recommendations (Study Group XV)
- **Fascicle III.5:** Integrated services digital network (ISDN). Series I Recommendations (Study Group XVIII)

(Continued)

BOX 4.2 *(Continued)*

Volume IV (four fascicles, sold separately)

- **Fascicle IV.1:** Maintenance—general principles, international transmission systems, international telephone circuits. Recommendations M.10-M.762 (Study Group IV)

- **Fascicle IV.2:** Maintenance—international voice frequency telegraphy and facsimile, international leased circuits. Recommendations M.800-M.1375 (Study Group IV)

- **Fascicle IV.3:** Maintenance—international sound program and television transmission circuits. Series N Recommendations (Study Group IV)

- **Fascicle IV.4:** Specifications of measuring equipment. Series O Recommendations (Study Group IV)

Volume V

- Telephone transmission quality. Series P Recommendations (Study Group IV)

Volume VI (13 fascicles, sold separately)

- **Fascicle VI.1:** General recommendations on telephone switching and signaling; interface with the maritime mobile service and the land mobile service. Recommendations Q.1-Q.118bis (Study Group XI)

- **Fascicle VI.2:** Specifications of signaling systems Nos. 4 and 5. Recommendations Q.120-Q.180 (Study Group XI)

- **Fascicle VI.3:** Specifications of signaling system No. 6. Recommendations Q.251-Q.300 (Study Group XI)

- **Fascicle VI.4:** Specifications of signaling systems R1 and R2. Recommendations Q.310-Q.490 (Study Group XI)

- **Fascicle VI.5:** Digital transit exchanges in integrated digital networks and mixed analog-digital networks; digital local and combined exchanges. Recommendations Q.501-Q.517 (Study Group XI)

- **Fascicle VI.6:** Interworking of signaling systems. Recommendations Q.601-Q.685 (Study Group XI)

- **Fascicle VI.7:** Specifications of signaling system No. 7. Recommendations Q.701-Q.714 (Study Group XI)

- **Fascicle VI.8:** Specifications of signaling system No. 7. Recommendations Q.721-Q.795 (Study Group XI)

- **Fascicle VI.9:** Digital access signaling system. Recommendations Q.920-Q.931 (Study Group XI)

BOX 4.2 *(Continued)*

- **Fascicle VI.10:** Functional specification and description language (SDL). Recommendations Z.101-Z.104 (Study Group XI)
- **Fascicle VI.11:** Functional specification and description language (SDL). Annexes to Recommendations Z.101-Z.104 (Study Group XI)
- **Fascicle VI.12:** CCITT high-level language (CHILL). Recommendation Z.200 (Study Group XI)
- **Fascicle VI.13:** Man-Machine Language (MML). Recommendations Z.301-Z.341 (Study Group XI)

Volume VII (three fascicles, sold separately)

- **Fascicle VII.1:** Telegraph transmission. Series R Recommendations (Study Group IX); Series S Recommendations (Study Group IX)
- **Fascicle VII.2:** Telegraph switching. Series U Recommendations (Study Group IX)
- **Fascicle VII.3:** Terminal equipment and protocols for telematic services. Series T Recommendations (Study Group VIII)

Volume VIII (seven fascicles, sold separately)

- **Fascicle VIII.1:** Data communication over the telephone network. Series V Recommendations (Study Group XVII)
- **Fascicle VIII.2:** Data communication networks—services and facilities. Recommendations X.1-X.15 (Study Group VII)
- **Fascicle VIII.3:** Data communication networks—interfaces. Recommendations X.20-X.32 (Study Group VII)
- **Fascicle VIII.4:** Data communication networks—transmission, signaling and switching, network aspects, maintenance and administrative arrangements. Recommendations X.40-X.181 (Study Group VII)
- **Fascicle VIII.5:** Data communication networks—open systems interconnection (OSI), system description techniques. Recommendations X.200-X.250 (Study Group VII)
- **Fascicle VIII.6:** Data communication networks—interworking between networks, mobile data transmission systems. Recommendations X.300-X.353 (Study Group VII)
- **Fascicle VIII.7:** Data communication networks—messsage-handling systems. Recommendations X.400-X.430 (Study Group VII)

(Continued)

BOX 4.2   *(Continued)*

Volume IX

- Protection against interference. Series K Recommendations (Study Group V). Construction, installation, and protection of cable and other elements of outside plant. Series L Recommendations (Study Group VI)

Volume X (two fascicles, sold separately)

- **Fascicle X.1:** Terms and definitions
- **Fascicle X.2:** Index of the Red Book

Common Carriers

A telecommunications common carrier, such as AT&T or Western Union, is a company that furnishes communication services to the general public. For communication between data communication equipment, common carriers often employ protocols devised by standards organizations, such as the CCITT or ISO. Many common carriers offer advanced features, such as electronic mail, that go far beyond simply transporting raw data back and forth between user machines. In some cases common carriers have devised their own network architectures to define the standards and protocols that govern their own advanced data networks. This is changing as the standardized network architectures are gaining in acceptance throughout the world.

Computer Manufacturers

Computer manufacturers began providing advanced data communication capabilities long before the development of today's standardized network architectures. For this reason, computer manufacturers were forced to develop their own architectures to give an overall cohesiveness to their product lines. The most commonly used manufacturer's network architecture is IBM's Systems Network Architecture (SNA). The first products that conformed to the SNA architecture were released in 1975. SNA is introduced later in this chapter and is described in more detail in Chapter 39. Computer manufacturers' architectures are specifically designed for data communication systems that are built from components supplied by that manufacturer. Since an individual organization often owns and implements its own network, often from components obtained from a single vendor, a manufacturer's architecture may allow systems to be built that meet the user's specific needs.

However, a manufacturer's architecture can make it difficult to interconnect machines offered by other competing vendors. The protocols used by communicating machines are often highly complex and are often completely different from one manufacturer to another. It may be relatively easy to hook a simple terminal from one manufacturer to a computer from another. It is quite difficult, however, to connect a computing system that conforms to Digital Equipment Corporation's DECNET to an SNA network. (Many computer manufacturers do, however, provide facilities called *gateways* that allow such connections to be made.)

Now that we have described network architectures in general, we will examine the software layers defined by two important network architectures: the OSI reference model and IBM's SNA.

THE OSI REFERENCE MODEL

The OSI reference model, often simply called the OSI model, was developed by a committee of the International Standards Organization (ISO). The OSI model defines an overall architecture for the complex software that modern computer networks require. This architecture describes how communicating machines can communicate with one another in a standardized and highly flexible way by defining the layers of software that should be implemented in each communicating machine.

There is no requirement on the part of any hardware or software vendor to adhere to the principles set forth by ISO's architecture. However, there is a worldwide trend in the computer industry today toward acceptance and conformance to the OSI model. The OSI model was adopted first by organizations outside the United States, but now U.S. computer manufacturers are increasingly working toward an acceptance of the OSI model.

The OSI model defines the seven independent software layers that are shown in Fig. 4.20. Each layer performs a different set of functions and is independent of any other layer. The OSI model does not define the software itself, nor does it define detailed standards for that software; it simply defines the broad categories of functions that each layer should perform. The OSI model can incorporate different sets of standards at each layer that are appropriate for given situations. In a very simple data communication system, for example, one that uses a simple point-to-point link, the software at many of the higher-level layers might be very simple or even nonexistent. In very complex systems, all seven layers can be implemented, some of which may contain highly complex software. Many alternative standards already exist for the various layers, and more are under development. Box 4.3 contains brief descriptions of the functions performed by each of the seven layers in the OSI model.

BOX 4.3   OSI Model software layers

- **Layer 7—Application.** The outermost layer, the one that user processes plug into, is the *application* layer. The application layer in a computer might consist of query software that an operator could use to request the retrieval of a person's salary from a personnel database. The application layer in a terminal might implement those control mechanisms that allow a person to enter a request for salary information and display the answer.

- **Layer 6—Presentation.** Software in the computer in the *presentation* layer might compress data or encypher it for security. Presentation-layer software in a terminal might reexpand the data and add screen formatting information.

- **Layer 5—Session.** Software in the *session* layer performs services that make possible an interaction between users. For example, the terminal user might start a session by specifying that payroll information is required.

- **Layer 4—Transport.** The *transport* layer pretends that there is a direct connection between the terminal control mechanisms and our query program. Software running in this layer is responsible for transmitting a message between one network user and another. For example, the salary request message entered by the terminal operator might be divided by transport-layer software into smaller units called *packets* for transmission through the network.

- **Layer 3—Network.** Software running in the *network* layer is responsible for transmitting a message, or an individual packet, from its source to its destination. Layer 3 provides a simple, standard interface to what might be a complex network. Layer 3 software might take a single packet of our salary request message and transmit it through the network from the location of the terminal to the location of the query program. The most commonly used standard for layer 3 and the layers below it is published by the CCITT and is called *Recommendation X.25. X.25* is widely used today in the implementation of networks that use a technique called *packet* switching. Packet switching and *Recommendation X.25* are discussed in detail in Chapter 37.

- **Layer 2—Data Link.** Software or hardware control mechanisms in the *data link* layer handle the physical transmission of frames over a single data link. A commonly used standard for the data link layer is called *high-level data link control* (HDLC). HDLC, one of the bit-oriented protocols described in Chapter 23, specifies the rules that must be followed in transmitting a single frame between one device and another over a single data link.

- **Layer 1—Physical.** Control mechanisms in the *physical* layer handle the electrical interface between a terminal and a modem. A commonly used standard for the physical layer is the EIA RS-232-C interface. It describes the electrical characteristics of 25 signals that can be used to connect a terminal to a modem.

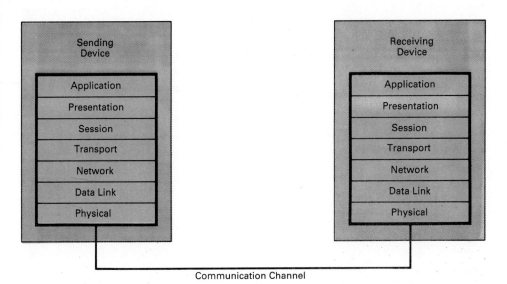

Figure 4.20　OSI model software layers

SYSTEMS NETWORK ARCHITECTURE

IBM's Systems Network Architecture (SNA) is an important network architecture because it is currently more widely used than any other. However, this is likely to change as support for the OSI model grows.

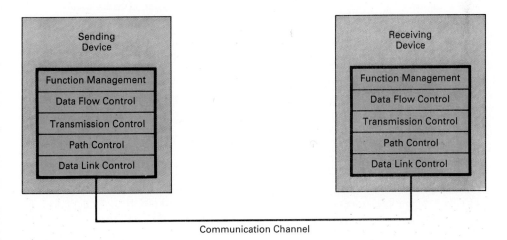

Figure 4.21　SNA software layers

SNA is similar to the OSI model in that it is an architecture for data communication systems that defines a framework into which a number of protocols fit. Many of the functions performed by SNA software have counterparts in the OSI layers. However, SNA software functions are divided up between the various layers somewhat differently. Figure 4.21 shows the major layers of software that are used in systems that conform to SNA. Box 4.4 contains brief descriptions of the functions performed at each of the six major SNA layers.

In addition to the five software layers that are defined by the SNA architecture, two other software layers, which operate outside of SNA's architectural

BOX 4.4   SNA software layers

- **Layer 5—Function Management.** The *function management* layer coordinates the interface between network users and the network, presents information to the user, controls and coordinates the activities of the network, and provides high-level services to the layers below it.

- **Layer 4—Data Flow Control.** The *data flow control* layer is concerned with the overall integrity of the flow of data during a session between two users. This can involve determining the mode of sending and receiving, managing groups of related messages, and determining what type of responses to use.

- **Layer 3—Transmission Control.** The *transmission control* layer keeps track of the status of sessions between users, controls the pacing of data flow, and sees that units of data are sent and received in the proper sequence. The transmission control layer also provides an optional data encryption/decryption facility.

- **Layer 2—Path Control.** The *path control* layer is concerned with routing data from one node to the next in the path that a message takes through the network. In a complex network, this path often passes over many separate data links through several nodes.

- **Layer 1—Data Link Control.** The *data link control* layer of SNA is comparable to the data link layer of the OSI model and is responsible for the transmission of data between two devices over a single physical link. A primary function of the data link control layer is to detect and recover from the transmission errors that inevitably occur. A standard for SNA's data link control layer is the *synchronous data link control* (SDLC) protocol. SDLC, another of the bit-oriented protocols described in Chapter 23, is a functional subset of HDLC used at the data link layer of the OSI model.

definition, are important when discussing an SNA system. The following are brief descriptions of these two software layers:

- **Physical Control.** Operating below SNA's lowest layer is a still-lower-level layer generally called the *physical control* layer. The physical control layer is comparable to the physical layer of the OSI model and addresses the transmission of bit streams over a physical circuit. The techniques used for physical transmission, although important, are defined outside the SNA architecture.

- **Application.** The *application* layer operates above the function management layer of SNA. The application layer represents the users—the application programs and the people that interface with the SNA network. As with the physical control layer, the application layer is not defined by the SNA architecture. Although this layer is important, it is defined outside SNA's architectural definition.

Do not be mislead because we have described seven software layers in discussing both the OSI model and SNA. Although the two architectures are quite similar at the physical and data link layers, they are quite incompatible at higher-level layers and distribute functions among the higher layers in different ways. It is possible that SNA and the OSI model will become more compatible over the years, especially as IBM supports more products that conform to the OSI reference model. But for the foreseeable future, the OSI model and SNA represent two fundamentally different network architectures.

This concludes our general discussion of today's data communication environment. The data communication systems of today are powerful and complex, and they employ many components. In Part II we begin a discussion of one of the most important components in any data communication system—the communication channel itself.

PART **II** CHANNEL
CHARACTERISTICS

5 THE CHANNEL AND ITS CAPACITY

Imagine someone with a long fire hose going into a building. Now let us suppose that this is not a firefighter, but an espionage agent who is trying to transmit data to an accomplice outside the building. Our espionage agent can send the data by means of a piston. As the piston at one end of the hose is pushed and pulled, the pulses are transmitted to a receiving piston at the other end.

Now, if the hose were absolutely rigid and the water in it absolutely incompressible, the movement of the receiving piston would follow exactly the movement of the sending piston. And if the water had no viscosity and moved completely without friction, the piston would be able to transmit pulses at a very high speed. However, a hose is not rigid; it is slightly elastic. And the water contains air bubbles and is slightly compressible. So the receiving piston does not follow exactly the movement of the transmitting piston. Furthermore, viscosity and friction prohibit the piston from moving and transmitting at a limitless speed. A communication line has properties that are loosely analogous to those of our fire hose.

THE IDEAL COMMUNICATION CHANNEL

What we would really like in constructing a data communication facility is a channel similar to our incompressible fire hose. Such a channel would have characteristics similar to those of the extremely high speed buses that connect the various pieces of equipment in the computer room. A device at one end of the connection generates a stream of bits that are transmitted at millions of bits per second to the other end, where they are interpreted correctly.

The purpose of a data communication channel is the same. We want to take a bit stream from a data processing machine at one location, and transmit that bit stream without error to another data processing machine at a distant location. If we had communication channels with capacities as high as the computer room buses, it would be possible to construct computing systems where the CPU might reside at one location with the disk drives located thousands of miles away.

**CHANNEL
CHARACTERISTICS**
Technical and economic factors generally make it necessary to transmit the bit streams much more slowly than data can be transmitted over the connections in the computer room. Electrical properties called *capacitance, resistance,* and *inductance* cause transmitted data to be distorted, just as data flowing along a fire hose would be distorted. A clean square-edged data pulse becomes distorted because of these factors as it travels down the communication path. When beginning, a pulse stream looks similar to this:

It ends up looking similar to this, with all the voltage transitions slurred:

At a slow transmission speed, we can still recognize each pulse and re-create the original square-edged signal. However, as the transmission speed increases, the signal distortion becomes greater and it becomes more and more difficult to detect the pulses without error. Furthermore, the impulses fade away as they travel down the line.

It might be possible to transmit data quite successfully at 5 bps over a 1000-foot fire hose, but if the hose were 3 miles long, the same technique would not work. Only a very slow bit rate would be detectable (see Fig. 5.1). In addition, there is *noise* on the line. Suppose that the fire hose is vibrating be-

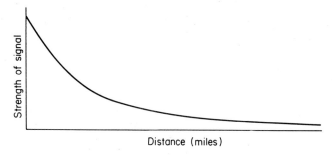

Figure 5.1 Signal strength versus distance

cause of the motion of a nearby pump. At high transmission speeds, the strength of the received pulses becomes comparable in magnitude with this vibration noise, and errors in the interpretation of the data will occur.

THERMAL NOISE   In all electronic circuitry, there is a constant background of random noise. The atoms and molecules of all substances vibrate constantly in a minute motion that causes the sensation of heat. The higher the temperature, the greater the vibration. As the atoms vibrate, they send out electromagnetic waves of all frequencies, forming what is called *thermal noise*. Thermal noise results in an unavoidable background to all electronic processes.

Data signals must be sent along with this small, but ceaseless random variation in signal strength. When heard, it sounds similar to a hiss. If the volume of an FM radio is turned up when no signal is being received, the hiss of this noise can be heard. If the signal falls in strength too much, it becomes irretrievably mixed up with the thermal noise. Once this happens, the two can never again be separated. If the signal is amplified, the noise will be amplified with it. Some processes in nature are irreversible, and this is one of them.

DIGITAL COMMUNICATION CHANNELS   Now, given these factors, how would a channel for transmitting computer data over long distances be built? Since we can transmit high bit rates only for relatively short distances before the noise and distortion interfere with the signal, we might provide *bit repeaters* at frequent intervals along the line.

A bit repeater is a device that detects the bits that are being sent and then retransmits them with their original strength and sharpness. The bit repeater catches the bit stream before it is submerged in the noise, and then separates it from the noise by creating it afresh. A very high bit rate can be transmitted over unlimited distances provided that the bit repeaters are sufficiently close together (see Fig. 5.2). In practice, the repeaters are small, solid-state devices that are very inexpensive when mass produced. A line that uses bit repeaters is called a digital line because it is designed to transmit bits. It cannot transmit music or speech unless they are first somehow converted into bits.

ANALOG COMMUNICATION CHANNELS   Unfortunately, most of the lines that are used to transmit data do not work this way. The most commonly used data communication channel is the ordinary telephone circuit. Its major function is to transmit the human voice, not computer data. With analog lines, *amplifiers* are used

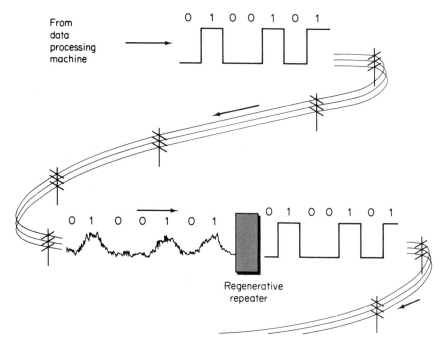

Figure 5.2 Regenerative repeaters

instead of bit repeaters. When the signal becomes too weak, it is amplified and sent on. The problem with amplifiers is that they amplify the noise and distortion as well as the original signal.

MODEMS

To use an analog line to transmit the discrete voltage levels that a data processing machine creates, the bits must first be converted into a continuous range of frequencies. As we learned in Chapter 1, the device that performs this conversion is called a *modem,* short for *modulator/demodulator.* The process of converting a digital bit stream into an analog signal is called *modulation.* The process of performing the opposite conversion at the other end is called *demodulation.* To connect two digital machines using an analog line, there must be a modem between the data machine and the line at each end (see Fig. 5.3).

THE CAPACITY OF A COMMUNICATION LINE

The capacity of a line is measured differently depending on whether the line is analog or digital in nature. A digital line is specifically designed to carry a given *bit rate,* so the capacity of a digital line is measured in *bits per second.* Some digital services

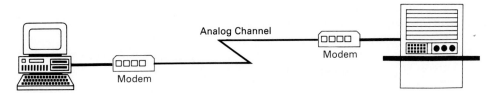

Figure 5.3   Modems

that are available today for data transmission transmit bits at 56,000 bps. And, as we have seen, the digital carriers used by common carriers for long-distance transmission of telephone traffic have capacities of millions of bits per second.

BANDWIDTH   Analog lines are designed to carry specific ranges of frequencies. The capacity of an analog line is measured by the range of frequencies that the line is designed to carry. This is called its *bandwidth*. For example, a standard telephone line is designed to carry the range of frequencies required to transmit human speech. This range is approximately from 300 to 3100 hertz (see Fig. 5.4). *Hertz* (Hz) is the term used for "cycles per second," which is the measure of frequency.

The difference between 3300 Hz and 300 Hz is 2800 Hz, or approximately 3 kilohertz (kHz), the bandwidth of a normal telephone line. (The bandwidth of a telephone channel is actually 4 kHz, but part of that bandwidth is used to

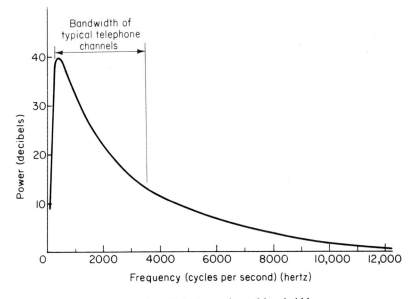

Figure 5.4   Telephone channel bandwidth

provide adequate separation between the channels when multiple channels share the same transmission facility.) The bandwidth of an analog channel is always the difference between the upper and lower limits of the frequencies it is designed to carry. If a line is designed to carry the frequencies between 80,300 and 83,100 Hz, its bandwidth is still approximately 3 kHz.

The number of bits per second that an analog line can carry is closely related to the line's bandwidth. However, the design of the modem also influences the bit rate. But in general, the higher the bandwidth, the higher the bit rate that can be carried. The relationship between bandwidth and bit rate is explored in more detail in Chapter 5.

THE ADVANTAGES OF DIGITAL TRANSMISSION

Just as there are modems to convert bit streams to and from analog signals, there are also devices called *codecs* that convert analog signals, such as telephone calls, to and from bit streams for transmission over digital circuits. Most of the world's telecommunications plant is analog in operation at present, and much of it will remain so for years to come because of the billions of dollars tied up in such equipment. But it is now clear that if we had it to do all over again, we would use digital transmission even for our telephone calls. Today, much of the long-distance telephone traffic is carried in digital form. When more and more of our telephone circuits are converted to digital transmission, the availability of high-speed, low-cost, data communication circuits will increase.

6 BASEBAND TRANSMISSION

When signals are carried on a transmission line in their original form, this is known as *baseband* signaling. The local loops of the public telephone network, which connect subscribers with their switching offices, typically carry baseband signals. Other lines, such as the links between toll offices, do not carry baseband signals. They use higher frequencies to carry many signals simultaneously. Privately laid wires in an office or factory may also carry baseband signals. In this chapter we discuss dc (direct-current) signals carried in a baseband fashion. As we will see, dc voltages can be used to transmit data directly in digital form without first converting the data into analog signals.

We sometimes use the terms *mark* and *space* to refer to the two line conditions that are used to carry digital data directly. For example, a mark might refer to the *presence* of a voltage and a space as the *absence* of a voltage. In another scheme, a mark might refer to a negative voltage and a space to a positive voltage. Many implementations of dc signaling use the mark condition on the line to represent a one bit and the space condition to represent a zero bit. There are more sophisticated systems that use a *transition* from a mark to a space or from a space to a mark to represent a one bit and the absence of a transition to represent a zero bit.

There is one advantage to sending signals in a dc form—it is simple and inexpensive. If the signals from a data processing machine are converted to an analog form in which they are "carried" by higher frequencies, modems are needed at each end of the line to convert the signals to analog form and then to convert them back again after transmission. If dc signaling is used, the cost of the modems can be avoided.

Dc signals can be sent over wire pairs of a few miles in length at speeds of up to 300 bps without harmful distortion. The speed can be increased enormously by using coaxial cables rather than wire pairs or by installing a regenerative repeater every few thousand feet on a wire pair. Baseband dc signals cannot be sent over lines that use amplifiers.

As the square-edged pulses travel along the communication line, they become distorted. The pulses received at the other end are far from square edged, and if the line is too long, the signals too weak, or the transmitting speed too great, the received signal may be unrecognizable and wrongly interpreted by the machine at the other end. The factors mainly responsible for the distortion are the *capacitance, inductance,* and *leakage* associated with the line used for transmission.

LINE CAPACITANCE

Let us first discuss the capacitance of the line. This is the main cause of distortion. The cable acts rather like the fire hose from Chapter 5. Because of the cable's "capacity," when electricity is applied at one end, we can think of it as if a certain amount is needed to fill it up before the result is detectable at the other end. Let us suppose that a short section of line is represented by the resistance, R, and electrical capacity, C, as shown in Fig. 6.1.

As is shown in elementary electricity books, when a battery of voltage V is connected across a capacitor of capacity C and resistance R, the current, I, flows until the capacitor is fully charged. It starts at a high value, momentarily $I = V/R$, and falls until it approaches zero, at which time the capacitor is fully charged. The equation for the current at a time, t, after the voltage was applied is

$$I = \frac{V}{R} e^{-t/RC}$$

Similarly, the current, I, received in Fig. 6.1, is

$$I = \frac{V}{R} (1 - e^{-t/RC})$$

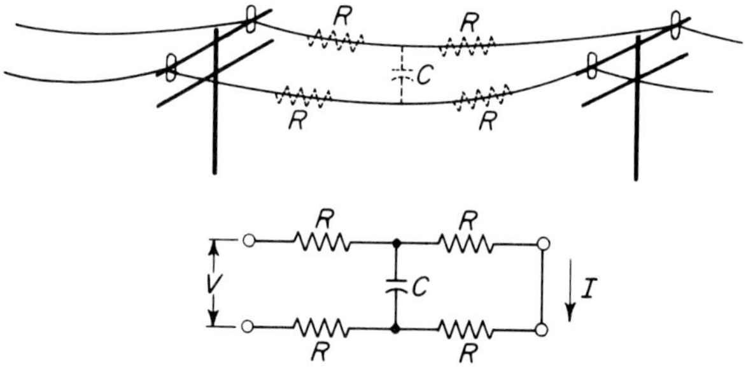

Figure 6.1 Line capacitance

If the voltage at the sending end is now suddenly removed, the current at the receiving end does not cease instantly but dies slowly because of the discharge of the capacitance. The equation for the falling current is

$$I = \frac{V}{R} e^{-t/RC}$$

This buildup and decay of current is shown in Fig. 6.2. The square-edged pulse transmitted is nothing like square edged when it is received at the other end.

The constant RC in the preceding equations is referred to as the *time constant* of the circuit and is a measure of the time taken for the current to build up to $1 - 1/e = 0.6321$ of its final value, or to decay to $1/e = 0.3669$ of its original value. The time of buildup or decay of these levels is thus proportional to both the resistance and the capacitance of the line.

Where the transmission line consists of an open pair of wires hanging from telegraph poles, the capacitance in question is between these two conductors separated by several inches of air. As in the case of an ordinary electrical capacitor, the capacitance is larger if the size of the conductors is larger and also when the distance between the conductors is smaller. If the wires are in a cable, as is now usually the case, the capacitance will be much greater because the wires are closer together and the insulating material has a higher dielectric constant than air. When the first submarine cables were laid in the sea, they had a much poorer performance than was anticipated because the presence of seawater increased the effective capacitance of the cable.

The preceding illustration is oversimplified. However, it serves to demonstrate the point that if the pulses representing data are too short in duration, or if there are too many pulses sent per second, the pulses become indistinguishable when they are received, as illustrated in Fig. 6.3.

In practice, there will be resistance across the receiving end, such as the resistance of the receiving equipment. The transmitting end will also have some resistance. Both of these increase the time constant.

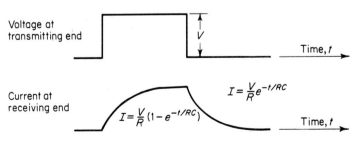

Figure 6.2   Distortion of a dc pulse due to capacitance

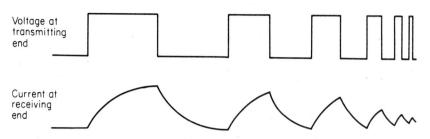

Figure 6.3   Capacitance versus transmission speed

LINE INDUCTANCE

In addition to capacitance and resistance, there is inductance associated with the line, although this is generally of less importance than the capacitance. Inductance in a circuit resists the sudden buildup of current. Current in an inductive circuit produces a magnetic field. A coil of wire in a circuit is an inductance; it is a much stronger inductance if it surrounds magnetic material. Large inductances that form part of electronic circuits are constructed by wrapping many thousands of turns of fine wire around a heavy, laminated, highly magnetic core. When a battery of voltage V is applied across a circuit with resistance R and inductance L, the current grows as shown in the equation

$$I = \frac{V}{R}\left(1 - e^{-(R/L)t}\right)$$

When the battery is removed, the current does not cease immediately but dies away slowly as the magnetic field built up by the current collapses. The energy stored in the magnetic field is dissipated in the circuit. The current falls as shown in the equation

$$I = \frac{V}{R}e^{-(R/L)t}$$

ARRIVAL CURVE

The properties of a given dc communication line are somewhat more complex than would be suggested by the preceding simple equations, and the transient effects of resistance, capacitance, inductance, and leakage from the line due to not-quite-perfect insulation may be summarized in an *arrival curve*. Such a curve is illustrated in Fig. 6.4. This shows the growth of current at the receiving end of a line when a steady voltage is suddenly applied across the transmitting end. The right-hand side of the diagram shows the decay of current when the voltage is then suddenly removed. There is an interval between the switching-on of the voltage and the start of the current growth at the other end. This is referred to as the *propaga-*

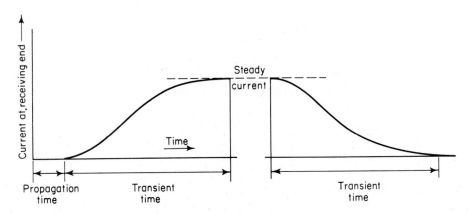

Figure 6.4   Arrival curve

tion time and is, in effect, the time the signal takes to pass down the line. The periods during which the current is building up, or decaying, are called the *transient times*. From the shape of the arrival curve for a particular line, its response to any voltage change can be evaluated. The exact shape of the arrival curve is difficult to calculate theoretically for a particular line, but it can be measured experimentally, and it can be recorded with an oscillograph.

Knowing the shape of the arrival curve for a given line, the distortion that a bit pattern will suffer can be plotted by adding, then subtracting the arrival curve for the various input voltage changes. This is done in Fig. 6.5. The resulting current at the receiving end can be used to operate a relay. The threshold

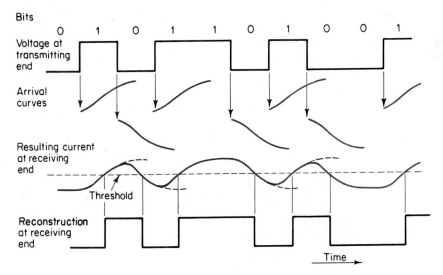

Figure 6.5   Baseband transmission of data

currcnt for rclay opening and closing is the dashed line through the curve of received current in Fig. 6.5. When the current is greater than this, the relay closes, thus reconstructing a sharp voltage change equivalent to the input.

If the bit rate transmitted were twice as great as that in Fig. 6.5, it would not be possible to set a threshold level for relay operation that would give the resulting correct bit pattern. The input pulse duration would be too small relative to the transient time of the line. This was a condition that prevented the correct operation of some of the early submarine cables. The first cable from England to France was laid in 1850 after some difficulty. A receiving device was connected to it by an excited group on the French coast, and a message was sent from the founder of the cable-laying company to Prince Louis Napoleon Bonaparte. The transient time of the cable in water was greater than had been anticipated, however, and to the group's bewilderment the receiver produced gibberish. Before the reason for the trouble was discovered, moreover, a fisherman's anchor pulled on the line, and the fisherman hauled it aboard his ship in astonishment and cut out a section to show his friends!

KELVIN'S LAW

The transient time is affected mainly by the capacitance, resistance, and length of the line. In 1855, Kelvin produced a famous law of telegraphy saying that for a line of negligible inductance and leakage and negligible terminal impedance, the maximum operating speed is inversely proportional to CRl^2, where C is the capacitance per unit length, R is the resistance per unit length, and l is the length. So to transmit at a given rate, a given line must not exceed a certain length. If it is desired to transmit over a distance greater than this, a repeater must be inserted in the line.

As we learned in Chapter 5, a device that reconstructs and retransmits a dc signal is called a *regenerative repeater*. This is true of modern electronic circuits as well as of the older relay circuits. A repeater that is not regenerative simply amplifies the signal and corrects certain types of distortion that have occurred but does not reconstruct a new, sharp-edged pulse train.

BIAS DISTORTION

Because of the shape of the arrival curve, distortion can occur in the length of the bits received. This is illustrated in Fig. 6.6. As a mark changes to a space there will be a slight delay in the falling off of the received voltage, so the receiving machine will begin its space slightly late. Similarly, the buildup of voltage when a space changes to a mark will not be instantaneous, so the receiving machine will begin its mark slightly late. Let us suppose that the sampling threshold of the receiving circuit is set too high. As shown in Fig. 6.6, this will cause the space-to-mark transition to be slightly later than the mark-to-space transition. Hence the re-

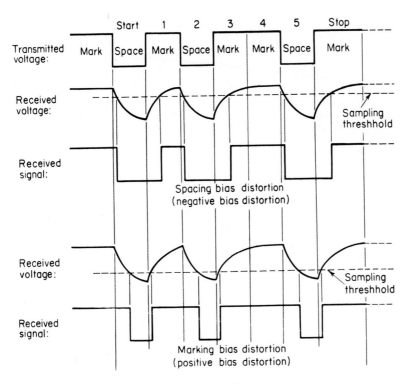

Figure 6.6   Bias distortion

ceived spaces will be longer than the marks. Similarly, if the threshold is set too low, the marks will be elongated at the expense of the spaces.

This effect will be greater the higher the transmission speed and the higher the value of CRl^2. It may also become bad when there are several telegraph links in tandem. If the bias distortion becomes too bad, this will result in incorrect reception of data.

LOADING   Losses of the type described above are much higher in twisted-wire-pair circuits than in open-wire lines because the capacitance is greater. There are a number of ways of reducing CR, and hence of reducing the loss. The resistance can be decreased by using larger cable conductors. The capacitance can be decreased by increasing the separation of the conductors. Both of these approaches are used on wires strung between telegraph poles, but there is a practical limit as to how far apart the wires can be and how heavy or expensive they can be. In cables, enlarging the conductor or the spacing between conductors decreases the number of separate circuits that can be carried in one cable, so again there is a limit to what can be done.

In 1886, Heaviside proved that the distortion can be minimized by causing the relationship between the inductance and capacitance of the line to satisfy the equation

$$RC = LG$$

where L is the inductance per unit length, R the resistance per unit length, C the capacitance per unit length, and G the shunt conductance per unit length, sometimes known as the *leakance*, a measure of the leakage between conductors on the line.

RC has already been made as small as possible, but it is still large compared with LG on a conventional telegraph or telephone line. The inductance and leakage are both very small. It is undesirable to increase the leakage of the line, as this would diminish the signal; therefore, to satisfy the equation $RC = LG$, the inductance is increased.

The first important application of Heaviside's work was to submarine cables. These had no repeaters, so distortion was a severe problem. To increase their inductance, iron wire was wound around their core. At a later date, materials with better magnetic properties were discovered, and today more modern cables have a thin permalloy or mumetal tape wrapped helically around the conducting core. This has a high magnetic permeability. By this means, cable transmission speeds can generally be increased by a factor of 4. Some of the early cable designs were speeded up 8 to 10 times.

Adding inductance to a cable is referred to as "loading" it. Wrapping magnetic tapes or wires around a cable is too expensive for most purposes, and it is found satisfactory to insert loading coils at intervals along the cable. The inductance of, and the distance between, loading coils are chosen to minimize the distortion on the line and so permit high-speed transmission over the line. Often, the loading coil consists of a ring of powdered permalloy of high magnetic permeability wrapped around with copper wire. Such coils are often fitted at intervals of a mile or so on cable circuits. Open-wire pairs are not normally loaded because their capacitance is much smaller and because their characteristics tend to change with adverse weather conditions. In general, for any type of communication line, a lessening of distortion on the line means that a higher transmission rate can be achieved, and the likelihood of errors is less.

DIGITAL CHANNEL CHARACTERISTICS

As we have already discussed, most of the world's telecommunications facilities are analog in nature, mainly for historical reasons. There are two principal reasons why it is economically advantageous for common carriers to switch from analog to digital transmission in the telephone network. First, the circuitry used to switch and multiplex digital signals is much cheaper than are the complex amplifiers and filters used to handle analog signals. As the cost of microelectronics drops, digital techniques become more attractive. Second, the use of data transmission is increasing rapidly. It is obviously more efficient to carry computer data in its original digital form. The transmission facilities that use digital techniques and the methods used for carrying telephone signals in the form of bit streams are discussed in Chapter 13.

Now that we have discussed the relatively simple techniques of baseband signaling, in Chapter 7 we discuss the more commonly used technique of carrying analog signals using carrier frequencies.

7 ANALOG TRANSMISSION

Light, sound, radio waves, and analog signals passing along telephone wires are all described in terms of *frequencies*. In all these means of transmission, the *instantaneous amplitude* of the signal at a given point oscillates rapidly, just as the displacement of a plucked violin string oscillates. The rate of oscillation is referred to as the frequency and described in terms of *cycles per second,* or *hertz,* abbreviated Hz. One thousand cycles per second is called a kilohertz (kHz), and 1 million cycles per second is called a megahertz (MHz).

With light we see different frequencies as different *colors*. Violet light has a higher frequency than green; green has a higher frequency than red. With sound, higher frequencies are heard as higher *pitch*. A flute makes sounds of higher frequency than those produced by a trombone.

HARMONICS

Normally, the light and sound reaching our senses do not consist of a single frequency but of many frequencies: in fact, a continuous band of frequencies traveling together. A violin note has many *harmonics* that are higher than the basic frequency with which the violin string is vibrating. The human voice consists of a jumble of different frequencies. When we see a red light, it is not one frequency but a collection of frequencies that combine to give this particular shade of red. The same is true of the electrical and radio signals of telecommunications. Usually, we will not be discussing a single frequency but a collection, or band, of frequencies occupying a given range.

THE SPEECH SPECTRUM

The human ear can detect sounds over a range of frequencies; in other words, it can hear sounds of different pitch. A sensitive ear can hear sounds of frequencies ranging from about 30 Hz up to about 20,000 Hz, although most people have a range somewhat less than this.

When the sound of a given frequency is referred to, this means that the air is vibrating with that number of oscillations per second. To transmit this sound, the microphone of a telephone converts the sound into an equivalent number of electrical oscillations per second. Then the telephone channels over which we wish to send data are designed to transmit electrical oscillations of a range equivalent to the frequencies of the human voice. However, these frequencies are often changed for transmission purposes.

TELEPHONE CIRCUITS As we discussed earlier, telephone circuits do not transmit the entire range of the human voice. This is unnecessary for the understanding of speech and recognition of the speaker. Figure 7.1 illustrates the characteristics of human speech and shows that its strength is different at different frequencies. (The strength of a signal is measured in *decibels*. We discuss decibels in more detail later.)

Most of the energy of human speech is concentrated between the frequencies 300 and 3100 Hz, and each telephone channel is designed to transmit approximately this range. Telephone companies made this decision based on economics. It permits the maximum number of telephone conversations to be sent at one instant over a transmission medium while still making the human voice intelligible and the speaker recognizable.

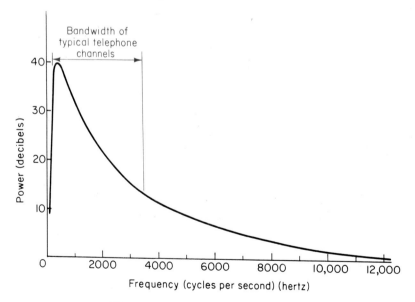

Figure 7.1 Spectrum of human speech

THE SINE WAVE   A signal of a given frequency can be represented mathematically by a diagram of a *sine wave*. Two typical sine waves are shown in Fig. 7.2. The vertical axis of each sine-wave diagram plots the *amplitude* of each signal. The horizontal axis plots a time interval. The number of peaks that occur in the sine wave in each second define the *frequency* of the signal.

    The two sine waves in Fig. 7.2 each depict signals of identical frequency. However, notice that their *peaks* occur at different times along the horizontal axes of the diagrams. These two signals are said to be different in *phase*.

SIGNAL STRENGTH   The unit normally used for expressing the *strength* of a signal in telecommunications is the *decibel* (dB). This unit is also used to quote gains and losses in signal strength. Spectrum diagrams such as the one we looked at in Fig. 7.1 normally plot decibels on the vertical axis. The unit measures *differences* in signal strengths, not the absolute strength of a signal. The decibel is a logarithmic unit, not a linear one.

    The decibel was first used as a unit referring to sound. It makes sense to refer to sound levels by a logarithmic unit because the response of the human ear is proportional to the logarithm of the sound energy, not to the energy itself. If one noise sounds twice as great as another, it is approximately 2 dB greater but is much more than twice the power. The sound energy reaching someone's ears in a New York subway train might be 10,000 times greater than in a quiet room, but it does not sound 10,000 times greater. It actually sounds about 40

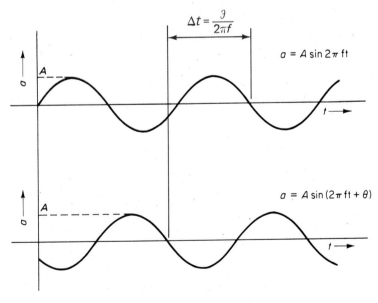

Figure 7.2   Two sine waves

times greater—someone would have to shout 40 times harder to be heard by a person some distance away. Ten thousand times the sound energy is called ''40 dB greater.''

Figure 7.3 shows the intensities of some common sounds measured in decibels relative to the threshold of human hearing. As with sound, the relative strength of electronic signals is referred to using logarithmic units because the signal strength falls off logarithmically as it passes down a cable.

BANDWIDTH

Whereas a frequency range of 300 to 3100 Hz is satisfactory for voice transmission, music transmitted with only these frequencies would sound poor because it would be clipped of the higher and lower frequencies which give it its quality. To reproduce faithfully the deep notes of a double bass, we need to go down to 30 Hz. To reproduce the high harmonics that make instruments sound realistic, a frequency of up to 15,000 Hz, or better, 20,000 Hz, is desirable. It is toward these extremities that high-fidelity enthusiasts strive.

AM radio transmits sound frequencies up to 5 kHz and thus is capable of reproducing music that does not sound too distorted, but could hardly be called ''high-fidelity.'' FM radio can produce the entire range needed for high-fidelity reproduction. We say that AM radio uses a *bandwidth* of 5 kHz, whereas FM has a *bandwidth* of approximately 18 kHz.

As we noted in Chapter 5, the bandwidth of an analog channel refers to the *range* of frequencies that are transmitted. A telephone channel capable of sending signals from 300 to 3100 Hz has a bandwidth of approximately 3 kHz. The bandwidth of a channel does not have anything to do with the actual frequencies that are used for transmission, but only with the difference between the lower and upper limits of the range. For example, the waves of FM radio do not actually travel at frequencies of 30 to 18,000 Hz. The transmission occurs at frequencies of approximately 100 million hertz. A similar consideration is true with AM radio and with high-frequency media used as carriers of telephone signals.

CARRIER FREQUENCIES

The transmission media can work efficiently only at high frequencies of approximately 70 to 150 MHz. Somehow this high frequency must be made to carry the lower frequencies. This is done through the process of *modulation*. The low frequencies *modulate* the high frequency, which is known as the *carrier frequency*. In this way, the modulation process produces a signal that can be transmitted efficiently and from which, after transmission, the original lower frequencies can be recovered.

Let us suppose that a bandwidth of 4000 Hz is to be used for voice transmission, and that the carrier frequency is 30 kHz. The conversion process might

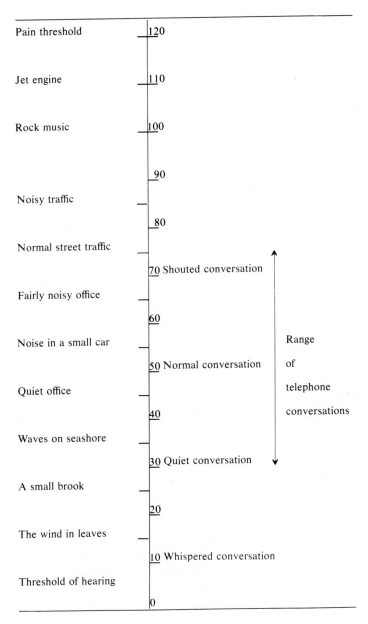

Figure 7.3 The intensity of common sounds

change the frequency band from 0 to 4000 Hz to 30,000 to 34,000 Hz. The bandwidth is still 4000 Hz and will still carry the same quantity of information, whether voice or data.

MULTIPLEXING

The physical cables and radio links that common carriers use for transmitting signals have a high bandwidth—many times higher than the 4-kHz bandwidth needed for telephone speech. To use them economically, many speech channels are transmitted together as a single signal occupying all the available bandwidth of the physical facility. For efficiency, the speech channels are packed together as tightly as possible, like sardines in a tin. Each speech channel occupies no more than 4 kHz of the available bandwidth.

The term *multiplexing* refers to any process that permits more than one separate signal to be transmitted simultaneously over a single physical channel. One type of multiplexing is called *space-division multiplexing*. With this simple multiplexing method, multiple physical circuits are carried in the same cable. For example, a telephone cable may contain 100 or more wire pairs, each of which carries a separate signal. In another method that is commonly used, called *frequency-division multiplexing*, each speech channel is raised in frequency to a 4-kHz slot assigned to it (see Fig. 7.4). All of these slots can then be carried simultaneously over a single circuit. We describe it, and other multiplexing methods, in detail in Chapters 9 and 27.

MODULATION

As we have already noted, speech frequencies are converted to the higher frequencies necessary for transmission through a process called *modulation*. A sine wave at the high frequency is modified by the speech to be transmitted in such a way that the higher frequencies "carry" the speech frequencies. In Fig. 7.4 three carriers are shown, having frequencies of 30, 34, and 38 kHz. Each is modulated by the speech band at frequencies of 300 to 3100 Hz, to form a block of frequencies slightly higher than the carrier frequency. The 30,000-Hz carrier is modulated to give a signal in the range 30,300 to 33,100 Hz, and so on. These three signals are transmitted together in a block of frequencies ranging from 30,000 to 42,000 Hz (or larger). After transmission, the signals are separated and demodulated to give three signals again, each ranging from 300 to 3100 Hz. Of course, in actual practice, many more than three different signals would be carried together over a channel of much higher bandwidth than in this example.

MODULATION TECHNIQUES

There are several methods that can be used to modulate a carrier frequency. The techniques used in AM and FM radio illustrate two of the most common

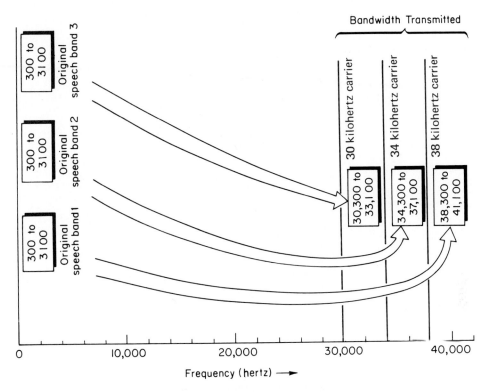

Figure 7.4 Telephone multiplexing

methods. *AM* and *FM* stand for *amplitude modulation* and *frequency modulation,* respectively. *Tuning* is the process of selecting one channel from the many that are received simultaneously at different frequencies. Amplitude modulation and frequency modulation, as well as other modulation methods, are also used for sending data over telecommunications links. Different modulation methods have different advantages, depending on the system needs, and the system planner might be faced with having to choose between modulation methods.

THE BANDWIDTH OF A TELEPHONE CHANNEL A telephone call can pass through many different multiplexing processes between its source and its destination. The multiplexing is engineered to precise standards, however, and the properties of the channels that users perceive are remarkably similar, no matter what processes were used to provide the channel.

Figure 7.5 shows the properties of a typical channel that has passed through multiplexing equipment. It shows how the signal strength varies with frequency. There is little attenuation of the signal between 300 and 3100 Hz,

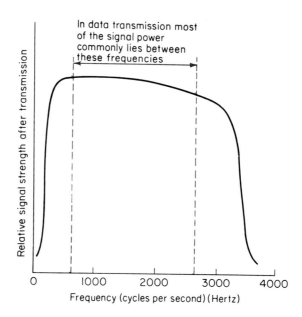

Figure 7.5   Telephone signal amplitude variation

but outside those limits its strength falls off rapidly. The main energy of human speech lies within this frequency range.

The electronics of the telephone plant have deliberately chopped the signal up into the shape of Fig. 7.5 so that it fits completely into 4-kHz slices. As we have mentioned, 4 kHz is a slightly larger slice than is absolutely necessary to carry human speech. This safety margin is used to provide comfortable gaps between the channels. The gaps are needed to minimize interference, or *cross-talk,* between channels.

LOCAL LOOPS   Normally, multiplexing is used only between tele-
                        phone switching offices. If a local call is made, em-
ploying only local loops to the telephone exchange, a much larger bandwidth than 4 kHz could be obtained. However, some lengthy local loops have *loading coils* connected to them that reduce the potential bandwidth of the local loops. Loading coils provide a means of decreasing the attenuation of a wire-pair line and holding it close to constant over a given frequency range. Its main purpose is to combat the effect of the capacitance between the wires. Local loops from subscriber to central office can have loading coils spaced about every 6000 feet. Figure 7.6 shows the difference in signal attenuation between a loaded wire pair operating at voice frequencies and the same wire pair unloaded.

For a certain band of frequencies, it is obvious that the attenuation on the loaded line is less than on the unloaded line and is also fairly constant. Above

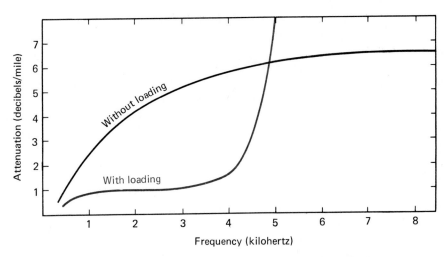

Figure 7.6   The effect of loading on a wire-pair local loop

a certain frequency, however, the attenuation rises fast. The combination of the capacitance of the line and the inductance of the loading coil causes the line to act like a low-pass filter. In other words, it transmits signals of frequencies up to a given cutoff point, and above that attenuation increases greatly. The loading coil must be selected for the particular frequency band that is to be transmitted. It would be quite different on a line that is to carry one voice channel from a line that carries several.

If the loading coils are removed from a local loop, frequencies up to 1 MHz or so can be transmitted. But the local loop would then not be as useful for normal voice transmission. In fact, when AT&T initiated Picturephone service, it removed the loading coils from the local loops that supplied service to its Picturephone customers. To transmit such high frequencies, the signal levels must be coordinated carefully to avoid interference with other services that can be using the higher frequencies on other wire pairs in the same cable. Generally, the *gain,* or *amplification,* has to be equalized at short intervals.

A data transmission rate of 250,000 bps is generally attainable over local loops on which the telephone company has removed the loading coils. This type of local loop provides the local distribution of the AT&T *Dataphone Digital Service,* which we discuss in Chapter 16. This service provides users with bit rates up to 56,000 bps. In effect, the lines that were initially constructed to carry analog signals are modified to carry a digital signal instead.

CAPACITIVE COUPLING   A second factor that limits high-speed digital transmission over local loops is the capacitive coupling between the wire pairs carrying high data rates and the other wire pairs in the same cable. To avoid this problem, rules are necessary to select which wires in the cable are permitted to be used for high-speed data.

In most cases, whether or not a line is loaded is strictly the concern of the common carrier. However, in some instances, the system designer might have to take loading into consideration on short lines. Some computer manufacturers' specifications for short-distance line equipment state that the lines must be non-loaded. This is generally intended for lines less than about 8 miles in length.

SENDING DATA THROUGH TELEPHONE CHANNELS

When data is sent over ordinary telephone channels, the digital data must be converted into analog signals that must fit into the 4-kHz bandwidth that we have been discussing. Because telephone channels are so widespread, it is desirable to have a method that will enable the highest data rate to be squeezed into the available bandwidth, but without incurring an excessive error rate.

This is normally achieved through another modulation process, similar to the process used by the telephone company in converting the speech spectrum into the frequency range used in the transmission medium. This time, however, the modulation process converts the bit stream produced by a data machine into audible tones that can be transmitted over a standard telephone channel.

MODEMS

As we discussed earlier, the device used to do this is called a *modulator/demodulator,* or *modem* for short (see Fig. 7.7). Some telephone companies, AT&T for one, have referred to the modem as a *data set.* This is an unfortunate choice of terminology, since in many operating systems, the term *data set* is used to refer to data files. Fortunately, this use of the term is now seldom seen.

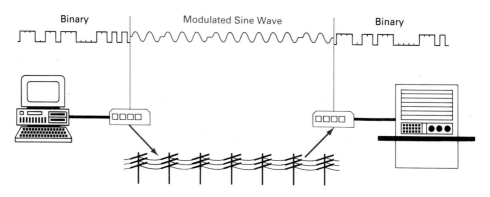

Figure 7.7 Modulation and demodulation

A modem to be used on a speech channel converts the bit stream produced by a data processing machine into a modulated sine-wave carrier that fits within the allowable frequencies that can be sent over a standard 4-kHz speech channel. Modems designed to operate on speech channels generally transmit data at speeds up to 9600 bps.

Modems are designed and manufactured both by common carriers and by manufacturers of data processing equipment. Many data processing machines, including many personal computers, have built-in modems.

TWO SEPARATE MODULATION PROCESSES

It is interesting to note that the bits that are sent between two data processing machines over a standard telephone channel must undergo two quite separate modulation processes. The first process is carried out on the user's premises in modems that allow the data processing machines to transmit digital information over the analog telephone channel. The telephone company then subjects this resulting analog signal to another modulation process in the multiplexing equipment that converts the speech frequencies into the high frequencies used for actual transmission.

The user can exercise control over only one of these processes, which is in the choice of the modem to be used. What the telephone company does with the signal after it enters their lines is not under the user's control.

THE EFFECT OF LIMITED BANDWIDTH

To perceive the effect of limited bandwidth on data transmission, let us discuss what might happen if we tried to transmit the sound of a violin over channels having different bandwidths. The sound of a middle C note has a frequency of 200 Hz. If we want to transmit the sound produced by the middle C violin string with absolute accuracy, we must not only transmit the frequency 200 Hz, but we must transmit all of its harmonics as well. In addition to vibrating at the frequency of 200 Hz, the violin string is also vibrating at 400 Hz, 600 Hz, 800 Hz, and so on. In practice, we need not transmit *all* of the harmonics, as the amplitudes of the higher harmonics are quite small and become much smaller as they become higher and higher in frequency. So we can transmit a reasonable facsimile of the original sound by transmitting only a subset of the harmonics, which are those that are greater than some given amplitude.

The middle C violin note sounds very realistic when reproduced over a hi-fi unit with a bandwidth of 18,000 Hz. It is still quite recognizable as a violin when transmitted over an AM radio channel with a bandwidth of 5000 Hz. If someone played the violin over the telephone, where the effective bandwidth is about 2800 Hz, the sound would be barely recognizable as a violin. If a violin were listened to over an even-lower-bandwidth channel, say 600 Hz, the note would definitely not be recognizable as being produced by a violin, but would still be recognizable as middle C.

BANDWIDTH AND BIT RATE

A similar situation exists in data transmission as well. We have a limited bandwidth available, and we want to transmit the maximum number of bits per second over it. We do not, therefore, transmit all the harmonics, only enough for the bits to be recognizable as such.

Figure 7.8 shows how bits are likely to become distorted on an actual transmission system. Suppose that pulses are transmitted such as those shown at the top of the diagram. The data rate is 2000 bps. If we transmit the fourth harmonic, as shown at the bottom of the figure, the resulting pulse shape is reasonably close to the original. It would be much closer if we, for example, transmitted the eighth harmonic. To transmit the fourth harmonic, a bandwidth of about 8000 Hz is needed, and for the eighth harmonic, about 16,000 Hz. With a bandwidth of 4000 Hz, the pulses are reasonably like the original, and with good equipment, a 2000-Hz bandwidth could still be detected as consisting of one bits or zero bits. At 1000 Hz, the pulses bear little resemblance to their original shape, but skillfully designed detection equipment might recover the original bits. At 500 Hz there is no hope of reconstructing the original.

NOISE AND DISTORTION

The diagram we have been using does not show the effects of noise and distortion; only the effects of limited bandwidth are shown. Noise and distortion can change the shape of the pulses, sometimes severely. The probability of error in the recognition of the bits will be greater with misshapen bits transmitted over smaller bandwidths.

In actual practice, it is generally possible to transmit bits at the rate of 9600 bps over a standard 4000-Hz telephone channel. But at this high rate a leased line is generally required. This is because the noise and distortion can be better controlled over a leased line. Also, more of 4-kHz bandwidth is actually available. When switched lines are used, some of the frequencies in the 4-kHz range are used for control and switching purposes. When the circuit is connected permanently, as it is on a leased line, these switching frequencies can be used by the modem for the transmission of data.

A data rate of up to 9600 bps can be sent over switched lines, but at the expense of a higher error rate. As we will explain later, errors in the bits can be detected, and the data resent. However, when some of the same messages must be sent twice, an *effective* transmission rate results, which is less than the 9600 bps at which the bits are actually sent.

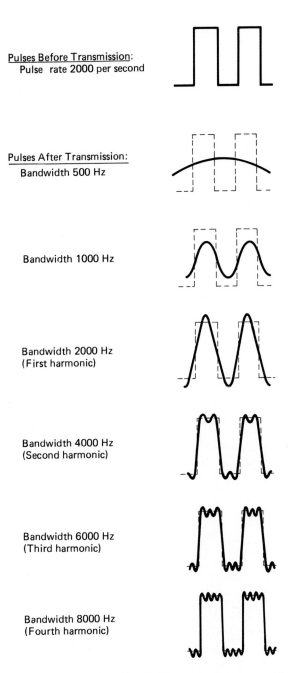

Pulses Before Transmission:
Pulse rate 2000 per second

Pulses After Transmission:
Bandwidth 500 Hz

Bandwidth 1000 Hz

Bandwidth 2000 Hz
(First harmonic)

Bandwidth 4000 Hz
(Second harmonic)

Bandwidth 6000 Hz
(Third harmonic)

Bandwidth 8000 Hz
(Fourth harmonic)

Figure 7.8　The effect of bandwidth on transmission quality

8 CHANNEL
       SPEEDS

One of the ways in which communication channels differ is in the speed at which data can be transmitted over them. In this chapter we examine the different uses that can be made of channels of various speeds. We also see what factors determine the maximum speed of a given channel.

Telecommunications channels of a wide variety of transmission rates, or bandwidths, are desirable. As we have seen, the most commonly used channels are the 4-kHz channels specifically designed for telephone speech. In the future, however, with data networks, private microwave channels, communications satellites, and optical fibers, a wide variety of channel speeds will be used.

HUMAN CHANNEL RATES
In many cases it is useful if transmission rates can be geared to the speed at which human beings can absorb information. Different transmissions for human consumption require different rates. The eye can absorb about 1000 times as much information as the ear, and high-fidelity stereophonic sound contains about 10 times as much information as telephone sound. "High-fidelity" wall-screen television would require 10 times the bandwidth of today's television—and today's television more than 10 times that of high-fidelity sound.

Figure 8.1 illustrates the human capacity for communication and storage of information. A young person's ear can hear about 20 kHz of sound, which could be coded into about 200,000 bps. With elaborate encoding, 10,000 bps can give intelligible speech input, with the speaker's voice being recognizable. The eye requires far more. Even with highly elaborate coding, more than 100 million bits per second would be required to represent the image we see—for example, to encode a wide-screen movie. Nevertheless, an interesting visual image can be transmitted with a channel speed of about 1 million bits per second.

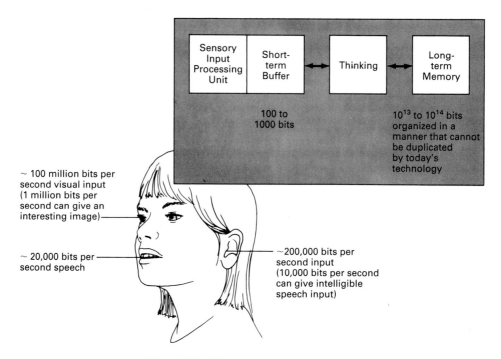

Figure 8.1   Human communication capacity

Sensory input is automatically processed and sifted before being stored in the brain's long-term memory. It appears to be stored in a highly compacted form with remarkable retrieval capabilities that we cannot imitate today with electronics. The brain has a limited capability to retain facts and figures as it receives them, and uses a *short-term buffer* for this purpose. This short-term buffer is part of the brain's sensory input apparatus and we use it heavily in conversation with other people and in dialogs with machines.

TRANSMISSION-RATE REQUIREMENTS   A given piece of information is conveyed to human beings, sometimes using a low transmission capacity and sometimes using a large capacity. For example, if we watch 5 minutes of a television talk show, a message might be conveyed to us. To transmit television signals digitally requires 92.5 million bps. The 5 minutes therefore requires 27.75 billion bits. The same message can be transmitted over a telephone line in 5 minutes of conversation. If the line is digital, operating at 56,000 bps, the message requires about 16.8 million bits.

Human conversation is highly redundant, and if the person with the message to convey is better organized, the message might be spoken in perhaps 120 words, taking about 1 minute. The message in this form requires only 3.36 million bits.

Taking yet another step, the 120 words could be sent using data transmission techniques. Using a typical coding scheme, this would take 4800 bits. If a tighter code is used, the message might be sent in 3000 bits. If message compaction techniques are used, the message could be sent in less than 1000 bits.

So, basically, the same message could be sent using 5 minutes of an extremely high capacity 92.5-million-bps television channel or slightly more than one-fifth of a second of a very ordinary 4800-bps data transmission channel.

CHANNEL SPEEDS   So in today's communications world, many different types of signals are transmitted. By their nature, they require widely differing transmission rates or bandwidths. So far, data communication applications have used a fairly restricted range of speeds. The most common speeds are the telegraph channel speeds of 45, 50, 75, and 150 bps, subvoice-grade lines outside North America of 200 bps, and speeds derived from voice lines of 300, 1200, 2400, 4800, and 9600 bps. Wideband data links operating at 19,200, 40,800, 48,000, and 50,000 bps are being widely used, although they are typically expensive. The AT&T Dataphone Digital Service (DDS) transmits bit rates of 2400, 4800, 9600, and 56,000 bps. Data transmission at speeds of 64,000 bps is being used, and this speed will be extremely important to data processing users as integrated services digital network (ISDN) technology is employed worldwide (see Chapter 41). The digital long-distance trunks that are employed by the common carriers of North America carry a bit rate of 1.544 million bps, and these facilities are now routinely employed by large organizations for data transmission.

As we mentioned earlier, analog and digital signals are interchangeable when the appropriate modems or codecs are used. We should keep this interchangeability in mind in discussing the speeds of telecommunications links. Computer data at 4800 bps can be converted to an analog form to travel over standard 4-kHz telephone channels. On the other hand, ordinary voice telephone signals can be digitized and represented by bit streams of 56,000 bps.

CHANNEL SPEED   The CCITT has recommended that data transmission
STANDARDS   speeds over telephone circuits should be 600N bits per second, where N is an integer between 1 and 18. In making the recommendation, it recognizes that in some countries, a data rate of 2000 bps is in common use and does not conform to the recommendation. Also, 300 bps is still very commonly used in the United States, especially with personal computers that employ inexpensive modems.

Of the recommended speeds, certain speeds are classed as "preferred" speeds. These are 600, 1200, 2400, 3600, 4800, 7200, and 9600 bps. Standardization of higher data rates is now necessary and should relate to the new hierarchy of digital PCM channels. CCITT has standardized the PCM sampling rate at 8000 samples per second, giving a 64,000-bps channel. AT&T derives 56,000 bps from its digitized speech channels, the remaining capacity being used for synchronization, signaling, and control.

The CCITT has standardized two PCM transmission rates of 1.544 and 2.048 million bps. It has been suggested that higher-capacity PCM channels should transmit at 2.048×2^N bits per second, where N is an integer. AT&T has standardized its own digital channel speeds as follows:

- Level 1:   1.544 million bps (T1 carrier)
- Level 1C: 3.2   million bps (T1C carrier)
- Level 2:   6.3   million bps
- Level 3:   45   million bps
- Level 4:   274   million bps (T4 carrier)

Although these differ from the CCITT recommendation, they have now become standard for North America.

RANGES OF CHANNEL SPEEDS

In the wide range of speeds at which transmission will take place, certain points stand out as being of particular importance. Some of these factors relate to human needs, such as the desire to make telephone sound intelligible; some relate to machine needs, such as the maximum speed of mechanical printers; and some relate to channel properties, such as the maximum capacity of a wire pair.

Let us look at the significant points in our range of speeds because they indicate requirements for communication channels. Eventually it will be desirable to have all these channels available on a dial-up or on-demand basis.

VERY SLOW TRANSMISSION

Some types of machines transmit *conditions* to each other and no bulk of data is transmitted. For example, a remote burglar alarm transmits a simple yes/no condition signal, and a vehicle detector in the street transmits simple pulses as cars go over it. Signals of these types require only a very small bandwidth.

HUMAN TYPING SPEEDS

The input speed on a keyboard is the maximum speed at which a human being can type. Fifteen characters per second is enough for the most nimble-fingered.

The output speed of a terminal need not be the same. Some printing terminals print at 15 characters per second, but many print at 55 characters, 120 characters, or more, per second. A very commonly used line speed for use with printing terminals is 300 bps. This is more than sufficient for terminals that print at 15 characters per second. But 300 bps is not fast enough for 55-character-per-second printers and is much too slow for those that print 120 characters and more per second. Line speeds of 1200 and 2400 bps are more appropriate for these faster terminals.

HUMAN READING SPEEDS   A fast reader might be able to read this page in less than a minute—in other words, at a speed of about 250 characters per second. If information is being displayed on a screen, it is desirable that it be transmitted at least as fast as it can be read. Doing so is a requirement of an efficient user interface.

Display screens operating today at 2400 bps (300 characters per second) on typical commercial applications allow an effective user interface to be employed. Computer output that is substantially slower than this tends to be frustrating for the user. On computer-based instruction systems, it has been commented that a lower-speed output is analogous to having a teacher with a speech impediment.

Sometimes a speed higher than 300 characters per second is desirable—for example, when pages are skip-read, and the terminal user quickly flashes from page to page. This practice is likely to be common in browsing or searching operations. In looking through a telephone directory, for example, every line is not read. Also, when tables are displayed, a fast operator can handle speeds somewhat higher than 300 characters per second. Many display screen terminals operate today using much higher speeds than 2400 bps. Speeds of 4800 bps, 9600 bps, and even 19,200 bps are common. These speeds may well become very commonly used speeds on digital data networks.

In some cases, for example, in word processing and text-editing applications, even a 19,200-bps data rate can seem slow. In these types of operations, the terminal operator scrolls quickly through pages of text, and experienced operators want pages to appear instantaneously on their screens.

It should be noted that although human beings can in many cases absorb information coming in at 4800 and 9600 bps, they cannot normally respond at this speed. A 150-bps return channel is adequate for most responses with foreseeable mechanical devices such as keyboards and light pens.

It might be the case that telecommunications channels that support different data rates in opposite directions will come into common use for data communication applications. Today, channels that support transmission in both directions normally provide the same data rate in each.

TELEPHONE CHANNELS The telecommunications channel we are all most familiar with was designed with the important economic constraint that the bandwidth used should not be larger than necessary—then, that the maximum number of telephone calls be multiplexed together over long-distance links or the trunk lines connecting switching offices. The result is that a bandwidth of about 4 kHz is used. This allows the caller to recognize the voices of the callers and comprehend what they say. The systems we design today are largely dominated by this bandwidth. Approximately 9600 bps is the highest practical speed that can be attained over standard 4-kHz analog channels.

MACHINE PRINTING AND READING SPEEDS Commonly used high-speed computer printers operate at about 1100 lines per minute—that is about 20,000 bps. It would be of value to have switched telecommunications lines which we could use to interconnect high-speed printers with other computing equipment. Because of mechanical improvements, the input/output speeds will increase even more. Many line printers now run at 2000 lines per minute, and xerographic laser printers run at speeds of 20,000 lines per minute or more. Optical document reading can also require higher speeds. Standard wideband channels that are in increasing use in the United States operate at about 50,000 bps.

DIGITAL VOICE CHANNELS A digital voice channel using PCM techniques transmits 56,000 bps. Many of the world's channels already use this form of transmission, and PCM transmission will be almost universal in the not-too-distant future. This rate is close to the speed requirement for high-speed printers and thus it would be valuable to have a switched public network supporting this data rate. AT&T's Dataphone Digital Service (DDS) provides leased digital channels supporting data rates of up to 56,000 bps, derived in part from PCM telephone channels.

A typical typewritten page can be transmitted, in a digitized facsimile form at 56,000 bps in about 4 seconds. Thus channels of this speed could form the basis for an interactive information retrieval or electronic mail system.

A HIGH-FIDELITY SOUND CHANNEL Telephone channels are restricted to a bandwidth of 4000 Hz. A bandwidth of 20,000 Hz is needed for full high-fidelity transmission, and twice that is required if the transmission is stereophonic. The telephone wires entering a private home are capable of carrying this range of frequencies; therefore, domestic distribution of high-fidelity music is technically feasible and could be done on a dial-up basis if desired. An analog channel engineered for high-fidelity transmission could carry about 10 times as much information as a telephone channel.

When a PCM channel is designed for high-fidelity transmission, more detectable signal levels (quantizing levels) are used than in speech transmission. Ten bits per sample might be used instead of the 7 bits used for speech. At 10 bits per sample, the total bit rate is about 320,000 bps. Stereophonic transmission can be carried by about 640,000 bps instead of 56,000 bps for telephone speech. Using more complex means of digitally encoding the stereo signal, a smaller number of bits can be used to carry music. This trade-off between bit rate and logical complexity of the digital encoding also applies to most other types of digital transmission.

THE MAXIMUM CAPACITY OF A WIRE PAIR

Multibillions of dollars worth of wire pairs are laid down under the streets and along the highways. In recent years, the wire pair has been made to carry a bit rate of a few million bits per second by using regenerative repeaters at appropriately close intervals on the line. These repeaters are used to implement the AT&T T1 carrier, which sends 1,544,000 bps over wire pairs with repeaters every 6000 feet. These are normally used to transmit 24 telephone conversations simultaneously. This has become a standard that is likely to remain for decades to come.

As we discussed earlier, the T1 carrier is commonly used for data transmission by many large organizations. Such high bit rates are appropriate for communication between computers in distributed processing applications for transmission of large quantities of data from one location to another. This type of facility is playing a major role in data communication systems because it provides extremely high bit rates while making the most effective use of the ubiquitous twisted-wire pairs.

Even higher bit rates can be sent over a twisted-wire pair. The T2 carrier transmits 6.312 million bps, which is close to the maximum rate practical on a wire pair. The T2 carrier was used by AT&T to implement the Picturephone service that was introduced in the 1960s. The Picturephone service encoded signals in a digital form that required about 6 million bps. Picturephone service was not a commercial success; however, the T2 carrier has become one of the main short-haul trunks of the United States and will be used for many different types of transmission, including the transmission of computer data. Four T1 signals are multiplexed together to travel over one T2 channel.

TELEVISION SIGNALS

The next step in speed relating to human communication is television, which requires about 4 to 6 MHz of bandwidth when transmitted over analog circuits.

Television is transmitted over analog trunks together with large groups of telephone calls. As with every other type of signal, it can be carried over a digital channel. A channel operating at 92.5 million bps is required for television. Such a channel is planned in the AT&T's hierarchy of digital channels.

The television screen itself can eventually become larger and of higher fidelity. If the number of lines on the screen is doubled, four times the bandwidth will be needed. If we have a 5-foot wall screen for television, or perhaps eventually a screen that occupies most of one wall, the resolution per inch will probably not need to be quite as good as that on today's sets. Ten times the present bandwidth will probably be enough for even the most spectacular home screens. This would give approximately the resolution gotten from a slide projector using a 6-foot screen. Such transmission would probably not use 10 times the bit rate of today's television because powerful signal-compression techniques can be used with digital transmission.

The ultimate requirement of visual transmission outside ultralarge-screen theaters can, then, be about 50 MHz. The T4 carrier of 274 million bps probably could be made to carry this video signal. Coaxial cables, like those laid into homes today to carry cable TV, could also be engineered to carry these signals, but such high bit rates are best carried by optical fibers.

In all probability, we will eventually find uses for this high transmission speed in data communication applications. Signals to and from many terminals can be multiplexed onto such channels. Responses to terminals on some systems take the form of pictures as well as alphanumeric responses. Data banks will be remote from the machines using the data. Time-sharing systems of immense versatility will be able to call in programs from remote locations. Small machines will be able to handle highly elaborate applications, using sophisticated graphics, by use of data networks employing such channels.

HIGH-SPEED DIGITAL CHANNELS

There are already many digital channels in existence with extremely high capacities. They will become even more widespread. We have already mentioned the AT&T T4 carrier that transmits 274 million bps. A similar type of channel is implemented in Canada as the LD4 coaxial system. The AT&T WT4 waveguide system transmits 60 of the T4 bit streams through a single pipe giving a total throughput of 16 billion bits per second. Designs for communications satellites have been discussed with total satellite throughputs of billions of bits per second. Optical fibers are capable of transmitting a billion bits per second, and many such fibers normally are packed into one cable.

COMMUNICATION SPEEDS

Figure 8.2 summarizes the main landmarks in this wide range of usable bit rates. Bit rates corresponding to human transmissions of various types, such as

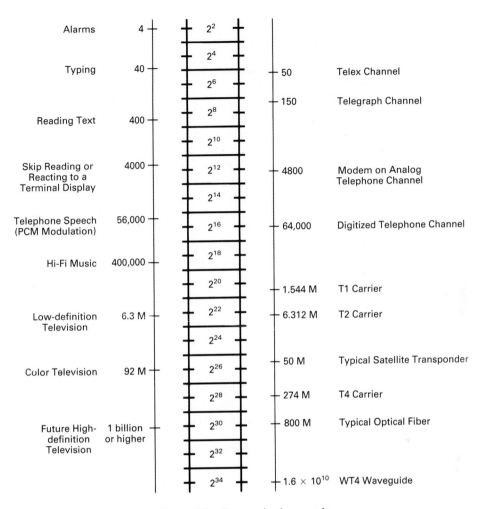

Figure 8.2   Communication speeds

typing, telephone, hi-fi music, and television are on the left. Bit rates of physical channels, ranging from the slow rate of telex to the high rate of AT&T waveguides, are on the right.

DESIGN TRADE-OFFS

It is clear that physical facilities are emerging that are capable of transmitting much higher bit rates than those in common use today. We will discuss some design trade-offs that relate to channel speeds. In designing a system that uses telecommunications facilities, a number of trade-offs can be exercised in the use of the available channel capacity. We will summarize a number of these trade-offs, some of which could, and should, have major effects on the design of systems that use data communication facilities.

**ENCODING
COMPLEXITY**
First, there is a trade-off between the number of signals that can be packed into a given channel and the complexity of their encoding. As we have already discussed, telephone companies often digitize the telephone voice today using simple PCM encoding. As we discussed earlier, this requires 56,000 bps with AT&T standards. More complex encoding techniques can achieve the same telephone sound quality with half the number of bits per second. Also, dynamic allocation of the bit stream can double the number of telephone calls that can be transmitted over the same physical channel.

Using dynamic allocation and more complex encoding techniques, the T1 carrier, which today carries 24 telephone calls, could be made to carry 96 calls. These techniques, of course, need more complex circuitry. As the complexity of the circuitry increases, so does its cost. But the cost of complex encoding circuitry is dropping as the technology of large-scale integration matures.

SWITCHING
The second trade-off that can be made is between switching and channel sharing. For example, if a network connects many points and the channels are not shared, extensive use of switching is required. Usually, large networks have more than one level of switching office. The higher levels in the hierarchy, for example the toll switching offices in a telephone network, have high-capacity trunks interconnecting them with a high degree of sharing. This greatly reduces the total channel mileage and the total number of switching offices needed. On the other hand, the local loops of a telephone network connect each subscriber, generally with no sharing, to the local telephone office. This results in a very large cable mileage. If the cables used in apartment buildings or dense subscriber groupings could be shared, a great reduction in cable mileage could result.

**DISTRIBUTED
STORAGE**
The third trade-off involves channel capacity versus distributed storage. Much of the data transmission used in computer systems is designed to obtain information from distant data storage facilities. The paperwork files in branch offices are often replaced with communication links to a centralized computer with a

database. The cost of small storage units is dropping fast and their reliability is increasing. Consequently, it is becoming economical to store some data in peripheral storage units and avoid the data transmission.

DISTRIBUTED INTELLIGENCE

The fourth trade-off is between channel capacity and distributed intelligence. Computer systems designed for computer terminal users need to be psychologically appropriate for the user. This requires a large number of bits going to and from the computer that performs the dialog processing. A trend in the computer industry is to use terminals or personal computers that are ''intelligent'' enough to carry out some of the dialog processing at the terminal location. The greater the level of programmed function at peripheral locations, the less data that needs to be transmitted to the central computer. Much of the motivation for using distributed intelligence has resulted from the fact that the data transmission links required for good interactive system design were too expensive, unavailable, or unreliable.

MIX OF SIGNALS

A final trade-off involves the mix of signals transmitted over the communication channels. An objective of telecommunications design ought to be to achieve a high utilization of the channels. Much of the difficulty in achieving high utilization stems from the fact that most users want to employ the channels at random times—times of their own choosing—and then want the channel to be available to them almost immediately when they request it. The probability of a user being refused a channel is ordinarily set at a very low level, for example, 0.01 or lower on the public telephone network.

A variety of mechanisms is employed to allocate channels to users when they need them. In general, higher channel utilization will be achieved if more channels can be grouped together for allocation purposes. Higher grouping is possible if a larger number of users share the group. Rather than construct data networks separately for each application, it would be more economical to combine the data networks and share the channels. It would be still more economical to combine voice and data networks, which is the goal of the integrated services digital networks that are beginning to emerge.

CHANNEL CAPACITY

We can describe the *capacity* of a communication channel as the maximum rate at which we can send information over it without error. For data communication purposes, this can be measured in *bits per second,* and this is the unit of measure we have been using and will continue to use throughout this book.

In the remainder of this chapter we explore in more detail the factors that limit the maximum bit rate that a given channel is capable of carrying and discuss the theoretical maximum capacity of a communication channel.

BIT RATE AND BANDWIDTH

As we mentioned earlier, one of the factors that influences a channel's speed is the channel's *bandwidth*. In 1928 a researcher named Hartley proved that the amount of information that can be sent over a channel in a given amount of time is directly proportional to the channel's bandwidth. And in 1924 and 1928, a researcher named Nyquist published papers concerning the transmission of information over a theoretical noiseless channel. Nyquist proved that a channel whose bandwidth is W can carry $2W$ separate voltage values per second. If we use one voltage value to represent a 0 and the another to represent a 1, we can transmit $2W$ bits per second over a line whose bandwidth is W.

As an example, a line whose bandwidth is 4000 Hz theoretically can carry a maximum of 8000 bps using this simple way of encoding the bits. Of course, this is a theoretical maximum, and assumes a noiseless channel, which does not exist. In reality, when we use two separate voltage levels to transmit data, a much lower bit rate than 8000 bps actually can be sent over a channel whose bandwidth is 4 kHz.

DIBITS AND TRIBITS

We explained previously that it is possible to send data over a normal telephone channel at the rate of 9600 bps. This appears to exceed the theoretical maximum. In fact, it does not, because when high bit rates are required, more voltage levels than two are used. For example, we can send 2 bits, called a *dibit,* simultaneously by having *four* possible voltage levels at any given instant. In this way, our 4-kHz channel now has a *theoretical* maximum capacity of 16,000 bps. If we construct equipment that generates and detects *eight* different voltage values, rather than four or two, we can send *tribits,* each consisting of 3 bits. This gives our 4-kHz channel a theoretical maximum capacity of 32,000 bps. Expressed as a mathematical formula, the channel capacity, $C,$ in the absence of noise, is

$$C = 2W \log_2 L$$

Thus the following question arises: How many voltage, or signaling, levels can be transmitted and be separately distinguishable at the receiver? Noise and distortion on the line, fluctuations in attenuation, and limits on the signal power that can be used all restrict this.

BAUD

The term *baud* is sometimes used in data communication literature in quoting the speed of a transmission line. A certain transmission line is said to have a speed of so many *baud*. In actual fact, the term *baud* should not be used in quoting the *capacity* of a line, but rather its *signaling speed*. The two are not synonymous. Signaling speed, or baud, refers to *the number of times in each second the line condition changes*. If the line condition represents the presence or absence of one bit, then the line's signaling speed in *baud* is the same as the line's capacity in *bits per second*.

MULTIPLE-STATE SIGNALING

If, however, the line can be in one of *four* possible states, then one line condition represents a dibit and the bit rate in bits per second will then be two times the line's speed in baud. For example, many modems transmit data in dibits; each pair of bits is coded as one of four possible line conditions. If the signals are coded into eight possible states, then one line condition represents a tribit and 1 baud equals 3 bps.

Remember that some literature uses the term *baud* to mean *bits per second*. Although this is true with many lines because they use two-state signaling, it is definitely *not* true in general. For any line not using two-state signaling, it is wrong. Since the term *baud* can be confusing, we avoid using it in this book.

This discussion seems to indicate that the capacity of a channel can be increased indefinitely simply by increasing the number of signal levels that are transmitted. In fact, there is a theoretical limit to this also, because in the real world, no channel is noiseless. Next, let us talk about the maximum capacity of a real-world channel—one with noise.

SIGNALING ON A CHANNEL WITH NOISE

In 1948, twenty years after Nyquist, a researcher named Shannon proved, again mathematically, that a channel has a finite maximum capacity. He discussed a continuous channel as well as one transmitting discrete values. His work relates first to a noiseless channel, and then, more interestingly in our case, to a channel with noise.

SHANNON'S LAW

Shannon proved that if signals are sent with a signal power S over a channel perturbed by random white noise of power N, the capacity C of the channel in bits per second is

$$C = W \log_2\left(1 + \frac{S}{N}\right)$$

This formula expresses what is called *Shannon's law*. It gives the maximum signaling rate over a communication channel in terms of three important parameters that are known or measurable. Shannon's law is one of the most fundamental laws of telecommunications. It relates to the *completely unpredictable* sequence of transmitting bits. If the sequence of some of the bits can be predicted, then a faster communication rate could be achieved by taking advantage of the predictability. But for an unpredictable sequence of bits, there is no way of exceeding the quantity of information given by Shannon's formula. Very ingenious modulation techniques and elaborate coding systems can be designed, but no amount of effort will ever send more than this number of bits over a given channel unless either the bandwidth or the signal-to-noise ratio is increased.

MAXIMUM CAPACITY OF A VOICE CHANNEL

Let us look at an example. A typical value for the signal-to-noise ratio of a switched telephone channel is 30 dB. This means that the noise on the line is 1/1000 as strong as the signal that is transmitted. It is also typical that the available bandwidth that can be used for data transmission is 2600 Hz. The remaining frequencies in the 4000-Hz bandwidth are reserved for switching and control functions and to separate the channel from adjacent channels sharing the same physical circuit. Plugging those into Shannon's formula gives the following:

$$C = 2600 \log_2\left(1 + \frac{1000}{1}\right) = 25,900 \text{ bps}$$

So the maximum possible transmission rate using these channel parameters is 25,900 bps.

The only way to improve on this is to make fundamental changes in the construction of the line. For example, the common carrier could increase the power of the amplifiers, increase the bandwidth, or reduce the noise. But there is nothing that can be done in the design of the modems or terminal equipment that would give a bit rate higher than 25,900 bps. If a common carrier provides a line of given characteristics, Shannon's law tells us the maximum transmission rate that we could ever achieve.

Occasionally, ingenious inventors propose a scheme that would provide better results than the capacity given by Shannon's formula. However, Shannon's law is so fundamental that any such scheme should be treated with the same attitude as inventions for perpetual-motion machines. Somewhere in the scheme there is a flaw, and we can say with assurance that it will not work.

Systems in practice on voice lines work at speeds very much lower than the theoretical limit specified by Shannon's formula. It is common to find transmission schemes operating at 300, 1200, and 2400 bps on voice lines. Even on a good-quality line, with the full bandwidth available, normally the maximum practical speed is not greater than 9600 bps. There are modems available that are capable of operating at 19,200 bps. However, these modems always implement fallback schemes that automatically cause the modem to reduce its transmission speed to a lower value if the line is less than perfect. On normal dial-up lines, it is rare for such a modem to operate at full capacity for long periods of time.

One reason that it is difficult to approach Shannon's limit is that as one approaches the Shannon maximum, the necessary encoding becomes very complex, with longer and longer word lengths. This causes more and more delay in encoding and decoding. Also, the cost of the modem increases with the speed of transmission, as shown in Fig. 8.3. The cost becomes very high long before the speed reaches the limit set by Shannon's law. At some point it simply becomes more economical to use a channel of higher bandwidth than to squeeze a high transmission rate out of a low-bandwidth channel.

DIGITAL CHANNELS

As we discussed earlier, the electronics on a wire-pair line can be changed so that it becomes a high-speed digital channel rather than an analog circuit. We explained that it is common to transmit more than 1.5 million bits using PCM techniques. This bit rate is much higher than if all the available analog channels on the same telephone wire transmitted data at the Shannon limit. Does this violate Shannon's law? The answer is no. What is happening on digital PCM channels is that much higher frequencies are being transmitted than are

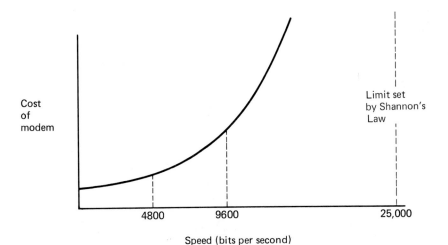

Figure 8.3 Modem cost

used on analog lines. This gives a much *higher* bandwidth, but a much *worse* signal-to-noise ratio.

Two factors compensate for this reduction in signal-to-noise ratio. First, the repeaters are close together, so the signal does not sink into the background of noise. Second, only binary bits are sent, so only the presence or absence of a bit need be detected—not the wide range of amplitudes needed in analog transmission. Also, Shannon's equation shows that while capacity increases in direct proportion to bandwidth, it increases only as the *log* of the signal-to-noise ratio. So a 10-fold increase in bandwidth compensates for a 1000-fold decrease in signal-to-noise ratio.

9 SHARING CHANNEL CAPACITY

In many systems that use data transmission facilities, the cost of the communication channels themselves represents a large percentage of the total cost of the system. The channels must be shared as much as possible to ensure that their capacity is fully utilized. As we will see in this chapter, the sharing of transmission lines can be carried out in a variety of ways. Basically, two problems are involved. The first is the technical problem of combining different transmissions on the same line. This is relatively easily solved. If several separate transmissions are sent over the same line *at the same time,* this is referred to as *multiplexing.* The second problem is that of bringing together a sufficient number of users to fill the group of channels that has been derived from the line. Sometimes there are enough users within one organization. They can be brought together to share a leased line. Often this is not the case, however.

DIFFERENT USERS OF ONE SYSTEM   On a system with many terminals, the communication network will be organized so that lines are shared between the terminals. A simple arrangement could be that shown in Fig. 9.1. Here a group of terminal users do not have a computer in their building. They use a distant computer by means of a voice line that is shared between them. Sometimes the terminal users are in different buildings, scattered geographically. In this case, unshared lines may connect them to a point at which sharing begins. A network of this type may link many users, as shown in Fig. 9.2. A variety of different devices and techniques to facilitate sharing are available. These are discussed in Chapter 27. It is the job of the systems analyst to select the best for each particular system, and this can be a complex job.

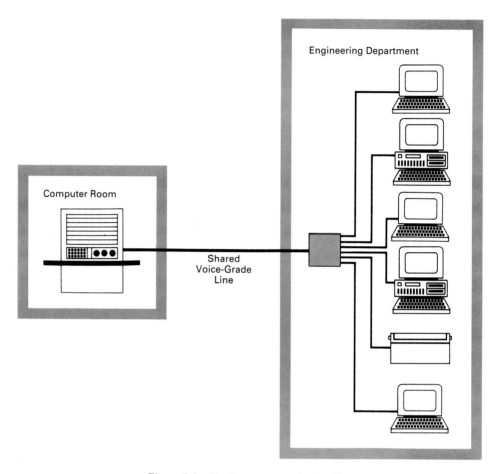

Figure 9.1   Sharing a communication line

DIFFERENT USERS   Organizations that are up to date in their use of data
WITHIN ONE   processing have a proliferation of different systems.
ORGANIZATION   A data communication network that is shared by dif-
                       ferent system users can be set up within the organi-
zation. In some cases this may simply be a facility that enables leased lines that
normally carry the organization's telephone traffic, sometimes called *tie lines*,
to be used for data. A leased wideband link can be split, using multiplexing
equipment, into many separate lower-capacity links, used for separate purposes.
The links so derived need not necessarily be of the same data rate. A variety of
such multiplexing equipment is on the market.

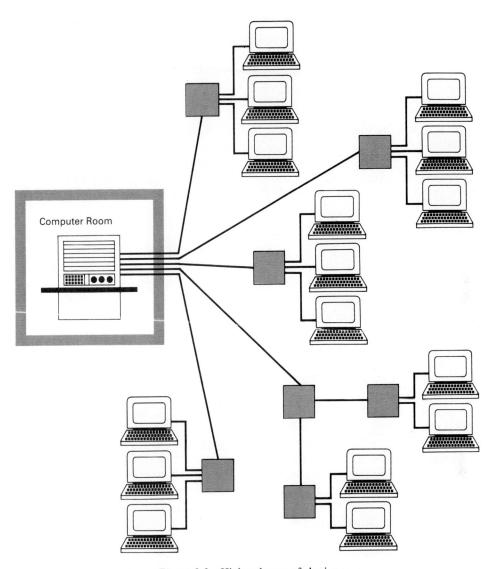

Figure 9.2   Higher degree of sharing

**SHARING
BETWEEN
SEPARATE
ORGANIZATIONS**

A higher utilization of shared facilities can often be achieved if several different organizations combine in the sharing. A network of leased lines and private switching facilities could serve an association of several organizations at a lower cost per user than if it were designed for one organization. Unfortunately, this is not permitted by the regulations controlling the use of telecommunications in most countries. In the United States, it is permitted only in certain special cases.

LINE BROKING

An organization might operate a *line broking* business in which it leases lines, attaches equipment to them that permits them to be shared, and then sells the subchannels so derived to individual users. The line broker may be a major telecommunications user with capacity to spare. This would be a very valuable service in data transmission because, again, it would greatly lessen the wastage and hence the cost to the user. Unfortunately, line broking is also prohibited in most countries.

PUBLIC DATA NETWORKS

In many cases there are no other users available with whom to share lines. Thus they may be used in a wasteful manner. Such is often the case today, especially when public telephone lines are used for data. To avoid this inefficiency, a switched public network, designed specifically for data transmission, might be constructed. Such a network might make use of high-capacity trunks that carry many millions of bits per second. The telex and TWX networks are examples of switched public networks, but these can operate only at low speeds. It is desirable that a switched public data network should operate at speeds ranging from about 300 bps to 56,000 bps or higher.

Most public data networks that are in operation today use a technique called *packet switching* to transmit data from one location to another. In a packet switching network, the physical connections remain fixed, and a message is routed from one location to another by passing it from one network node to the next until the message reaches its destination. The term "packet switching" is used because, with this type of network, messages are divided into smaller *packets* for transmission efficiency. Public data networks are introduced in Chapter 36, and the packet switching techniques used by these networks are discussed in Chapter 37.

THE EVOLUTION OF COMPUTER NETWORKS

The need for communication line multiplexing is a basic factor in achieving economic usage of remote computers. A *very* high degree of multiplexing is necessary to take advantage of the digital transmission media that today's technology makes possible. Common carriers routinely use microwave links and coaxial cables that carry a billion bits per second. Consequently, data transmission networks are passing through the following stages.

- **Private Single-Use Networks.** First, we have seen private networks in which terminals are linked to one system designed for one set of functions—for example, today's airline and banking systems, and time-sharing systems, each using its own computer center.

- **Private Networks Interlinking Systems.** Next, we see private networks in which more than one system is interlinked within an organization. For example, a private network might interlink separate time-sharing facilities or database systems or might connect multiple computer centers.

- **Private Shared Networks.** Then come private networks in which systems in different organizations share data network facilities. In this category are interbank systems or interairline systems in which network facilities are shared. This type of network might interconnect time-sharing systems or the computer centers in different organizations.

- **Limited Public Networks.** Next, came the proliferation of public data transmission networks that offered services in large metropolitan areas. Unlike the telephone network, these have been built to take advantage of digital technology and multiplexing so that the user pays a fee proportional to the data rate. Public networks such as these are available now, but for cost reasons they often allow local access only in certain areas—those with a high density of users.

- **Nationwide Public Networks.** It is then a logical step to nationwide public networks in which access is provided virtually everywhere in a country. It may be some time before public data networks become as ubiquitous as the telephone network, but eventually terminals and personal computers in most homes and offices will be interlinked.

- **International Public Networks.** The next step is toward international public data networks. The problems we are now creating with international incompatibility will have to be solved with interface computers. Political problems will also have to be overcome. The work being done toward the creation of international telecommunications standards is a step in the right direction toward the creation of international public networks.

- **Integrated Services Digital Network (ISDN).** A future goal of networking is to have universal access to an integrated network that allows a user anywhere to plug in any type of device—telephone, data terminal, computer, facsimile machine, or video equipment—and to communicate with a similar device anywhere in the world. A channel with the appropriate bit rate will be assigned automatically by the network. ISDN development is actively under way in a number of countries, including the United States, and pilot ISDNs are in operation on a limited basis; within the foreseeable future this goal of a universal ISDN may be realized. ISDN technology is discussed in Chapter 41.

GREATER DEGREES OF SHARING

The further we progress toward nationwide data networks, the less wastage of bandwidth there will be. There are now many millions of terminals in use in the United States, and their numbers are growing at a fantastic rate. Most of these use their communication lines inefficiently, and the wastage of the available lines is appalling. It is certain that sufficient communication lines to support the usage of all the terminals that will be used in the next decade could not be provided using traditional methods. The use of private data networks would be somewhat less wasteful. However, many separate private networks overlaid geographically would require a much greater number of communication lines than would a universal public data network with digital microwave links or coaxial cables and a very high level of multiplexing. Such a data network is needed and will be an extremely important national resource.

We turn our attention next to the technology that is used in sharing communication facilities.

MULTIPLEXING

A channel of given capacity can be split up into a number of lesser subchannels. We have already seen that on an analog line, a given bandwidth or range of frequencies can be split up into smaller bandwidths by a technique called *frequency-division multiplexing*. Similarly, on a digital line, a bit stream can be subdivided to carry lesser bit streams with their bits interleaved—for example, every tenth bit in a high-speed stream might be a bit from one subchannel. The bit after that is from the second channel and so on, until 10 subchannels are derived. This process is called *time-division multiplexing*. We discuss multiplexing techniques in more detail in Chapter 27, but in the meantime we shall refer to this process frequently, saying, for example, that one pair of wires carries 12 voice channels or that 100 music channels can be sent over one television channel.

When frequency-division multiplexing is used, some space is needed between the channels to avoid interference; this is called the *guard band*. As we have seen, for telephone traffic, the world's transmission media are divided into slices of about 4 kHz, even though the usable bandwidth is closer to 2800 Hz. If ten 20-kHz hi-fi channels are packed into a bandwidth of 200 kHz, only about 18 kHz of each channel will remain (more than enough for most human ears). About 2 kHz between each channel would be required to separate the channels. Time-division multiplexing is also less than 100 percent efficient and requires some housekeeping bits among the information bits. Some sawdust is inevitable when a tree is cut into logs.

SWITCHING

Another way to share communication channels between many users, but for a different purpose, is to interconnect them by means of *switching*. The user has a line to a telephone exchange, and there the user's line can be connected to that of another subscriber. The switching can take place in the network facilities, for example in a telephone exchange, or it can take place on the subscriber's premises, enabling many users to share a small number of access lines.

The type of switching used on the public telephone network in interconnecting subscribers is not the only kind of switching that can be used. In general, there are four types of switching:

- **Conventional Circuit Switching.** With this technique, all the lines are connected to exchanges, or switching offices. The exchanges are used to connect, on demand, any subscriber to any other subscriber. Although this type of switching is most often associated with the telecommunications common carriers, individual subscribers can also use conventional telephone switching techniques. Individual users can lease telephone channels and install switches to construct private switched networks of their own. This is often done by large organizations.

- **Fast-Connect Circuit Switching.** This technique is logically similar to conventional circuit switching. All the lines are connected to switching centers, and circuits are established on demand between any two subscribers. However, with telephone switching it may take as long as 30 seconds to establish a connection. With fast-connect switching a typical connection is established in a fraction of a second. The extremely fast switching time makes this switching technique particularly well suited to data transmission.

- **Message Switching.** With *message switching* users can be interconnected on demand without using circuit switches. Messages that enter a message switching system each have a *destination address* attached to them. They are then *forwarded* to their final destinations. Electronic mail systems have been built that use message switching techniques to route letters and memos between users.

- **Packet Switching.** As discussed earlier, *packet switching* is a particular form of message switching that is often used to interconnect all types of users on a general-purpose public data network. Messages are divided into smaller *packets,* which are routed independently through the network for transmission to their final destinations.

All of the switching techniques discussed above are described in detail in Chapter 28. Packet switching is a particularly important technology for data communication and is described further in Chapter 37. Box 9.1 describes the operation of Telenet, a typical packet switching public data network. Telenet is discussed in detail in Chapter 36.

MULTIPOINT LINES   Figure 9.3 illustrates the difference between using multiple *point-to-point* connections and a single *multipoint* connection to interconnect devices. When a point-to-point connection is used, data can be exchanged only between devices that are directly connected, unless data is relayed from one device to another as in the packet switching

BOX 9.1 The Telenet public data network

The public data network operated in the United States by General Telephone and Electronics (GTE) is called *Telenet*. The Telenet network consists of a large number of specialized network computers interconnected with high-speed data links. The network computers at each node of the network are installed in Telenet central offices (TCOs), of which there are more than 350 nationwide. The following diagram (simplified for clarity) shows the general structure of the Telenet network.

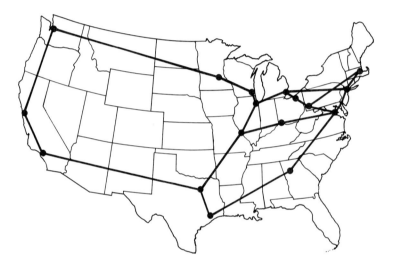

Notice that there are a number of possible network paths between any two nodes. However, no circuit switches are used; all connections are connected permanently.

The Telenet network can be used to connect a terminal to a distant computer in a manner similar to the way the public telephone network might be used to do so. A computer is generally permanently attached to its local TCO via a leased line; a terminal user typically gains access to the local TCO by using an ordinary dial-up telephone connection. In effect, the computer is connected to one node of the network, and the terminal is connected to another.

BOX 9.1 *(Continued)*

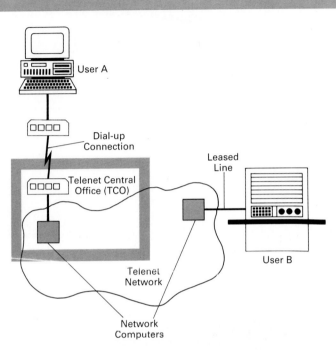

User A

Dial-up
Connection

Leased
Line

Telenet Central
Office (TCO)

User B

Telenet
Network

Network
Computers

Let us suppose that user A (a terminal) is sending a message to user B (a computer). User A's terminal first carves the message up into smaller pieces, attaches a destination address to each piece, and delivers the resulting packets to a Telenet network computer at the TCO to which user A's terminal is attached. The network terminal at the TCO then uses information it has about traffic conditions on the network to choose the next node to send each packet to. Since network conditions change from instant to instant, it may choose a different path for each packet. As each packet enters each new node, that node examines its destination address, and repeats the process of sending it along to the most appropriate next node. Finally, each packet reaches its destination TCO and is passed to user B. User B then waits until all the packets arrive and reassembles them into the original message.

It is also possible to attach a terminal or computer to the Telenet network that is not capable of carving messages up into packets. The packet assembly and disassembly (PAD) functions can be handled by

(Continued)

BOX 9.1 *(Continued)*

a specialized processor provided either by the user or by Telenet. The PAD facility can be on either the user's or Telenet's premises.

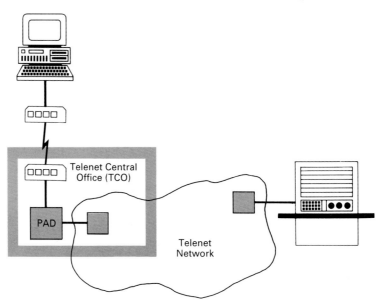

The transmission of a complete message generally takes place in a small fraction of a second. Thus it appears to the terminal user as if there is a two-way direct connection between the terminal and the computer, just as if a long-distance telephone line were being used. This imaginary connection is referred to as a *virtual circuit*. It appears to the user as if a circuit exists, even though each piece of each message may take a completely different path through the network.

Users that generate large message volumes, such as users that connect mainframe computers to the network, are generally charged based on message volume, although connect time may also be a factor in determining charges. Users that generally have only small message volumes, such as the typical user of an information utility (see Chapter 36), may be charged based on actual connect time alone.

Interestingly, with most public data networks, including Telenet, distance plays no part in the charging algorithm. Consequently, the charges for a typical interaction with a computer using Telenet can be a small fraction of what they would be if a normal toll telephone connection were used. The longer the distance, the more attractive is a public data network to the data transmission user.

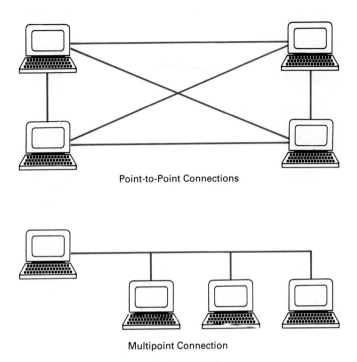

Point-to-Point Connections

Multipoint Connection

Figure 9.3   Point-to-point versus multipoint connections

network described above. The situation is different when multipoint connections are used. (A multipoint line is sometimes referred to as a *multidrop line*.) When data is transmitted from the terminal on the left using a multipoint line, all three of the other terminals receive the transmission. Therefore, more complex procedures are needed to ensure that each terminal ignores all transmissions that are not intended for it.

The use of multipoint lines can often make it possible to reduce line costs substantially. It would be much more expensive to interconnect a group of terminals fully with point-to-point connections, especially if the distances involved are long (see Fig. 9.4).

DYNAMIC CHANNEL ALLOCATION   The use of *dynamic channel allocation* is another method for increasing the utilization of an expensive channel. Common carriers often use this method when a telephone line is long and expensive, such as a trans-Atlantic cable. With this technique, the link is subdivided into many channels in both directions. When you talk, a circuit detects that you are talking and allocates a channel to you. When you stop talking, even for a second or two, the channel is made available to other users. When the party you are talk-

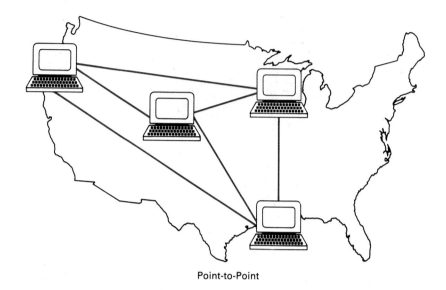

Point-to-Point

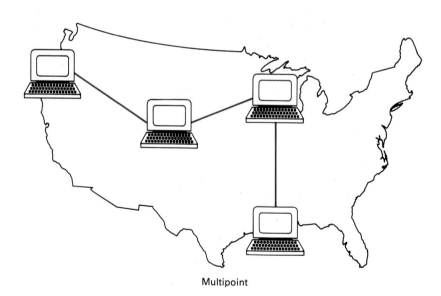

Multipoint

Figure 9.4   Multipoint cost advantage

ing to replies, a channel is dynamically allocated in the opposite direction. The channel allocations are done at electronic speed within a tiny fraction of a second. One technique used on analog lines, *time assignment speech interpolation* (TASI), can greatly increase the effective capacity of the line.

When the speech travels in a digitized form, digital channel capacity can be allocated to it as required, by computer-like circuits. One technique for this is called *digital speech interpolation* (DSI). When a speaker says a word, channel space is assigned for it. When the speaker is silent, the channel space is taken away. With digital circuitry, this process can occur at high speed. Channel capacity can be assigned to speech just as memory blocks are allocated dynamically to users in a computer.

Most telephone speakers spend about 55 percent of their time pausing or listening. Dynamic channel space allocation done very rapidly can more than double the capacity of a channel. The front of some words will be removed, as the channel allocation cannot be done instantaneously. Usually, only a few milliseconds (ms) is removed, but occasionally many milliseconds are lost because, by chance, most persons are speaking in one direction and there is no free channel space until one of them pauses briefly. If no more than about 50 ms is chopped off the front of every word spoken, most speech is still quite intelligible and recognizable.

REALTIME OR NON-REALTIME

Many additional methods can be used to share telecommunications facilities when a distinction is made between realtime and non-realtime traffic. *Real-time* usage of a channel means that the receiving party or machine receives the signal at approximately the same time that it originates. In practice, there will always be a small transmission delay. This delay should be sufficiently small so that the channel can be used as though there were zero delay. Thus telephone transmission is realtime. The receiving party reacts to the signal as though there were no delay in its transmission. Telegram transmission, on the other hand, is an example of *non-realtime* use of telecommunications facilities. The receiving party sees the telegram perhaps hours after it was sent.

Live television of a ball game is realtime; a broadcast of a program recorded the previous night is non-realtime. Batch data transmission of computer data is non-realtime; transmission permitting interactive use of a terminal, as with an airline reservation system, is realtime. When a terminal operator uses a distant computer, there could be a transmission delay of several seconds and we would still refer to it as *realtime* because the operator uses the terminal in effectively the same way as if there were no delay.

SLOW SCAN

When realtime transmission is needed, the bandwidth of the channel used must be at least as great as the bandwidth of the signal. When the transmission is non-realtime, the channel bandwidth could be smaller, and the signal might be stored until it is transmitted.

Realtime television transmission in America, for example, needs a bandwidth of 4.6 MHz. Prior to the use of communications satellites, the telecommunications links across the Atlantic or Pacific, the suboceanic cables, did not have channels of that bandwidth. Television was therefore slowed down and transmitted non-realtime over smaller bandwidth cables. It was stored on videotape machines and then rebroadcast. This technique is called *slow-scan transmission*.

Hi-fi music could be transmitted over ordinary telephone channels in a similar manner. It would be slowed down, for example, by playing a 15-inch-per-second tape at 1⅞ inches per second, and raising it in frequency by about 400 Hz to fit into the central part of the telephone channel bandwidth.

MIXED REALTIME AND NON-REALTIME TRAFFIC

The fact that channels for realtime traffic are often unutilized a large percentage of the time presents an opportunity. These channels could be made to carry non-realtime traffic in their idle moments, provided that it did not interfere in any way with the realtime traffic. A corporate tie-line network, for example, handling mainly telephone calls, could be designed so that non-realtime messages or data could be sent whenever a channel did not have a telephone call being transmitted over it. The most idle time occurs at night and on weekends. When a telephone call is made, or other realtime signal is sent, it must be given a channel if at all possible. Non-realtime traffic has to wait if a realtime signal comes along. Storage is therefore needed for the non-realtime traffic. It is rather like shunting railroad cars onto a siding to make way for the express.

Given suitable control mechanisms, then, a network can be made to handle a mixture of realtime and non-realtime traffic, and so achieve a higher channel utilization. Box 9.2 lists some of the types of non-realtime traffic that could be sent over a network, such as the one we have been describing.

GRADE OF SERVICE

The *grade of service* that a network provides is an especially important consideration when a high degree of sharing is implemented. When switching is used, as on the public telephone networks, or when many users *share* a smaller number of channels, there is a certain probability that a user will not be able to obtain a connection when one is needed. This happens when all the channels are *busy*. When this happens on the telephone network, the user receives a *network busy* signal (an *engaged* signal in British parlance). This signal can be distinguished from the normal *called party* busy signal because it is faster.

The probability of receiving a network busy signal is referred to as the

BOX 9.2   Non-realtime traffic

- Telegraph messages
- Facsimile transmission of documents
- Electronic mail messages
- Mailgrams
- Electronic funds transfer transactions
- Voicegrams (one-way spoken telephone messages)
- Electronic transmission of news photographs
- Batch data transmission
- Data collection signals
- Computer data entry
- Computer message generation
- Recorded video programs

grade of service of the network. As an example, many telephone systems are engineered to provide a grade of service of 0.002. This means that 99.8 percent of all calls made will be connected to the called telephone (which itself may be busy). Some congested areas have a grade of service that is not this good. Corporate tie-line networks are usually engineered more frugally, often with a grade of service between 0.01 and 0.05.

With realtime signals, such as telephone calls, a good grade of service can only be achieved if the average utilization of the channels is substantially less than 100 percent. For a given number of channels and a given average utilization, the grade of service can be calculated. The acceptable channel utilization increases as the number of channels increases. For 10 channels, with enough traffic to use five of them on average, the grade of service is 0.018. To achieve a grade of service of 0.001 with that traffic, 14 channels are needed. Similarly, with realtime data transmission, a mean channel utilization substantially lower than 100 percent is used in order to achieve an acceptably fast response time.

Now that we have completed our examination of the general characteristics of communication channel, in the final chapter of this part we discuss standards for the physical layer of a data communication system.

10 PHYSICAL LEVEL STANDARDS

As we have seen, the simplest type of point-to-point data link takes the form of a cable that connects two communicating stations. Figure 10.1 shows a direct cable connection between the serial I/O port of a small computer and a serial printer. We will use this simple form of connection to summarize the functions performed by the physical layer in a data communication system. The following are the major functions of the physical layer:

- To provide an electrical connection between two devices
- To transmit electrical signals over the electrical connection
- To detect electrical path failures

PHYSICAL LAYER STANDARDS

As discussed in Chapter 4, the *Electronic Industries Association* (EIA) publishes standards that are analogous to those developed by the CCITT in Geneva, Switzerland. A common EIA standard for the physical layer is called *RS-232-C*. The RS-232-C standard has CCITT counterparts called *Recommendation V.24* and *Recommendation V.28* that together are equivalent to the RS-232-C standard. We will refer to this standard by its EIA designation in the remainder of this discussion.

THE RS-232-C STANDARD

The RS-232-C standard defines 25 circuits that can be used to connect two communicating stations and describes the electrical characteristics of the signals carried over those circuits. CCITT *Recommendation V.24* defines those same 25 circuits, and *Recommendation V.28* defines the electrical characteristics of the signals. The 25 circuits are defined in the standards by circuit number. This

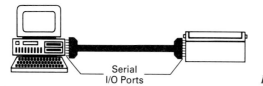

Figure 10.1   Direct cable connection

Serial
I/O Ports

interface allows for serial transmission at speeds up to about 20,000 bps at a typical distance of 50 feet or less. Each of the circuits is assigned a specific function. These functions can be divided into four groups:

- Data
- Control
- Timing
- Ground

Figure 10.2 shows some of the commonly used functions of the interface and the pins to which those functions are assigned. Although the connector itself is not specified in the standard, a 25-pin connector, such as that shown in Fig. 10.3 has become a generally accepted standard for implementing an RS-232-C connection. Note that RS-232-C is a *physical layer standard,* and does not define functions that are performed in the higher-level layers in a data communication system. For example, the RS-232-C standard does not specify how bits are generated or detected, nor does it specify how bits are to be grouped into

Pin	Description	Ground	Data	Control	Timing
1	Protective ground	●			
7	Signal ground	●			
2	Transmitted data		●		
3	Received data		●		
4	Request to send			●	
5	Clear to send			●	
6	Data set ready			●	
20	Data terminal ready			●	
22	Ring indicator			●	
8	Received line signal detector			●	
21	Signal quality detector			●	
23	Data signal rate selector			●	
24	Transmitter signal element timing (DTE)				●
15	Transmitter signal element timing (DCE)				●
17	Receiver signal element timing				●

Figure 10.2   RS-232C Interface pin functions

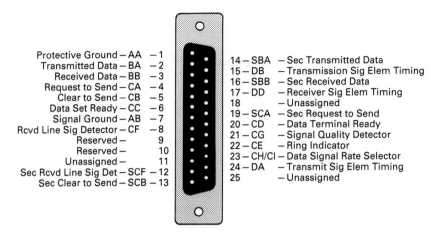

Protective Ground — AA   — 1
Transmitted Data — BA   — 2
Received Data — BB   — 3
Request to Send — CA   — 4
Clear to Send — CB   — 5
Data Set Ready — CC   — 6
Signal Ground — AB   — 7
Rcvd Line Sig Detector — CF   — 8
Reserved —   9
Reserved —   10
Unassigned —   11
Sec Rcvd Line Sig Det — SCF — 12
Sec Clear to Send — SCB — 13

14 — SBA   — Sec Transmitted Data
15 — DB   — Transmission Sig Elem Timing
16 — SBB   — Sec Received Data
17 — DD   — Receiver Sig Elem Timing
18   — Unassigned
19 — SCA   — Sec Request to Send
20 — CD   — Data Terminal Ready
21 — CG   — Signal Quality Detector
22 — CE   — Ring Indicator
23 — CH/CI — Data Signal Rate Selector
24 — DA   — Transmit Sig Elem Timing
25   — Unassigned

Figure 10.3   RS-232-C cable connector

characters. These concerns are handled by software or firmware in the data link layer.

When two devices communicate using the RS-232-C standard, they each contain circuitry that can generate and detect the voltages specified by the RS-232-C standard. They also typically use a cable that connects two 25-pin connectors in a standard way. There are many different implementations of the RS-232-C standard. For example, not all 25 circuits need be used by the two communicating devices. As few as three of the circuits, and thus three conductors, can be used for communication between two devices and still be in conformance to the standard. However, some devices use more than the minimum three. One of the difficulties in using the RS-232-C recommendation is that the two communicating devices must agree in advance as to which circuits will be used. Since devices that use the RS-232-C standard are designed and manufactured by a great many competing companies, the proper wiring of an RS-232-C cable and its two connectors has been referred to by some writers as a "black art."

**COMMUNICATING
OVER LONGER
DISTANCES**

Communicating over an RS-232-C cable is limited to a distance of less than 50 feet. So it would appear that the RS-232-C standard is much too restrictive to be of use in data communication applications, where distances are sometimes measured in hundreds or thousands of miles. However, when we introduce the true purpose of the RS-232-C standard, the applicability of the standard will become more clear. The RS-232-C standard is designed for connecting a device in a class called *data terminal equipment* (DTE) to a device in a complementary class called *data circuit-terminating equipment* (DCE). The communication ports in terminals and computers are common examples of DTEs; modems are common examples of devices that contain DCEs.

Figure 10.4 illustrates a typical long-distance implementation of a physical connection between two communicating stations. In this case, the computer on the left has circuitry installed in it that performs the functions of a DTE. It is connected via a cable that uses two 25-pin RS-232-C connectors to a complementary device that has circuitry installed in it that perform the functions of a DCE. On the right, the printer also has a DTE that is connected by another RS-232-C cable to a DCE. The DCEs are connected to each by a telephone line of arbitrary length. In this example, the DTE on the left consists of a communication port installed in the computer, the two DCEs are implemented in a pair of compatible modems, and the DTE on the right consists of a communication port installed in the printer.

Notice that there are three physical connections in this configuration. The DTE on the left is connected to its DCE by an RS-232-C cable, the two DCEs are connected by a telephone line, and the DTE on the right is connected to its DCE by another RS-232-C cable.

ANALOG AND DIGITAL SIGNALS

As we saw in Chapter 5, when communicating over long distances, it is often necessary to convert the digital signals used by the DTEs to analog signals that can be transmitted over an ordinary telephone circuit. An RS-232-C connection is intended to carry *digital* data. A positive voltage on the appropriate RS-232-C circuit indicates a zero bit, and a negative voltage indicates a one bit. In order to send digital signals over analog telephone lines, modems (short for "modulator/demodulator") are used to convert the voltages generated by the DTE into analog signals. The analog signals are continuous audio tones that are similar to the tones generated by a pushbutton telephone.

VIRTUAL CHANNEL

When two communicating devices (DTEs) are connected using two modems and a telephone line, it

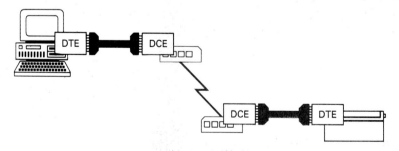

Figure 10.4   Telephone line with modems

appears to the two DTEs as if a simple hard-wired cable connects them. In effect, the two modems and the telephone line are transparent to the two DTEs; the modems implement a virtual channel between the two devices that appears just as if a simple cable connects them. When the DTE on the left in Fig. 10.4 generates a bit stream, its DCE converts the bit stream to a continuous analog signal and transmits it to the DCE on the right. The DCE on the right reconstructs the original bit stream and applies the appropriate voltages to the cable connected to its DTE. The DTE on the right has no way of knowing that the voltages were not generated directly by the DTE on the left. In effect, the physical connection appears just as though a very long RS-232-C cable were used to connect the two DTEs. The use of two modems and a telephone line is *transparent* to the two DTEs. They implement a simple, point-to-point *virtual channel,* as shown in Fig. 10.5. We can change the modems, perhaps using exotic technology to increase transmission speed, and this change would not be apparent to the two communicating devices. We could even substitute a digital communication line of arbitrary length for the two modems and the telephone line, and the two DTEs would still communicate in the same manner.

The important thing to note here is that the level above the physical level—the data link level—is not aware of the complexities of the physical link. The firmware operating at the data link level simply assumes that the bit stream it sends down to the firmware operating at the physical level will somehow appear in its original form at the firmware operating at the data link level in the device at the opposite end of the data link.

DIRECT RS-232-C CONNECTIONS

Direct RS-232-C connections are often used to connect communicating devices. For example, Fig. 10.1 showed how we might connect a small computer to a printer via a direct RS-232-C cable connection. As we mentioned earlier, the RS-232-C standard is meant for connecting a DTE to a DCE. However, if the serial ports in both devices happen to be wired as DTEs (as shown in Fig. 10.6) or perhaps both as DCEs, they can still be connected simply by using a cable

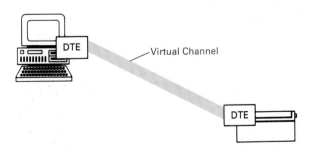

Figure 10.5   Virtual channel

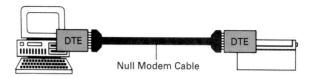

Figure 10.6　Connecting a DTE to a DTE

that has the appropriate circuits crossed. An RS-232-C cable that has its circuits crossed in the appropriate way is sometimes known as a *null modem* because it simulates the presence of a pair of modems connected by an analog circuit.

Notice that the direct cable connection in Fig. 10.6 is conceptually identical to the virtual channel in Fig. 10.5. The computer and printer need have no knowledge of how the physical connection is implemented. The two devices function in an identical manner whether they are in the same room connected by a 6-foot cable or in separate cities connected using modems and a telephone connection.

The RS-232-C standard is used quite often in connecting devices to personal computers. In Chapter 29 we discuss the use of the RS-232-C standard in the personal computer environment and provide cable wiring charts that can be used in a number of personal computer data communication applications.

OTHER PHYSICAL STANDARDS

There are many other U.S. and international standards that are commonly used to connect communicating devices at the physical layer. As we have mentioned, the CCITT V.24 and V.28 recommendations are equivalent to the EIA RS-232-C standard. The following are brief descriptions of the purposes and characteristics of some other physical layer standards.

THE RS-422 STANDARD

The RS-422 standard (also published by the EIA) specifies an alternative method for connecting a DTE to a DCE. The RS-422 standard specifies a more electrically stable method for generating positive and negative voltages in the range of from 2 to 6 volts. The standard states that these techniques can be used to implement equipment capable of transmitting and receiving data at up to 10 mbps. However, many implementations are limited to speeds much less than this. For example, the Apple Macintosh computer implements a variation of the RS-422 standard in its serial communication ports; these ports can handle speeds up to 230,400 bps.

CCITT MODEM RECOMMENDATIONS

The RS-232-C and RS-422 standards define the interface between a DTE and a DCE. A number of additional standards govern the way modems generate signals for transmission over analog telephone channels. Box 10.1 lists the CCITT series V recommendations for modem signaling. In Chapter 26 we discuss modem standards further.

CCITT RECOMMENDATION X.21

The standards above all apply to situations where modems are used to transmit data over telephone circuits. There now exist many public data networks that use digital rather than analog circuits for data transmission. Examples of these in the United States are the Telenet and Tym-

BOX 10.1   CCITT Series V modem recommendations

- **Recommendation V.21:** 300 bps duplex modem standardized for use in the general switched telephone network
- **Recommendation V.22:** 1200-bps duplex modem standardized for use on the general switched telephone network and on leased circuits
- **Recommendation V.23:** 600/1200-baud modem standardized for use in the general switched telephone network
- **Recommendation V.26:** 2400-bps modem standardized for use on 4-wire leased circuits
- **Recommendation V.26bis:** 2400/1200-bps modem standardized for use in the general switched telephone network
- **Recommendation V.27:** 4800-bps modem with manual equalizer standardized for use on leased telephone-type circuits
- **Recommendation V.27bis:** 4800/2400-bps modem with automatic equalizer standardized for use on leased telephone-type circuits
- **Recommendation V.27ter:** 4800/2400-bps modem standardized for use in the general switched telephone network
- **Recommendation V.29:** 9600-bps modem standardized for use on point-to-point leased telephone-type circuits
- **Recommendation V.35:** data transmission at 48 kbps using 60–108-kHz group band circuits
- **Recommendation V.36:** modems for synchronous transmission using 60–108-kHz group band circuits

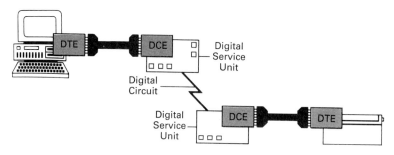

Figure 10.7   Digital circuit

net networks. Public data networks will become increasingly important as data transmission occupies a greater proportion of the total traffic being transmitted over the world's telecommunications facilities. A typical configuration where a digital circuit is used is shown in Fig. 10.7. Notice that the diagram is conceptually similar to the diagram showing two modems communicating over an analog circuit. However, in this case, the two DCEs are not modems. Instead, they are simple devices, sometimes called *service units, signal converters,* or *line drivers,* that provide an interface between a digital device and a digital line. The *CCITT Recommendation X.21* defines the electrical interface between a DTE and a DCE that is often used for communication over digital lines in much the same way as the RS-232-C standard defines the interface between a terminal and a modem.

Readers that are interested in specific details of the many physical-level standards that govern data communication can consult the appropriate fascicles of the CCITT Red Book or *McGraw-Hill's Compilation of Data Communication Standards* (see Chapter 4).

The chapters in Part II have been concerned mainly with the general characteristics of communication channels of all types. In the chapters in Part III we discuss the technology of data transmission and examine the actual transmission facilities that are available from common carriers.

PART **III** TRANSMISSION
FACILITIES

11 THE PUBLIC TELEPHONE NETWORK

In the years ahead, telecommunications channels of enormous capacity will change the way people communicate. Behind much of the development in telecommunications are two fundamental changes. These changes are so powerful that it will be necessary to rethink almost all aspects of the technology.

The first is a continuing and rapid increase in the *capacities* of the channels in use. The television cables now being laid into homes have 1000 times the information-carrying capacity of the existing telephone lines.

In 1940, long-distance cables carried 60 telephone calls. Many of AT&T's transmission links carry 108,000. The optical fiber cables that are in use have a much higher capacity than that. Communications satellites offer the prospect of very high capacity channels whose cost is independent of distance.

The other dominant trend in telecommunications is of special interest to users of data transmission facilities. This is the trend toward the use of computers and computer-like logic in our telecommunications links. Computer logic and storage chips are increasing in capacity and complexity at a staggering rate. We are in the era of *very large scale integration* (VLSI). What this means in economic terms is that if many thousands of logic or memory circuits are needed, they can be manufactured at very low cost, even if an exceedingly complex circuit is required. Once the mask for an LSI circuit is set up, huge quantities of the circuit can be produced rather like newspaper printing.

Increasing channel capacities and decreasing logic costs are a potent combination. Both changes are happening fast. The technical press calls it a revolution. But we have barely begun to grasp the implications. We should no longer think of telecommunications as meaning telephone and telegraph facilities. Almost every means of communication known to man, except perhaps love at first sight, can be converted to an electronic form.

Box 11.1 lists some of the major trends in the telecommunications industry, both in end-user equipment and in the channels that common carriers provide, that affect the user of data communication services.

143

BOX 11.1   Trends in telecommunications

Trends in End-User Equipment

- Higher levels of multiplexing
- Increasing complexity of control mechanisms that permit different signals to be transmitted together
- Conversion to digital rather than to analog form for transmission
- More complex information encoding
- Greater degrees of signal compression and data compaction
- Greater use of intelligence in terminal equipment

Trends in Telecommunications Channels

- Increasing channel capacities
- Increasing transmission carrier frequencies
- Decreasing cost of long-distance channels
- Larger number of signals occupying the same physical channel
- Channels increasingly designed for digital rather than for analog transmission
- Channels with higher levels of noise and distortion used for cost reasons, with more complex signal encoding to protect the signal from the noise and distortion

CLASSIFYING COMMUNICATION CHANNELS

It will be helpful to establish a framework for a detailed study of communication facilities by classifying communication links according to the following criteria:

- Analog or digital
- Channel capacity
- Switched versus leased lines
- Transmission mode
- Physical transmission medium

ANALOG OR DIGITAL
As discussed in Part II, telecommunications channels can be designed to carry analog signals or can carry digital data directly. This is a fundamental difference that has much to do with the way the communication link is engineered. Most of today's telecommunications links are analog in nature, but this is rapidly changing, and digital links will become much more common in the future. Computer data can be carried on either analog or digital channels, but as we have already seen, data is carried much more economically on a channel that has been designed with digital data in mind.

CHANNEL CAPACITY
As we discussed in Chapter 8, the transmission rates that are available today range from just a few bits to millions of bits per second. For convenience, we generally separate transmission lines into three categories. In the first category are *subvoice-grade* lines, those that transmit at rates from about 45 to 600 bps. These are lines that do not have sufficient capacity to carry telephone calls. Some telegraph circuits consist of subvoice-grade lines.

In the second category are *voice-grade* lines, which are generally normal telephone channels. They are typically used at speeds of from 1200 to 9600 bps. The highest bit rates on voice lines are paid for with a penalty of increased error rates. Speeds of 300 bps, or even slower speeds, are also often used over voice-grade lines because the user equipment is so inexpensive. Voice-grade facilities are discussed in this chapter.

In the third category are *wideband* lines, those that have higher capacities than normal telephone channels: 19,200, 48,000, and 56,000 bps are commonly used on wideband channels. Some of the long-distance communication channels in use today support bit rates much higher than these, sometimes as high as millions of bits per second. But most of these high-capacity links are used only by common carriers to multiplex large numbers of voice channels or to transmit television signals. Extremely high bandwidth lines are available to the user today, but at high cost. Wideband facilities are discussed in Chapter 12.

SWITCHED VERSUS LEASED LINES
When you dial a telephone call, you make use of a *public, switched line*. When you dial, a communication line is made available to you through the facilities of switching offices between you and your destination. As soon as you hang up, the switches disconnect your circuit and it can be used by someone else.

When a *leased line* is used, the common carrier establishes a permanent circuit between one user and another, and a fixed monthly charge is assessed for the connection. The line may still go through the switching offices, but the switches are permanently set so the circuit is always connected.

As discussed in Chapter 9, many other options exist for switching other than the circuit switching used by the telephone company. As we have seen, one switching technique that is particularly well suited for many data transmission applications is packet switching (see Chapter 37), used by many public data networks (see Chapter 36). When you use a public data network, you do not pay for a communication channel. Instead, you pay the common carrier to transmit a group of bits from here to there. You are charged for access to the network and for the quantity of data that you transmit rather than for the length of time that a circuit is connected. It is up to the carrier to manage and maintain the network. In most cases the organization that operates the public data network leases lines from other common carriers to handle the data transmission.

TRANSMISSION MODE

There are basically three modes of transmission. These are *simplex, half-duplex,* and *full-duplex*. In designing a data transmission system, the designer must decide whether the lines must transmit in one direction only or in both directions.

As shown in Fig. 11.1, a *simplex* line is capable of transmitting in only one direction. A *half-duplex* line can transmit in both directions, but only in one direction at a time. A *full-duplex* line can transmit in both directions at once.

Most communication lines that are used today for data transmission are either half-duplex or full-duplex. Simplex lines are not very useful because even

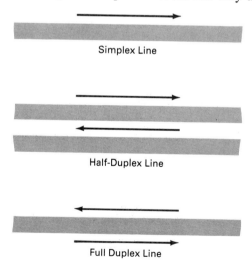

Simplex Line

Half-Duplex Line

Full Duplex Line

Figure 11.1 Transmission modes

in the simplest data communication application, where data is transmitted in only one direction, control signals must periodically flow the opposite way.

When ordinary switched telephone circuits are used for data transmission, half-duplex transmission is normally used. Some leased lines are full-duplex. It sometimes costs only about 10 percent more for a full-duplex leased line instead of a half-duplex one. However, much equipment cannot make effective use of a full-duplex line.

PHYSICAL TRANSMISSION MEDIUM

As far as data transmission is concerned, the three classification methods we have looked at so far—classification by *transmission rate, switching technique,* and *transmission mode*—are all that are necessary for choosing a line for data transmission purposes. Our final method of classification is of more interest to the common carrier. We discuss it here because it shows how far we have come in the last 100 years in telecommunications technology. With this classification method we look at the *physical medium* that is used to construct the communication channel.

Early telecommunications systems used relatively thick wires that were capable of carrying signals a long distance without amplification. Most of these, called *open-wire pairs*, have been replaced with cables containing a number of *twisted-wire pairs*. These cables use thinner wire and use amplifiers spaced closer together. It is common for a single twisted-wire pair to carry either 12 or 24 simultaneous telephone calls. Wire pairs have a limited bandwidth because as the frequencies transmitted increase, the current tends to flow on the outer skin of the wire, and the effective resistance of the wire increases.

To carry higher frequencies, and hence deliver a higher bandwidth, *coaxial cables* can be used. A coaxial cable consists of a wire surrounded by a hollow copper cylinder. The wire is insulated from the cylinder by air or plastic. Several coaxial cables are often bound together with a number of twisted-wire pairs in a single cable. A special form of coaxial cable is used in the submarine cables used for overseas communication.

In many cases *radio* is used as the transmission medium. Regular high-frequency radio communication is used for mobile telephone service and ship-to-shore operations. Microwave radio channels span the nation and carry much of our long-distance telephone traffic. The disadvantage of microwave radio is that transmission must be on a line-of-sight basis with the microwave towers relatively close together. *Tropospheric scatter circuits* use the reflective nature of the earth's troposphere to make possible radio communication over long distances.

Very high frequency radio waves can be used in rectangular and helical *waveguides*. Their advantage is that the higher frequencies used allow for extremely high bandwidths. But almost as soon as waveguides were publicly used, *optical fibers* made them appear obsolete. As we discussed earlier, optical fibers, lasers, and communications satellites represent the most dramatic new technologies for telecommunications. These technologies are discussed further in Chapter 14.

NETWORK COMPONENTS   There are four major parts to the telecommunications networks that provide the voice-grade facilities that are employed for the vast majority of voice and data communication. These parts are *instruments, local loops, switching,* and *trunks.*

- **Instruments.** These are the devices that subscribers use to originate and receive signals. The vast majority of instruments in use are ordinary telephone handsets. Today, however, an endless array of other devices are being attached to the telephone lines, including the terminals and computers used for data transmission.

- **Local Loops.** These are the cables that connect the subscriber's premises to the local switching office. Telephone and telegraph local loops today consist of twisted-wire-pair cables. Every subscriber normally has a separate pair of wires to the central office, and nobody else uses these, unless it is a party line. Coaxial cables are now being laid into many people's homes for the distribution of cable television. These cables have many potential uses other than television because of their extremely high capacity compared to the twisted-wire cables used for telephone local loops.

- **Switching.** These are the facilities that permit users to be interconnected on demand. Most switching is done by the world's vast network of telephone exchanges, although today, important new types of switching, such as packet switching, are being used for computer data and new forms of telecommunications.

- **Trunks.** These are the channels that carry calls between the switching offices, sometimes over long distances. In most cases, one trunk carries many calls simultaneously.

CHANGING COSTS   In the public telephone network, the cost breakdown among the four areas listed above is approximately as follows:

- Instruments: 23 percent
- Local loops: 15 percent
- Switching: 45 percent
- Trunks: 17 percent

New technology, however, is changing these costs.

COST REDUCTIONS IN THE TRUNKS The fastest change is in long-distance transmission. The capacity of such systems is increasing greatly without a proportional increase in cost. Techniques in the laboratory today portend much greater economies of scale in the years ahead. The investment cost of adding a channel mile to a typical telephone network is dropping rapidly as the channel capacity of the links used increases. Satellites and new terrestrial technology will probably lower the cost of long-distance bandwidth to one tenth of its present cost. On the other hand, the traffic volumes are rising, and some signals, mainly video signals, require much more bandwidth than do telephone signals. The costs for the other three parts of the network are not dropping as fast.

COST REDUCTIONS IN SWITCHING The largest portion of the telephone cost is that of switching, which contributes 45 percent to the cost of an average telephone call; the switching-cost percentage is 54 percent for a typical long-distance call on the AT&T network. Only 28 percent of the cost of an average call is in the switching equipment; the remainder is in operator salaries.

The key to switching economy lies in the use of computers. If used fully, they can reduce the cost of operator salaries. Computers and electronic circuitry, like computer circuitry, have already largely replaced electromechanical devices in most telephone exchanges. The cost of computer circuitry is dropping rapidly, and its maintenance costs will be much lower than those of the vast arrays of electromechanical switches.

COST REDUCTIONS IN LOCAL LOOPS The local loops in the telephone networks are unlikely to come down much in cost, although the use of concentrators may drop their cost somewhat. A concentrator enables the signals from a number of subscribers to be sent over one pair of wires. It is possible that with digital transmission and efficient multiplexing techniques, a quite different configuration of local loops could be built that would be much lower in cost. However, the vast investment sums tied up in today's wiring inhibit too drastic a change.

A change that has great potential, however, *is* occurring. The local telephone loops can be made to carry a much higher bandwidth. When ISDN services become commonplace, a wide range of digital channel capacities will be made available to the subscriber over the local loops that now carry a single analog voice channel. In addition, other channels of enormous capacity are now being wired into homes to carry cable TV. These are not switchable as is a telephone channel; still, in the future, new forms of switching could be used in which many subscribers communicate at once over the same coaxial cable.

COST REDUCTIONS IN INSTRUMENTS

The cost of the telephone set (23 percent of the total) is the least likely to drop; already, telephone sets are available for less than $10. Instead, many new forms of terminal, some of which are relatively expensive compared to the telephone handset, are now commonly used. These include facsimile machines, personal computers, display terminals, and voice answer-back devices.

The cost of terminals can be expected to drop as markets increase and logic circuitry mass-production techniques are perfected. If a true mass market for data terminals develops, it is conceivable that they could drop to very low costs. For example, many personal computers use an ordinary television set as a display screen, thus allowing the consumer to use an existing piece of equipment as a part of a data terminal. The telephone handset itself can be used as a data terminal for some simple applications. It is probable that in the near future, a high proportion of telephone extensions will have data capability.

12 WIDEBAND CHANNELS AND TRUNKS

The wideband analog telecommunications facilities that allow data communication systems to carry high bit rates of 50,000 bps and more are derived mainly from the high-capacity trunks that carry telephone signals over long distances. We begin this investigation of wideband facilities by examining the nature of these high-capacity analog trunks. In Chapter 13 we examine digital transmission facilities.

The main telecommunications highways of the world carry many different signals simultaneously, and these signals are gathered together into standardized groupings. The composition of a grouping is precisely defined in terms of the number of channels, the frequencies used, the carrier frequencies, and the multiplexing techniques employed to form the grouping.

A standardized grouping may travel over a variety of different physical facilities that are differently structured, such as coaxial cable routes, microwave routes, satellites, and so on. It is necessary that the structures be standardized so that groupings of signals can pass from one type of transmission facility to another, and can pass from one common carrier to another, without having to demultiplex the grouping into its constituent channels and remultiplex them. To a major extent, international standardization has been achieved, but some of the North American standards are different from the CCITT standards adopted by much of the rest of the world. This is because many of the North American high-capacity facilities were designed and installed before the international standards came into existence.

NORTH AMERICAN CHANNEL GROUPS   Figure 12.1 shows the main blocks of channels that form the standards for North American common carriers. At the bottom of the diagram is the telegraph channel. Either twelve 150-Hz telegraph channels or twenty-four 50-bps telex

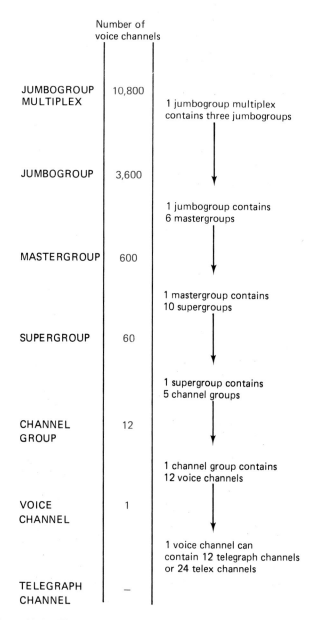

Figure 12.1 Hierarchy of AT&T frequency-division multiplex groups

channels can be derived from one voice channel. Twelve voice channels can be multiplexed together to form a *channel group,* sometimes called simply a *group.* This was the highest level of multiplexing in the 1930s; since then larger and larger blocks have come into use, as follows:

- Five channel groups are combined to form one *supergroup.*
- Ten supergroups are combined to form one *mastergroup.*
- Three mastergroups are sometimes combined to form one *mastergroup multiplex.* (This grouping is used only by some common carriers and is not shown in Fig. 12.1.)
- Six mastergroups are combined to form one *jumbogroup.*
- Three jumbogroups are combined to form one *jumbogroup multiplex.*

The jumbogroup multiplex is used on one high-capacity coaxial cable link and consists of 10,800 voice channels. This carrier physically consists of 22 coaxial tubes—10 carry signals in one direction, 10 in the opposite direction, and 2 are spares that are used if one or two of the others fails. Each tube carries a jumbogroup multiplex of 10,800 voice channels. The cable thus carries a total of 108,000 voice channels in both directions simultaneously.

CCITT STANDARD GROUPS

The CCITT international standards are the same as the North American ones for the group and supergroup but are different for higher-capacity groups. Consequently, a mastergroup or higher cannot travel directly from North Amer-

Number of Voice Channels	CCITT Standard	AT&T Standard
12	Group	Channel group (sometimes called "Group")
60	Supergroup	Supergroup
300	Mastergroup	
600		Mastergroup
900	Supermaster group (sometimes called "Mastergroup" or "Hypergroup")	
1800		Mastergroup multiplex
3600		Jumbogroup
10,800		Jumbogroup multiplex

Figure 12.2 CCITT and North American standards for multiplex groups

ican to European telephone networks. They must first be demultiplexed down to the supergroup level and then remultiplexed using CCITT groupings. The CCITT groupings are shown in Fig. 12.2.

FREQUENCIES USED

Figure 12.3 shows the frequencies used for the North American channel groupings. The voice channel might be regarded as the first building block. Telegraph signals multiplexed into the voice channel frequencies can travel over voice channels everywhere.

The channel group enables 12 voice channels to travel as a unit in a band of 60 to 108 kHz. This frequency band is used throughout most of the world as a standard. The band 12 to 60 kHz is also used. Many of the world's wire-pair cables and their associated plant are designed for 60 to 108 kHz. Without this standardization, international telephone transmission would be much more expensive.

The supergroup, containing five channel groups, occupies frequencies of 312 to 523 kHz. The telephone companies thus manufacture another subdivision of transmission facilities to carry this band of $5 \times 12 = 60$ telephone channels. The frequencies 312 to 552 kHz are generally agreed upon internationally. However, several different pilot frequencies (the carrier frequency used for modulation) are used by different countries.

To carry the mastergroup in North America, 10 supergroups are multiplexed together to carry a total of $10 \times 5 \times 12 = 600$ voice channels. This is suitable for the bandwidth available on a coaxial cable or microwave link. Television transmission requires the bandwidth of two master groups. Consequently, the mastergroup multiplex block of frequencies, shown in the center of Fig. 12.3, is generally used for television transmission.

The first coaxial cable systems were originally built by AT&T to carry either three mastergroups and a supergroup (total of 1860 voice channels) or one mastergroup, a supergroup, and a television channel. Today, television is transmitted separately to achieve the higher transmission quality needed for color. Most microwave facilities similarly carry the mastergroup multiplex block. The massive growth of commercial television in the United States has been a spur to the building of such wideband facilities to carry the programs across the nation. Fortunately, television peak broadcasting periods do not coincide with the time of day when people are using their telephones the most, so the same bandwidth is often used for television transmission in the evening and for telephone calls by day.

The larger capacity and more recent coaxial cable systems needed the jumbo group and then the jumbogroup multiplex. Figure 12.4 shows the frequencies used on one of AT&T's carrier systems. On this carrier system, most of the spectrum is occupied by 10,800 voice channels. These are arranged in three jumbogroups, each containing six 600-channel mastergroups. Other por-

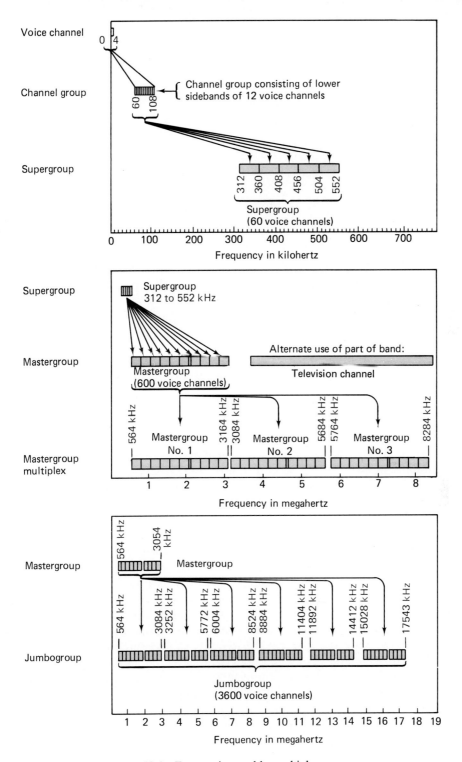

Figure 12.3 Frequencies used by multiplex groups

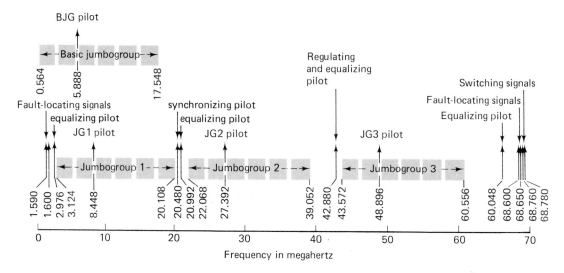

Figure 12.4   Frequencies used by the L5 carrier system

tions of the spectrum are dedicated to test and control signals that perform such functions as regulation, equalization, fault location, synchronization, and protection.

NORTH AMERICAN TRANSMISSION SYSTEMS

AT&T gives letter designations to its various transmission systems, or carriers. The coaxial systems mentioned above are referred to as the L carrier systems: L1, L3, L4, and L5. Microwave transmission systems are referred to as TD, TH, TM, TJ, and TL carriers. Twisted-wire-pair systems are called K and N carriers. Open-wire-pair systems are called O carrier systems. The long-distance carriers that compete with AT&T have similar facilities, which they describe with their own designations.

The physical transmission systems used by the various common carriers in North America have widely differing physical characteristics, but all carry the standard blocks of channels referred to in this chapter. Making the structures of the groups of channels independent of the physical structures of transmission systems is an architectural concept that has served the common carriers well. (It is a little like separating logical and physical structures in a computer system.) Table 12.1 summarizes the main transmission systems of North America and Fig. 12.5 illustrates the relative cost per circuit on different systems.

So far we have discussed *analog* transmission systems, which multiplex the signal by dividing the available bandwidth into various frequency bands.

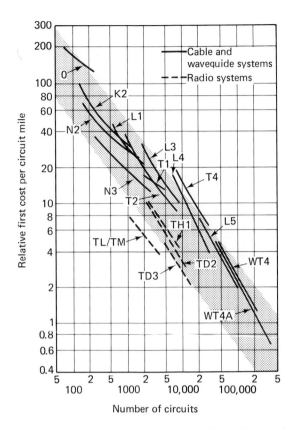

Figure 12.5　Relative cost per circuit mile for various carriers

Some of the most interesting systems for the computer industry are AT&T's *T* carrier systems, which are *digital* in nature and not analog. We discuss these digital carrier systems in Chapter 13.

LINKING OF DIFFERENT FACILITIES

Figure 12.6 shows three small towns and illustrates the types of facilities that might be used to link them. The towns may be many hundreds of miles apart.

Suppose first that subscriber A at the bottom left of the figure calls a subscriber in the same town. Both are connected to the same local switching office on dedicated two-wire subscriber loops. The telephone conversation undergoes no multiplexing. The signals travel at voice frequency.

Now consider what happens when subscriber C telephones subscriber D, both of them living in town 2. These two are not connected to the same switch-

Table 12.1 North American transmission systems

	ATT Name of Transmission System	Main Application	Today's Usage	Analog (A) or Digital (D)	Frequency Band Used	Number of Voice Circuits per Wire Pair
Open-wire pair	O carrier	Short haul	Declining	A	Up to 200 kHz	4-24
Twisted-wire pair	K carrier	Short haul	Medium	A	Up to 300 kHz	12
	N1 carrier	Short haul	Declining	A	Up to 300 kHz	12
	N2 carrier	Short haul	Medium	A	Up to 300 kHz	12 Many wire pairs in one cable.
	N3 carrier	Short haul	Large	A	Up to 300 kHz	24
	T1 carrier	Up to 50 miles	Large	D		24 (1.544 million bps)
	T2 carrier	Up to 500 miles	Large	D		96 (6.3 million bps)

	ATT Name of Transmission System	Main Application	Today's Usage	Analog (A) or Digital (D)	Frequency Band Used	Number of Voice Circuits per Tube	Number of Voice Circuits per Cable System
Coaxial cable	1.1 carrier	Long haul	Declining	A	Up to 3 MHz	600	1,800
	1.3 carrier	Long haul	Large	A	Up to 10 MHz	1,800	9,000
	1.4 carrier	Long haul	Large	A	Up to 20 MHz	3,600	32,400
	1.5 carrier	Long haul	Becoming large	A		10,800	108,000
	T4 carrier	Long haul or short haul	Large	D		274 million bps per channel	

						Number of Voice Circuits per Radio Channel	Typical Number of Voice Circuits per Route
Microwave radio	TD-2 carrier	Long haul	Large	A	3.7-4.2 GHz	600-1200	12,000
	TD-3 carrier	Long haul	Large	A	3.7-4.2 GHz	1200	12,000
	TH-1 carrier	Long haul	Large	A	5.925-6.425 GHz	1800	10,800
	TH-3 carrier	Long haul	Large	A	5.925-6.425 GHz	1800	10,800
	TM-1 carrier	Short haul	Large	A	5.925-6.425 GHz	600-900	3,600
	TJ carrier	Short haul	Low	A	10.7-11.7 GHz	600	1,800
	TL-1 carrier	Short haul	Medium	A	10.7-11.7 GHz	240	720
	TL-2 carrier	Short haul	Medium	A	10.7-11.7 GHz	600-900	2,700

						Total Digital Bit Rate	Number of Voice Circuits per Waveguide
Waveguide	WT-4 carrier	Long haul	Small	D		1.6×10^{10}	234,000

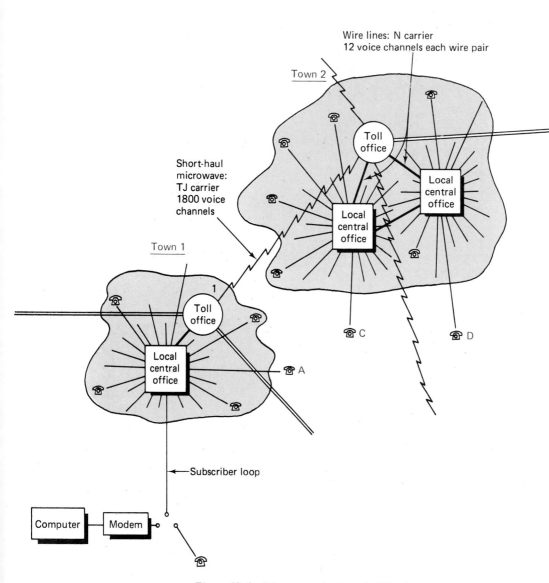

Wire lines: N carrier
12 voice channels each wire pair

Town 2

Toll
office

Short-haul
microwave:
TJ carrier
1800 voice
channels

Local
central
office

Local
central
office

Town 1

1

Toll
office

☎ C

☎ D

Local
central
office

☎ A

← Subscriber loop

Computer — Modem

☎

Figure 12.6   Telecommunications facilities between three towns

160

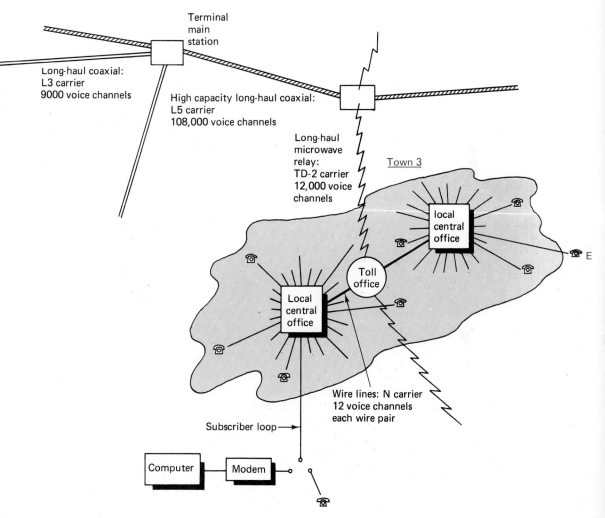

Terminal
main
station

Long-haul coaxial:
L3 carrier
9000 voice channels

High capacity long-haul coaxial:
L5 carrier
108,000 voice channels

Long-haul
microwave
relay:
TD-2 carrier
12,000 voice
channels

Town 3

local
central
office

E

Toll
office

Local
central
office

Wire lines: N carrier
12 voice channels
each wire pair

Subscriber loop

Computer

Modem

Figure 12.6 (Continued)

ing office. The call must therefore be routed from one central office to another on an interoffice trunk. Most of the time this trunk route will be handling several calls from people in that town talking to each other. Therefore, multiplexing equipment might be used. The interoffice trunk might consist of a number of wire pairs, each carrying a channel group of 12 voice channels, or it could be a number of nonmultiplexed pairs in a cable if that is more economical.

When subscriber A telephones subscriber C the situation is more complex, since there is no direct connection between the local switching offices to which they are attached. This is often the case even within one town. A large town with several central offices would have an additional exchange called a *tandem office* for switching lines between central offices. In Fig. 12.6 subscriber A's call will travel to the town where subscriber C lives over the short-haul microwave system connecting the towns. This is connected in both of these towns to a toll office. A's call goes over the local loop to the local central office, and this routes it to the toll office on a toll connecting trunk (or terminal trunk). Like the interoffice trunk, this trunk may be one of a channel group, and it travels with two other mastergroups between towns 1 and 2. The toll office of the receiving town demultiplexes it and sends it to the appropriate central office on a toll-connecting trunk in a channel group. From there it goes at voice frequency on to subscriber C via the local loop.

When subscriber A telephones subscriber E in town 3 there is another stage in the process because the link to subscriber E's town goes over two long-haul coaxial cable systems, an L3 carrier, carrying a mastergroup multiplex, and an L5 carrier, carrying a jumbogroup multiplex. The call then goes over a microwave relay to the toll office of town 3.

The same complex route would be taken if subscriber A were using a computer terminal for communicating with a computer in subscriber E's town. Suppose that subscriber A has a computer terminal and dials the distant computer. The data that travels in the ensuing dialog undergo the same multiplexing processes as a voice conversation would. The data, however, may be more seriously affected by noise and distortions along the route. The design of the modem is the key to tailoring the signal so that it can travel over this network without errors other than those caused by unavoidable noise.

At the switching offices that interconnect different trunk systems, the signals must be demultiplexed to lower-level groups or to a voice channel because different signals have different destinations.

**RELATIVE
ATTENUATION**
A long-distance telephone call thus goes through many stages of multiplexing and demultiplexing and may be transmitted over many different carrier systems. It is a triumph of modern electronics that the telephone voice can pass through all these manipulations and emerge unharmed. The curve of relative

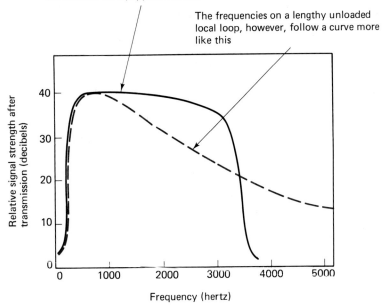

Figure 12.7   Voice channel characteristics

signal strength against frequency remains approximately the curve of Fig. 12.7, and hence a telephone voice from the other side of the nation usually sounds much the same as it would from across the street.

MICROWAVE TRUNKS

The frequencies allocated for radio transmission of common carrier signals are much higher than those of mastergroups and jumbogroups. Table 12.2 lists the microwave transmission frequencies. The bands most commonly used are the bands at 3.7 to 4.2 GHz and 5.925 to 6.425 GHz. These bands each have a bandwidth of 500 MHz, which is much greater than the 3-MHz bandwidth of the master group or the 18-MHz bandwidth of the jumbogroup. Several channels each containing a high-level multiplexed block are therefore transmitted over a microwave route. The TH systems, for example, have six active radio channels (with additional backup channels in case of failure), and each channel carries a mastergroup multiplex block. The route capacity is thus 10,800 voice channels.

The mastergroup multiplex block occupies frequencies up to 9 MHz. It is frequency modulated as a unit into a carrier of intermediate frequency, about 60 to 80 MHz. This band is shifted again to the correct transmitting frequency in

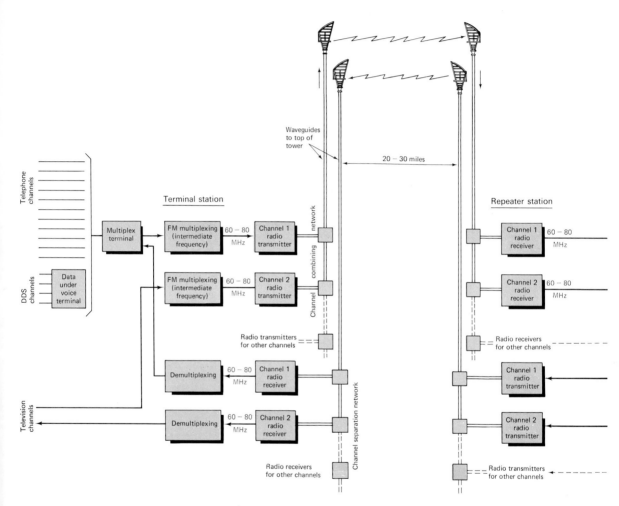

Figure 12.8 Microwave equipment

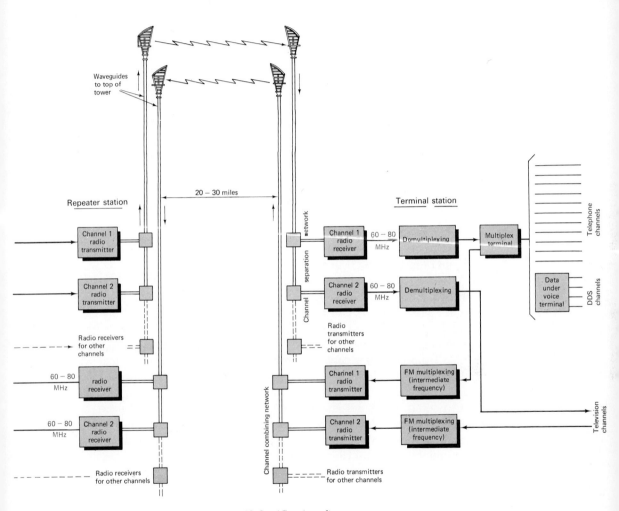

Figure 12.8 (Continued)

Table 12.2   Microwave frequencies allocated by the FCC

Band (MHz)	Bandwidth (MHz)
2110–2130	20
2160–2180	20
3700–4200	500
5925–6425	500
10,700–11,700	1000

the gigahertz band and amplified. A waveguide carries it up to the antenna, where it is radiated. Figure 12.8 shows the equipment that is typically used to implement a microwave circuit.

WIDEBAND CHANNELS

Most common carriers lease their channel groups and supergroups, as well as leasing individual channels, to provide a wideband service. Three grades of wideband services in North America are listed in Table 12.3. The series 8000 channel is thus equivalent to one channel group, the type 5700 channel to a supergroup, and the type 5800 to four supergroups.

When an organization leases a wideband channel, such as these, it will also lease appropriate channel terminals. A variety of terminating equipment is available. The channels can be used as wideband channels or they can be subdivided by the user into private channels of lower bandwidth to be used for telephone calls or for data transmission. The various channel groupings that are available from common carriers can use terminating equipment that will enable the channel to be used for a number of different purposes. Some of these are listed in Box 12.1.

Providing wideband analog transmission facilities to end users is difficult because most installed wideband systems link only the toll offices. It is usually the case that there are no commonly used facilities wider than the voice channel linking individual subscribers to the local switching office. Special arrangements, therefore, have to be made to bring wideband channels onto the user's

Table 12.3   Three grades of wideband service available from AT&T

	Equivalent Bandwidth (kHz)	Equivalent Number of Voice Channels
Series 8000 channel	48	12
Type 5700 channel	240	60
Type 5800 channel	1000	240

BOX 12.1   Common uses of channel groupings

Channel Group Uses

1. Twelve telephone channels between two points

2. Forty-eight 150-bps channels between two points

3. 144 teletype channels between two points

4. Equivalent combinations of the above

5. Data transmission at 40,800 bps, plus one telephone channel for coordination purposes

6. Two-level facsimile signals in the frequency range of approximately 29 to 44 kHz plus one telephone channel for coordination purposes

7. Two-level facsimile signals requiring up to 50,000 bps plus one telephone channel

8. A channel of bandwidth up to 20 kHz of high quality (i.e., only minor deviations in gain and delay characteristics)

Supergroup Uses

1. Data transmission at approximately 105,000 bps plus a control channel and a telephone channel for coordination purposes

2. Two-level facsimile requiring up to 250,000 bps plus four channels of teletype grade for control and coordination

3. A channel of bandwidth up to 100 kHz having only minor deviations in gain and delay characteristics

premises. As discussed in Part II, the local loop can carry a bandwidth much higher than that of the voice channel if the loading coils are removed.

In this chapter we have discussed the wideband analog transmission facilities that are used by common carriers. As we have already introduced, however, high-speed digital transmission facilities now dominate the long-haul facilities of common carriers. For a subscriber to obtain digital transmission at rates higher than those of the voice channel with modems, the techniques and transmission facilities discussed in Chapter 13 are extremely important.

13 DIGITAL TRANSMISSION FACILITIES

For half a century, telecommunications has been dominated by analog transmission and frequency-division multiplexing. Multibillions of dollars are tied up in such equipment. However, if the telecommunications industry were to start again today building the world's transmission links, frequency-division multiplexing would have limited use, and trunks would transmit *digital* bit streams instead of analog signal. Most links, with the possible exception of local loops, would be incapable of transmitting analog signals without conversion to digital form. As we will see in this chapter, the technique used most often to transmit analog signals in digital form is called *pulse code modulation* (PCM). The telephone voice becomes a bit stream looking like computer data.

Whether a telecommunications link is converted to digital technology is determined by economic considerations. When an entire nation's telephone system is considered, vast sums of money are involved. The links that can benefit most profitably are converted first. With many links, it is still cheaper to use analog transmission. However, the cost of digital transmission is dropping.

COMPUTER DATA   The swing to digital transmission is good news for the computer industry. If digital bit streams form the basis of telecommunications, computer data will no longer need to be converted to analog form for transmission. In other words, there will be no need for modems at each terminal. This can be seen today in AT&T's *Dataphone Digital Service* (discussed in Chapter 15), which performs end-to-end digital transmission. The user has a *service unit* instead of a modem, which contains a buffer from which the data is transmitted.

On the other hand, analog information, such as the sound of the human voice, needs to be converted to digital form before it can be transmitted over digital links. This conversion is done with a *codec* (short for *coder/decoder*), which in a sense is the converse of the modem. Ironically, instead of the computer industry having to convert its data with a modem to travel over the telephone lines in an analog form, the telephone industry now has to convert its analog signals with a codec to travel over digital lines.

A telephone call, when digitized using PCM techniques, 64,000 bps for transmission (56,000 bps for the voice signal and 8000 bps for control functions on AT&T digital carriers). This rate is much higher than 4800 or 9600 bps, which represent typical maximum rates at which data travels over analog telephone lines. The balance of cost between telephone voice transmission and data transmission is thus swinging substantially in favor of data.

ADVANTAGES OF DIGITAL TRANSMISSION

What are the advantages of transmitting the telephone voice in digital form? Oddly enough, one of the major advantages existed on early teletype links, but when several teletype channels were multiplexed into one voice circuit the advantage was lost. Now the changing economics are bringing it back. With analog transmission, whenever the signal is amplified, the *noise is amplified with it*. As the signal passes through its many amplifying stations, the noise is cumulative. With digital transmission, however, each repeater station *regenerates* the pulses. New, clean pulses are reconstructed and sent on to the next repeater, where another cleaning-up process takes place. So the pulse train can travel through a dispersive, noisy medium, but instead of becoming more and more distorted until eventually parts are unrecognizable, it is repeatedly reconstructed and thus remains impervious to most of the corrosion of the medium. Of course, an exceptionally large noise impulse may destroy one or more pulses so that they cannot be reconstructed by the repeater stations. As we will see in Part IV, techniques are used with computer data for detecting such errors and causing lost data to be retransmitted automatically. With voice signals, only a few milliseconds of the conversation are typically lost when severe noise occurs on a digital circuit, and the loss is barely noticed.

A major disadvantage of digital transmission would appear to be that much greater bandwidth is required. However, because the signal is reconstructed at frequent intervals down the line, it can tolerate much more battering than if it had to travel a long distance without reconstruction. It can survive traveling over a channel with a high level of distortion and with a poor signal-to-noise ratio.

There is a trade-off between bandwidth and signal-to-noise ratio. A given transmission link, such as a pair of wires, can be operated at a higher bandwidth (i.e., higher frequencies can be transmitted over it), but the resulting signal will be more distorted and the signal-to-noise ratio will be lower. The trick that makes digital transmission worthwhile is to *reconstruct* the signal sufficiently often so that it survives the bad distortion. A high bit rate can then be transmitted.

Consider a telephone wire pair under the streets of a city. With analog transmission it can typically carry a *channel group*—12 voice channels. Now suppose that we transmit digitally over the same wire pair. The digital signal becomes distorted as it is transmitted, as shown in Fig. 13.1. We catch it before it becomes too distorted to recognize whether a bit is zero or one. The bit stream is then reconstructed, retimed, and retransmitted. The faster the bit stream is transmitted, the greater will be the distortion and the closer the spacing of repeaters necessary to reconstruct the signal correctly. If, for the sake of argument, repeaters reconstructed the signal every 100 feet, then a *very* high bit rate could be transmitted. The wire pair would be handling a high bandwidth. The distortion would be severe, but the bit stream would get through. However, we cannot normally space the repeaters that close together. The cost would be too high and the wires may not be accessible. How closely can they reasonably be spaced? If the wires are carried on poles, they can be spaced any desired distance apart. In a typical city, where wires are carried underground, there is at least one access to the wires about every 6000 feet. In practice, this is the distance at which loading coils were typically spaced on analog circuits. To reengineer an analog line for digital transmission, the loading coils are simply replaced with regenerative repeaters, using this same 6000-foot spacing.

In North America, conservative engineering allows 1.544 million bps, thus carrying 24 speech channels instead of the 12 typically carried over analog circuits. When carefully adjusted modern lines are used, 6.3 million bps can be carried, thus allowing for 96 speech channels. Much higher bit rates can be carried over coaxial cables or waveguides that are specifically engineered to carry digital signals.

ECONOMIC FACTORS

The economic circumstances favoring digital transmission stem from several factors. First, the cost of digital circuitry produced in large quantities is dropping fast due to VLSI (very large scale integration) technology. Telecommunications networks employ large quantities of any circuit used and so can benefit from the mass-production economics of VLSI.

Second, as we have seen, it is becoming economical to build channels of higher bandwidth. Satellites, waveguides, and optical fibers provide much higher bandwidths. A high level of multiplexing is needed to make use of high-capacity channels. When many callers are packed in a high bandwidth, the cost of a voice channel mile drops greatly, but the cost of the increasing number of multiplexing and routing operations becomes high. Frequency-division multiplexing uses fairly expensive circuit components, such as filters. When thousands of telephone conversations travel together over coaxial cable or microwave links, they must be demultiplexed, switched, and then multiplexed together again at each switching point. Although there is great economy of scale in the *transmission,* there is not in this multiplexing and switching operation.

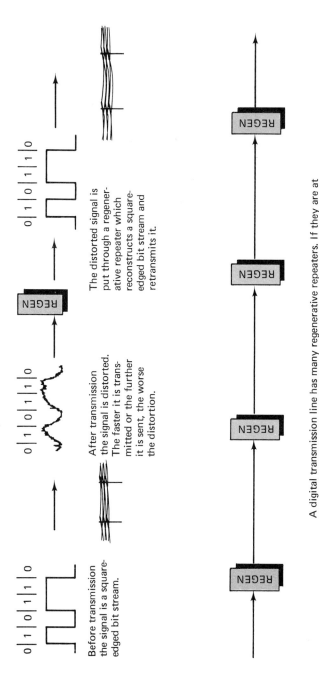

0|1|0|1|1|0

Before transmission the signal is a square-edged bit stream.

0|1|0|1|1|0

After transmission the signal is distorted. The faster it is transmitted or the further it is sent, the worse the distortion.

0|1|0|1|1|0

The distorted signal is put through a regenerative repeater which reconstructs a square-edged bit stream and retransmits it.

A digital transmission line has many regenerative repeaters. If they are at sufficiently frequent intervals, a much higher bit rate can be transmitted than with analog transmission.

Figure 13.1 Regenerative repeaters

As the channel capacities increase, so the multiplexing and switching costs assume a greater and greater proportion of the total network cost.

Digital circuitry, on the other hand, is dropping in cost at a high rate. Where digital rather than analog transmission is used, this increasingly low cost circuitry handles the multiplexing and switching. The telecommunications network becomes in some aspects like a vast digital computer.

Third, the use of digital transmission makes it possible to operate on links with a poor signal-to-noise ratio. On links with a wide-ranging trade-off between signal-to-noise ratio and bandwidth, a somewhat larger number of voice channels can be derived by PCM techniques than by analog circuitry. This is the case on today's wire-pair telephone lines and satellite channels, for example.

Fourth, digitization of voice channels can be done with more complex techniques than PCM, which will permit the speech to be encoded into fewer bits.

Finally, an additional economic factor is the rapidly increasing use of data transmission. Although data transmission still employs only a small proportion of the total bandwidth in use, it is increasing much more rapidly than other uses of the telecommunications networks. Data can be transmitted over digital voice links with a total equipment cost that can be as low as a tenth of that for transmission over analog links with modems.

In terms of the immediate economics of today's common carriers, pressed for capacity, digital transmission is appealing for short-distance links because with relatively low cost electronics it can substantially increase the capacity of existing wire pairs. This is particularly important in the congested city streets.

An important long-term advantage is the fact that all signals—voice, television, facsimile, and data—become a stream of similar-looking pulses. Consequently, they will not interfere with one another and will not make differing demands on the engineering of the channels. In an analog signal format, television and data are much more demanding in the fidelity of transmission than speech and create more interference when transmitted with other signals. As we have already mentioned, the goal of ISDN development is an integrated network in which all signals travel together digitally (see Chapter 41).

Since most traffic that is carried over telecommunications links is analog in nature (telephone voice) and not digital (computer data), techniques are used to carry analog signals in digital form. Although these techniques are not used with data transmission, they are important to us because they affect the way digital data is carried on a line that is also used to transmit speech in digital form.

PULSE AMPLITUDE MODULATION   To convert an analog signal, such as speech, into a pulse train, a circuit must sample it at periodic intervals. The simplest form of sampling produces pulses, the amplitude of which is proportional to the amplitude of the signal at the

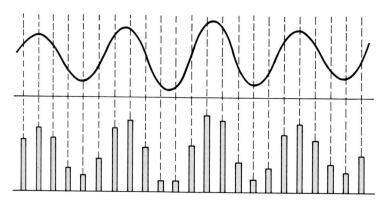

Figure 13.2 Pulse amplitude modulation (PAM)

sampling instant (see Fig. 13.2). This process is called *pulse amplitude modulation* (PAM). Compare the PAM illustration in Fig. 13.2 with that for amplitude modulation of a sine-wave carrier (see Chapter 7). Envelope detection can be used for demodulating the PAM signal in much the same way as described in Chapter 7 for amplitude modulation.

The pulses of Fig. 13.2 still carry their information in analog form, since the amplitude of the pulse is continuously variable. If the pulse train were transmitted over a long distance and subjected to distortion, it might not be possible to reconstruct the original pulses. To avoid this, a second process called *pulse code modulation* (PCM) is employed that converts the PAM pulses into unique sets of equal-amplitude pulses, in other words, into a binary bit stream. The receiving equipment then need only detect whether a bit is 0 or 1; it detects the presence or absence of a pulse, not its size.

PULSE CODE MODULATION

With PCM, the input signal is first quantized, and the signal amplitude at a particular instant in time is represented by a number. This process is illustrated schematically in Fig. 13.3. Here the signal amplitude can be represented by any one of the eight values ranging from binary 000 through binary 111. The amplitude of the pulses will therefore be one of these eight values. An inaccuracy is introduced by rounding values in a computation. Figure 13.3 shows only eight possible values of the pulse amplitude. If there were more values, the "rounding error" would be less. In systems in actual use today on the public telephone network, 128 pulse amplitudes are used (127 to be exact, for the zero amplitude is not transmitted).

1   The signal is first "quantized" or made
    to occupy a discrete set of values

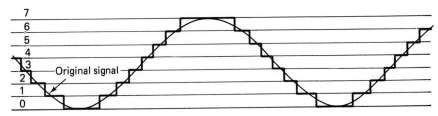

2   It is then sampled at specific points. The
    PAM signal that results can be coded
    for pulse code transmission

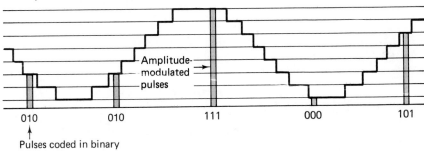

010   010   111   000   101

Pulses coded in binary

3   The coded pulse is transmitted
    in a binary form

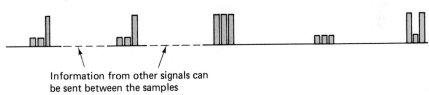

Information from other signals can
be sent between the samples

Figure 13.3   Pulse code modulation (PCM)

THE BIT STREAM   As shown above, with only eight possible ampli-
                       tudes, 3 bits are required to transmit each sample.
With 128 quantizing levels, 7 bits are needed for each sample. The resulting
train of pulses passes through frequent repeater stations that reconstruct the
pulse train and is impervious to most types of telecommunications distortion
other than major noise impulses or signal interruptions. The mere presence or
absence of a pulse can be recognized easily even when distortion is present,

whereas determination of pulse magnitude would be more prone to error. However, the original analog signal can never be reproduced exactly because of the quantizing error that was introduced when the bit stream was created. This deviation from the original signal is sometimes referred to as *quantizing noise*. The quantizing noise can be reduced to any desired level by increasing the number of sampling levels. Using 7 bits for each sample, 128 resulting levels are enough to produce telephone channels having a signal-to-noise ratio comparable to that achieved on today's analog voice channels.

The number of sampling levels, as well as the number of samples that are taken each second, can be varied. The more samples we take, the more accurately we can reproduce the signal, and the more bits that must be transmitted. Together, the number of quantizing levels used, and the number of samples taken per second, determine the bit rate that must be transmitted.

HOW MANY SAMPLES ARE NEEDED?

The pulses illustrated in Figs. 13.2 and 13.3 are sampling the input at a limited number of points in time. The question therefore arises: How often do we need to sample the signal to be able to reconstruct it satisfactorily from the samples? The less frequently we can sample it, the lower the number of pulses we have to transmit in order to send the information, or conversely, the more information we can transmit over a given bandwidth.

Any signal can be considered as being a collection of different frequencies, but the bandwidth limitation on it imposes an upper limit to these frequencies. When listening to a violin, you hear several frequencies at the same time, the higher ones being referred to as "harmonics." As discussed in Chapter 6, you hear no frequencies higher than 20,000 Hz because that is the upper limit of the human ear. (Like any other channel, the ear has a limited bandwidth.) When listening to a full orchestra, you are still hearing a collection of sounds of different frequencies, although now the pattern is much more complex. Similarly, other signals that we transmit are composed of a jumble of frequencies. A digital signal can be analyzed by Fourier analysis into its component frequencies.

It can be shown mathematically that if the signal is limited so that the highest frequency it contains is W hertz, then a pulse train of $2W$ pulses per second is sufficient to carry it and allow it to be completely reconstructed.

Therefore, the human voice, if limited to frequencies below 4000 Hz, can be carried by a pulse train of 8000 PAM pulses per second. The original voice sounds, below 4000 Hz, can then be *completely* reconstructed. Similarly, 40,000 samples per second could carry hi-fi music and allow complete reproduction. (If samples themselves were digitized with PCM, the reproduction would not be quite perfect because of the quantizing error.) Table 13.1 shows the bandwidth needed for four types of signals for human perception, plus the digital bit rate used or planned for their transmission with PCM.

Table 13.1　Bandwidths and equivalent PCM bit rates

Type of Signal	Analog Bandwidth Used (kHz)	Number of Bits per Sample	Digital Bit Rate Used or Needed (1000 bps)		
Telephone voice	4	7	$4 \times 2 \times 7 =$		56
High-fidelity music	20	10	$20 \times 2 \times 10 =$		400
Picturephone	1000	3	$1000 \times 2 \times 3 =$		6000
Color television	4600	10	$4600 \times 2 \times 10 =$		92,000

In telephone transmission, the frequency range encoded in PCM is somewhat less than 200 to 3500 Hz; 8000 samples per second are used. Each sample is digitized using 7 bits so that $2^7 = 128$ different volume levels can be distinguished. This gives $7 \times 8000 = 56,000$. (As mentioned earlier, in actual practice a PCM speech channel in North America carries 64,000 bps; the other 8000 bps is used for control purposes.) High-fidelity music with five times this frequency range would need five times as many samples per second, and to achieve subtle reproduction, more bits per sample.

TIME-DIVISION MULTIPLEXING　　As noted, $4000 \times 2 \times 7 = 56,000$ bps is needed to carry telephone voice signals. However, all the transmission facilities that this bit stream is likely to be sent over can carry a much higher bit rate than this. It is therefore desirable to send many telephone signals over one physical path. This is done by interleaving the "samples" that are transmitted by using *time-division multiplexing*. If four voice signals are to be carried over one pair of wires, the samples are intermixed as follows:

> sample from speech channel 1
> sample from speech channel 2
> sample from speech channel 3
> sample from speech channel 4
> sample from speech channel 1
> sample from speech channel 2
> sample from speech channel 3
>
> .
> .
> .

This is illustrated in Fig. 13.4. By sampling the signals at the appropriate instant in time, a train of PAM pulses is obtained; these pulses are then digitally encoded. For simplicity, only a 4-bit code is shown in the diagram. Each PAM

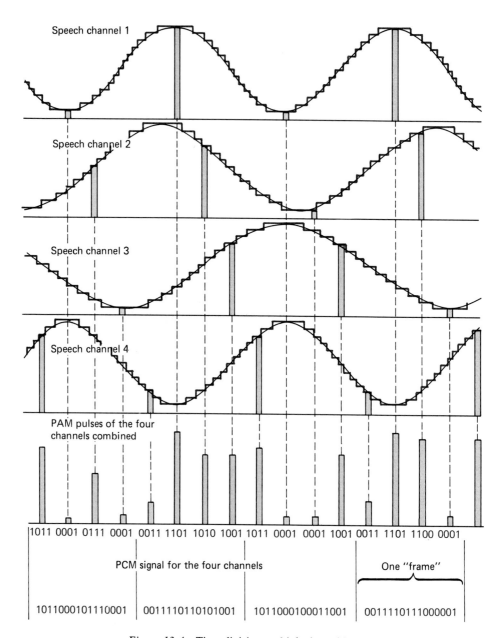

Speech channel 1

Speech channel 2

Speech channel 3

Speech channel 4

PAM pulses of the four channels combined

1011 0001 0111 0001 0011 1101 1010 1001 1011 0001 0001 1001 0011 1101 1100 0001

PCM signal for the four channels   One "frame"

1011000101110001   0011110110101001   1011000100011001   0011110111000001

Figure 13.4   Time-division multiplexing with PCM

178

pulse is encoded as 4 bits. The result is a series of *frames,* each of 16 bits. Each frame contains one sample of each signal.

To decode the signal, it is necessary to be sure where each frame begins. The signals can be reconstructed with this knowledge. The first 4 bits relate to speech channel 1, the second 4 to channel 2, and so on. A synchronization pattern must also be sent in order to know where each frame begins. This, in practice, can be done by the addition of 1 bit per frame. The added bits, when examined alone, form a unique bit pattern that must be recognized to establish the framing. This process takes place at electronic speeds in low-cost, computer-like circuits.

COMPANDING

If the signal being transmitted were of low amplitude, the procedure illustrated in Fig. 13.3 would not, of itself, be so satisfactory. The quantizing noise, still the same absolute magnitude, would now be larger relative to the signal magnitude. The quantizing error is a function of interval between levels and not of the signal amplitude; therefore, the signal-to-quantizing-noise ratio is lower for low-amplitude signals. For this reason a *compandor* is normally used.

A compandor is a device that compresses the higher-amplitude parts of a signal before modulation and expands them back to normal again after demodulation. Preferential treatment is therefore given to the weaker parts of a signal. The weaker signals traverse more quantum steps than they would otherwise, so

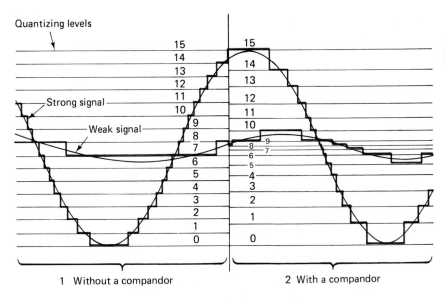

Figure 13.5　Use of a compandor

the quantizing error is less. This is done at the expense of the higher-amplitude parts of the signal, for these cover less quantum steps.

The process is illustrated in Fig. 13.5. The effect of companding is to move the possible sampling levels closer together at the lower-amplitude signal values. Figure 13.5 shows the quantizing of a weak signal and a strong signal. The right-hand side of the diagram is with companding, and the left-hand side without. Notice that on the left-hand side, the ratio of signal strength to quantizing error is poor for the weak signal; on the right-hand side it is better. Furthermore, the strong signal is not impaired greatly by the use of the compandor. In practice, the PAM pulses are companded, and one device serves all the channels that are being multiplexed together.

REGENERATIVE REPEATERS

As we have seen, the main reason that high bit rates can be achieved on wire-pair circuits using pulse code modulation is that repeaters are placed at sufficiently frequent intervals to reconstruct the signal. A regenerative repeater has to perform the following three functions, sometimes referred to as the three "R"'s:

- Reshaping
- Retiming
- Regeneration

When a pulse arrives at the repeater, it is attenuated and distorted. It is first passed through a preamplifier and an equalizer to reshape it for the detection process. A timing recovery circuit provides a signal to sample the pulse at the optimum point and decide whether it is a one or a zero bit. The timing circuit controls the regeneration of the outgoing pulse and ensures that it is sent at the correct time and is of the correct width.

AT&T DIGITAL CARRIERS

As we have seen, in telephone transmission on AT&T digital channels, 8000 samples per second are used. With 128 sampling levels using 7 bits per channel, this gives a bit rate of about 56,000 bps. Another 8000 bps is used for control purposes, giving a total of about 64,000 bps. In AT&T there are standards defined for four different levels of digital transmission channels. These are referred to as the T1, T2, T3, and T4 carriers. These same standards are used by many of the other long-distance common carriers in the United States.

THE T1 CARRIER

The most widely used transmission system at present that uses PCM and time-division multiplexing is the

T1 carrier. This carrier uses wire pairs with digital repeaters spaced 6000 feet apart to carry 1.544 million bps. As we have seen, 24 speech channels are encoded on this bit stream. The T1 carrier is used for short-haul transmission over distances of up to 50 miles. It has been highly successful, and millions of voice-channel-miles of it are in operation. Most readers of this book have talked over a digital T1 carrier without knowing it.

The AT&T T1 PCM system uses the technique discussed earlier for encoding telephone voice. Seven bits are used for coding each sample. The system is designed to transmit voice frequencies up to 4 kHz, and therefore 8000 samples per second are needed, and 8000 frames per second travel down the line. Each frame, then, takes 125 microseconds (μs). A T1 transmission frame is illustrated in Fig. 13.6. It contains 8 bits for each channel. The eighth bits form a bit stream for each speech channel that contains network signaling and routing information: for example, to establish a connection and to terminate a call. There are a total of 193 bits in each frame, giving 193 × 8000 = 1.544 million bps.

The last bit in the frame, the 193rd bit, is used for establishing and maintaining synchronization. The sequence of these 193 bits from separate frames is examined by the logic of the receiving terminal. If this sequence does not follow a given coded pattern, the terminal detects that synchronization has been lost. If synchronization does slip, the bits examined will probably be speech bits and

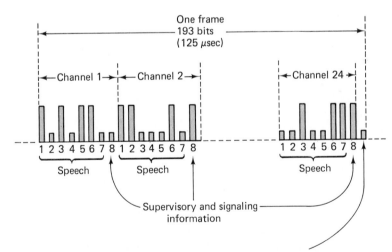

Framing code. The 193rd bits on successive frames follow a pattern which is checked to ensure synchronization has been maintained. If synchronization is lost this pattern is scanned for to re-establish it. The pattern used is 010101. . . repeated.

Figure 13.6   T1 carrier transmission frame

will not exhibit the required pattern. There is a chance that these bits will accidentally form a pattern being sought. The synchronization pattern must therefore be chosen so that it is unlikely that it will occur by chance. If the 193rd bit was always made to be a 1 or always a 0, this could occur by chance in the voice signal. It was found that an alternating bit pattern, 0 1 0 1 0 1 ..., never occurs for long in any bit position. Such a pattern would imply a 4-kHz component in the signal, and the input filters used do not pass this frequency. Therefore, the 193rd bit transmitted is made alternately a 1 and a 0. The receiving terminal inspects it to ensure that this 1 0 1 0 1 0 ... pattern is present. If it is not, then it examines the other bit positions that are 193 bits apart until a 1 0 1 0 1 0 ... pattern is found. It then assumes that these are the framing pulses.

This scheme works very well with speech transmission. If synchronization is lost, the framing circuit takes 0.4 to 6 milliseconds (ms) to detect the fact. The time required to reframe is about 50 ms at worst if all the other 192 positions are examined, but normally the time will be much less, depending on how far out of synchronization it is. This is quite acceptable on a speech channel, where the error would probably not even be noticed. It is more of a nuisance when computer data is sent over the channel, where the error would necessitate the retransmission of one or more blocks of data. Retransmission is required from time to time whenever data is transmitted, however, because of noise on the line.

PRIVATE T1 FACILITIES

When T1 facilities were first introduced by AT&T, they were installed mainly in the public telephone network to implement connections between switching offices; these high-speed facilities were not initially available to individual subscribers. The T1 carrier has been so successful, however, that individual users of telecommunications can now lease T1 facilities from a variety of common carriers. These leased T1 communication facilities are now routinely used to implement communication links where high data rates are required.

HIGHER-CAPACITY PCM

The T1 carrier was only the beginning. A hierarchy of interlinking digital channels is used in the public telephone network. The next step up is the T2 carrier, which takes the signals from four T1 carriers and operates at 6.3 million bps. Millions of T2 voice-channel-miles are operational. The T2 carrier typically uses wire-pair circuits that are specifically engineered for digital transmission.

The T3 and T4 carriers are too fast for wire-pair circuits. They must use more sophisticated transmission media. The T3 carrier is approximately seven times the capacity of the T2 carrier and can carry 672 telephone channels. This carrier standard is actually used very little in actual practice and serves mainly as a bridge between the T2 and T4 carriers.

The T4 carrier has a capacity roughly 42 times that of the AT&T T2 carrier and can carry 4032 PCM voice channels. It is coming into common use for long-haul circuits and can be carried by a variety of transmission media, including coaxial cable, microwave relay, waveguide, satellite, and optical fiber.

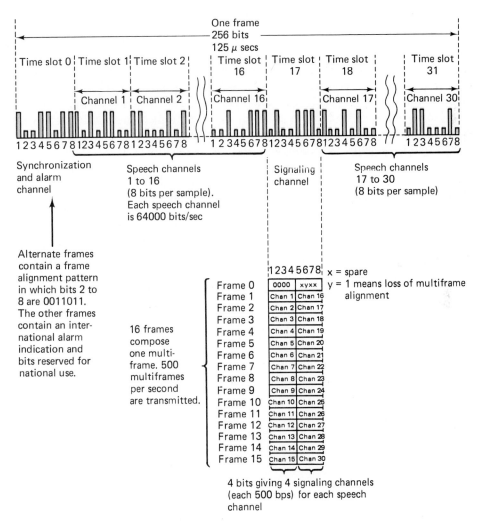

Figure 13.7   CCITT recommendation for PCM transmission frames

CCITT
RECOMMENDATIONS The CCITT has made two recommendations for PCM transmission, one for transmission at the T1 carrier speed of 1.544 million bps and one for transmission at 2.048 million bps, which can be achieved over most telephone wire pairs. As is often the case, the CCITT recommendation for 1.544-million-bps transmission is slightly different from the North American standard set by AT&T. It employs a 193-bit frame with 8 bits per channel, as in Fig. 13.6, but the frame alignment bit is the first bit, not the 193rd bit as in Fig. 13.6, and it carries a different synchronization pattern. Twelve such frames are grouped together to form one *multiframe*.

If separate signaling is provided for each channel, *two* signaling bit streams are derived from the eighth bits and only every sixth frame contains signaling bits. This gives a smaller bit rate for signaling but leaves 8 bits per channel in five-sixths of the frames for carrying speech or information.

Figure 13.7 shows the CCITT 2.048-million-bps recommendation, which most of the world outside North America uses for PCM transmission. With this standard, 16 frames of 256 bits each form a multiframe. There are thirty-two 8-bit time slots in each frame, giving 30 speech channels of 64,000 bps each, one synchronization and alarm channel, and one signaling channel. The signaling channel is submultiplexed to give four 500-bps signaling channels for each speech channel.

The difference between the CCITT and North American standards will be a major impediment for the implementation of ISDN techniques. Current ISDN standards development does acknowledge the existence of incompatible standards for PCM transmission and is attempting to reconcile these conflicting techniques, thus paving the way for the creation of international integrated services digital networks.

14 SATELLITES AND FIBER OPTICS

A great many complex technologies are used to implement the world's telecommunications facilities. We have already touched on many of these in the preceding chapters. Two of the newest technologies for telecommunications are having a major impact on the reduction in cost of long-haul transmission. These are the technologies of communications satellites and optical fibers. These two technologies are so important that they deserve a chapter to themselves in this part.

COMMUNICATIONS SATELLITES

A *communications satellite* provides essentially a very high capacity cable in the sky. The unique thing about a satellite link is that the cost of a channel can be independent of distance. We can illustrate the power of satellites for the computer industry by means of a simple calculation. When you use a computer terminal you do not transmit continuously at the full capacity of the channel. Instead, you transmit sporadically in short bursts. In a typical interactive application, about 10 bps, on average, pass back and forth. Today's communications satellites support a number of high-capacity channels. For example one RCA satellite can transmit up to 60 million bps over each channel, and supports 24 such channels. Figuring a conservative 15% utilization, this would give us a usable capacity of 216 million bps.

Let us take the combined population of the United States and Canada to be about 240 million people and make the assumption that every person makes substantial use of data transmission. We will assume that working people will transmit data using a terminal or personal computer an hour a day and a nonworking person only a half-hour. This gives us a total of 160 million hours of interactive usage. If we assume that in the peak hour the usage is three times the daily average, the total data rate in the peak hour would be about 200 million bps. This means that a single satellite has more than enough transmission capacity to provide every man, woman, and child in the United States and Canada with access to data transmission facilities.

On April 6, 1965, the world's first commercial satellite, Early Bird, rocketed into the evening sky at Cape Kennedy. The success of the transmission experiments that followed this has been spectacular. Before long, earth stations were being built around the world, and new and more powerful satellites were on the drawing boards.

TRANSPONDERS   A communications satellite is really no more than a microwave relay in the sky. It receives microwave signals from equipment on the earth in a given frequency band and retransmits them at a different frequency. It must use a different frequency for retransmission; otherwise, the powerful transmitted signal would interfere with the weak incoming signal. The receiver, transmitter, and antenna used on the ground is referred to as an *earth station*. The power of satellites lies in the fact that they can handle a large amount of traffic and relay it between earth stations located almost anywhere on the earth.

The device in the satellite that receives a signal, amplifies it, changes its frequency, and retransmits it is called a *transponder*. Most satellites have multiple transponders. The bandwidth handled by a transponder has differed from one satellite design to another, but many contemporary satellites have transponders with a bandwidth of 36 MHz. How this bandwidth is used depends on the nature of the earth station equipment. For example, a typical transponder can carry any of the following:

- One color television channel
- 1200 voice channels
- One channel of 50 million bps
- 16 T1 channels of 1.544 million bps
- 400 channels of 64,000 bps
- 600 channels of 40,000 bps

**WORLD
COVERAGE**   Communications satellites are stationed at a very special position in space, in a *geosynchronous orbit* about 23,000 miles above the equator. In this unique orbit they revolve around the earth in exactly the time it takes for the earth to rotate, and hence appear to hang stationary in the sky. Because they are so high, they can transmit to much of the earth. Three satellites can cover all of the inhabited regions of the earth, with the exception of a few dwellings close to the poles.

The cost of satellite channels is dropping remarkably fast. A main thrust of the technology is to find ways to make the receiving equipment on earth cheap and mass producible. Costs have already dropped sufficiently that many corporate and government organizations have their own earth stations.

THE CHANGING PERCEPTION OF SATELLITES

The perception of the value of communications satellites has changed since the first satellites were launched. At first, satellites were perceived largely as a means to provide isolated places with communication facilities. Most of the world's population is not served by the telephone and television networks that so greatly influence Western society. The cost of lacing Africa and South America with AT&T-style engineering would be unthinkable. Satellites were perceived as a counter technology, and earth stations began to appear in the remotest parts of the world. Countries with only the most primitive telecommunications put satellites on their postage stamps.

As satellites dropped from their initial exorbitant cost, it was realized that they could compete with the world's suboceanic cables; satellites then had a part to play in the industrial nations, linking the continental landmasses. The owners of the suboceanic cables took political steps to protect their investments at the expense of satellites, but soon more transoceanic telephone calls were made by satellite than by cable. Television relayed across the oceans via satellite is now common.

It soon became clear that there were major economies of scale in satellites. A big satellite could give a much lower cost per channel than a small one. To take advantage of these economies of scale, satellites need to be employed where the traffic volume is heaviest. Nowhere is it heavier than in U.S. domestic telecommunications, so it began to appear, contrary to the earlier view, that there was more profit in domestic satellites than in international ones. A further perceptual change was soon to follow, after it was found that satellites can also be used for broadcasting.

SATELLITE BROADCASTING

While corporations and computer users perceived the satellite as providing two-way channels between relatively few earth stations, broadcasters, or would-be broadcasters, perceived satellites as a potentially ideal way to distribute one-way signals. Television or music sent up to a satellite could be received over a vast area. If a portion of the satellite capacity were used for sound channels for education or news, a very large number of channels could be broadcast. The transmitting earth station would be large and expensive, but the receiving antennas could be small and numerous. The Musak Corporation envisioned small receiving antennas on the roofs of their subscribers' buildings. Satellites offer the possibility of broadcasting television to vast areas of the world that have no television today. If powerful satellites are launched, television could be broadcast directly to the hundreds of millions of homes in industrial countries. A Japanese broadcast satellite now beams programs directly to Japanese homes, which use relatively inexpensive home receivers. With satellites of lesser power, television is today being distributed to hundreds of regional stations for rebroadcasting over today's cable television links.

A CABLE IN THE SKY?

Broadcasting is usually thought of as having one transmitter and many receivers. However when a satellite is used for two-way signals, a form of broadcasting is taking place in which there are many transmitters. Each earth station is, in effect, a broadcasting transmitter because its signal reaches all the other earth stations, whether they want it or not. Because of this broadcasting nature of satellites, it is limiting to think of a statellite as a *cable in the sky*. It is much more than that. A signal sent up to the satellite comes down everywhere over a very wide area. To maximize the usefulness of the satellite for telecommunications, any user in that area should be able to request a small portion of the vast satellite capacity at any time, and have it allocated at that moment if it is free.

Just as with the telephone network, to make it really useful, any user should be able to call any other user. However, it is not desirable to put a telephone exchange in the satellite, at least not yet. The equipment in the satellite needs to be simple and reliable because equipment failures cannot be easily repaired. The equipment also needs to be light and consume as little power as possible. To achieve this desirable *multiple-access* capability, ingenious ways have been devised of allocating satellite capacity to geographically scattered users, permitting them to intercommunicate.

SATELLITES FOR DATA

Since this is a book on data communication, we are especially interested in a satellite's usefulness for the transmission of computer data. For the first decade of communications satellite operation, most of the capacity of the satellites was used for *telephone traffic* and *television*. The technology has evolved, however, so that in a sense, satellites are much more powerful for the transmission of *data* between computers and computer users.

As we have already discussed, it is technically desirable to carry telephone traffic, and even television, in a digital form. Normal telephone voice channels require a bit rate of 64,000 bps for transmission. A channel for data communication transmitting a bit rate that high would be extremely useful. Such bit rates make telephone voice appear expensive by comparison with data transmission as a means of transmitting information.

The example that began this chapter showed how a single, relatively simple satellite could be used to provide enough transmission capacity to provide data transmission capabilities to every man, woman, and child in North America. Despite the satellite's power for data transmission, it would not be a sound business operation to launch a satellite solely for use with computers. Of all the traffic that might be sent by satellite, a relatively small proportion of it is computer traffic. Whatever the mix in the future, most of today's traffic is *plain old telephone service* (POTS). To maximize its potential profit, a satellite should be capable of carrying many different types of signals—realtime and non-realtime, voice, data, facsimile, and video. For all of these signals, it should be regarded as a broadcasting medium accessible from anywhere beneath it, not as a set of cables in the sky.

The following summarizes how the various perceptions of communications satellites have changed as we have gained experience with them. Communications satellites have been perceived as:

- A means to reach isolated places on earth
- An alternative to suboceanic cables
- Long-distance domestic telephone and television links
- A data facility capable of interlinking computer terminals everywhere
- A new form of broadcasting
- A multiple-access facility capable of carrying all types of signals on a demand basis

PROPERTIES OF SATELLITE LINKS

Satellite channels have unique properties. Some of these properties have an effect on how those channels can be employed for data communication. Box 14.1 lists some of the properties of satellite channels. Two of the characteristics listed in Box 14.1 deserve further discussion. These are the costs of satellite channels, and the 270-ms propagation delay inherent in satellite links.

SATELLITE CHANNEL COSTS

One of the favorable characteristics of a communications satellite channel is its potentially very low cost. Figure 14.1 shows how the investment cost per satellite channel has been dropping dramatically. This chart plots only the cost per satellite voice channel per year for the satellite only, including its launch. The cost to a subscriber will be much higher because it must include the earth station and links to it, and must take into consideration the fact that the average channel utilization may be low. The extraordinary cost reduction shown in Fig. 14.1 will probably continue, but not at such a spectacular rate. Massive reductions in cost per voice channel could result if satellites with a much higher capacity than today's were launched.

The satellites and their launch costs are referred to as the *space segment* of satellite communication. The comment is sometimes made among system

BOX 14.1   Characteristics of satellite channels

- Transmission cost is independent of distance. A link from Washington to Baltimore costs the same to engineer as a link from Washington to Vancouver.

- There is a 270-ms *propagation delay* of the signal due to the great distance the signal must travel.

- Very high bandwidths or bit rates are available to users if they can have an earth station at their premises, or a microwave link to an earth station, thereby avoiding the local loops.

- A signal sent to a satellite is transmitted to all receivers within range of the satellite.

- Because of the broadcast property, dynamic assignment of channels is necessary between geographically dispersed users.

- Also because of the broadcast property, security procedures are extremely important.

- Most satellite transmissions are sent in digital form. Digital techniques can therefore be used to manipulate and interleave the signals in a variety of ways. The high bit rates make possible new uses of telecommunications not economical on terrestrial links.

- A transmitting station can receive its own transmission and hence monitor whether the satellite has transmitted it correctly. This fact can be utilized in certain forms of transmission control.

planners that the space segment costs are dropping to such a low level that the overall system costs will be dominated by the organization of the ground facilities. The cost of an earth station, however, has dropped more spectacularly than that of a satellite. Early earth stations cost more than $10 million and some early experimental earth stations cost several times that. Costs have now dropped to a small fraction of that, especially for small receive-only stations.

TOTAL INVESTMENT COST   Combining the dropping costs of both the satellite and its launch, plus the earth stations, gives us the total investment cost per voice channel. Figure 14.2 shows how this cost has been dropping.

There is a trade-off between the cost of the satellite and the cost of its earth station. If the satellite has a large antenna and considerable power, smaller earth stations can be used. If the satellite makes more efficient use of its fre-

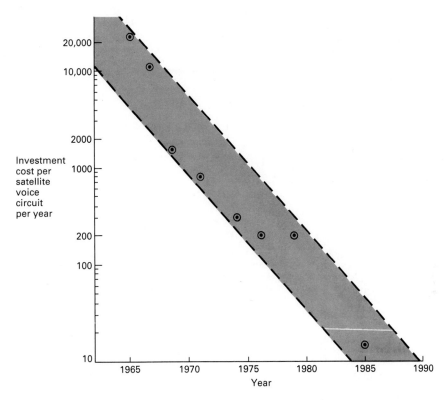

Figure 14.1   Drop in cost of satellite circuits

quency allocation, the cost per channel will be lower. There is a limit to satellite efficiency, so the main effect of increasing satellite cost will be to reduce earth station size and cost. As earth facilities drop in cost, more antennas will be constructed and more traffic sent, making it economical to use more powerful satellites. This will make earth facilities drop in cost even further. If satellites use large numbers of small earth stations, however, the overall system architecture that permits the earth stations to share the satellite is extremely important and eventually will dominate the cost of satellite systems.

PROPAGATION DELAY   A disadvantage of satellite transmission is that a delay occurs because the signal has to travel far out into space and back. The signal propagation time is about 270 ms, and varies slightly with the earth station locations. If you make a telephone call that uses a satellite link in both directions, you wait for the reply of the person you are talking to for an extra 540 ms. This delay of more than half a second can be annoying in telephone conversations, but most people who regularly use satellite circuits for voice communication get used to it. The delay

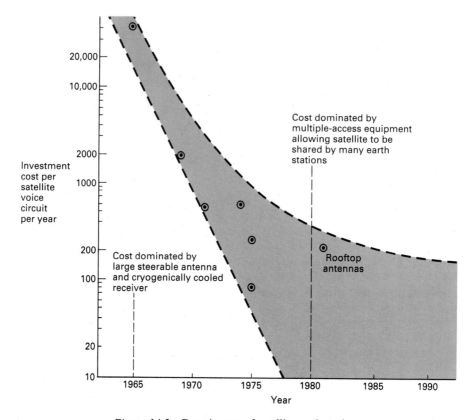

Figure 14.2   Drop in cost of satellite earth stations

has more serious consequences for the users of data communication. In interactive data transmission via satellite, a terminal user will experience a constant increase in response time of 540 ms. A system designer has to take this into account in determining the overall system response time.

In many interactive systems it is desirable that the mean response time for certain interactions be no greater than 2 seconds. This is achieved satisfactorily on many interactive systems using satellites today. However, appropriate line control procedures have to be used on satellite channels. Some of the common equipment for data transmission over telephone lines performs very poorly if used on a satellite channel because it uses a control procedure that is inappropriate if the channel has a long delay.

Two control procedures that should not be used on satellite circuits are *polling* (in which a control station asks each station on the line if it has something to transmit) and *stop-and-wait* error control (in which the transmitting station stops after each message sent and does not transmit another message until it hears that the previous one was received correctly). There are alternative forms of line control that perform efficiently on satellite channels; we discuss them in Chapter 23.

We discuss next the other technology that is revolutionizing telecommunications—the *optical fiber*. In some ways, the optical fiber is an even more important technology for telecommunications than the communications satellite.

OPTICAL FIBERS AND LASERS

The optical fiber has two advantages over traditional forms of terrestrial telecommunications circuits. First, the fiber can be manufactured at lower cost than traditional copper wire or other types of cable. Second, since the frequency of a light beam is much higher than other forms of electromagnetic radiation, an optical fiber can support a much higher bandwidth. The frequency of light is 10 million times greater than the frequencies used on coaxial cables. Furthermore, a coaxial cable has 10,000 times the cross-sectional area of the glass fibers used for optical transmission, so many more fibers than coaxial tubes can be packed together into one cable. A diagram illustrating the construction of an optical fiber cable is shown in Fig. 14.3.

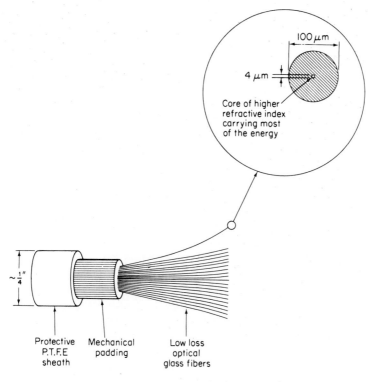

Figure 14.3 Optical fiber construction

ABSORPTION

In the early stages of optical fiber development, fibers worked successfully for telecommunications only over short distances. The main reason for this was the *absorption* that occurred in the glass. In the 1970s and 1980s, however, phenomenal progress occurred in glass fiber manufacture. It is now clear that optical fibers are one of the most important technologies of telecommunications. Optical fiber transmission links are now in common use throughout the world.

When light travels 1 m through ordinary window glass, it loses about two-thirds of its power (a 5-dB loss). Through good-quality optical glass, it can travel 5 meters before suffering the same loss. Through the glass fibers now being manufactured, it can travel between 1 and 2 km with that loss. Digital repeaters on such cables could be more than 10 km apart. Figure 14.4 shows the loss in decibels per kilometer of a typical glass fiber for different frequencies, or colors, of light.

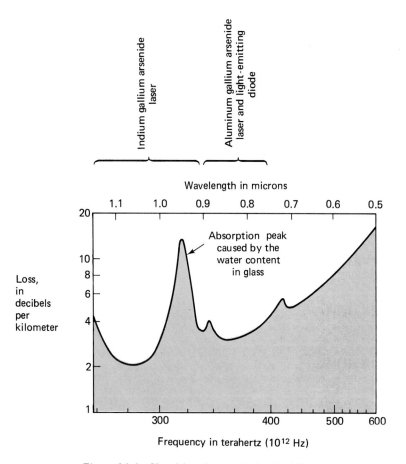

Figure 14.4   Signal loss in a typical optical fiber

REFLECTION   Why does the light stay inside the fiber? It travels down a cylinder of glass that is surrounded by a substance, usually also glass, of low refractive index. When the beam strikes the edge of the cylinder, it is totally reflected and remains inside, as shown in Fig. 14.5. This total internal reflection occurs in a similar manner at the surface of a pond. If you put your head under the water and look at the surface some distance away, it will appear to be a totally reflecting mirror. A ray of light is not refracted out of the pond at all because of its low striking angle but is reflected back into the water.

The light beam travels down a fiber and is confined within it by total internal reflection. However, it will be absorbed somewhat by the fiber and, consequently, it must periodically be amplified or processed by a bit repeater. Light beams of different frequencies can travel together down the same fiber, and a bundle of such fibers, thin enough to be highly flexible, are normally bound together to form one cable.

DISPERSION   The potentially usable bandwidth of glass fibers is very high. If the potential bandwidth could be fully utilized, one fiber could transmit on the order of 10^{14} bps. The glass fibers in use today transmit bit rates that are far below this theoretical maximum. One factor that limits the transmission capacity is *dispersion* of the signal as it travels down the fiber.

Rays of light traveling down a fiber can be transmitted by different paths, as shown in Fig. 14.5. A ray traveling straight down the axis of the fiber will reach its destination before a ray that bounces down the fiber with many reflections. A very short pulse transmitted down a fiber will therefore be spread out in time, as shown in Fig. 14.6. The farther it is transmitted, the more it will be spread out.

In a typical fiber of 100-micrometer (0.1-millimeter) diameter, the axial ray is transmitted 1 km in several nanoseconds less time than the ray that takes the longest path. Pulses less than a few nanoseconds apart will interfere with one another and become indistinguishable. If the repeaters on the fiber are to be 10 km apart, this pulse spreading limits the transmission rate to well below 100 million bps per fiber.

Light rays are reflected down a glass fiber with total internal reflection at the surface:

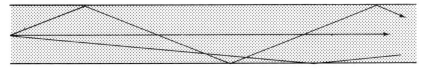

Figure 14.5 Reflection of light rays in an optical fiber

However some light rays travel by shorter paths than others,
This causes the signal to become increasingly dispersed:

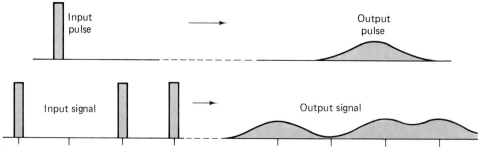

This dispersion puts an upper limit on the signaling rate of a
glass fiber. Fibers can be constructed with very low dispersion
and such fibers can carry a very high information rate.

Figure 14.6   Effects of dispersion in an optical fiber

LASERS

It is necessary to have a source of light with a long-enough life to act as a transmitter and that can be modulated to carry a high information rate. Glass fibers can carry either ordinary light or laser beams. Most of today's fibers are designed to work with laser beams.

Laser stands for *light amplification by stimulated emission of radiation*. A laser produces a narrow beam of light that is *coherent*. A coherent light beam has all of its waves traveling in unison, like the waves traveling away from a stone dropped in a pond. The beam is also sharply *monochromatic;* that is, it occupies a single color or frequency, or consists of multiple monochromatic emissions.

An analogy with sound waves is somewhat inexact, but it will help you visualize the difference between a laser beam and an ordinary beam of light. The sound from a tuning fork consists of waves that are of one frequency and are reasonably coherent. On the other hand, if you put a hammer through your window, the sound waves would be neither monochromatic nor coherent. The former may be compared to a laser beam and the latter with ordinary light.

CREATING THE
LASER BEAM

A laser beam is formed by a molecular process somewhat analogous to the vibration of a tuning fork. It is possible to make certain molecules oscillate with a fixed frequency. The electrons in an atom can only move in certain fixed orbits; associated with each orbit is a particular energy level. The electrons can be induced to change orbits, and when this happens, the total energy associated with the atom changes. The atom can therefore take on a number of discrete energy levels—a fact that is well known today from quantum mechanics.

Certain processes can induce the atom to shift from one energy level to another. When this happens, the atom either absorbs or emits a quantum of energy. In this way, radio waves, or other electromagnetic radiation is emitted in discrete quantums.

When ordinary light is emitted, the mass of molecules switch their energy levels at random. A random jumble of noncoherent waves is produced. Under the lasing action, however, the molecules are induced to emit in unison; the substance oscillates at a given frequency, and a stream of coherent waves at this single frequency results. This could range from a microwave frequency, to a light frequency, or higher. X-ray lasers are used in some applications.

RESONANCE   When a laser beam produced by certain lasing molecules falls on other molecules of that type, it can produce an oscillation in them. A form of *resonance* is set up. You might imagine a huge pendulum much too heavy to move far by a single hard push. If you give it a series of relatively gentle pushes, however, you can set it swinging. You can go on pushing at just the right point in the swing, and the length of the swing increases until the pendulum builds up great power. This is resonance; your gentle pushes have built up massive oscillations. In a similar manner (and again the analogy is helpful but not exact), a weak laser beam can fall on a lasing substance and cause resonance in it. It sets the molecules oscillating so that a powerful laser beam is emitted. The laser beam has thus been amplified. In this way, a very intense beam of a single frequency or several frequencies can be emitted.

A beam of ordinary light, even a beam that we describe as monochromatic, actually consists of a small spread of frequencies, each of which would be bent differently by a prism or lens. A laser beam, however, is not dispersed by a prism and optical arrangements can be built for it so precisely that beams of laser light have been shone onto the moon and have illuminated only a small portion of its surface. A beam can be concentrated with a lens into a minute area, and the intense concentration of energy in such a small area causes very localized heating to occur. This fact can be used to create a cutting or welding tool with miniature precision far beyond the dreams of Swiss watchmakers. The surgeon can be provided with a microscopic scalpel; the general with a potential death ray.

LASER LIGHT   Box 14.2 summarizes the ways in which laser light
CHARACTERISTICS   differs from ordinary light. The wide variety of applications of the laser are based on one or more of the properties listed there. For telecommunications, the laser provides a highly controllable beam of great intensity. This light beam has a frequency 100,000 times higher than today's microwave signals, and its potential information-car-

BOX 14.2   Characteristics of laser light

- Laser light is sharply monochromatic. It may, however, have more than one monochromatic frequency (color). By using filters, a single frequency can be separated from the others.
- The light is coherent, the waves being regularly arranged and in phase with each other.
- The light can have very great intensity, so great that it could blind a person instantly.
- Lasers emit light in a parallel beam rather than in all directions like a light bulb filament.
- Because a laser beam is parallel and monochromatic, it can have a low dispersion; it can be accurately directed by lenses and prisms. Laser light pulses suffer little spreading when they pass down a suitable fiber.

rying capacity is thousands of times greater than microwave. It has been said that lasers portend a revolution in telecommunications as fundamental as the invention of radio.

LASERS WITH OPTICAL FIBERS   A problem with optical fibers is how to get a powerful signal inside such a tiny fiber. The beam for a typical fiber must be shone down the very central portion of the glass fiber in a beam as narrow as 5 micrometers (0.005 millimeter) in diameter. Lenses and mirrors could be used but much of the light from an incoherent source would be lost. As we have seen, a laser can provide a very tiny but intensely bright source that emits light in a narrow parallel beam and can be attached directly to the fiber.

SEMICONDUCTOR LASERS   A particularly interesting type of laser for this purpose is the *semiconductor laser*. It is tiny and inexpensive to manufacture, using methods similar to those that are used for producing today's microelectronic chips. Figure 14.7 shows the construction of a typical semiconductor laser. It consists of a tiny rectangular slab of gallium arsenide coated with alternating layers of aluminum gallium arsenide and gallium arsenide. At the top and bottom are layers of metal that act as electrical contacts. The layers consist of *n*-type and *p*-type regions. The *n*-type regions contain mobile electrons—negative current carriers. The *p*-

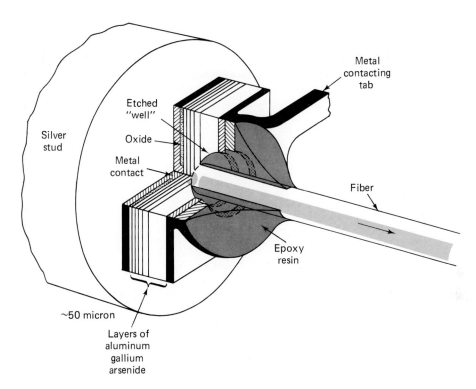

Figure 14.7 Typical semiconductor laser construction

type regions contain positive current carriers that are, in effect, the absence of electrons from the molecular structure. These are referred to as *holes*.

When an electrical current is applied to the contacts, electrons from the n-type layers are injected into the p-type layers. In the central p-type gallium arsenide layer, electrons combine with the holes, and the excess energy is emitted as light. The lasing action takes place in this central layer. The light generated is mostly confined to that layer because the adjoining aluminum gallium arsenide layers are of lower refractive index. The edges of the block are mirror-like so that they reflect the light back into the layer. The light then stimulates the generation of more light. This stimulates yet more light until an intense beam of coherent radiation is emitted.

The lasing action is confined to the central thin layer of gallium arsenide. To produce a hair-thin beam, all but the central strip of that layer is made semi-insulating by bombarding it with protons during the manufacturing process. The laser chip then emits an intense narrow beam, small enough to enter an optical fiber.

As in production of LSI circuitry, quantities of such chips are produced simultaneously by depositing the various chemical layers on a wafer of the substrate material, and then dicing the wafer into many chips.

A major problem with the early semiconductor lasers was that their lifetime was short. Research indicated that the processes that eventually led to their failure began at defects in the crystalline structure. The defects might be there after manufacture and might be introduced by strain on the laser. The lifetime of lasers has been increased from minutes to years by careful avoidance of crystalline defects. The lasers now being manufactured have a long enough life for wide application in telecommunications.

15 TELECOMMUNICATIONS COMMON CARRIERS

In this chapter we examine the common carriers, telecommunications administrations, regulatory authorities, and other organizations that make up the telecommunications industry. We begin with the largest class of organizations, the common carriers that make up the telephone companies of the United States.

U.S. COMMON CARRIERS

The companies in North America that furnish communication services to the public are referred to as *common carriers*. Legally, the name applies to all companies that undertake to carry goods for all persons indiscriminately. Reference to the communication companies by this name dates back to days when messages were carried by a stagecoach clattering through the sagebrush. The telecommunications common carriers offer facilities for the electronic transmission of information of all types, including voice, data, facsimile, television, and telemetry. Some of them are now offering computer services also, and it is likely that their business could branch out widely in this direction. Many computer manufacturers and independent companies are also offering online computer services to the general public and so run the risk of being classed as public utilities for this part of their business in the future and being subject to the various government controls on public utilities.

It is surprising that there are thousands of telecommunications common carriers in the United States. Many other countries have only one such organization, which is run by the government. Most of the common carriers in the United States are very small; only about 250 of them have more than 5000 subscribers.

BELL OPERATING COMPANIES

The *American Telephone and Telegraph Company* (AT&T) had for years operated one of the largest telecommunications networks in the world. The network was called the *Bell System* after Alexander Graham Bell, the inventor of the telephone. In 1982, a federal court forced AT&T to divest itself of the Bell operating companies (BOCs) that provided local loop telephone service to individual subscribers. The divestiture officially began on November 21, 1983, and the former Bell System is now organized as AT&T and seven regional holding companies (RHCs). The RHCs together operate the 23 Bell operating companies. The new organization of AT&T and the RHCs is described in Box 15.1. The RHCs must now provide

BOX 15.1 The Bell System breakup

- **AT&T.** The *American Telephone and Telegraph Company* no longer controls the Bell operating companies (BOCs) that install and maintain the telephone local loops that provide telephone service to individuals, corporations, and government organizations. AT&T continues to operate Bell Laboratories, AT&T's research and development organization, and Western Electric, AT&T's manufacturing organization. The BOCs are now organized in the form of the seven regional holding companies (RHCs) described below.

- **Ameritech.** *American Information Technologies* (Ameritech) owns the five Midwestern BOCs that provide telephone service to Illinois, Indiana, Michigan, Ohio, and Wisconsin.

- **Pacific Telesis.** *Pacific Telesis* owns the BOC that provides telephone service to California and Nevada.

- **Bell South.** *Bell South* owns the BOCs that provide telephone service to Alabama, Florida, Georgia, Kentucky, Louisiana, Mississippi, North Carolina, South Carolina, and Tennessee.

- **Bell Atlantic.** *Bell Atlantic* owns the BOCs that provide telephone service to Connecticut, Delaware, Maryland, New Jersey, Pennsylvania, West Virginia, and Virginia.

- **NYNEX.** *NYNEX* owns the BOCs that provide telephone service to Maine, Massachusetts, New Hampshire, New York, Rhode Island, and Vermont.

- **Southwestern Bell Corporation.** *Southwestern Bell Corporation* owns the BOCs that provide telephone service to Arkansas, Kansas, Missouri, Oklahoma, and Texas.

- **US West.** *US West* owns the BOCs that provide telephone service to Arizona, Colorado, Idaho, Iowa, Minnesota, Montana, Nebraska, New Mexico, North Dakota, Oregon, South Dakota, Utah, Washington, and Wyoming.

equal access for their customers to any of the various long-distance telephone common carriers (described later in this chapter) that now offer long-distance services in competition with AT&T.

THE AMERICAN TELEPHONE AND TELEGRAPH COMPANY

Up until the divestiture, AT&T was affectionately known as "Ma Bell" and was the world's largest corporation. It employed over 1 million people and its assets were over three times greater than General Motors, America's largest industrial corporation. The Bell System once referred to the vast network of telephone and data circuits with many switching offices and to the television and other links that were operated across the United States by AT&T and its subsidiaries and associated companies. AT&T is now prohibited by law from using the name "Bell" or the familiar "Bell" logo in advertising any of its products or services; the "Bell" name and logo are for the exclusive use of the seven regional holding companies that own the Bell operating companies.

Although AT&T does not now own any portion of the 23 Bell operating companies, it still operates its *Long Lines Department,* which provides much of the U.S. interstate long distance service. AT&T still also owns the Western Electric company, its main manufacturing company. It manufactures and installs most of the equipment that AT&T uses in providing long-distance telephone service. AT&T and Western Electric together own the Bell Telephone Laboratories.

Bell Labs, which is claimed to be the world's biggest research organization, has done much of the development work that has made today's telecommunications possible. It was there that the transistor was invented, Shannon's work on information theory was done, the solar battery was invented, and the first communications satellite, Telstar, was designed and built.

In addition to providing telecommunications products and services, the divested AT&T currently also manufactures and markets a wide range of computing equipment, including many personal computer and minicomputer models. AT&T also provides a series of Accunet digital communication services, including an Accunet public data network packet service. The Accunet services are described later in this chapter.

GENERAL TELEPHONE AND ELECTRONICS CORPORATION

The network of the *General Telephone and Electronics Corporation* (GTE) is known as the *General System.* This organization operates approximately 8 percent of American telephones. General System equipment is compatible with the equipment of the Bell operating companies in most areas, to allow direct interconnection. The General System has quite complete vertical and horizontal integration and manufactures all the major components in a telephone system except cable. It buys cable and some other equipment from Western Electric. Its two manufacturing subsidiaries are the *Automatic Electric Company* and the *Lenkhurt Electric Company*. GTE now operates the Telenet public data network and the US Sprint long-distance telephone service. Both of these services are described later in this chapter.

THE INDEPENDENTS

All other telephone companies are referred to as *independent* telephone companies. These serve more than half of the U.S. geographical area and operate about 17 percent of the telephones. The number of independents has been decreasing ever since 1920, when there were 9211 of them, but their combined revenue has been growing more rapidly than that of AT&T and the Bell operating companies. The independents today are bigger than AT&T was in 1940. Virtually all the independents interconnect with the rest of the public telephone system and transmit signals compatible with it.

THE UNITED STATES INDEPENDENT TELEPHONE ASSOCIATION

Most of the independent companies are members of the *United States Independent Telephone Association* (USITA), which coordinates their practices. Most states also have independent telephone associations. These and the USITA are highly influential and have played an important part in the development of the independent telephone industry.

WESTERN UNION

The *Western Union Telegraph Company* has provided America with telegraph links since the days of the Wild West. It operates a national telegraph message service to all parts of the United States. Western Union also leases private communication links, and it operates two public dial-up telegraph networks, a *telex* network, compatible with the worldwide telex network, and the *TWX* (Teletypewriter Exchange) network, which it bought from AT&T. The number of telegrams in the United States is falling rapidly, but as this business declines, the telex and TWX business is growing. The Western Union leased-line facilities now include voice, data, and facsimile services of a wide range of speeds.

Western Union has done much experimenting with online computer systems and offers a wide range of computer services. It also acquired the *PS Newswire Association*. To do this it had to form a holding company, *Western Union Corporation,* which is separate from the common carrier, the Western Union Telegraph Company. *Western Union International Inc*. is also a separate company that handles international cablegrams and data traffic. Western Union distinguished itself in 1974 by having the United States' first two domestic satellites launched, the Westar satellites. Western Union leases satellite channels as well as using them to carry its subscriber traffic.

GOVERNMENT AGENCIES

With so many common carriers, many of which monopolize the services they offer, it is necessary to have some regulating authority. There is at least one such authority for each American state, as well as a national authority for controlling interstate lines and foreign facilities originating in the United States. The latter is the *Federal Communications Commission* (FCC).

THE FEDERAL COMMUNICATIONS COMMISSION

The FCC is an independent federal agency that regulates radio, television, telephone, telegraph, and other transmissions by wire or radio. The powers of the FCC are defined in the Communications Act of 1934. It was created to "regulate interstate and foreign commerce in communication by wire and radio so as to make available, so far as possible, to all people of the United States a rapid, efficient, nationwide wire and radio communications service with adequate facilities at reasonable charges."

Figure 15.1 shows the organization of the FCC. The FCC has jurisdiction over *interstate* and *foreign* telecommunications but not telecommunications within a state. The latter are regulated by *state public utility commissions*.

THE STATE PUBLIC UTILITY COMMISSIONS

What the FCC does for interstate links and foreign links originating in the United States, the state public utility commissions do for links within one state. Different states have different tariffs for the same grade of service, and there can be a wide difference in the price of facilities from one state to another. Interstate tariffs, however, are uniform across America.

THE OFFICE OF TELECOMMUNICATIONS POLICY

The *Office of Telecommunications Policy* (OTP) was set up by President Nixon in 1970 because telecommunications technology was advancing so rapidly that it was outpacing the ability of government to formulate policy. The OTP was created to formulate plans, policies, and programs designed to maximize the value of telecommunications to the public interest, the U.S. economy, and national security.

The OTP has no executive authority. It can issue recommendations, not directives. Its recommendations appear to have influenced the FCC to stimulate more competition in an industry that monopolistic practices might make sloth-

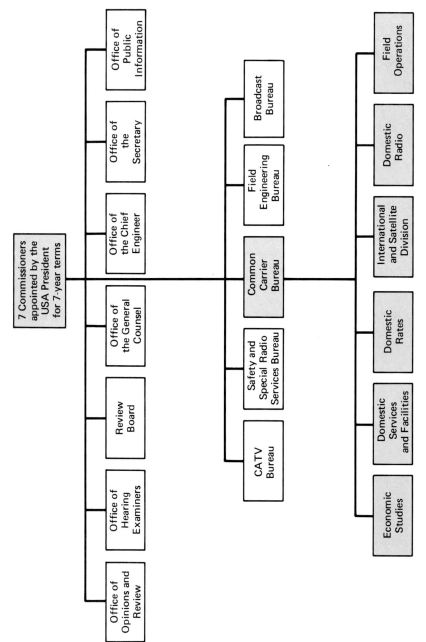

Figure 15.1 Organization of the United States FCC

ful. It appears to have stimulated the launching of domestic communications satellites, the growth of the specialized common carriers, the rise of the value-added common carriers, and the regulations encouraging the growth of cable television operators. We discuss the specialized common carriers and the value-added common carriers later in this chapter.

THE INTERCONNECT INDUSTRY

Prior to 1968 it was illegal for subscribers to connect their own devices to the public telephone network. After a long legal battle, the "Carterphone ruling" permitted the *Carter Electronics Corporation* to connect its mobile radio system directly to the telephone network. The FCC concluded,

> A customer desiring to use an interconnecting device . . . should be able to do so, so long as the interconnection does not adversely affect the telephone company's operations or the telephone system's utility for others. . , The appropriate remedy is to . . . permit the carriers if they so desire to propose new tariffs which will protect the telephone system against harmful devices and they may specify technical standards if they wish.

It was then permitted to connect devices to the public telephone network via a small white box on the wall called a *direct-access adapter* (DAA). The DAA was essentially an isolation transformer designed to protect the telephone network from potentially damaging voltages. The need to use a DAA was later eliminated in most situations.

A large new industry began to grow after the Carterphone ruling. Everything from computers to decorator telephones can now be connected to the telephone network. Terminal and personal computer manufacturers are putting modems under the covers. Computerized telephone exchanges, monitoring equipment, and network control equipment are being manufactured by organizations other than the common carriers. The entire telecommunications facilities of a corporation can now be independently designed to service the overall communication needs of the corporation. The interconnect decision gave would-be telecommunications users the freedom to invent.

TELECOMMUNICATIONS ORGANIZATIONS IN OTHER COUNTRIES

In a few countries, telecommunications is organized in a manner similar to its organization in the United States. In others, it is quite different. We next look at the organizations that control telecommunications in some representative countries, beginning with Canada.

CANADA The structure of the telecommunications industry in Canada is somewhat similar to the United States, except that some of Canada's 1600 common carriers are government owned. A value-added or "intelligent" data network is being operated by the Trans-Canada Telephone System (TCTS), a company owned by Canada's eight largest regional telephone companies. The TCTS provides users with the DATAPAC service for sending data. TCTS plans and coordinates joint system efforts and allocates toll revenues among members. Another nationwide telecommunications carrier is Canadian National/Canadian Pacific Telecommunications (CN/CPT). CN/CPT offers private services and public message telex and telegraph service.

Sixty-nine percent of Canada's telephones are operated by Bell Canada, which is entirely separate from AT&T or the Bell operating companies in the United States. Twelve percent of the telephones are operated by GTE. Four percent are operated by small independent common carriers and almost 16 percent by provincial or municipal governments.

Telsat Canada, a mixed private- and government-owned corporation, established the free world's first domestic communications satellite system in 1972.

THE BRITISH POST OFFICE CORPORATION In many countries the job of delivering mail and providing telecommunications is undertaken by the same organization. This came about because the first use of telecommunications was in telegraph message delivery, which was an extension of the mail. This type of organization may make sense again, before long, as it becomes cheaper to transmit letters via electronic mail than to deliver them physically. The *British Post Office Corporation* (BPOC) consists of one organization for handling mail and a separate organization for handling telecommunications. In 1969, the BPOC changed its status from a government department to a nationalized commercial company. It has its own research laboratories, although most of its equipment is manufactured by private industry.

For data transmission, the BPOC offers a variety of links under the heading of *datel services*. It operates a telex system of dial-up teleprinters and paper tape machines. The BPOC provides facilities for sending data over the dial-up public telephone network, and it offers private leased lines of varying speeds. It provides private wideband circuits with a capacity of 12 to 60 times that of voice circuits. The waiting period necessary for obtaining these facilities, however, is sometimes much greater than in the United States. The lines are not always compatible with the American ones, and sometimes equipment that works well in the United States cannot be installed in Britain.

OTHER COUNTRIES

Most of the countries of the world have a government-controlled monopoly providing their telecommunications, such as Britain's BPOC, and offering facilities for data transmission that are broadly similar. In some countries, the organization is a civil service department. In others it is a nationalized corporation. In Germany there is the *Deutschen Bundepost* and in France the *Postes Téléphonique et Télégraphique*. In most countries, financing comes from government, not public, sources. For the *Swedish Telecommunications Administration*, for example, the state, through the Riksdag (Parliament), decides the amount of investments and makes the necessary grants. Some countries manufacture most of their own telecommunications equipment; others import it. For example, India tries to manufacture as much as possible internally. The *Indian Posts and Telegraphs Department* has an active research organization that works closely with private firms, such as *Indian Telephone Industries Ltd.* and *Hindustan Cables Ltd.*, to produce modern equipment at low cost.

THE INTERNATIONAL TELECOMMUNICATIONS UNION

Although incompatibilities exist, the degree of *compatibility* that exists in the world's telecommunications facilities is remarkable. This is largely due to the *International Telecommunications Union* (ITU), which we introduced in Chapter 4. This organization, centered in Switzerland, has over 100 member countries throughout the world. Its consultative committees carry out very detailed studies of world telecommunications and make recommendations for standardization. The recommendations are put into practice widely throughout the world, with some notable dissensions.

ORGANIZATIONS IN THE ITU

There are three main organizations within the ITU: the *International Frequency Registration Board*, which attempts to register and standardize radio-frequency assignments and to assist in the elimination of harmful radio-frequency interference on the world's radio communication circuits; the *Consultative Committee on International Radio* (CCIR), which deals with other standards for radio, especially long-distance radio telecommunications; and the *International Telegraph and Telephone Consultative Committee* (CCITT). Figure 15.2 shows the organization and functions of the ITU. The organization within the ITU of most interest to us with regard to data transmission is the CCITT.

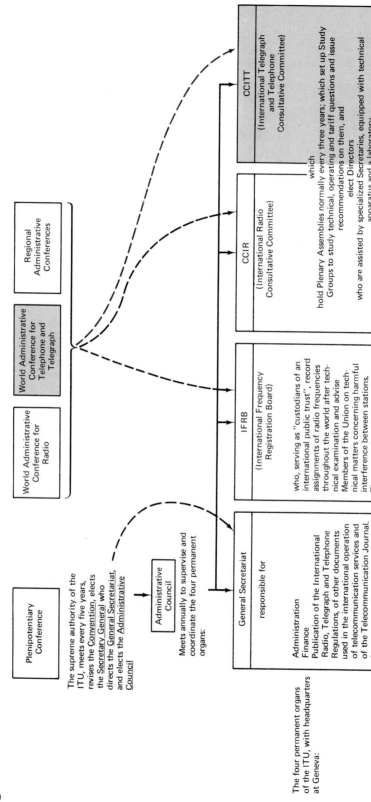

Plenipotentiary Conference

The supreme authority of the ITU, meets every five years, revises the <u>Convention</u>, elects the <u>Secretary General</u> who directs the <u>General Secretariat</u>, and elects the <u>Administrative Council</u>

Administrative Council

Meets annually to supervise and coordinate the four permanent organs:

The four permanent organs of the ITU, with headquarters at Geneva:

World Administrative Conference for Radio

World Administrative Conference for Telephone and Telegraph

Regional Administrative Conferences

General Secretariat

responsible for

Administration
Finance
Publication of the International Radio, Telegraph and Telephone Regulations, of other documents used in the international operation of telecommunication services and of the Telecommunication Journal. Arrangements for conferences. Technical cooperation.

IFRB

(International Frequency Registration Board)

who, serving as "custodians of an international public trust", record assignments of radio frequencies throughout the world after technical examination and advise Members of the Union on technical matters concerning harmful interference between stations. They are assisted by a specialized Secretariat.

CCIR

(International Radio Consultative Committee)

CCITT

(International Telegraph and Telephone Consultative Committee)

which

hold Plenary Assemblies normally every three years; which set up Study Groups to study technical, operating and tariff questions and issue recommendations on them, and elect Directors

who are assisted by specialized Secretaries, equipped with technical apparatus and a laboratory.

Figure 15.2   Organization of the International Telecommunications Union

INTERNATIONAL TELEGRAPH AND TELEPHONE CONSULTATIVE COMMITTEE The CCITT, which we discussed in Chapter 4, is divided into a number of study groups that make recommendations on various aspects of telephony and telegraphy. There are study groups, for example, on telegraphy/transmission, performance, telegraph switching, alphabetic telegraph apparatus, telephone channels, telephone switching and signaling, noise, and several others. The study group that is the most concerned with the topics discussed in this book is the special committee on data transmission. It has produced reports of great thoroughness, giving recommendations for standards for data transmission that are widely accepted throughout the world.

NEW BREEDS OF COMMON CARRIERS In the 1970s the telecommunications industry of the United States changed from being a somewhat placid growth industry to an industry in upheaval. In the 1980s, the breakup of the Bell System caused further far-reaching changes in the telecommunications industry. Changes in the regulatory climate encouraged three new breeds of common carriers to come into existence. These are the long-distance telephone common carriers, the satellite carriers, and the value-added carriers. All are extremely important to the users of data transmission services. Major legal battles and regulatory slowness have impeded the new carriers. Nevertheless, the new carriers have a flexibility and inventiveness that permit them to move in a nimble fashion while the old large carriers are bogged down by vast capital investments, obsolete equipment, huge pension commitments, massive bureaucracy, and inappropriate depreciation policies. New management taking control of one of the old carriers publicly described the job of adapting it to modern electronics as "like trying to turn around an elephant in a bathtub."

The new "specialized" common carriers seized on the rigidity of the U.S. telephone system, claiming that separate microwave and other transmission links were needed for specialized purposes, including business telephone and data transmission. In 1970, the FCC, summarizing the conclusion of a lengthy inquiry into computers and telecommunications, stated that there was "dissatisfaction on the part of the computer industry and by many data users who had been attempting to adapt their requirements to existing [communications] services."

In 1971, the FCC commissioners voted favorably on the concept of the specialized carriers, saying: "The entry of new carriers would have the effect of dispersing somewhat the burdens, risks and initiatives involved in supplying the rapidly growing market for new and specialized [communications] services." This sudden injection of competition into an industry, which for decades had little competition, has been dramatic in its effect. Many aspiring new carriers triggered new tariffs and service offerings from the old carriers. It is possible that the most major effect of the new carriers will be edging the massive old carriers into competitive response.

REASONS FOR SUCCESS

There are major economies of scale in telecommunications, and the large carriers have often quoted this fact to say that it is not economically beneficial for the country to have small carriers operating on the same routes. Why, then, can the specialized carriers charge lower rates?

The first reason is that the old established carriers have tended to install high-quality but expensive equipment. The formula regulating their profits tends to encourage high capital expenditure. A typical microwave tower of a specialized common carrier is much lower in cost than a typical AT&T microwave tower.

The second reason is that there is a certain range of traffic volumes, which are handled by microwave, for which economies of scale do not apply. There appears to be a kink in the microwave curve between 4000 and 10,000 circuits. Beyond a certain traffic volume, a major increase in equipment is needed. This is a very temporary reason. It is true, and likely to remain true, that the cost per call on a trunking system handling 100,000 calls or more is substantially less than on a microwave route handling fewer than 10,000 calls.

A third reason, and perhaps the most important, is that the new carriers are better able to introduce new technology such as satellites, small private earth stations, new switching techniques, CATV interconnections, and so on. The new carriers can also introduce *new services,* competitive with the old.

In view of the economies of scale and advantages inherent in an integrated technology, the final argument in favor of the specialized carriers probably has to be a belief in the ultimate virtues of competition, the low overheads of small corporations, and the initiative of private entrepreneurs.

LOCAL LOOPS

Although it is possible to compete with the giant telephone companies in long-haul transmission, it would be difficult to compete with them in local signal distribution—the copper wire pairs that go into homes and offices. Because of this the telephone companies will have less immediate competition in home telephone distribution, although there is great scope for the introduction of new home telephone instruments, conference devices, intercoms, telephone answering machines, and so on.

The specialized common carriers all have a problem in local distribution. Today the local distribution usually has to be done by having an interconnect agreement with the telephone company. This works satisfactorily but limits the link capacities to those of the telephone loops. It therefore precludes very high speed data transmission or video applications. To achieve these valuable applications, the specialized common carriers could someday forge links with CATV companies, or build new types of local distribution links, including short high-capacity radio links at frequencies above 10 GHz. Most specialized carriers are concentrating on voice transmission and data transmission up to 9600 bps because this is where most of the business revenue exists, and telephone interconnect agreements are satisfactory for these applications.

An AT&T tariff specifies what transmission facilities it will provide to other common carriers. In particular, it specifies characteristics of local loops. There are three grades of wire pair line specified for digital transmissions:

- Type W1: 2400 or 4800 bps
- Type W2: 9600 bps
- Type W3: 56,000 bps

The tariff also specifies voice-grade and television-grade interconnections. We will next further discuss the three new categories of specialized common carriers that now inhabit the telecommunications industry.

LONG-DISTANCE TELEPHONE CARRIERS

A long-distance telephone carrier does not provide the broad range of telecommunications services as do the conventional common carriers. Instead, they provide specialized transmission facilities that are designed to compete with the long-distance telephone services originally offered only by AT&T.

Microwave Communications Incorporated

The pioneer and pacesetter of the specialized common carriers is *Microwave Communications Incorporated* (MCI). In 1969, after six years of legal battling (the telecommunications lawyers are making a fortune), the FCC gave MCI permission to build a microwave system between St. Louis and Chicago. This historic decision triggered a flood of new microwave station applications.

MCI was soon a very large group of corporations building a nationwide microwave network and selling a wide variety of bandwidths to any customer who could use them. MCI's prices, like those of the other specialized carriers, were just sufficiently lower than those of the established carriers to attract customers.

AT&T bitterly accused MCI of "cream-skimming," that is, providing service only to those parts of the country where there would be maximum profit, whereas AT&T had to provide a similar service to its entire geographical area. The FCC ruled that in order to enable new corporations to come into business, they were indeed allowed to operate in selected areas. Today, MCI's network is truly nationwide and provides long-distance services to and from any telephone in the country, just as AT&T's network does.

MCI originally described themselves as a "nontelephone" common carrier. It soon became clear, however, that their main business revenue was to come from corporate telephone service, and their marketing drive is now oriented largely toward this.

US Sprint

Another extremely successful long-distance telephone carrier began operations in 1970 as the *Southern Pacific Communications Company* (SPC). SPC began its operations by offering telecommunications services whose circuits used the Southern Pacific Railroad's right-of-way between California and the Southwest. In 1978, SPC began offering a low-cost long-distance service called *Sprint* to the general public. In 1983, SPC was acquired by General Telephone and Electronics, and today the Sprint long-distance telephone service is known as US Sprint. The majority of US Sprint's long-distance calls are transmitted over fiber optic circuits, and the company's advertising has stressed the high quality of signals that the US Sprint network provides, in addition to the lower cost.

THE SATELLITE CARRIERS

A particularly interesting form of specialized common carrier is that constructing a satellite network.

Several new corporations obtained permission to become satellite carriers, but the first domestic satellites were launched by already existing organizations such as Western Union, RCA, and COMSAT. The Canadian ANIK satellite—the first domestic satellite—and later Canada's CTS satellite, were planned and launched by the Canadian government. *Satellite Business Systems* (SBS) will enable organizations to have their own earth stations on their premises.

Satellite carriers, like the other specialized carriers, are restricted by the local distribution facilities. A high-bandwidth signal could be sent via the transponder but cannot be delivered to the end user in many cases because the local wiring going to the end user is telephone copper wire cables organized so as to restrict the user to telephone bandwidths.

Satellite carriers can, however, bypass the local loop bottleneck by taking the signal directly to subscribers and giving them antennas on their premises. This is now being done for many large organizations.

VALUE-ADDED COMMON CARRIERS

The value-added carriers are different from other common carriers in that they are not ordinarily in the business of building new communication channels. Instead, they lease channels from other common carriers and then provide additional services to customers using these leased channels. The networks operated by the value-added common carriers are normally referred to as *public data networks*. When you use the services of a public data network, you do not pay for a communication channel. Instead, you pay the carrier to transmit a given number of bits from here to there. As discussed in Chapter 9, the equipment of most public data networks carves up the user's data into segments called packets, and then routes the packets over its network between one location and another, reassembling them into their original form on the other end.

The first value-added common carrier to receive FCC approval was *Packet Communications Inc.* (PCI). PCI intended to build a network providing packet-switched data communication and later went out of business.

The second FCC approval for a value-added common carrier went to Graphnet Systems Inc., which intended to provide a network to interconnect facsimile machines, and to transmit from computers, telegraph machines, and data terminals to facsimile machines. In January 1975, Graphnet became the first operational value-added common carrier.

The third FCC approval was for the *Telenet Communications Corporation* network. This, like PCI's proposal, was for a packet-switched data network providing fast-response transmission between computers and terminals. The Telenet network was based on the previously existing ARPA network, built with Department of Defense (DARPA) funds to interconnect university computing locations with a few other research establishments. The network of the Telenet Communications Corporation was later acquired by General Telephone and Electronics.

Box 15.2 lists the four most widely used public data networks in North America, including one operated by AT&T. These networks all implement packet switching techniques that conform to *CCITT Recommendation X.25*. These networks are described in more detail in Chapter 36, and packet switching and *Recommendation X.25* are discussed in Chapter 37. The widespread availability of the services of public data networks promises to revolutionize data transmission. These networks are already spreading throughout the world, and a wide variety of services will be available from many carriers.

CHARACTERISTICS OF PUBLIC DATA NETWORKS

The public data networks take advantage of economies of scale. When many users share the same wideband communication channels, they can communicate more cheaply. The wider the bandwidth they share, the faster the response time of the network. Also, the communication path can be made more reliable because the network can be designed to bypass failures. Users who could not otherwise communicate, because they have incompatible machines, can be interconnected. For example, the Telenet network routinely interconnects all varieties of incompatible computers and terminals.

BOX 15.2   North American public data networks

- **Telenet.** The *Telenet Public Data Network* is the oldest value-added network in operation in the United States. It began operation in 1975 as the Telenet Public Data network, and GTE acquired Telenet in 1979. In addition to offering general packet-switched communication services, Telenet also offers an electronic mail service called Telemail. Information about Telenet can be obtained from Telenet Communications Corporation, 8229 Boone Boulevard, Vienna, VA 22180; telephone: (703)442-1000.

- **Tymnet.** The *Tymnet* network is operated by a wholly owned subsidiary of McDonnell Douglas Automation. The Tymshare network was originally developed to support the time-sharing services marketed by Tymshare, Inc. and has evolved to a general-purpose public data network. Like Telenet, Tymnet also offers an electronic mail service, called On-Tyme-II. Information about Tymnet can be obtained from Tymnet, Inc., 2710 Orchard Parkway, San Jose CA 95134; telephone: (408)946-4900.

- **ADP Autonet.** The *ADP Autonet* network is operated by a subsidiary of *Automatic Data Processing, Inc.* (ADP). The ADP Autonet network evolved from a private network that ADP developed to service its own clients. ADP Autonet operates an electronic mail service that it calls Auto Mail. Information about ADP Autonet can be obtained from ADP Autonet, 175 Jackson Plaza, Ann Arbor, MI 48106; telephone: (313)769-6800.

- **AT&T Accunet Packet Service.** The *AT&T Accunet* Packet Service is the newest of the five major packet-switched public data networks described here. Unlike the other packet-switched services, AT&T's packet switching network does not allow simple terminals to be connected to the network that do not provide their own packet assembly and disassembly (PAD) facility. A terminal or computer must support the *CCITT Recommendation X.25* interface in order to operate on the network. (See Chapter 37 for more information about X.25.) Information about the Accunet Packet Service can be obtained from AT&T Communications, 295 North Maple Avenue, Basking Ridge, NJ 07920.

A public data network does not ordinarily *process* the messages that it transmits and stores. They may, however, enhance the messages, such as adding a corporate letterhead and logo to messages sent in alphanumeric form. Similarly, signatures can be added to certain documents if tight security controls are used.

BOX 15.3   Possible value-added services

Message Delivery

- Telegrams
- Facsimile
- Electronic mail
- Interactive and batch computer data
- Interconnecting incompatible data machines
- One-way voice messages
- Monetary transfers and bank card traffic

Broadcasting

- Data broadcasting
- Weather and marine forecast services
- News broadcasting by data, voice, or video
- Financial information services
- Music delivery

Message Enhancement

- Adding forms to computer data
- Adding corporate logos and letterheads
- Adding signatures under tight security control
- Form letters customized with recipient's name
- Message editing
- Word processing functions

Message Storage

- Document filing services
- Secure storage service for vital records

Message Retrieval

- Library services
- Information retrieval and search services
- Financial information services
- Data bank services
- Newspaper morgue searching
- Music library

NEW TELECOMMUNICATIONS SERVICES

The specialized common carriers are in the business of providing new *services* to society and industry that the traditional carriers do not provide. There are many possible opportunities for new types of services. Box 15.3 lists some examples.

Many different types of value-added services are possible and we may see the specialized common carriers develop in new directions. A carrier that transmits and stores facsimile messages could also transmit and store voice messages. A carrier that transmits packets of interactive computer data could equally relay telex conversations or provide a fast message delivery service. The more diverse types of traffic a value-added network handles, the better, because of the economies of scale. Telenet today delivers messages faster and cheaper than telegrams. If the traffic volumes were high enough, it could handle mail at delivery costs lower than those of the postal service.

The specialized common carriers can also offer new services, such as setting up video conferencing studios, or transmitting bulk data at high speed. Using manual pickup and delivery, a file of say 10^9 bits could be sent across the country from one computer center to another in an hour or so. A service that would be attractive to some corporations is the complete analysis of their communication needs, traffic monitoring, and the design of an optimum corporate network. "Turnkey" corporate network management could have great appeal if done in a highly professional fashion with the latest equipment and tools. Several specialized carriers are moving into this business. Much of the future of the specialized carriers may lie in their offering innovative services that the telephone companies do not supply.

16 COMMON CARRIER TARIFFS

In the United States, the services offered by a telecommunications common carrier are described in *tariffs,* which are documents that a common carrier files with a regulating authority. As we discussed in Chapter 15, the Federal Communications Commission (FCC) regulates all interstate telecommunications facilities, and the state public utilities commissions control intrastate communications. By law, a tariff must be registered and approved by one of these regulating bodies before a service can be made available to the public. In most other countries, the telecommunications facilities are set up by government bodies and thus are directly under their control. These government bodies are often referred to as PTTs (for "postal, telephone, and telegraph").

In this chapter we examine some of the tariffs that are of particular interest to users of data transmission services. The examples we will use in this chapter are taken from the United States. The offerings of other countries are broadly similar. In general, countries with less well developed telecommunications facilities than the United States have less to offer in the way of wideband facilities. But in some cases, many European countries are ahead of the United States in the construction of public data networks. This is due primarily to political difficulties, not to problems with the technology.

COMMUNICATION RATES

In the United States, the subject of communication rates has become very complex. The amount and structure of charges differ from one state to another. In most other countries, the rates for more conventional channels remain relatively straightforward; however, often the carriers are government organizations who are not obliged to publish tariffs for all their facilities. The price for less common channels, such as wideband links, may have to be obtained by special request to the carrier. In general, it is desirable, when designing a system, that the organization in question be called in to quote a price for the facilities needed.

GUIDE TO COMMUNICATION SERVICES

A particularly useful source of current information on telecommunications services is a book called the *Guide to Communication Services* published by the *Center for Communications Management, Inc.,* P.O. Box 324, Ramsey, NJ 07446. This reference guide contains a description of all currently available telecommunications tariffs along with their costs. The CCMI Guide is published in looseleaf form on an annual subscription fee basis and is kept up to date with monthly replacement pages.

CATEGORIES OF LINE

One way to categorize communication lines is according to three speed categories: *subvoice grade, voice grade,* and *wideband*.

Subvoice Grade

There is some overlap in the speeds that are available in the subvoice-grade and voice-grade categories. But, in general, these are lines designed for telegraph and similar machines transmitting at speeds ranging, in the United States, from 45 to 150 bps. Some countries have telegraph lines of higher speed. Britain, for example, has its DATEL 200 service operating at 200 bps. Most industrialized countries outside North America have a similar 200-bps service; in fact, the 200-bps rate is a CCITT standard. We will consider a channel that supports speeds up to about 600 bps to be a subvoice-grade line. Today, all these lines are commonly obtained by subdividing ordinary telephone channels through multiplexing techniques.

Voice Grade

At present, telephone channels can normally transmit data at speeds ranging from 300 to 9600 bps. Dial-up telephone lines are commonly used today for speeds of up to 4800 bps. A speed of 9600 bps is possible but requires elaborate modem design and powerful facilities for error correction. Normally, this speed is used only over leased lines. Telephone organizations in some other countries have not yet permitted the use of such high speeds over their telephone lines. In many countries, 1200 or 2400 bps is still the maximum allowable bit rate.

Wideband Lines

Wideband analog lines (sometimes called *broadband* lines) give speeds much higher than those of voice channels. They typically use facilities that would otherwise carry many simultaneous telephone calls. Speeds up to 500,000 bps are in common use over analog channels, and higher bit rates are possible if required.

PHYSICAL FACILITIES

All the line types discussed above can be channeled over a variety of physical facilities, generally at the discretion of the common carrier. In fact, the tariffs themselves typically say nothing about the medium used for transmission, other than to make a distinction between terrestrial and satellite circuits. A given terrestrial channel might be implemented via twisted pair, coaxial cable, microwave radio, or optical fiber. A given link might well use a combination of different transmission media at different points in the circuit.

The transmission over different media is organized in such a way that the channels obtained have largely the same properties—the same capacity, the same noise level, and the same error rate. The user is generally not able to tell whether a microwave link, coaxial cable, or pairs of wires stretched between telephone poles are being used. Only satellite transmission requires different data-handling equipment because of the propagation delay and because the satellite can be used as a broadcast rather than a point-to-point facility.

SWITCHED VERSUS LEASED LINES

When you dial a friend and talk on the telephone, you speak over a line connected by means of the public exchanges. This line, referred to as a *public* or *switched* line, can also be used for the transmission of data by using appropriate modems. Alternatively, a *private* or *leased* line could be connected permanently, or semipermanently between the transmitting machines. The private line might be connected via the local switching office, but it is not ordinarily connected to the switching gear and signaling devices of that office. An interoffice leased connection does use the same physical links as the switched circuits. It would not, however, have to carry the signaling that is needed on a switched line. This frees up the signaling frequencies for use by the subscriber, thus making slightly more bandwidth available than is available over a public, switched connection.

Just as you can either dial a telephone connection or have it permanently wired, so it is with some other types of lines. Telegraph lines, for example, which have a much lower speed of transmission than is possible over voice lines, may be permanently connected or may be dialed like a telephone line via a switched public network. Telex is such a network; it exists throughout most of the world, permitting transmission at 50 bps. Some countries have a switched public network that operates at a somewhat higher speed than telex but at less speed than telephone lines. In the United States, the TWX network gives speeds up to 150 bps. TWX lines can be connected to telex lines for overseas calls.

Facilities for switching wideband channels are also in operation in some locations, although most wideband channels today are permanent connections. Certain countries are building up a switched network for very high speed connections. In the United States, Western Union installed the first sections of a system in which a user can indicate in the dialing sequence the bandwidth that is required.

MEASURED-USE SERVICES

The switched public telephone network is an example of a *measured-use service*. The telephone company keeps track of the time a circuit is connected, and thus "measures the use" of the circuit. The public telephone network provides a very high degree of flexibility for data transmission, as a computer can be dialed from practically any telephone in the world. There are other measured-use services that common carriers provide. Box 16.1 lists some of the more popular measured-use services in the United States.

HOT-LINE SERVICE

An interesting type of measured-use service, called a hot-line service, is offered by some carriers. A hot line gives the impression that a dedicated channel exists between two points. When a subscriber picks up the phone at one end, a particular phone at the other end rings automatically. In fact, a switched connection is automatically established between the two points as soon as the receiver is picked up. The user is billed for a monthly service fee plus a measured-use charge based on the amount of time the circuit is actually used. In some cases, a hot-line service can be used for data transmission when instant communication is required between two data machines but where the cost of a private line is not justified.

WIDE-AREA TELEPHONE SERVICE

Another measured-use tariff in the United States provides dial-up facilities for a fixed monthly fee and is called WATS, the *wide-area telephone service*. When a company is given an *OUTWATS* access line, people in that company may make as many calls as desired to a specified zone. With an *INWATS* line, anyone in a specified zone is permitted to call into that line without being charged for the call. These would be two separate lines. On either, there are two alternative methods of charging. One uses a flat monthly charge and the other uses a fixed hourly rate with a minimum of 10 to 15 hours.

Suppose that your company is in New York and you wish to have a WATS

BOX 16.1   Measured-use services

- **Toll telephone:** the public telephone service.

- **WATS (Wide-Area Telephone Service):** an AT&T reduced-rate, bulk-billing, long-distance, telephone service in which the United States is divided into billing zones; there are tariffs for either measured-time or full-period charges

- **Hot Line:** a service providing fixed point-to-point telephone-grade connections on a measured-time basis

- **Broadband Exchange Service:** a Western Union service in which the user can dial the bandwidth required

- **Telex:** the international 50-bps service used over much of the world

- **TWX (Teletypewriter Exchange Service):** a Western Union 150-bps teletypewriter service with dial-up connections like telex

- **Infomaster** [formerly Telex Computer Services (TCS)]: a message switching service for Western Union telex subscribers, offering telex-to-TWX conversion

- **Public data networks:** networks that generally use packet switching techniques to transmit messages between two subscribers

line to the West Coast of North America. You can pay a certain fixed charge for this line and you are then free to make whatever calls you like to the West Coast or to WATS zones that are nearer than the West Coast. The whole of the United States is divided up into six WATS zones based largely on state boundaries. Figure 16.1 shows these zones as viewed from New York. The charge for zone 2 is greater than that for zone 1, zone 3 greater than 2, and so on. If the subscriber pays for access to zone 4, calls can be made to zones 1, 2, and 3 for that same charge, but not to zones 5 and 6.

The zone numbering of Fig. 16.1 is applicable only to New York. Another state would have a map with different numbering and different charges. Figure 16.2 shows the WATS zone numbering as applicable to the state of Missouri.

WATS permits data transmission using the same types of modems that are used with normal telephone lines. It is not possible to make person-to-person, conference, third-party, credit, or collect calls under the WATS tariff.

WIDEBAND SWITCHED SERVICES

The main drawback to using a normal switched circuit for data transmission purposes is that most of the services available use standard telephone circuits of

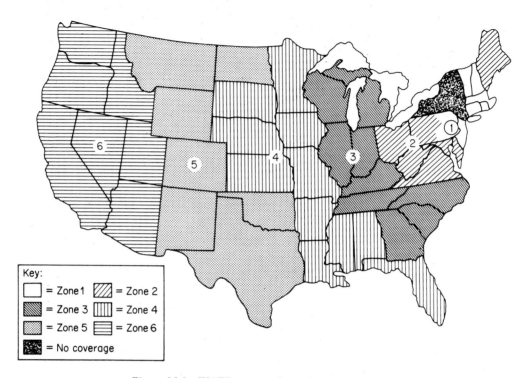

Figure 16.1　WATS zone configuration for New York

4-kHz bandwidth. The highest practical bit rate normally used on this type of channel is 4800 bps. Although 9600 bps is sometimes achievable, it is only at the cost of a higher error rate. However, there are switched services available that allow much higher bit rates. For example, AT&T offers a switched service that provides 48-kHz channels into customer location and is available in most of the larger cities over the access lines operated by the local telephone company. Such a wideband channel can be used for economical data transmission at bit rates up to about 50,000 bps.

Measured-use wideband services will become more and more important to data transmission as switched services supporting high bit rates become more widespread. But today, the most common way of providing high-speed data transmission channels between two points is via leased lines.

LEASED LINES　　　　A subscriber can acquire a private line by leasing a channel from a common carrier, usually on a monthly basis. The private channel is permanently connected, and the subscriber

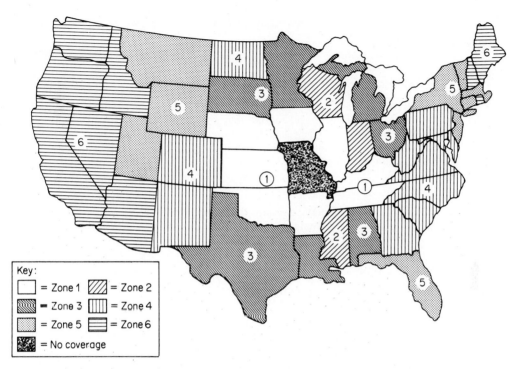

Key:
- ☐ = Zone 1
- ▨ = Zone 2
- ▩ = Zone 3
- ⊞ = Zone 4
- ▦ = Zone 5
- ☰ = Zone 6
- ▪ = No coverage

Figure 16.2   WATS zone configuration for Missouri

can use the channel at any time without incurring additional usage charges. The most commonly used leased line is a normal telephone channel of 4-kHz bandwidth. Leased voice lines have certain advantages over switched telephone connections for data transmission. Box 16.2 lists some of the advantages of both leased and switched lines.

LINE CONDITIONING

Since a leased channel is permanently connected, the subscriber can pay extra for special *line conditioning* that improves the quality of the channel. With proper conditioning and appropriate modem equipment, bit rates of 9600 bps, and sometimes higher, are achievable with acceptable error rates. AT&T has two types of conditioning, referred to as *C* and *D* conditioning (see Box 16.3). There are several categories of C conditioning, and several categories of D conditioning. Each is labeled with a C or D followed by a digit, for example C3. Since C and D conditioning controls different types of distortion, both may be used on the same circuit.

BOX 16.2 Leased versus switched lines

Advantages of Leased Lines

- **Cost.** If a line is to be used for more than a given number of hours per day, the leased line is less expensive than the switched line. If it is used only for an hour or so per day, it is more expensive. The break-even point depends on the actual charges, which in turn depend on the mileage of the circuit, but is likely to be on the order of several hours per day. The cost factor is clearly an important consideration in designing a data transmission network.

- **Lack of Switching Delay.** Because the leased line is permanently connected, there is no switching delay associated with using the line. Leased lines are, therefore, better than telephone switching systems for applications requiring *fast* access to a distant computer. The same argument does not apply to fast-connect or packet-switched systems.

- **Conditioning.** Private lines can be specially treated, or *conditioned,* to compensate for the distortion that is encountered on them. The common carriers charge extra for conditioning. In this way the number of data errors can be reduced, or alternatively, a higher transmission rate can be made possible. Switched connections cannot be conditioned beforehand in the same way, because it is not known what path a circuit will take. Dialing at one time is likely to set up a quite different physical path from that obtained by dialing at another time.

- **Bandwidth.** Although the bandwidth of leased and public lines are the same—4 kHz—switched lines usually carry signaling within the bandwidth that is used for data. Data transmission machines must be designed so that the form in which the data is sent cannot interfere with the common carrier's signaling. With some machines, this operation also makes the bandwidth available for data transmission somewhat less than over a leased voice line.

- **Noise and Distortion.** A leased line may be less perturbed by noise and distortion than a switched line. The switching gear can cause impulse noise that results in errors in the data. This is another factor that contributes to a lower error rate for a given transmission speed on private lines.

Advantages of Switched Lines

- **Cost.** If the terminal or terminals at a given location have only a low usage, switched lines will give a lower overall cost than leased lines for those terminals.

BOX 16.2 *(Continued)*

- **Flexibility.** The ability to access multiple distant machines using a switched network gives great flexibility. Many different machines offering different services and with different databases may be dialed by a terminal user.

- **Reliability.** If a leased line fails, its users may be cut off from the facilities to which it connects. With a switched system, the user or using machine can redial and may be able to obtain an alternative path to the facilities.

- **Load Sharing.** If a computer is overloaded or under repair, its users may be able to dial an alternative computer. If leased lines are used, there may be no access to alternative equipment.

- **Simplicity.** Leased-line systems often become complex because of the techniques used, such as polling, concentrators, and multipoint lines, which allow separate users to share the line.

BOX 16.3 C-type and D-type conditioning

- **C-Type Conditioning.** A line ideal for data transmission would have an equal drop in signal voltage for all frequencies transmitted. Also, all frequencies would have the same signal propagation time. This is not so in practice. Different frequencies suffer different attenuation and different signal delay. C conditioning attempts to equalize the attenuation and delay at different frequencies. Standards are laid down in the tariffs for the measure of equalization that must be achieved. The signal attenuation and delay at different frequencies must lie within certain limits for each type of conditioning. The higher the conditioning number, the narrower are the limits. The result of the conditioning is that a higher data speed can be obtained over the line, given suitable modems.

- **D-Type Conditioning.** D conditioning controls the signal-to-noise ratio and the harmonic distortion. It is intended for voice-grade lines operating at 9600 bps.

CHANNEL GROUPS If a higher bandwidth than that of a telephone channel is desired, *channel groups* can be leased. A group of 12 channels provides a total bandwidth of about 48 kHz. A group of 24 channels provides a total bandwidth of about 96 kHz. A supergroup of 60 voice channels, for a total bandwidth of 240 kHz, is also generally available. With private analog channels, it is up to the user to decide how to use the available bandwidth, and generally, voice and data can be combined. Various types of modems are available to support various bit rates up to as high as 230,400 bps when a supergroup is used.

TARIFFS FOR WIDEBAND LINES AND BUNDLES The North American common carriers offer several tariffs for leased wideband lines. Some of these can be subdivided by the carrier into bundles of lower bandwidth. They can also be subdivided into channels for voice transmission, teletypewriter, control, signaling, facsimile, or data. With some tariffs, the user pays a lower price for the bundles than for the individual channels.

TYPES 5700 AND 5800 TARIFFS The type 5700 line provides a capacity equivalent to 60 full-duplex voice channels. The type 5800 line provides a capacity equivalent to 240 voice channels. The full capacity of these lines can be used as a single channel for data transmission at very high bit rates, or the voice channels can be used by the customer individually. In addition, each of the voice channels can itself be subdivided in a number of ways to provide multiple subvoice-grade subchannels.

THE SERIES 8000 TARIFF Series 8000 is another *bulk* communications service of AT&T that offers wideband transmission of high-speed data or facsimile at rates up to 50,000 bps. The customer has the alternative of using the channel for voice communication up to a maximum of 12 circuits. A type 8801 link, part of this series, provides a data link at speeds up to 50,000 bps with appropriate modems. An additional voice channel is provided with this link for coordination purposes. The type 8803 tariff provides a data link with a fixed speed of 19,200 bps and leaves a remaining capacity that can be used either for a second simultaneous 19,200-bps channel or for up to five voice channels.

Many other North American common carriers and the telecommunications administrations of many other countries also offer tariffs similar to the series 8000. In most locations quotations for higher speeds can be obtained on request. Obtaining a wideband link in many such countries can be a slow process. This is particularly so if the termination is required in a small town or rural area rather than in a city where such links already exist. Undoubtedly, as the demand for such facilities increases, the service of the common carriers in providing them will improve.

USES FOR WIDEBAND LINES

Wideband lines serve two purposes. First, they provide a wideband channel over which data can be sent at a much higher rate than over a voice channel. Second, they provide a means of offering groups of voice or subvoice lines at reduced rates—a kind of discount for bulk buying.

Suppose that a company requires a 50,000-bps link between two cities, together with 23 voice channels and 14 teletypewriter channels. Then it would be likely to use the type 5700 tariff. In leasing these facilities, it would have some unused capacity. If it wishes, it can make use of this capacity for no additional mileage charge, although it may incur additional charges if it adds terminal equipment.

SHARING WIDEBAND BUNDLES

In the United States, government agencies and certain firms in the same business whose rates and services are regulated by the government (e.g., airlines and railroads) are able to *share* bundled services. Airlines, for example, pool their needs for voice and teletypewriter channels. An intercompany organization purchases the bundled services and then apportions the channels to individual airlines. Most of the lines channeling passenger reservations to a distant office where bookings can be made are type 5700 or type 5800 lines and so are the lines carrying data between terminals in those offices and a distant reservations computer.

SATELLITE CHANNELS

Another type of leased-line channel that is now available from several common carriers, including AT&T, is a leased satellite channel. Satellite channels are generally more economical than terrestrial channels of equivalent capacity. Bandwidths as great as 1.2 MHz are available, and this type of channel can provide bit rates into the millions of bits per second for those users that require them. A satellite channel has the capability of dropping in cost much more rapidly than high-capacity channels of most other types.

DIGITAL CHANNELS

Most leased channels, including those supplied by many satellite carriers, are analog in nature and require modems for data transmission. But many carriers are also supplying channels that are designed specifically for digital transmission. AT&T offers a number of options for digital data transmission in its Accunet group of digital services. Some of the available AT&T Accunet services are described in Box 16.4. Modems are not required, and users are connected to the network via digital adapters. AT&T calls these adapters *digital service units* (DSUs). The digital adapters can usually be acquired from the common carrier that offers the digital service or from a variety of telecommunications equipment vendors.

Unlike the other AT&T tariffs, the Accunet lines themselves are digital and so cannot transmit analog signals such as voice (unless it is first digitized using the techniques discussed in Chapter 13). The error rate on AT&T digital lines is generally better than that on voice lines because they are designed specifically for digital transmission.

As we have discussed, common carriers are in the process of swinging from analog to digital transmission for many telephone trunks. The Accunet

BOX 16.4   AT&T Accunet Services

- **Dataphone Digital Service.** The Dataphone Digital Service (DDS) provides leased digital lines at bit rates of 2400, 4800, 9600, or 56,000 bps.

- **Accunet Switched 56 Service.** The Accunet Switched 56 Service provides digital data transmission at the bit rate of 56,000 bps via a switched network. The network is accessed via a dedicated digital line to a local Accunet switching office. A subscriber can access any other subscriber to the Switched 56 Service in a similar manner to placing a long-distance call.

- **Accunet Packet Service.** The Accunet Packet Service, introduced in Chapter 15, provides a packet-switched public data network that can be accessed via dedicated lines that operate at 2400, 4800, or 56,000 bps.

- **Accunet T1.5 Service.** The Accunet T1.5 Service offers leased digital lines that operate at the speed of the T1 carrier—1.544 Mbps. The service can be used for data transmission as well as for conventional telephone channels, color video, audio, facsimile, and graphics signals for video teleconferencing applications.

- **Accunet Reserved 1.5 Service.** The Accunet Reserved 1.5 Service offers the same T1 channel as the Accunet T1.5 Service, but allows the subscriber to schedule the use of the channel in half-hour increments whenever the channel is required, rather than leasing a dedicated line on a monthly basis. A request can be made for a channel as little as an hour in advance of when the channel will be required.

collection of services is a by-product of this process of voice digitization. The T1 and T2 carriers discussed in Chapter 13 are used in the Accunet network.

DIGITAL CHANNEL ADVANTAGES

The use of digital channels such as those provided by the Accunet services can have several advantages over using telephone channels, including:

- Lower cost
- No modems
- Higher speeds
- Lower error rate
- Higher availability

Unfortunately, these digital channels are available only in certain locations. Depending on where the subscriber is located, it may not be possible to obtain a local channel to such a network. The alternative is to use a telephone connection to the nearest access point of the digital network. When this is done, however, many of the advantages listed above are lost. If a telephone connection is needed at each end, a total of four modems are required, where two would suffice had an ordinary telephone line been used to implement the entire connection. It can be expected that the digital networks will grow and become more widespread so that increasing numbers of users will be able to connect to them directly.

PRIVATE SYSTEMS

Some communication lines are wholly owned by their users rather than being leased from a common carrier. Individual users are generally prohibited from installing their own cables across public highways, and most privately installed communication links are wholly within a user's premises—for example, within a factory, office building, or laboratory. Railroads have their own communication links along their tracks. Some companies have point-to-point microwave transmission links or other radio links. Recently, infrared and optical links have been used for the transmission of data; line-of-sight links can be established at low cost, capable of carrying up to several million bits per second. Such links require no license, as do private microwave links. They could be used in cities for transmission between rooftops. Their main drawback is that the link can be put out of operation for brief periods by rain downpours of abnormal intensity—and for longer periods by thick fog. Relatively inexpensive millimeterwave radio equipment is also coming into use for short line-of-sight links. Small dishes often mounted on rooftops transmit at extremely high frequencies and have the potential of carrying a very high bandwidth over distances of a few miles.

SWITCHED PRIVATE SYSTEMS

Many firms have private lines that are switched with private exchanges. In this way they build their own switched systems, which are often called *corporate tie-line networks*. The lines that are used can be either privately owned or leased from common carriers. The reason for designing a switched private system is either to lower the total telephone bill or to have a switched system of higher bandwidth than the telephone system.

Telephone companies facilitate the building of private switched networks within organizations by providing *common control switching arrangements* (CCSAs). Such an arrangement uses switching equipment at telephone exchanges to switch calls in a private leased network. All stations connected to the private network may call one another without having to use the public toll facilities.

VALUE-ADDED COMMON CARRIERS

As discussed in Chapter 15, value-added common carriers provide a very different type of tariff structure than those discussed above. Operators of public data networks do not charge for a communication channel; instead, they charge by the message or by the packet. In general, the resulting price is much lower than with dialed or leased telephone lines if the quantity of data is low. In a sense, the value-added carriers are enabling the small user to obtain some of the economies of scale that a large user obtains with leased lines.

Chapter 17 begins Part IV, where we discuss the procedures that are used in controlling data transmission over a communication channel.

PART IV DATA LINK PROTOCOLS

17 DATA LINK CHARACTERISTICS

When data transmission devices send data to each other, a variety of control signals must pass to and fro between the devices to ensure that they are working in step with one another. For example, the sending machine must tell the receiving machine when it is about to start transmitting data. The receiving machine must tell the sending machine whether it is ready to receive. Throughout the transmission, exact synchronization must be maintained and slippages in synchronization must be corrected. When the receiving machine detects errors, it must notify the sending machine, and the erroneous data must be retransmitted.

An important set of standards, generally called *data link protocols,* govern the way in which communicating machines interact at the data link level. A data link protocol is a set of rules that all devices on the data link follow in controlling transmission over that link. Several commonly used data link protocols are introduced later in this chapter, including *asynchronous* protocols, the *binary-synchronous* protocol, and the *bit-oriented* protocols that are used with today's computer networks.

NETWORK USERS

We refer to any component of the system that sends a message into the network or accepts a message from it as a *network user,* or simply a *user*. There are many types of network users. They may be complex ones, such as a program that is running in a large mainframe; or they may be simple ones, like the control mechanisms of a simple asynchronous terminal. As introduced in Chapter 4, we often refer to the logical links between network users as *virtual channels*.

VIRTUAL CHANNELS

Virtual channels can be implemented simply, as with a single point-to-point physical circuit; or in complex ways, as with a nationwide packet switching network. Figure 17.1 shows a complex network in which a number of physical links are used to implement a single virtual channel. When we discuss data communication, we must distinguish between the virtual channels that appear to exist between users and the physical links that actually exist between devices.

Network users consist of processes, such as software components running in a computer or firmware control mechanisms running in terminals. When we discuss the virtual channels that connect users, we are looking at the network from the users' perspective—we are discussing *what* the network does for them. From this perspective, many of the complexities of the network become transparent. For example, it does not matter to a user whether a message is going over a phone line or whether it is being routed across the country through packet switches, as long as the message gets to its destination in an acceptably short time.

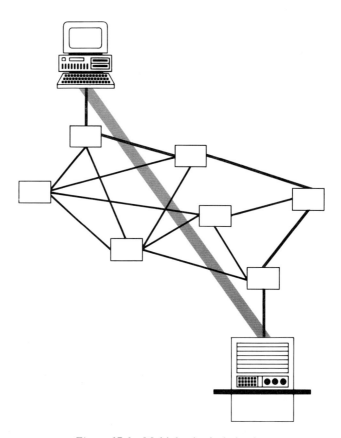

Figure 17.1   Multiple physical circuits

PHYSICAL CIRCUITS

We must sometimes look at a data communication system from the *network's* perspective. We do this when we examine the devices and communication links that make up the network. As we have seen, the physical circuits that implement a network are different from the virtual channels that connect users. Virtual channels are imaginary; they do not actually exist, at least not in the way that users perceive them. But the physical circuits do exist. They consist of the wire pairs, microwave links, satellite channels, and so on, that we discussed in Part III.

When we take the user's perspective, we are interested in the functions of the network; when we take the network's perspective, we are interested in understanding the processes that are carried out within the network. The network's perspective is the one we take in the chapters in this part. We are interested here in the operation of the physical connections between network machines and the rules these machines follow in transmitting data over physical circuits.

DATA LINKS

We use the term *virtual channel* to describe a *logical* communication path between network users. We use the term *data link* to describe a *physical* connection between two hardware components. A data link consists of a communication channel and the hardware needed to transmit data over it. In discussing data links, the terms *DTE*, for *data terminal equipment,* and *DCE,* for *data circuit-terminating equipment,* are important. We introduced these two terms in Chapter 10 when we discussed physical layer standards.

DATA TERMINAL EQUIPMENT

Data terminal equipment (DTE) is that portion of a data processing machine that is capable of transmitting digital data over a communication circuit. It can take the form of a communications adapter installed in a computer, a separate communications controller, a mid-network device, such as a packet switch, or it can consist of communications hardware installed in a simple terminal. From the network's perspective, a DTE is any device that converts a message into a collection of bits suitable for transmission over a digital communication channel. Since, in most cases, only a small portion of the hardware that makes up a terminal or other piece of computing equipment actually performs the function of a DTE, we often draw a data link and its associated equipment as shown in Fig. 17.2. The communication channel and its DTEs together determine the operational characteristics of the data link.

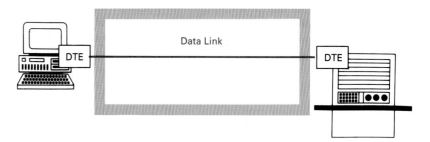

Figure 17.2   Data link connecting two DTEs

**DATA CIRCUIT-
TERMINATING
EQUIPMENT**

Data circuit-terminating equipment (DCE) is often used in implementing a data link, although they are not required on all data links. If DCEs are used, they form part of the data link itself, as shown in Fig. 17.3. A DCE is any device that performs a signal conversion that allows a digital bit stream to be transmitted over a physical channel. If an analog telephone channel is being used, the DCEs are typically modems. If an AT&T DDS line is being used, the DCEs are AT&T service units. When a data link does not use DCEs to perform signal conversion, the two DTEs are connected directly together.

Whether or not DCEs are used to implement a data link, it appears to the DTEs as if a simple connection exists between them. In other words, the use of DCEs in implementing the connection is transparent to the DTEs. The control mechanisms in a modem or service unit that perform signal conversions operate at the *physical* level. The control mechanisms that operate in the DTEs to implement a data link operate at the *data link* level. Because of the principle of

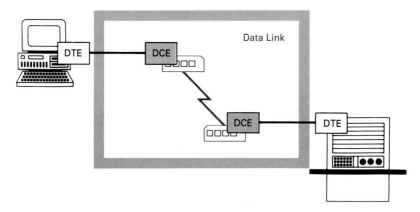

Figure 17.3   Data link with DCEs

layer independence, all functions that operate at the physical level are transparent to the data link layer.

In these chapters, we will ordinarily think of a data link as consisting of two or more DTEs connected by a simple, direct connection. The physical nature of the connection, and whether or not DCEs are used to implement it, are of no concern to the data link layer. At this level, we simply assume that a bit stream sent out by a DTE at one end of the connection will be received by a DTE at the other end of the connection. However, as we will see in Chapter 20, we do *not* yet assume at the data link level that an *error-free* connection exists.

DATA LINK CONFIGURATIONS

There are three data link configurations that are in common use. These are the *point-to-point, multipoint,* and *loop* configurations.

Point-to-Point Configuration

A point-to-point data link, shown in Figure 17.4, is the simplest and the easiest to control. When one station transmits, the station at the other end of the link must receive. Since no other stations are attached to the data link, there are no problems associated with determining for whom a message is intended. In some systems that use point-to-point links, one station on the link is designated as the *primary* station (often a computer) and the other is designated as the *secondary* station (often a terminal). The terms *master* and *slave* or *tributary* are sometimes alternatively used to describe the relationship between stations. In a system in which a primary/secondary relationship exists, only the primary station is capable of originating an exchange of messages; the secondary station can transmit only after the primary station has given it permission. In other systems, the two stations are *peers,* and either can initiate an exchange of messages. These relationships are discussed in more detail in later chapters in this part when we examine specific data link protocols.

Figure 17.4   Point-to-point configuration

Multipoint Configuration

As discussed in Chapter 9, when the communication lines used to implement a data transmission system are expensive and the terminals are in use only a fraction of the time, it is often usual to have several terminals attached to the same data link. A data link that has more than one DTE attached to it is called a *multipoint* data link, as shown in Fig. 17.5. (An older term that is still sometimes used instead of multipoint is *multidrop*.) The terminals might be all in one location, or the communication line might wander in a zigzag fashion between different locations. In most cases, one of the stations on a multipoint data link is designated as the primary station (often a computer) and the others as secondary (often terminals).

In Chapter 5 we used a fire hose analogy to describe data flowing along a communication line. In that analogy, an imaginary espionage agent sent data down a fire hose by modulating the stream of water with a piston. An accomplice at the other end detected the data with a receiving piston. By carrying the analogy a step further, we can see that if our espionage firefighter had several agents connected to the fire hose over which data were being sent, only one of them could be transmitting at once. The espionage agent, in fact, must have some way of maintaining discipline over the other agents. They must have a carefully worked out procedure for who transmits when and for determining for whom a particular message is meant. When the agent sends a pulse down a multipoint fire hose, it will be detected by all the agents connected to that hose. Discipline is needed on multipoint data links for the same reason.

Loop Configuration

Some systems allow devices to be connected to one another in the form of a loop. This technique often uses a high-speed pulse stream, traveling in a constant and unbroken fashion, over links that are generally installed on the user's premises. Loops are not generally used with systems that use common carrier

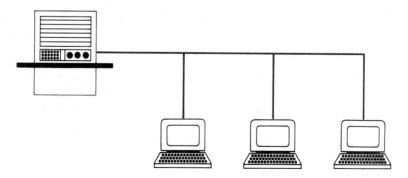

Figure 17.5   Multipoint configuration

facilities for data communication. The loop configuration has the advantage that both the terminals and the communication links can be relatively inexpensive. Bits can be carried at a very high rate over a simple pair of wires if regenerative digital repeaters are used with sufficiently close spacing. The bit rate can, in fact, be so high that the bits can be used in a wanton fashion if this helps lower the cost of terminal equipment.

The wires can be arranged in a loop, as in Fig. 17.6, that originates at a computer or controlling machine, wanders around various data-handling machines, and then returns to the computer. In one such system, the loop carries a train of fixed-length blocks that convey messages to or from the terminal devices. If a terminal at a particular instant has a message to transmit, its controller waits for an empty block, then places the message in it. You might picture this as being similar to a never-ending train of railroad cars. Each car can carry one message. The terminal looks at the *address* on each car to see if that car is carrying a message for it. If so, it takes the contents of that car. Similarly, if the station has a message to send to the computer, it looks for the next *empty* car. It places the message into that car along with the terminal address. The terminals can transmit continuously or sporadically. The train will always be going by.

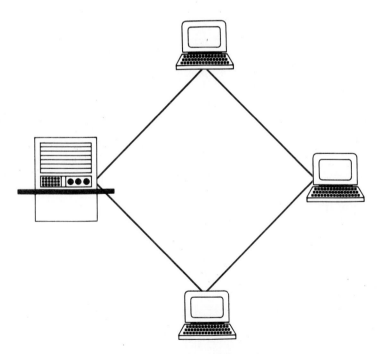

Figure 17.6 Loop configuration

TRANSMISSION STATES

With most data link protocols, it is useful to distinguish between four status conditions that a station can be in at any given time:

- **Transmit Control.** A station is in this state when it is transmitting commands that control the data link rather than characters that make up the text of a message.
- **Transmit Text.** A station is in this state when it is transmitting message text.
- **Receive Control.** A station is in this state when it is receiving, or ready to receive, commands that control the data link.
- **Receive Text.** A station is in this state when it is receiving, or ready to receive, message text.

These status conditions determine the types of messages or commands that a given station can send or receive at any given instant. Commands that flow back and forth over the data link cause stations to change their status as required.

MODES OF TRANSMISSION

A variety of techniques can be used for transmitting data over a given data link. Each technique uses a different method for organizing the signals sent so that they convey the information in question. For each transmission technique, there are families of devices built to operate in this manner. We discuss next some of the modes of transmission that can be used in implementing data links.

DATA LINK TRANSMISSION MODE

We have already seen that a given physical transmission facility supports either simplex, half-duplex, or full-duplex transmission. There are three interrelated factors that determine the transmission mode of the data link itself. These are the transmission mode that the communication line itself supports, the transmission mode supported by the DCEs used in implementing the link, and the data link protocol used by the DTEs that implement the link.

Communication-Line Transmission Mode

A communication channel that is either built by the organization that will use it, or leased from a common carrier, can be either a simplex, half-duplex, or full-duplex facility. Since simplex lines are not generally used in computer communication, we will not discuss them here.

A half-duplex communication facility supports transmission in one direction at a time. Communication lines that operate in this fashion are often referred to as *two-wire circuits*. They have the characteristics of a single twisted-wire pair. Full-duplex communication channels that allow transmission in both directions at once are sometimes referred to as *four-wire circuits*. In fact, they are sometimes implemented by two physical twisted-wire pairs.

A full-duplex circuit, however, is not required to implement a full-duplex data link. It is possible for full-duplex transmission to take place over a half-duplex communication channel if appropriate DCEs are used. On the other hand, without proper supporting equipment, full-duplex transmission may be impossible over a four-wire transmission facility. The transmission mode that is actually used over the transmission facility may be determined by the other two factors that we listed above.

DCE Transmission Mode

For full-duplex transmission to take place over an analog circuit, modems must be employed that are specifically designed to transmit in both directions at once. Full-duplex modems operating over full-duplex channels actually operate as if there were two modems under the covers of each device. On each end of the data link, one set of circuits in the modem transmits while another set of circuits receives. In essence, the data link operates as if it were made up of two independent half-duplex links.

Simultaneous transmission in two directions can be obtained on a channel that is half-duplex in nature by using two separate frequency bands. One is used for transmission in one direction and the other for transmission the other way. By keeping the signals strictly separated in frequency, they can be prevented from interfering with each other. The two bands need not be of the same bandwidth. A much larger channel capacity may be needed for sending data than for sending the return signals that control the flow of data. If, therefore, data is to be sent in one direction only, the majority of the line bandwidth can be used for data. One modem that has been used in the past permitted transmission of data at 3600 bps in one direction and provided a simultaneous return path for control signals at 150 bps.

Neither a four-wire circuit nor full-duplex modems are useful for full-duplex transmission unless the DTEs are also designed to use a full-duplex data link protocol.

DTE Transmission Mode

Over a given data link, the terminal equipment may be designed so that it uses a *data link protocol* that can transmit either in *full-duplex* mode or in *half-duplex* mode. The type of transmission mode supported by the data link protocol determines the transmission mode of the data link. As an example, the binary-synchronous protocol is a half-duplex protocol. No matter what type of DCEs and communication channel is used, the binary-synchronous protocol will support only half-duplex transmission over the data link. However, equipment can be used to create two or more half-duplex data links using the same physical communication channel. But each is considered to be a separate binary-synchronous data link. The bit-oriented protocols discussed in Chapter 23, on the other hand, can support full-duplex transmission over the same data link. To take advantage of the full-duplex capabilities of bit-oriented protocols, appropriate communication channels and DCEs must be used to connect the two DTEs.

PARALLEL VERSUS SERIAL TRANSMISSION

Another way to classify data links is by whether data is transmitted over the link in a parallel or a serial fashion. As we have seen, one of the functions of a DTE is to convert messages into bit streams for transmission over a communication channel. It is not always necessary in all cases to transmit the bits serially, bit by bit. Although most data transmission is done on a serial basis, digital data can be sent over a data link in a parallel fashion. The stream of data is often divided into characters, the characters being composed of bits. This stream may be sent either serial by character and serial by bit, or serial by character and parallel by bit.

Let us suppose that the characters are composed of 8 bits each. The serial-by-character, parallel-by-bit system must then transmit 8 bits at once. This is done on some terminals by using eight separate physical circuits, as shown in Fig. 17.7. In practice, there would usually be additional circuits for control purposes. This is not likely to be done on long-distance, low-speed lines, for it would be more expensive than other means. However, this method is often used for connecting local devices to a computer. For example, one type of data link that transmits data in a parallel fashion uses a protocol called the *Centronics interface* (named for the company that first standardized it). The Centronics interface is very often used to connect printers to personal computers. Box 17.1 shows the circuits that are used to control data transmission when the Centronics interface is used to implement a data link. Because the Centronics interface is so often used in conjunction with personal computers, it is described in detail in Chapter 29.

Parallel-wire transmission does have the advantage that it can lower the cost of the DTEs. No circuitry is needed in the terminals for deciding which bits are which in a character, and synchronization is very easy to control. Parallel-wire transmission is therefore commonly used over short distances where the wires are laid down by the user. Some machines are designed for parallel-by-bit transmission, but separate parallel wires are not used to connect them.

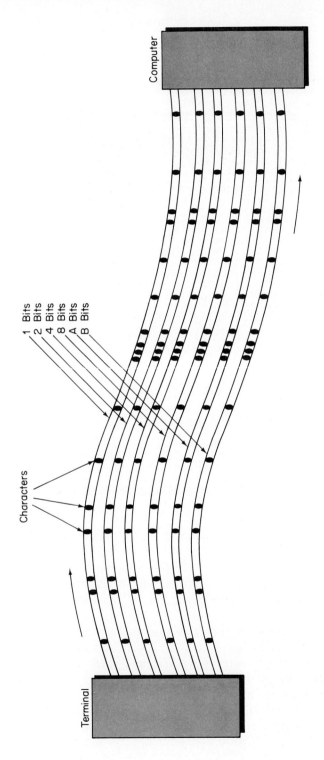

Figure 17.7 Parallel transmission

BOX 17.1   Centronics interface

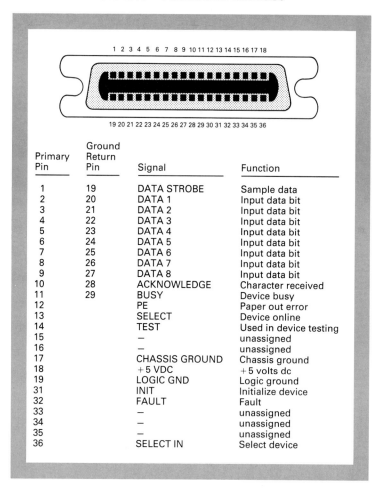

Primary Pin	Ground Return Pin	Signal	Function
1	19	DATA STROBE	Sample data
2	20	DATA 1	Input data bit
3	21	DATA 2	Input data bit
4	22	DATA 3	Input data bit
5	23	DATA 4	Input data bit
6	24	DATA 5	Input data bit
7	25	DATA 6	Input data bit
8	26	DATA 7	Input data bit
9	27	DATA 8	Input data bit
10	28	ACKNOWLEDGE	Character received
11	29	BUSY	Device busy
12		PE	Paper out error
13		SELECT	Device online
14		TEST	Used in device testing
15		–	unassigned
16		–	unassigned
17		CHASSIS GROUND	Chassis ground
18		+5 VDC	+5 volts dc
19		LOGIC GND	Logic ground
31		INIT	Initialize device
32		FAULT	Fault
33		–	unassigned
34		–	unassigned
35		–	unassigned
36		SELECT IN	Select device

Instead, the bits travel simultaneously, using different frequency bands on the same wire. One physical channel is split up into several effective channels, each operating on a different frequency band. This is often referred to as *multitone transmission*.

Some systems using multitone transmission use the tones generated by a pushbutton telephone (see Fig. 17.8). A Touchtone telephone keyboard can transmit eight audible frequencies: 697, 770, 852, 941, 1209, 1336, 1477, and 1633 Hz. The pressing of any one key produces a discordant combination of two of these frequencies, one from the first four and one from the second. Some modems are designed to use these same eight frequencies for data transmission.

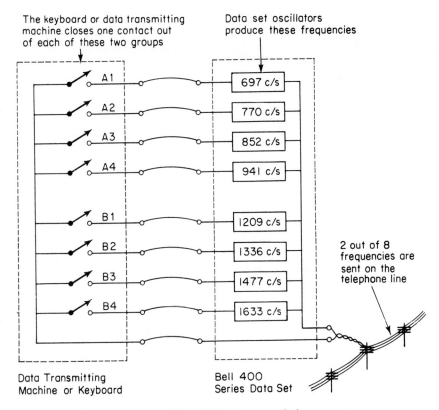

The keyboard or data transmitting machine closes one contact out of each of these two groups

Data set oscillators produce these frequencies

A1 — 697 c/s
A2 — 770 c/s
A3 — 852 c/s
A4 — 941 c/s

B1 — 1209 c/s
B2 — 1336 c/s
B3 — 1477 c/s
B4 — 1633 c/s

2 out of 8 frequencies are sent on the telephone line

Data Transmitting Machine or Keyboard

Bell 400 Series Data Set

Figure 17.8   Multi-tone transmission

SYNCHRONOUS VERSUS ASYNCHRONOUS TRANSMISSION

Data transmission can be either *asynchronous* or *synchronous*. With asynchronous transmission, sometimes called *start-stop* transmission, one character is sent at a time. Relatively simple equipment can be used, because the two stations must be in synchronization only for the time it takes to transmit and receive a single character. With synchronous transmission, characters are sent in a continuous stream. A block of perhaps 100 characters or more can be sent at one time, and for the duration of the entire block the receiving terminal must be exactly in synchronization with the transmitting terminal.

Asynchronous Transmission

Asynchronous transmission is usually used for slow-speed transmission, for example with keyboard devices that do not have a buffer and with which the operator sends characters along the line at more-or-less random intervals. Each transmitted character begins with a *start* bit and ends with one or more *stop* bits. The start bit indicates the beginning of a transmission, and there can be an indeterminate interval between transmitted characters. Characters are transmitted when the operator's fingers press the keys.

The receiving machine has a clocking device that starts when the start bit is detected and operates for as many bits as there are in a character. With this, the receiving machine can distinguish which bit is which. In many cases, two stop bits are used at the end of each character in case the receiver's clock was not operating at quite the same speed as the transmitter's.

Synchronous Transmission

When machines transmit to each other continuously, with regular timing, *synchronous* transmission can give much more efficient data link utilization. Here the bits of one character are followed immediately by those of the next. Between characters, there are no start or stop bits and no pauses. With synchronous transmission, the stream of characters is divided into blocks called *frames*. All the bits in the frame are transmitted at equal time intervals. The transmitting and receiving machines must be exactly in synchronization during the time it takes to transmit a complete frame. To permit synchronous transmission, however, terminals must have buffers, and thus they are more expensive than asynchronous devices.

Devices that use synchronous transmission employ a wide variety of frame lengths. The frame size may vary from a few characters to many hundreds of characters. A period of time is taken up between the transmission of one frame and the next, so the larger the frame length, in general, the faster the overall transmission. On the other hand, the larger the frame, the higher the probability that it contains an error and will have to be retransmitted. A compromise between these two factors must be made.

The synchronization of the transmitting and receiving machines on many systems is controlled by oscillators. Before a frame is sent, the oscillator of the receiving machine must be brought exactly into phase with the oscillator of the transmitting machine. This is done by sending a synchronization pattern at the start of the frame. If this were not done, the receiving device would not be able to tell which bit received was the first bit in a character, which the second, and so on.

Synchronous transmission can give better protection from errors than asynchronous transmission. At the end of each frame, an error-checking sequence is generally transmitted that is constructed by putting the data bits in the frame through an algorithm. The algorithm selected for generating the error-checking sequence is chosen to provide a high degree of error detection. In addition to the error code at the end of the frame, each character may also have a parity bit for error checking. This, however, is often not done, and an end-of-frame check is used alone.

Parity bits provide extremely useful protection against loss of bits in the circuits of a computer because there it is likely that only one bit will be lost at a time. On a communication line, however, several bits are often lost at once because of a noise impulse or dropout, so parity bits are not very useful as a method for detecting transmission errors. Where 2, 4, or 6 bits are changed in a character, a parity check will not detect this. Some form of frame check that can detect the loss of several consecutive bits is therefore desirable. The faster the transmission, the more likely is the loss of 2 or more adjacent bits, and thus the frame check becomes more important. We discuss error detection and correction in detail in Chapter 20.

DATA LINK PROTOCOLS

The DTE at one end of a physical link must follow a specific set of rules in converting a message into a serial bit stream and transmitting it over the channel. The DTE at the other end must follow a similar set of rules in correctly reconverting the bit stream into a copy of the original message. If the DTEs do not follow the same rules, communication is not possible. As we introduced earlier, the rules that the control mechanisms running in DTEs must follow are called *data link protocols*.

Each specific data link protocol that is in use today performs a different set of functions and performs them in different ways. However, there is a standard set of basic functions that any data link protocol must perform to be considered a true data link protocol:

- **Synchronization.** The protocol must be capable of establishing and maintaining synchronization between the sender and the receiver. This means that the receiver must be capable of determining where each bit and each character begins and ends.

- **Framing.** The protocol must be capable of marking the beginning and the end of each transmission frame.

- **Control.** The protocol must perform some minimum set of control functions. For example, on a multipoint link, the sending station must be capable of identifying the receiving station to which it is transmitting data.

- **Error Detection.** The protocol must be able to perform some degree of error detection in order to implement error recovery.

The functions above are those that all data link protocols must perform. However, some data link protocols implement additional functions, including the following:

- **Addressing.** In some systems, the manipulation of network addresses is performed by the data link protocol.

- **Retransmission of Frames.** In some protocols, when errors are detected, the protocol specifies rules for retransmitting frames.

- **Pacing.** Some data link protocols have provision for controlling the rate at which data is transmitted to accommodate the situation where the sender is capable of sending data faster than the receiver is capable of receiving it.

- **Status Inquiry.** Some protocols implement control functions that allow one station to inquire about the status of other stations.

TYPES OF DATA LINK PROTOCOLS

Data link protocols fall into two major categories. The following are brief descriptions of these categories:

- **Character-Oriented Protocols.** A character-oriented protocol uses a particular code set for transmission, with some of the characters in the code set reserved for control functions. With character-oriented protocols, special provision must be made for transmitted messages that contain, in their text, characters ordinarily reserved for control functions.

- **Bit-Oriented Protocols.** A bit-oriented protocol is independent of any particular code set, and no character codes are reserved for control functions. Messages consist simply of bit streams, and no special significance is attached to any of the bit configurations in the message.

The asynchronous protocol and the binary-synchronous protocol are examples of character-oriented protocols. The most modern protocols that are used in implementing computer networks are bit-oriented protocols. As we will see in Chapter 23, most bit-oriented protocols share a common set of characteristics and are more flexible and efficient than character-oriented protocols.

ASYNCHRONOUS PROTOCOLS

Asynchronous protocols represent a class of data link protocols that use similar techniques for coordinating transmission. As we have seen, asynchronous, or start-stop, transmission is commonly used for slow-speed applications. There are many protocols that use asynchronous transmission. They all use similar techniques but differ in the character code that is used, the number of stop bits, whether or not parity bits are sent, the specific interpretation of control characters, and a number of other factors. Asynchronous protocols are examined in detail in Chapter 21.

With one commonly used asynchronous protocol, illustrated in Fig. 17.9, the data link is in either of two conditions, with the two conditions representing the binary values zero and one. When no data is being transmitted, the data link is in the one condition. Data is sent over the data link one 7-bit character at a time. When the sending machine has a character to send, its DTE starts by

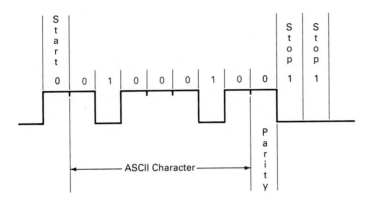

Figure 17.9   Asynchronous transmission character

transmitting a zero bit (the *start* bit). Then comes the 7 bits that make up the character, followed by a parity bit. Finally come two one bits (the *stop* bits) to signal the end of the character. If there is an interval between characters, the line remains in the "one" condition.

The DTE in the receiving machine has a clocking mechanism that starts when the line's condition changes to zero and counts the number of bits that follow. The scheme works because the receiving machine knows that each separate transmission will consist of exactly 11 bits. After the 11 bits arrive, the DTE in the receiving machine waits for the next zero bit, which signals the beginning of the next character.

Start-stop transmission has many advantages. It is simple, uses uncomplicated equipment, and is well suited for transmission between a slow terminal and a computer. Since characters can be sent as they are typed, no buffer is required, and the operator can enter characters at any rate (up to some maximum speed determined by the speed of the channel itself). On the other hand, there are many disadvantages to asynchronous transmission. Each transmitted character carries up to 4 overhead bits with it, and some systems that use asynchronous transmission echo back each character after it is sent. When the operator presses a key, a character is sent down the line. At the other end, the character is echoed back and displayed on the screen. This means that a line turnaround may be required with the transmission of each separate character. A communication line using asynchronous transmission can use channel capacity very inefficiently. Of course, for many applications this does not matter.

THE BINARY-SYNCHRONOUS PROTOCOL

The binary-synchronous protocol is used on much of IBM's older high-speed communication equipment and is discussed in detail in Chapter 22. The binary-synchronous protocol requires that the DTEs have more logic capability and some buffer storage. Characters are assembled in the sending DTE into transmission units called *frames*. Figure 17.10 shows one possible frame format that can be used with binary-synchronous transmission.

As long as the line is active, but no data is being transmitted over the data link, the sending DTE transmits a synchronization pattern to the receiving DTE. This keeps the clocks in the two DTEs in step with one another. The sending DTE starts each transmitted frame with control characters that indicate to the receiving DTE that data follows. The end of the frame is indicated by another set of control characters that are followed by two error-checking bytes. Then the synchronization pattern starts again.

If a received frame is found to be in error, the receiving DTE sends back a negative acknowledgment. This causes the sending DTE to retransmit the frame. Since entire frames are transmitted at a time, binary-synchronous transmission is better suited than asynchronous protocols for high-speed transmission.

BIT-ORIENTED PROTOCOLS

An example of a bit-oriented protocol is *high-level data link control* (HDLC), the data link protocol that is recommended by the International Standards Organization (ISO). *Synchronous data link control* (SDLC) is another bit-oriented protocol that is used by IBM with equipment that conforms to the SNA architecture. The characteristics of bit-oriented protocols are examined in detail in Chapter 23. With a bit-oriented protocol, as with the binary-synchronous protocol, an entire frame is transmitted at a time, as shown in Fig. 17.11. A frame starts with a flag that has the bit configuration 01111110. The flag is followed by control information, the text of the frame, and error-checking bits. The frame's end is signaled by another flag.

Three bits in the control portion of each frame are used for frame sequencing. The 3 sequence bits allow the sending DTE to transmit up to seven frames before the receiving DTE needs to send an acknowledgment. Thus a single acknowledgment can signal the correct receipt of up to seven frames. Variations of many bit-oriented protocols use 7 bits for sequencing. A 7-bit sequence number allows up to 127 frames to be sent before an acknowledgment is required. Because multiple frames can be sent between acknowledgments, bit-oriented protocols can achieve higher data link efficiency than the binary synchronous or asynchronous protocols.

Figure 17.10 Binary-synchronous transmission frame

Figure 17.11   Bit-oriented protocol transmission frame

DATA LINK EFFICIENCY

It is not difficult to see that asynchronous transmission would be extremely inefficient for high-speed transmission between intelligent machines. Only a single character at a time is transmitted. Binary-synchronous is better, but to achieve high efficiency, very long frames must be used. With bit-oriented protocols, high efficiency can be achieved even with short frames because multiple frames can be sent with a single acknowledgment. This is especially important for data links that have high propagation delays, such as those that use satellite circuits.

Now that we have examined the general characteristics of data links and introduced data link protocols, in Chapter 18 we discuss the character codes that are used in transmitted data over a data link.

18 DATA CODES

It is desirable to have internationally agreed-upon alphabets for the transmission of data so that computers and terminals from different manufacturers can inter-communicate. During the 1960s an alarming proliferation of data transmission codes developed. Some of these codes have now dropped into disuse, and the following three codes predominate:

- **International Alphabet No. 2.** This is a 5-bit code that has been standardized by the CCITT. It is based on the Murray code used decades ago for telegraphy. The International Alphabet No. 2 is now used primarily for telex transmission around the world. In the United States, the International Alphabet No. 2 is known (incorrectly) as the Baudot code.

- **International Alphabet No. 5.** This is a 7-bit code that has been standardized by both the CCITT and by ISO. U.S. ASCII *(American Standard Code for Information Interchange)* is a variation of this code.

- **The EBCDIC Code.** This is an 8-bit code that was introduced by IBM in the 1960s with the System/360 computing system. The EBCDIC code is used less often for data transmission than the two above, but it is nonetheless an important character code due to the widespread use of IBM equipment.

BITS PER CHARACTER

The three character codes above each use a different number of bits for representing a character of data. If we transmit n bits, such as the ON and OFF pulses of telegraphy, we can, in theory, code 2^n different combinations in these pulses. The "characters" that are sent by data transmission often contain 5, 6, 7, or 8 bits. Five bits can give 32 different characters, 6 bits, 64; 7 bits, 128; and 8 bits, 256. Some of these combinations are typically reserved for special-purpose *control characters,* which have such functions as indicating the end of a record, requesting a printer carriage return, and a variety of other operations. Therefore, an n-bit code is often capable of representing substantially less than 2^n different data characters.

INTERNATIONAL
ALPHABET NO. 2

Figure 18.1 shows a code chart for the *International Alphabet No. 2*. Notice that two conditions in five positions are used to represent 32 different characters. The conditions are indicated in the chart as *A* and *Z;* however, they could be interpreted as meaning *zero* and *one,* and could be represented by voltage changes on a communication line. Alternatively, the *A* condition could be a *magnetic spot* on a diskette or magnetic tape and the *Z* condition *no spot.* There are several binary conditions that the CCITT recommends should be regarded as equivalent, and these are shown at the bottom of the diagram.

North American practice in telecommunications frequently differs slightly from the rest of the world, often for the reason that the North American carriers led the world and then had too much invested to change when the world finally formulated standards. There are some minor differences between the telegraph codes used in North America and elsewhere. Figure 18.2 shows the American variants of International Alphabet No. 2.

ESCAPE
CHARACTERS AND
FUNCTION
SEQUENCES

International Alphabet No. 2 provides for only 32 bit combinations; however, letters-shift and figures-shift characters are used to extend the range of characters. When a *figures-shift* character is sent, the characters that follow it are interpreted as uppercase characters until a *letters-shift* character is sent. Similarly, the characters following a letters-shift are interpreted as letters until a figures-shift is sent. The letters-shift and figures-shift characters must be recognized no matter which option is in effect.

The use of the letters-shift and figures-shift characters is an example of an *escape* mechanism in a code. The letters-shift and figures-shift characters are referred to as escape characters. By using escape characters, the total number of possible characters in a code can be greatly increased. Sometimes the escape character changes the meaning of all the other characters following it until an additional escape character is received, as in the example above. In other codes, the escape character changes the meaning of only the one character that follows it.

Character

Letters shift	Figures shift	Number of symbol	5-unit international code No. 2 (used by telex machines)
A	—	1	Z Z A A A
B	?	2	Z A A Z Z
C	:	3	A Z Z Z A
D	Who are you?	4	Z A A Z A
E	3	5	Z A A A A
F	*	6	Z A Z Z A
G	*	7	A Z A Z Z
H	*	8	A A Z A Z
I	8	9	A Z Z A A
J	Bell	10	Z Z A Z A
K	(	11	Z Z Z Z A
L	)	12	A Z A A Z
M	.	13	A A Z Z Z
N	,	14	A A Z Z A
O	9	15	A A A Z Z
P	0	16	A Z Z A Z
Q	1	17	Z Z Z A Z
R	4	18	A Z A Z A
S	'	19	Z A Z A A
T	5	20	A A A A Z
U	7	21	Z Z Z A A
V	=	22	A Z Z Z Z
W	2	23	Z Z A A Z
X	/	24	Z A Z Z Z
Y	6	25	Z A Z A Z
Z	+	26	Z A A A Z
< Carriage return		27	A A A Z A
≡ Line feed		28	A Z A A A
↓ Letters		29	Z Z Z Z Z
↑ Figures		30	Z Z A Z Z
■ Space		31	A A Z A A
(Not used)		32	A A A A A
Signal repetition			—
Signal α			(Permanent A polarity)
Signal β			(Permanent Z polarity)

*: Not used internationally; reserved for national allocation.

EQUIVALENT MEANINGS OF THE ABOVE A AND Z CONDITIONS

	A Condition	Z Condition
Bits:	0	1
Start-stop code:	Space (start condition)	Mark (stop condition)
Holes (perforations) in paper tape:	No hole	Hole
Single-current signaling:	No voltage	+ ve voltage
Double-current signaling:	− ve voltage	+ ve voltage
Amplitude modulation	Tone-off	Tone-on
Frequency modulation	High frequency	Low frequency
Phase modulation with reference phase	Opposite phase to reference phase	Reference phase
Differential phase modulation	Inversion of the phase	No inversion

Figure 18.1 CCITT International Alphabet No. 2

Code signals:

Start	1	2	3	4	5	Stop	Letters shift	Figures shift
	●	●				●	A	—
	●			●	●	●	B	?
		●	●	●		●	C	:
	●			●		●	D	Who are you?
	●					●	E	3
	●		●	●		●	F	Note 1
		●		●	●	●	G	Note 1
			●		●	●	H	Note 1
		●	●			●	I	8
	●	●		●		●	J	Bell
	●	●	●	●		●	K	(
		●			●	●	L	)
			●	●	●	●	M	.
			●	●		●	N	,
				●	●	●	O	9
		●	●		●	●	P	0
	●	●	●		●	●	Q	1
		●		●		●	R	4
	●		●			●	S	'
					●	●	T	5
	●	●	●			●	U	7
		●	●	●	●	●	V	=
	●	●			●	●	W	2
	●		●	●	●	●	X	/
	●		●		●	●	Y	6
	●				●	●	Z	+
						●	Blank	
	●	●	●	●	●	●	Letters shift	↓
	●	●		●	●	●	Figures shift	↑
			●			●	Space	■
				●		●	Carriage return	<
		●				●	Line feed	≡

● Denotes positive current or the Z condition

Figure 18.2 U.S. version of International Alphabet No. 2

The most commonly used form of data transmission today uses 7 bits per character. International Alphabet No. 5 is a widely accepted 7-bit code that permits minor national variations. This code is shown in Fig. 18.3. Following are notes that explain the characters indicated with a circled number.

1. The FE_2 through FE_5 codes are *format effectors* that are intended for equipment in which horizontal and vertical movements are effected separately. If equipment requires the action of carriage return to be combined with a vertical movement, the format effector for that vertical movement may be used to effect the combined movement. For example, if new line (symbol NL, equivalent to CR + LF) is required, FE_2 will be used to represent it. This substitution requires agreement between the sender and the receiver of the data. The use of these combined functions may be restricted for international transmission on general switched telecommunications networks (telegraph and telephone networks).

2. The symbol £ is assigned to position 2/3 and the symbol $ is assigned to position 2/4. In a situation where there is no requirement for the symbol £, the symbol # (number sign) may be used in position 2/3. Where there is no requirement for the symbol $, the symbol ¤ (currency sign) may be used in position 2/4. The chosen allocations of symbols to these positions for international information interchange must be agreed upon between the communicating parties. It should be noted that unless otherwise agreed between sender and recipient, the symbols £, $, or ¤ do not designate the currency of a specific country.

3. These are the national use positions. The allocations of characters to these positions lies within the responsibility of national standardization bodies. These positions are primarily intended for alphabet extensions. If they are not required for that purpose, they can be used for symbols.

4. Positions 5/14, 6/0, and 7/14 are provided for the symbols upward arrowhead, grave accent, and overline. However, these positions can be used for other graphical characters when it is necessary to have eight, nine, or ten positions for national use.

5. Position 7/14 is used for the graphic character ‾ (overline), the graphical representation of which may vary according to national use to represent ~ (tilde) or another diacritical sign, provided that there is no risk of confusion with another graphical character included in the table.

6. The graphic characters in positions 2/2, 2/7, 2/12, and 5/14 have, respectively, the significance of quotation mark, apostrophe, comma, and upward arrowhead; however, these characters take on the significance of the diacritical signs diaresis, acute accent, cedilla, and circumflex accent when they are preceded or followed by the backspace character (0/8).

INTERNATIONAL ALPHABET NO. 5 VARIATIONS   As the chart indicates, 10 characters can be varied to produce *versions* or *dialects* of the code. The codes shown in Fig. 18.3 show a variation used for international transmission. Figure 18.4 shows the United States national version of International Alphabet No. 5, which is known as the U.S. ASCII code. ASCII is the most widely used code for data transmission and telegraphy in North America. Box 18.1 lists the meanings of the various control codes in the ASCII code.

THE EBCDIC CODE   A great many of those who work with IBM equipment are familiar with the EBCDIC code (short for *Extended Binary Coded Decimal Interchange Code*). The EBCDIC code is an 8-bit code that is used internally in much of IBM's computing equipment. In many cases, a computing system may use the EBCDIC code internally, but will have equipment that automatically translates between EBCDIC and ASCII for data transmission. Some systems, on the other hand, use the EBCDIC code directly for data transmission. A code chart for the EBCDIC code is shown in Fig. 18.5. Notice that the EBCDIC code provides for more control functions than International Alphabet No. 5. These control codes are listed in Box 18.2. IBM was never successful in its attempt to make EBCDIC a universally accepted character code (other than as an internal code used with IBM equipment). In some ways this is unfortunate, since many data transmission systems would benefit from an 8-bit code.

Bit positions 5, 6, 7:

Bit positions 1, 2, 3, 4:		000	100	010	110	001	101	011	111
		0	1	2	3	4	5	6	7
0000	0	NUL	TC_7 (DLE)	SP	0	@ ③	P	` ④	p
1000	1	TC_1 (SOH)	DC_1	!	1	A	Q	a	q
0100	2	TC_2 (STX)	DC_2	" ⑥	2	B	R	b	r
1100	3	TC_3 (ETX)	DC_3	# ②	3	C	S	c	s
0010	4	TC_4 (EOT)	DC_4	¤ ②	4	D	T	d	t
1010	5	TC_5 (ENQ)	TC_8 (NAK)	%	5	E	U	e	u
0110	6	TC_6 (ACK)	TC_9 (SYN)	&	6	F	V	f	v
1110	7	BEL	TC_{10} (ETB)	' ⑥	7	G	W	g	w
0001	8	FE_0 (BS)	CAN	(	8	H	X	h	x
1001	9	FE_1 (HT)	EM	)	9	I	Y	i	y
0101	10	FE_2 ① (LF)	SUB	*	:	J	Z	j	z
1101	11	FE_3 ① (VT)	ESC	+	;	K	[③	k	{ ③
0011	12	FE_4 ① (FF)	IS_4 (FS)	, ⑥	<	L	\ ③	l	| ③
1011	13	FE_5 ① (CR)	IS_3 (GS)	–	=	M	] ③	m	} ③
0111	14	SO	IS_2 (RS)	.	>	N	^ ④ ⑥	n	‾ ④ ⑤
1111	15	SI	IS_1 (US)	/	?	O	_	o	DEL

Figure 18.3 CCITT International Alphabet No. 5

Bit positions 1, 2, 3, 4:		000 / 0	100 / 1	010 / 2	110 / 3	001 / 4	101 / 5	011 / 6	111 / 7
0000	0	NUL	DLE	SP	0	@	P	`	p
1000	1	SOH	DC1	!	1	A	Q	a	q
0100	2	STX	DC2	''	2	B	R	b	r
1100	3	ETX	DC3	#	3	C	S	c	s
0010	4	EOT	DC4	$	4	D	T	d	t
1010	5	ENQ	NAK	%	5	E	U	e	u
0110	6	ACK	SYN	&	6	F	V	f	v
1110	7	BEL	ETB	'	7	G	W	g	w
0001	8	BS	CAN	(	8	H	X	h	x
1001	9	HT	EM	)	9	I	Y	i	y
0101	10	LF	SUB	*	:	J	Z	j	z
1101	11	VT	ESC	+	;	K	[	k	{
0011	12	FF	FS	,	<	L	\	l	¦
1011	13	CR	GS	−	=	M	]	m	}
0111	14	SO	RS	.	>	N	^	n	~
1111	15	SI	US	/	?	O	_	o	DEL

Figure 18.4 The U.S. ASCII code

BOX 18.1   ASCII control codes

NUL (Null): no character. Used for filling in time or filling spaces when there is no data

SOH (Start of Header): used to indicate the start of a message heading that may contain address or routing information

STX (Start of Text): used to indicate the start of the text of a message and to indicate the end of the header

ETX (End of Text): used to terminate the text that was started with STX

EOT (End of Transmission): indicates the end of a transmission

ACK (Acknowledge): a character transmitted by a receiving device as an affirmative response to a sender

BEL (Bell): used to sound an alarm or actuate other attention device

BS (Backspace): moves the print mechanism or display cursor one position backward

HT (Horizontal Tab): moves the printing mechanism or display cursor to the next preassigned TAB position

LN (Line Feed): moves the printing mechanism or display cursor to the next line

VT (Vertical Tab): moves the printing mechanism or display cursor to the next series of preassigned lines

FF (Form Feed): moves the printing mechanism or display cursor to the beginning of the next page or screen

CR (Carriage Return): moves the printing mechanism or display cursor to the beginning of the same line

SO (Shift Out): indicates that the code combinations that follow should be interpreted as outside the standard character set until a SI (Shift In) code is received

SI (Shift In): indicates that the code combinations that follow should be interpreted according to the standard

DLE (Data Link Escape): changes the meaning of one or more characters that follow

DC1, DC2, DC3, and DC4 (Device Controls): characters used to control ancillary devices or special terminal features

NAK (Negative Acknowledgment): character transmitted by a receiving device as a negative response to the sender

SYN (Synchronous/Idle): used to achieve synchronization

ETB (End of Transmitted Block): indicates the end of a block of data for communication purposes

CAN (Cancel): indicates that the data that precede it should be ignored or discarded

EM (End of Medium): indicates the physical end of the storage medium

SUB (Substitute): substituted for a character found to be erroneous or invalid

ESC (Escape): character intended to change the meaning of one or more characters that follow

FS (File separator): most inclusive information separator

GS (Group separator): next most inclusive information separator

RS (Record separator): next most inclusive information separator

US (Unit separator): least inclusive information separator

SP (Space): nonprinting character used to separate words or to move the printing mechanism or display cursor forward one character

DEL (Delete): used to obliterate unwanted characters

Figure 18.5 The EBCDIC code

		00				01				10				11			
		00	01	10	11	00	01	10	11	00	01	10	11	00	01	10	11
		0	1	2	3	4	5	6	7	8	9	A	B	C	D	E	F
0000	0	NUL	DLE	DS		SP	&	−						{	}	\	0
0001	1	SOH	DC1	SOS		RSP		/		a	i	~		A	J	NSP	1
0010	2	STX	DC2	FS	SYN					b	k	s		B	K	S	2
0011	3	ETX	DC3	WUS	IR					c	l	t		C	L	T	3
0100	4	SEL	RES/ENP	BYP/INP	PP					d	m	u		D	M	U	4
0101	5	HT	NL	LF	TRN					e	n	v		E	N	V	5
0110	6	RNL	BS	ETB	NBS					f	o	w		F	O	W	6
0111	7	DEL	POC	ESC	EOT					g	p	x		G	P	X	7
1000	8	GE	CAN	SA	SBS					h	q	y		H	Q	Y	8
1001	9	SPS	EM	SFE	IT				\	i	r	z		I	R	Z	9
1010	A	RPT	UBS	SM/SW	RFF	¢	!	|	:					SHY			
1011	B	VT	CU1	CSP	CU3	.	$	,	#								
1100	C	FF	IFS	MFA	DC4	<	•	%	@								
1101	D	CR	IGS	ENQ	NAK	(	)	_	'								
1110	E	SO	IRS	ACK		+	;	>	=								
1111	F	SI	IUS/ITB	BEL	SUB	|	¬	?	"								EO

Bit Positions 4, 5, 6, 7

Second Hexadecimal Digit

Bit Positions 0,1
Bit Positions 2, 3
First Hexadecimal Digit

BOX 18.2   EBCDIC code chart

ACK	Acknowledge	IUS/ITB	Interchange Unit Sep./ Intermediate Text Block
BEL	Bell		
BS	Backspace	LF	Line Feed
BYP/INP	Bypass/Inhibit Presentation	MFA	Modify Field Attribute
		NAK	Negative Acknowledge
CAN	Cancel	NBS	Numeric Backspace
CR	Carriage Return	NL	New Line
CSP	Control Sequence Prefix	NUL	Null
CU1	Customer Use 1	POC	Program-Operator Comm.
CU3	Customer Use 3		
DC1	Device Control 1	PP	Presentation Position
DC2	Device Control 2	RES/NEP	Restore/Enable Presentation
DC3	Device Control 3		
DC4	Device Control 4	RFF	Required Form Feed
DEL	Delete	RNL	Required New Line
DLE	Data Link Escape	RPT	Repeat
DS	Digit Select	SA	Set Attribute
EM	End of Medium	SBS	Subscript
ENQ	Enquiry	SEL	Select
EO	Eight Ones	SFE	Start Field Extended
EOT	End of Transmission	SI	Shift In
ESC	Escape	SM/SW	Set Mode/Switch
ETB	End of Transmission Blk	SO	Shift Out
ETX	End of Text	SOH	Start of Heading
FF	Form Feed	SOS	Start of Significance
FS	Field Separator	SPS	Superscript
GE	Graphic Escape	STX	Start of Text
HT	Horizontal Tab	SUB	Substitute
IFS	Interchange File Sep.	SYN	Synchronous Idle
IGS	Interchange Group Sep.	TRN	Transparent
IR	Index Return	UBS	Unit Backspace
IRS	Interchange Record Sep.	VT	Vertical Tab
IT	Indent Tab	WUS	Word Underscore

19 CONTENTION AND POLLING

As we have seen, when multiple DTEs are connected to the same data link, no two of them may transmit at once. We can think of a half-duplex data link, no matter what its physical nature, as though it were a pair of copper wires that connect the computer to the different terminals on it. We may think of a full-duplex data link as though it were two pairs of wires, one for input and one for output. If we send an output pulse down the line, it will reach all the terminals. If one terminal sends an input pulse, this will travel down the line, not only reaching the computer, but also reaching all the other terminals. It is clear, then, that if two terminals transmitted at once, the pulses from them would be mixed up. We need a line discipline that prevents this.

Equally important, each terminal must have a means of recognizing which signals are meant for *it;* otherwise, it will react to the messages that are sent to and from the other terminals on the data link. If a message is sent from the computer to a terminal, the message might contain the address of the terminal for which the message is destined. The terminal whose address this is recognizes it and takes appropriate action. All the other terminals on the data link ignore it. On some systems it is not the message itself that contains this address, but rather a preliminary request that is sent down the line to say, in effect: "Terminal number *X,* I have a message for you. Are you ready to receive it?" The terminal replies "yes" or "no" by sending back a response. If it replies "yes," the computer sends the data, and all terminals but that one ignore it.

The preliminary request causes the data link to become, in effect, a point-to-point connection for a limited period of time. All of the other terminals ignore what is transmitted until a further signal is sent that ends the private interconnection. The request that releases the interconnection is called an *end-of-transmission* or *end-of-message* signal. Once this request is sent, all terminals on the data link reset and listen for the next request to be sent.

A system for permitting the computer to send a message to one terminal on a multipoint data link is referred to as *selective calling*. In addition to having the ability to address one terminal, some systems also have *group* codes that allow selected sets of terminals to receive messages and a *broadcast* code that can cause a message to be accepted by all terminals.

To recognize its address and carry out the various line control functions needed, the terminal must contain some logic capability. With some terminals this logic is built into the terminal; with others, it resides in a terminal control unit. These logic circuits make the terminal somewhat more expensive than otherwise. A terminal without them cannot be used on a multipoint data link.

OVERLOADING

When a realtime response is needed and a multipoint data link is used, we have to be careful in the design not to overload the data link. Suppose that the six terminals in Fig. 19.1. are part of a realtime system. All six operators may be carrying on a dialog with the computer at the same time. All of them want a fast response. We must take into consideration the extent to which the response to one operator will be delayed by the transmissions to and from the others.

BUFFERED TERMINALS

Suppose that the terminals in question operate on a low-speed half-duplex data link at 15 characters per second, that the average number of total characters, including control characters, in a message to the computer is 30, and that the number in its response is 60. Suppose that the operator sends one such message on the average every 100 seconds. The remainder of the time is "think" time or time when the transaction is being discussed with a client. The total transmission time per message is $(30 + 60)/15 = 6$ seconds.

If six terminals each transmit for a total of 6 seconds every 100 seconds, the line is clearly not overloaded. This assumes, however, that the terminal can transmit to the computer at its full speed. If transmission involves a continuous action, such as sending the contents of a buffer, this is true. If, however, it is

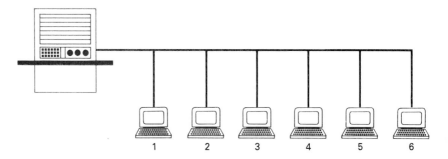

Figure 19.1   Multipoint data link

asynchronous transmission from a keyboard on an unbuffered terminal, the characters are sent as the operator presses the keys, and this input could tie up the line for a lengthy period.

If the terminal is unbuffered, we have to take into consideration the typing speed of the operator. This can vary over a surprisingly wide range. A figure often used by systems analysts for the speed of a touch typist operating a terminal is 3 characters per second. The transmission of 30 input characters then ties up the data link for about 10 seconds rather than the 2 seconds if the characters are transmitted from a buffer. It is often, however, much worse than this. The terminal operator may be a one-finger typist who is lucky to average 1 character per second. Worse still, the operator may stop and "think" in the middle of a transmission, reading documentation or composing what is to be typed next. If the terminal is unbuffered, all other users will be excluded from the data link during the pauses—probably without the operator knowing it.

CONTROLLING TRANSMISSION

Schemes have been devised for locking the keyboard during a terminal operator's pauses. If no character is received for more than a given time, say 5 seconds, the computer may suspend transmission from that device to see whether there is anything to transmit for any other terminal. The keyboard might be locked until the computer returns its attention to that terminal. This scheme does not, however, take into account the ingenuity of the terminal operator.

In one such system, the news went around the operators that during a period of pause they should idly move the SHIFT key up and down, and this would prevent their keyboard's locking. Thus a steady stream of shift-change characters were sent to the computer. This did not, in effect, alter the message content, but the computer never had 5 seconds without receiving a character and so did not lock out the operator. The other terminal users on that data link, however, had a long wait.

Suppose that an operator types at 3 characters per second with no pauses. The total transmission time for the input and output will be $30/3 + 60/15 =$ 14 seconds. If this timing applies to each of the six terminals, there will be a total of 84 seconds line occupancy every 100 seconds. The data link will be tied up 84 percent of the time. (It will actually be occupied for a higher percentage than this because of control characters that the terminal transmits in addition to the data entered by the operator.) Queuing theory indicates that it is inadvisable to load a communication line more than about 70 percent; otherwise, high queues build up and the response time is degraded.

If all our operators typed at 1 character per second, the total transmission time for one terminal would be $30/1 + 60/15 = 34$ seconds. With six such terminals the data link would clearly be overloaded.

In this case it would be unwise to recommend that the data link have six terminals, even if the operators were touch typists, unless buffered terminals were used. With a buffer it does not matter how slowly an operator types or whether there are lengthy pauses. The terminal buffer can be filled slowly; its contents are always transmitted at the full line speed.

RESPONSE TIME   Without buffering we might, perhaps, be able to support three of these terminals on one multipoint data link. The lack of buffering will, however, mean that a terminal will sometimes give a poor response time. A 1-character-per-second operator will tie up the line for 30 seconds, and more if the think time is substantial. Another operator may be held up for this time before being able to start, or if it is a half-duplex data link, the reply may be held up by this amount. If the data link is shared with *two* 1-character-per-second colleagues there is a small probability that the delay will be twice this long.

Occasionally, on the other hand, the response will be received very fast because the operator's colleagues are not transmitting at that moment. The system will therefore appear to be somewhat erratic in its performance—sometimes keeping the operator waiting half a minute, but sometimes reacting very quickly. The situation would be worse if instead of our 30-character input, we had a much longer one.

Some multipoint terminals are designed so that many can be put on one line. Clearly, we cannot take advantage of this without careful examination of response times. Buffered terminals should always be used on such data links when the response time is critical.

CONTENTION   Most techniques for controlling transmission on a
TECHNIQUES   multipoint data link involve designating one of the
                        stations on the multipoint link as the *primary* station
and the others as *secondary* stations. One method that can be used for controlling a multipoint data link is called *contention*. When the contention technique is used for controlling transmission, any station on the data link is free to make a request to transmit. If the data link is available, transmission proceeds. If the data link is in use, the station must wait. When contention is used, queues of "contention requests" are normally built up. This queue is then scanned by the primary station. The queue can be scanned in a prearranged sequence or in the sequence in which the requests were made.

ROLL-CALL   Far more common than contention are various *polling*
POLLING   techniques. The simplest form of polling is called
                        roll-call polling. With roll-call polling, the primary
station asks the secondary stations, one by one, whether they have anything to transmit. The primary station sends a polling message down the line to one of

the secondary stations, asking "Terminal X, have you anything to transmit? If so, go ahead." If terminal X has nothing to send, it may send a negative reply and the next polling message will be sent: "Terminal Y, have you anything to transmit? If so, go ahead."

Normally, the primary station consists of a computer, or its communications controller, that organizes the polling; the secondary stations may consist of terminals. The primary station may have in its storage a polling list indicating the sequence in which the secondary stations should be polled (see Fig. 19.2). The polling list and its use determine the priorities with which the secondary stations are scanned. Certain important stations may have their address more than once on the polling list so that they are polled more frequently than the others. Once a polling message has established an interconnection between a secondary station and the primary station, the transmission can proceed much as point-to-point transmission does.

**CONTROL
FUNCTIONS**
To control transmission on a multipoint data link, various characters or sequences of characters sometimes have special meanings during transmission. In some systems, certain characters are reserved as control characters. A variety of these are seen in the ASCII and other codes (see Chapter 18). Special characters or character sequences may also be used for terminal addressing. An address

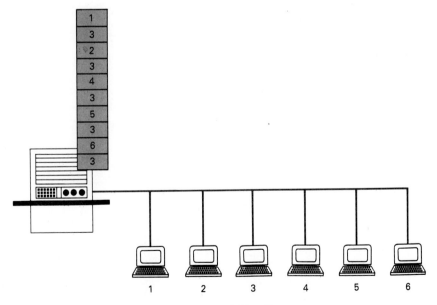

Figure 19.2 Polling list

must be specified when the primary station is sending a message to an individual secondary station.

As shown in Chapter 18, transmission codes with 7 or 8 information bits per character, such as ASCII and EBCDIC, usually use some of the character codes to help in controlling transmission. ASCII uses the EOT character to mean "End of Transmission" and the STX character to mean "End of Address" or "Start of Text." Similarly, systems that use a code, such as ASCII, sometimes use a single character to specify the address of a secondary station. In other cases, a secondary station may consist of several interconnected devices, and an extra character may be needed after the terminal address to indicate which device on that station is being addressed.

HUB POLLING

An alternative polling technique to roll-call polling is called *hub go-ahead* or simply *hub* polling. Hub polling is often used in conjunction with expensive long-distance lines and on lines with fast turnaround time and many terminals. Figure 19.3 shows an example of hub polling. With this technique, the primary station addresses only the secondary station at the far end of the data link, and the secondary stations pass the polling message down the line from one secondary station to the next. The computer polls the farthest terminal, terminal A, and says: "Have you anything to send?" If A does not, A passes the polling signal to its neighbor B. If B has nothing, it sends it to C. C sends it to D, and so on, until it arrives back at the computer.

During normal operation, hub polling at its simplest requires only two types of message: the *polling* message and the *data* message. If no data is being sent, the polling message travels from station to station on the data link. When a station has data to send, it sends the data to the primary station before passing the polling signal on to the next secondary station.

The main disadvantage of hub polling is that more logic capability is needed in the secondary stations. They must have the ability to send the polling

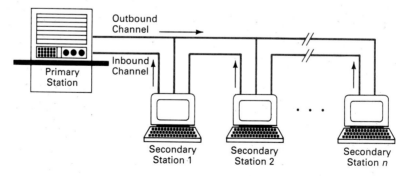

Figure 19.3   Hub go-ahead configuration

messages on to the next station. A second disadvantage is that, on an analog line, an extra modem, or at least that half of a modem that receives data, is needed at each terminal. Each terminal must be able to receive data from either the output line or the input line. A disadvantage that is usually of less importance is that hub polling does not easily allow one or more of the secondary stations to be given preferential treatment when they have a greater load or need a faster response.

The main advantage of hub polling lies in lessening the number of line turnarounds that are required in order to perform an entire scan of the secondary stations. When fast transmission is used, it may take as long to turn the line around as it does to transmit hundreds of characters.

The number of control messages flowing on the data link when hub polling is used is less than would be the case where roll-call polling is used. The data link can therefore handle a higher throughput. This is especially significant if the messages are short, as on many realtime systems, and the response-time requirement is high.

LOOP OPERATION

In addition to the contention and polling techniques that we have discussed, a loop configuration can be used instead of a conventional multipoint configuration. Figure 19.4 shows an example of a data link configured as a loop. When loop operation is used, each

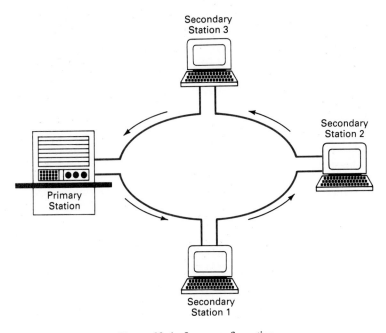

Figure 19.4   Loop configuration

secondary station on the loop acts as a repeater and relays every frame it receives to the next station on the loop.

One form of loop operation is supported by some bit-oriented protocols. With a loop, each secondary station on the loop examines the address of every frame and captures those frames that are addressed to it. When a station originates a frame, it briefly suspends its repeater function and transmits its frame. A secondary station is permitted to do this only after it receives a special "go-ahead" bit pattern. The primary station, usually a computer or communications controller, begins a cycle by transmitting a go-ahead pattern around the loop. If no terminal wants to transmit, the go-ahead pattern eventually arrives back at the primary station. It then transmits another go-ahead pattern.

When a station that wants to transmit receives the go-ahead pattern, it changes the go-ahead pattern to a starting flag pattern that it uses as the beginning of frame it transmits. It then follows the frame, or frames, that it transmits by sending another go-ahead pattern. When that go-ahead pattern reaches the primary station, the cycle starts again. In this way the go-ahead patterns keep the terminals from interfering with one another's transmissions.

20 ERROR DETECTION AND CORRECTION

Transmission errors invariably occur when data is transmitted over telecommunications channels. Noise on the lines can destroy bits, switch a one bit to a zero, and vice versa. In addition to the continuing background of thermal noise, there are sharp noise *impulses,* occasionally of high magnitude. They are caused by ill-protected switching equipment, crosstalk, pickup from electrical cables, atmospheric static, and a variety of other factors. If you listen down a telephone line when nobody is talking, you can occasionally hear crackles, hums, clicks, and whistles. I once heard violin music. These stray noises are usually of low intensity but occasionally are loud enough to damage the data being sent.

NUMBERS OF ERRORS

On a good-quality telephone line with conservatively designed modems, a typical error rate is 1 bit incorrect in 100,000. If the modems are designed to maximize the data rate, the receiving machine has to recognize smaller changes in signal condition and so is more prone to misinterpret noise conditions and cause errors. Some typical error rates that are experienced with data transmission over the public telephone network are cited in Table 20.1. The figures for data rates above 2400 bps on a voice line are subject to fairly wide variation because the modulation techniques used become far more sensitive to noise and distortion than at the lower speeds.

When communication lines are constructed especially for data, much lower error rates than these are achieved. One error in 10 million bits or 100 million bits is more common for digital circuits, such as AT&T's Dataphone Digital Service. Unfortunately, many of our systems today must be linked together using data links that were not designed with the transmission of computer data in mind. The high error rate is part of the price we pay for the compromise of using lines intended for something else. There are, however, steps that we can take to make the communication channel *appear to the user* as error free as we

Table 20.1 Typical telephone circuit
error rates

Transmission Rate (bps)	Bit Error Rate
300	1 in 700,000
1200	1 in 200,000
2400	1 in 100,000
4800	1 in 10,000 to 100,000*
9600	1 in 1,000 to 10,000*

*Before error-correcting codes are applied
by the modem.

like. All data link protocols use one or more of these methods to transform the
error-prone communication channel into an essentially error-free virtual channel
between users.

THE EFFECT OF ERRORS

On many data transmission systems, the control of errors is of vital importance. On some, it is not of great significance. Some systems transmit vital information, such as accounting data, financial figures, military orders, encoded medical data, or programs. These must be letter perfect (or bit perfect). Other systems transmit the information that an operator is keying in at a terminal. The operator is likely to make far more errors in entering the data than the communication line makes in transmitting it, especially an unskilled one-finger operator. In this case, there is no point in worrying too much about the line—we must protect our system from the operator. Accuracy controls can be devised for human input. On many systems a tight network of controls is necessary to stop abuse or embezzlement. It is also important to ensure that nothing is lost or double-entered when hardware failures occur on the system or when switchover takes place.

CUMULATIVE FILE ERRORS

In designing any computer system, it is important to know what error rate is expected. Calculations should then be done to estimate the effect of this error rate on the system as a whole. On some systems, the effect of infrequently occurring errors is cumulative, and it is in situations such as these that special care is needed in eliminating errors. For example, if messages cause the updating of a database, and an error in the message causes an error to be recorded in a record, it is possible on some systems that as the months pass the database will accumulate a greater and greater number of inaccuracies.

Suppose, for example, that transactions coming in over telecommunications lines that have 1 bit in 100,000 in error are used to update a database containing 10,000 records. Suppose that on the average, an item is updated 100 times a month, and that if any one of twenty 5-bit characters is in error in the transmission, the item will be updated incorrectly. After six months no fewer than 4500 file records will be incorrect. If an error-correction procedure on the telecommunications lines reduces the rate of undetected errors to 1 bit in 10 million, then 60 of the file records are likely to be incorrect at the end of six months. With 1 bit in 100 million, six records are likely to be wrong. Probability calculations of this type need to be done on various aspects of the system when it is being designed.

A number of approaches can be used to deal with noise on transmission lines. All the approaches that we will discuss in this text are found on data transmission systems in use today.

IGNORING ERRORS

The first and easiest approach is to ignore the errors. Surprisingly, this is often done. The majority of telegraph links in operation now, for example, have no error-checking facilities at all. Part of the reason is that they normally transmit English-language text that will be read by human beings. Errors in ordinary text caused by the changing of a bit or of a small group of bits are usually obvious to the human eye, and we correct them in the mind as we read the material. Telegrams that have figures as well as text in them commonly repeat the figures or spell them out. This inexpensive approach is also taken on computer systems where the transmission handles verbal text. For example, on administrative message switching systems, it is usually acceptable to have transmission to and from unchecked simple terminals. If the text turns out to be unintelligible, the user can always ask for a retransmission.

An error rate of 1 bit in 100,000 is possibly not quite as bad as it sounds. Suppose that we consider transmitting the text of this book, for example, and coded it using 7-bit ASCII. If 1 bit in 100,000 were in error in the text of this book, there would be about 120 letters that were wrong. The book would certainly still be readable, and the majority of its readers would not notice most of these errors. The human eye has a habit of passing unperturbed over minor errors in text. This text was first set in galley proofs by the compositor. The proofs were checked by a proofreader. It was then divided into pages and page proofs were produced. By now most of the errors should have been removed from the text, but, in fact, those remaining correspond to an error rate of 1 bit in about 50,000, an error level higher than that which would be found on unchecked telegraph transmission.

In any case, on most systems *some* of the errors are ignored. An error-detection procedure that catches all of them is too expensive. Many systems in current use might raise the level of undetected errors from 1 bit in 100,000 to 1 bit in 10 or 100 million. It is possible to devise a coding scheme that gives very much better protection than this. In fact, there are coding schemes that give an undetected error rate as low as 1 bit in 10^{14}.

For example, the error-correcting coding scheme used to store data on the CD/ROM optical disks that are based on compact audio disk technology gives an undetected error rate that is less than 1 incorrect bit in 10^{13}. This corresponds to one single-bit error in about 2000 CD/ROM disks, each of which stores up to 600 megabytes of data. This low error rate is achieved using a physical medium that is more error prone than some telecommunications lines (microscopic pits on an imperfect plastic surface).

An error-detection rate of 1 bit in 10^{13} or 10^{14} is much better than is needed for most practical purposes in data transmission systems. For example, if we transmitted using an error rate of one error in 10^{14} bits over a voice line at 2400 bps, for a normal working week (no vacations), since the time of Christ, we would probably not have had an error yet! By using sufficiently powerful error-detecting codes, virtually any measure of protection from transmission errors can be achieved.

DETECTING ERRORS

To *detect* communication errors, we must build some degree of redundancy into the messages transmitted. In other words, more bits must be sent than need be sent for the coding of the data alone. Redundancy can be built into individual characters or into an entire transmitted block.

VERTICAL REDUNDANCY CHECKING

Some data transmission systems use vertical redundancy checking (VRC) in which each transmitted character is accompanied by a parity bit. If odd parity is used, the transmitter sets the parity bit to either 0 or 1 in order to make the total number of one bits between the start and stop bits an odd number. If even parity is used, the transmitter sets the parity bit so

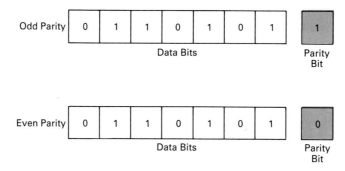

Figure 20.1   Vertical redundancy checking

that the total number of one bits between the start and stop bits is even. (Examples of odd and even parity are shown in Fig. 20.1.) Then if the receiver detects a parity error in a received character, it knows that a transmission error has occurred.

The problem with parity checking is that if more than 1 bit is changed, it is possible that the parity bit will still be set correctly, even though the data is incorrect. A parity check is not very useful for detecting transmission errors, especially at high transmission speeds, because it is likely that when an error occurs, many adjacent bits will be changed.

LONGITUDINAL REDUNDANCY CHECKING

When a longitudinal redundancy checking (LRC) method is employed, redundant bits are used to check the accuracy of an entire transmitted frame (see Fig. 20.2). In this form of error detection, the transmitter passes the entire message through an arithmetic algorithm to generate a number that is sent with the message. Then, when the receiver receives the message, it passes the message through the same algorithm and compares its generated value with the value received with the message. If the two values match, the receiver assumes that the message is correct. If the two values do not match, an error is assumed. Typically, when an LRC error occurs, the receiver asks the transmitter to retransmit the message.

Some transmission schemes use both the VRC and LRC methods—for example, a parity bit on each character in addition to a check on the entire frame. It can be shown, however, that much more efficient error detection results from using all the redundant bits for frame checking only.

CORRECTING ERRORS

Once the errors have been detected, the question arises: What should the system do about them? It is generally desirable that it should take some automatic action to correct the fault. Some data transmission systems, however, do not do so and leave the fault to be corrected by human means at a later time. For

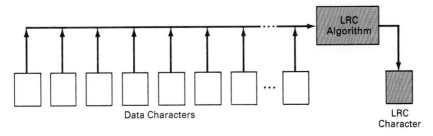

Figure 20.2   Longitudinal redundancy checking

example, some early systems that transmitted data to be punched into cards caused a card to be sent to a different stacker when an error was detected. The cards in the error stacker were later picked out by the operator, who then arranged for retransmission.

In some realtime terminal systems, automatic retransmission has not been used because it is easy for the terminal operator to reenter a message or request retransmission. In general, it is much better to have some means of automatic retransmission rather than a manual procedure, and it is usually less expensive than employing an operator for this purpose. Most modern data transmission systems do cause messages in error to be retransmitted. This is an automatic function of all modern data link protocols, such as binary synchronous and the bit-oriented protocols.

However, on some systems, it is possible to ignore incorrect data, but it is important to know that a given message *is* incorrect. On such systems error detection takes place with no attempt to correct the errors. This could be the case with statistical data where erroneous samples can be discarded without distortion. It is used on systems for reading remote instruments where the readings are changing slowly and an occasional missed reading does not matter.

The advantage of a detection-only scheme is that it requires a channel in only one direction. In systems with telephone and telegraph lines, this is not a worthwhile advantage because such channels are almost always half or full duplex. However, it is a great advantage with certain tracking and telemetry systems that use simplex transmission because of the great expense of the channels. With these we find detection-only schemes.

FORWARD-ERROR CORRECTION   Automatic error correction can take a number of forms. First, sufficient redundancy can be built into the transmission code so that the code itself permits *automatic error correction* as well as detection. As no return path is needed, this is sometimes referred to *forward-error correction*. To do this effectively in the presence of *bursts* of noise can require a large proportion of redundant bits. Codes that give safe forward-error correction are therefore inefficient in their use of communication-line capacity. It is interesting to note that the coding scheme used with CD/ROM disks does handle automatic error correction. The physical medium is very error prone, and once the data is stored, there is no opportunity for repeating it. So the system is designed with the assumption that a great many errors will occur that must automatically be corrected if the storage system is to have the required degree of reliability.

If a communication line permitted the transfer of information in one direction only, then forward-error correction techniques, such as those used with CD/ROMs, would be extremely valuable. However, a typical transmission channel is typically not as error prone as a CD/ROM disk and supports half-duplex or full-duplex transmission. In general, error-*correcting* codes alone on voice-grade lines do not give us as good value for money, or value for bandwidth, as error-*detecting* codes coupled with the ability to automatically retransmit data that is found to contain an error. Most modern data link protocols use error correction techniques with automatic retransmission of those transmission frames found to be in error.

Forward-error correction becomes advantageous when the number of errors is so high that the retransmission of data necessary would substantially degrade the throughput. On higher-speed links, the argument for forward-error correction becomes stronger because the time taken for reversing the direction of transmission might be equivalent to many hundreds of bits of transmission. This time is relatively high on wideband links and on half-duplex, voice-grade links with high-speed modems.

In some special cases, for example with some high-speed modems, forward-error correction is handled in the modems themselves. But this is generally backed up by the normal error-handling methods used by the data link protocol. When this is done, the transmission errors that are corrected by the modems are transparent to the data link protocol. Those errors that get by the modems are handled by the error-detection and automatic-transmission procedures of the data link protocol. This results in less data having to be retransmitted.

LOOP CHECK

One special-purpose method of detecting errors does not use an error-detecting code at all. Instead, all the bits received are retransmitted back to their sender, and the sending machine compares them against the original to see that they are still intact. If not, the item in error is retransmitted. This scheme, sometimes referred to as a *loop check* or *echo check,* is normally used on a full-duplex data link or on a continuous loop line. Again, it uses the channel capacity less efficiently than would be possible with an error-detection code, although in many systems the return path of a full-duplex line is underutilized anyway, for the system does not produce enough data to keep the channel loaded with data in both directions. Loop check techniques are most commonly found on short lines and in-plant systems where the wastage of channel capacity is less costly. One important advantage of this technique is that it gives a degree of protection that is more certain than most other methods.

RETRANSMISSION OF DATA IN ERROR

Many different forms of error *detection* and *retransmission* are built into data-handling equipment. In early paper-tape transmission systems, a "vertical" parity check—that is, a parity check on each character—was used along with a "horizontal" checking character at the end of a block of characters. At the end of each block, the receiving station would send a signal to the transmitting station saying whether the block has been received correctly or whether an error has been detected. If any error was found, both the transmitting tape reader and the receiving tape punch would go into reverse and run backward to the beginning of that block. The punch would then erase the incorrect data by punching a hole into every position—the *delete character* code. The block would then be retransmitted. If transmission of the same block was attempted several times (four times on much equipment) and was still incorrect, the equipment would notify its operator by means of a warning light and bell or buzzer. Other automatic facilities were usually used to detect broken or jammed paper tape and to warn when the punch was running short of tape. Where data is being transmitted to a computer, automatic retransmission is sometimes handled under control of a program and sometimes by circuitry external to the main computer.

HOW MUCH IS RETRANSMITTED?

Systems differ in how much they require to be retransmitted when an error is detected. Some retransmit only one character when a character error is found. Others retransmit many characters or even many messages. There are two possible advantages in retransmitting a *small* quantity of data. First, it saves time. It is quicker to retransmit 5 characters than 500 when an error is found. However, if the error rate is one character error in 100,000 (a typical figure for telephone lines) the percentage loss in speed does not differ greatly between these two cases. It *would* be significant if a block of 5000 had to be retransmitted.

Second, when a large block is retransmitted, it has to be stored somewhere until the receiving machine has confirmed that the transmission was correct. This is often no problem. In transmitting from paper tape, for example, the tape reader merely reverses to the beginning of that block. The paper tape is its own message storage. The same is true with transmission from magnetic tape or disk.

With transmission from a keyboard, however, an auxiliary storage unit, or *buffer,* is needed if there is a chance that the message may have to be retransmitted automatically. On some input devices, a small semiconductor storage unit constitutes the buffer. On others, the keys themselves are the storage. They remain locked down until successful transmission is acknowledged. Again several input devices may share a common control unit, and this contains the buffer storage.

The *disadvantages* of using small blocks for retransmission are first that the error-detection codes can be more efficient on a large block of data. In other words, the ratio of the number of error-detection bits to the number of the data bits is smaller for a given degree of protection if the quantity of data is large. Second, where blocks of data are sent synchronously, a period of time is taken up between acknowledgments in control characters and line-turnaround procedures. The more data transmitted between acknowledgments, the less significant is this wasted time. The well-designed transmission system achieves the best compromise between these factors.

Retransmission of One Character

Here, characters are individually error checked, as with a parity check or other type of code. As soon as a character error is detected, retransmission of that character is requested. This is likely to be used only on a very slow data link, for example, one using asynchronous transmission.

Retransmission of One Word

Some types of computing equipment manipulate *words* that consist of small blocks of characters. The block might use a parity bit for each character and also for each word. A transmitting terminal might have a buffer that holds two such words. Should the receiver detect an error in row or column parity, retransmission of that word can be requested.

Retransmission of a Frame

A word of the type described above is both short and fixed in length. Many machines retransmit complete *frames* at one time that are much longer than a typical word and that more often than not are variable in length. They may have a format in which an end-of-transmission character terminates the text, which is followed by error-checking characters. This is the retransmission unit used by the binary-synchronous and bit-oriented protocols.

Frames are normally retransmitted from a variable-length area in the storage of a computer or from a buffer in a control unit attached to the transmitting station, and there may be a maximum size for the frame that can be retransmitted. If a complete message exceeds that size, it may be broken into separate frames that are linked together.

Retransmission of a Block of Messages

When the transmission speed is high, it becomes economical on many systems to transmit the data synchronously in large blocks. In this case, frames may contain not one message or record, but several. On most systems, when an error occurs in any of the records, the whole frame is retransmitted. By using machines with good logic capabilities it is possible to resend only the faulty record and not all the other records in the frame. This is beyond the capability of most protocols that are used today.

Retransmission of a Group of Frames

This is the system used with bit-oriented protocols. As you learned earlier, with bit-oriented protocols, groups of frames may be sent with a single acknowledgment. With most bit-oriented protocols, up to eight frames may be sent between acknowledgments; some protocol variations allow up to 128 frames to be sent. If all the frames are found to be error free, a single positive acknowledgment is sent. When a frame is found to be in error, all frames sent since the previous acknowledgment are retransmitted automatically.

Retransmission of a Batch of Separate Records

Sometimes a control is placed on a whole batch of records. As with the controls conventionally used in batch data processing, the computer adds up account numbers and/or certain fields from each record to produce *hash totals*. These totals are accumulated at the sending and the receiving end and are then compared. This form of error detection can also be used in systems where one computer sends a program to another computer. It is vital that there should be no undetected error in the program, so the words or groups of characters might be added up into an otherwise meaningless hash total. This hash total can be transmitted with the program, and only if the receiving computer obtains the same total in *its* addition is the program accepted.

Some form of batch control of this type is often used, where applicable, *as well* as other automatic transmission controls as an overriding safety precaution. Its use is entirely in the hands of the systems analyst and can be made as comprehensive and secure as necessary.

Retransmission at a Later Time

The batch totals we just discussed are ordinarily checked immediately; the transmission is complete, and the sender is notified whether they were correct or not. Some forms of validity check might not be capable of being used until the items are processed. They may, for example, necessitate comparing transactions with a master tape. They are, nevertheless, valuable error controls, and an originating computer might keep the data in its files until a receiving computer has confirmed this validation.

TRANSMISSION ERROR CONTROL   To govern the automatic retransmission of data in which an error has been detected, a number of special characters *(control characters)* are sometimes used. For example, with the binary-synchronous protocol, characters representing a positive acknowledgment are sent by the receiver to signal the transmitter that a frame has been received correctly. Similarly, codes representing a negative acknowledgment are sent by the receiving terminal to tell the transmitter that a frame received had an error in it. When the transmitter sends a frame on most systems, it waits before it sends the next one until the acknowledgment control characters are received from the transmitter. If a positive acknowledgment is received, the transmitter proceeds normally; if the acknowledgment is negative, it resends the frame in error.

The transmitter itself commonly does some error checking on what it sends. It is possible that the circuits doing this may detect an error in a frame on which transmission has already begun. The transmitter must then cancel the frame, so it sends a Cancel code. The transmitting and receiving machines may have circuits designed to detect these special characters.

In more sophisticated protocols, entire frames flow back and forth between the communicating stations to monitor error control procedures. In some cases, normal data frames can carry control bits that allow them to be used as positive acknowledgments. In this way, when a positive acknowledgment is required, a normal data frame can be used for this purpose, thus reducing the amount of overhead transmission that is required when no errors have occurred.

ODD-EVEN RECORD COUNT

It is possible that the control characters or control frames themselves or the end-of-transmission characters could be invalidated by a noise error. If this happens, there is a danger that a complete transmission frame might be lost or two frames joined together inadvertently. It is possible that during the automatic retransmission process a frame could erroneously be sent twice. To prevent these errors, an odd-even count is sometimes kept of the records transmitted.

With some protocols, a control character is sent that indicates whether this is an odd-numbered or an even-numbered block. On some systems two alternative *start-of-transmission* characters are used. With other schemes, it is the ACK characters that contain this odd-even check. With the binary-synchronous protocol, two different positive acknowledgment signals are sent: ACK0 and ACK1. In the ASCII code there is only one ACK character, so when ASCII is used, a two-character sequence is employed for positive acknowledgments. If an odd-numbered acknowledgement does not follow an even-numbered acknowledgement, the previous block is retransmitted.

FRAME SEQUENCE NUMBERS

It is very improbable indeed that two blocks could be lost together or that two blocks are transmitted twice in such a manner that an odd-even count would not detect the error. However, to avoid this possibility, most modern protocols use a *sequence number* to check that this has not happened, instead of an odd-even count. As we have already mentioned, either 3-bit or 7-bit sequence numbers are used with bit-oriented protocols. These bits are part of the control information sent with each transmission frame. In addition to providing better protection against lost or duplicated frames, these sequence numbers also allow more data to be sent before an acknowledgment is required.

MINIMUM NUMBER OF BITS FOR ERROR RECOVERY

It is interesting to note that error control need not have elaborate transmission of control characters back and forth. Some transmission schemes seem unnecessarily burdened by their use of control messages. On very simple systems, error control *could* be achieved with two control bits only, one for saying whether a message had been received correctly or not, and one as an alternation bit giving an odd-even count.

On multipoint lines it is difficult to recover from *addressing* errors with certainty by means of answerback schemes with control characters. The simplest method is a scheme with positive acknowledgments *only*. The receiver simply ignores incorrect messages. The transmitter sends a message with an odd–even block count and waits for acknowledgment of its correct receipt. If no acknowledgment is received after a specified time, it resends the message, with the same odd-even count. One of two things might have gone wrong. First, the message might have been received with an error. In this case, it is resent, as would be required. Second, the positive acknowledgment might have been destroyed. In this case, when the receiver receives a second copy, the positive acknowledgment will be sent again. Provided that all errors are detected by error-detecting codes, this simple scheme will be infallible on relatively slow-speed point-to-point or multipoint lines that do not require the sophistication of today's modern data link protocols.

Now that we have discussed the general characteristics of data link protocols and the error-detection techniques they employ, in Chapters 21 through 23 we provide detailed descriptions of commonly used protocols, including asynchronous protocols, the binary-synchronous protocol, and bit-oriented protocols.

21 ASYNCHRONOUS PROTOCOLS

As we introduced in Chapter 17, *asynchronous* (also known as *start-stop*) transmission is used with systems in which characters are sent one at a time with no fixed time relationship between one character and the next. In the following list we describe many of the characteristics of data link protocols that use asynchronous transmission:

- Protocols that use asynchronous transmission are half-duplex in nature.
- Asynchronous transmission techniques are simple and permit very inexpensive terminals to be designed.
- The use of start and stop bits results in a relatively high percentage of overhead bits being transmitted.
- Asynchronous protocols have little standardization; each asynchronous protocol has its own conventions for control functions.
- Asynchronous communication techniques are oriented to computer-to-terminal communication where transmission speeds are relatively low, typically less than 20,000 bps.

In a typical application of an asynchronous data link protocol a terminal is connected to a computer (see Fig. 21.1). When the terminal operator is keying a message on the terminal's keyboard, each keystroke results in a character being sent to the computer. The receiving station must reestablish synchronization for every character by being able to recognize the first bit of each character. This is accomplished by having the transmitting station precede each character with a *start* bit. A typical character format used with asynchronous transmission is shown in Fig. 21.2.

The receiving station detects start bits by monitoring the line, which can be in either the 1 state or the 0 state. When the line is idle (the time between characters when no data is being transmitted), it is conventional to leave the

Figure 21.1　Terminal and computer

line in the 1 condition. This is sometimes called the *mark* or *marking* condition. The opposite line status, the 0 condition, is sometimes known as the *space* or *spacing* condition. In the idle state, the transmitter sends a continuous series of 1's.

When the transmitting station wishes to send a character, it changes the line status from mark to space, in effect sending a *start* bit. The start bit tells the receiving station that data bits follow. One possible implementation of asynchronous transmission is shown in electrical terms in Fig. 21.3. The receiving station is resynchronized at the beginning of each character when it detects the start bit. The receiving station then samples the line each bit time for a zero or one data bit. In this example, the bit rate is 2400 bps, making each bit time 0.0004166 second. A character can be made up of any number of data bits; however, each character must be made up of the same number of bits, the number being agreed upon between the sender and the receiver. Typical implementations of asynchronous transmission use 5, 7, or 8 data bits per character. After sending the requisite number of data bits, the transmitting station sends one or more *stop* bits to allow the receiving station to prepare for the next character to be received.

**ASYNCHRONOUS
TRANSMISSION
CONVENTIONS**

There is very little standardization in the specific details concerning asynchronous transmission. For the most part, all aspects of asynchronous line control are determined by the design of specific terminal equipment. For example, the communication circuitry in the terminal and the computer must both be in agreement on the following when using an asynchronous protocol:

- The line status that indicates an idle condition
- The line status that indicates a zero bit and the line status that indicates a one bit

Start Bit	Data Bit	Data Bit	Data Bit	Data Bit	Data Bit	Data Bit	Data Bit	Data Bit	Stop Bit

Figure 21.2　Typical character format

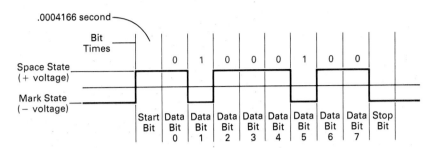

Figure 21.3   Asynchronous transmission

- The amount of time that elapses in transmitting a single bit
- How many bits make up a single character
- Whether 1 or 2 stop bits are used to indicate the end of a transmitted character

Note that none of the above information is standardized for asynchronous protocols; all that is required is that both the sender and the receiver use the *same* conventions.

RS-232-C TRANSMISSION

As we have seen, asynchronous line control is nothing more than a general method that is used to control transmission. There are actually a collection of protocols that all employ asynchronous techniques for delimiting the beginning and end of each transmitted character and for controlling each character's transmission and receipt. Box 21.1 lists the conventions that might be followed by a particular asynchronous protocol that employs an RS-232-C link at the physical layer.

If the conventions listed in Box 21.1 are used, Fig. 21.3 illustrates how a single character is transmitted over the physical RS-232-C connection. The sender begins with the line set at a negative voltage (mark condition), indicating that it is in an idling condition. To send a character, the sender changes the line to a positive voltage (space condition) for one bit time to send the start bit. Immediately following the start bit, the sender transmits the 8 bits that make up a character. To transmit a zero bit, the sender sets the line to a positive voltage (spacing condition); to transmit a one bit, the sender sets the line to a negative voltage (marking condition). The sender has a clock that allows it to change the line condition at the appropriate times.

As indicated above, if the sender is transmitting at 2400 bps, each bit time is approximately 0.0004166 second. The receiver knows where each bit begins and ends because it also has a clock that tells it when to sample the line condition to interpret each bit. When the line is in the marking condition for a bit

BOX 21.1   Typical asynchronous protocol conventions

- A negative current on the line between transmitted characters indicates an idle condition.
- During data transmission, a negative voltage indicates a one bit, and a positive voltage indicates a zero bit.
- Data is sent at 2400 bps, indicating that a single bit is transmitted in approximately 0.0004166 second.
- The ASCII code is used, with each transmitted character consisting of 7 data bits followed by a parity bit.
- One stop bit is transmitted at the end of each transmitted character.

time, the receiver interprets this as a one bit; when the line is in the spacing condition for a bit time, the receiver interprets this as a zero bit. The sender's and receiver's clocks need only stay in synchronization for the duration of a single character because the start bit allows the receiver to be resynchronized with the sender at the beginning of each character.

Finally, after all the bits that make up a character have been transmitted, the transmitter places the line back into a marking condition for at least 1 bit time. The bit that follows the bits of data is called a stop bit because it marks the end of a transmitted character. After transmitting the stop bit, the sender places the line back into the marking condition until the next character is ready to be sent.

CHARACTER CODES

Asynchronous techniques can be used to transmit the characters of any desired character code. All that is required is that both the sender and the receiver use the same code. Figure 21.4 shows how asynchronous transmission is used with a number of different character codes. Typically, in modern applications, ASCII or EBCDIC data is sent using 1 start bit and 1 stop bit; however, when very slow transmission speeds are used with simple equipment, 2 stop bits are sometimes used to ensure that the receiver receives at least 1 stop bit, even if the receiver has slipped slightly out of synchronization with the sender.

DATA LINK MESSAGE EXCHANGES

In a typical asynchronous protocol, certain characters from the character set that is used by the communicating devices are reserved for data link control func-

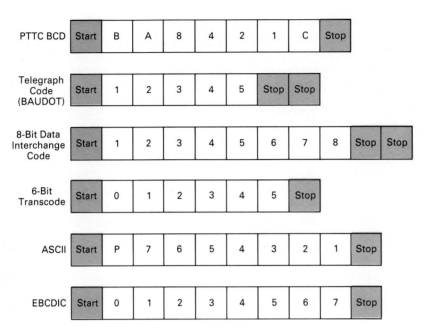

Figure 21.4   Asynchronous encoding for various codes

tions. A sending station places itself into transmit control mode when these characters are to be transmitted. Similarly, a station must be in receive control mode in order to receive one of these characters. Figure 21.5 shows a typical set of control codes that might be used to control data transmission for simple terminal devices. The particular characters that are used to implement each of these functions are not important for this discussion; they must simply be agreed upon by convention between the communicating stations. Since these codes perform control function, they must not appear in the text of any message that is sent.

Mnemonic	Function
SOA	Start of Addressing
EOA	End of Addressing
EOB	End of Block
EOT	End of Transmission
ACK	Positive Acknowledgment
NAK	Negative Acknowledgment

Figure 21.5   Line control codes

Recall from Chapter 17 that a station attached to a data link is always in one of the following four status conditions during the time that it is operational.

- Transmit Control
- Transmit Text
- Receive Control
- Receive Text

In the remainder of this chapter, we will see how these status conditions change by looking at some examples of typical message flows that take place over data links that use asynchronous transmission. Keep in mind as you examine these message flows that they are meant as examples only; each asynchronous data link protocol uses its own conventions for control functions.

POINT-TO-POINT MESSAGE EXCHANGE

As we saw in Chapter 17, the simplest type of data link consists of a point-to-point connection between two stations. In the example shown in Fig. 21.6, a primary station (a computer) is communicating with a single secondary station (a terminal) over a point-to-point data link. With this type of connection, the requirement for control functions is minimal. Box 21.2 shows a typical message exchange that might occur over the point-to-point data link in Fig. 21.6.

MULTIPOINT DATA LINK MESSAGE EXCHANGE

Figure 21.7 shows a more complex data link in which a primary station (a host computer with a locally attached communications controller) is connected to multiple secondary stations (terminals) using a single multipoint data link. The multipoint link has two secondary stations attached to it, each of which contains multiple devices. Each device attached to the data link has an address that is made up of two parts: a station identifier (A or B) and a device number (1, 3, or 5). Box 21.3 illustrates a typical message

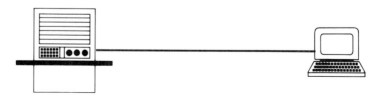

Figure 21.6   Point-to-point data link

BOX 21.2　Point-to-point message exchange

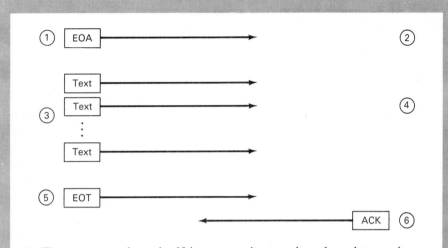

1. The computer places itself into transmit control mode and transmits an End of Addressing (EOA) command to the terminal.

2. The terminal receives the EOA command and places itself into receive text mode.

3. The host computer transmits the characters that make up a message, one character at a time.

4. The terminal receives each character of the message and performs a parity check as it receives each character.

5. The computer goes into transmit control mode and transmits an End of Transmission (EOT) command, indicating the end of the message.

6. The terminal receives the EOT command, performs LRC error checking on the received message, and finds the message to have been received correctly. The terminal then transmits an ACK command back to the host, places itself into receive control mode, and waits for the next control character from the computer.

exchange that might take place on the multipoint data link in Fig. 21.7 when the communications controller in the primary station asks one of the devices on a secondary station if it has any data to send.

Notice in Box 21.3 that when the addressed device receives the two-character address, the fact is *implied* that these address characters constitute a poll request. This is because in our simple example, the addressed device happens to be a machine that can only transmit data from the remote station back to the host; for example, it might be a keyboard. Later in this chapter, we show ex-

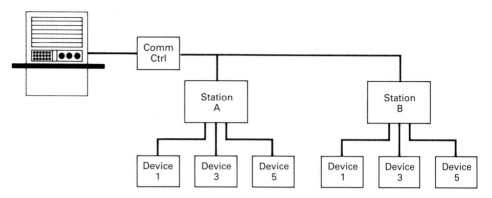

Figure 21.7   Multipoint data link

amples of *selection* sequences in which data is sent in the opposite direction. For example, the addressed device might be a printer. If the host addresses a printer, the device knows that this is a selection and not a poll because the printer only *receives* data and does not send it.

The protocol illustrated in Boxes 21.2 and 21.3 is very simple and may be

BOX 21.3   Multipoint link message exchange

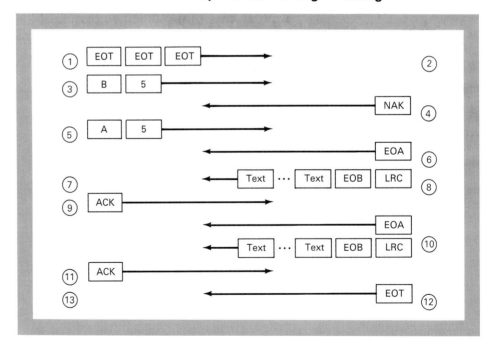

BOX 21.3 *(Continued)*

1. The communications controller attached to the host computer sends a sequence of three EOT commands.

2. All devices on the data link receive the EOT commands and place themselves into receive control mode.

3. The host communications controller transmits a B followed by a 5. These two address characters constitute a *poll* sequence that asks if device 5 on station B has any data to send.

4. All devices other than device 5 on station B ignore the poll. Device 5 on station B accepts the poll and transmits a Negative Acknowledgment (NAK) command back to the communications controller.

5. The communications controller receives the NAK command, which tells it that device 5 on station B has no data to send. The host communications controller then consults its polling list and transmits an A followed by a 5 to poll the next device on its list (in this case, device 5 on station A).

6. Device 5 on station A has data to send, so it transmits an EOA command.

7. The communications controller receives the EOA command and places itself into receive text mode.

8. Device 5 on station A transmits its message text and then sends an End of Block (EOB) command and an LRC character for error checking. Device 5 places itself back into receive control mode.

9. The communications controller receives the message. The EOB command marks the end of the message and indicates that the next character contains the LRC value. The communications controller computes an LRC value using the received text and compares the received LRC value against the value that it computes. In this example, it determines that the message was received correctly. It then transmits a Positive Acknowledgment (ACK) command.

10. Device 5 now transmits a second message back to the communications controller using the same sequence of events as above.

11. The communications controller attached to the host again receives the message correctly and responds with an ACK.

12. Device 5 transmits an EOT, indicating that it has no more data to send.

13. All devices on the data link receive the EOT command and place themselves into receive control mode. The host communications controller is now ready to issue the next poll sequence.

BOX 21.4   Multipoint poll—transmission error

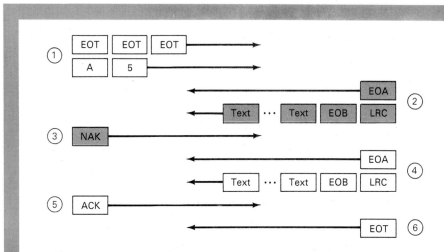

1. The host communications controller sends a sequence of three EOT commands following by the A5 address characters.

2. Device 5 on station A has data to send, so it sends an EOA command, the message text, an EOB command, and an LRC character. A transmission error occurs during the sending of the message text.

3. The communications controller receives the message, performs the LRC computation, and finds that its computed LRC value does not match the value in the LRC character that it received. The communications controller transmits a NAK command, which constitutes a negative acknowledgment to the message.

4. Device 5 retransmits the original message, including another EOB and an LRC value.

5. The communications controller receives the message and performs the LRC verification procedure. This time the message is received correctly and the communications controller transmits an ACK.

6. Device 5 transmits an EOT, indicating that it has no more data to send.

well suited to a particular application. However, as a general protocol, it has many shortcomings. First, a great many things must be agreed upon by convention and must be hard-wired into each device. For example, all devices must know that addresses are two characters in length; the protocol does not use any explicit method of delimiting the addresses that are transmitted. Also, each device must either send or receive data; they cannot do both. For general-purpose applications this is too simplistic. Even keyboards can both send and receive data; for example, the keyboards used on many personal computers receive data from the system unit to set their status lights on or off.

The next three examples show additional message exchanges that can occur on multipoint lines where polling is implied by the device type that is addressed. After that are four message exchanges in which selection is implied.

MULTIPOINT POLL— TRANSMISSION ERROR

The message exchanges discussed thus far all assume that message text is transmitted and received correctly. In actual practice, transmission errors will occur that cause messages to be received incorrectly. With the protocol discussed above, an LRC character is transmitted that the receiver uses in detecting transmission errors. Box 21.4 shows the message exchange that takes place when a transmission error occurs and the receiving station detects a mismatch between the LRC value it receives and the value it generates.

BOX 21.5　Multipoint poll—no response

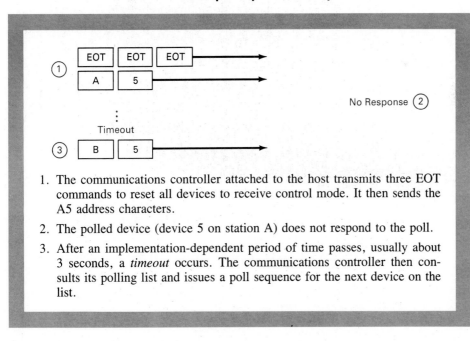

1. The communications controller attached to the host transmits three EOT commands to reset all devices to receive control mode. It then sends the A5 address characters.

2. The polled device (device 5 on station A) does not respond to the poll.

3. After an implementation-dependent period of time passes, usually about 3 seconds, a *timeout* occurs. The communications controller then consults its polling list and issues a poll sequence for the next device on the list.

MULTIPOINT POLL—NO RESPONSE   The message exchange in Box 21.5 shows what happens when the communications controller in the primary station issues a poll request, and the polled device does not respond to the poll. This might occur when the polled device is powered off or otherwise unavailable.

MULTIPOINT POLL—INQUIRY   Some applications use *piggybacked responses* to eliminate the need for positive acknowledgments when an inquiry from the terminal is usually followed by a response from the host. This message exchange is illustrated in Box 21.6.

BOX 21.6   Multipoint poll—inquiry

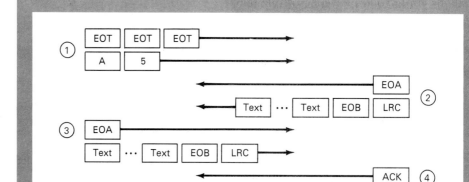

1. The communications controller attached to the host computer transmits three EOT commands followed by the address characters.
2. The polled device sends an EOA, the message text, the EOB command, and the LRC character.
3. The communications controller receives the message correctly and transmits a message of its own back to the polled device. The message itself serves as a positive acknowledgment to the message that was received.
4. The polled device replies with an ACK command (positive acknowledgment).
5. The communications controller transmits three EOT commands to reset all devices to receive control mode.

At point 3 in Box 21.6, a positive acknowledgment would normally be sent to the host communications controller from the polled device. However, in this case, the communicating devices have agreed, again by convention, that a message instead of an ACK command serves the same purpose as an explicit acknowledgment. This eliminates the need for two line turnarounds. In this data flow, if a transmission error occurs at point 2, the host responds with a NAK command, as in Box 21.4, and the message is retransmitted in the conventional fashion.

MULTIPOINT SELECTION MESSAGE FLOW

The foregoing multipoint message exchanges all illustrate polling situations, in which the host communications controller issues a request for one of the

BOX 21.7   Multipoint selection message flow

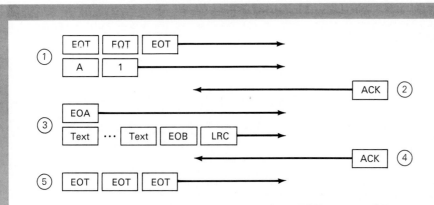

1. The host communications controller sends three EOT commands to reset all devices to receive control mode and sends the address characters A1 to address device 1 on station A.

2. Device 1 on station A responds to the selection with an ACK command, indicating that it is ready to receive data.

3. The host communications controller transmits a message in the normal fashion by sending an EOA, the message text, an EOB, and an LRC character.

4. Device 1 on station A performs the LRC verification procedure and responds with an ACK command.

5. The host communications controller transmits three EOT commands to reset all devices to receive control mode.

terminals to send data back to the host. In a selection situation, the data transfer occurs in the opposite direction. If the host communications controller addresses a device that is designed to receive data instead of send it (a printer, for example), the address operation is called a selection sequence rather than a poll. A typical selection message exchange is illustrated in Box 21.7.

**MULTIPOINT
SELECTION—
NEGATIVE
RESPONSE**

In some situations, a selected device may not be prepared to receive data from the host at the time that it is selected. For example, a printer might be out of paper. To handle this, a device may respond with a negative acknowledgment to a selection sequence. Box 21.8 illustrates the message exchange for a negative response to a selection.

**MULTIPOINT
SELECTION—
TRANSMISSION
ERROR**

As with the polling message exchanges examined earlier, a transmission error may occur in sending data from the host to the selected device. The message exchange that occurs when a transmission error is detected by the selected device is illustrated in Box 21.9.

BOX 21.8   Multipoint selection—negative response

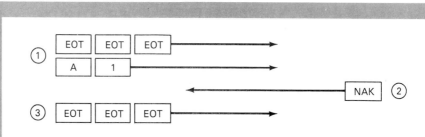

1. The host communications controller sends three EOT commands to reset all devices to receive control mode and then addresses device 1 on station A.

2. Device 1 on station A responds to the selection with a NAK command, which indicates that it is not currently ready to receive data.

3. The host communications controller transmits three EOT commands to reset all devices to receive control mode. The host might then try again after some implementation-dependent period of time.

BOX 21.9 Multipoint selection—transmission error

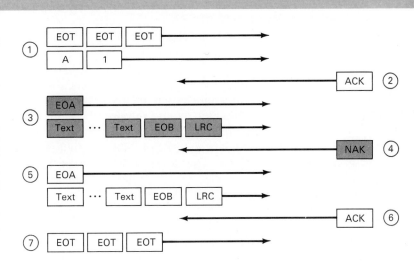

1. The host communications controller sends three EOT commands to reset all devices to receive control mode and then selects device 1 on station A.

2. Device 1 on station A responds to the selection with an ACK, which indicates that it is ready to receive data.

3. The host communications controller transmits a message in the normal fashion by sending an EOA, the message text, an EOB, and an LRC character. A transmission error occurs during the sending of the message text.

4. Device 1 on station A performs the LRC verification procedure and detects a mismatch between the generated LRC value and the value received with the message. It responds by transmitting a NAK.

5. The host communications controller responds to the NAK by retransmitting the message.

6. Device 1 on station A correctly receives the message and transmits an ACK.

7. The host communications controller transmits three EOT commands to reset all devices to receive control mode.

MULTIPOINT SELECTION—NO RESPONSE

A selected device may be powered down, or otherwise unavailable, at the time that the host device attempts to select it. In this case no response is received by the host. The message exchange that occurs when no response is received to a selection is illustrated in Box 21.10.

PACING TECHNIQUES

Some implementations of asynchronous communication techniques require the use of pacing techniques. For example, suppose that a particular device, such as a printer, is capable of receiving data at a rate of 2400 bps, but is not capable of actually printing the data that fast. The device might contain a quantity of buffer storage that fills up as the device prints. When the buffer fills up, the device needs to have a method of notifying the sender of that fact, so the sender can temporarily stop transmitting new data until the device empties its buffer.

One technique to control pacing uses two control codes. These codes are called Transmitter On (XON) and Transmitter Off (XOFF). Most implementations use the ASCII DC1 code to represent the XON function and the DC3 code to represent XOFF. Box 21.11 illustrates the use of XON and XOFF to control pacing.

Asynchronous communication techniques are well suited for some data communication applications and will continue to be used now and in the future.

BOX 21.10   Multipoint selection—no response

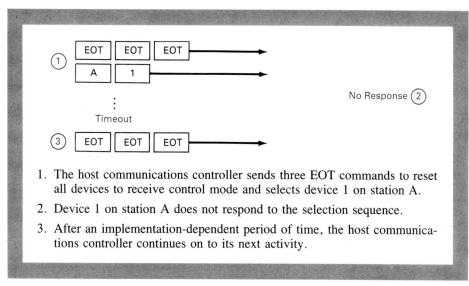

1. The host communications controller sends three EOT commands to reset all devices to receive control mode and selects device 1 on station A.

2. Device 1 on station A does not respond to the selection sequence.

3. After an implementation-dependent period of time, the host communications controller continues on to its next activity.

BOX 21.11   XON/XOFF pacing message flow

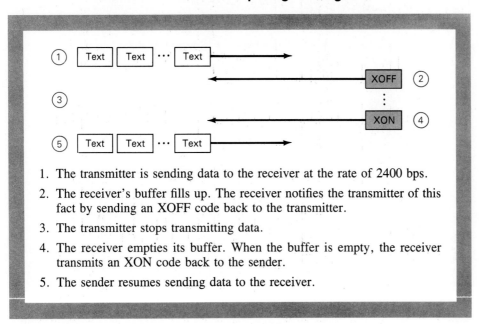

1. The transmitter is sending data to the receiver at the rate of 2400 bps.

2. The receiver's buffer fills up. The receiver notifies the transmitter of this fact by sending an XOFF code back to the transmitter.

3. The transmitter stops transmitting data.

4. The receiver empties its buffer. When the buffer is empty, the receiver transmits an XON code back to the sender.

5. The sender resumes sending data to the receiver.

However, some forms of data communication, especially when higher transmission speeds are required, require more efficient and reliable data link protocols. Chapter 22 examines the binary-synchronous protocol, which was developed by IBM to overcome some of the drawbacks of asynchronous transmission techniques.

22 THE BINARY-SYNCHRONOUS PROTOCOL

As we saw in Chapter 21, asynchronous protocols are protocols in which synchronization must be established by the sending and receiving DTEs before each character is transmitted. The start and stop bits are the mechanism by which this synchronization is established. The binary-synchronous protocol is different from asynchronous protocols in that bit synchronization is established for a much longer duration, usually for the time it takes to transmit several thousand bits. The binary-synchronous protocol requires more complex circuitry that allows the clocks in the sending and receiving stations to remain in synchronization for long periods of time. There are many other differences between the asynchronous protocols and the binary-synchronous protocol. Some of these are listed in Box 22.1. These differences point out some of the general characteristics of the binary-synchronous protocol.

SYNCHRONIZATION With asynchronous transmission, sending and receiving stations are synchronized for the transmission of each character. As already mentioned, with the binary-synchronous protocol synchronization takes place at the beginning of each message. Figure 22.1 illustrates the synchronization process. The following steps take place to bring two communicating stations into synchronization with one another:

- **Bit Synchronization.** To achieve synchronization, two characters called *PADs* are sent before each message to ensure that the sending and receiving stations are in bit synchronization before transmission begins. The PAD characters consist of sequences of characters that contain alternating zero and one bits. These characters are sequences of either hexadecimal AA (10101010) or hexadecimal 55 (01010101).

BOX 22.1 Asynchronous/binary-synchronous differences

- With the binary-synchronous protocol, no start and stop bits are needed with each character. This results in less transmission overhead. Instead of start and stop bits, a sequence of special characters is transmitted to get the transmitter and receiver in bit synchronization and an entire transmission frame is sent. With asynchronous transmission, start and stop bits occupy about 25 percent of the transmission capacity. Control bit overhead with binary-synchronous is typically 5 percent or less.

- There is very little standardization in asynchronous transmission; each application defines its own control procedures. The binary-synchronous protocol is better defined but is still not fully standardized. When discussing the binary-synchronous protocol, a specific product name is generally used to establish which variation of the protocol is meant. For example, 3270 binary-synchronous is somewhat different from 3780 binary-synchronous.

- The binary-synchronous protocol is capable of supporting three different character sets. The two most commonly used today are EBCDIC and ASCII. The third is a little used 6-bit code called *six-bit transcode.*

- The binary-synchronous protocol is capable of providing for a greater range of transmission speeds than start-stop and supports higher line utilization.

- The binary-synchronous protocol provides for better error-detection methods than are generally used with start-stop transmission.

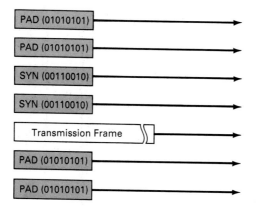

Figure 22.1 Synchronization

- **Character Synchronization.** After the PAD characters are sent, a sequence of two SYN characters (hexadecimal 3232) are sent to establish character synchronization between the sending and receiving stations.

- **Frame Transmission.** After the two SYN characters are sent, the sending station then transmits the frame itself.

- **Synchronization Maintenance.** During the transmission of a long frame, the sending station maintains synchronization with the receiving station by inserting an additional SYN pattern into the data stream approximately every second. The receiver detects and discards these SYN patterns. The SYN characters that are inserted into the data stream allow the clocks to be brought back into synchronization during the transmission of long messages.

- **Frame End.** After the frame is transmitted, two more PAD characters are sent.

LINE CONTROL CHARACTERS

Figure 22.2 lists the codes that are used to control binary-synchronous transmission. The codes in the column labeled "binary-synchronous mnemonic" are the mnemonic codes that are used to identify each line control function. Each mnemonic represents a general binary-synchronous function that is implemented differently depending on the character set that is being used. For example, each

Control Code Function	BSC Mnemonic	EBCDIC Code	ASCII Code
Start of Heading	SOH	SOH	SOH
Start of Text	STX	STX	STX
End of Transmission Block	ETB	ETB	ETB
End of Text	ETX	ETX	ETX
End of Transmission	EOT	EOT	EOT
Enquiry	ENQ	ENQ	ENQ
Negative Acknowledge	NAK	NAK	NAK
Synchronous Idle	SYN	SYN	SYN
Data Link Escape	DLE	DLE	DLE
Intermediate Block Character	ITB	IUS	US
Even Acknowledge	ACK0	DLE (70)	DLE 0
Odd Acknowledge	ACK1	DLE /	DLE 1
Wait Before Transmit	WACK	DLE ,	DLE ;
Mandatory Disconnect	DISC	DLE EOT	DLE EOT
Reverse Interrupt	RVI	DLE @	DLE <
Temporary Text Delay	TTD	STX ENQ	STX ENQ

Figure 22.2   Binary-synchronous control codes

binary-synchronous function is implemented by one or more characters in either the EBCDIC or ASCII character sets.

In some cases a particular character set, such as ASCII, uses the same mnemonic as the corresponding binary-synchronous mnemonic to implement a particular function. For example, the binary-synchronous *Start of Text* function has the binary-synchronous mnemonic STX. This is implemented in both the EBCDIC and ASCII character sets by the STX code. (Figures 18.7 and 18.8 show the ASCII and EBCDIC code charts.)

In many cases, a particular binary-synchronous mnemonic has no corresponding mnemonic in the particular character set being used. For example, the binary-synchronous function *Intermediate Block Character* has the binary-synchronous mnemonic ITB. There is no ITB mnemonic in either the ASCII or EBCDIC code charts. In EBCDIC, the ITB function is represented by the IUS code (hexadecimal 1F). In ASCII, the ITB function is represented by the code US (also hexadecimal 1F).

Some of the binary-synchronous functions are represented by a combination of two characters. For example, binary-synchronous uses two ACK functions: ACK0 *(Even Acknowledge)* and ACK1 *(Odd Acknowledge)*. Neither of these binary-synchronous functions uses the ACK codes that are included in both EBCDIC and ASCII. ACK0 is implemented in ASCII by the DLE character followed by the digit 0; ACK0 is implemented in EBCDIC by a DLE character followed by a byte containing hexadecimal 70.

Throughout this chapter we reference binary-synchronous control functions using binary-synchronous function names and/or binary-synchronous mnemonics. To avoid complicating the discussion, the specific codes that are used to implement these functions in EBCDIC or ASCII are not shown.

BINARY-SYNCHRONOUS TRANSMISSION FRAME

Figure 22.3 shows the format of a typical frame that is transmitted when using the binary-synchronous protocol. Box 22.2 shows the sequence in which the parts of a frame are sent. Note that the protocol itself supports variable-length frames of any size. However, each specific implementation of the binary-synchronous protocol may limit frame length based on a variety of factors, including the availability of buffer storage. A primary reason for limiting frame length to a reasonable value is that the longer the frame, the higher the chance that an error will occur in transmitting the frame.

Figure 22.3   Binary-synchronous frame format

BOX 22.2 Binary-synchronous frame transmission

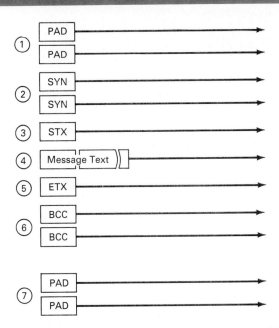

1. The sending station transmits two PAD characters to establish bit synchronization with the receiving stations.

2. The sending station transmits a sequence of two SYN characters to establish character synchronization with the receiving station.

3. The sending station transmits a *Start of Text* (STX) code to mark the beginning of a transmission frame.

4. The sending station transmits the text of the message, which can consist of any number of text bytes.

5. The sending station transmits an ETX character to mark the end of a transmission frame.

6. The sending station transmits a *Block Check Character* (BCC) sequence (two characters), which the receiver uses to verify that the frame was received correctly.

7. The sending station sends a final set of two PAD characters.

ALTERNATIVE FRAME FORMATS

A number of alternative frame formats are supported by the binary-synchronous protocol. Descriptions of some of these alternative frame formats follow.

- **Multiple-Frame Message.** Figure 22.4 shows the format of frames when multiple transmission frames are used to transmit a long message. The message text in each frame, other than the last, is terminated by *End of Transmission Block* (ETB) instead of *End of Text* (ETX). The message text in the final frame of the message is terminated by an ETX code.
- **Multiple Blocks in a Single Frame.** The protocol allows for multiple blocks of data to be embedded in a single transmission frame, as shown in Fig. 22.5. The message text in each block, other than the last, is terminated by *Intermediate Block Character* (ITB); the message text in the last block is terminated by ETX. Notice that each block has its own individual BCC sequence.
- **Message Headers.** A header can also be used in conjunction with the message text, as shown in Fig. 22.6. When a header is used, the *Start of Header* (SOH) code and the text of the header precedes the STX code that marks the beginning of the message text.

ERROR CHECKING

Each of the frame formats above shows that transmission frames contain one or more BCC sequences that are used by the receiving station to verify that the frame was received correctly. The specific techniques that are used in handling error detection are dependent on the specific binary-synchronous implementation and the character set that is used.

- **Error Checking with ASCII.** Implementations of binary-synchronous that use ASCII generally use two forms of error detection. The first form is a *vertical redundancy check* (VRC) consisting of a parity bit sent with each byte in the

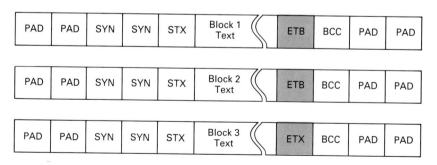

Figure 22.4   Multiple frame message

Figure 22.5　　Multiple block frame

message text. The second form consists of either a *longitudinal redundancy check* (LRC) that takes the form of a 1-byte BCC sequence or a *cyclical redundancy check* (CRC) that takes the form of a 2-byte BCC sequence. Figure 22.7 shows how VRC and LRC bits are generated for a message consisting of 5 bytes when odd parity is used. Notice that the bit in the lower right-hand corner of the diagram is the VRC of all the LRC bits.

● **Error Checking with EBCDIC.** EBCDIC transmission with the binary-synchronous protocol does not use vertical redundancy checking. With EBCDIC, a CRC method is used to generate a 2-byte BCC sequence. The two BCC bytes provide the only form of error detection. However, the CRC method is a more powerful form of error detection than the VRC/LRC combination sometimes used with ASCII.

BCC SEQUENCE GENERATION

To generate the 1- or 2-byte BCC sequence, the sending station passes the entire binary-synchronous frame through an arithmetic algorithm. The details of the specific algorithms used to generate BCC sequences using LRC and CRC methods are beyond the scope of this book.

After all of the bytes have been examined, the result of the LRC or CRC algorithm is a value that is sent with the frame in the BCC sequence. On the receiving end, the frame being received is passed through the identical algorithm to generate a corresponding value. The receiving station compares the generated BCC value to the value contained in the received BCC sequence. If the two values are the same, it is likely that the frame was received correctly. If the two values are different, one or more of the received bytes are not the same as the bytes that were transmitted, and the receiver can request that the frame be retransmitted.

Note that binary-synchronous provides for error detection only; it does not attempt to correct frames that are received incorrectly. Errors are corrected by the simple expedient of requesting retransmission of the entire frame that was found to be in error.

Figure 22.6　　Message with header

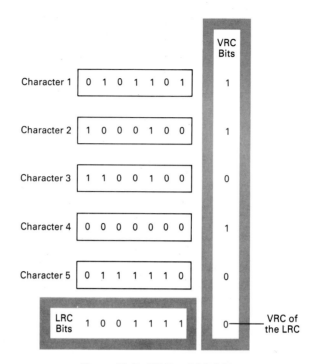

Figure 22.7   VRC and LRC bits

TRANSMISSION STATES

A binary-synchronous station can be in one of four transmission states at any given time:

* Transmit control mode
* Transmit text mode
* Receive control mode
* Receive text mode

Whether a station is currently transmitting or receiving data determines whether the station is in one of the two transmit modes or one of the two receive modes.

* **Transmitting Station States.** A transmitting station starts a transmission in transmit control mode and remains in that mode until it transmits the STX character. Then it changes to transmit text mode to transmit the text of the

frame. Finally, it changes back to transmit control mode and transmits the ETX characters and the two BCC bytes.

- **Receiving Station States.** A receiving station starts out in receive control mode until it receives the STX character. Then it changes to receive text mode so that it can receive the text of the frame. The receiver changes back to receive control mode after it receives the ETX character.

We now continue by examining a number of exchanges of messages that can occur on a point-to-point data link. We then discuss procedures used to control multipoint data links.

POINT-TO-POINT CONTENTION

When two stations are connected by a point-to-point connection, the configuration is called a *point-to-point contention* link. The flow of data between the two stations is controlled by firmware operating in the two DTEs. Between data transfers, the line is in an idle condition. In order to begin data transmission, one of the two stations on the line must initiate a *bid* procedure. Box 22.3 shows the message exchange that takes place between two DTEs over a point-to-point contention link in initiating a bid and in completing a normal transfer of data.

Note that Box 22.3 does not show the PAD and SYN characters that are sent preceding each individual transmission. For example, before station 1 initiates the bid, it must first have sent PAD characters to get the stations into bit synchronization, followed by the two SYN characters to get the stations into character synchronization. Similarly, before station 2 responds to the bid, it also must have sent the PAD characters and the two SYN characters. The transmission of a complete frame, which may contain any number of bytes of message text, is also preceded by a single sequence of PAD and SYN bytes. A small transmission involves the sending of a high percentage of overhead bytes, but the transmission of longer messages, which may often contain hundreds of bytes, incurs a relatively low percentage of overhead bytes.

MULTIPLE-BLOCK MESSAGES

The message exchange in Box 22.3 showed the transmission of three complete messages, each contained in a single transmission frame. The binary-synchronous protocol also allows for the transmission of large messages that in some

BOX 22.3 Point-to-point contention

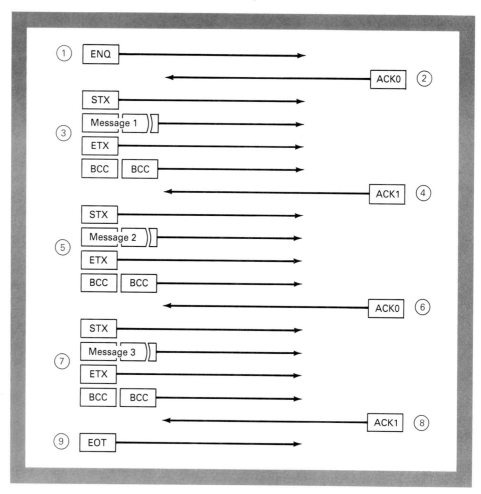

BOX 22.3 *(Continued)*

1. Station 1 indicates to station 2 that it has data to send by transmitting an *Enquiry* (ENQ) code. The ENQ in effect asks station 2 if it is ready to receive a message.

2. Station 2 responds to the ENQ by transmitting an *Even Acknowledge* (ACK0) code. This informs station 1 that station 2 is ready to receive the message.

3. Station 1 sends a complete message in a single frame across the data link. The message begins with a *Start of Text* (STX) code and is followed by the text of the message. The end of the text of the message is marked by an *End of Text* (ETX) code and is followed by the two *Block Check Character* (BCC) bytes.

4. After the message has been received, station 2 passes the text of the message through its CRC algorithm and compares the computed value with the value contained in the two BCC bytes it has received. If the values are the same, station 2 assumes that it has received the frame correctly and transmits a positive acknowledgment. Since the positive acknowledgment code that it used previously was an *Even Acknowledge* (ACK0), it transmits an *Odd Acknowledge* (ACK1) code this time.

5. The receipt of the positive acknowledgment indicates to station 1 that it can now send the second message.

6. Station 2 receives the message correctly and transmits an ACK0.

7. Station 1 transmits the third message.

8. Station 2 responds positively with an ACK1.

9. Station 1 signifies that it has finished sending data by transmitting an *End of Transmission* (EOT) code. At this point the line reverts to an idle condition and either station is free to send an ENQ code to initiate another message transfer sequence.

BOX 22.4 Multiple-block message

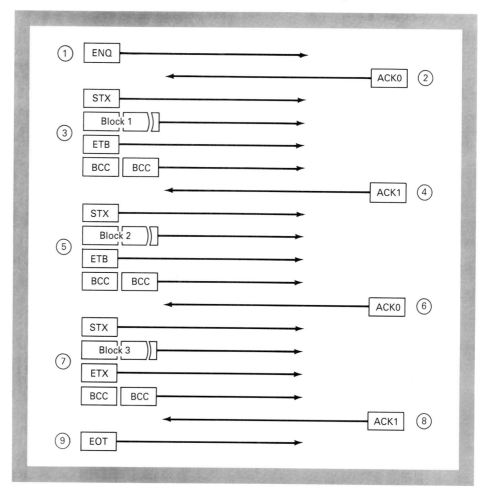

BOX 22.4   *(Continued)*

1. Station 1 initiates a bid by transmitting an *Enquiry* (ENQ) code.

2. Station 2 responds to the ENQ by transmitting an *Even Acknowledge* (ACK0) code.

3. Station 1 sends the first block of the message. The block begins with a *Start of Text* (STX) code and is followed by the text of the message. The end of the first block is marked by an *End of Transmission Block* (ETB) code and is followed by the two *Block Check Character* (BCC) bytes.

4. After verifying the BCC bytes, station 2 transmits an ACK1.

5. Station 1 sends the second block of the message.

6. Station 2 responds positively with an ACK0.

7. Station 1 sends the third block of the message. This is the final block because it ends with an *End of Text* (ETX) code rather than an ETB.

8. Station 2 responds positively with an ACK1.

9. Station 1 signifies that it has finished sending data by transmitting an *End of Transmission* (EOT) code.

implementations may require multiple transmission frames. Box 22.4 shows the transmission of a message that consists of three transmitted blocks. ETB codes mark the end of all but the last message block; an ETX code marks the end of the last block.

The transmission of individual frames is controlled in the same way whether ETB or ETX codes are used to terminate the frames. The difference between a frame that is terminated by an ETB and a frame that is terminated by an ETX is of significance to a higher layer of software above the data link protocol level.

MESSAGES WITH HEADERS   Box 22.5 shows the message exchange that takes place when the text of the message is preceded by a *header*. The *Start of Header* (SOH) code and the text of the message header precede the STX code that normally indicates the beginning of a transmission frame. The sequence of events that occurs in sending this type of frame is similar to sending frames without headers.

BOX 22.5   Message with header

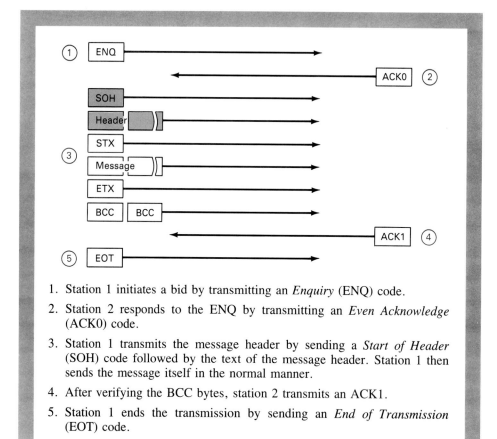

1. Station 1 initiates a bid by transmitting an *Enquiry* (ENQ) code.

2. Station 2 responds to the ENQ by transmitting an *Even Acknowledge* (ACK0) code.

3. Station 1 transmits the message header by sending a *Start of Header* (SOH) code followed by the text of the message header. Station 1 then sends the message itself in the normal manner.

4. After verifying the BCC bytes, station 2 transmits an ACK1.

5. Station 1 ends the transmission by sending an *End of Transmission* (EOT) code.

As in the message exchange in Box 22.4, the presence or absence of a message header is determined by a layer of software operating above the data link layer. The header can contain any desired information, such as a network address, the length of the text portion of the message, identification information, time or date information, security information, and so on. The interpretation of the information contained in the header is not the responsibility of the data link protocol.

BOX 22.6 Negative response to a bid

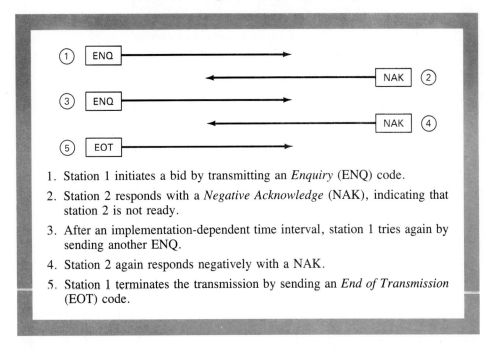

1. Station 1 initiates a bid by transmitting an *Enquiry* (ENQ) code.

2. Station 2 responds with a *Negative Acknowledge* (NAK), indicating that station 2 is not ready.

3. After an implementation-dependent time interval, station 1 tries again by sending another ENQ.

4. Station 2 again responds negatively with a NAK.

5. Station 1 terminates the transmission by sending an *End of Transmission* (EOT) code.

NEGATIVE RESPONSE TO A BID

Box 22.6 shows the message exchange that occurs when station 1 initiates a bid and station 2 is not ready to receive a message. After the negative response, depending on the particular implementation, station 1 may then try again and send another ENQ. If station 2 responds again with a NAK, station 1 may disconnect by sending an EOT.

TRANSMISSION ERROR

As we discussed earlier, each transmission frame is accompanied by a 2-byte block check character sequence that is generated by putting the message text through a CRC algorithm. A receiving station puts the text of each message it receives through an identical CRC algorithm and then compares the calculated value with the received value. If the values do not match, retransmission is requested. Box 22.7 shows the message exchange that occurs when a transmission error occurs in sending data from station 1 to station 2.

BOX 22.7 Transmission error

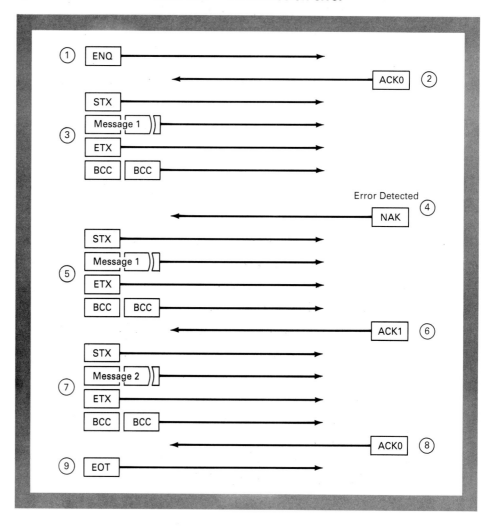

BOX 22.7   *(Continued)*

1. Station 1 initiates a bid by transmitting an *Enquiry* (ENQ) code.

2. Station 2 responds to the ENQ by transmitting an *Even Acknowledge* (ACK0) code.

3. Station 1 sends a complete message across the data link. A transmission error occurs during transmission of the message text.

4. Station 2 performs its CRC calculations, compares the resulting value with the value contained in the BCC bytes it received, and finds that they do not match. Station 2 then assumes that a transmission error has occurred and transmits a *Negative Acknowledge* (NAK) code.

5. The receipt of the negative acknowledgment indicates to station 1 that it should retransmit the original message.

6. Station 2 receives the message correctly and this time responds positively with a positive acknowledgment (ACK1).

7. Station 1 transmits the next message.

8. Station 2 responds positively with an ACK0.

9. Station 1 ends the transmission by sending an *End of Transmission* (EOT) code.

STATION NOT READY

In the message exchange shown in Box 22.8, station 1 transmits a two-block message to station 2, but station 2 is not ready to receive the message. This indicates that station 1 should try again after some implementation-dependent period of time. The WACK has many uses. For example, it might be used to

BOX 22.8 Station not ready

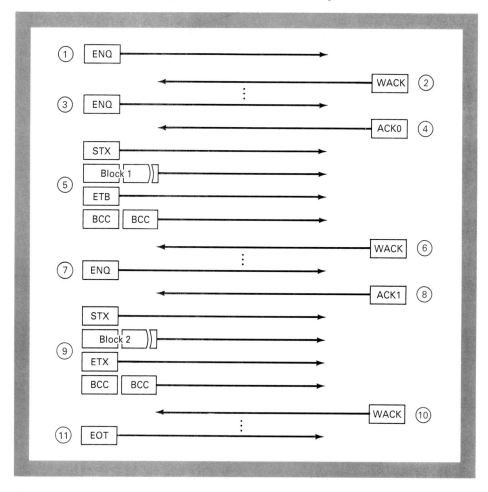

BOX 22.8   *(Continued)*

1. Station 1 initiates a bid by transmitting an *Enquiry* (ENQ) code.

2. Station 2 responds to station 1's bid by sending a *Wait Before Transmit Positive Acknowledgment* (WACK) code.

3. After a time interval, station 1 initiates another bid by sending a second ENQ.

4. Station 2 responds positively with an ACK0.

5. Station 1 transmits the first block of a multiple-block message.

6. Station 2 responds positively with a WACK code, indicating that it has received the first block of the message correctly, but that it is not yet ready to receive the next block.

7. After a time interval, station 1 sends another ENQ.

8. Station 2 responds with an ACK1, indicating that it is ready for the next block.

9. Station 1 sends the second block of the message, which happens to be the final block because it ends with an *End of Text* (ETX) code.

10. Station 2 replies with another WACK, indicating that it has received the block correctly but is not ready for the next message.

11. Station 1 has no more data to send and ends the transmission by sending an *End of Transmission* (EOT) code.

indicate that station 2 has full buffers or is experiencing some other type of temporary difficulty. The WACK code can be used to implement a simple form of *flow control* or *pacing* between two stations.

TEMPORARY TEXT DELAY   Box 22.9 shows an example of another type of wait that the transmitting station can request. Station 1 is transmitting a two-block message to station 2. The transmission of the first message block and its receipt by station 2 proceeds normally. But station 1 then decides that it must wait before sending the second block. The *Temporary Text Delay* (TTD) code is used to inform the receiving station that there will be a delay between message blocks.

BOX 22.9 Temporary text delay

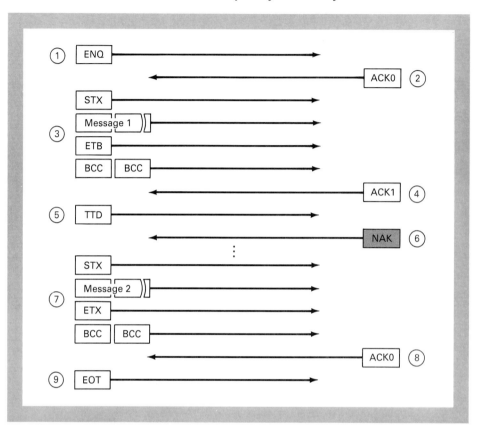

BOX 22.9   *(Continued)*

1. Station 1 initiates a bid by transmitting an *Enquiry* (ENQ) code.

2. Station 2 responds to the ENQ by transmitting an *Even Acknowledge* (ACK0) code.

3. Station 1 transmits the first block of a multiple-block message.

4. Station 2 responds positively with an ACK1.

5. Station 1 responds to station 2's positive acknowledgment with a *Temporary Text Delay* (TTD) code. The TTD code indicates that more data is to follow, but that station 1 is not ready to send it.

6. Station 2 responds to the TTD with a NAK. In this case the NAK code is used as a positive acknowledgment signifying receipt of the TTD code.

7. When station 1 is ready to transmit, it begins by immediately transmitting the STX code followed by the second block of the message. Notice that station 1 begins when it is ready without having to initiate another bid sequence.

8. Station 2 responds positively with an ACK0.

9. Station 1 ends the transmission by sending an *End of Transmission* (EOT) code.

MESSAGE TRANSMISSION INTERRUPTION

Box 22.10 shows the message exchange that may occur as station 1 attempts to send a long message, perhaps consisting of many transmission frames. During the transmission, station 2 wishes to interrupt the message transfer in order to get into temporary communication with station 1. The *Reverse Interruption* (RVI) code is sent by the receiving station in order to interrupt a message being sent.

INTERMEDIATE TEXT BLOCK

The message exchange in Box 22.11 shows how a number of separate data blocks can be sent in a single transmission frame. Each individual block is terminated by an *Intermediate Block Character* (ITB) code and is followed by its own BCC sequence. However, all three blocks are sent as a unit and are all

BOX 22.10 Message transmission interruption

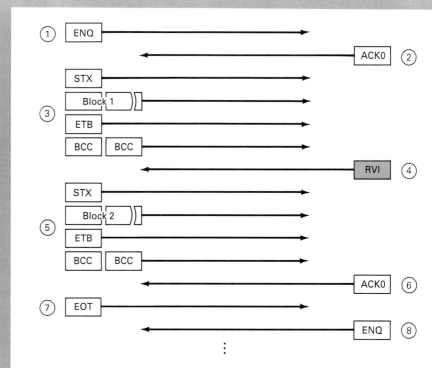

1. Station 1 initiates a bid by transmitting an *Enquiry* (ENQ) code.

2. Station 2 responds to the ENQ by transmitting an *Even Acknowledge* (ACK0) code.

3. Station 1 transmits the first block of a multiple-block message.

4. Station 2 responds with a *Reverse Interrupt* (RVI) code. This is a positive acknowledgment and indicates that the frame containing the first message block was received correctly. The RVI indicates that station 2 may not be ready to receive the entire message that station 1 wishes to send, and that for some reason station 2 wishes to get into communication with station 1. The RVI tells Station 1 to stop transmission as soon as possible.

5. Station 1 may not stop transmitting immediately. In this case it first sends the second block of the message.

6. Station 2 responds positively with an ACK0.

7. Station 1 now temporarily suspends transmission by sending an *End of Transmission* (EOT) code.

8. Station 2 now initiates a bid of its own by sending an ENQ code to station 1, thus beginning data transmission in the opposite direction.

BOX 22.11. **Intermediate text block**

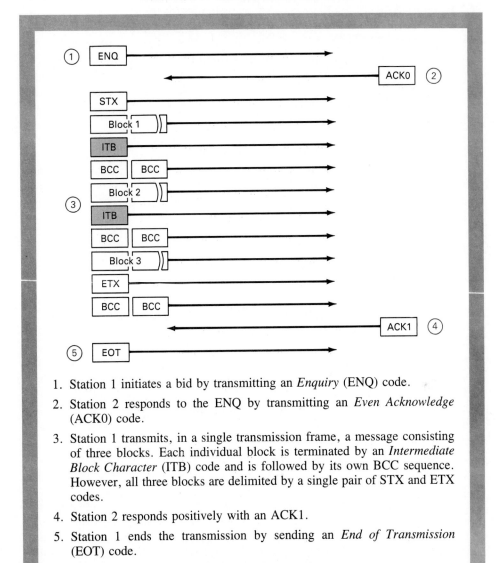

1. Station 1 initiates a bid by transmitting an *Enquiry* (ENQ) code.
2. Station 2 responds to the ENQ by transmitting an *Even Acknowledge* (ACK0) code.
3. Station 1 transmits, in a single transmission frame, a message consisting of three blocks. Each individual block is terminated by an *Intermediate Block Character* (ITB) code and is followed by its own BCC sequence. However, all three blocks are delimited by a single pair of STX and ETX codes.
4. Station 2 responds positively with an ACK1.
5. Station 1 ends the transmission by sending an *End of Transmission* (EOT) code.

delimited by a single pair of STX and ETX codes. The interpretation of the individual blocks that make up the frame when ITB codes are used is not the responsibility of the data link protocol; the decision to use ITBs is made in a higher level of software.

TRANSPARENT TEXT TRANSFER

In all of the preceding message exchanges, a number of the codes from the character set being used (i.e., EBCDIC or ASCII) are used to control the flow of messages between the two stations. To enable the DTEs to interpret control codes correctly, it is important that the text that makes up the message or block being transmitted not contain any of the codes that are used to control transmission. For example, if the text of a message contains an ETX code, the message will be terminated prematurely and the 2 bytes that follow the stray ETX will be interpreted as the BCC sequence.

In some applications, however, such as in the transmission of executable code, it is desirable to be able to send sequences of bytes containing any bit configuration. To permit this, the binary-synchronous protocol has a mode, supported by some implementations, called *transparent text* mode. Transparent text mode allows a station to send a message whose text can consist of any sequence of bits, including bit sequences that contain the same bit patterns as binary-synchronous control codes. Box 22.12 shows a message exchange involving transparent text transfer.

Once transparent text mode has been entered, the receiving station does not interpret bytes in the message text that contain binary-synchronous control codes as control functions; it interprets them instead as ordinary data. Transparent text mode is terminated when station 1 sends the 2-byte sequence DLE ETX (or something similar, such as DLE ETB).

The technique used by the binary-synchronous protocol to implement transparent text is called *character stuffing*. The receiver must be able to recognize that the 2-byte sequence DLE ETX (or some other combination, such as DLE ETB) at the end of the message is, in fact, a control sequence rather than data. Remember, true transparency must allow the data portion of the message to contain sequences of DLE ETX, DLE ETB, or any other combination of characters. To handle this, whenever the transmitting station detects a DLE character in the text stream, it sends a sequence of two DLE characters instead of only one. Then, when the receiving station receives a sequence of two DLE characters, it discards one of them.

Because of character stuffing, a sequence of DLE ETX that is embedded in the text is sent as DLE DLE ETX. Only when the receiving station receives an actual DLE ETX rather than DLE DLE ETX does it determine that transparent text mode has ended and that the DLE ETX sequence is, in fact, a control sequence indicating the end of the message text.

CONVERSATIONAL PROCESSING

If the two stations support the *limited conversational mode,* which is an optional feature that is not supported by all implementations, higher line utilization can be achieved by eliminating some of the positive acknowledgments and bid

BOX 22.12   Transparent text transfer

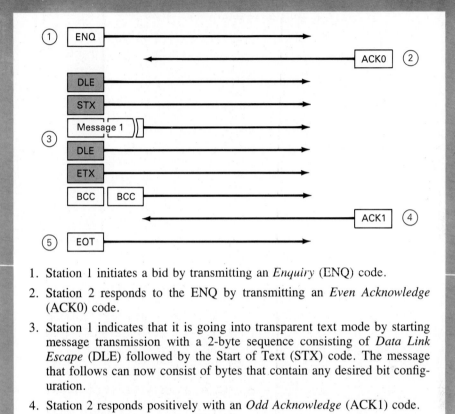

1. Station 1 initiates a bid by transmitting an *Enquiry* (ENQ) code.

2. Station 2 responds to the ENQ by transmitting an *Even Acknowledge* (ACK0) code.

3. Station 1 indicates that it is going into transparent text mode by starting message transmission with a 2-byte sequence consisting of *Data Link Escape* (DLE) followed by the Start of Text (STX) code. The message that follows can now consist of bytes that contain any desired bit configuration.

4. Station 2 responds positively with an *Odd Acknowledge* (ACK1) code.

5. Station 1 ends the transmission by sending an *End of Transmission* (EOT) code.

sequences that are normally required. Box 22.13 shows a message exchange in which station 1 transmits a single-frame message to station 2, followed by a single-frame message flowing from station 2 back to station 1. The message flowing from station 2 back to station 1 constitutes a positive acknowledgment to the first message. The limited conversational mode is useful when two stations often alternately exchange a pair of messages.

STATION IDENTIFICATION

When the binary-synchronous protocol is used over switched lines, it is sometimes desirable for two stations to exchange identification sequences as part of

BOX 22.13   Conversational processing

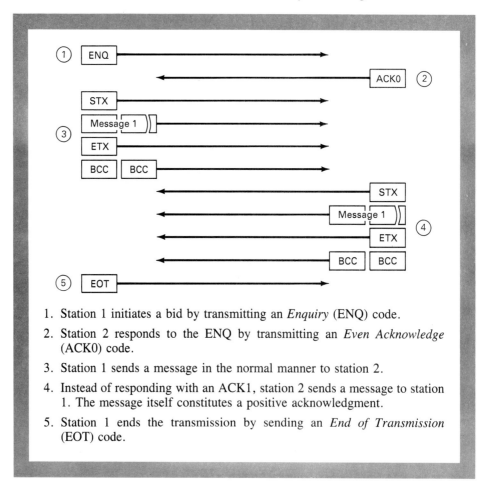

1. Station 1 initiates a bid by transmitting an *Enquiry* (ENQ) code.
2. Station 2 responds to the ENQ by transmitting an *Even Acknowledge* (ACK0) code.
3. Station 1 sends a message in the normal manner to station 2.
4. Instead of responding with an ACK1, station 2 sends a message to station 1. The message itself constitutes a positive acknowledgment.
5. Station 1 ends the transmission by sending an *End of Transmission* (EOT) code.

the bid process. Box 22.14 shows how a sequence of identification characters can be sent before the initial *Enquiry* (ENQ) code. Station 2 then precedes its positive acknowledgment with its own identification sequence. An identification sequence can consist of from 2 to 15 characters. If only a single character of identification is required, it is sent twice.

LEADING GRAPHICS   *Leading graphics* is an optional feature of the protocol that allows stations to provide additional information with positive and negative acknowledgments (ACK0, ACK1, and NAK). When this feature is implemented, a station can

BOX 22.14   Station identification

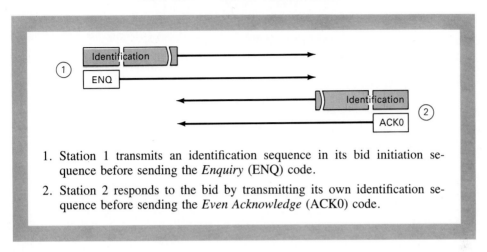

1. Station 1 transmits an identification sequence in its bid initiation sequence before sending the *Enquiry* (ENQ) code.
2. Station 2 responds to the bid by transmitting its own identification sequence before sending the *Even Acknowledge* (ACK0) code.

send from one to seven characters of data preceding each acknowledgment, as shown in Box 22.15.

FORWARD ABORT   The forward abort feature, which is also optional, allows a station to terminate a transmission before a complete message has been sent. As shown in Box 22.16, the message being sent does not terminate normally with an ETX and a BCC sequence. Instead, station 1 terminates transmission by sending an ENQ code. The normal response to this by station 2 is to send a NAK, indicating that it is ignoring the part of the message just sent. Station 1 then responds with an EOT, which puts the line back into an idle condition.

TIMEOUT   In all the message exchanges examined thus far, positive acknowledgments alternate between *Even Acknowledge* (ACK0) and *Odd Acknowledge* (ACK1). This provides for message sequence control in the event of certain types of errors, such as the timeout situation illustrated in Box 22.17. A timeout occurs when one station sends a message and the other station fails to respond. This can occur for one of two reasons:

- The receiving station did not receive the ETX that ended the message.
- The receiving station actually sent an acknowledgment, but the sending station did not receive it.

BOX 22.15 Leading graphics

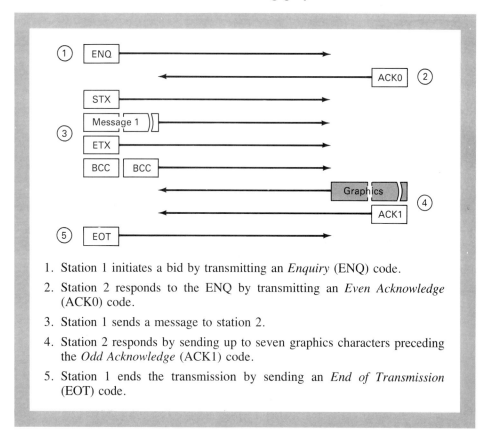

1. Station 1 initiates a bid by transmitting an *Enquiry* (ENQ) code.
2. Station 2 responds to the ENQ by transmitting an *Even Acknowledge* (ACK0) code.
3. Station 1 sends a message to station 2.
4. Station 2 responds by sending up to seven graphics characters preceding the *Odd Acknowledge* (ACK1) code.
5. Station 1 ends the transmission by sending an *End of Transmission* (EOT) code.

After a period of time, the sending station transmits an ENQ, in effect asking the receiving station which type of ACK it last transmitted. Given the situation shown in Box 22.17, there are four possible responses from station 2:

- **ACK1 Response.** If station 2 responds with ACK1, station 1 knows that the last positive acknowledgment sent by station 2 was an ACK1, and that the last frame received correctly by station 2 was message 1. This means that station 2 did not receive the end of message 2 sent at point 5. Station 1 responds by retransmitting message 2.

- **ACK0 Response.** If station 2 responds with an ACK0, it is probable that station 2 correctly received message 2 and responded to it by sending an ACK0 back to station 1. In this situation, station 1 probably did not correctly receive the ACK0 from station 2. Station 1 now continues by sending message 3.

BOX 22.16   Forward abort

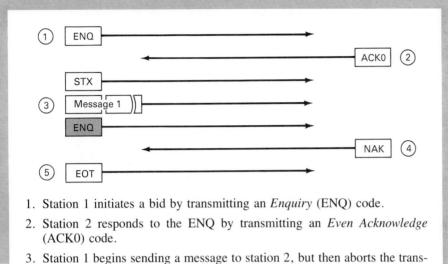

1. Station 1 initiates a bid by transmitting an *Enquiry* (ENQ) code.

2. Station 2 responds to the ENQ by transmitting an *Even Acknowledge* (ACK0) code.

3. Station 1 begins sending a message to station 2, but then aborts the transmission by sending an ENQ code before the message has been completely transmitted.

4. Station 2 responds positively by sending a *Negative Acknowledge* (NAK) code, indicating that it is ignoring the part of the message just sent.

5. Station 1 ends the transmission by sending an *End of Transmission* (EOT) code.

- **NAK Response.** If station 2 responds with a NAK, it is probable that station 2 received message 2, but that it detected a transmission error and sent a NAK that station 1 did not correctly receive. In this case, station 1 responds by retransmitting message 2.

- **Timeout.** If station 1 receives no response to the ENQ, another timeout occurs and station 1 assumes that station 2 is experiencing a failure.

MULTIPOINT LINES   When implementing the binary-synchronous protocol with multipoint lines, one station is known as the *control station;* the other stations on the line are called *tributary stations.* With multipoint lines, mechanisms implemented in the control station are required for *polling* the tributary stations on the line and for *selecting* a tributary station to which a message is being sent. Corresponding mechanisms are implemented in the tributary stations for responding to polling and selection sequences.

BOX 22.17 Timeout

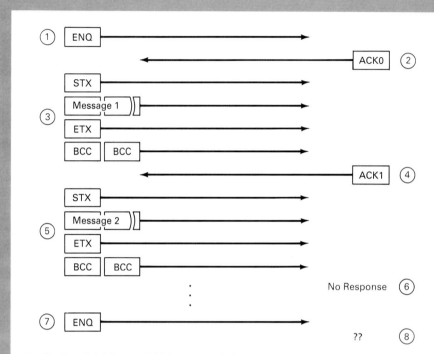

1. Station 1 initiates a bid by transmitting an *Enquiry* (ENQ) code.

2. Station 2 responds to the ENQ by transmitting an *Even Acknowledge* (ACK0) code.

3. Station 1 sends a message to station 2.

4. Station 2 responds positively transmitting an *Odd Acknowledge* (ACK1) code.

5. Station 1 sends another message to station 2.

6. Station 2 does not respond to the message.

7. After an implementation-dependent period of time, station 1 responds by initiating a new bid and transmitting an *Enquiry* (ENQ) code to station 2.

8. The response from station 2 indicates to station 1 what type of failure caused the lack of a response at point 6.

334

BOX 22.18   Polling sequence

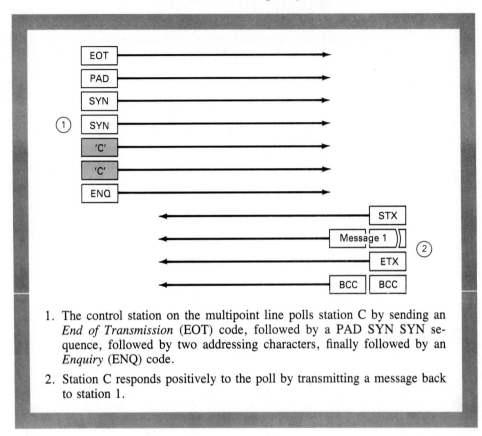

1. The control station on the multipoint line polls station C by sending an *End of Transmission* (EOT) code, followed by a PAD SYN SYN sequence, followed by two addressing characters, finally followed by an *Enquiry* (ENQ) code.
2. Station C responds positively to the poll by transmitting a message back to station 1.

**POLLING
SEQUENCES**

On a multipoint line, the control station sends a polling sequence to determine if a particular tributary station on the line has a message to send back to the control station. Box 22.18 shows a polling sequence on a multipoint line. The control station sends an EOT, followed by a PAD SYN SYN sequence, followed by from one to seven addressing characters, finally followed by an ENQ. The number of addressing characters used and the interpretation of the addressing characters is implementation dependent.

In some binary-synchronous implementations, a single addressing character is used, which is sent twice preceding the ENQ. In Box 22.18, the control station is polling the tributary station identified by the addressing character ''C.'' If station C has a message to transmit, it responds by immediately transmitting its message.

BOX 22.19 Negative response to a poll

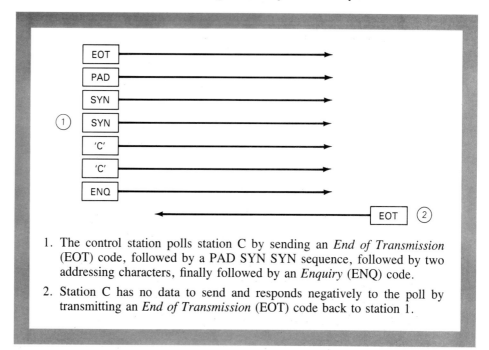

1. The control station polls station C by sending an *End of Transmission* (EOT) code, followed by a PAD SYN SYN sequence, followed by two addressing characters, finally followed by an *Enquiry* (ENQ) code.

2. Station C has no data to send and responds negatively to the poll by transmitting an *End of Transmission* (EOT) code back to station 1.

NEGATIVE RESPONSE TO A POLL

Box 22.19 shows a polling sequence in which the tributary station being polled (again station C) does not have a message to send. Station C responds to the polling sequence by transmitting an EOT. The control station then consults its polling list and polls the next tributary station in sequence.

SELECTION SEQUENCES

The contents of the addressing characters determine whether the addressing sequence represents a poll or a selection. A selection sequence is used when the control station has a message to send to a particular tributary station.

Box 22.20 shows the control station selecting station B. The lowercase "b" is used as an addressing character rather than the uppercase addressing characters used for polling. This is one mechanism that is used by some terminal types for distinguishing a polling sequence from a selection sequence. Other types of equipment use more complex methods.

BOX 22.20   Selection sequence

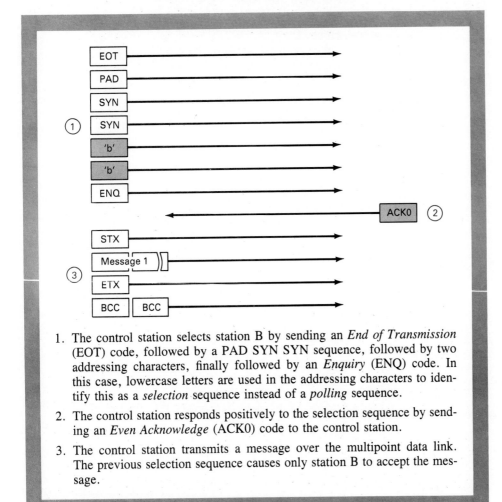

1. The control station selects station B by sending an *End of Transmission* (EOT) code, followed by a PAD SYN SYN sequence, followed by two addressing characters, finally followed by an *Enquiry* (ENQ) code. In this case, lowercase letters are used in the addressing characters to identify this as a *selection* sequence instead of a *polling* sequence.

2. The control station responds positively to the selection sequence by sending an *Even Acknowledge* (ACK0) code to the control station.

3. The control station transmits a message over the multipoint data link. The previous selection sequence causes only station B to accept the message.

   In conclusion, the binary-synchronous protocol is an efficient data link protocol that provides significant advantages over simpler, asynchronous forms of line control. However, modern data communication systems that support high-speed data links between computing systems and intelligent workstations have a need for even more efficient data link protocols. Chapter 23 introduces the bit-oriented protocols that have been developed as higher-performance alternatives to character-oriented protocols such as binary-synchronous.

23 BIT-ORIENTED PROTOCOLS

All modern network architectures provide for the use of bit-oriented protocols for data link control procedures. Bit-oriented data link protocols have evolved to overcome the inherent deficiencies of character-oriented protocols, such as the binary-synchronous protocol described in Chapter 22. A major deficiency of character-oriented data link protocols is that they are not well standardized. Each individual line of terminal equipment implemented a slightly different version of the protocol. Bit-oriented protocols were developed in conjunction with the major standards organizations of the world, and are today highly standardized.

Box 23.1 describes the major bit-oriented protocols that are in use today. They are all similar, and differ only in small details; the principles described in this chapter apply to all the bit-oriented protocols listed in Box 23.1. Standardization of the bit-oriented protocols began in 1968 with the development of ADCCP by ISO and of HDLC by the CCITT. Many major computer manufacturers worked closely with the CCITT in the development of HDLC; as a result, IBM's SDLC, first described in 1973, is today a compatible subset of HDLC. Box 23.2 lists some of the advantages that bit-oriented protocols have over the binary-synchronous protocol. In general, transmission over a data link controlled by a bit-oriented protocol is considerably faster than transmission over a binary synchronous link.

Bit-oriented protocols provide for a number of operating modes, only some of which may be supported by a specific protocol. The three major operating modes are described in Box 23.3. The most commonly used operating mode, supported by all the bit-oriented protocols, is called *normal response mode*. When a data link operates in normal response mode there are two types of link stations: *primary stations* and *secondary stations:*

BOX 23.1 Bit-oriented protocols

- **High-Level Data Link Control (HDLC).** The standard for HDLC was developed by the International Standards Association (ISO) and is documented in ISO Standards 3309 and 4335.

- **Link Access Protocol (LAP) and Link Access Protocol—Balanced (LAPB).** The protocols for LAP and LAPB document the data link layer functions of *Recommendation X.25* of the International Telegraph and Telephone Consultative Committee (CCITT). LAP and LAPB are compatible subsets of ISO's HDLC.

- **Synchronous Data Link Control (SDLC).** SDLC is the main data link protocol that is used to implement networks that conform to IBM's System Network Architecture (SNA). SDLC is a compatible subset of ISO's HDLC, and is similar to the LAP protocol of the CCITT.

- **Advanced Data Communication Control Procedures (ADCCP).** The standard for ADCCP was developed by the American National Standards Association (ANSI) and is documented in ANSI Standard X3.66 and in Federal Standard 1003. ADCCP is very similar to HDLC.

BOX 23.2 Bit-oriented protocol advantages

- A character-oriented protocol treats the data stream as a continuous stream of characters, some of which have a special significance to the protocol. A character-oriented data link protocol is sensitive to particular characters that appear in the data stream.

- A bit-oriented protocol does not perceive the data stream as a string of characters; instead, it perceives it as a continuous bit stream. A bit-oriented protocol attaches no significance to the specific character set being used.

- The binary-synchronous protocol operates only in half-duplex mode; bit-oriented protocols can accommodate half-duplex or full-duplex links.

- The binary-synchronous protocol requires messages to be acknowledged individually. Bit-oriented protocols allow multiple messages to be sent before expecting an acknowledgment. This advantage is particularly important on satellite links that have long propagation delays.

BOX 23.3 Bit-oriented protocol operating modes

- **Normal Response Mode (NRM).** In this mode a secondary station cannot initiate transmission without first receiving permission from the primary station.

- **Asynchronous Response Mode (ARM).** In this mode a secondary station can initiate transmission without receiving permission from the primary station.

- **Asynchronous Balanced Mode (ABM).** In this mode there is no distinction between primary and secondary stations, and each station is capable of initializing and disconnecting the data link and for recovering from error conditions.

- **Primary Station.** This is the station that initiates a data transfer and is in control during the exchange of messages. It notifies each secondary link station when it can transmit data and when it should expect to receive data.

- **Secondary Station.** This is a station that is contacted by the primary station and is controlled by the primary station during the exchange of frames.

There can be only one primary link station on a data link at a given time; however, there can be multiple secondary stations. All communication on a link takes place between the primary station and a secondary station; secondary link stations cannot communicate directly with each other. Link stations that are able to communicate with each other are known as *adjacent link stations*. Thus a primary link station and each of its secondary link stations are adjacent link stations. For any secondary link station, only its primary link station is adjacent. Since a secondary link station cannot directly communicate with any other secondary link stations, they are not considered adjacent to one another.

A secondary link station is able to send data to the primary link station only after it receives notification from the primary station that it is allowed to send. The primary station uses a polling procedure to notify each secondary link station that it can send data.

DATA LINK CONFIGURATIONS   There are four configurations that are typically used to connect a primary station and one or more secondary stations. The following are brief descriptions of each of the configurations:

- **Point-to-Point.** In the *point-to-point* configuration shown in Fig. 23.1, a single primary station is connected by a point-to-point link to a single secondary station. Each station in this configuration can send data to the other.

- **Multipoint.** In the *multipoint* configuration shown in Fig. 23.2, a single primary station is connected to two or more secondary stations. The primary station can send data that is addressed to one or more of the secondary stations. A secondary station can send data only to the primary station; one secondary station cannot send data to one of the other secondary stations.

- **Loop.** In the *loop* configuration shown in Fig. 23.3, the primary station is directly connected only to the first and last secondary stations on the loop. The primary station passes data to the first secondary station, which in turn passes it to the next secondary station, and so on, until the data arrives back at the primary station. Like the multipoint configuration, the primary station can send data to one or more of the secondary stations; a secondary station can send data only to the primary station.

- **Hub Go-Ahead.** The *hub go-ahead* configuration, shown in Fig. 23.4, is a little-used configuration that is typically supported only by some implementations of IBM's SDLC. In the hub go-ahead configuration, two channels are used: an inbound channel and an outbound channel. The primary station communicates with any and all of the secondary stations via the outbound channel. A secondary station can communicate only with the primary station via the inbound channel, which is daisychained from one secondary station to the next.

LINK STATION ADDRESSES

Each secondary link station has associated with it a set of *receive addresses* and a single *send address*. When the primary link station sends a frame, an address is included as part of it. If that address is included in the receive address set of a particular secondary link station, that station recognizes and accepts the frame. Allowing each secondary link station to have a set of receive addresses allows a primary station to send frames to a group of secondary stations on the data link.

Figure 23.5 illustrates a situation in which each secondary has multiple receive addresses. In this example the primary station has seven different addresses that it can use for transmission. If the primary station needs to send a frame to only one of the four secondary stations, the primary station will include in the frame a *station address*. Valid station addresses in this example are A,

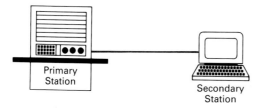

Primary
Station

Secondary
Station   *Figure 23.1*   Point-to-point configuration

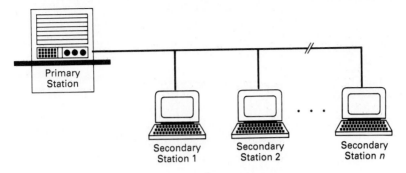

Figure 23.2   Multipoint configuration

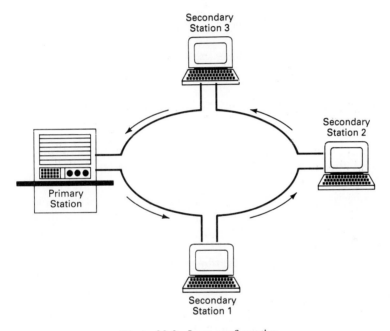

Figure 23.3   Loop configuration

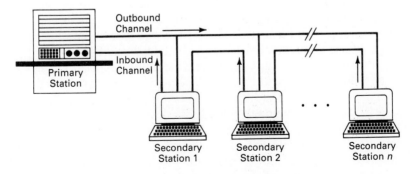

Figure 23.4   Hub go-ahead configuration

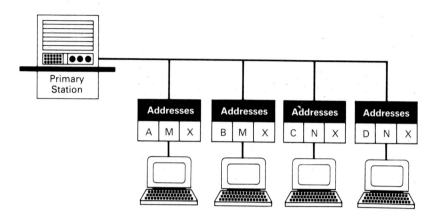

Figure 23.5 Secondary stations with multiple addresses

B, C, and D. If, however, the primary station wishes to send a frame to all of the stations, it might use address X. Address X is called a *broadcast address*. Since all of the stations have X in their receive address sets, they will all recognize and accept the frame.

Suppose that secondary station 1 and 2 perform one type of function and stations 3 and 4 perform a different type of function. In this case it is possible that the primary station may need to send data or control information to both stations 1 and 2 and to both stations 3 and 4. To send the same message to both stations 1 and 2, the primary station need only send a single frame using address M. Both stations 1 and 2 will accept the message, while stations 3 and 4 will reject it. Similarly, if the primary station needs to send the same data to stations 3 and 4, it can send a single frame using address N. Addresses M and N are called *group addresses*.

Any address value can be defined as a broadcast address or as a group address as long as all stations on the link interpret address values in the same way. Two address values are defined by the architecture. An address value of all zeros is interpreted as referring to no station; thus an address value of zero cannot be assigned as a station address. An address value that consists of all one bits is reserved for use as a broadcast address; however, a specific implementation may use other address values as broadcast addresses as well.

It is important to distinguish between the addresses used by the data link protocol and the network addresses and network names that are used in the higher layers of software. The higher-level layers work with network addresses and network names that uniquely identify nodes in the total network. Station addresses are used by the data link protocol to identify uniquely the stations that are attached to a single data link. In many cases, an individual data link connects only two stations. In other cases, such as with multipoint data links and loops, several stations may share the same data link. However, it is rare for a single data link to be shared by more than a few stations, so the limit imposed by the 256 different bit configurations in a single-byte data link address is seldom reached in actual practice.

TRANSMISSION STATES

A data link connection can be in one of four *transmission states* at any given time. The following are brief descriptions of these transmission states:

- **Active.** In the *active* state, control bits or bits representing message text are actively flowing between the primary station and a secondary station on the link connection.
- **Idle.** In the *idle* state, no information is being transmitted. A continuous sequence of 1 bits is transmitted when the line is in the idling condition.
- **Transient.** The *transient* state represents the transition that takes place between the time that the primary station transmits a frame to a secondary station and the time that the secondary station transmits a frame back to the primary station.
- **Disconnected.** The line is in the *disconnected* state when the secondary station is physically disconnected from the primary station, such as when a secondary station connected to a switched line is *on-hook*.

TRANSMISSION FRAMES

The message unit that is transmitted over a data link is normally called a *frame*. Some frames are originated by the data-link-level software itself and are used to control the operation of the data link. Other frames consist of data or control information that is passed down from a higher software layer. As shown in Fig. 23.6, each frame is divided into three major parts: a header, a variable-length information field, and a trailer. Control information is carried in the header and the trailer. Frames originated by the data-link-level software sometimes use the variable-length information field in the frame to contain control information. Other frames use the information field to carry messages that are passed down from higher-level software layers. Box 23.4 provides brief descriptions of the fields that make up a transmission frame.

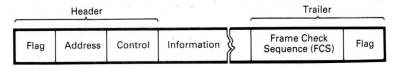

Figure 23.6   SDLC transmission frame

BOX 23.4 Transmission frame fields

- **Beginning Flag Field.** A frame begins with a flag field, consisting of a single byte that contains the unique bit configuration 0111 1110. A *bit-stuffing* technique (discussed later) guarantees that the only place where 6 consecutive one bits will occur is in a flag field.

- **Address Field.** The field that follows the flag field, normally a single byte in length, is interpreted as the data link address. The position of this field within the frame (the byte immediately following the beginning flag) defines this field as the address field. The address field contains the link address of the secondary station that is sending or receiving the frame. An extension to the architecture allows multiple-byte data link addresses, but this extension is seldom implemented.

- **Control Field.** The control field, normally a single byte in length, defines what type of information is carried by the frame. This byte determines the type of frame being transmitted, conveys information necessary for the proper sequencing of frames, and carries control and polling information. The position of the control field within the frame (the next 8 bits after the address field) defines this byte as the control byte. Extensions to most bit-oriented protocols, which are implemented by some device types, allows for frames that carry 2-byte control fields.

- **Information Field.** A variable-length information field in the frame is used to carry the data portion of the frame. It consists either of control information or of a message that has been passed from a higher-level software layer. Some frames that are originated by the data-link-level software do not use an information field. There are no minimum or maximum length restrictions on information fields, but IBM's SDLC does require that the length be some multiple of 8 bits; with other bit-oriented protocols, the information field can be any number of bits in length. The receiving station knows where the first byte of the information field begins because it always immediately follows the control field. The information field can contain any desired bit configurations other than the flag configuration (0111 1110).

- **Frame Check Sequence (FCS) Field.** The frame check sequence contains a 16-bit cyclic redundancy check (CRC) value that is used for error detection. Error checking is performed on all bits in the transmission frame, including the bits in the address field, the control field, and the information field.

- **Ending Flag Field.** Another flag field (0111 1110) terminates each transmission frame.

Notice that a single byte is normally used to contain the address in a frame. This address field always contains the address of a secondary station. Since all communication on the link takes place between a primary and a secondary station, the address of the secondary station is all that is needed to identify the source and destination of a frame; the address of the primary station is always implied. When the primary station is transmitting, the address field defines the address of the secondary station that is to receive the message. When a secondary station is transmitting, the address field contains the address of the secondary station that originates the message.

In many cases, the address specified by the primary station is a station address that identifies a single secondary station. As described earlier in this chapter, however, the address might alternatively be a broadcast address that allows a single frame to be recognized by all secondary stations on the link, or it might be a group address that is recognized by a specific group of secondary stations.

A considerable amount of control information must be carried in each frame. Not only must the frames be received by the proper devices, but they must also be sequence numbered so that multiframe transmissions can take place without the danger that lost frames will be undetected. Frames must carry information to control polling and error detection. Communication must be able to take place on links that have many users as well as those that have just a few. All this must be accomplished with the lowest possible ratio of control information to user data.

Transmission frames can be divided into two major categories: *commands* and *responses*. A *command* is a frame that flows from the primary station to one or more secondary stations. A *response* is a frame that flows from a secondary station to the primary station. Normally, when the primary station sends a command, it expects a response or string of responses in reply. Some commands and responses are used to carry data; others are used to perform control functions.

All commands and responses have the same basic format. The following are descriptions of each field in a transmission frame.

Beginning Flag Field

A *flag field,* shown in Fig. 23.7, begins each transmission frame. A flag consists of a single byte that has the following bit configuration: 0111 1110. A *bit-stuffing* technique, described in detail later in this chapter, guarantees that the only place where six consecutive one bits occurs is in a flag field.

Address Field

The *address field,* shown in Fig. 23.8, is present in all frames; however, on point-to-point links, the address field is not used and contains binary zeros. When the primary station is transmitting on a multipoint link or a loop, the

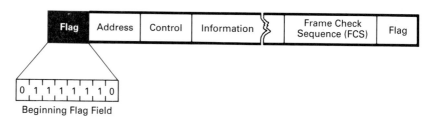

Figure 23.7 Beginning flag field

address field of the frame contains the address of the secondary station that is to receive the message. As discussed earlier, the address field can address a single secondary station, a group of secondary stations (group function), or all the secondary stations (broadcast function). When the secondary station is transmitting, the address field contains the secondary station's own address.

As we have already seen, the address field normally consists of a single byte. However, extensions to some bit-oriented protocols, which are seldom implemented in practice, allow for a multiple-byte address field. When the architectural extension is used, a one in bit position 7 of an address byte indicates that another address byte follows. Bit position 7 of the final address byte contains a zero. This allows for an address field of any desired length, as shown in Fig. 23.9.

Control Field

The control field, shown in Fig. 23.10, is normally a single byte in length and defines the type of information that is carried by the frame. An extension to the architecture (which is implemented more frequently than multiple-byte addresses) allows for frames that carry 2-byte control fields. The format of frame control fields will be examined later when we discuss the three types of transmission frames.

Information Field

The information field in a transmission frame is used to carry the data portion of the message (see Fig. 23.11). With most bit-oriented protocols, the infor-

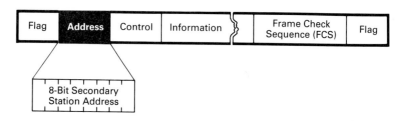

Figure 23.8 Address field

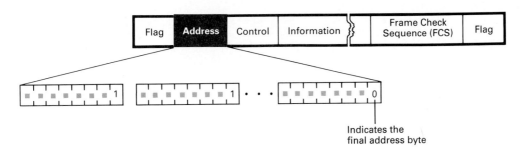

Figure 23.9   Multiple-byte address field

mation field can be any number of bits in length; with IBM's SDLC, the size must be some multiple of 8 bits. With all the bit-oriented protocols, the size can be zero bits for some commands and responses. Although no bit-oriented protocol specifically defines a maximum length, a particular device may set limits on the size of the information field based on the size of the buffer that is available. The contents of the information field is of no significance to the data link protocol and is interpreted by higher software layers. It can consist of any sequence of bits, using any desired character set.

Frame Check Sequence Field

The frame check sequence field contains a 16-bit cyclic redundancy check (CRC) value that is used for error detection. This 2-byte sequence, shown in Fig. 23.12, is generated by the sending station. The address, control, and information fields are all included in the CRC computation.

Ending Flag Field

The end of a transmission frame is marked by another flag field that contains the same bit configuration as the beginning flag field (0111 1110). The ending flag field is shown in Fig. 23.13.

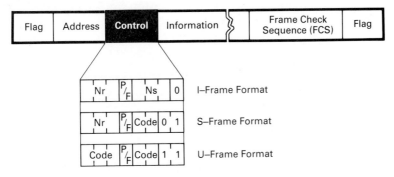

Figure 23.10   Control field

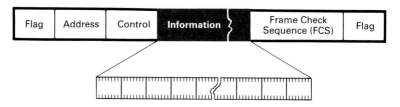

Figure 23.11   Information field

TRANSPARENT OPERATION

Bit-oriented protocols always operate in *transparent mode*, meaning that any desired bit configurations can be carried in the data that is contained in the frame's information field. Transparency is easier to achieve with bit-oriented protocols than in character-oriented protocols, such as the binary-synchronous protocol. This is primarily because the bit configurations for control functions, such as the functions performed by the address byte and the control byte, always appear in a fixed place in the frame. Therefore, any desired bit configuration can appear in any of the fields of the frame without confusion. The only requirement for achieving full transparency is to ensure that flag bytes (bytes that contain 6 consecutive one bits) are not transmitted in any part of the frame other than in the beginning and ending flag field positions. If a flag field appeared anywhere else in the frame, stations would have no way of knowing where a frame begins and ends. If the protocol is to be fully transparent, however, frames must be capable of containing bit sequences of any desired bit configuration, including bytes that contain the flag configuration (0111 1110). To handle data streams that contain any desired bit configuration, a technique called *zero-bit insertion* (sometimes called *bit stuffing*) is used.

ZERO-BIT INSERTION

In transmitting the data between a beginning and ending flag, the transmitter inserts an extra zero bit into the data stream each time it detects a sequence of 5 one bits. The transmitter turns off the zero-bit insertion mechanism when it

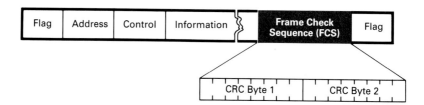

Figure 23.12   Frame check sequence field

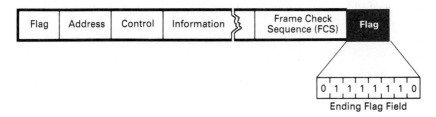

Figure 23.13   Ending flag field

transmits an actual beginning or ending flag. In this way, no consecutive sequence of 6 one bits is ever transmitted except when an actual flag is sent over the link.

A complementary technique called *zero-bit deletion* is used by the receiver in removing the extra zero bits. Whenever the receiver detects 5 one bits followed by a zero bit, it discards the zero bit, thus restoring the bit stream to its original value. The bit-stuffing technique ensures that 6 one bits in a row will never occur except in a flag field. When the receiver detects 6 consecutive one bits, it knows that it has received an actual flag field.

SYNCHRONIZATION   In addition to making transparency possible, bit stuffing also helps link stations maintain synchronization. Many devices that implement bit-oriented protocols stations use a technique called *non-return-to-zero encoding* (NRZI) in transmitting data. This technique is also sometimes called *zero-complemented differential encoding*. With this technique, a transition on the line occurs only when a zero bit is transmitted. Each time a one bit is transmitted, the line remains in the same state. The NRZI transmission technique is shown in Fig. 23.14. Since the receiving station is in synchronization with the sending station, it knows where each bit is in relation to time. Transitions are interpreted as zero bits; the lack of a transition is interpreted as a one bit.

Since transitions occur only for zero bits, very long sequences of one bits can cause long periods of time during which no transitions occur on the line. Zero-bit insertion ensures that no more than 5 consecutive one bits will ever be transmitted (except when transmitting a flag). This ensures that a transition will occur at least every five or six bit times, making it easy for the stations to stay in synchronization.

Figure 23.14   NRZI encoding. 0 bit = transition. 1 bit = lack of transition.

FRAME AND CONTROL FIELD FORMATS

There are three types of transmission frames. Each of these conforms to the same general format, but they have format variations that allow them to be used for different purposes. The following are brief descriptions of each frame type:

- **Information Frames.** The primary function of an information frame (I-frame) is to carry user data. However, I-frames also carry some control information.

- **Supervisory Frames.** Supervisory frames (S-frames) are used to carry information necessary for supervisory control functions rather than user information. These functions include requesting transmission, requesting a temporary suspension of transmission, and performing control functions such as requesting polls, acknowledging the receipt of I-frames, and reporting on status. Normal, routine transmission over a data link involves only I-frames and S-frames.

- **Unnumbered Frames.** Unnumbered frames (U-frames) are sometimes used to carry data, but are most often used for special functions such as performing initialization procedures, controlling the data link, and invoking diagnostic sequences.

I-Frame Format

Figure 23.15 illustrates the format of I-frames and shows how the control field bits are interpreted. Bit positions 6 and 7 in the control field identify the type of frame. An I-frame always has a 0 in bit position 7. The remainder of the bits in the I-frame control field are used to contain a receive count, a send count, and a poll/final bit. With 1-byte control fields, the two 3-bit count fields allow up to seven frames to be sent between acknowledgments. The poll/final bit is used for two different purposes depending on whether the transmitting station is the primary station or a secondary station. A primary station turns on the poll/

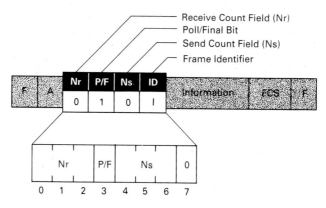

Figure 23.15   I-frame control field format

final bit to indicate that the primary station is *polling* the addressed secondary station. A secondary station turns on the poll/final bit to indicate that the frame is the *last frame* it intends to transmit back to the primary station.

S-Frame Format

Figure 23.16 illustrates the format of S-frames showing the control field layout. Notice that S-frames do not carry information fields. (No information field is a valid format variation since the information field is defined as consisting of any number of bits, including no bits.) When bit position 7 of the control field is 1, bit position 6 further identifies the frame as being either an S-frame or a U-frame. A 01 in bit positions 6 and 7 identifies the frame as an S-frame. The remainder of the bits in the S-frame control byte are interpreted as containing a receive count, a poll/final bit, and a 2-bit function code. The function code bits identify the type of command or response the frame represents.

U-Frame Format

Figure 23.17 shows the format of U-frames, showing details for the control field. Some U-frame commands and responses have information fields; others do not. A bit configuration of 11 in bit positions 6 and 7 identifies the frame as a U-frame. Bit position 3 is the poll/final bit. The remainder of the bits are interpreted as function code bits. The function code bits in a U-frame identify the type of command the frame represents. The five function code bits allow for up to 32 different bit configurations. A particular function code bit configuration can have a different interpretation depending on whether the frame contains a *command* that is being sent from the primary station to a secondary station or a *response* that is being sent from a secondary station back to the primary station. Thus the five bits can be used to represent up to 64 different functions, only some of which are actually used in any given implementation.

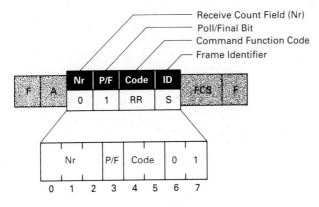

Figure 23.16   S-frame control field format

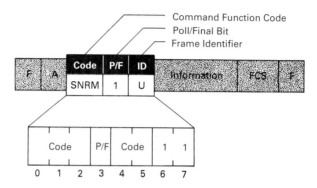

Figure 23.17   U-frame control field format

TWO-BYTE   Most bit-oriented protocols define an optional mode
CONTROL FIELDS   that supports 2-byte control fields. This mode is hard-
                          ware defined, and both the transmitting station and
the receiving station must be operating in this mode in order for frame control
fields to be properly formatted and interpreted. Figure 23.18 shows the formats
of I-frame, S-frame, and U-frame control fields when the stations are operating
in 2-byte control field mode. Notice that in this mode, 7 bits are used for count
fields rather than 3 bits. This mode allows up to 127 frames to be sent before
the transmitting station must wait for an acknowledgment. Two-byte control
fields are often used over channels with long propagation delays, such as satellite links.

FRAME   We will next examine exchanges of frames that take
EXCHANGES   place between primary and secondary stations over a
                          data link when a bit-oriented protocol is used. The
examples all assume that the stations on the link are capable of supporting the
normal response mode. We begin by examining the simplest case involving an
acknowledgment after the receipt of each frame. After that, more complex
frame exchanges involving multiple frames between acknowledgments and various types of error situations are presented.

ACKNOWLEDGMENTS   One of the primary responsibilities of any data link
                      protocol is to detect errors and when an error is
detected, to cause retransmission of the affected frames. To achieve this, frames
that are transmitted require acknowledgments from the receiving station indicating whether or not frames were received correctly. In earlier data link protocols,
a sending machine needed to receive an acknowledgment for each frame it trans-

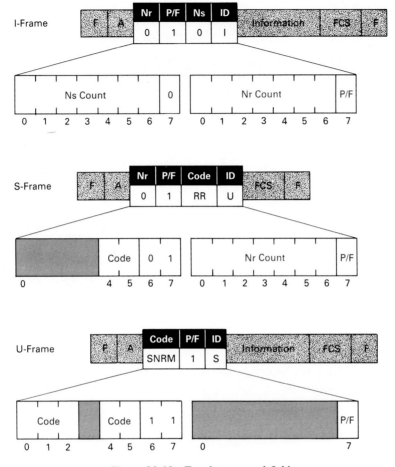

Figure 23.18 Two-byte control fields

mitted before it could send the next one. This procedure slowed down the traffic somewhat, especially on half-duplex links or when there was a lengthy propagation delay or long line turnaround time. In today's data communication environment, with more extensive use of high-performance links, it is particularly desirable to avoid frame-by-frame acknowledgment. The capability for transmitting multiple frames before requiring an acknowledgment is one of the primary reasons that bit-oriented protocols can achieve higher throughput than earlier protocols, such as binary-synchronous. With 1-byte control fields, a transmitting station can send up to seven frames before an acknowledgment is required. With 2-byte control fields, up to 127 frames can be transmitted between acknowledgments.

FRAME SEQUENCE NUMBERS   To ensure that no frames are lost and that all frames are properly acknowledged during a transmission, a system of *sequence numbering* is employed to control frame transmission. All link stations maintain counters that keep track of two counts: a *send count* (Ns) and a *receive count* (Nr) (see Fig. 23.19). These two internal counters are used to update the count fields in the control byte of the I-frames and S-frames that the station transmits. Figure 23.20 shows the format of an I-frame and an S-frame with some sample control field contents. I-frames carry both an Ns and an Nr field; S-frames carry only an Nr field. The transmitter always keeps track of how many frames it has sent, and the receiver keeps track of how many frames it has received. We will look now at how the send count and receive count fields are used to monitor and control data transmission.

INDIVIDUAL ACKNOWLEDGMENTS   The first frame exchange we will examine is a simple one in which individual I-frames are sent by the primary station, each of which is acknowledged individually by an S-frame from the secondary station. This frame exchange is illustrated in Box 23.5. The numbers in the illustration in Box 23.5 correspond to the step numbers in the description of the frame exchange. For simplicity, the steps in the frame exchange omit the FCS field verification step for each frame. Assume that this step is performed after each frame is received and that no transmission errors occur in this frame exchange. Each I-frame that the primary station sends has the poll/final bit set. This indicates that the secondary station must send a response back to the primary station after each I-frame is received. The process described in Box 23.5 can continue as long as the primary station desires to send frames to the secondary station using this procedure. A similar procedure can be used in sending I-frames in the opposite direction.

NR AND NS COUNT FIELD VALUES   Notice in Box 23.5 that the Nr counter in the primary station and the Ns counter in the secondary station remain set to 0 throughout the entire process. This is because frames are being transmitted in only one direction. The information flowing back from the secondary station to the primary

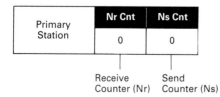

Figure 23.19   Send and receive counters

I–Frame Format

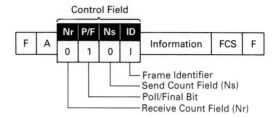

S–Frame Format

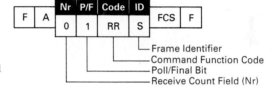

Figure 23.20   SDLC I-frame and
S-frame formats

station consists only of S-frame acknowledgments. Only I-frames cause the Ns and Nr counts to be updated. Since only S-frames are flowing from the secondary station to the primary station, the Nr count in the secondary station and the Ns count in the primary station remain the same. In more complex frame exchanges, in which the receipt of I-frames by one station are acknowledged by I-frames flowing in the opposite direction, both sets of counters are updated and cause message sequencing to be checked in both directions.

**MULTIPLE FRAMES
BETWEEN
ACKNOWLEDGMENTS**
When individual acknowledgments are required, the sending station turns on the poll/final bit in each I-frame, indicating that the secondary station should send an acknowledgment after the receipt of each frame. However, individual acknowledgments are not required. If the poll/final bit is off in a received I-frame, the receiving station does not reply with an acknowledgment; instead, it simply waits for the next frame. The next frame exchange, shown in Box 23.6, demonstrates how a sequence of multiple I-frames can be sent with an acknowledgment requested only after the entire sequence of frames is sent. In this frame exchange, the primary station sends a sequence of three I-frames, only the last of which has the poll/final bit set. The secondary station replies with an S-frame only after the third I-frame is received. This frame exchange again assumes that the FCS field value is correct

BOX 23.5   Individual acknowledgments

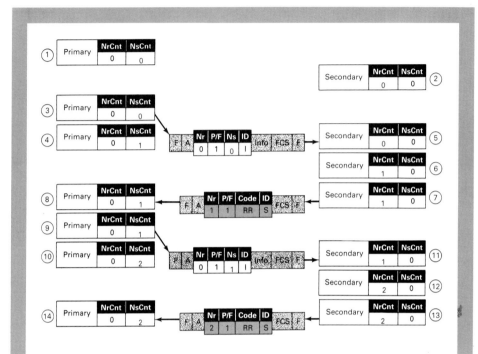

1. The primary station begins with its Ns counter set to zero, indicating that the next frame it will *send* is frame 0. The value in the sender's Nr counter is not significant in this example, and its value is shown as 0.

2. The secondary station begins with its Nr counter set to zero, indicating that the next frame it expects to *receive* is frame 0. The value in the receiver's Ns counter is not significant in this example and its value is also shown as 0.

3. The primary station formats an I-frame by setting the Ns and Nr count fields in the I-frame to the values in its internal counters (both currently 0) and turning on the poll/final bit. It then transmits frame 0. A 1 in the poll/final bit in a *command* (a frame sent from the primary station to a secondary station) indicates that the primary station is requesting a response to this frame.

4. The primary station adds 1 to its internal Ns counter, indicating that the next frame it will send is frame 1.

5. The secondary station receives frame 0. It compares the Ns count field in frame 0 with the value in its internal Nr counter. These two values are the same, which indicates that frame sequencing is correct.

BOX 23.5 *(Continued)*

6. The secondary station adds 1 to its internal Nr counter, indicating that the next frame it expects to receive is frame 1.

7. Since the poll/final bit in the received I-frame was on, the secondary station formats an S-frame as a positive acknowledgment for frame 0 and transmits the S-frame back to the sender. The secondary station turns on the poll/final bit in the S-frame response. A value of 1 in the poll/final bit in a *response* (a frame sent from a secondary station back to the primary station) indicates that this is the last frame the secondary station intends to send. The Nr field in the S-frame indicates to the primary station that the next frame the secondary station expects to receive is frame 1. It is important to note here that only the transmission of I-frames cause the Nr and Ns internal counter values to be updated; counter values are not updated when transmitting S-frames.

8. The primary station receives the S-frame acknowledgment and compares the received S-frame Nr field value with the value contained in its own internal Ns count value. Since they both contain the value 1, the primary station assumes that frame sequencing is correct and that frame 0 was successfully received by the secondary station.

9. The primary station formats a second I-frame by setting the Ns and Nr count fields to the value in its internal counters and again turning on the poll/final bit. It then transmits frame 1.

10. The primary station adds 1 to its internal Ns counter, indicating that the next frame it will send is frame 2.

11. The secondary station receives frame 1. It compares the Ns count field in the received frame with the value in its internal Nr counter. These two values are now both 1, indicating that it has received the proper frame.

12. The secondary station adds 1 to its internal Nr counter, indicating that the next frame it expects to receive is frame 2.

13. Since the poll/final bit in the received frame was again on, the secondary station formats another S-frame as a positive acknowledgment for frame 1 and transmits it back to the primary station. The Nr field in the S-frame indicates to the primary station that the next frame the secondary station expects to receive is frame 2.

14. The primary station receives the S-frame acknowledgment and compares the received S-frame Nr field value with the value contained in its own internal Ns counter. Since they both contain 2, the primary station assumes that frame sequencing is correct and that frame 1 was successfully received by the secondary station.

BOX 23.6 Multiple frames with no acknowledgment

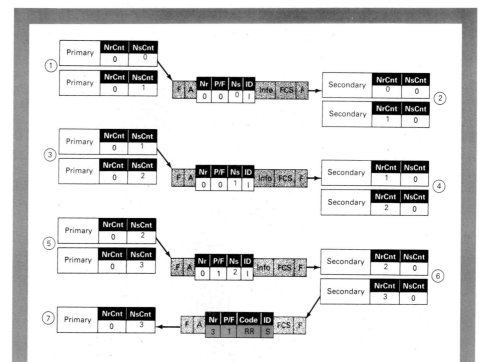

1. The primary station formats an I-frame by setting the Ns field to the current value of its Ns counter and turning off the poll/final bit. It then transmits frame 0 to the secondary station and updates its Ns count.

2. The secondary station receives the I-frame and compares the Ns field value to its Nr count. Since they are both 0, frame sequencing is correct. Since the poll/final bit was off, the secondary station simply updates its internal Nr counter and waits for the next frame.

3. The primary station formats frame 1 and sends it, again with the poll/final bit off and updates its Ns count.

4. The secondary station receives frame 1 and compares the Ns field value with its internal Nr counter value. Since they are now both 1, frame sequencing is again correct. The poll/final bit was off, so the secondary station updates its Nr counter and waits for the next frame.

5. The primary station formats frame 2, sends it, and updates its Ns count. This time it turns on the poll/final bit, requesting a response from the secondary station.

BOX 23.6   *(Continued)*

6. The secondary station receives frame 2, verifies the Ns field value, updates its Nr counter, and examines the poll/final bit. Since the poll/final bit is on, the secondary station sends an S-frame acknowledgment back to the primary station.

7. The primary station receives the S-frame acknowledgment and compares the received S-frame Nr field value with the value contained in its internal Ns count. Since they both contain the value 3, the primary station assumes that frame sequencing is correct and that the three frames it sent were all successfully received by the secondary station.

after each frame is received. Notice again that the Nr count in the primary station and the Ns count in the secondary station remain unchanged, since no I-frames are flowing from the secondary station back to the primary.

ONE-BYTE AND TWO-BYTE CONTROL FIELDS
When a data link uses 1-byte control fields, it functions using *modulo-8* operation; when a data link uses 2-byte control fields, it functions using *modulo-128* operation. Figure 23.21 shows the I-frame control field formats for both 1-byte and 2-byte control fields. In the following sections we describe the differences between modulo-8 and modulo-128 operation.

Modulo-8 Operation

When stations operate in single-byte control field mode, Nr and Ns field values consist of 3-bit values. Three-bit count values allow Nr and Ns values to range from 0 through 7. Modulo-8 operation allows a sending station to transmit up to seven frames in sequence before it must turn on the poll/final bit and request an acknowledgment.

Modulo-128 Operation

When stations operate in 2-byte control field mode, Nr and Ns field values consist of 7-bit values, allowing values from 0 through 127. Modulo-128 operation allows a sending station to transmit up to 127 frames in sequence before the poll/final bit must be turned on to request an acknowledgment. Stations use modulo-128 operation when channels with long propagation delays, such as satellite channels, are employed. It is important to note that a link station must be

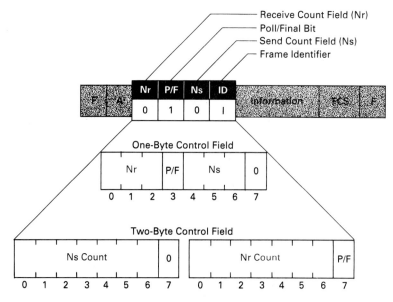

Figure 23.21   I-frame format

specifically designed to operate with 2-byte control fields, and modulo-128 operation is not supported by all link stations. Also, if a primary station is operating with 2-byte control fields, all secondary stations on that data link must also be capable of modulo-128 operation and must also use 2-byte control fields.

Trade-Offs

In deciding how many frames should be transmitted between acknowledgments, the hardware or software designer must evaluate several trade-offs. When channels with high error rates are used, relatively few frames should be sent between acknowledgments. This is because the frame sequencing scheme only enables the receiver to inform the sender of the last frame that was received correctly. If an error occurs early in the transmission of a long sequence of frames, all the frames that are sent after the error is detected will have to be retransmitted. If a channel with a low error rate but a long propagation delay is used, a relatively large number of frames should be sent between acknowledgments, because the turnaround time required to send a high percentage of acknowledgments can cause line utilization to be unacceptably low.

**SUPERVISORY
FRAMES**
In the previous frame exchanges S-frames were used as positive acknowledgments. In actual operation, S-frames can be used in a variety of additional ways to control the operation of the data link. Figure 23.22 shows the frame format for

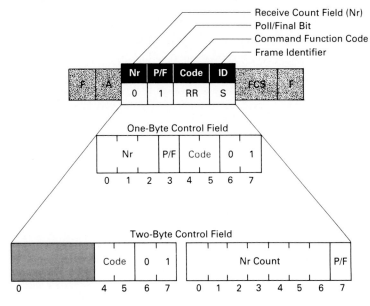

Figure 23.22   S-frame format

S-frames showing the control field layout for both modulo-8 and modulo-128 operation. Notice that the 2 bits provided for the function code allow up to four different S-frame commands and four different S-frame responses. Box 23.7 describes the three most commonly used S-frame commands and responses.

The next sections examine typical frame exchanges that involve the transmission of S-frames in both directions along the data link. These flows illustrate the use of S-frames that carry the RR and RNR command/response codes.

BOX 23.7   S-frame commands and responses

- **Receiver Ready (RR):** used as a command by the primary station for polling and as a response by the secondary station to indicate that the receiver is ready to accept additional I-frames

- **Receiver Not Ready (RNR):** used to indicate that the secondary station is not able to accept additional frames from the primary station

- **Reject (REJ):** used to indicate certain types of errors in the Ns count field

RR-POLLING— NORMAL FLOW
The RR-polling frame exchange is used to exchange messages between the primary and secondary stations. With RR-polling, the primary station begins by sending a frame to the secondary station that has the poll/final bit set. A frame sent by the primary station that has the poll/final bit set performs the function of a poll, which asks the secondary station if it has data to send. If the secondary does not have data to send, it replies with a negative acknowledgment; if it has data to send, it sends the data in the form of I-frames. Box 23.8 shows a typical RR-polling data exchange. The receiving station is shaded in each step of the flow. Each poll that the primary station initiates is followed by a response from the secondary station. The frame exchange shown in Box 23.8 illustrates how RR-polling can be used to control the transfer of data in both directions on a point-to-point data link.

BOX 23.8   RR-polling—normal flow

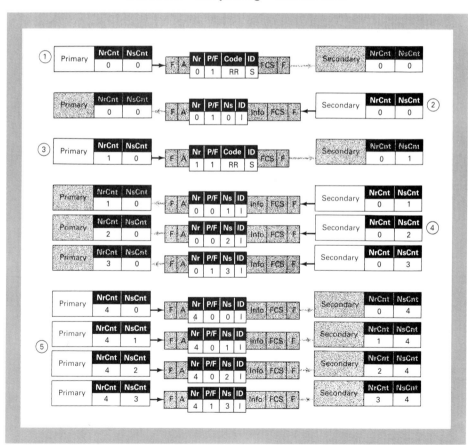

BOX 23.8   *(Continued)*

1. The primary station sends an S-frame RR command to the secondary station, asking if it has data to send. Notice that the poll/final bit is on, indicating that this is a poll.

2. The secondary station has a single I-frame of data to send, so it transmits it back to the primary station. Notice that the poll/final bit is on, indicating that this is the last I-frame the secondary station wishes to send.

3. The primary station acknowledges the receipt of the single I-frame, and sends another S-frame RR command. Again, the poll/final bit is on, asking the secondary station if it has any more data to send.

4. The secondary station this time responds by transmitting a sequence of three I-frames. Notice that the poll final bit is on only in the last of the three I-frames. Also notice how the Ns count is updated after each frame is transmitted to control frame sequencing.

5. The primary station this time has data of its own to send, and it responds by transmitting four I-frames. Again, the poll/final bit is on only in the last frame sent, which serves the same purpose as the above S-frame RR command poll and asks the secondary station if it has any data to send.

The next three frame exchanges show the data exchanges that take place when various types of errors occur. Each type of error causes a slightly different exchange of I-frames and S-frames.

RR-POLLING— RECEIVER NOT READY

In the frame exchange illustrated in Box 23.9 an error occurs that causes a receiver-not-ready condition in the receiving station. A receiver-not-ready condition may be caused by some event, such as a station's internal buffer filling up. This may cause one or more received frames to be discarded by the receiver, creating a mismatch between the receiver's Ns counter and the Nr count field in the last correctly received frame. In this frame exchange, the secondary station signals that it is not ready by transmitting an RNR S-frame to the primary station. This indicates that the receiver-not-ready condition has occurred, and the Nr count value in that frame indicates with which frame retransmission should begin. The primary station replies with another RR S-frame poll, which asks the secondary station if it is now ready to transmit. If the secondary station replies positively, the primary station then retransmits the frames that the secondary station missed.

BOX 23.9 RR-polling—receiver not ready

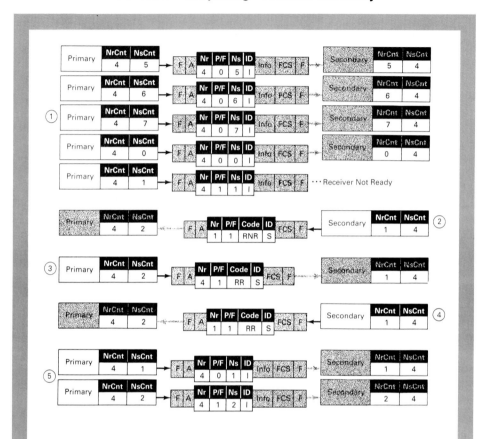

1. The primary station sends a sequence of five I-frames to the secondary station. Notice that the Ns counts in the I-frames are sent in the sequence 5, 6, 7, 0, 1; there is no special significance to the count wrapping around from 7 to 0. In single-byte control field mode in which 3 count bits are used, this indicates normal frame sequencing. Notice also that the poll bit is turned on in frame 1, which asks the secondary station for a response.

2. The secondary station receives the frames correctly but was not able to accept the final frame, possibly due to a buffer overflow. It responds by sending a *Receiver Not Ready* (RNR) I-frame, indicating in the Nr count field that the next frame it expects to receive is frame 1. Since the primary station has already transmitted frame 1, this indicates that the secondary station was able to handle frames 5, 6, 7, and 0, but that it would like frame 1 sent again.

BOX 23.9 *(Continued)*

3. The primary station responds by issuing another poll request that, in effect, asks the secondary station if it is now ready.

4. The secondary station is now ready, and it responds to the poll with a Receiver Ready (RR) S-frame, again indicating that the next frame it expects to receive is frame 1.

5. The primary station resets its internal Ns count field back to 1 and then retransmits frame 1 followed by any additional I-frames it may have to send.

FRAME SEQUENCING ERROR

The S-Frame Reject (REJ) command or response is issued by a station that detects an error in frame sequencing. A frame sequencing error can occur when a transmission error causes one or more frames to be completely missed by the receiving station. A typical frame exchange associated with a frame sequence error is illustrated in Box 23.10. Here the secondary station has missed a frame, and it sends a REJ S-frame command to the primary station, which tells the primary station with which frame retransmission should begin. The primary station then responds immediately by retransmitting the requested frames.

FCS ERROR

In all the previous frame exchanges, we have assumed that the CRC value contained in the FCS field of each received frame matches the calculated CRC value that the receiving station generates. When transmission errors occur while a frame is being sent, these values will not match. The receiving station must ask for that frame, and any sent after it, to be retransmitted. A typical frame exchange associated with this type of error situation is illustrated in Box 23.11. This time, the error occurs while the secondary station is transmitting I-frames to the primary station. After the complete sequence of frames has been received, the primary station sends an RR S-frame poll that indicates the number of the frame with which the secondary station should begin retransmission.

FULL-DUPLEX OPERATION

Prior to the use of distributed processing and computer networks, half-duplex operation of physical links was common, and full-duplex operation was ex-

BOX 23.10   RR-polling—frame reject

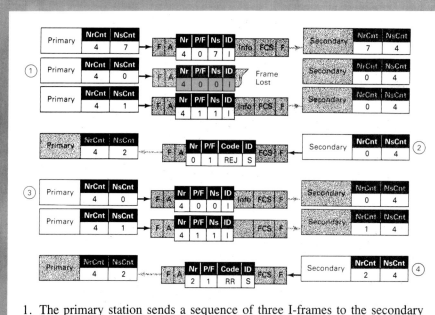

1. The primary station sends a sequence of three I-frames to the secondary station. Transmission errors occur during the data transfer, which causes one of the frames to be lost.

2. The secondary station compares its internal Nr count with the value in the Ns count field in the last frame it received correctly and finds that they do not match. This indicates that a frame sequencing error has occurred. The secondary station responds by sending a Reject (REJ) S-frame response back to the primary station. The REJ frame indicates that the next frame that the secondary station expects to receive is Frame 0.

3. The primary station receives the REJ S-frame, examines the Nr count in the S-frame, and resets its Ns counter back to 0. It then retransmits frame 0 and frame 1.

4. The secondary station this time correctly receives the two I-frames and responds with a positive acknowledgment.

ceptional. However, with complex networks, it is desirable to be able to transmit frames in both directions at once on many of the physical links. Figure 23.23 shows how a data link operates in full-duplex mode. This rather complex example shows the middle of a transmission sequence in which data messages are traveling in both directions. The user information flowing in one direction

BOX 23.11   RR-polling—FCS error

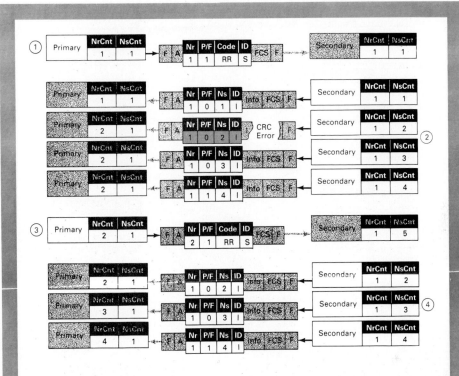

1. The primary station initiates a poll by transmitting an RR S-frame to the secondary station.

2. The secondary station transmits a sequence of four I-frames back to the primary station. In this particular case, a transmission error occurs during the transmission of the second frame (frame 2).

3. The primary station detects a CRC error in frame 2 when it compares the value it generates by putting the frame through the CRC algorithm against the value contained in the FCS bytes received with the frame. It then stops updating its Nr count value for that and all subsequent I-frames. After it receives the final frame from the secondary station (frame 4 that has the poll/final bit on) it sends a *Receiver Ready* (RR) S-frame to the secondary station, indicating that the next frame it expects to receive is frame 2.

4. The secondary station compares the value in the Nr count in the received frame with the value in its own internal Ns counter. Since these do not match, the secondary station resets its Ns counter back to 2 and retransmits frames 2, 3, and 4.

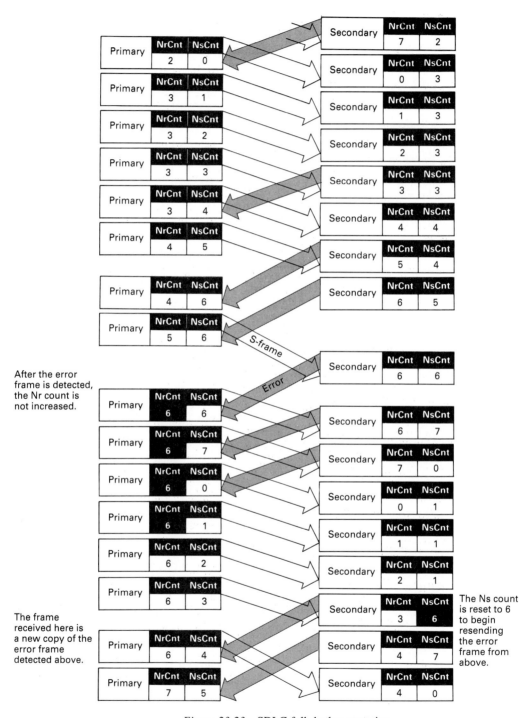

After the error frame is detected, the Nr count is not increased.

The frame received here is a new copy of the error frame detected above.

The Ns count is reset to 6 to begin resending the error frame from above.

Figure 23.23 SDLC full-duplex operation

is independent of the flow of frames in the other direction. The vertical dimension represents time and the shaded areas represent the frames that are flowing between the two stations.

We can assume that the transmission sequence shown in Fig. 23.23 has been going on for some time, since the sequence numbers at the beginning (top) of the sequence are not set at zero. The I-frame that is being transmitted from the secondary station at the top of the illustration has a send sequence number (Ns) of 2 and a receive sequence number (Nr) of 7; thus it must have already transmitted at least two frames (Ns = 0 and Ns = 1). Since the receive sequence number of this frame is 7, we can infer that when the secondary station began transmitting this frame, the last *complete* frame that it had received from the primary station had a sequence number of 6. During the course of the transmission of frame Ns = 2, the secondary station received a frame from the primary station with a send sequence number of 7, so the second frame that the secondary transmits in this illustration has a receive sequence number of 0.

There is only one S-frame shown in this example because most of the signals controlling the exchange of information are piggybacked on the information frames. Each I-frame carries both its own send sequence number (Ns) and the receive sequence number (Nr) of the frame to be received next. When an error occurs in frame Ns = 6, transmitted by the secondary station, the primary station detects the error and so does not update its Nr count. It keeps its Nr count at 6 in all the frames that it transmits from that point, indicating that the next frame it expects to receive should have a send sequence number (Ns) of 6. When the secondary station finally receives a frame from the primary station that has the poll/final bit set, it resets its Ns count field to the value contained in that frame (Ns = 6) and begins retransmitting frames from that point.

MULTIPOINT
OPERATION

On multipoint lines such as that illustrated in Fig. 23.24 it is sometimes advantageous to interleave transmissions to several different secondary stations.

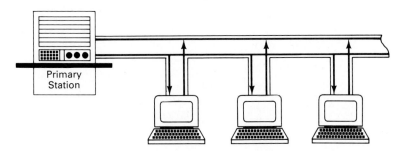

Figure 23.24   Full-duplex multipoint line

When this occurs a primary station does not send a whole group of frames to one secondary station before sending another group to a different secondary. Rather, the primary station may send the first frame in a group to one secondary station, then the first frame in another group to a second secondary, and so on, until parts of several frame groups are sent to several different secondary stations. The primary might then proceed to send subsequent frames to each of the secondary stations in turn. This practice is particularly helpful when the speed of the secondary machines is considerably lower than that of either the primary station or the physical link. On a multipoint link that uses full-duplex lines, interleaved transmissions in both directions can occur simultaneously.

U-FRAME COMMANDS

The frame exchanges that we have examined in this chapter are typical of the flows that occur during operation of a data link that connects stations operating in Normal Response Mode. In addition to the supervisory functions that are performed by using S-frames, stations also transmit U-frame commands and responses to perform additional functions in initializing and controlling the data link.

Figure 23.25 shows the general format of a U-frame. Some U-frames have information fields and others do not. Notice that the control field in a U-frame has no count fields, thus freeing up 5 bits for the function code field. A 5-bit function code allows for up to 32 commands and 32 responses; however, not all 32-bit configurations are currently used by any given implementation. Box 23.12 provides brief descriptions of the most commonly used U-frames.

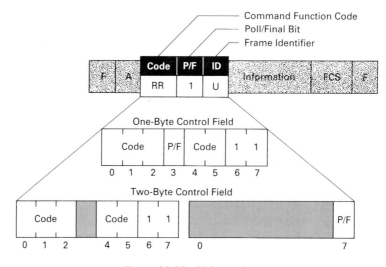

Figure 23.25   U-frame format

BOX 23.12 U-frame commands and responses

- **Unnumbered Information (UI).** A UI U-frame is used as a command or a response as a vehicle for transmitting information between stations under certain circumstances.

- **Set Normal Response Mode (SNRM).** An SNRM U-frame is sent from the primary station to a secondary station to place the secondary station into the normal response mode.

- **Request Disconnect (RD).** An RD U-frame is sent from a secondary station to the primary station to request that the secondary station be disconnected and placed offline.

- **Disconnect (DISC).** A DISC U-frame is sent from the primary station to a secondary station to place the secondary station offline.

- **Disconnect Mode (DM).** A DM U-frame is sent from the secondary station to the primary station as a positive acknowledgment to a DISC command to indicate that the secondary station is now in the disconnect mode.

- **Request Initialization Mode (RIM).** An RIM U-frame is sent from the secondary station to the primary station to request initialization. A typical initialization procedure may consist of downloading code from the primary station to the secondary station.

- **Set Initialization Mode (SIM).** An SIM U-frame command is sent from the primary station to the secondary station to begin initialization procedures.

- **Unnumbered Acknowledgment (UA).** A UA U-frame is sent from a secondary station to the primary station as a positive acknowledgment to an SNRM, DISC, or SIM command.

- **Frame Reject (FRMR).** Normal flows use the REJ and RR S-frames to indicate problems with frame sequencing and CRC errors. These are normal flows. The FRMR command and response are used to indicate abnormal conditions. The command contains bits that indicate the reason for the rejection, such as an invalid or unimplemented command function code, a frame with an information field that should not have one, or a frame with an information field that is too big for the station's buffer.

- **Test (TEST).** TEST U-frames are exchanged as commands and responses in performing diagnostic procedures.

- **Exchange Station Identification (XID).** XID U-frames are sent as commands and responses in exchanging identification sequences between a primary and a secondary station. XID U-frames are most often used on switched lines to identify secondary stations that are requesting connection to the data link.

DATA LINK OPERATING MODES

A typical use for U-frames is to set the operating mode of a secondary station. Following are brief descriptions of three commonly used secondary station operating modes.

Initialization Mode

A station is in the initialization mode before it actually becomes operational. Special U-frame commands are used to change the station from this mode to the normal response mode. The primary station places a secondary station into the initialization mode when it is necessary to perform some hardware-specific initialization procedure, such as downloading program code to the secondary station after powering up.

Normal Disconnected Mode

Disconnected mode is needed when a secondary station is to be prevented from appearing on the link unexpectedly while another interchange is taking place. In the normal disconnected mode the station is logically and/or physically disconnected from the data link. No frames that carry user data can be transmitted or accepted, although the station may transmit or accept certain types of control frames in order to change the mode, cause the secondary station to identify itself, or poll the secondary station. A secondary station assumes the normal disconnected mode at these times:

- When the station is first powered on or is enabled for data link operation
- Following certain types of failures, such as when a power failure occurs
- When a secondary station is first connected to the primary station on a switched line
- After a secondary station receives a Disconnect (DISC) command from the primary station

On a dial-up line, the DISC command causes the secondary station to place itself "on hook," thus freeing up the line for use by some other secondary station. On a leased line, the secondary station remains physically attached to the line, but is logically disconnected until an SNRM U-frame is received.

Normal Response Mode

When the data link is in the normal response mode, one of the link stations is designated the primary station and the others are designated as the secondary stations. Figure 23.26 shows how a primary station places a secondary station into the normal response mode. This is typically done immediately after a secondary station has been powered up or attached to a switched data link. After the SNRM/UA exchange, the secondary station is able to receive S-frames, I-

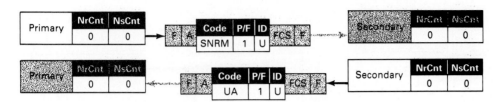

Figure 23.26   Setting normal response mode

frames, and U-frames in normal operation. In the normal response mode, one of the stations is identified as the primary station (the one that sends the SNRM command) and the other is defined as the secondary station (the one that receives the SNRM command and responds with the UA response).

When a secondary station is operating in the normal response mode, the secondary station transmits data only after receiving a poll from the primary station. As seen earlier, a poll consists of a frame from the primary station that has the poll/final bit on. The secondary station's response may consist of one or more frames, and the station must indicate the last frame of the response. It then cannot transmit again until it receives another poll.

POLLING AND LOOP OPERATION

Throughout this book we have stated that the primary station initiates communication over a link either by sending an I-frame or by polling a secondary with a receive ready S-frame. Most of the examples we have shown so far have been relatively simple and have used point-to-point links. The polling that takes place on a multipoint link is somewhat more complex than the frame exchanges we have examined thus far. On a multipoint data link, roll-call polling is the polling technique that is most often used.

ROLL-CALL POLLING

As discussed in Chapter 19, with roll-call polling, the primary station sends a poll request to each secondary station in turn to ask whether that station has something to send. Figure 23.27 shows an example of roll-call polling over a multipoint data link, in which a primary station polls three secondary stations. The primary first polls secondary station 1 with an RR S-frame. In the example, station 1 has data to send, and it responds with an I-frame. Next, the primary polls station 2, which responds with an S-frame indicating that it has no data to send. Finally, the primary station sends a poll request to station 3, which responds with an I-frame.

This process is likely to be repeated over and over again. The primary will continue to poll the other stations in sequence, and when it completes the circuit

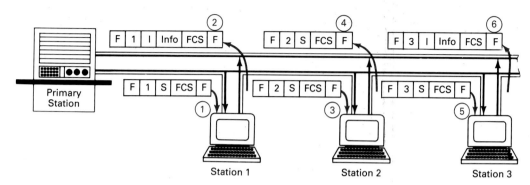

Figure 23.27 Roll-call polling

and returns to the secondary station that has sent I-frames, it will acknowledge those frames and poll the station for more frames.

This simple sequence is appropriate when all of the secondary stations on a link transmit with approximately the same frequency. On many links, however, one secondary station transmits more often than another. For example, if station 1 sends more data than the other two stations, the primary station might use the following polling sequence instead of the sequence shown above:

1. Poll station 1
2. Poll station 2
3. Poll station 1
4. Poll station 3

The polling sequence can be set by the primary link station with information gathered from a polling list maintained in its storage.

LOOP OPERATION   The frame exchanges examined thus far have been flows associated with point-to-point and multipoint links. There are additional U-frame commands that support operation over data links that are configured as loops. The loop configuration described here is a loop that operates using IBM's SDLC protocol in an SNA environment. In an SNA loop configuration, only the primary station or one of the secondary stations transmits at any one time. The secondary stations transmit sequentially, as required, according to their physical sequence on the data link.

PRIMARY STATION   When the primary station transmits on the loop, it
SENDING   sends command frames that are directed at an individual secondary station or any group of secondary

stations on the loop. Each frame transmitted by the primary station carries in its address field the address of the secondary station or stations to which the command is directed. When the primary station finishes transmitting, it begins transmitting a continuous sequence of one bits, which constitute a "go-ahead" signal.

SECONDARY STATION RECEIVING

Each secondary station on the loop receives each frame transmitted by the primary station. Each station decodes the address field in the frame and accepts only commands intended for it. Each secondary station also serves as a repeater to relay each frame to the next station on the loop. All frames are relayed to the next station on the loop, including commands that are accepted by the station and those that are not.

SECONDARY STATION SENDING

Before a secondary station can transmit on the loop, it must have received a frame intended for itself that constitutes a poll (poll/final bit on). It then formats its response and waits for the go-ahead signal from the primary station (continuous one bits). When the first secondary station on the loop that has a response detects the go-ahead signal, it converts the seventh of a sequence of 7 one bits to a zero bit, thus creating a flag. It then sends its response down the loop to the next station, where it will eventually be relayed to the primary station.

The secondary station that sent the response then begins relaying the go-ahead signal down the loop to the next station. Other secondary stations down the loop each gets a similar opportunity to send a response to the primary station. When the primary station receives frames from all the secondary stations on the loop that responded and again detects the go-ahead signal, it transmits its next frame to one or more secondary stations.

LOOP COMMANDS

Three additional U-frames are defined in the SNA architecture as commands and/or responses for loops. These are described in Box 23.13. The primary station on a loop can use the UP U-frame command to poll the secondary stations. Unlike a conventional poll, the UP U-frame can have the poll/final bit set either to 0 or to 1. When a secondary station receives a UP command addressed to it with the poll/final bit set to 0, that station can decide whether or not it should respond to the poll; if it has no response at that time, it normally does not respond to the poll. If a secondary station receives a UP U-frame with the poll/final bit set to 1, that station must respond. The UP command is particularly useful on loops since it reduces the number of negative acknowledgments to polls that would result if normal RR-polling sequences were used on the loop.

BOX 23.13   Loop U-frame commands

- **Unnumbered Poll (UP).** A UP U-frame is used by the primary station to poll the secondary stations. The poll/final bit indicates whether or not the secondary station must respond.

- **Configure (CFGR).** The Configure U-frame is used as both command and response to perform loop configuration functions. A number of Configure subcommands are defined to control loop operation.

- **Beacon (BCN).** A secondary station begins transmitting a sequence of Beacon U-frame responses when it detects loss of signal at its input. This allows the primary station to locate the source of a problem on the loop.

PART **V** **DATA COMMUNICATION HARDWARE**

24 HARDWARE REQUIREMENTS

Today, with the tremendous advances that are being made in microelectronics, it is possible to put a substantial amount of computing power in almost every place in the system where it might be useful. Most terminals already have microprocessors under their covers. Today, a very powerful microprocessor can be bought for less than $10. That is an insignificant cost compared to the purchase price of even the simplest display terminal. This is causing systems that use data transmission to be designed very differently from the early systems in which a collection of simple terminals communicated with a central computer.

INCOMPATIBILITIES There are a number of incompatibilities that exist between data processing users and equipment and the communication channels with which they must interface. First, there are incompatibilities in electrical signals. As we have seen, the data processing machine produces, and interprets, digital signals; most communication lines operate with continuously varying analog signals. Second, there are incompatibilities in speeds. The computer operates at one speed, the communication line at another, the terminal at yet another, and the human operator at still another. These incompatibilities cause the need for various different pieces of hardware in data communication systems.

HARDWARE LOCATIONS There are three general places that devices can be used in data transmission systems. The two most obvious places are at the two ends of a data link. The third place is in the communication network that implements the data link (see Fig. 24.1). In each of these three locations different types of devices can be used. The typical data transmission system today looks like the one shown in Fig. 24.2. A central mainframe is isolated from the communication lines by a

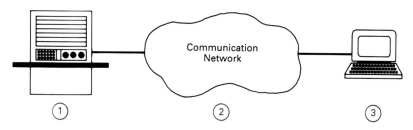

Figure 24.1   Hardware locations

specialized processor to which all of the communication lines are attached. Then at the user locations, each line is connected to another specialized processor that controls the functions of a number of terminals.

TERMINAL EQUIPMENT In a system that supports a dialog between a human operator and a computer, terminal features form an essential element of the dialog. The terminal is very important to the user. It is typically the only component of the system that the user sees. Users may form their impressions of the system entirely from the terminal. A poorly planned terminal configuration can have a serious effect on the efficient operation of the system. It can slow the system down, introduce

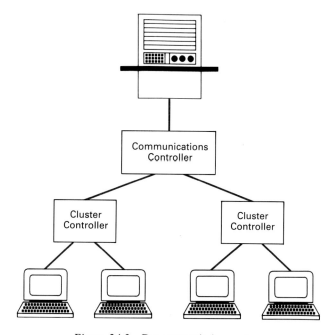

Figure 24.2   Data transmission system

errors, lessen its usefulness, and significantly add to the system's overall cost. At worst, it can reduce users to a state in which they want to put their fists through the screen.

For efficient operation, the terminal must be as unconfusing as possible and must give a suitably fast response time. For most uses it should be operable with one hand. If it has a display screen, the screen should be large enough to support the user interface, and there should be an easy way of responding to the screen contents.

There are any number of different types of terminal devices available. They range from simple teletypewriter devices, which combine a typewriter-like keyboard and a slow speed character-by-character printer, to display screen terminals that support alphanumeric displays, and with the more expensive devices, graphic displays as well. In today's environment, a very commonly used terminal device is a personal computer, more often than not of the IBM or IBM-compatible variety. A very important characteristic of a personal computer used as a terminal is that the personal computer can be programmed in a variety of ways to support the interaction between the central computing system and the user. The storage and processing power of the personal computer are extremely important assets in the implementation of an efficient user interface.

Many types of special-purpose terminal devices are also available, including devices that read the bar code printed on all items for sale in supermarkets and banking terminals designed to be used by the consumer.

A commonly used device, used in all but the simplest data communication system, is the *cluster controller*. It often consists of a small computer whose sole job is to control the operation of a group, or *cluster,* of terminals. Instead of attaching each terminal directly to the central computer using a separate communication link, cluster controllers are used at each remote location. This allows a single link to connect all the terminals to the central computer. The cluster controller can also free the central computer from performing many functions that are better done at the remote location itself. For example, the cluster controller may have disk storage capabilities and may run application programs that perform functions such as screen formatting and data collection (see Fig. 24.3). The use of cluster controllers is a step in the direction of distributed processing, where computing power is used at each point in the system where it can serve some need. Terminals and cluster controllers are discussed in Chapter 25. The use of personal computers in a data transmission system is discussed in Chapter 29.

LINE TERMINATION EQUIPMENT

As we discussed earlier, there is a third place in the system (other than at the ends of the data link) where hardware can be used. This is in the implementation of the data links themselves. The most familiar of these devices are the modems. As we discussed in Part II, an analog communication line requires a

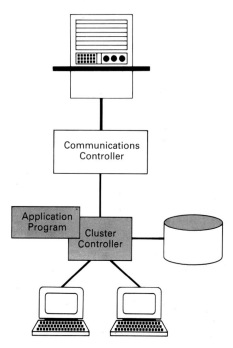

Figure 24.3   Cluster controller capability

modem at each end in order to send digital information over it. Modems are available in a wide range of speeds, generally ranging from 300 to 9600 bps for use with voice-grade channels up to hundreds of thousands of bits per second for use with wideband leased lines. Modems and other types of line termination equipment are discussed in Chapter 27.

LINE CONTROL EQUIPMENT   Suppose that we had to connect 10 terminals to a single computer, but that on average, only about three of the 10 terminals would be in use at one time. We might choose to use, say, four lines, to provide a measure of extra capacity. A concentrator is one type of device that could be used to connect the 10 devices to four available lines. It allows any of the terminals to be used, as long as no more than four of them are active at any given time.

A multiplexor is a related device but serves a different purpose. A multiplexor carves up a channel of high bandwidth into several channels of smaller bandwidth. It is as if a single large-diameter fire hose were subdivided by a number of smaller tubes (see Fig. 24.4). There are several ways of doing this, and various types of multiplexors can be used.

Most data transmission systems today use some sort of intelligent *com-*

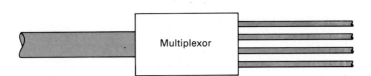

Figure 24.4   Multiplexor

munications controller at the location of the central computer to perform communications control functions. These were functions that had to be performed on the central computer in early data transmission systems. A communications controller normally takes the form of a minicomputer that runs specialized programs to handle line control functions. Concentrators, multiplexors, and communications controllers are discussed in Chapter 27.

SWITCHING   Another category of device includes switches of var-
EQUIPMENT   ious types. A circuit switch allows an incoming chan-
                       nel to be switched to any one of several outgoing
channels. Circuit switches are used in telephone exchanges to switch phone calls
from one subscriber to another. Circuit switches of various types can also be
used in implementing data communication systems.

Another type of switching device is called a packet switch. As we introduced in Chapter 9, a packet switch is a specialized processor whose job it is to read a header on each packet coming into it on an inbound channel, and on the basis of the information contained in the header, choose an appropriate outbound path for it. In this way messages can be routed through a network in the most efficient manner and delivered via the packet switches to their destinations. In a packet switching network, all channels are permanently connected via packet switching computers, and no circuit switches are used. Switching equipment is discussed in Chapter 28.

25 TERMINAL EQUIPMENT

Terminals can be devices into which data is entered by human operators or devices that collect data automatically from instruments. Terminals designed for human use may permit a fast two-way "dialog" with the computer or may be a remote equivalent of the computer-room input/output devices. For example, keyboards, magnetic tape drives, or diskette readers can be used to provide input over communication lines. Printers and display screens of various types can be used to provide output.

TELEGRAPH EQUIPMENT

In the early days of data transmission, the most commonly used terminal combined a typewriter-like keyboard and a slow-speed printer. The telecommunications industry has produced a range of such machines for telegraphy. In North America, these are generally called *teletype* machines. The word *teleprinter* is common elsewhere. Teletype machines transmit at a speed much lower than the capacity of a voice line. Common teletype speeds in North America are 75 and 150 bps. Common speeds elsewhere in the world are 100 and 200 bps. The international telex network and many European lines operate at 50 bps.

Telegraph signals are formed simply by switching an electrical current on and off or by reversing its direction of flow. Figure 25.1 shows a *single-current* telegraph signal, in which the information is coded by switching the current on and off at particular times, and a *double-current* telegraph system in which positive and negative potentials are applied at one end of the line. The means for producing these current changes are some form of make-and-break contact. The instruments for sending signals, such as teleprinters or paper-tape readers, make or break the circuit at appropriate times. The on and off pulses form a code that is appropriately interpreted by the receiving device. Single-current telegraph signaling is also known as *neutral* or *unipolar* signaling. Double-cur-

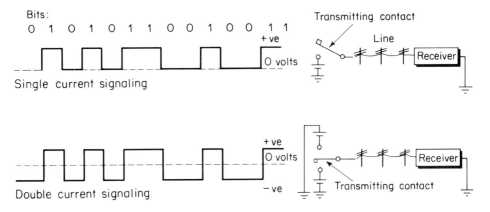

Figure 25.1   Single-current and double-current telegraph signaling

rent signaling is called *polar* or *bipolar*. In the United States, neutral signaling is more common than bipolar signaling. In Europe, bipolar (there usually called *double-current*) signaling is more common. The adapters for connecting telegraph equipment to computers can use either neutral or bipolar signals, whichever is appropriate.

At one time most telegraph signals were carried on overhead wires. In Wall Street the sky was once filled with such overhead wires. When telephony grew up, it soon outgrew telegraphy, and when there were more telephone circuits than telegraph it became economical to send the telegraph signals over telephone links. Today this trend has gone much further, and many telegraph signals can travel together over one path, being manipulated by the complex electronics that are part of today's telephone plant.

DISPLAY TERMINALS

Today, the vast majority of terminals combine a keyboard and a display screen to form what is commonly referred to as a *display terminal*. Many display terminals today take the form of personal computers that are doing double duty by functioning also as display terminals in mainframe-based online systems. The hardware aspects of this use of a personal computer as a terminal is discussed separately in Chapter 29. The software that is used in personal computer data communication applications is discussed in Chapter 33.

ASYNCHRONOUS DISPLAY TERMINALS

The most commonly used and generally least expensive form of display terminal communicates with a host computer using asynchronous transmission. These terminals do not ordinarily use buffers and transmit characters one at time between the host computer and the terminal using the same type of protocol that is used by a teletype machine. In fact, simple asynchronous display terminals are sometimes referred to as ''glass teletypes.'' When the terminal operator presses a key, the corresponding character is transmitted to the host computer. When the host computer transmits a character, it is displayed on the terminal's screen.

ANSI DISPLAY TERMINAL STANDARDS

Literally thousands of different types of asynchronous terminals are available in the marketplace, with each type generally supporting its own set of control codes. In an attempt to eliminate the confusion caused by the thousands of incompatible terminal control code schemes, the American National Standards Institute (ANSI) has defined a standard set of terminal control codes that could be used to control the standard functions performed by most asynchronous display terminals. Many of today's asynchronous terminals support the ANSI standard codes, sometimes as an option in addition to the terminal manufacturer's own set of terminal controls. Box 25.1 shows a few of the ANSI standard codes for controlling the functions of an asynchronous display terminal.

BOX 25.1 ANSI standard terminal codes

In the following control code descriptions, ESC stands for the ASCII Escape character and the symbol # stands for an integer value.

Code	Function
ESC[#,#H	Moves the display cursor to the position indicated by the two numeric values. The first value indicates the row and the second the column.
ESC[#A	Moves the display cursor up the number of rows specified by the numeric value.
ESC[#B	Moves the display cursor down by the number of rows specified by the numeric value.
ESC[#C	Moves the display cursor forward by the number of columns specified by the numeric value.
ESC[#D	Moves the display cursor back by the number of columns specified by the numeric value.
ESC[2J	Erases the screen and moves the display cursor to the home position (row 1, column 1).
ESC[K	Erases from the position of the display cursor to the end of the line.

PROTOCOL ADAPTERS

Many asynchronous terminals are attached directly to host computers or host computer communications controllers over asynchronous communication facilities, as shown in Figure 25.2. To avoid the inefficiencies of asynchronous transmission, protocol converters are available that function as cluster controllers for groups of asynchronous terminals (see Fig. 25.3). They allow multiple asynchronous terminals to be attached to the adapter using asynchronous transmission. The device then handles the transmission of data between the adapter and the host computer in the form of synchronous transmission frames using either the binary-synchronous or a bit-oriented data link protocol. Such a device performs a line concentration function as well as a protocol conversion function. The use of such a protocol converter allows inexpensive terminals to be used in a system while still gaining the advantages of synchronous transmission between the remote location and the host computer.

THE 3270-TYPE TERMINAL

One of the most widely used types of terminal for IBM mainframe applications is the 3270-type display terminal marketed by IBM. Many other terminal manufacturers now offer terminals that are compatible with 3270-type equipment, and due to the extremely large numbers of 3270s and 3270-compatible computers that are now installed, the 3270 has become somewhat of a standard terminal design. The 3270 is a buffered terminal that generally uses synchronous transmission in communicating with a host computer. Data is sent from the host computer to the terminal a screen at a time. When the operator enters data at the keyboard, the data is stored in a buffer at the terminal location until an attention key (such as ENTER) on the terminal is pressed.

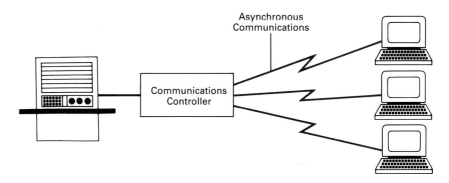

Figure 25.2 Individual asynchronous connections

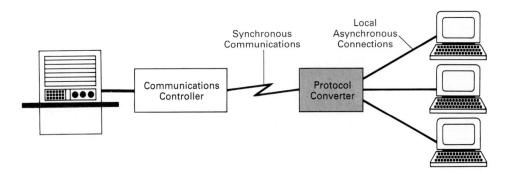

Figure 25.3 Using a concentrator/protocol convertor

In most applications, multiple 3270 terminals are attached to a control unit that functions as a cluster controller. The control unit can be connected directly to a host computer's I/O channel, or synchronous modems can be used to connect a control unit at a remote location to the host computer's communications controller using a communication line. Terminal models are also available with integral control units when a single terminal is required at a given location. These options are shown in Fig. 25.4.

In Chapter 29 we discuss add-on circuit boards that allow personal computers to emulate 3270 terminals. One such board is a communications adapter that allows a personal computer to plug into a 3270 control unit. Another type of communications adapter contains an integral synchronous modem that allows the personal computer to emulate a 3270 cluster controller directly and to communicate directly with the host computer's communications controller over a communication line.

THE 3270 TERMINAL SCREEN
When referring to the 3270 terminal screen, we usually refer to display positions in terms of *rows* and *columns*. Several screen sizes are supported by the 3270 family of terminals, and both monochrome and color display capabilities are provided. The following are the most popular display screen sizes:

- 24-row by 80-column screen
- 32-row by 80-column screen
- 43-row by 80-column screen
- 27-row by 132-column screen

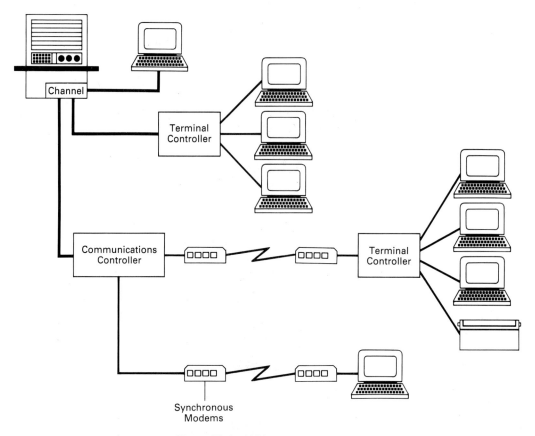

Figure 25.4   3270 terminal connection options

3270 TERMINAL SCREEN FIELDS

Information is displayed on the 3270 terminal screen in various *fields*. Terminal screen fields are generally of the following two types:

- **Literal fields.** This type of field has a predefined value and is generally written to the screen as part of a display that provides information to the terminal operator.
- **Variable fields.** This type of field (sometimes called a *data field*) is defined without a specific value and is often used to contain data entered by the terminal operator.

3270 FIELD ATTRIBUTES

Each field on the terminal screen begins with a single byte called an attribute byte. The attribute byte occupies a screen position but is not displayed on the screen. It describes the field's physical characteristics, such as the type of data the field can contain, the brightness at which the field should be displayed, whether the field should blink, and so on. Box 25.2 describes the various attributes that a field can have.

THE 3270   The keyboards of 3270-type terminals vary in layout
KEYBOARD   from one model to another. However, they all have
                      keys similar to those shown in Fig. 25.5. The keys
on any 3270 keyboard can be divided into the following three categories:

- **Data Character Keys.** These include the keys for letters, numbers, and special characters. They are similar to the corresponding keys on a typewriter keyboard and are used to enter data into fields on the 3270 screen.

- **Cursor Movement Keys.** These include the up, down, left, and right arrow keys, and the various tab keys. They move the display cursor from place to place on the screen and determine where data is entered on the screen.

- **Attention Keys.** These include ENTER, CLEAR, Program Attention (PA), and Program Function (PF) keys. They cause data to be transmitted from the screen buffer to the host computer.

BOX 25.2   3270 field attributes

The following attributes are supported by all terminals of the 3270 variety:

- **Alphanumeric/Numeric.** This attribute determines the types of characters a terminal operator can enter into a variable field. For a *numeric* field, an operator can enter only the characters 0 through 9, the period (.), and the hyphen (-). For an *alphanumeric* field, the operator can enter any characters.

- **Skip/Noskip.** The 3270 keyboard has keys that cause the display cursor to move backward and forward from one field to another. The *skip* attribute causes the cursor to skip over a field when the cursor is moved from the field preceding or following this one in sequence. The *noskip* attribute causes the cursor to stop at the field. Literal fields, containing data that is simply displayed for the operator, are normally given the *skip* attribute; variable fields, into which the operator is to enter data, are normally given the *noskip* attribute.

(Continued)

BOX 25.2 *(Continued)*

- **Modify/Nomodify Data Tag.** This attribute sets the *modify data tag* (MDT) on, causing the contents of a variable field to be transmitted to the host computer regardless of whether the terminal operator modified the field. If the *no modify data tag* option is chosen, the MDT is not set unless the terminal operator modifies the field. This option is useful in minimizing the amount of data transmitted each time an attention key is pressed.

  Detectable/Nondetectable. This attribute determines whether a field is detectable by a light pen (provided that the terminal supports the light-pen feature).

- **Protected/Nonprotected.** This attribute determines whether a terminal operator is allowed to enter information into a field. Literal fields generally are given the *protected* attribute since they are not ordinarily modified. Variable fields are normally given the *unprotected* attribute, since the operator is usually expected to key information into variable fields.

- **Display/Bright/Dark.** This attribute determines the visual characteristics of a field. *Display* causes the field to be displayed at normal intensity. *Bright* causes the field to be displayed at a brighter intensity. A field that has the *dark* attribute occupies screen positions, and its data is stored in the screen buffer, but the data is not displayed on the screen.

- **Delimit/Nodelimit.** This attribute determines whether the operator will be prevented from keying past the end of the field.

The following additional attributes are generally supported by color terminals only:

- **Blink/Noblink.** A field that has the *blink* attribute flashes on and off at a constant rate.

- **Reverse Video/Normal Video.** A field displayed in *normal video* is represented as illuminated characters against a dark background. A field displayed in *reverse video* is represented as dark characters against an illuminated background.

- **Underscore/Nounderscore.** A field that has the *underscore* attribute is written on the screen with underscores under all the characters in the field.

- **Blue/Red/Pink/Green/Turquoise/Yellow/White/No Color.** This attribute determines the field's color.

Figure 25.5 Typical 3270 keyboard layout

3270 TERMINAL I/O OPERATIONS   As mentioned earlier, the 3270 terminal hardware supports a screen buffer that can store an entire screen of data within the terminal. The cursor control and data character keys allow the terminal operator to enter data into the screen buffer, and modify it as required, without causing the data to be transmitted to the host computer. When finished entering data and possibly editing it for correctness, the operator presses one of the attention keys. This sends to the host computer, in a single transmission frame, selected fields from the screen buffer. Transmission takes place using a synchronous data link protocol. Both the binary-synchronous and the SNA SDLC protocols are supported by various terminal models (see Chapter 23).

THE 3270 WRITE CONTROL CHARACTER   When the 3270 screen is transmitted to the terminal from the host computer, a single byte, called the *write control character* (WCC), accompanies the screen. The WCC provides the 3270 control unit with information about the functions it is to perform as it displays the information on the screen. The control unit (cluster controller) to which one or more 3270 terminals are attached can also control a printer device. The WCC controls three display functions and three print functions. These are described in Box 25.3.

SPECIALIZED TERMINALS   Most computer peripherals can be taken out of the computer room and attached to a communication line. With the addition of a control console, they can make up an offline data preparation terminal, or with a cluster of manual-input devices, they can form a data-collection system. Tape cartridges or small diskette devices can be added. Logic circuitry and memory can be added in varying quantities to form various types of *intelligent terminals*. Microprogramming can

BOX 25.3   3270 WCC functions

WCC Display Functions

- **Alarm/Noalarm.** This WCC function controls whether the terminal's audible alarm is sounded (if this feature is installed in the terminal) as the information is displayed on the screen.

- **Lock/Unlock.** This WCC function controls whether the keyboard will be unlocked automatically after data is transmitted to the terminal. Normally, the keyboard is locked by the 3270 hardware when the operator transmits data from the terminal and is unlocked when the system displays the next screen. If LOCK is specified, the keyboard does not unlock after the data is transmitted.

- **Reset/Noreset MDT.** This WCC function determines whether the modify data tags (MDTs) for each field are reset for each field on the screen.

WCC Print Functions

- **Start Printer.** This WCC function causes the printer device on the control unit to be started.

- **Start New Line.** This WCC function causes the printer to advance the paper to the next line.

- **Set Printer Line Length.** This WCC function is used to set the logical page length of the printer device.

be used or a stored-program minicomputer or microprocessor. The endless variations on these terminal possibilities are further proliferated by the fact that the components can be supplied from many hundreds of peripheral equipment manufacturers. The units are often built in a modular fashion so that, as with a hi-fi system, a variety of different devices may be added. The user's choice can be complex.

ONLINE OR OFF-LINE OPERATION   The information, whether from automatic devices or from manually operated keyboards, can be transmitted immediately to the computer or it can be stored on some medium for transmission at a later moment. The preparation of data, in other words, can be *online* or *offline*. Readings of instruments, for example, can be transcribed onto a magnetic medium and the data later transmitted to the computer. Similarly, data collected from manually operated devices can be stored on a diskette. In this case, the diskette device is the terminal. The output

BOX 25.4   Specialized terminals

- Bank teller terminals
- Supermarket bar code readers and checkout stations
- Fast-food computerized cash register terminals
- Consumer check verification terminals
- Consumer airline ticketing terminals
- Stock quote terminals that read radio data broadcasts
- Factory floor data collection terminals
- Rapid-transit automatic ticketing terminals
- Credit-card verification terminals
- Police radio terminals for car license verification
- Radio terminals supporting field engineering personnel

can also make use of an interim medium, such as magnetic tape, or it can directly control the environment in question. Very often it is necessary to make a printed copy of the computer output for later analysis. In this case, part of the terminal equipment may be a printer of some kind.

Many types of specialized terminals are today used for various applications. In many cases, these specialized terminals are operated by the general public. A few of these specialized terminal types are listed in Box 25.4.

In Chapter 26 we discuss the equipment used at each end of a communication line that allows data processing equipment to transmit data over the line.

26   LINE TERMINATION
         EQUIPMENT

We have now seen that the signal we send down a communication line can travel to its destination by a wide variety of possible means. When it disappears into our wall plaster on its telephone or telegraph wires we are not necessarily sure how it is going to travel. It may go in solitude on a wire circuit, or it may be huddled with hundreds of other signals on coaxial cable or microwave. It may race 25,000 miles into space to be beamed back by a satellite. When a terminal screen flashes back a response after a pause of a second or so, its operator does not know how the data was transmitted.

Whatever way the signal has traveled, though, for a telephone trunk the curve of attenuation against frequency is approximately that in Fig. 26.1. Telephone channels are engineered to this specification whether they are satellite channels or open-wire pairs singing in the wind between poles. It is therefore into this frequency range that in today's data transmission environment we must fit our signals if we are going to use a standard telephone channel for data transmission.

In this chapter we explore the different types of *line termination equipment* that can be used for data transmission. As we have already discussed, the most common form of device that is used at each end of a communication channel is a *modem*. It is the primary function of a *modem* to convert a binary data signal into a set of frequencies that fit into the transmission space shown in Fig. 26.1. Before we discuss modems, let us review how we might transmit digital signals on telephone lines without using modems.

**DATA
TRANSMISSION ON
LOCAL LOOPS**

A telephone local loop, or any channel on which frequency-division multiplexing is not used, has properties different from those in the diagram. Figure 26.2 shows the characteristics of a typical local loop. It can transmit higher frequencies or a higher bit rate. As we saw in Chapter

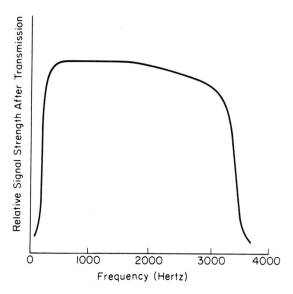

Figure 26.1   Telephone trunk circuit characteristics

16, AT&T often transmits 56,000 bps without modems on local telephone loops to provide the high-speed Dataphone Digital Service. As we indicated in Chapter 6, to achieve this speed the loading coils, if they are present, must be bypassed. Most local loops today do not have loading coils.

BASEBAND   As we have seen, the typical output of a data pro-
SIGNALING   cessing machine consists of dc signals in the form of
                    a set of rectangular pulses as shown in Fig. 26.3.
Such pulses cannot be sent down a telephone trunk circuit in their original, or baseband, form. They must first be converted to fit as efficiently as possible into the transmission space of the standard telephone channel.

However, the dc pulses of a data processing machine can be sent down the *local loops* in baseband form. However, as we saw in Chapter 6, if they are transmitted too fast, they become excessively distorted—much more so on a loaded than on an unloaded loop. On a loaded loop, a baseband signal of 300 bps can be sent several miles without modems. On an unloaded loop a signal of 56,000 bps can be sent several miles, as is done with DDS. As we saw in Chapter 13, if the loading coils are replaced with regenerative bit repeaters, twisted-pair wires can handle a bit rate of several million bits per second, as is done with the ubiquitous T1 and T2 carriers.

Usually today, line termination equipment is designed not only for local loop transmission but for transmission to anywhere on the telephone network. Therefore, the signal must be tailored to fit within the characteristics of the

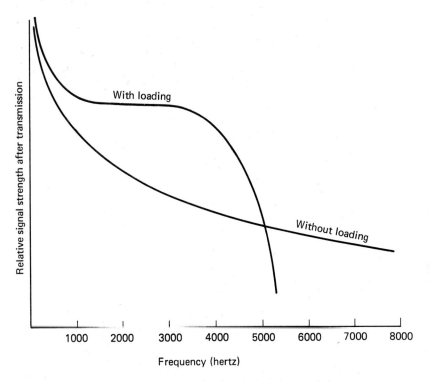

Figure 26.2   Local loop transmission characteristics

standard telephone channel. When this is done, the transmission is generally limited to a bit rate of 9600 bps or less. As we have already pointed out, this limitation makes clear the need for, and indicates the potential of, public data networks, possibly employing digital PCM trunks.

The need for modems can be eliminated in some cases by using private telecommunications channels rather than those supplied by a common carrier.

IN-PLANT AND Many computer users have privately owned lines on
OUT-PLANT LINES their own premises linking terminals to computers.
The term *in-plant* is used for these lines to distinguish them from the *out-plant* lines that are supplied by common carriers. *Out-plant* refers to common carrier lines connecting separate premises. *In-plant* refers to lines or systems within one building or complex of buildings. In-plant lines are most commonly copper wire pairs, but they can be coaxial cables in some cases. They may be installed by an organization's own engineers or by a telecommunications company.

In many cases, private lines can be specifically engineered to a company's own specifications so that they require no modems for data transmission. They

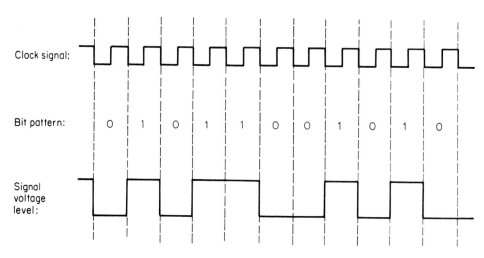

Figure 26.3   Digital signal

may use baseband digital signaling at speeds ranging from telegraph speeds to several million bits per second. For high speeds, digital repeaters are used every 1000 feet or so. In-plant lines can be used to handle ordinary data communication, in which point-to-point, multipoint, or loop data links are constructed using the private facilities. But more often in today's data communication environment, they are used to construct *local area networks* (LANs), in which very high speed transmission facilities connect data processing machines in a more flexible way to create *resource sharing networks*. Local area networks are the subject of Chapter 40.

FULL-DUPLEX VERSUS HALF-DUPLEX   Over a given physical line, the line termination equipment must be designed so that it can transmit either in both directions at once—full duplex transmission—or else in either direction but not both at the same time—half-duplex. Simplex transmission is also possible, but this is rarely used in data transmission, as there is no easy way of controlling the flow of data or requesting retransmission after errors or failures. All transmission lines using four wires are capable of full-duplex transmission, although they are sometimes used in half-duplex mode. Many private, leased lines are four-wire circuits. Some lines using two wires can operate only in a half-duplex mode.

A terminal or modem will work somewhat differently depending on which of the foregoing possibilities is used. Where full-duplex transmission is employed, it can be used either to send data streams in both directions at the same time or to send data in one direction and control signals in the other. The control signals might govern the flow of data and might also be used for error control. Data at the transmitting end might be held until the receiving end indicates that they had been received correctly. Control signals might be used to ensure that no two terminals transmit at once on a line with many terminals and might organize the sequence of transmission.

As we discussed in Chapter 17, simultaneous transmission in both directions can be obtained on a two-wire line by using two separate frequency bands. One band is used for transmission in one direction and the other band for transmission in the opposite direction. By keeping the signals strictly separated in frequency, they can be prevented from interfering with each another. Many full-duplex modems provide a full-speed data channel in each direction. Generally, only equipment that uses a sophisticated bit-oriented data link protocol is capable of fully using such full-duplex line termination equipment.

FACTORS GOVERNING TRANSMISSION MODE

As we saw in Chapter 17, there are many factors, singly or in combination, that govern the mode of transmission that can be used over a communication link. Simply because a communication line is capable of full-duplex operation does not mean that full-duplex transmission will take place. The following is a summary of the factors that control transmission mode. All of these factors must be designed for full-duplex operation if the full-duplex transmission mode is to be used.

- Engineering of the communication channel
- Design of the modem
- Characteristics of the communicating devices
- Capabilities of the data link protocol

FUNCTIONS OF LINE TERMINATION EQUIPMENT

The equipment at the ends of a communication line carries out several functions. In general, this equipment could perform all of the functions listed in Box 26.1. Often, however, the modem or other device carries out only the first four functions. Dialing the call may be done by the terminal or computer operator. The protection of the line may be done by an external device, such as the *data access arrangement* (DAA) that was required at one time to connect a device to the telephone network. The error detection is sometimes done by the software that runs above the physical level, in the data link layer. And automatic diagnosis of failures is too often not done at all. The most economical and efficient approach is for all of these functions to be carried out in an integrated fashion "under the cover" of the terminal or other data processing device.

BOX 26.1   Modem functions

- Handling the initial setting up of the connection; this procedure is sometimes called *handshaking*
- Transmitting and receiving digital bit streams over the physical circuit to which it is attached
- Converting digital signals into a form suitable for transmission over the physical circuit
- Converting signals back again after transmission
- Protecting the transmission facilities from harmful signals or voltages
- Possibly initiating calls by automatically sending dialing pulses and accepting responses to them
- Possibly detecting some forms of data errors and taking action to correct them
- Possibly detecting transmission or equipment failures and diagnosing where they occurred so that action can be taken

CHOOSING A MODEM

There is a wide variety of different types of modems. They vary in many ways, but there are four main criteria that can be used for choosing between them. These criteria are:

- The speed of transmission that is required
- The maximum cost
- The number of transmission errors that can be tolerated
- The turnaround time of the line that is used

Obviously, the needs of the application will dictate the relative importance of each of these criteria.

MODEM STANDARDS

It is desirable that independent organizations be able to design and manufacture modems and data processing equipment that have modems integrated into them. To permit this, various standards exist for modem design that permit modems of different manufacturers to communicate with one another. It is desirable that modem standards be internationally accepted, and they should permit international transmission. The CCITT has published a series of V-series recommendations for modems. These are listed in Box 26.2. Box 26.3 describes the signaling system documented in *CCITT Recommendation V.27* for a 4800-bps modem. Similar standards are specified for modems operating at other bit rates. As long as a modem manufacturer conforms to the standards in designing a modem, modems of different manufacturers will be able to communicate with one another over communication channels.

BOX 26.2   CCITT V-series recommendations

- **Recommendation V.1:** equivalence between binary notation symbols and the significant conditions of a two-condition code
- **Recommendation V.3:** international Alphabet No. 5
- **Recommendation V.4:** general structure of signals of International Alphabet No. 5 code for data transmission over the public telephone network
- **Recommendation V.5:** standardization of data signaling rates for synchronous data transmission in the general switched telephone network
- **Recommendation V.6:** standardization of data signaling rates for synchronous data transmission over leased telephone-type circuits
- **Recommendation V.10:** electrical characteristics for unbalanced double-current interchange circuits for general use with integrated-circuit equipment in the field of data communication
- **Recommendation V.11:** electrical characteristics for balanced double-current interchange circuits for general use with integrated-circuit equipment in the field of data communication
- **Recommendation V.21:** 300-bps duplex modem standardized for use in the general switched telephone network
- **Recommendation V.22:** 1200-bps duplex modem standardized for use on the general switched telephone network and on leased circuits
- **Recommendation V.23:** 600/1200-baud modem standardized for use in the general switched telephone network
- **Recommendation V.24:** list of definitions for interchange circuits between data terminal equipment and data circuit-terminating equipment
- **Recommendation V.25:** automatic calling and/or answering equipment on the general switched telephone network, including disabling of echo suppressors on manually established calls
- **Recommendation V.26:** 2400-bps modem standardized for use on four-wire leased circuits

(Continued)

BOX 26.2   *(Continued)*

- **Recommendation V.26bis:** 2400/1200-bps modem standardized for use in the general switched telephone network
- **Recommendation V.27:** 4800-bps modem with manual equalizer standardized for use on leased telephone-type circuits
- **Recommendation V.27bis:** 4800/2400-bps modem with automatic equalizer standardized for use on leased telephone-type circuits
- **Recommendation V.27ter:** 4800/2400-bps modem standardized for use in the general switched telephone network
- **Recommendation V.28:** electrical characteristics for unbalanced double-current interchange circuits
- **Recommendation V.29:** 9600-bps modem standardized for use on point-to-point leased telephone-type circuits
- **Recommendation V.31:** electrical characteristics for single-current interchange circuits controlled by contact closure
- **Recommendation V.35:** data transmission at 48 kbps using 60–108-kHz group band circuits
- **Recommendation V.36:** modems for synchronous transmission using 60–108-kHz group band circuits
- **Recommendation V.54:** loop test devices for modems

An important form of standard, especially in the United States, are those ad hoc standards that have arisen simply because certain types of modems have become very widely used. Standards for these modems are important at two levels:

- The signals that are used for transmitting data over the physical circuit
- The command set that is used by the data processing machine to control the functions of the modem

Signaling System

Two of the most commonly used modem signaling system standards have been set by AT&T. Almost all of the modems used today with personal computers in North America support data transmission at 300 bps using the form of signaling employed by the AT&T Model 103 data set, an obsolete modem that is little used today. The signaling system used by the Model 103 modem is discussed later in this chapter when we show an example of modem operation.

BOX 26.3 CCITT Recommendation V.27

CCITT Recommendation V.27 documents a signaling system that can be used to implement a 4800-bps modem. Many of the modems that are available today for transmission at this bit rate over telephone lines follow this standard. Modems following this standard are intended for synchronous transmission on leased telephone circuits. They are capable of operating in either full-duplex or half-duplex mode. When full-duplex is chosen, the modem can optionally support a backward channel of up to 75 bps that can transmit simultaneously with the forward transmission of 4800 bps. The directions of these channels can be simultaneously reversed.

The 4800-bps signal modulates a single carrier of 1800 ± 1 Hz. It is assumed that there may be a frequency drift up to ±6 Hz in the transmission; hence the receiver must be able to accept errors of ±7 Hz in the received frequencies. The modulation rate is 1600 baud (i.e., 1600 separate line condition changes per second). The data is divided into groups of three consecutive bits (tribits). Each tribit is transmitted as one change in line condition, thus giving 4800 bps. The bit rate, and hence the modulation rate, are held constant to ±0.01 percent.

Each tribit is encoded as a phase change relative to the phase of the immediately preceding tribit. The encoding is done according to the following scheme:

Tribit	Phase Change (degrees)
001	0
000	45
010	90
011	135
111	180
110	225
100	270
101	315

The receiving modem detects these phase changes and converts them into the appropriate groups of 3 bits. Notice that a data stream 0 0 1 0 0 1 0 0 1. . . could result in no phase changes, and this could result in loss of synchronization between the transmitting and

(Continued)

BOX 26.3 *(Continued)*

receiving modems. Certain other repetitive bit patterns might also cause problems. To avoid the transmission of repetitive bit patterns, the bit stream is scrambled before modulation and unscrambled by the receiving modem. The procedure for scrambling is specified as part of the CCITT recommendation.

The reverse channel of up to 75 bps is an optional feature of the modem. The reverse channel is organized in the same manner as standard voice-frequency telegraph channel that uses frequency-shift modulation: 390 Hz represents a one bit or a *mark* condition; 450 Hz represents a zero bit or a *space* condition. The use for this reverse channel is to permit control signals, especially error control signals, to be sent simultaneously with the transmission of data in the opposite direction.

Another obsolete AT&T modem, the Model 212A data set, supported data transmission at either 300 bps using the Model 103 signaling system, or at 1200 bps using a different signaling system. Modems that are compatible with the two signaling systems of the Model 212A modem are very commonly used. A third type of modem is also commonly used for data transmission at 2400 bps. The signaling system most often used by the manufacturers of 2400-bps modems is that described by the CCITT in the form of *Recommendation V.26bis*. Most of these 2400-bps modems also support data transmission at 300 and 1200 bps using the two AT&T 212A signaling systems.

Command Set

A modem manufacturer can employ any desired command set that the data processing equipment must employ in controlling the modem. Many manufacturers of sophisticated modems use their own command sets to control the unique features of their modems. Users of these modems must employ custom software that is able to employ these command sets. Often the modem manufacturer supplies the necessary software. However, most manufacturers of standard modems that communicate at 300, 1200, or 2400 bps, using the signaling systems discussed above, use the command set that was first introduced by the Hayes Corporation for its 300-bps *Smartmodem*. This command set, generally referred to as the *AT* command set, is now a standard, simply because it has become so widely used. The advantage of using a modem that employs the Hayes AT command set is that almost all general-purpose data communication software that is available for personal computers can work with any modem that employs the Hayes AT command set.

By using modems that use one of the three signaling systems discussed above and the Hayes AT command set, the personal computer user can be assured of compatibility with generally available data communication software and with the modems used by other personal computer users and by the major suppliers of information services. These issues are discussed further in Chapters 29, 33, and 36.

MODEM OPERATION

Some data transmission links need a human operator at each end of the link to establish the connection. Many machines, however, are capable of *unattended operation,* and so, when called, the modem must place its associated data-handling machine into operation without human intervention.

Figure 26.4 illustrates the opening sequence of events on a typical system that uses asynchronous transmission. The frequencies quoted in this diagram are those of AT&T's Model 103A signaling system, which uses frequency-shift keying on two separate frequency bands, one for each direction of transmission. In this way full-duplex transmission can be achieved over switched voice lines, but at the relatively low speed of 300 bps. These modems transmit in a binary fashion sending either a mark or a space frequency ("1" or "0"). These frequencies are audible, and if the telephone handset is picked up, the user will hear the whistle of data rushing along the line.

The first step in establishing the connection is to dial the distant machine. This might be done automatically by the modem (if the modem implements an *autodial* feature) or manually by the user. Most modems that use the Hayes AT command set support an autodial feature. When the connection is made, the answering modem must be placed into its data mode so that it is ready to receive and transmit data. Depending on the modem used at the opposite end, this might be done automatically (if the modem implements an *autoanswer* feature) or it might be done manually by the user at the other end. Again, most modems that support the Hayes AT command set are capable of answering a data call.

A short time after the establishment of data mode, the answering modem places a mark frequency on the line. If the originating call was dialed manually, this will be heard as a high-pitched whistle. When the originating modem is placed into the data mode, the tone may no longer be heard because the telephone has probably been disconnected from the circuit to prevent the handset from causing data errors. If the call was originated automatically by the modem, the modem will place itself into the data mode. A short pause before answering is used to avoid interfering with certain tone-signaling actions that are used on the telephone network. A similar pause occurs after the originating modem is placed in *data* mode, and it then places its mark frequency on the line (a different frequency because these modems are designed for full-duplex operation).

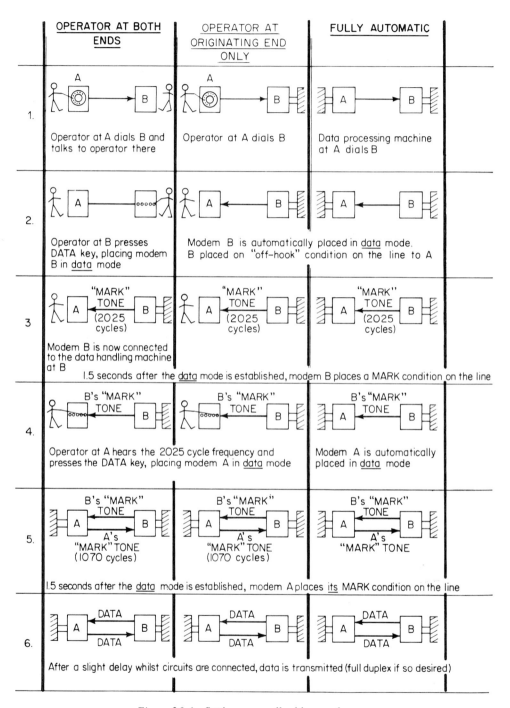

OPERATOR AT BOTH ENDS	OPERATOR AT ORIGINATING END ONLY	FULLY AUTOMATIC
1. Operator at A dials B and talks to operator there	Operator at A dials B	Data processing machine at A dials B
2. Operator at B presses DATA key, placing modem B in *data* mode	Modem B is automatically placed in *data* mode. B placed on "off-hook" condition on the line to A	
3. Modem B is now connected to the data handling machine at B	1.5 seconds after the *data* mode is established, modem B places a MARK condition on the line	
4. Operator at A hears the 2025 cycle frequency and presses the DATA key, placing modem A in *data* mode		Modem A is automatically placed in *data* mode
5.	1.5 seconds after the *data* mode is established, modem A places *its* MARK condition on the line	
6.	After a slight delay whilst circuits are connected, data is transmitted (full duplex if so desired)	

Figure 26.4 Setting up a call with a modem

Both modems, once they receive the other set's mark frequency, then place their transmitting circuits under the control of the data-handling machine. Thus the connection for full-duplex data transmission has been set up.

PARALLEL TRANSMISSION   Most modems are designed to transmit information serially, character by character and bit by bit. Some modems, however, send a character at a time, transmitting the bits of each character in parallel. Parallel transmission is usually employed by inexpensive terminals and modems, often for data collection systems in which many terminals are needed and the data flow is in one direction.

The cheapest form of data terminal is a simple pushbutton telephone. Each button pressed transmits a pair of frequencies that travel well within the telephone bandwidth. A computer receiving the data may respond to the telephone user either with tones or with voice answerback. *CCITT Recommendation V.30* documents a system that can be used for parallel transmission over the public telephone network.

Telephone networks use signaling schemes that employ frequencies inside the telephone bandwidth, and these frequencies must be avoided by multifrequency transmission devices. The frequencies used by Touchtone telephones are suitable for North America, but unfortunately telephone networks in many other countries use different signaling frequencies. The *CCITT Recommendation V.24* avoids all these different national signaling frequencies with the result that a closely bunched group of 12 frequencies is used, as shown in Fig. 26.5. These frequencies exclude the use of a normal pushbutton telephone set.

The 12 frequencies are grouped as follows:

Group A:	920 Hz	1000 Hz	1080 Hz	1160 Hz
Group B:	1320 Hz	1400 Hz	1480 Hz	1560 Hz
Group C:	1720 Hz	1800 Hz	1880 Hz	1960 Hz

It is desirable to be able to transmit either 16, 64, or 256 different character combinations using these 12 frequencies. For a 16-character system, groups A and B are used; for a 64-character system, all three groups are used. For a 256-character system, each character is split into two half-characters, and two groups of frequencies are used.

A backward channel can be used in conjunction with the above frequencies, at 420 Hz. This can be used for either audible signals or amplitude-modulated digital signals at a rate up to 5 baud. The CCITT recommends that speeds up to 40 characters per second be used with the 16-character system if two of the frequencies are used for a separate binary timing channel. If there is no such

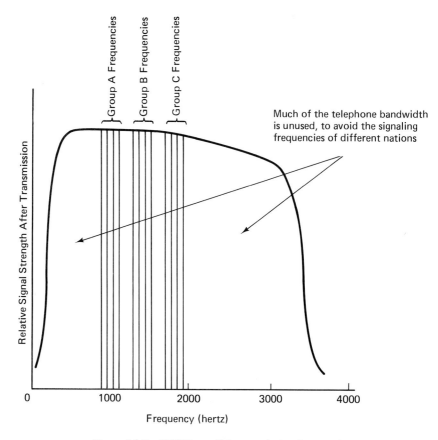

Figure 26.5   CCITT parallel transmission frequencies

timing channel, an intercharacter rest condition is recommended, with a speed up to 20 characters per second. Speeds up to 20 characters per second are recommended with the 64- and 256-character systems.

ACOUSTICAL   Where audible tones are used, there is no need to
COUPLING   have a direct wire connection to the communication
                        line. Instead, the modem can use a technique called
acoustical coupling. With a typical acoustical coupler, the telephone handset fits into a special cradle. The device converts data signals into audible tones that are picked up by the microphone of a telephone handset. The earpiece of the telephone instrument at the other end sends these same tones into another acoustical coupler, where the signals are converted back into data signals.

An advantage of acoustical coupling is that it allows data transmission to take place anywhere there is a standard telephone. Acoustical couplers were once very widely used, but have fallen out of favor. This method of connection to the public telephone network is somewhat less efficient than a direct wire connection. It is also more expensive and can be used only for transmitting between relatively slow machines. A very commonly used speed with acoustical couplers is 300 bps. Some more expensive models allow transmission at 1200 bps. Speeds higher than 1200 bps are not generally used with acoustical couplers. Today, because of the widespread use of the standard modular telephone jack, it is much easier than in days past to connect a modem directly to the telephone network. Acoustical couplers are most often used today where direct connection to the public telephone network may be difficult, such as where data calls must be placed using public call boxes.

Although there is no electrical connection to the telephone lines, it is still possible for acoustically coupled machines to interfere with the public network's signaling, as with a directly coupled device. Also, severe crosstalk can be caused on a multiplexed link by the transmission of a continuous frequency, as with a repetitive data pattern. It is therefore desirable that the coupling device randomize the signal before it is sent, although not all devices do so. The CCITT recommends that acoustical couplers not be used for permanent installations

HIGH-SPEED LINE TERMINATION

As we saw in Part II, communication lines with a bandwidth much greater than that of a telephone line can be leased. For example, the bandwidth of a *12-channel group* can be leased, giving a bandwidth of 48 kHz instead of the 4 kHz of a standard telephone channel. Channels of even higher bandwidths are routinely used for data transmission. Modems are available from various manufacturers for wideband transmission. *CCITT Recommendation V.35* is for a 48,000-bps modem operating in the band 60 to 104 kHz.

With the spread of digital circuits, it is more common today for high-data-rate links to operate over digital lines and hence not need modems. T1 links are very widely used today, both by common carriers for the transmission of telephone signals and by individual users for data transmission. The approach of some common carriers is to provide their customers with an *interface unit* that can contain different facilities depending on the nature of the transmission link. Sometimes it contains a modem; sometimes it contains a digital baseband signaling unit. The customer does not necessarily need to know what it contains. The customer needs to know merely how it interfaces with the data processing equipment.

For wideband transmission, AT&T provides devices called *data stations,* which contain either modems or digital line drivers. These devices can operate over various types of local and toll facilities, including analog, T1, and T2 digital carriers. They are routinely used to transmit data synchronously at rates from 19.2 to 460.8 kbps. A commonly used data station provides a full-duplex

Box 26.4 AT&T DDS data service unit functions

- Samples the data it receives synchronously
- Recovers the timing of the bits
- Transmits the bits in an appropriately coded way
- Generates and recognizes control signals
- Formats the data and control signals as required; any combination of bits can be sent
- Protects the telephone network from harmful voltages and signals
- Provides a remote loopback facility so that end-to-end testing can be performed on the link
- Equalizes the line to improve its transmission properties

data circuit plus a voice channel for coordination purposes. The equipment can permit a customer to use either wideband data transmission or multiple voice circuits, and to switch between these at the user's discretion. When such equipment transmits high-speed data in analog form over local telephone loops, special conditioning of the local loops is sometimes used. This conditioning employs wideband amplifiers with equalizers to provide flat response over the required bandwidth.

DIGITAL LINE TERMINATION
As we discussed in Chapter 16, the AT&T Dataphone Digital Service (DDS) provides a digital channel and hence requires no modems. The digital channel operates at speeds of 2400, 4800, 9600, or 56,000 bps using either half-duplex or full-duplex transmission. Instead of a modem, AT&T provides the user with a device called a *data service unit*. The data processing machine passes data to, and receives data from, this device. Some of the functions that the data service unit performs are listed in Box 26.4.

The data service unit is designed so that the user's terminal or data processing equipment connects to it with the same plug that would be used with a modem on an analog line. For transmission at 2400, 4800, or 9600 bps, this is the 25-pin plug that conforms to the *EIA RS-232-C* interface standard. The data service unit used for 56,000-bps transmission uses the 34-pin plug conforming to *CCITT Recommendation V.35* for wideband modems.

27 LINE CONTROL EQUIPMENT

When I was writing the first edition of the book *Introduction to Teleprocessing,* I happened to be at a conference in Europe. At that conference I needed to demonstrate some points by accessing a computer in the United States. I used a simple asynchronous terminal and was able to get a dial-up connection to a computer in the United States with no difficulty. At the end of half an hour's time, I looked at the printout and estimated that no more than 3000 characters had been transmitted in total, in both directions. This is about typical when a start–stop device is used as a terminal. That voice line was capable of transmitting 4800-bps with a fairly inexpensive modem. So in half an hour, then, it could transmit 8,640,000 bits. In fact, fewer than 21,000 bits were transmitted. We can calculate the efficiency of my use of that line by dividing 21,000 by 8,640,000—about 0.0024. You might say that this was certainly a poor way to use such an expensive facility. The purpose of this chapter is to examine the characteristics of equipment that can be used to optimize the use of expensive communication facilities.

DATA LINK CONNECTIVITY

A single data link is made up of one communication channel and the related equipment necessary for transmitting data over it. There are many ways that data links can be used to interconnect data processing equipment, each providing a different level of line sharing.

SEPARATE PHYSICAL LINKS

Figure 27.1 shows the first way we might implement logical connections between a group of terminals and a mainframe computer. Here we are using a separate physical data link for each terminal. This has the advantage that each terminal

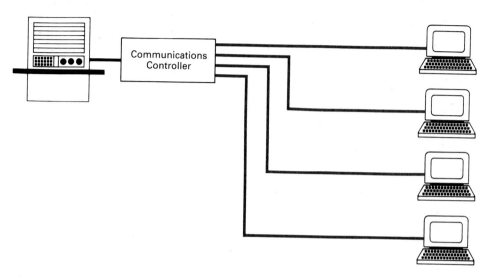

Figure 27.1   Individual point-to-point links

can communicate with the mainframe at any time, but there is no line sharing involved. As we have seen, this is an expensive way to implement the data links, especially when they are long.

MULTIPOINT DATA LINKS

As we discussed in Chapter 17, one method we might use to introduce line sharing is to use a single multipoint data link to connect the terminals to the computer. In Fig. 27.2, each terminal can communicate with the computer as long as only one of the terminals transmits or receives at a time. All DTEs on the data link receive all the messages that are transmitted over it. An addressing scheme must be used to identify the intended recipient of each message, and all the DTEs on a multipoint data link must be intelligent enough to implement the addressing scheme. Also, multipoint data links are not well suited to asynchronous transmission, so the terminals generally should have buffers and be capable of using a synchronous data link protocol, such as binary-synchronous or one of the bit-oriented protocols.

RISKS ASSOCIATED WITH MULTIPOINT DATA LINKS

A major risk involved with multipoint data links is one of degraded response time. If a terminal wants to transmit to the computer, it must wait until no other terminal is using the data link. Only one terminal on the data link can transmit at any given time. Occasionally, and by chance, all the devices may be ready to transmit at once; one

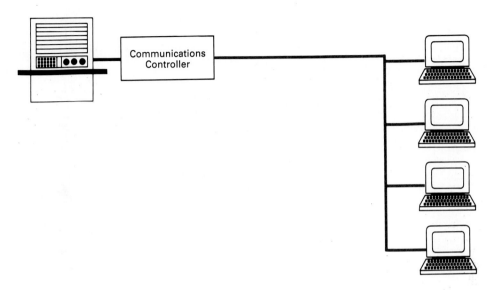

Figure 27.2   Multipoint data link

terminal will have to wait until all the others have finished. The response time, then, will be uneven.

If every terminal has a buffer and uses a synchronous datalink protocol, the wait may never be very long. When the terminals do not have buffers and use asynchronous transmission, the time it takes to send a message depends on the rate at which the operator types it. The risk is therefore much greater when the terminals use an asynchronous protocol. For a realtime system in which a fast response time is necessary, the risk of unbuffered terminals on a multipoint line is generally not worth running.

MULTIPLEXORS   Other methods of line sharing use devices of various types to interconnect data links in a variety of ways. Instead of connecting the terminals to the mainframe using a single multipoint data link, we can use a single high-capacity data link and a multiplexor to provide a separate channel for each terminal. In Fig. 27.3, each terminal has a separate 1200-bps line to the multiplexor. A single 4800-bps data link connects the multiplexor at the terminal's end to another multiplexor at the computer's end. This splits the 4800-bps data link back into the four original 1200-bps channels for input to the computer.

The multiplexor's main job is to combine the data being transmitted over a number of low-bandwidth data links for transmission over one or more channels of higher bandwidth. The net effect here is of a single 1200-bps channel

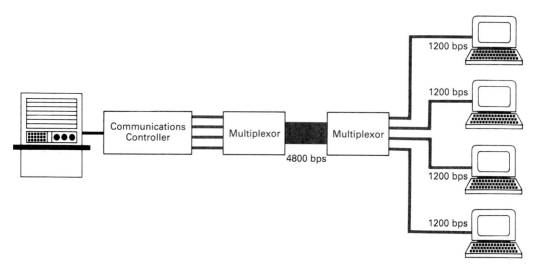

Figure 27.3   Using a multiplexor

between each terminal and the mainframe. But a single 4800-bps data link is used to implement them.

     This is especially advantageous if the high-capacity data link is long, say coast to coast, while the low-capacity links are short, say in the same building. Here we trade the cost of the lines against the cost of the multiplexing equipment. A variety of techniques may be used to implement multiplexors, but they all fall into two general categories—frequency division or time division.

FREQUENCY-DIVISION MULTIPLEXING

Frequency-division multiplexing, shown in Fig. 27.4, is generally used with analog channels. A multiplexor at one end of a group of low-capacity lines combines these lines into a single high-bandwidth channel. It does this by assigning a different range of frequencies to each of the incoming signals. Generally, some of the bandwidth is lost in separating the subchannels. A multiplexor at the other end splits each of these frequency ranges back into the original group of lower-capacity channels.

     When frequency-division multiplexing is used at the location of a terminal or a computer, a device is generally used that performs the functions of a normal modem, but in addition carries out the multiplexing function. The device, instead of using a single carrier, as with ordinary modems, uses several carriers, one for each of the signals that are to be transmitted in parallel. (Sometimes one carrier is used for two signals.)

MULTIPLEX
MODEM
EXAMPLES

A simple frequency-division multiplex modem might be designed to send four independent 150-bps signals over a single voice channel. The four subchannels operate over approximately the following frequency ranges:

- Subchannel 1: 820–990 Hz
- Subchannel 2: 1230–1400 Hz
- Subchannel 3: 1640–1810 Hz
- Subchannel 4: 2050–2220 Hz

These frequencies fit easily into that part of the voice channel best suited for data transmission and they avoid the public telephone system signaling frequencies in North America. It is interesting to note, however, that they would not avoid the signaling frequencies used in Britain and some other countries, so this machine would not be permitted on Britain's public telephone lines.

Frequency-shift keying might be used in each subchannel, with a one bit being represented as a low frequency and a zero bit being represented by a high frequency. Each subchannel would probably be filtered to prevent stray signals from interfering with the four subchannels. The characteristics of the filters and the frequencies used are shown in Fig. 27.5. Notice that a substantial *guard band* between the subchannels is used to prevent interference.

TIME-DIVISION
MULTIPLEXING

With *time-division multiplexing,* the time available is divided up into small slots and each of these is occupied by a piece of one of the signals to be sent. The multiplexing apparatus scans the input in a round-robin fashion. Only one signal occupies the channel at one instant. It is thus quite different from frequency-division multiplexing, in which all of the signals are sent at the same time, but each occupies a different frequency band.

Time-division multiplexing operates in a manner similar to a commutator. Consider the commutator shown in Fig. 27.6. The mechanically driven arm of this device might be used to sample the output of eight instruments. Provided that the values of the voltages from the instruments are not varying too rapidly compared with the rotation time of the arm, the individual inputs can be reconstructed from the composite signal.

Such a device is used in the telemetering. To separate the signals when they are received, a commutator similar to the one shown might be used, but with the input and output reversed. The receiving commutator must be exactly synchronized with the transmitting commutator. The time-division-multiplexing devices we see in telecommunications today are normally electronic and of

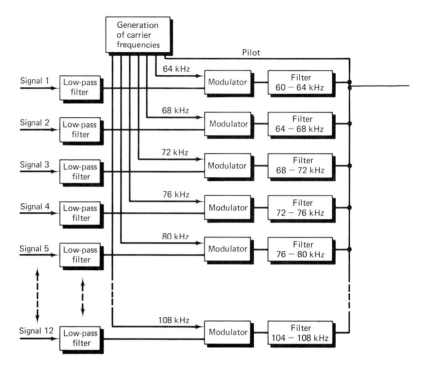

Figure 27.4   Frequency-division multiplexing

much higher speed, but in principle operate in a manner similar to the commutator.

Time-division-multiplexing, shown in Fig. 27.7, is generally used on digital channels. The multiplexor reads each of the incoming low-speed bit streams and interleaves them to form a single high-speed bit stream. Similar equipment at the other end separates the bits from the high-speed bit stream and recreates the original lower-speed ones.

The net effect of either technique is to combine several slow-speed transmissions into a single high-speed transmission. Because of the economies of scale in telecommunications, the high-speed channel is nearly always cheaper than the equivalent number of slower channels.

TIME-DIVISION-MULTIPLEXING EXAMPLE

A relatively simple method can be used to take several low-speed bit streams and combine them into one high-speed bit stream. Figure 27.3 showed a typical arrangement. A group of relatively inexpensive terminals (no buffering, no multipoint logic, asynchronous operation) are each attached to a low-speed line. The low-speed signals are multiplexed together to

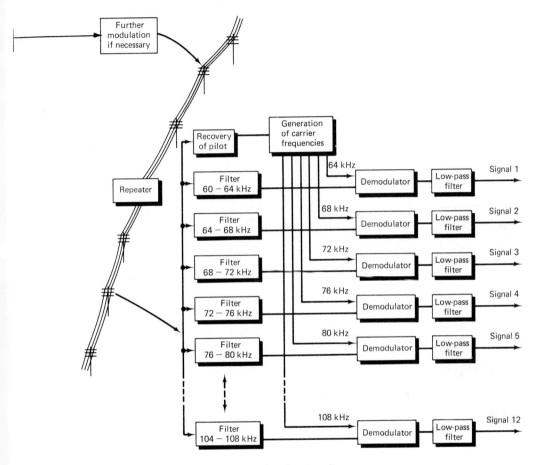

Figure 27.4   (Continued)

travel over a leased voice line to the computer center. The low-speed lines are half-duplex, but the high-speed line is full-duplex, so some of the terminals can be transmitting at the same time as others are receiving. Such a scheme can be used where its overall cost is lower than that of taking low-speed lines directly from the terminals to the computer center.

In Fig. 27.3, the voice line is shown entering a multiplexing device at the computer center, which is identical to the remote one. Low-speed lines then enter the computer system as though they were linked directly to the terminals. An alternative would be to take the high-speed lines directly into the computer, which could then assemble and disassemble the high-speed bit stream.

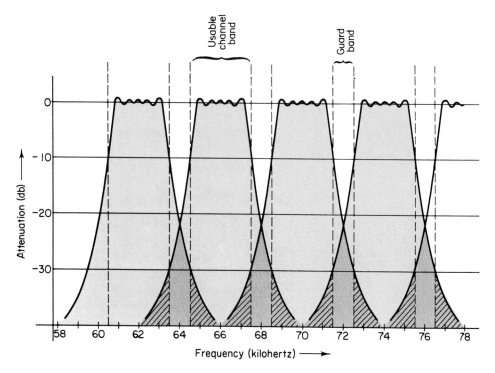

Figure 27.5   Frequency-division multiplexing filter characteristics

MULTIPLEXING WITH MULTIPOINT LINES

Any characters traveling on a group of low-speed lines can be multiplexed into a high-speed bit stream using the multiplexing techniques discussed above. The low-speed lines can therefore take on any configuration that they would have had if the multiplexing device had not been present. In particular, such configurations are often found with multipoint lines. Figure 27.8 illustrates this. It requires a complex calculation to work out the lowest-cost configuration of lines and the optimum location of a multiplexing unit for a network such as that shown in Fig 27.8.

ADVANTAGES OF MULTIPLEXING

The straightforward multiplexing methods we have discussed thus far have a number of advantages over the other means of improving line utilization. Following are a few of them:

● They are relatively inexpensive—certainly more so than the concentration techniques we discuss later in this chapter.

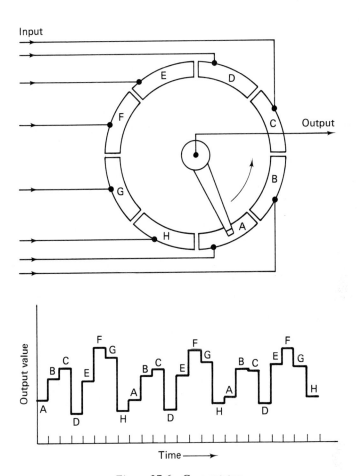

Figure 27.6   Commutator

- They do not affect the programming in any way. The multiplexors are "transparent" to the programs that send and receive data and control signals.

- Being simple, the multiplexing devices generally have a high reliability.

- If it is desired to send a long continuous stream of data on some of the lines, as in remote batch operation, the multiplexors can handle this without interruption of the data stream or interference with other users.

- Multiplexors cause no significant increase in response time.

- The low-speed lines can be connected to the computer center at all times. When permanently connected lines are used, there is no wait to obtain a line as there often is with dial-up public lines or with systems that use a private branch exchange (PBX).

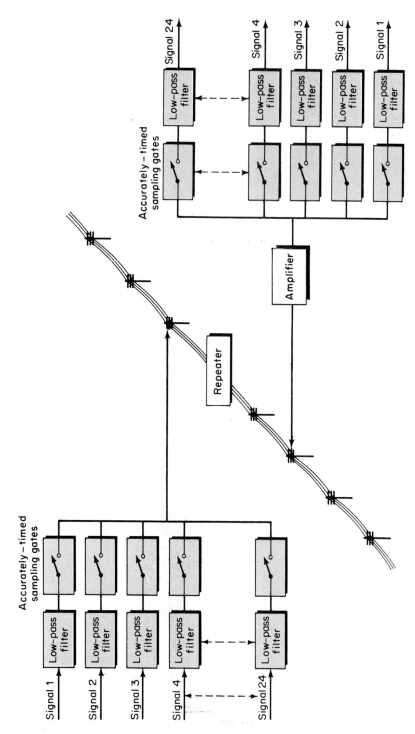

Figure 27.7 Time-division multiplexing of analog signals

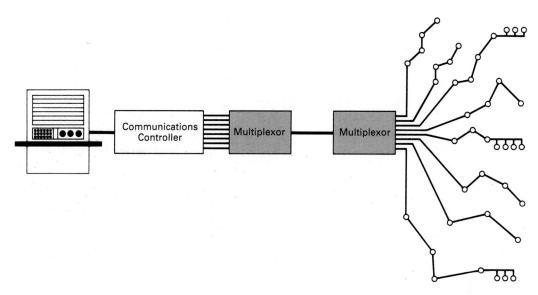

Figure 27.8   Multiplexors and multipoint lines

CONCENTRATORS   With simple multiplexing *all* the terminals can transmit *all* the time, because each has its own dedicated subchannel. In most systems, terminals do not need this capability. When an operator is carrying on a dialog using a terminal, the data flows in bursts, often small compared with the amount of data that would be sent if the line transmitted continuously. Furthermore, when an operator uses a keyboard, the resulting character rate is usually far less than that of the line. An input rate of 3 characters per second would be faster than that of most terminal operators, but this is a fraction of the 300- or 1200-bps rate that is used for many applications.

If the low character rate is taken advantage of, a number of terminals might be handled without the need of a higher-speed line. This can be done with a concentrator. In a concentrator network, we would attach each terminal to a concentrator, as shown in Fig. 27.9. The concentrator is then connected to the main computer, with one or more data links, possibly having the same capacity as those used for the terminals. The concentrator generally has enough intelligence to allow multiple terminals to communicate simultaneously. The concentrator uses buffer storage to store messages for transmission and uses the data link between it and the mainframe more efficiently. All the terminals act as if they have a dedicated circuit to the mainframe. They get acceptable response time as long as the combined transmissions of all the terminals do not overload the links between the concentrator and the mainframe.

Concentration functions are often performed in a cluster controller, which attaches a group of terminals to one or more data links connected to a host

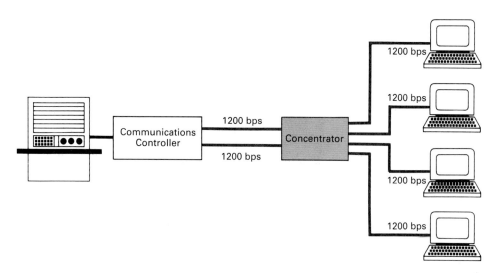

Figure 27.9   Using a concentrator

computer. But concentrators can be used anywhere in a network. In Fig. 27.10, several concentrators, each controlling several terminals, tie into a mid-network concentrator, which, in turn, ties into a host computer's communications controller.

CONCENTRATOR
OPERATION

To perform its function, the concentrator needs to have storage that is flexibly allocated to the different terminals. Storage must be sufficient to absorb the temporary overload that will occur when, fortuitously, all the operators happen to pound away at their keyboards simultaneously and for a while generate data at a higher rate than the line can handle.

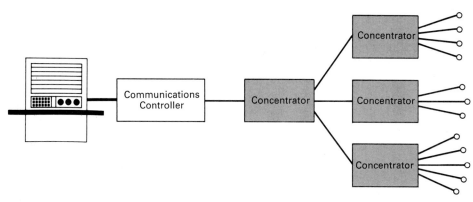

Figure 27.10   A concentrator network

A concentrator can be used to collect the characters arriving from a number of asynchronous terminals and send them onward in synchronous transmission frames. Separate frames are used for each terminal. The characters on the lines connected to terminals are widely scattered, but on the line from the concentrator to the computer they are packed together. It is rather like people driving to a bus station, one person per car, and all getting into a bus. Both the cars and the bus use the same road facilities, but the bus uses the road facilities more efficiently than the individual cars. In effect, this type of concentrator converts a number of transmissions using an inefficient asynchronous data link protocol into a single transmission using a more efficient protocol, such as binary-synchronous or one of the bit-oriented protocols. Systems that use this type of equipment must be able to determine from which terminal a transmission frame comes. Conversely, blocks traveling to the concentrator must indicate to which terminal they are bound.

Half-duplex lines could be used to connect the terminals to the concentrator, but a full-duplex line could be used to connect the concentrator to the computer. Although simultaneous two-way transmission between each individual terminal and the computer might not increase throughput, two-way transmission between the concentrator and computer would increase the total capacity of the system as a whole and might make it possible to increase the number of terminals connected to the concentrator.

RISKS ASSOCIATED WITH CONCENTRATORS

A system that uses a concentrator may avoid the cost of a high-speed line but is taking a risk that input data will occasionally have to be reentered or that a keyboard will have to be locked because of a temporary overload when all the terminal operators enter data at once.

In the design of transmission networks, there are other such risks that the system planners sometimes take in order to lower the cost of the transmission facility. In some cases, the design uses line switching and runs the risk of giving terminal operators busy signals, thus blocking their ability to transmit. In other cases, the design will result in lengthened response times when an occasional overload occurs.

System designers must plan their risk taking to minimize the frustration it causes for terminal operators. A bad form of risk would be that of losing data. Equally frustrating is to be cut off in the middle of a terminal interaction, especially if it is one in which it will be difficult to pick up the threads.

CONCENTRATOR AND MULTIPLEXOR DIFFERENCES

Multiplexors and concentrators perform similar functions, but the way in which they do it, and their real purposes, are fundamentally different. The main distinguishing characteristic of a simple multiplexor is that the total bandwidth entering the device is roughly equivalent to the total bandwidth leaving it. All it does is chop up a high-capacity channel into several smaller subchannels. With a concentrator, on the other hand, the total bandwidth entering is normally different from the bandwidth leaving it. It uses computer logic and memory to combine several inefficient transmissions into one, or several, more efficient ones. It can give a much better utilization of the available bandwidth than a multiplexor.

Today, devices are available that perform the functions of both concentrators and multiplexors. For example, a device called a *statistical multiplexor* combines several low-speed channels into one or more high-speed channels whose total bandwidth is less than the total of the lines entering it.

CONCENTRATOR AND MULTIPLEXOR COMBINATIONS

In complex networks, various combinations of concentrators and multiplexors can be used to create almost any kind of configuration. In Fig. 27.11 cluster controllers perform concentration functions for small groups of terminals. Each of the concentrators ties into a multiplexor at some convenient location for transmission over higher-capacity channels to the location of the computer. Then multiplexing equipment there splits out the individual subchannels used by each concentrator.

Multiplexors can also be used to combine computer and noncomputer traffic. Multiplexors can be used to split a single wideband transmission facility into a number of voice channels. Some of the voice channels might be used for data transmission, with others being used for normal voice traffic.

CONCENTRATORS WITH MULTIPOINT LINES

A variety of combinations of the preceding techniques are possible. A channel derived by dividing up the bandwidth of a larger channel could itself be

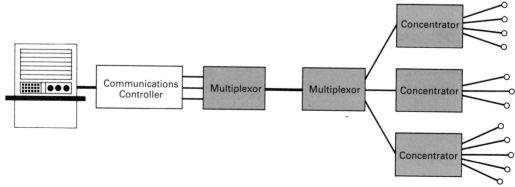

Figure 27.11   Using multiplexors and concentrators

used for multipoint operation. A multiplexed line could link into a concentrator. A concentrator could occupy one channel of a multiplexed line. Multipoint lines could link into a concentrator, or concentrators themselves could be attached to a multipoint line.

COST TRADE-OFFS   If communication lines are long and therefore expensive, it is generally worthwhile to use elaborate techniques to reduce the number of lines needed. The larger computer networks of today would be unthinkably expensive without the concentrators, multiplexors, and switching devices that they use, and without the sometimes elaborate data link protocols they employ.

On the other hand, if the lines are very short or inexpensive, the emphasis should be on lessening terminal and equipment cost rather than line cost. When the lines are very short—for example, all in one plant, one office block, or one campus—their cost is of little significance in the design, and we often find their bandwidth being used quite wantonly.

Where a system has a very large number of terminals, the terminal cost may dominate the design. For this reason, many systems have used asynchronous transmission from the terminals and no buffering. This has made possible an inexpensive terminal design, as with simple ASCII display terminals. Buffering and conversion to synchronous transmission are then sometimes done in a concentrator.

The cost of placing logic and storage (such as buffers) in the peripheral parts of the network is dropping rapidly, largely through the use of microprocessors and other types of integrated circuits. As this happens, there will be an increasing number of systems that use multiplexors, concentrators, and other remote mechanisms for lowering the overall network cost.

COMMUNICATIONS
CONTROLLERS   The third type of device that is used to perform line control functions in a data transmission system is the *communications controller,* which we have shown in the preceding network examples. The major purpose of a communications controller is not to optimize the use of the transmission facilities, but to optimize the use of the host computer to which it is attached. As we have seen, digital information is normally transmitted over communication lines a ''bit'' at a time. The messages to be transmitted must therefore be broken into bits, and these bits must be sent at the speed of the line. Similarly, on receiving a message, bits are assembled one at a time into characters and the characters are assembled into messages. Both the characters and messages must be error checked and the errors corrected, if possible. Suitable control signals must be generated for op-

erating the distant terminals at the correct times. The way these functions are performed is closely related to the way in which data links are connected to the host computer:

- They may go directly into the main computer, so that bits arriving are stored directly in the main memory. This approach may result in many interruptions and "cycle stealing" from the main operations. It is often restricted to systems with low-volume transmission requirements.

- They may terminate in a *communications controller*. Such a device is sometimes called a *transmission control unit,* a *line-control computer,* or a *front-end processor*. A communications controller may feed characters to the main computer and accepts data characters and control characters from it. The main programs will then be interrupted only to assemble characters into messages or to feed characters to the line-control equipment.

- The communications controller may pass frames, rather than characters, to the main computer and may receive frames from it. There is then less time taken from the main computer programs.

- The communications controller may itself be a stored program computer, which feeds complete, checked-out, edited messages to the computer and receives complete messages for transmission. The communications controller might assume responsibility for maintaining discipline on the lines and leave the main machine free to do the processing.

The choice among these approaches may be indicated to some extent by the number of communication lines that must be handled. If the system has only one communication line, the line may go straight into the computer or into a device with a buffer storage, which automatically assembles or disassembles a complete message. If, however, there are 50 or 100 communication lines, these may best be terminated in a separate communications controller.

COMMUNICATIONS CONTROLLER ADVANTAGES   The value of a stored-program computer in controlling communication functions lies in its adaptability. It must handle messages of any length; therefore, dynamic memory allocation is desirable. It might control differing numbers of lines with different devices. It will often have to change the sequence in which it accepts messages from terminals, as terminals are shut down and opened up. It may have to dial out to terminals and accept calls dialed in. Diagnostic programs will be run in it to detect network faults and help in terminal checkout.

The communications controller most often has an instruction set that is different from conventional computers and designed for handling communication lines. It may have the facility to log messages on its own disk drives or magnetic tape units. It may send English-language messages to the terminal operators as part of its control procedures. Because it is a programmable unit, its procedures may be modified as circumstances demand.

CODE   An additional function of the communications con-
CONVERSION   troller might be code conversion. The transmission
                                   line often uses a different means for encoding char-
acters than the main computer. Seven-bit ASCII is a very commonly used code for transmission of data over communication lines, whereas the 8-bit EBCDIC code is used in the internal circuitry of IBM mainframe computers. Either the communications controller or the main computer may have to translate back and forth between EBCDIC and ASCII. This step is now often done by hardware or microprogramming in the communications controller.

Now that we have examined line termination and line control equipment, in Chapter 28 we examine the various switching alternatives that can be used in constructing data communication networks.

28 SWITCHING EQUIPMENT

Let us suppose that we want to interconnect a great number of intelligent machines so that any machine in the network can establish a logical connection to any other machine. With point-to-point connections, we need a great many data links. To interconnect three machines, three data links are required. But to interconnect eight machines, 28 separate data links are required (see Fig. 28.1). Multiplexors cannot help in this situation because all they do is provide a more economical means for implementing individual data links. A concentrator network could be built, but then one of the machines would have to be in charge of the network and handle the setting up of the various logical connections that might be required.

A common technique is to use one or more switches to interconnect the various users. For example, each intelligent machine might be connected to the public telephone system with voice-grade channels, as shown in Fig. 28.2. For any machine to contact any other, all that is needed is the other user's telephone number.

PRIVATE BRANCH EXCHANGES When an organization has many telephones, it may have its own switching facility that interconnects these telephones with one another and also with the public network or other lines leaving the premises. These private switching facilities can also be used for data communications by employing appropriate modems and other line termination equipment. A private switching facility is called a *private branch exchange* (PBX). Today, most PBXs are fully automatic as opposed to being manually controlled by operators; an automatic PBX is often referred to by the term *private automatic branch exchange* (PABX). Most large PABXs today are computer controlled, and each extension attached to the system ordinarily has its own individual telephone number (sometimes called *Centrex* service). Some PABXs are specifically designed to support users of data

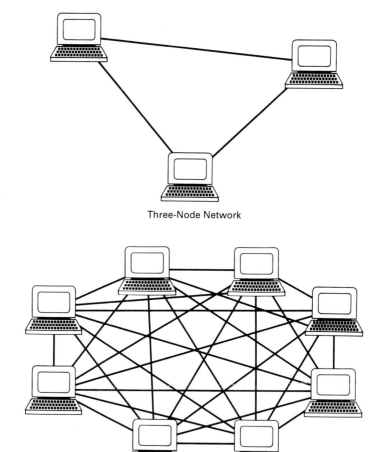

Three-Node Network

Eight-Node Network

Figure 28.1 Network interconnection with point-to-point data links

communication services and use digital technology. A digital PABX can often be used to connect data processing equipment directly with digital circuits, thus avoiding the use of modems.

DISADVANTAGES OF CONVENTIONAL SWITCHING

The conventional switching techniques used in the public telephone network and in PBXs are better suited to conventional telephone users than to users of data communication services. Some of the differences between telephone users and data users are listed in Box 28.1.

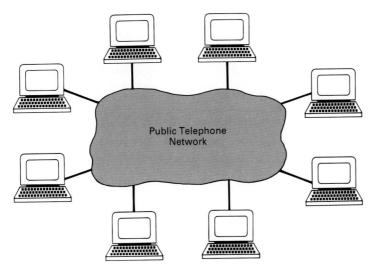

Figure 28.2　Network interconnection with public telephone network

BOX 28.1　Characteristics of telephone and data users

Telephone Users	Data Users
Fixed channel capacity	Wide range of channel capacities
Two-way conversations	One-way or two-way transmissions
Tolerant to channel noise	Data must be delivered without error
Continuous transmission	Burst or continuous transmission
Immediate delivery of signal	Delivery time can often be delayed
Constant transmission rate	High peak-to-average ratio
Switching can be done in seconds or minutes	Switching should be done in milliseconds
Session switching required	Item switching is desirable
Manual dialing	Automatic dialing
Simple compatible instruments	Wide range of incompatible machines

Perhaps the most important difference in handling telephone traffic versus data traffic is that telephone users talk or listen more or less *continuously*, whereas typical users of data communication transmit and receive *bursts* of data with relatively long periods of silence between the bursts. Figure 28.3 shows a single terminal using a transmission line in a typical interactive fashion. Notice that the line is idle the majority of the time. When a telephone line is used by a single interactive computer terminal, the line is used inefficiently because of the long gaps between transmissions.

To overcome these disadvantages a network designed specifically for data transmission should be able to handle sporadic bursts of transmission rather than continuous transmission. The *transmission* facilities in existence for telephone traffic are well suited to such a network, but the *multiplexing* and *switching* facilities need to be different. Such a network needs *burst multiplexing* and *burst switching* rather than continuous-channel multiplexing and switching.

PEAK-TO-AVERAGE RATIO

How strongly burst switching and multiplexing is advantageous over continuous-channel switching and multiplexing depends on how bursty the traffic is. A useful measure of this is the ratio of peak-to-average data rate of the transmis-

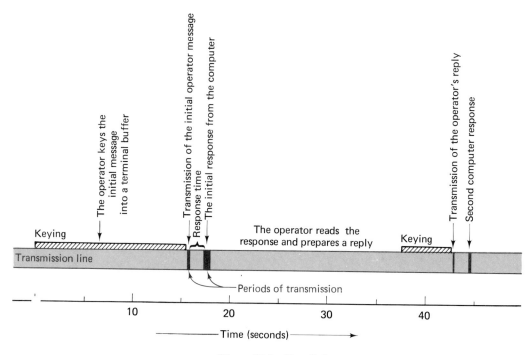

Figure 28.3 Data link usage

sion from one user. The peak-to-average ratio can be assessed for any specific application of data transmission. Box 28.2 shows some sample peak-to-average ratios.

The *average* bit rate of these applications is calculated from the total number of bits that pass to and from the terminal. The *peak* rate is calculated for the period of maximum desirable data flow to or from that terminal. The peak might occur, for example, when a screen is being filled with information. Some of the applications need a fast response time if they are to be effective and hence a screen must be filled with information in a second or two. Implementations of almost all typical user interfaces have a peak-to-average ratio greater than 10.

Most dialogs that use a buffered display screen unit have a peak-to-average ratio greater than 100; some greater than 1000. The trend to intelligent programmable terminals and personal computers tends to reduce the *average* data flow because more interactions can take place at the terminal location. Nevertheless, the peak data flow often remains the same; hence the peak-to-average ratio is often greater with intelligent terminals. To make things worse, graphics are now commonly used to enhance the capability of people to grasp and manipulate information at terminals. Graphics dialogs require a much higher bit rate to the screen than is common in alphanumeric applications—again in the form of high-speed bursts.

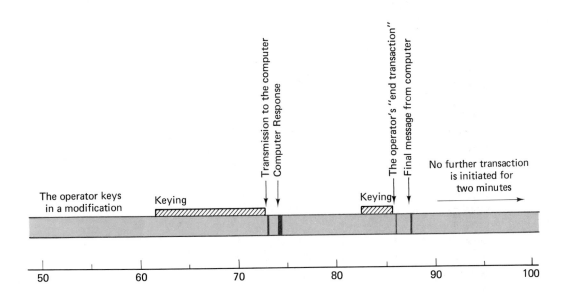

Figure 28.3　(Continued)

BOX 28.2   Peak-to-average ratios of typical dialogs

Application	Average Rate (bps)	Peak Rate (bps)	Peak/Average Ratio
Calculation in BASIC using a printer terminal	8	100	12.5
Stock analysis using a printer terminal	10	150	15
Airline reservations using a display terminal	10	1,500	100
Processing sales orders			
Simple display terminal	40	4,000	100
Programmable terminal	2	4,000	2,000
Data entry—form filling on screen	15	1,500	100
Circuit design using a personal computer connected to a mainframe	200	200,000	1,000

The continuous-channel switching and multiplexing used for conventional telephone traffic thus has two disadvantages for computer terminals. First, it causes inefficient utilization of the facilities because of the high peak-to-average ratio. Second, the transmissions are restricted to the maximum speed of the telephone channels, when in some cases faster burst of transmission would be beneficial.

SWITCHING TECHNIQUES

In examining the nature of a communication channel, we find that there are basically two methods that can be used for dividing up a channel's capacity. These are shown in Fig. 28.4. The horizontal line represents the traditional methodology; a portion of the bandwidth or capacity is allocated to one user for as long as it is needed. The vertical lines represent burst subdivision. A user is given the whole capacity for a brief period, whenever it is needed. The two methods of operation apply both to the multiplexing process and to the switching. In some cases, these two methods can be used together, as shown in Fig. 28.5. Some networks operate using continuous subchannels that are leased from the telephone companies, but the channels are subdivided using burst multiplexing

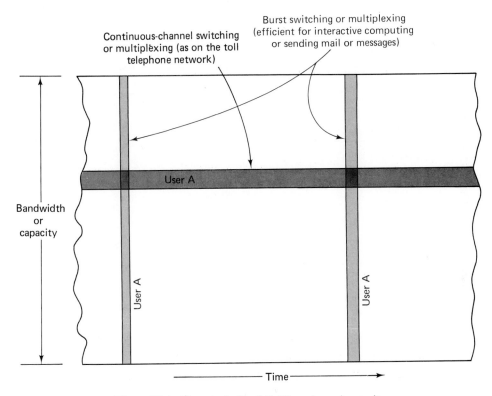

Figure 28.4   Two methods of dividing channel capacity

and burst switching. The two ways of dividing up channel capacities lead to four different methods that can be used for switching:

- Conventional circuit switching
- Fast-connect circuit switching
- Message switching
- Packet switching

**CONVENTIONAL
CIRCUIT
SWITCHING**
The first switching method is the method we have already discussed. We have seen that conventional circuit switching is wasteful of both switching and transmission capacity when the traffic consists of short or high-speed bursts. It may take many seconds to complete the circuit, but then a data message may take only a few milliseconds to travel to its destination. Because the switching time is so long relative to the transmission time,

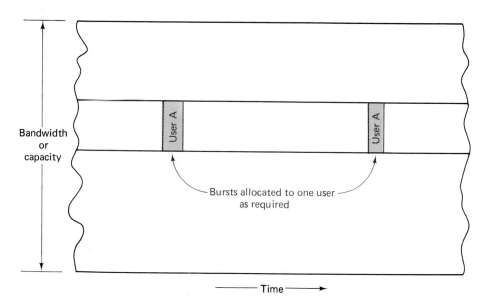

Figure 28.5   Combining continuous channel and burst multiplexing

the circuit usually remains connected for an entire terminal session. It would be unreasonable to ask terminal operators to dial up the computer each time they press the ENTER key.

FAST-CONNECT CIRCUIT SWITCHING

Fast-connect circuit switching is a form of burst switching that is more efficient with sporadic rather than continuous traffic. Since the circuit is connected very fast (a few milliseconds), it is feasible to establish a new connection each time there is new data to transmit. Since the circuits remain connected only briefly, busy signals are less of a problem. A terminal connected to a fast-connect circuit switching network might be programmed to dial the appropriate computer automatically each time the ENTER key is pressed.

There have been public data networks implemented that use fast-connect circuit switching, and they solve many of the problems associated with conventional switching. However, experience has shown that the two other switching methods—message switching and packet switching—are better suited to the handling of large volumes of data traffic on complex networks.

MESSAGE SWITCHING

Our last two switching categories represent a fundamentally different type of switching than the first two. With circuit switching, the physical transmission path is switched; with message switching and packet switching, circuits remain permanently connected and messages are received at a switching center and are routed onward to the requisite destination. The user of a data network would like to tie into the network and have a simple way of sending a message to another network user. In the ideal situation, the user should not have to know any of the details of how the network is implemented. The message should contain the network address of the destination user, and the network should take care of delivering it.

With a typical message switching system, terminals are connected to a central computer that performs the message storage and message switching functions, as in Fig. 28.6. The central computer accepts messages coming into the network from network users, examines their destination addresses, and sees that they are properly delivered to the appropriate user at the other end. Figure 28.7 shows a large message switching system that uses a mesh-structured rather than a star-structured network. Each node in the network may implement storage in which messages are retained for a period of time.

Message switching networks can give better line utilization than if the same network was operated with circuit switching. Although the cost of the message switching computers is often higher than that of conventional circuit switches, the total line cost is lower, since a greater degree of sharing can be achieved. Message switching therefore tends to be economical on a large network with long lines and many terminals.

A message switching computer carries on three functions continuously: it receives messages, stores them, and sends them to their destinations. Message switching can form a "nonblocking" network that never fails to accept traffic

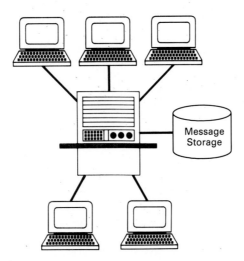

Figure 28.6   Message switching network

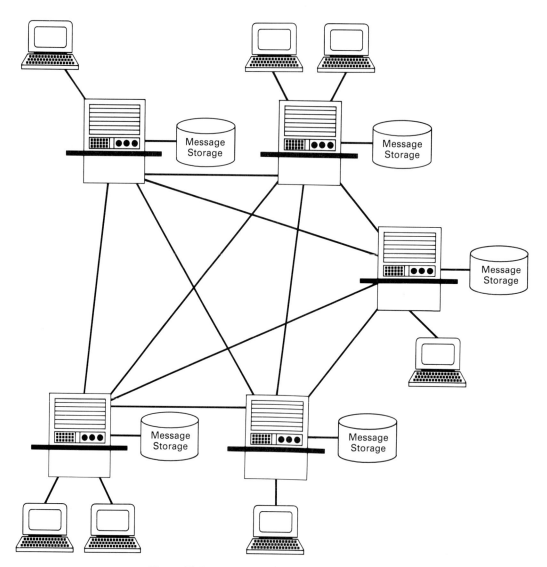

Figure 28.7   Mesh-structured message switching network

unless there is a breakdown. The *risk* with message switching is not of busy signals, as with circuit switching, but of a lengthened delivery time.

Message switching systems have traditionally been used to relay messages that need to get to their destinations in perhaps a few seconds or even a few minutes. When fast delivery times are essential, such as a small number of milliseconds, a special form of message switching called *packet switching* is typically used.

PACKET SWITCHING

Most of today's public data networks use packet switching techniques. In a packet switching network, the terminals or computers are linked to the network via small *interface computers* that are designed to work with small units of data, called *packets,* that are no larger than some fixed maximum size. As shown in Fig. 28.8, a packet switching network is similar in structure to a mesh-structured message switching network. What is different is that the terminals and computers that are connected to a packet switching network must have enough intelligence to break long messages into *packets* for transmission through the network. The packets are given to the interface computers for transmission to their final destinations. The computer or terminal at the destination then reassembles the individual packets into their original messages. Less capable terminals can be attached to a packet switching network through an intermediary device that implements a *packet assembly and disassembly* (PAD) function. The device that performs the PAD function can be supplied by the user and can be on the user's premises or it can be supplied by the network operator and can be installed at the location of a network interface computer.

Wideband communication links are normally used to interconnect the interface computers, the network being designed so that if one of the lines fails, there is always an alternative path to the destination. Thus the interface computers form the nodes of a multipath network. They determine the routing for the packets, and the packets are passed very quickly from one node to another.

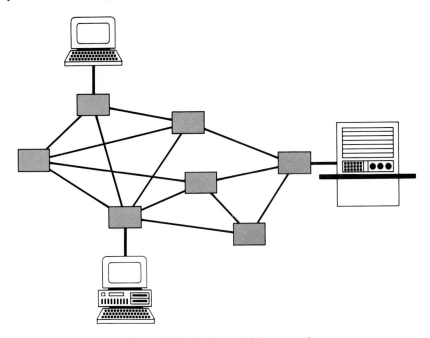

Figure 28.8 Packet switching network

Typical packet switching networks do not retain the packets or messages once they have been delivered correctly. The network acts simply as a mail service. A message switching network, on the other hand, generally *files* messages for possible retrieval at a later time. In Chapter 37 we discuss packet switching in detail and describe *CCITT Recommendation X.25,* which documents a set of standards and protocols that is widely used in implementing packet switching data networks. In Chapter 29, the final chapter in this part, we discuss the use of personal computers in implementing data communication systems.

29 PERSONAL COMPUTER
DATA COMMUNICATION HARDWARE

Personal computers of all types are seen today performing many tasks that required more specialized hardware in days past. For example, the personal computer has become one of the most widely used terminal devices in many of today's data transmission systems. In this chapter we discuss the hardware that is used in conjunction with personal computers to implement data communication functions. We use IBM personal computers in most of our examples, but the principles are the same for most other types of personal computers as well.

PARALLEL
COMMUNICATION
The simplest application of data communication with personal computers involves parallel communication between the personal computer and a printer. Most personal computers, including all IBM and IBM-compatible systems, have a parallel communication port that is most often used to communicate with a local printer. This port is sometimes installed on the circuit board that is used to control the personal computer's display screen. This parallel port normally implements a form of parallel interface that was standardized a number of years ago by the *Centronics Corporation,* a supplier of computer printers. The *Centronics interface* is generally implemented in printers using a 36-pin connector, as shown in Fig. 29.1.

Many personal computers do not use the 36-pin connector used in printers. Instead, they use a 25-pin RS-232-C connector for this purpose. Many feel that this is an unfortunate choice, because it is often difficult to tell which connector on the back of the computer is the one for the parallel port. In most cases, the parallel port uses a female connector, and the connectors for other adapters use a male connector, but this is by no means standard on all computers. Figure 29.2 shows how a cable can be wired to connect the 36-pin connector used in most printers to the 25-pin connector used in many personal computers.

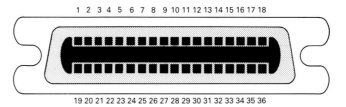

Figure 29.1   36-pin parallel port connector

In most cases, the length of the cable that is used to implement a parallel connection should be limited to about 25 feet or so to avoid data errors. When a parallel printer must be located at a distance greater than this, adapters can be used that convert the parallel data into a serial bit stream that can be sent without error over a much longer cable (see Fig. 29.3). Such devices can be used to extend a parallel connection up to a mile or so.

SERIAL COMMUNICATION

Parallel communication is used most often for attaching a printer to a personal computer, but most other data communication applications use serial commu-

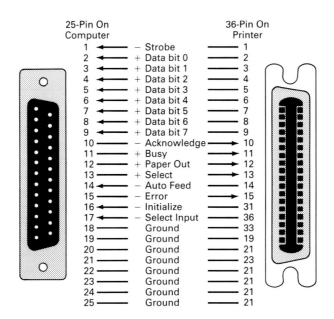

Figure 29.2   IBM parallel printer cable

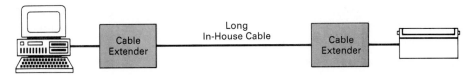

Figure 29.3   Parallel cable extenders

nication. For example, serial communication is used most often for connecting a personal computer to a remote mainframe using modems. In the remainder of this chapter we discuss some of the types of serial communication applications that are used with personal computers.

ASYNCHRONOUS COMMUNICATIONS ADAPTERS

The simplest type of data communication functions generally require the installation of some type of *asynchronous communications adapter* in the personal computer. These adapters generally implement the RS-232-C interface that was introduced in Chapter 10. Many personal computers have such an adapter installed as original equipment. For example, many Apple Macintosh models implement two serial communication ports that can be used for asynchronous communication. Many IBM and IBM-compatible personal computers have an adapter installed as standard equipment that implements both parallel and serial communication ports. The original IBM Personal Computer and Personal Computer XT, on the other hand, did not have such adapters as standard equipment.

To install a serial communication adapter on a computer that is not already equipped with one requires the insertion of an add-on circuit board. There are many such add-on boards available. One is the *asynchronous communications adapter* marketed by IBM. What is more prevalent in the personal computer marketplace, however, are *multifunction boards* that provide the asynchronous communication function on the same circuit board that provides other facilities as well, such as added memory and a clock/calendar function. The asynchronous communication circuits on these multifunction boards generally perform in a manner identical to the IBM asynchronous communications adapter, and provide a more cost-effective way of gaining a serial communication port.

The asynchronous communications adapters that are available allow the user to attach the personal computer to all types of devices that support asynchronous communication. Common examples of such equipment are serial printers and modems. Most asynchronous communications adapters, including IBM's asynchronous communications adapter, terminate in a standard 25-pin RS-232-C connector. A notable exception to this is the parallel/serial adapter installed in the PC/AT, which uses a 9-pin connector instead of the standard 25-pin plug. The functions of the various pins in IBM's 25-pin plug and 9-pin plug are shown in Fig. 29.4.

DTE VERSUS DCE Most asynchronous communications adapters are wired as DTEs, which allows them to be connected with a standard RS-232-C cable to any device that is wired as a DCE, such as a modem. [The distinction between *data terminal equipment* (DTE) and *data circuit-terminating* equipment (DCE) is introduced in Chapter 10.] Typical wiring charts for constructing typical RS-232-C cables for connecting asynchronous adapters to modems are shown in Fig. 29.5. Many adapters provide jumper wires or internal switches that allow the adapter to be configured as a DCE instead of a DTE. Configuring the adapter as a DCE allows it to be connected with a standard cable to a device that is configured as a DTE, such as a printer, a display terminal, or an asynchronous adapter in another personal computer.

If it is necessary to connect an asynchronous adapter that is configured as a DTE to a device that is also configured as a DTE, such as when connecting together two personal computers, a special cable called a *null modem* can be used. The null modem cable simply crosses the appropriate circuits to simulate the presence of two modems between the two DTEs.

Typical simple null modem cables are shown in Fig. 29.6. These show the minimum circuits that are required for communicating over an RS-232-C con-

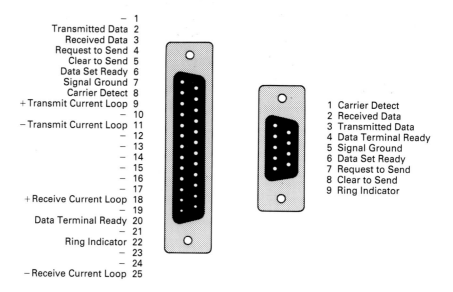

Figure 29.4 IBM 25-pin and 9-pin RS-232-C connectors

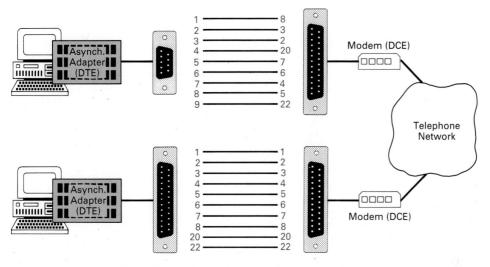

Figure 29.5 Connecting a computer to a modem

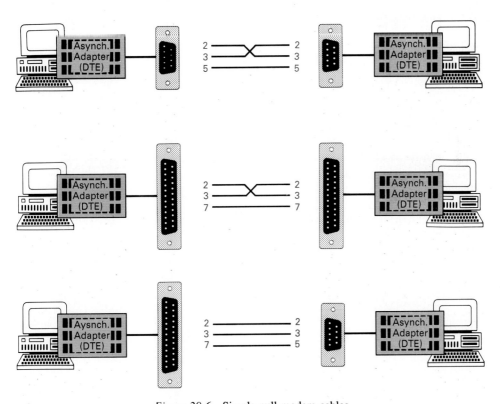

Figure 29.6 Simple null modem cables

nection. This type of cable generally suffices for connecting two personal computers that communicate using uncomplicated software.

The RS-232-C specification defines many more circuits that are used for various types of functions. If the software that is employed sets and tests some of these circuits, a more elaborate cable may be required. Examples are shown in Fig. 29.7.

Even more elaborate cables are required for some applications, which is why the wiring of RS-232-C cables has sometimes been referred to as a black art. The documentation for the device in question generally contains information about the RS-232-C circuits that are used and the type of cable that is required. Various types of null modem cable adapters that cross the appropriate circuits are also commercially available. The reader interested in learning more about the RS-232-C interface and the types of connections that are used for various applications can consult *RS-232 Made Easy* by Martin D. Seyer, (Englewood Cliffs, NJ: Prentice-Hall, Inc., 1984).

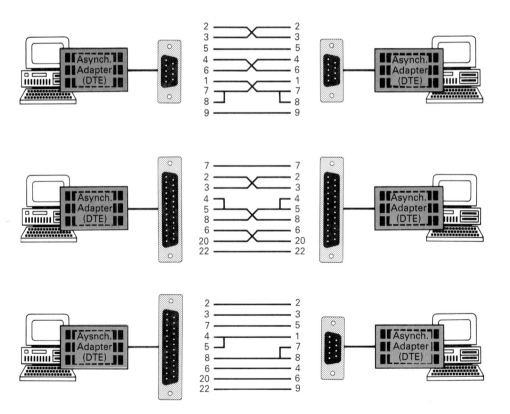

Figure 29.7   More elaborate null modem cables

FILE TRANSFERS   A common application of asynchronous communications adapters and a null modem cable is to connect together two personal computers for the purposes of transferring files from one computer to the other. When the two computers are located in the same place, a simple RS-232-C cable can be used to connect the asynchronous adapter in one personal computer to the adapter in the other computer. If the communications adapters in the two computers are both wired as DTEs, a null-modem cable must be used as discussed above. An ordinary RS-232-C null modem cable can be used over distances of up to about 50 feet. If a longer cable must be used, simple, short-distance modems can be used to transmit the data over privately installed cables that are up to about a mile or so in length. If the two computers are widely separated, a conventional modem can be used at each location to connect the computers via the telephone network. (See Fig. 29.8 for examples of these configurations.)

A special software package is generally used to handle file transfer operations. File transfer software must read the appropriate file from the first computer, format the data for transmission, and send it out over the modem. A

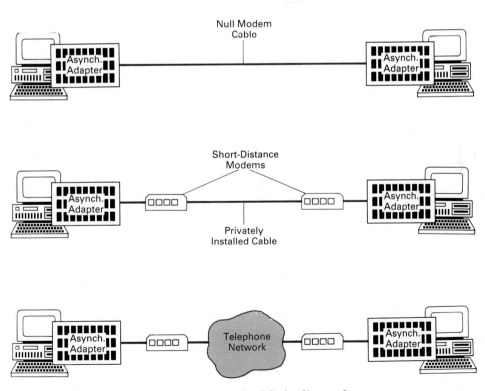

Figure 29.8 Connecting PCs for file transfer

complementary software package running in the second computer receives the data, checks for transmission errors, and reconstructs the original file. This type of software is discussed in detail in Chapter 33.

INTERNAL MODEMS

The connection to communication facilities can be simplified by using an internal modem instead of an asynchronous communications adapter connected to an external modem. An internal modem contains circuitry that performs the functions of both an asynchronous communications adapter and a modem on the same circuit card. The interface between the adapter and the modem is implemented directly on the circuit board itself, and the circuit board terminates in a standard modular telephone jack that can be connected directly to the telephone network (see Fig 29.9).

ASYNCHRONOUS TERMINAL EMULATION

The most common use of a personal computer and a modem is to emulate an asynchronous terminal. Such a hardware configuration is combined with a software package that makes the personal computer appear to the device to which it is attached as if it were a simple asynchronous terminal. The simplest such software simply monitors the personal computer keyboard and sends out over the modem the character corresponding to each key that is pressed. The software also monitors the communication line and displays on the screen each character that is received by the modem. The software may also interpret control sequences that are received in order to perform certain terminal control functions, such as clearing the screen and moving the display cursor. This type of software also often supports additional functions that use the personal computer's memory and disk storage to perform many of the functions normally associated with intelligent terminals. Terminal emulation functions and file transfer functions are often combined in the same data communication software package.

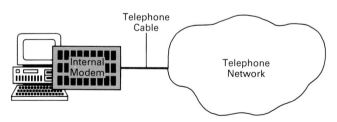

Figure 29.9   Internal modem

SYNCHRONOUS COMMUNICATIONS ADAPTERS

Although most data communication applications of personal computers use an asynchronous protocol for communication, a synchronous protocol is sometimes used for higher-performance applications. IBM offers two communication adapters that support synchronous communication; other vendors supply similar add-on circuit cards. The IBM *binary synchronous communications adapter* uses the binary-synchronous protocol for communicating with devices that use this line control procedure. The IBM *synchronous data link control (SDLC) communications adapter* uses the SDLC protocol for communicating with devices in the SNA environment. Both of these adapters use a standard 25-pin RS-232-C connector to allow the adapter to be attached to a synchronous device, such as a high-speed synchronous modem.

3270 EMULATION

As we mentioned in Chapter 25, a very widely used type of terminal is the IBM 3270 display station. More data communication applications in the IBM mainframe environment have been written for this type of terminal than for any other. Since many people who may require access to mainframe applications already have personal computers on their desks, it is common to use these same personal computers to emulate the functions of 3270 display stations. As with asynchronous terminal emulation, a combination of a circuit board and a software package is required for this type of terminal emulation.

A widely used communications adapter for 3270 emulation is the *IRMA*

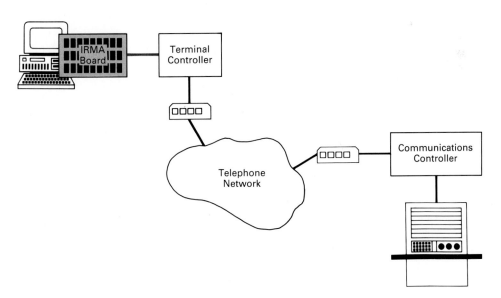

Figure 29.10   3270 emulation with IRMA board

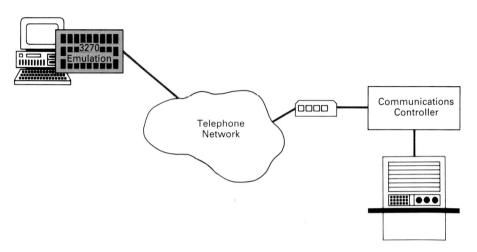

Figure 29.11   3270 emulation with integral controller and modem

board marketed by *Digital Communications Associates,* 1000 Alderman Drive, Alpharetta, GA 30201. The IRMA board plugs into the personal computer in the same manner as an asynchronous adapter and comes with software that handles all standard 3270 terminal functions. The IRMA board circuitry terminates

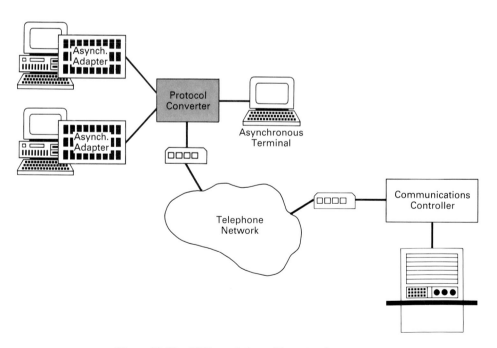

Figure 29.12   3270 emulation with protocol converter

with a standard 3270 coaxial cable connector that allows the adapter to be attached to a 3270 cluster controller in the same manner as an ordinary 3270 terminal (see Fig. 29.10).

Other 3270 emulation adapters go further than the IRMA board and perform the functions of a 3270 terminal, a controller, and a synchronous modem. This type of device terminates in a standard modular telephone connector that allows the personal computer to communicate directly with an IBM host communications controller over a telephone circuit (see Fig. 29.11).

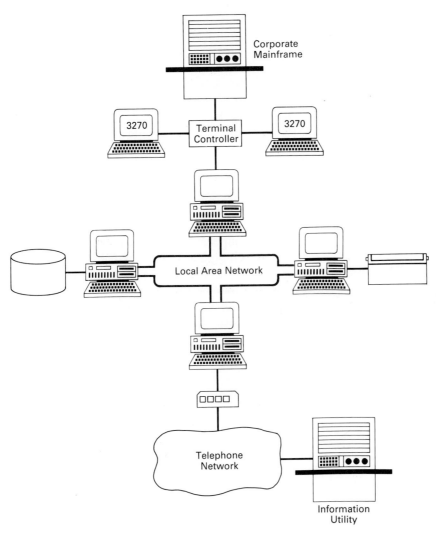

Figure 29.13   Resource sharing using a local area network

Another method of handling 3270 terminal emulation is through the use of a protocol converter. For example, IBM markets a device called the *3708 protocol converter,* to which one or more personal computers can be attached via conventional asynchronous communications adapters. The 3708, in turn, communicates with a host communications controller using a synchronous protocol as if it were a 3270 cluster controller (see Fig. 29.12). Other vendors also supply devices that perform concentration and protocol conversion services. These devices were introduced in Chapter 27.

LOCAL AREA NETWORKS

In addition to the uses of conventional serial and parallel communication discussed above, flexible resource sharing networks can be created by using *local area network* (LAN) techniques. To use a local area network, an LAN adapter is installed in each personal computer, and these adapters are wired together so that each personal computer can communicate with all the others. Using LAN techniques, it is possible for each personal computer to share the devices and communications adapters installed on the other systems. For example, it is possible to create a network such as the one shown in Fig. 29.13. Each of the personal computers on the network can share the resources installed on the other computers, such as the 3270 emulation board installed in the PC on top, the printer attached to the PC on the right, the asynchronous adapter and modem installed in the PC on the bottom, and the high-capacity disk connected to the PC on the left.

Local area networks generally support high transmission speeds, such as a million or more bits per second. Such high speeds allow the network to make it appear to the user as if the shared devices are actually attached to the user's own personal computer. Local area networks are discussed in detail in Chapter 40.

Now that we have examined the hardware that is used in constructing data communication systems, in the chapters in Part VI we discuss the various types of software that are required to support data transmission applications.

PART **VI** **DATA COMMUNICATION SOFTWARE**

30 DATA COMMUNICATION SOFTWARE FUNCTIONS

One of the issues that complicates the software environment surrounding data transmission systems relates to the various locations at which software functions can be run in a communication network. The intelligence in a network, as discussed earlier, can reside almost entirely in a host computer or it can be scattered throughout the network. Logic functions can have their home in the following places:

- In a terminal
- In a cluster controller
- In a concentrator or other mid-network node
- In a communications controller
- In a host computer

Any of the logic operations performed on the data transmitted can be carried out by programming if the device in question is a stored-program machine, as all the devices noted above can be. On the other hand, the operations can be performed by logic circuitry permanently wired into the machines or by microprogramming in which the built-in logic is modifiable.

Because of this diversity of options, the programming required for control of the transmission of data varies substantially from one selection of hardware to another. The software packages available for assisting the programmer also vary widely. On some systems the programmer must handle the movement of every bit or character on the communication lines; on others software packages take care of all the functions associated with data transmission.

CATEGORIES OF FUNCTIONS

We begin this chapter by reviewing the functions that must be accomplished in order to control the transmission of data. We continue by discussing the various ways these functions can be assigned to hardware logic, microprogramming, software packages, or code written specifically for an application system. First we examine the basic data transmission functions that are likely to be performed in a simple online system. A variety of other functions relating to more complex network control—line control, user interface processing, and so on—are then listed.

BASIC TRANSMISSION FUNCTIONS

When I/O is performed with any input/output unit, such as a tape drive or disk device, the main programs in the computer receive, or prepare for output, a complete logical record. A short routine writes or reads the record and checks that it has been done correctly. This operation is also required when I/O is performed using a communication line instead of an ordinary I/O device, but here the input/output routine might be more complicated.

The digital information is normally transmitted over a communication line a "bit" at a time. The messages to be transmitted must therefore be broken into bits, which are sent at the speed of the line. Similarly, on receiving a message, bits are assembled one at a time into characters, and the characters are assembled into messages. Both the characters and the messages must be error checked and the errors corrected if possible. Suitable control signals must be generated for operating the distant terminals at the correct times. Box 30.1 lists some of the basic transmission functions that might be performed by hardware or software mechanisms in controlling data transmission.

If programs in the main computer carry out all the basic transmission functions described in Box 30.1, the application programs will be interrupted very frequently and the performance of the computer will be degraded. If there are many communication lines or a high data rate, the degradation will be severe. As we have already mentioned, it is usual, therefore, to perform some of the foregoing functions in peripheral devices. Such devices can assemble the bits into characters and feed characters to the main computer. They can also assemble the characters into words or blocks. To do so substantially reduces the number of interrupts. The peripheral devices might store entire messages, recognize the end-of-transmission characters, and only then interrupt the main computer.

The choice among these approaches is determined to some extent by the number of communication lines that must be handled. If the system has only one communication line, this line can go straight into the computer or into a device with a buffer storage, which automatically assembles or disassembles complete messages. However, if there are 50 or 100 communication lines, they are best terminated in a separate communications controller, as is usually the case with today's mainframe-based data communication systems.

BOX 30.1   Transmission functions

1. **Data reception.** Control mechanisms may be required to initiate and control the reception of data over communication lines. The lines might operate at different speeds. Many lines might be transmitting or receiving at once. The terminals may have to be polled to see when they are ready to transmit.

2. **Message assembly.** Control mechanisms are required to assemble the bits into characters and characters into messages.

3. **Code conversion.** Control mechanisms might be required to convert the coding of the characters. The coding used in transmitting data over communication lines is sometimes different from that used by the computer. The lines, for example, might use ASCII, whereas the computer might use EBCDIC.

4. **Error detection.** Control mechanisms are normally used to check for errors, both in the characters, by means of a parity check, and in the transmission frames by means of error detection bits. If an error is detected, the same frame is normally sent again.

5. **Message editing.** Control mechanisms are sometimes used to edit the messages. For example, an operator might make mistakes in typing on the keyboard and transmit backspace or erase characters to correct them. The message must be edited into its correct format before it is ready for processing. The backspace or erase characters must be recognized and removed.

6. **Control character recognition.** Control mechanisms may be required to recognize end-of-record or end-of-transmission characters and carry out necessary housekeeping, preparing for another transmission if necessary.

7. **Message delivery.** Control mechanisms might deliver messages to the main programs, one at a time, edited and converted.

8. **Message transmission.** Control mechanisms can accept messages from the main programs when they are ready for transmission to the terminals.

9. **Message output.** Control mechanisms can prepare messages for output. It might be necessary to convert them from computer code to communication line code and control characters might have to be added.

10. **Transmission initiation.** Control mechanisms are sometimes used to initiate the transmission of messages.

11. **Transmission monitoring.** Control mechanisms might monitor the sending process, repeating characters or messages if the terminal detects errors in transmission.

12. **End-of-transmission signaling.** Control mechanisms can signal end-of-transmission to the terminal and carry out necessary housekeeping and line control functions.

BOX 30.2 Polling and dialing functions

1. **Terminal dialing.** Control mechanisms can dial a telephone number and establish contact with a terminal or with another computer. If the dialed station is busy, the request for the operation can be stored and acted on later.

2. **Terminal scanning.** A group of terminals can be automatically scanned by the hardware to see whether any of them have data to send.

3. **Automatic answering.** When a dialed call is received from a terminal or another computer, control mechanisms can be used that automatically establish a connection with the device, using the requisite protocol, and might notify the necessary application program.

4. **Software polling.** When a line is polled, this can be done entirely by programming. The program might have a list giving the terminal addresses and the polling sequence.

5. **Hardware polling.** Where an external polling device is used, the software might not send the polling messages itself; instead, it might give instructions to the polling device.

6. **Loop Line Control.** Where several devices are attached to a looped line using synchronous transmission, control mechanisms can assemble and disassemble the necessary bits and characters.

POLLING AND DIALING

Software requirements increase in complexity when an elaborate configuration of communication lines is used. Box 30.2 describes some of the additional functions required to control the functions of complex networks.

Once again, the foregoing polling and dialing functions can be handled in the central computer or in a separate communications controller. For flexibility, the communications controller is most often a programmable device that is capable of handling messages of any length and is capable of controlling different numbers of lines. It most often has an instruction set that is specially designed for the control of communication functions. It may have the facility to log messages on its own direct-access devices or tape units. It might send English-language messages to the terminal operators as part of its control procedures. Because it is a programmable unit, its procedures can be modified as circumstances demand.

BASIC DATA COMMUNICATION SOFTWARE

In the preceding sections we discussed the basic functions that are required for controlling communication lines. Some software systems for the control of communication functions perform only these basic functions and do little else. They relieve the programmers of the need to assemble bits into characters, convert codes, and perform the other functions discussed earlier. Little else is required on simple systems. On larger or more complex systems, more functions are needed concerning the efficiency of both the central computer and the communication network.

BOX 30.3 Scheduling and resource allocation functions

1. **Dynamic Buffer Allocation.** When variable-length messages are received and transmitted, the buffers that hold them can be organized in several different ways. The dynamic allocation of buffer storage in blocks can lessen the total storage requirement. The blocks can be chained together as required; and as soon as a block becomes free, it can be allocated again to the pool of available blocks.

2. **Line Message Queuing.** On a polled communication line, a queue of transactions can build up, if it is permitted to, waiting for transmission. On some simple systems, no queuing is permitted; that is, no program can send a message on a line when one is already waiting to be sent. This procedure will sometimes hold up the processing, so a queuing mechanism is desirable.

3. **Program Message Queuing.** Similarly, queues of input messages build up, if permitted, waiting for the attention of certain programs. A similar queuing mechanism can handle output messages.

4. **Destination Routing.** A message can be routed, not to one but to many destinations. Rather than occupying many queues simultaneously, which is wasteful, there can be one copy of the message. Control entries referencing the message would then be put into the various queue control areas.

5. **Priority Scheduling.** Some messages can be given priority over others. In this case, a queue mechanism that handles multiple priorities is needed.

6. **Multitasking.** When software functions have to wait for telecommunications operations to be completed, it is desirable that the computing equipment be able to switch its attention to other work. The ability to switch easily to lower-priority tasks, and back, is needed not only in host computers, but in other communication-related devices as well.

SCHEDULING AND RESOURCE ALLOCATION   Concern for efficient use of the central computer is likely to lead to a variety of functions relating to the scheduling of computing facilities and the allocation of hardware and software resources. Box 30.3 lists some of these scheduling and allocation functions.

NETWORK DEVICE CONTROL   As we discussed in Part V, a variety of devices can be used to implement a data communication system. These devices include multiplexors, concentrators, and various types of switches. The software might format data or control messages so as to interface with such devices. Box 30.4 provides a list of the functions that might be performed in relation to the control of these devices.

LOGGING AND STATISTICS GATHERING   Any communication-based system must perform some functions that relate to the logging of messages and the gathering of statistics regarding the overall operation of the system. Box 30.5 describes two of these two important functions.

BOX 30.4   Network device control functions

1. **Data Blocking.** In some systems there is an optimum block length for transmission. Individual records or messages can therefore be gathered together in one block. In some cases, the network devices handle a fixed-length block or packet size, or a range of sizes. Software in remote devices can reformat the data to be transmitted, as required, and can extract individual records from the blocks received.

2. **Multiplexing.** Where multiplexors are used that interleave characters from different terminals, the various devices that perform multiplexing and demultiplexing functions can handle these functions either in software or in hardware.

3. **Data compression.** A variety of techniques can be used for compressing the transmitted information so that it can be sent in a smaller number of characters.

4. **Store-and-forward operations.** Some systems, such as packet switching networks, file messages for later transmission or later retrieval by a terminal. Software control of these operations is needed.

5. **Message switching.** All the functions normally carried out by a message switching system can be built into the software.

BOX 30.5   Logging and statistics-gathering functions

1. **Message logging.** On some systems all messages are logged on tape or disk, for possible reference later.
2. **Statistics gathering.** An important but often neglected function is the gathering of statistics on traffic volumes, line errors, and line failures.

BOX 30.6   Failure recovery functions

1. **Failure Recording.** When a line or terminal fails, the programs might record information to assist in recovery.
2. **Message Numbering.** Messages can be given sequential numbers to assist in recovery procedures when failures occur. The sequential numbers are transmitted with the messages and are verified by the receiving equipment.
3. **Central Computer Failure Assistance.** Software in a transmission control unit can record data needed for recovery when the central computer fails. It can then automatically send responses to the terminals.
4. **Recovery Processing.** Software to assist in recovery from failure is necessary. These routines might be implemented in data communication software or they might be contained in application programs. They might make use of message logs or sequential numbering schemes.
5. **Diagnostic processing.** The correct functioning of various parts of the system can be checked by using diagnostic programs in the central computer and in other devices. For example, the correct operation of a terminal and its connection to the computer might be tested by calling a diagnostic program from the terminal, which checks all possible conditions.
6. **Component testing.** The software and hardware might provide facilities for *cross patching*, sometimes called *wraparound*. With this technique, each line leaving the computer can be patched so that it immediately reenters the computer. By sending data out and then immediately in on such a line, the capability of the computer to transmit and receive correctly can be tested. By using such methods, the cause of incorrect functioning can be pinpointed, and software to do this automatically has proved of great value.

BOX 30.7 External response-generation functions

1. **Data Formatting.** An external unit can store details of forms, tables, or charts to be printed or displayed. Information from the computer will cause the form to be generated and filled with relevant data. Often such a unit will be part of the terminal itself. A personal computer used as a terminal can easily be programmed to perform such functions.

2. **Voice Answerback.** Instructions can be given to a voice-answerback unit to generate selected spoken words. The central computer might send a coded reference to each word or phrase to be sent. With more sophisticated devices, a string of bits is sent, which the voice-answerback unit can use to synthesize a spoken response.

BOX 30.8 Security functions

1. **Terminal Identification.** Many terminals designed with security in view have the capability to transmit a unique terminal-identification number. The system can check this number when queries are being received. Sometimes, when data is being sent, the software will first check the identification of the device to which it is about to send.

2. **User Identification.** The terminal user can be identified by various means. The most common method uses a unique number, or password, which is checked by the computer. The password is normally changed periodically. The user might alternatively insert into the terminal, or an associated device, an identification card that causes a user number to be transmitted. The programs can then check whether this user is authorized to have access to the requested functions.

3. **Message Encoding and Decoding.** As protection against wiretapping or accidental misrouting of sensitive data, cryptography can be used. Data transmission control mechanisms often automatically do the encryption and decryption of messages.

4. **Security Violation Monitoring.** When violations of security procedures occur, the software might automatically lock a terminal and notify a security officer. All potential violations should be logged by the software for later analysis or inspection.

FAILURE RECOVERY
As we have already seen, communication-based systems are especially susceptible to various types of failures. Box 30.6 lists some of the functions that hardware or software in various parts of the system might perform in dealing with failures of various types.

EXTERNAL-RESPONSE GENERATION
Devices might be used that store responses to be sent to terminals. The use of such devices frees the host computer from having to perform functions relating to these preprogrammed responses. Such external devices can be installed at the computer location, in the middle of the network, or at the location of a terminal. Box 30.7 describes some of the functions relating to two types of external response-generating equipment.

SECURITY
Security features desirable in data communication software include the ability to identify positively the

BOX 30.9 User-interface processing functions

1. **Reasonableness Checking.** Range values can be placed on certain fields to assist in the detection of miskeying.

2. **Completeness Checking.** A record can be assembled entry by entry and then checked to ensure that no entry has been omitted.

3. **Data Inspection.** Some inspection of data can take place without the data being processed in any way. This can be done using standard features in hardware or software, without recourse to central computer application programs. File records can be inspected. A mass of data in many "pages" can be scanned or page-flipped with a display terminal. An index can be scanned, and so on.

4. **Preliminary Dialog Handling.** A precisely defined preliminary dialog can be used before the application programs are entered. This dialog might step through a series of menu screens to determine which application program should be used. It might request a series of data entries from the operator to build up a record ready for the application program.

terminal with which the computer is communicating and the operator of that terminal. Other security-related functions are also desirable. Box 30.8 provides a list of some important functions that relate to security.

USER-INTERFACE   Some functions related to the interface with the end
PROCESSING   user can be built into hardware and/or software.
                            These functions, however, are likely to be more application-oriented than the features discussed above. Box 30.9 lists some important functions relating to the interface between the terminal user and the data communication system.

In the remaining chapters in this part we discuss the various software components that are used in implementing data communication systems. In Chapter 31 we discuss the category of software subsystems called *telecommunications access methods*.

31 TELECOMMUNICATIONS ACCESS METHODS

As we introduced in Chapter 1, telecommunications access methods run in a host computer and make up a software layer that operates above the level of the operating system. The functions provided by telecommunications access methods can be accessed, if desired, directly by application programs. Such applications are generally complex programs that are typically written in assembler language. More commonly, the functions performed by telecommunications access methods are accessed by intermediary software subsystems that are called *teleprocessing (TP) monitors*. Application programs, written in any desired language, then make high-level requests of the TP monitor, which in turn request telecommunications access method services as required. These software subsystem relationships are summarized in Fig. 31.1.

IBM TELECOMMUNICATIONS ACCESS METHODS

Because of the dominance of IBM equipment in the mainframe computing environment, it is useful to examine the telecommunications access methods that are provided to support data transmission using IBM mainframes. There are three IBM telecommunications access methods that are used most often in the IBM mainframe environment. All conform to the SNA network architecture.

- ACF/TCAM: Advanced Communications Function for the Telecommunications Access Method
- ACF/VTAM: Advanced Communications Function for the Virtual Telecommunications Access Method
- ACF/VTAME: Advanced Communications Function for the Virtual Telecommunications Access Method—Entry

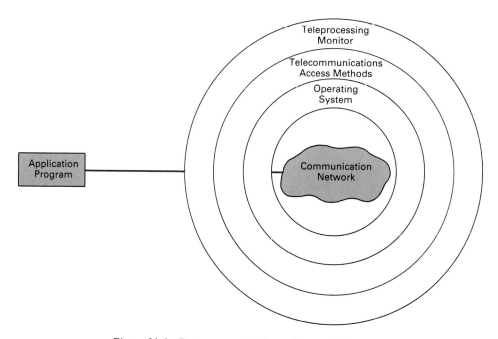

Figure 31.1   Data communication software relationships

     Each of the above three access methods performs similar functions. ACF/ TCAM and ACF/VTAM (often called simply TCAM and VTAM) are designed to be run under the control of an MVS-type operating system; ACF/VTAME (often referred to simply as VTAME) runs under the control of the VSE operating system and is the VSE counterpart of ACF/VTAM. ACF/TCAM supports a number of advanced features that are not provided by either ACF/VTAM or ACF/VTAME.

     The predecessor to VTAM and VTAME was a system called BTAM, which stands for *Basic Telecommunications Access Method*. BTAM was used with the non-virtual-storage systems, such as MVT and MFT. The predecessor to TCAM was QTAM, for *Queued Telecommunications Access Method*. Neither BTAM nor QTAM are typically used with today's virtual storage operating systems.

BASIC ACCESS METHOD FUNCTIONS   The fundamental purpose of a telecommunications access method is to give application programs, or teleprocessing monitor programs, direct access to the messages that are going out or coming in over communication lines. The access method performs polling functions and provides READ- and WRITE-level support for communication functions.

READING FROM COMMUNICATION LINES

Coding a READ instruction in an application program results in a linkage to an access method routine, which may address the indicated communication line or network node and start the transmission of data. After the READ instruction has been executed, the application program can continue if desired with other processing. Eventually the program reaches a point where it can go no further until the message is read in. At this point, a WAIT request can be issued. When the conditions of the WAIT are satisfied—in other words, when the message has been read in and is ready to be processed—control is passed back to the waiting application program. This type of facility gives the programmer complete control over communication functions. However, as indicated earlier, the programs that issue the READ and WAIT instructions tend to be quite complex and generally must be written in assembler language.

POLLING

If the terminal is on a polled line, the READ instruction may result in the line being polled; and when a terminal indicates that it has a message, this message is read. To do so, the application program may have a polling list telling it the addresses of the terminals and the sequence in which they must be polled.

WRITING TO COMMUNICATION LINES

An application programmer can send a message to a terminal by means of a WRITE instruction. As with READ, the WRITE instruction initiates the write operation. A WAIT instruction can be used at the point in the program where the write operation must be completed.

HANDLING TRANSMISSION ERRORS

When error-detecting codes are used, with automatic retransmission of erroneous messages, the access method code may ensure that retransmission is initiated when necessary. In many cases, the code that implements the data link protocol, which operates at a lower level than the access method software, may handle error detection and retransmission. If correct transmission has not been accomplished after a specified number of retries, the access method code may notify the application program so that it can take appropriate action.

ORGANIZING BUFFER POOLS

A telecommunications access method normally allocates blocks of buffers dynamically as required. If a message is being received and fills the block allocated to it, another block will be chained to the first. This chaining process continues until the entire message is received. The converse process takes place on output. As soon as a block is no longer needed, it is made free again in the pool of available blocks.

DIALING AND   When the terminal is on a dial-up line, a WRITE
ANSWERING   instruction can cause the access method code to carry
CALLS   out the dialing operation. One form of WRITE in-
struction might cause the computer to dial a terminal, establish a connection, and transmit a message. Another form of WRITE might cause it to transmit the data without dialing, because the connection is already established. When a busy signal is obtained for a terminal that is dialed, the access method code may notify the application program.

Similarly, a READ instruction may dial a terminal to see whether it has anything to send. In some cases, a dialing list will be given to the access method software, which will then dial the terminals on the list, as in a polling operation. When a terminal user dials the computer, the telecommunications access method can be set up to accept the call, establish contact with the terminal, and notify the application program that the call has been received.

There are a number of additional functions that most telecommunications access methods perform. Box 31.1 describes some of them.

HIGHER-LEVEL   Some of today's advanced telecommunications ac-
FUNCTIONS   cess methods provide additional facilities over and
above the basic functions discussed above and in Box 31.1. For example, some access methods maintain queues of messages that allow higher-level requests, such as GET and PUT, to be made instead of the more basic READ and WRITE facilities. To send messages to terminals, the application programmer codes PUT instructions. To obtain messages from terminals, GET instructions are used. Messages are typically stored in queues and are actually transmitted by the access method software when it is most efficient to do so. No WAIT instructions are necessary when using GET- and PUT-level support.

An advanced telecommunications access method may also implement its own *message control program,* which schedules the traffic-handling operations. Interrupts and instructions in the calling programs cause control to be given to the message control program at appropriate times. The message control program generally resides in one region or address space in the system and is executed as one of the high-priority tasks.

Application programs and the teleprocessing monitor are normally executed as lower-priority tasks. Messages reaching the message control program are routed by it to the requisite destination, which may be a terminal, some

BOX 31.1   Additional telecommunications access method functions

- **Converting Character Codes.** Telecommunications access methods normally provide a translation routine and a set of translation tables that convert between the codes employed by the computer and the various codes employed by terminals. The user may be able to define new sets of terminal codes and give these translation tables to the access method routines.

- **Keeping Error Statistics.** Telecommunications access methods generally maintain statistics regarding transmission errors that are detected. This aids in evaluating the performance of the communication network. Often, application systems contain special programs that are designed to organize, display, and evaluate error statistics.

- **Providing Testing Facilities.** Telecommunications access method software sometimes provides online diagnostics that facilitate the testing of terminal equipment. These facilities are helpful in the maintenance of the communication network.

- **Performing Initialization Procedures.** Telecommunications access methods generally allow programmers to use instructions such as OPEN to activate a communication path. This must be done before any message can be sent or received. Similarly, a CLOSE instruction shuts down a path.

other device in the network, or an application program. Often the required communication line or program will be occupied, so the message control program organizes queues of items waiting for these facilities.

MESSAGE SWITCHING   An advanced telecommunications access method may have the capability of handling some incoming messages by itself without needing to pass them to an application program or the TP monitor. Such is the case when the message is merely to be routed to another terminal or computer, as in a message switching system. An advanced telecommunications access method may in fact carry out by itself all the functions that would be found in a message switching system.

DATA COLLECTION   Similarly, some advanced access methods are able to carry out data collection functions without requiring application programs. Terminal operators may key in data that is to be collected for subsequent batch processing. The access method might either store the data in a queue for a particular application program or else write it in secondary storage independently of an application program. In the latter case, the data may be read for batch processing later by data management software unrelated to the telecommunications access method. The message control program thus serves as an intermediary between application programs and terminals, between network devices and other network devices, and sometimes between network devices and secondary storage devices.

MESSAGE ROUTING

Because of the different routing possibilities, some messages need to have a *header* which the message control program will use in directing the message to appropriate destinations. The header might contain such information as:

- Source address
- Destination address
- Message type
- Sequence number
- Priority

Many systems do not use a header at all on the incoming messages because all messages are destined for the same application program. In others, a destination address or transaction code may be used to select the appropriate application program.

QUEUING

Messages may arrive at random times. Often, they are not processed immediately because the CPU is occupied. When they have been processed, a response may not be sent immediately because the line is occupied. The message control program, attempting to maintain high utilization of both the CPU and the lines, may build queues of items waiting for these facilities. The queues can be either in the computer's main memory or in secondary storage.

NETWORK CONTROL PROGRAMS

As we have seen, a central computer generally uses a communications controller to perform many communications-related functions that would otherwise require the attention of the central computer itself. The communications controller runs a software subsystem that directly supports the functions performed by the telecommunications access method. In the IBM mainframe environment, the software that runs in the communications controller is called a *network control program* (NCP). The primary IBM network control program is called ACF/NCP (Advanced Communications Function for Network Control Program).

The NCP interfaces with the telecommunications access method running in the mainframe to control communication functions. The NCP controls the physical operation of the communication lines in a network and performs routine transmission functions. It also performs bit assembly and disassembly, code translation, polling, routing, error recovery, line tests, device tests, and other physical management functions. The telecommunications access method is generally responsible for downloading a copy of the NCP to the transmission control unit when the network is initialized.

Operating at a higher level than the telecommunications access method is the teleprocessing monitor and the application programs that use data transmission services. In Chapter 32 we examine the functions that are performed by teleprocessing monitors.

32 TELEPROCESSING MONITORS

As we discussed in Chapter 31, in most data transmission systems, application programs do not request the services of a telecommunications access method directly. Instead, they make requests of an intermediary software system called a *teleprocessing monitor* (TP monitor). Examples of teleprocessing monitors are IBM's CICS and IMS/DC and Cullinet Software's IDMS/DC. Although some application programs are written to request directly the services of a telecommunications access method, this approach is avoided today where possible because the programming necessary to interface directly with a telecommunications access method is much more complex than the programming needed to work with a TP monitor. Application programs that use TP monitors are often written in high-level languages, such as COBOL or PL/I. Some of today's fourth-generation languages also contain interfaces to the most popular TP monitors, thus allowing the traditional programming process to be bypassed in many cases.

TELEPROCESSING MONITOR FUNCTIONS

A teleprocessing monitor is a software package that serves as an interface between the messages that are sent and received over communication lines and the application programs that process those messages. The specific functions of each teleprocessing monitor are different, and the way in which they are used varies, but they all provide similar services. In general, a system programmer describes to the TP monitor the communication network environment, including the communication lines and the terminals attached to them. The system programmer also describes the application environment by assigning symbolic names to all the transaction types that the system uses and giving names to the application programs that process them. Some TP monitors also allow the system programmer to describe the file or database environment.

The teleprocessing monitor performs all the functions of sending and receiving messages over the communication network by requesting the services of the underlying telecommunications access method software. Three major functions are performed by a TP monitor in handling the communications-related aspects of the application systems under its control:

- Monitoring the communication network and using telecommunications access method software to read messages coming into the system
- Scheduling the appropriate application programs that are required to process input messages based on control information included in each message
- Accepting output messages from application programs and using telecommunications access method software to transmit them to their destinations

TP monitors operate in either of two ways. Some TP monitors read in each message and then immediately run the application program that is required to process it. Cullinet's IDMS/DC is an example of a TP monitor that normally operates in this manner. Other TP monitors store messages into queues that they maintain. Another task that operates concurrently with the message-reading task then selects messages from the queues based on a priority scheme and runs the appropriate application program to process each message. IBM's IMS/DC is an example of a TP monitor that uses message queues. Many TP monitors perform additional functions as well as those described above. For example, IBM's CICS provides functions that are related to the formatting of screens that are displayed on terminals. Box 32.1 briefly describes the two major TP monitor software subsystems that are available from IBM. Many software vendors supply TP monitors that perform services that are similar to those provided by IBM's TP monitor software.

IMS/DC

The remainder of this chapter examines the characteristics of a typical TP monitor. The one we use as an example is the particularly powerful IMS/DC TP monitor that is marketed by IBM. As we mentioned earlier, IMS/DC is an example of a TP monitor that uses a complex queuing scheme to separate the functions of reading transactions from terminals and selecting those transactions for processing by application programs.

IMS/DC RESOURCES

In the IMS/DC environment, all resources under the control of the IMS/DC software must be defined during system definition. There are two main categories of system resources that must be defined to IMS/DC: *application resources* and *data communications resources*. Application resources are those system re-

BOX 32.1 IBM TP monitors

- **IMS/DC.** IMS (short for *Information Management System*) is a family of software components whose main purpose is to provide database management services. However, one independent subsystem of IMS, called IMS/DC (short for *IMS/Data Communication*), is designed to provide teleprocessing monitor support. Although IMS/DC is designed to be run in conjunction with the database portions of the IMS software, the database portion, sometimes referred to as IMS/DB, and the data communications portion can be run separately and are separately priced by IBM. IMS/DC operates under the control of any of the MVS-type operating systems; there is no VSE version of IMS/DC.

- **CICS.** CICS (short for *Customer Information Control System*) is another IBM teleprocessing monitor. It provides roughly the same types of services as IMS/DC, although there is little compatibility between the two subsystems. The CICS software provides no direct database support, but does provide support for file operations on application files that are defined to the software; an interface is also provided that allows access to IMS databases. Like IMS/DC, CICS uses the services of a telecommunications access method in working with the communication-related resources of the system. Versions of CICS are available for both the MVS and VSE environments.

sources that are related to application programs that operate in the IMS/DC system. Specifically, these resources consist of *message processing programs* and *transactions*.

- **Message Processing Programs.** Message processing programs are application programs that are under the control of IMS/DC and are automatically loaded by IMS/DC at the appropriate time. Each MP program is assigned a unique one- to eight-character name.

- **Transactions.** A transaction is a message that has an MP program as its destination. Transactions can be sent to MP programs either from remote terminals or from other programs. Each transaction is assigned a unique one- to eight-character transaction code.

During IMS/DC system definition, names are given to MP program names and transaction codes, and each transaction code is associated with an MP program. Only one program can be assigned to process a given transaction; however, a given program can process more than one type of transaction.

A second category of resource that must be defined during IMS/DC system definition includes all the data communications hardware in the communications network. The following entities define the network to the IMS/DC software:

- **Communication Lines.** In an IMS/DC network, a single communication line can handle one or more remote terminals of a particular type. A line can be switched or nonswitched. Lines that connect terminals of a similar type can be grouped together into *line groups*.

- **Physical Terminals.** One or more physical terminals can be connected to each communication line through one or more levels of controllers. In a switched line network, each terminal can be connected to any one of several lines. In a nonswitched network, a terminal is always connected to the same line.

- **Logical Terminals.** MP programs do not communicate directly with physical terminals. Instead, messages that are destined for remote terminals include a one- to eight-character logical terminal name. When a logical terminal name message is sent, the physical terminal currently assigned to that logical terminal name receives the message. The system operator has commands that can be used to change the logical and physical terminal assignments at any time.

MESSAGE QUEUES   All messages that flow through IMS/DC are stored in *message queues*. IMS/DC maintains a separate message queue for each transaction code and for each logical terminal. As shown in Fig. 32.1, a separate task running in the IMS/DC region or address space selects transactions from the message queues for processing by MP programs. Because the queues often contain more transactions than can be processed at one time, a priority scheme is used in determining which transaction to select first from the various queues. Messages destined for logical terminals are also selected from the appropriate message queues and transmitted to the appropriate physical terminal at appropriate times.

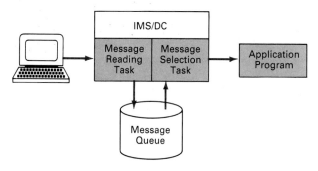

Figure 32.1   Message queues

OPERATING ENVIRONMENT

Multiple operating system regions or address spaces are normally used for running the IMS/DC software and the various MP programs. IMS/DC supports three region types: the IMS control region, MP regions, and BMP regions. Figure 32.2 shows a typical IMS/DC region configuration.

The IMS Control Region

The IMS control region handles all communication between IMS/DC and remote terminals and contains the IMS/DC software. The software running in the IMS control region controls the allocation of the various MP regions in the system. The IMS control region also contains the database management system software if the DBMS portion of IMS is also being used.

Message Processing Regions

The scheduling of MP programs into the MP regions is handled by the IMS/DC software. Each of the transaction codes defined to IMS/DC is assigned to a *transaction class* identified with a number from 1 to 255. Each MP region is set up to process transactions from up to four of the transaction classes. Each time an MP region becomes available, IMS/DC checks the message queues to see if a transaction of the appropriate class is available. If none is available, the region remains idle. If there are multiple transactions to choose from, IMS/DC uses a priority scheme to select the highest-priority transaction.

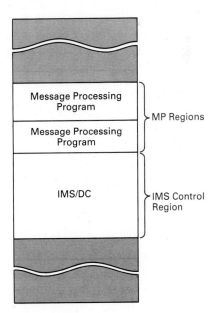

Figure 32.2 IMS/DC region configuration

Batch Message Processing Regions

A *batch message processing program (BMP program)* is a special type of message processing program that is designed to operate in the batch mode. The system operator initiates a BMP program in one of the BMP regions. IMS/DC does not automatically start BMP programs. A BMP program might be used when each transaction of a particular type might require substantial processing. Normally, MP programs are designed so that they occupy a message processing region for as short a time as possible. In cases that require lengthy processing times but not immediate responses, a BMP program might better suit the application requirements. Batch message processing programs are often used when it is desirable to submit input from a terminal but an immediate response back to the terminal is not required.

MESSAGE PROCESSING

IMS/DC messages can be divided into multiple segments, each of which contains up to 130 bytes of text. As shown in Fig. 32.3, the text of a message segment is preceded by a 2-byte-length field and 2 bytes of control information. In general, a message segment consists of a particular line of the total message. For example, if a terminal operator is required to send a message that consists of five individual lines, that message consists of five segments. For a program to send a message consisting of seven lines of data to a terminal or remote printer, the message will contain seven segments.

When a message processing program is loaded into a message processing region and control is passed to the MP program, there will be a transaction in the message queue waiting for it that has one of that program's assigned transaction codes. An MP program normally begins its processing by reading the first segment of the waiting message.

An MP program retrieves message segments by issuing CALL statements in a conventional programming language, such as COBOL, PL/I, or assembler language. CALLS to IMS/DC reference a number of parameters that describe the function to be performed. Among these parameters is a four-character *function code* that describes the type of service that is desired. Box 32.2 lists four IMS/DC services, with their associated function codes, that are commonly used in writing MP programs that send and receive messages.

The interface between the MP program and IMS/DC is designed so that

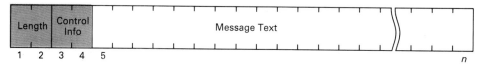

Figure 32.3   IMS/DC message segment

BOX 32.2   CALL statement function codes

- **Get-Unique (GU):** used to retrieve the first segment of a message from the message queue
- **Get-Next (GN):** used to retrieve the second and all subsequent message segments from the message queue
- **Insert (ISRT):** used to send a message to a logical terminal or to another MP program
- **Purge (PURG):** used to establish a synchronization point from which restart can begin should a system failure later occur

the message queue behaves in a manner similar to a sequential file. Each message retrieval CALL statement reads a new message segment until there are no more segments available in the message queue for that message. A status code value that is returned by IMS/DC tells the program when the end of the message has been reached.

IMS/DC DATA FLOW

To see how IMS/DC processes messages, we will walk through a simple example to see how data flows through the system. We will examine the sequence of events that occurs within the system after a terminal operator enters a message at a terminal.

Message Input

The terminal operator sends a message by entering it at the terminal and pressing the ENTER key. Software running in the IMS control region works with the telecommunications access method to handle the transmission of the message from the remote terminal to the central computing system. Each received message is accompanied by a transaction code and possibly a password. The transaction code and password are entered by the terminal operator or are supplied by software running either in the terminal equipment or in the central computing system.

After the message is received, the control region checks the transaction code against a list to see if the transaction code is valid; if required, it also verifies the password. If the transaction code and the password are valid, the message is stored in the appropriate message queue. As mentioned earlier, each transaction code and logical terminal name has its own message queue.

Message Selection

Another task running in the IMS control region selects messages from the message queues. When this task selects a message, it consults an internal list to see which MP program is associated with the message's transaction code. It then schedules that MP program for loading into an available MP region.

Message Processing

Once a message processing program is loaded into an MP region, a task is created, and control is passed to the MP program. The MP program then competes for system resources with all other tasks running in the system. The MP program begins by issuing a CALL statement to IMS/DC to retrieve the first message segment. The program then processes the data in that message segment, which may require making one or more file or database accesses. If the message consists of more than one segment, the program issues additional CALL statements to IMS/DC to retrieve the remaining message segments.

Message Output

If the MP program determines that a reply is necessary, the MP program issues CALL statements to IMS/DC to send one or more messages back to the originating terminal. Optionally, the program can send messages to other terminals, and can also put messages back into the message queues to be read by other MP or BMP programs.

IMS/DC MESSAGE SCHEDULING As we have seen, messages from terminals are stored into message queues before they are passed to message processing programs. IMS/DC uses a priority scheme in deciding which message to select next from the message queues. During IMS/DC system definition, the number of MP programs must be determined, and it must be decided which transaction codes each MP region should handle. Transactions are normally separated into classes based on their response time requirements. For example, a particular application system may have a particular transaction type that occurs very frequently and must be given a fast response time. One or more MP regions might be set aside for that transaction type only. The MP regions are set up based on the requirements of the individual MP programs that run in the system.

IMS/DC attempts to select a transaction for each of the message processing regions currently in operation. Each transaction type has two priorities associated with it: a *normal priority* and a *limit priority*. In addition, each transaction has a *limit count*.

Within each message queue, messages are queued serially by transaction code. When an MP region becomes available, IMS/DC examines the message queues to determine which messages can be handled by the available region. It then selects the transaction having the highest priority. To determine whether to use the normal priority or the limit priority, IMS/DC looks at how many transactions with each transaction code are stored in each message queue. If the number of transactions in a particular queue is greater than or equal to that transaction code's limit count, the limit priority is used. If the number of messages queued is less than the limit count, the normal priority is used.

MESSAGE FORMAT SERVICE

Message Format Service (MFS) is a powerful screen formatting facility that is part of the IMS/DC software. Messages to be sent to an MP program from a terminal often consist of entire screens of information. These screens often contain descriptive information that helps make the screen readable. When MFS is used, the MP program works only with certain predefined data fields. MFS inserts and removes fixed text, filler characters, and control codes that are required to format a screen at the terminal. MFS provides two control blocks, set up by macros, to separate out information of direct interest to the MP or BMP program.

One control block, called the *Message Input Descriptor* (MID), is used to describe an input message as the program would like to see it. The MID describes only those fields on the screen in which the program is interested. Another control block, called the *Device Input Format* (DIF), describes the screen format as the terminal operator formats it.

Two other MFS control blocks are used to help format screens that will be transmitted from an MP program to a terminal. The *Message Output Descriptor* (MOD) describes the message as the program formats it. Another control block, called the *Device Output Format* (DOF), describes the screen format as it will appear at the terminal. MFS uses the MOD and DOF to translate the data fields that the program places in the output message into a complete screen format as it will appear on the display screen.

MFS allows IMS/DC application programs to work with information on the data field level, avoiding concern over where on the screen the information is stored or should appear. It allows complex screen formats to be used without tying the MP program to the screen location where the pertinent information is stored.

In this and the preceding chapter, we have been discussing software that is used mainly in the mainframe data communication environment. The ubiquitous personal computer is playing an ever-increasing role in today's data processing environment. The software that is used to support data communication using personal computers is the subject of Chapter 33.

33 PERSONAL COMPUTER DATA COMMUNICATION SOFTWARE

We begin this chapter by examining the software that is available for implementing data communication applications on small computers. We end it by discussing what is lacking in today's software and predicting how this software is likely to evolve. No area of computing is growing and changing more rapidly than that of software for small computers. Our problem in writing this chapter is that much of what we say is likely to be obsolete by the time that it is read. For this reason we will not try to describe any particular software product or make specific recommendations. The realities of book publishing make it necessary for us to take a different approach here. We begin by examining the broad categories of software that can be used to create data communication applications using personal computers.

SERIAL PORTS   As we pointed out in Chapter 29, a popular hardware option for the IBM Personal Computer is the asynchronous communications adapter, often called a *serial port*. One or more serial ports can be an integral part of the small computer, as on many Apple Macintosh machines, or it can be implemented on a separate add-on circuit board, as is typical with many IBM personal computers. Such a board is marketed by IBM for those of its small computers that do not have serial ports as standard equipment. Many vendors of various other types of add-ons, such as additional RAM storage, also include a serial port on their boards. Other popular add-ons are available that combine a serial port and a modem on the same board. The various personal computer data communication hardware options are described in Chapter 29.

ASYNCHRONOUS TERMINAL EMULATION

The simplest asynchronous communication software packages are those that allow the personal computer to use a serial port to emulate an asynchronous terminal. The simplest of these software packages perform only the two functions shown in Fig. 33.1. A simple terminal emulation package monitors the keyboard and sends a character out the serial port each time a key is pressed; each time a character is received it is displayed on the computer's screen. The software at the other end of the communication line thinks it is communicating with an ordinary asynchronous terminal. Box 33.1 shows a program written in BASIC for the IBM personal computer that performs simple asynchronous terminal emulation.

ADVANCED FUNCTIONS

There are many commercially available programs that perform asynchronous terminal emulation. These programs, of course, are a good bit more sophisticated than the one shown in Box 33.1. In addition to emulating the input and output functions of a simple terminal, the commercially available programs generally perform many additional functions that allow the personal computer to function as an intelligent terminal. Some of these functions are listed in Box 33.2.

FILE TRANSFERS

A particularly useful function, performed by almost all asynchronous terminal emulation packages, is to transfer files between two personal computers or between a personal computer and a larger processor. In the mid-1970s, Ward Christensen, an early microcomputer user, developed a simple protocol to support file transfers, which he placed into the public domain. This protocol has become known as the *XMODEM* protocol, after the name of the original program that supported it. Over the years, the XMODEM protocol has become widely used, and most commercial software packages that perform file transfer operations support the XMODEM protocol. Even though more efficient and reliable

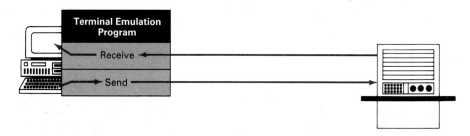

Figure 33.1   Terminal emulation program

BOX 33.1   Terminal emulation program

```
110 SCREEN 0,0
120 WIDTH 40
130 KEY OFF
140 CLS
150 CLOSE
160 DEFINT A-Z
170 FALSE=0
180 TRUE=NOT FALSE
190 XOFF$=CHR$(19)
200 XON$=CHR$(17)
210 OPEN "COM1:300,E,7" AS #1
220 OPEN "SCRN:" FOR OUTPUT AS #2
230 LOCATE ,,1
240 PAUSE=FALSE
250 ON ERROR GOTO 410
260 B$=INKEY$
270 IF B$<>"" THEN PRINT #1,B$;
280 IF EOF(1) THEN 260
290 IF LOC(1)>128 THEN PAUSE=TRUE
300 PRINT #1,XOFF$
310 A$=INPUT$(LOC(1),#1)
320 LFP=0
330 LFP=INSTR(LFP+1,A$,CHR$(10))
340 IF LFP>0 THEN MID$(A$,LFP,1)-" "
350 GOTO 330
360 PRINT #2,A$;
370 IF LOC(1)>0 THEN 290
380 IF PAUSE THEN PAUSE=FALSE
390 PRINT #1,XON$;
400 GOTO 260
410 PRINT "ERROR NO.";ERR
420 RESUME
```

This is a simple program, written in BASIC for the IBM personal computer, that performs asynchronous terminal emulation. It accepts characters entered at the keyboard and sends them out the COM1: serial port. It simultaneously monitors the COM1: port and displays on the screen each character that it receives.

protocols exist for file transfers, the XMODEM protocol has become some-what of a defacto standard for personal computers.

THE XMODEM PROTOCOL

When the XMODEM protocol is used, data is trans-mitted in fixed-size, 128-character blocks. A fixed-length format is used so that the 128 data bytes can contain any desired bit configuration with no danger of any of the characters being interpreted as control functions. Figure 33.2 shows the format of the

BOX 33.2 Terminal emulation software functions

- **Asynchronous Terminal Emulation.** All asynchronous terminal emulation packages perform the simple input and output functions that are performed by an asynchronous terminal.

- **Automatic Dialing.** The program may store a telephone number list and allow the user to automatically dial up a time-sharing service or computer utility.

- **Capture to Memory or Disk.** The program may allow the user to automatically capture for later use all the data that flows back and forth between the personal computer and the computer to which it is connected. The data can be captured in memory, and then later stored into a disk file, or it can be captured directly to disk.

- **Script Facility.** The program might implement some type of script facility that allows the user to create sequences of commands that are sent out automatically over the communication line. These scripts can be used to perform any type of processing, including automatic log-on sequences.

- **File Transfers.** The program might perform the error checking necessary to permit files to be transferred between computer systems.

- **Downloading Capabilities.** The program might allow the user to change the input source from the keyboard to a file in the midst of an interactive session. The computer to which the user is connected then accepts data from the file as if it were being keyed in by the user. This is useful in electronic mail applications where the user wishes to compose an electronic mail message offline before logging onto the electronic mail service.

blocks that are transmitted when using the XMODEM protocol. Each block begins with the SOH ASCII code. This is followed by a one-byte sequence number that is increased by one for each new block. The sequence number is followed by another character that contains the complement of the sequence number. Finally come 128 bytes of data. The 128-byte block of data is followed by a one-byte check sum. The technique used to develop the check sum consists simply of adding together the contents of the bytes that make up the 128 data characters and using the low-order 8 bits of that sum.

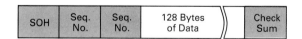

Figure 33.2 XMODEM transmission block format

Figure 33.3 illustrates how data flows between two computers when the XMODEM protocol is employed. In this example, the sender is transmitting two blocks of data to the receiver. The steps in the flow are as follows:

1. The receiver begins the data transfer operation by transmitting the ASCII NAK code to the sender. (See Chapter 18 for a discussion of the ASCII character code.)

2. The sender replies by transmitting a block of data in the format described above.

3. The receiver receives the block, performs the check sum calculation, and compares the calculated check sum to the check sum received at the end of the block. The values are the same, so the receiver transmits an ACK code back to the sender.

4. The sender adds one to the sequence number and sends the second block.

5. The receiver performs the check sum verification procedure and detects a mismatch. It responds by transmitting a NAK code back to the sender.

6. The sender retransmits the second block.

7. The receiver correctly receives the second block and replies by transmitting an ACK code.

8. The sender indicates that all data has been sent by transmitting an EOT code to the receiver.

9. The receiver acknowledges receipt of the EOT by transmitting an ACK back to the sender.

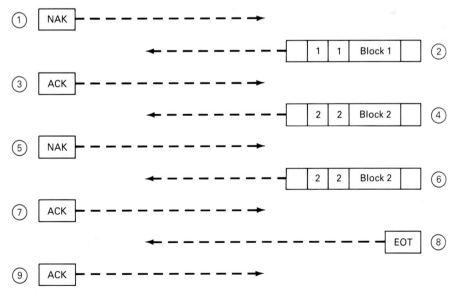

Figure 33.3   XMODEM data flow

SYNCHRONOUS TERMINAL EMULATION

Software that performs synchronous terminal emulation performs many of the same functions described earlier for asynchronous terminal emulation. Synchronous terminal emulation programs are generally supplied with the communication adapters that are designed to emulate certain types of synchronous terminals. For example, the IRMA card, described in Chapter 29, is supplied with a software package that allows the personal computer to perform all of the functions normally associated with a synchronous 3270-type terminal.

In many types of applications where mainframe programs must communicate with programs running in personal computers, or where personal computers must communicate with one another, asynchronous terminal emulation techniques are used to handle communication. This is because the protocols involved in communicating with 3270 terminals are widely used and well understood. In the future it is likely that protocols better suited to program-to-program communication will become more prevalent and will replace these more cumbersome terminal emulation techniques. An example of such a protocol is the protocol used by the *Advanced Program-to-Program Communication* (APPC) facility of SNA. This protocol is described further at the end of this chapter and is also discussed in Chapter 39.

MICRO-MAINFRAME LINK SOFTWARE

Many software packages are available that perform more advanced functions than terminal emulation and file transfers. These packages are generally referred to as *micro-mainframe link* packages. Unfortunately, the term "micro-mainframe link" has been much overused, to the point where it has now become almost meaningless. The term was originally used to refer to software that allows a personal computer to be hooked to a mainframe to perform such functions as downloading data. The downloaded data could then be used to perform data analysis functions on the personal computer. However, today, nearly any vendor which has software that allows a personal computer to be connected to a larger system refers to that software as a micro-mainframe link. This often includes the simplest terminal emulation and file transfer software.

We feel that for a package to be called a micro-mainframe link it should perform advanced functions over and above terminal emulation and file transfers. As an example of such advanced functions, some true micro-mainframe link packages allow virtual disk drives to be created on the mainframe. The personal computer user is allowed to access the virtual disk on the mainframe as if it were a disk drive attached directly to the personal computer. With a virtual disk, the communication functions that take place in moving data to and from the mainframe are transparent to the user. Another advanced function might be extracting selected data from a mainframe database and converting it into the personal computer format necessary for manipulating the data with conventional personal computer software, such as a spreadsheet program. Many other advanced micro-mainframe link functions are also possible.

INTEGRATED
SOFTWARE
Much more can be done with personal computer data communication software than terminal emulation, file transfers, and simple micro-mainframe links. To perform truly advanced functions, it is necessary to closely coordinate the functions that are performed by the personal computer and the functions that are performed by the software that runs in the mainframe or departmental processor to which the personal computer is attached. Figure 33.4 shows a hardware environment that is becoming commonplace. In this configuration, personal computers are attached directly to a host mainframe, which may itself be connected to a complex network of other mainframes. Figure 33.5 shows a second configuration in which a group of personal computers is connected to a departmental minicomputer, which in turn is connected to a larger mainframe network.

Although it is possible today to create all manner of distributed data processing configurations, the software to support such complex environments is lagging far behind the hardware. What is needed in complex environments that

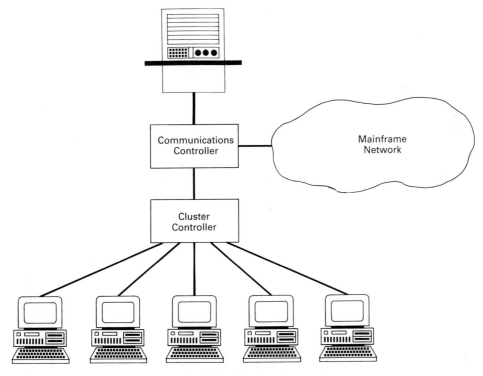

Figure 33.4   Mainframe network

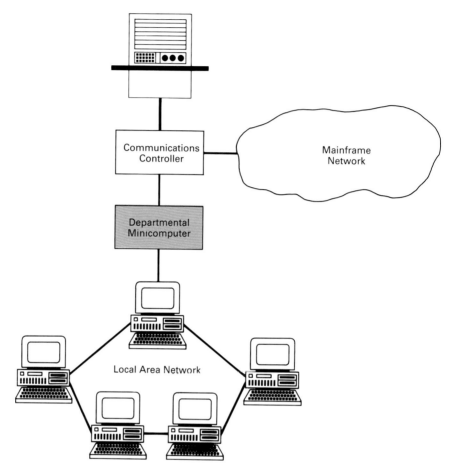

Figure 33.5   Departmental processor

have multiple levels of processors is *seamless integration* of functions. This seamless integration is extremely difficult to achieve. An example will help point out where we are now and the direction in which we should be heading.

A COMPLEX IBM NETWORK

While this book was being written, one of the authors had an opportunity to be present at a demonstration of the capabilities that IBM has for interconnecting its mainframes, departmental processors, and personal computers. The collection of hardware was quite impressive. Personal computers, System/36 and System/38 minicomputers, and some of IBM's largest mainframes, running in both the MVS/XA and the VM environments, were all connected together into a distributed processing configuration. The personal computers were connected to a token ring local area network (see Chapter 40), which was in turn connected to the various larger processors. Each personal computer was able to share peripheral devices, such as modems, printers, and large disk drives on the local area network (LAN), and were able to gain access to software running on the departmental processors and on the mainframes. The system worked rather well and demonstrated how IBM's various computer lines could be made to work together. However, once a number of day-to-day tasks were demonstrated, it became clear that the level of skill and knowledge required of a personal computer user on this network would be clearly beyond that of the average information worker.

AN ELECTRONIC MAIL EXAMPLE   In one demonstration of the IBM network, it was shown how a personal computer user could send an electronic mail message to another user. The personal computer we used in this demonstration was connected, via the local area network, to an IBM mainframe running MVS/XA. The personal computer of the user to whom we wanted to send the message was connected to a different large mainframe that was operating in the VM/CMS environment. The procedure went something like this:

1. We logged onto the personal computer and were greeted with the familiar ''C>'' PC-DOS prompt. We then used a PC-DOS command to load in the local area network software.

2. We next issued a command to the LAN software that allowed us to gain access to a modem card installed in another personal computer on the token ring LAN. We used a different menu structure and command set here than those used to communicate with PC-DOS.

3. We next loaded in a terminal emulation software package that allowed us to place a local telephone call to the mainframe. At this third level of software, we used yet another menu structure and command set.

4. Once the mainframe responded to our request for access, we issued a series of VTAM commands that put us in contact with the CICS teleprocessing monitor running on the mainframe. We were now at the fourth software level and saw different types of messages and used a fourth command set.

5. Once we were accepted by CICS, we were able to log onto the office automation and electronic mail software running on the MVS/XA mainframe. We accomplished this at the fifth software level by using yet another command set.

6. We next composed our electronic mail message and got it accepted into the mainframe messaging system. We accomplished this at the sixth software level by negotiating a different set of menus and using a different set of commands.

7. Finally, we issued a complex series of commands that caused the message to be routed from the MVS/XA mainframe to the VM/CMS mainframe, which ran similar but incompatible office automation and electronic mail software. This took place at the seventh level of software that, again, used a different command set.

To perform what should have been a simple task, it was necessary for us to have the necessary skill to work our way up the software hierarchy by communicating directly with seven distinctly different software entities, each of which issued its own messages or displayed its own menus. We were required to know, at least on a rudimentary level, how to issue commands to these seven software entities, each of which used a different command syntax. Figure 33.6 summarizes how the following software entities were involved in the message transmission above:

1. PC-DOS running on the personal computer
2. LAN software running on the personal computer
3. Terminal emulation software running on the personal computer
4. Telecommunications access method software running on the mainframe
5. Teleprocessing monitor software running on the mainframe
6. Office automation and electronic mail software running on the MVS/XA mainframe
7. Office automation and electronic mail software running on the VM/CMS mainframe

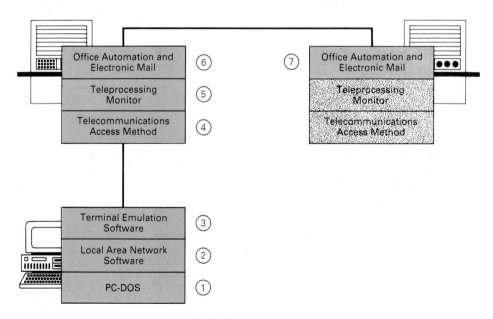

Figure 33.6 Seven software entities

It became very clear during the demonstration that it was not possible simply to log onto the personal computer, compose a message, and state its destination. We had to negotiate a complex series of menu- and command-oriented programs to perform this simple task. To be fair, a few of the interactions described above had been preprogrammed and were handled by automatic log-on sequences. However, while all the software was in a sense integrated and did allow us to perform the required function, the integration could in no sense be called seamless.

At each point in time, we had to know exactly what software entity we were interacting with and how to issue the necessary commands to get us to the next level of software. The people demonstrating this system, although they were quite knowledgeable and actually used this software on a day-to-day basis, made many errors as they went along, and it took 10 or 15 minutes to get the message sent to its destination.

SEAMLESS INTEGRATION

For a personal computer user to effectively use a distributed system, it must operate much more simply than the system described above. For electronic mail, the user should be required simply to compose the message, indicate the user ID or network address of the destination user, and send it on its way. The user of the personal computer should have one software package, with a simple user interface, that handles the interactions that are required with all the higher levels of software. If users are required to negotiate several complex layers of software and are required to memorize a different command syntax at each level, they will avoid using the system and will find other ways to accomplish their tasks. What is needed is software running at each of the levels described above that is better integrated and can easily be automatically controlled by software running in the personal computer.

To put things into perspective, there are many office automation systems available, both from IBM and from other vendors, that are easier to use than the system described above. But they are generally simpler systems that do not attempt to integrate diverse types of hardware. In today's environment, it is nearly always true that the more complex the hardware configuration, and the more diverse are the computing systems that are interconnected, the more difficult the system is to use.

To its credit, IBM understands the difficulties that users have with distributed systems and is taking steps to provide more seamless integration of software functions. For example, IBM is currently developing a complex series of application architectures whose aim is to standardize the application programming interfaces across its many product lines. However, this task is extremely complex and will take years to complete. Another tool that is being used to provide the required integration in a distributed environment is the *Advanced Program-to-Program Communication* (APPC) facility that is provided in the

SNA environment (see Chapter 39). APPC provides application developers on mainframes, minicomputers, and personal computers with a standard protocol that can be used in transferring messages between intelligent machines. As this book was nearing completion, the APPC protocols had just been adopted as one of the standards for the higher-level layers of the OSI reference model (see Chapter 35). Acceptance of the APPC protocols as an international standard makes it more likely that the machines of different vendors will be able to communicate in a compatible manner.

PART VII   DISTRIBUTED PROCESSING AND COMPUTER NETWORKS

34 HIGH-LEVEL STANDARDS AND PROTOCOLS

All advanced computer systems have software that has grown up in layers rather like the skins of an onion. Different layers relate to different types of functions and services. This applies to operating systems, to database software, and also to data transmission software. Each layer that is added is an attempt to increase the usefulness of the underlying hardware or to introduce modularity by dividing the complex set of functions into discrete layers.

COMPARISON WITH DATABASE

When data is transmitted over a communication line, or stored in a storage unit, it becomes a serial stream of bits. In both cases, layers of software exist between the user program and the physical storage unit or transmission system. Conversion between the data the user perceives and what is physically transmitted or stored ranges from simple to complex, depending on the sophistication of the system. Figure 34.1 shows the layers used in implementing database management systems. The layers closest to the user process provide user services and represent data in the form most useful to the user. As we move to the layers that are closer to the computer (the central layer), the data becomes more abstract. The bit streams stored or transmitted serve multiple applications and are manipulated to suit the diverse mechanisms employed. The bit streams may be sliced up or converted into different forms for reasons of economy, efficiency, reliability, or security.

DATA COMMUNICATION SOFTWARE LAYERS

For advanced data communication systems, in which intelligent machines are interconnected, layers of software (or hardware or microcode) are needed around the telecommunications links to make these

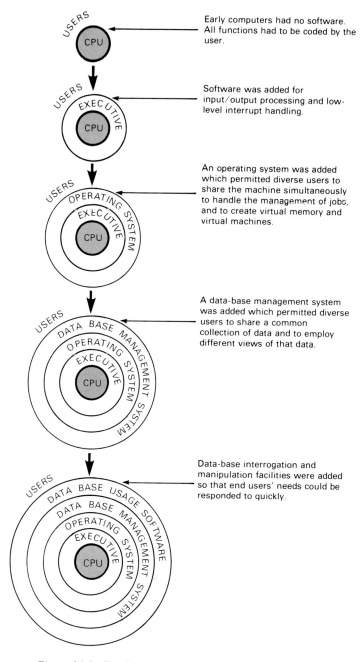

Early computers had no software. All functions had to be coded by the user.

Software was added for input/output processing and low-level interrupt handling.

An operating system was added which permitted diverse users to share the machine simultaneously to handle the management of jobs, and to create virtual memory and virtual machines.

A data-base management system was added which permitted diverse users to share a common collection of data and to employ different views of that data.

Data-base interrogation and manipulation facilities were added so that end users' needs could be responded to quickly.

Figure 34.1   Database management system software layers

more useful, to hide the complexity from the system's users, and to separate the functions into more manageable pieces. Figure 34.2 shows four layers of control that are fundamental to all advanced data communication systems.

Physical Connection

The innermost layer is the *physical connection* that must exist between machines. As we have seen in Chapter 10, this layer handles the physical transmission of bits over a physical connection.

Link Control

The next layer is the *link control* layer, which relates to how data is transmitted over a physical connection. As we saw in Part IV, throughout the history of teleprocessing there have been many different forms of link control. Some were character oriented, such as asynchronous control. Some were oriented to blocks of characters, such as the binary-synchronous protocol. More recently the bit-oriented link control procedures have emerged.

Transmission Control

The third layer, *transmission control,* in conjunction with the inner layers, provides the transmission network—the transmission subsystem. The transmission network can be regarded as an entity that the higher levels employ for moving data from one user machine to another through multiple intermediate nodes, such as concentrators, packet switches, and line controllers.

Session Services

The *session services* layer, external to the transmission subsystem in Fig. 34.2, provides a variety of services that are used to establish and operate sessions between the user machines. As we will see throughout the chapters in this part, a rich array of such services is possible and desirable.

EXISTING NETWORK ARCHITECTURES

The four layers discussed above are fundamental to data networking and distributed systems. They are found in all existing network architectures. Their detail differs somewhat from one architecture to another, especially in the outermost layer. The functions performed in the transmission control layer and the session services layer are themselves often split into multiple layers. Figure 34.3 shows the correspondence between the four fundamental layers discussed above and the layers defined for the OSI reference model and the layers of IBM's SNA. (The OSI reference model is discussed in Chapter 35, and SNA is described in Chapter 39.)

USERS
SESSION SERVICES
TRANSMISSION SUBSYSTEM
TRANSMISSION CONTROL
LINK CONTROL
PHYSICAL CONNECTION

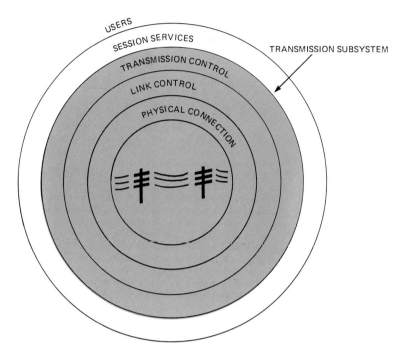

Figure 34.2 Data communication system software layers

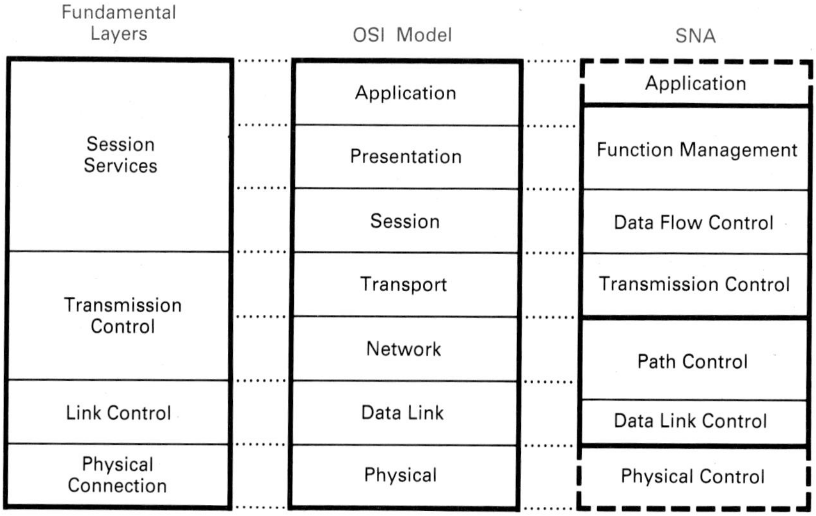

Fundamental Layers
OSI Model
SNA
Session Services
Transmission Control
Link Control
Physical Connection
Application
Presentation
Session
Transport
Network
Data Link
Physical
Application
Function Management
Data Flow Control
Transmission Control
Path Control
Data Link Control
Physical Control

Figure 34.3 Layer comparisons

However the layers are defined for a particular architecture, they form a standard for that architecture. When a particular computer manufacturer defines a network architecture, the many different machines of that manufacturer incorporate the same standard layers. They form the basis for communication between machines that are otherwise diverse. It is highly desirable that machines designed by *different* manufacturers should be able to communicate. For this to be possible the various machines have to use the same layers, and the formats of data and control messages that pass between the layers have to be compatible.

LAYERED ARCHITECTURE TRADE-OFFS

The main disadvantage of a layered architecture is that it increases the total overhead required for communication. The layer 2 frames, layer 3 packets, and higher-layer session messages each need headers, and the total of these headers often adds up to 100 bits or more. Many of the bits would be required whether or not a layered architecture were used. However, when each layer is designed to be of general use and is independent of the other layers, the overhead is usually higher, and the number of processing instructions needed to control the transmission is higher.

When general-purpose layers are used, there may be some overlap of functions. This may occur, for example, when the interfaces between the layers are standards adopted by a manufacturer or common carrier or by the standards organizations. This duplication of function is not a serious problem, merely an increase in overhead. In terms of processing cost it can be offset by placing some of the lower-level layers in peripheral microprocessors and other distributed systems.

In all layered architectures there is a trade-off between the advantages of layering and the increased overhead it incurs. The duplication of function is likely to be less if all the layers are designed by one design team to form part of a common architecture. The overhead can be lessened by designing the mechanisms and message headers so that the more complex functions are *optional*. Simple networks should have simple mechanisms. Complex networks have more elaborate mechanisms and longer message headers. The higher-level layers are not needed for all communication. They can therefore be designed so that they can shrink to nothing or almost to nothing when not needed. Simple communication should not be penalized by mechanisms designed for complex communication.

The advantages of layering are immense. They are summarized in Box 34.1. There is no doubt that layered architectures and standard interfaces between the layers will lead to a much greater interconnectibility of machines.

BOX 34.1   Layering advantages and disadvantages

Advantages of Layered Architectures

1. Any given layer can be modified or upgraded without affecting the other layers.
2. Modularization by means of layering simplifies the overall design.
3. Different layers can be assigned to different standards committees or different design teams.
4. Fundamentally different mechanisms can be substituted without affecting more than one layer (e.g., packet switching versus leased-line concentrators).
5. Different machines can plug in at different levels.
6. The relationships between the different control functions can be better understood when they are split into layers. This is especially true for those control actions that occur sequentially in time from layer to layer.
7. Common lower-level services can be shared by different higher-level users.
8. Functions, especially at the lower layers, can be removed from software and built into hardware or microcode.

Disadvantages of Layered Architectures

1. The total overhead is somewhat higher.
2. The communicating machines may have to use some functions that they could do without.
3. To make each layer usable by itself, there may be some small duplication in function between layers.
4. As technology changes, the functions may not be in the most cost-effective layer.

In general, the advantages are great; the disadvantages are slight.

REQUIREMENTS FOR HIGH-LEVEL STANDARDS AND PROTOCOLS

The time it takes to write programs and the shortage of programmers are perhaps the main factors discouraging a more comprehensive use of computers. Too much of the available talent is drowning in the problems of coding and debugging. The years ahead are going to be ones of ever-increasing complexity in the design of systems, and it will be increasingly important to protect application programmers from the monstrous complications that will entangle them if they venture into complex areas such as the control of integrated communication networks.

Running counter to this trend is the spread of minicomputers and personal computers. But even here one wonders how many small computers will exist in a decade's time without the capability to connect easily with distant library computers, databases, number crunchers, and other specialized services.

The overhead associated with systems that require complex software, such as systems that conform to network architectures like the OSI model and IBM's SNA, is going to become very high. This situation will no doubt meet with protests from persons such as those who objected to the overhead incurred by languages such as FORTRAN when they were first used, and then to the overhead of operating systems.

However, one force is moving us inexorably in the direction of increased software capability: The cost of the hardware is dropping fast. The numbers of machine instructions that can be executed, or the number of bits that can be stored, for $1 are increasing exponentially. New techniques now emerging in the research laboratories will ensure that a near exponential growth continues for many years to come. In 10 years' time we will probably be able to store 100 times as many bits and execute 100 times as many instructions as today—for the same price.

However, whereas machine capability is developing at this amazing rate, programmer capability is not. Programmers are, if anything, increasing in cost. Are there any conceivable techniques by which we could make an application programmer 100 times more productive?

HIGH-LEVEL LANGUAGES

The first essential is that high-level languages must be available for all data transmission applications. For programming realtime systems in the 1960s, the use of FORTRAN, ALGOL, COBOL, and PL/I was the exception rather than the rule. In the future, application programming in any language lower than those must become unthinkable, and the language arguments should revolve around fourth-generation languages that provide even greater levels of productivity.

Application programmers should be able to forget about the telecommunications network almost completely. They should use high-level instructions with symbolic names to specify communication paths or network devices, and software running in various network machines should take care of all transmission and network control questions. This will be an increasingly complex function as network structures become more complex.

TRANSPARENT FACILITIES

The concept of transparency is an important one in data transmission. It is important that complex facilities be made as easy as possible for programmers and users to employ. In Chapter 4 we gave a simple definition for the term *transparent*. As we indicated there, a transparent facility is one that appears not to exist, but in fact does. Three types of transparency are especially important: *network transparency, terminal transparency,* and *code transparency.*

NETWORK TRANSPARENCY

It is desirable that application programmers be isolated as completely as possible from the complexities of the transmission network. They should code high-level input/output instructions that specify symbolic network addresses and be unconcerned with how data reaches its destination. We will refer to this facility as *network transparency*. In effect, the communication network should be invisible to programmers. They should perceive the terminal and its relation to their programs, and know nothing about the layers in between. The terminal in this case could be either local or remote and it would make no difference to the application programs. The data would travel between the two with the same result.

In a system that implements network transparency, the application program could be transferred to a computer with a different communication network, and no change should be necessary. It should be possible to change the network drastically without affecting the application programs. The change may happen suddenly, for example, if a leased line fails and a dial-up connection is made, perhaps with quite a different line organization. To achieve network transparency, complex software for network control is needed. The more sophisticated the network, the more software features are required.

TERMINAL TRANSPARENCY

It may be desirable to have not only the *network* but also the *terminal* transparent. If the software provides *terminal transparency*, a terminal of one type can be substituted for a terminal of another type, given the same symbolic address, and no change would be needed in the application programs. A user could dial the same program from a printer terminal, a simple display terminal, or a complex intelligent terminal with data storage capability. The software might allow terminals of all different types to be interconnected.

Terminal transparency is probably not completely attainable between *all* terminals, because there is such a diversity of types. A few handle only digits; some only Yes/No or specially labeled lights. Some have elaborate editing logic and internal programming. Some handle graphics; some voice answerback.

It is possible, however, to divide all terminals into a number of categories such that transparency is attainable within a category. This would seem a worthwhile objective in view of the increasing proliferation of terminals on the market. Many attempts at standardization have worked but within a limited group of machines, and new reasons have emerged for designing machines outside the restrictions or for inventing yet another level of standardization. The mess, as some would call it, is likely to become worse, not better; therefore, there is great value in the concept of terminal transparency.

CODE TRANSPARENCY

A third form of transparency is *code transparency,* which occurs when a network and line-control scheme is able to transmit all possible combinations of bits. Some public data networks require certain bit patterns for network functions, and these patterns must be unique. Some data link control schemes attach special significance to certain bit patterns. As we have seen in Part IV, the most modern bit-oriented data link protocols provide code transparency and allow the transmission of random bit patterns over data links.

LOGICAL AND PHYSICAL TRANSMISSION

Most systems analysts are familiar with the concept of logical and physical records on tape or disk. The *logical record* is the input or output of an application program. The *physical record* is what is actually written on an external storage medium, and it often contains several logical records blocked together. In data transmission, too, the units of data that travel over the data links are generally different from the messages that are generated by programs, and they differ in more complex ways. In discussing these concepts further in this chapter, we will call the program's input/output item the *message* and the unit of data that is transmitted the *physical transmission frame*.

The message will have control characters and a destination address added to it in order that the destination device can receive it and interpret it correctly. We will call the combination of message, destination address, and control characters the *terminal transmission block*. The terminal transmission block will in some cases contain no user data. It might simply be requesting a controlling action, as in error control or addressing. It might sometimes have more than one address.

The *physical transmission frame* might contain several *terminal transmission frames*. It might also carry its own control bits, an address, and error detection bits.

LEVELS OF SOFTWARE

The levels of software producing the message, the terminal transmission block, and the physical transmission frame are completely separate in advanced data communication systems, such as public data networks and systems that conform to IBM's SNA architecture. The future trend in communication software is toward systems that conform to the seven-layer OSI reference model. In layered systems, each software layer is independent of all the other layers. Communication between layers is done by adhering to rigidly defined interface standards. This allows each layer to be changed and enhanced without the changes affecting the layers that surround it.

ROUTING AND JOB CONTROL

An increasing number of networks are likely to connect more than one computer. There are two main reasons for this. The first is that *similar* computers can be connected for load sharing. This technique can substantially decrease the turnaround time for batch jobs. The second is that computers with different facilities can be interconnected to make a wide range of capabilities available to the user. In some cases, a job given to a small local computer will automatically be passed on to a larger or faster machine. A job requiring a particular database can automatically be passed on to a machine having access to it.

DIRECTORY FUNCTIONS

Terminal users will often have many different computer services available to them. A user's first step will often be to find the right computer. At present a terminal user does this by dialing a known telephone number. It might be desirable to have directory services available to terminal users. Users might type in the name of the services they need and be automatically switched to them. They might carry on dialogs with directory routines to locate the required facilities. In the future, a user may have an entire ''yellow pages'' of computer services available on the terminal screen; and when a service is selected, the computer will automatically switch to the machine offering that service. ''Directory'' software may become a standard part of computer networks. Having selected a computer in this way, the user might not know where it is. The software in the machine to which the user's terminal is connected may automatically route messages to it.

In Chapter 35 we discuss the seven-layer architecture defined by the OSI reference model developed by the International Standards Organization (ISO). As mentioned above, the OSI model represents the future direction of advanced computer networking systems and provides an overall umbrella for the high-level standards and protocols that will be used in the future.

35 THE OPEN SYSTEMS INTERCONNECT MODEL

Given the immense proliferation of machines now occurring, one of the activities most important to the future of data processing is the setting of standards to enable machines of different manufacturers and different countries to communicate. As a start in the setting of such standards, the *International Standards Organization* (ISO), in Geneva, Switzerland, has defined a seven-layer architecture. The seven ISO layers define a generalized architecture called the *Reference Model of Open Systems Interconnection* (OSI reference model or OSI model). These are shown in Fig. 35.1. The ISO International Standard 7498 is the original source of documentation of the OSI reference model. The OSI reference model is also now documented in the CCITT X.200 series of recommendations (see Box 35.1). The ISO and CCITT versions of the OSI model are essentially identical. The primary purpose of the OSI model is to provide a basis for coordinating the development of standards that relate to the flexible interconnection of systems using data communication facilities. It is the plan of the CCITT, for example, to document in its X series of recommendations comprehensive standards and protocols for each of the seven OSI model layers, many of which are already documented in the CCITT Red Book (see Chapter 4).

CORPORATION FOR OPEN SYSTEMS

Many computer manufacturers, software companies, and telecommunications vendors are actively involved in the development of standards that support OSI, and over the years, will provide capabilities for coexisting with equipment and systems that conform to the OSI model. In 1985, an organization known as the Corporation for Open Systems (COS) was formed in the United States under the auspices of the Computer and Communications Industry Association. A number of large organizations, including IBM and many other computer manufacturers, have joined the COS. The COS

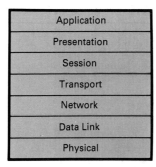

Figure 35.1   OSI reference model layers

has as its charter the monitoring of OSI standards development and also the monitoring of standards in the area of *integrated services digital network* (ISDN) development. ISDN standards have to do with the combining of all types of traffic, including voice, data, and images, over the same communication facilities.

BOX 35.1   CCITT OSI Model X-200 series recommendations

- **Recommendation X.200:** Reference Model of Open Systems Interconnection for CCITT Applications
- **Recommendation X.210:** Open System Interconnection (OSI) Layer Service Definition Conventions
- **Recommendation X.213:** Network Service Definition for Open Systems Interconnection (OSI) for CCITT Applications
- **Recommendation X.214:** Transport Service Definition for Open Systems Interconnection (OSI) for CCITT Applications
- **Recommendation X.215:** Session Service Definition for Open Systems Interconnection (OSI) for CCITT Applications
- **Recommendation X.224:** Transport Protocol Specification for Open Systems Interconnection (OSI) for CCITT Applications
- **Recommendation X.225:** Session Protocol Specification for Open Systems Interconnection (OSI) for CCITT Applications
- **Recommendation X.244:** Procedure for the Exchange of Protocol Identification during Virtual Call Establishment on Packet Switched Public Data Networks
- **Recommendation X.250:** Formal Description Techniques for Data Communication Protocols and Services

INTERCONNECTION OF SYSTEMS   The OSI model is concerned with the *interconnection of systems*—the way they exchange information—not the *internal functions* that are performed by a given system. In OSI terminology, a *system* is defined as "a set of one or more computers, the associated software, peripherals, terminals, human operators, physical processes, transfer means, etc., that forms an autonomous whole capable of performing information processing and/or information transfer."

The OSI model provides a generalized view of a layered architecture. With the broad definition that has been given for a system, the architecture can apply to a very simple system, such as the connection of a terminal to a computer, or to a very complex system, such as the interconnection of two entire computer networks. It can also be used as a model for a network architecture, which is how we will view it here. The development of the OSI model is still in progress. For some areas, specific standards have been defined in support of the model; in other areas, standards still need to be developed.

There are some basic concepts that underlie the layered architecture of the OSI model. The first is that of an *entity,* which is an active element within a layer. Two entities within the same layer are called *peer entities*. Entities in one layer provide services to entities in the layer above them, and in turn, receive services from entities in the layer below them. For example, entities in the presentation layer provide services to the application layer, and receive services from the session layer. A key part, then, of the definition of a layer is the set of services it provides. In addition, each layer performs a set of functions in providing its services. We will also discuss the functions that a layer performs in providing its services to the next-higher layer.

SERVICE-DATA-UNITS   The units of data that are handled by the various layers are defined by the OSI model as *service-data-units*. The name of each service-data-unit begins with the name of the layer with which it is associated. The service-data-units handled by the physical layer are called *physical-service-data-units,* the service-data-units handled by the data link layer are called *data-link-service-data-units,* and so on. The data units handled by the lower-level layers have come to have informal names that are often referenced in the literature. For example, data-link-service-data-units are often called *frames,* and network-service-data-units are typically called *packets*.

DEFINING THE LAYERS   The CCITT study group that was responsible for defining the OSI reference model began by establishing a number of principles that guided the development of the architecture. These principles are listed in Box 35.2. Although it may be difficult to prove that the seven layers selected represent the best possible so-

BOX 35.2   Principles of layering

- **Principle 1.** Do not create so many layers as to make the system engineering task of describing and integrating the layers more difficult than necessary.

- **Principle 2.** Create a boundary at a point where the description of services can be small and the number of interactions across the boundary are minimized.

- **Principle 3.** Create separate layers to handle functions that are manifestly different in the process performed or the involved technology.

- **Principle 4.** Collect similar functions in the same layer.

- **Principle 5.** Select boundaries at a point that past experience has demonstrated to be successful.

- **Principle 6.** Create a layer of easily localized functions so that the layer could be totally redesigned and its protocols changed in a major way to take advantage of new advances in architectural, hardware, or software technology without changing the expected services from and provided to the adjacent layers.

- **Principle 7.** Create a boundary where it may be useful at some point in time to have the corresponding interface standardized.

- **Principle 8.** Create a layer where there is a need for a different level of abstraction in the handling of data.

- **Principle 9.** Allow changes of functions or protocols to be made within a layer without affecting other layers.

- **Principle 10.** Create for each layer boundaries with its upper and lower layers only.

lution, the general principles listed in Box 35.2 guided the CCITT study group in answering the questions of where a boundary should be placed and how many layers there should be. Given the 10 principles, the following describes the rationale that was used in establishing each of the seven OSI layers:

- **Physical Layer.** It was established that the OSI model must be designed to support a wide variety of physical media for interconnection using suitable control procedures. Application of principles 3, 5, and 8 led to the identification of the physical layer as the lowest layer in the architecture.

- **Data Link Layer.** Some physical media require techniques for the error-free transfer data over a connection that has a relatively high error rate. Data link protocols already existed for handling transmission errors, and it was determined that the architecture should accommodate the use of these protocols. It was also recognized that the architecture should accommodate new physical communication media that may require new control procedures. Application of principles 3, 5, and 8 led to the identification of a data link layer in top of the physical layer in the architecture.

- **Network Layer.** It was recognized that some systems would act as the final destination of data, while others would act only as intermediate nodes that pass data on to its final destination. Application of principles 3, 5, and 7 led to the identification of a network layer on top of the data link layer. Network-oriented protocols, such as routing, are grouped in the network layer. The network layer provides a connection path between systems, including the case where intermediate nodes are involved.

- **Transport Layer.** The transport layer forms the uppermost layer of the data transport service defined by the architecture. The transport layer isolates higher-level entities from any concern with the transport of data from one system to another and makes the network transparent to users of the network.

- **Session Layer.** The need was recognized for a method of controlling and synchronizing the dialog that takes place between systems and for managing the exchange of data. Application of principles 3 and 4 led to the identification of a session layer on top of the transport layer.

- **Presentation Layer.** The only remaining functions that are general in nature and are not unique to a specific application are those concerned with the representation and manipulation of structured data for the benefit of application programs. Application of principles 3 and 4 led to the identification of a presentation layer on top of the session layer.

- **Application Layer.** The application processes that use the services of the lower six layers and the protocols by which they communicate make up the application layer, which is the highest layer of the architecture.

The resulting architecture with the seven layers listed above can be shown to obey principles 1 and 2. Now that we have presented the rationale that was used in defining the seven layers of the OSI model, we next discuss the characteristics of each layer.

THE PHYSICAL LAYER

The *physical layer* is responsible for the transmission of physical-service-data-units (actually *bits*) across a particular physical transmission medium that connects two or more data link entities. It involves a connection between two machines that allows electrical signals to be exchanged between them. Typically, the hardware consists of a cable, appropriate connectors, and two communicating devices, which are capable of both generating and detecting voltages on the connecting cables. Software consists of firmware permanently installed in the devices that controls the generation and detection of these voltages. Box 35.3

BOX 35.3   The OSI physical layer

Services to the Data Link Layer

- **Physical Connections:** transparent transmission of bit streams across physical connections

- **Physical Service-Data-Units:** definition of the unit of data that is handled by the physical layer (*one bit* for serial transmission and *n bits* for parallel transmission)

- **Physical Connection End Points:** definition of identifiers that are used by the data link layer to refer to physical connection endpoints

- **Data Circuit Identification:** definition of identifiers that are used by the data link layer to refer to physical circuits

- **Sequencing:** delivery of bits in the order in which they were transmitted

- **Fault Condition Notification:** notification of the data link layer when fault conditions occur

- **Quality-of-Service Parameters:** definition of parameters that define quality of service, including error rate, service availability, transmission rate, and transit delay

Physical Layer Functions

- Activating and deactivating physical connections upon request from the data link layer

- Transmitting bits over a physical connection in a synchronous or asynchronous fashion

- Handling physical layer management activities, including activation and error control

lists the services that the physical layer provides to the data link layer and describes some of the functions that the physical layer performs.

Protocols for the physical layer involve mechanical, electrical, functional, and procedural means for activating, maintaining, and deactivating physical connections. This includes the specification of physical connectors, cables, and electrical signals. At this level, hardware standards are extremely important. A computer must have an appropriate connector installed, to which the cable can be connected. The cable must have an appropriate connector attached to each end. A terminal must also have an appropriate connector. Also, the computer and the terminal must agree on the voltage levels that will be used to transmit signals between the two devices. Standards are also important for the simple software, or firmware, that runs in the physical layer. For example, the firmware that runs in the computer and the firmware that runs in the terminal must agree as to how long in duration each bit should be and how to tell the difference between a one bit and a zero bit. The physical layer must deliver bits in the same sequence they are submitted, and must notify the next-higher layer of any faults that are detected. A physical connection might involve the interconnection of a series of data circuits. The transmission alternatives addressed by the physical layer include:

- Duplex or half-duplex links
- Point-to-point or multipoint connections
- Synchronous or asynchronous transmission

If the user machine employs an analog circuit, such as a conventional telephone line, it will be connected to a modem. Its interface with the modem is defined by a generally accepted standard, such as the EIA RS-232-C and RS-449 standards or *CCITT Recommendation V.24*. If a digital circuit is used, a newer recommendation for the physical interface, such as *CCITT Recommendation X.21*, can be used. *Recommendation X.21* describes the interface that allows a terminal to operate in synchronous mode over a public data network.

THE DATA LINK LAYER

The *data link layer* is responsible for providing reliable data transmission from one network entity, or physical node, to another and for shielding higher layers from any concerns about the physical transmission medium. It is concerned with the error-free transmission of data-link-service-data-units, or *frames*, of data. Box 35.4 lists the services that the data link layer provides to the network layer and describes some of the functions the data link layer performs in providing those services. This layer is concerned with such functions as:

- Determining where each transmitted block starts and ends
- Detecting transmission errors
- Recovering from transmission errors to give the appearance of an error-free link
- Controlling transmission when several machines share the same physical circuit so that their transmissions do not overlap and become jumbled
- Addressing a message to one of several machines

A standard protocol that has been developed for the data link layer is high-level data link control (HDLC). HDLC is a bit-oriented, synchronous protocol for transmitting data. The SDLC protocol, which is the standard data link protocol defined by SNA, is effectively a subset of the HDLC protocol. SDLC and

BOX 35.4   OSI data link layer functions

Services to the Network Layer

- **Data Link Connection:** establishment of a data link connection between two or more entities defined by the network layer (data link connections are established and released dynamically)
- **Data Link Service-Data-Units:** definition of the unit of data handled by the physical layer (generally called a *frame* consisting of a sequence of bits)
- **Data Link Connection Endpoint Identifiers:** definition of identifiers that are used by the network layer to refer to data link connection end points
- **Sequencing:** delivery of frames in the same order in which they were transmitted
- **Error Notification:** notification of the network layer when unrecoverable errors occur
- **Flow Control:** dynamic control over the rate at which a network entity receives frames from a data link connection
- **Quality-of-Service Parameters:** definition of parameters that define quality of service, including mean time between unrecoverable errors, residual error rate, service availability, throughput, and transit delay

Data Link Layer Functions

- Establishing and releasing data link connections for use by the network layer
- Building a data link connection using one or more physical connections
- Delimiting data so that it can be sent as frames over a physical connection
- Synchronizing the receipt of data that has been split over multiple physical connections
- Maintaining the sequential order of frames that are transmitted over a data link connection
- Detecting and correcting transmission errors, with retransmission of frames if necessary
- Providing flow control, including dynamically altering the rate at which data units are accepted, and temporarily stopping transmission to a particular receiving entity upon request

HDLC are discussed in Chapter 23. The LAP and LAPB data link protocols that are part of *CCITT Recommendation X.25* are also compatible with the data link layer of the OSI model.

THE NETWORK LAYER

The network layer relates to *virtual circuits*. The path between computers may at one instant be via a number of physical communication links, as shown in Fig. 35.2. Each physical link spans two network machines, which must use at least the physical and data link layer procedures to exchange data. The users at either end of the network do not wish to know what route the data travels or how many physical data links it travels over. The user machines want a simple interface with a virtual circuit. The network layer of control creates the virtual circuit and provides the higher levels with an interface to it.

On some systems, the route over which data travels between two user machines varies from one instant to another. The network machine may require that messages be divided into slices called *packets,* no greater than a certain length. The packets must be reassembled into messages after transmission. On some networks the packets may become out of sequence during transmission. The rules for the network layer state that the network must deliver the packets to the user machine in the same sequence as that in which they were sent. There are many such complications in the implementation and operation of a virtual circuit. The network layer provides a standard interface with the virtual circuit and, as far as possible, hides the complex mechanisms of its operation from the higher layers of software.

The formal definition of the network layer states that this layer is responsible for establishing, maintaining, and terminating the network connection between two transport entities and for transferring data along it in a way that keeps any higher layer from being concerned about, or aware of, the nature of that connection. At any given time, there can be only one network connection between two given entities, although there can be multiple possible physical routes between the two transport entities. The network layer handles routing of data through any intermediate nodes that are necessary. If the route involves multiple networks, the network layer shields higher layers from dealing with any differences in transmission facilities, quality of service, or implementation technologies between the various networks. The services provided by the network layer to the transport layer, and many of the functions performed in providing those services, are listed in Box 35.5.

A commonly used standard that conforms to the guidelines established for the network layer is *CCITT Recommendation X.25* Level 3. *Recommendation X.25* has three levels, each of which addresses a different layer. Level 1 addresses the physical layer, level 2 the data link layer, and level 3, sometimes called the *packet level,* addresses the network layer. *Recommendation X.25* defines how a packet terminal interfaces with a packet-switched network.

BOX 35.5   The OSI network layer

Services to the Transport Layer

- **Network Addresses:** definition of network addresses to be used in identifying entities defined by the transport layer

- **Network Connections:** transfer of data between transport entities that are identified by network addresses (each network connection is point-to-point, and multiple network connections can exist between transport entities)

- **Network Connection Endpoint Identifiers:** definition of unique endpoint identifiers that are associated with the network addresses used by the transport layer

- **Network Service-Data-Unit Transfer:** definition of the unit of data that is handled by the network layer (generally called a *packet,* on which no maximum size limit is imposed by the architecture)

- **Quality-of-Service Parameters:** definition of parameters that define quality of service, including residual error rate, service availability, throughput, transit delay, and connection-establishment delay; a selected quality of service is maintained for the duration of the network connection

- **Error Notification:** notification of the transport layer when unrecoverable errors occur (error notification may or may not lead to the disconnection of network connection)

- **Sequencing:** delivery of frames in the same order in which they were transmitted if requested by the transport layer

- **Flow Control:** provision for stopping the transfer of packets upon request by the transport entity that is receiving packets

- **Expedited Network Service-Data-Unit Transfer:** an optional, expedited service for handling information exchange over a network connection

- **Reset:** an optional service that when requested by a transport entity, causes the network layer to discard all packets currently in transit and to notify the transport entity at the other end of the connection that a reset has occurred

- **Release:** release of a network connection upon request by a transport entity

Network Layer Functions

- Determining an optimum routing over the possible network connections that can exist between two network addresses and then relaying packets over the various point-to-point connections that make up that route

BOX 35.5   *(Continued)*

- Providing a network connection between two transport entities and transferring data over the network connection in a transparent fashion

- Multiplexing multiple network connections onto a single data link connection in order to optimize their use

- Segmenting and/or blocking packets for the purposes of facilitating the transfer of packets over network connections

- Detecting errors and recovering from them

- Selecting an appropriate quality of service and maintaining this quality of service even when a network connection spans subnetworks of dissimilar quality

- Handling network layer management activities, including activation and error control

THE TRANSPORT LAYER

The lowest three layers of Fig. 35.1 represent a common network that many machines can share, independently of one another, just as many independent users may share the postal service. It is possible that a postal service might occasionally lose a letter. To ensure that this has not happened, two users of the postal service might apply their own end-to-end controls, such as sequentially numbering their letters. The transport layer is concerned with similar end-to-end controls of the transmission between two users that are conducting a session.

Figure 35.2 illustrates that whereas the network layer is concerned with the interface between the user machine and the network, the transport layer (and the higher layers) is concerned with the end-to-end interaction between user processes. The functions executed in the transport layer may include end-to-end integrity controls to prevent loss or double processing of transactions, flow control of transactions, and addressing of end-user machines or processes. The transport layer, together with the three layers below it, provides a *transport service*. They are concerned with the transport of messages from one user process to another, but they do not manipulate the data contained in the messages.

The transport service may be implemented in a variety of ways; the OSI model does not specify implementation details. In some cases it may take the form of a packet switching network using *Recommendation X.25* for layers 1, 2, and 3. When X.25 is used, the transport layer must break each user message into packets for transmission through the network. In other cases, point-to-point circuits will be used, possibly with circuit switching, and in still other cases, satellite circuits might be employed. When these techniques are used, messages

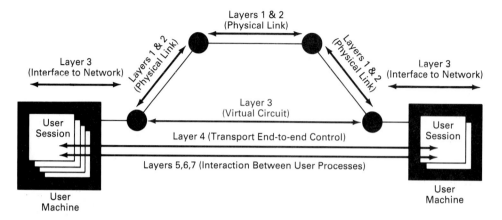

Figure 35.2   Path between user machines

may not have to be broken up into packets for transmission. The interface from higher layers or from user machines to the transport layer is intended to provide a standard interface to users of the transport service independent of what network type is used.

In the OSI model's formal definition, the transport layer is responsible for transferring transport-service-data-units (complete *messages*) between two session entities at an agreed-upon level of service quality. The transport layer is not concerned with the specific route that is used through the network; instead, it is simply concerned with reliable, cost-effective transfer of data. The transport layer is responsible for establishing transport connections between entities, transferring data, and releasing connections.

The transport layer offers a defined set of *service classes*. The service classes provide various combinations of factors, such as throughput, transit delay, connection setup delay, error rate, and availability. When a transport connection is established, a particular class of service is selected based on the type of service requested by the session entity. The transport layer is then responsible for monitoring transmission to ensure that the appropriate service quality is maintained, and if not, for notifying the appropriate entity of the failure or degradation. The services provided by the transport layer to the session layer, and many of the functions performed by the transport layer, are summarized in Box 35.6.

THE SESSION LAYER   The task of setting up a session between user processes can be complex because there are so many different ways in which machines can cooperate. Like two business managers agreeing to a joint venture, they must agree in advance on the rules of the game. In effect, they sign a contract stating the manner in

BOX 35.6   The OSI transport layer

Services to the Session Layer

- **Transport Connection Establishment:** establishment of a transport connection, of an agreed-upon quality of service, between two entities defined by the session layer (at the time of connection establishment, a class of service can be selected from a defined set of available classes)

- **Data Transfer:** transfer of data in accordance with the quality of service negotiated when the connection was established

- **Transport Connection Release:** release of a transport connection upon request by a session entity (the other session entity is also notified of the connection release)

Transport Layer Functions

- Converting transport addresses for entities into network addresses; multiple transport addresses can be associated with the same network entity, and thus multiple transport addresses might be mapped onto a single network address

- Multiplexing multiple transport connections onto a single network connection or splitting a transport connection over multiple network connections as needed to optimize use of network connections

- Sequencing of data units transferred to ensure that they are delivered in the same sequence in which they were sent

- Detecting and recovering from errors

- Segmenting, blocking, and concatenation of data units

- Controlling data flow to prevent overloading of network resources

- Handling transport layer supervisory activities

- Providing for expedited transfer of data units between session entities

which they will cooperate. The session layer standardizes the process of establishing a session and of terminating it. If something goes wrong in midsession, the session layer must restore the session without loss of data, or, if this is not possible, it must terminate the session in an orderly fashion. Error-checking and error-recovery procedures are thus functions that are carried out in this layer.

In some types of sessions a dialog takes place between machines, and a protocol must regulate who speaks when and for how long. In some cases the two machines transmit alternately. In others, one machine may send many messages before the other replies. In some sessions one machine may interrupt the other, in other cases not. The rules for how the dialog is conducted need to be agreed on when the session is set up.

The session layer focuses on providing a set of services that are used to organize and synchronize the dialog that takes place between presentation entities and to manage the session-service-data-units that are exchanged between them. The session layer maintains the dialog even if data is lost at the transport level. It is responsible for establishing, managing, and releasing session connections between presentation entities. There can be multiple concurrent session connections between a given pair of entities. A session connection can be mapped onto transport connections in a variety of ways. In the simplest case, a session connection uses a single transport connection. In more complex situations, one session might use a series of transport connections if, for example, a transport connection has to be terminated because of errors or failures. In other cases, a series of consecutive session connections might use the same transport connection.

As discussed above, a primary concern of the session layer is to manage dialog interaction. The session layer defines three types of dialog:

- Two-way, simultaneous interaction, where both entities send and receive concurrently
- Two-way, alternate interaction, where the entities take turns sending and receiving
- One-way interaction, where one entity only sends and the other only receives

Where the entities take turns sending and receiving, the changeover can be voluntary on the part of the entities, or it can be forced by the session layer upon request of the presentation entity. Box 35.7 lists the services that the session layer provides to the presentation layer and describes many of the functions that the session layer performs. There are additional functions that are currently not defined for the session layer, but considered to be candidates for future extensions. These include the following:

- Sequence numbering of session-service-data-units
- Brackets
- Stop-go transmission
- Security functions

THE PRESENTATION LAYER

The presentation layer performs functions that relate to the character set and data code which are used and to the way data is displayed on a screen or printer. A stream of characters reaching a terminal will result in certain actions that result in a meaningful and attractive display or printout. The

BOX 35.7 The OSI session layer

Services to the Presentation Layer

- **Session Connection Establishment:** establishment of a session connection between two entities defined by the presentation layer

- **Session Connection Release:** release of a session connection, in an orderly fashion and without loss of data, upon request of a presentation entity (this service permits either of the presentation entities to abort a session connection, in which case data might be lost; the release of session connection can also be initiated by one of the session entities supporting it)

- **Normal Data Exchange:** normal transfer of data between a sending presentation entity and a receiving presentation entity

- **Quarantine Service:** request by a sending presentation entity that a specific number of session data units be held and not made available to the receiving presentation entity until specifically released by the sending entity (the sending entity can later specify that the data units be discarded instead of being sent to the receiving entity)

- **Expedited Data Exchange:** transfer of data on an expedited basis for high-priority traffic

- **Interaction Management:** explicit control over whose turn it is to exercise certain control functions

- **Session Connection Synchronization:** definition by presentation entities of synchronization points (the session layer provides services to reset a session connection to a resynchronization point and to restore entities to a defined state)

- **Exception Reporting:** notification to presentation entities by the session layer about exceptional conditions

Session Layer Functions

- Providing a one-to-one mapping between a session connection and a presentation connection at any given instant; over time, however, a transport connection can use several consecutive session connections, and several consecutive transport connections might use a single session connection

- Preventing a presentation entity from being overloaded with data by using transport flow control (there is no explicit flow control in the session layer)

- Reestablishing a transport connection to support a session connection in the event of a reported failure of the underlying transport connection

- Handling session layer management activities

character stream may contain characters that cause editing of the data, line skipping, tabbing to position the data in columns, adding fixed column headings, highlighting certain fields, appropriate use of color, and so on. Formats may be displayed into which an operator enters data, and then only the entered data is transmitted. A coded number sent to an intelligent terminal may cause it to select a panel for display and enter variable data into that display. These are only a few of the many possible functions concerned with the presentation of data.

In some cases network users and application programmers perceive a *virtual terminal* or *virtual display space*. Input/output statements relate to this make-believe facility, and the presentation layer software must do the conversion between the virtual facility and the physical terminal that is being used. It is desirable that devices that use different character sets should be able to communicate. Conversion of character streams may therefore be a concern of the presentation layer. The character stream may also be compacted to save transmission costs and encryption and decryption for security reasons may be performed. These are also presentation layer functions.

The presentation layer is concerned with the syntax used both for representing data and for the formatting of data. Representation of data deals with character sets and coding structures. Formatting of data deals with the formats of data required by particular input and output devices. For either type of syntax, there can be up to three different types of syntax involved during a given session between two application entities:

- The syntax used by the sending entity
- The syntax used by the receiving entity
- The syntax used for the transfer of data

The three types of syntax can all be different, or any two, or even all three, can be the same. If they are different, the presentation layer is responsible for transforming from one syntax to another. Negotiations between the presentation entities that represent the application entities determine what transformations will be necessary and where they will be performed. These negotiations ordinarily take place when the session is initiated. Negotiations can also take place while the session is in progress. Box 35.8 lists the services that the presentation layer provides to the application layer and describes many of the functions that are performed in providing those services.

THE APPLICATION LAYER

The application layer is concerned with higher-level functions that provide support to the application or system activities: for example, operator support, the use of remote data, file transfer control, distributed database activities, higher-level dialog functions, and so on. The extent to which these are supported in

BOX 35.8   The OSI presentation layer

Services to the Application Layer

- **Session Services:** provision to the application layer of all the services provided by the session layer

- **Syntax Selection:** initial selection of a syntax and subsequent modification of the initial syntax selection

- **Syntax Transformation:** code and character set conversion and modification of data layout

Presentation Layer Functions

- Issuing a request to the session layer for the establishment of a session

- Initiating a data transfer from one application entity, or user, to another

- Negotiating and renegotiating the choice of a syntax to be used in the data transfer

- Performing any required data transformation or conversion

- Issuing a request to the session layer for the termination of a session

the network architecture and in the software external to the network architecture, such as database software, will differ from one system to another.

When distributed files and databases are used, various controls are needed to prevent integrity problems or deadlocks. Some of the types of controls for this are strongly related to networking, for example, the time stamping of transactions and delivery of transactions in time stamp sequence (sometimes called *pipelining*). Pacing is necessary with some processes so that the transmitting machine can send records continuously without flooding the receiving machine or so that an application can keep a distant printer going at maximum speed.

The application layer provides application processes with a point of access to the system. The application layer provides a means for application processes to access the system interconnection facilities in order to exchange information. It provides all functions related to communication between systems that are not provided by the lower layers. These functions include those performed by people as well as those performed by application programs. The application layer is the most difficult of the seven layers to standardize, and the OSI model does not currently define the specific functions that are performed by the application layer. However, it does divide the possible functions into two categories. Box 35.9 lists the services that the application layer provides to the application pro-

BOX 35.9 The OSI application layer

Services to the Application Process

- **Identification:** identification of the intended communication partners (e.g., by name, address, description, etc.)

- **Availability:** determination of the current availability of the intended communication partners

- **Authority:** establishment of the authority of the partners to communicate

- **Privacy:** agreement on the privacy mechanisms to be used in communication

- **Security:** authentication of the identity of the intended communication partners

- **Cost Allocation:** determination of cost allocation methodology to be used in communication

- **Resource Allocation:** determination of the adequacy of available resources

- **Quality of Service:** determination of the acceptable quality of service to be used with respect to such factors as response time, tolerable error rate, and cost

- **Synchronization:** synchronization of cooperating applications

- **Dialog Discipline:** selection of the dialog discipline to be used in communication, including the procedures to be used in initiation and release

- **Error Recovery:** agreement on responsibility for error recovery

- **Data Integrity:** agreement on the procedures for control of data integrity

- **Data Syntax:** identification of constraints on data syntax (character sets, data structures, etc.)

Application Layer Functions

- Performing *common application functions,* which are functions that provide capabilities that are useful to many applications

- Performing *specific application functions,* which are functions that are required to service the needs of a particular application

cess, or user, and describes the two broad categories of functions that are performed by the application layer.

Additional services, over and above those shown in Box 35.9, may also be provided. In addition, the application layer provides management services related to both management of the application processes and of the systems being interconnected. Management of application processes includes initializing, maintaining, and terminating the processes; allocating and deallocating resources; detecting and preventing deadlocks; and providing integrity, commitment, security, checkpoint, and recovery control. Again this list is not exhaustive. Management of systems might include activating, maintaining, and deactivating various system resources; program loading; monitoring and reporting status and statistics; error detection, diagnosis, and recovery; and reconfiguration and restart.

MESSAGE HEADERS   As data flows down through the various layers of software, headers are added to the original message that enters the system at the application layer. The data link layer typically adds a header and a trailer. These headers and trailers contain control information that the system at the opposite end uses in interpreting the information found in the transmission frame. This is shown in Fig. 35.3. Thus the final transmission frame that is transmitted over the physical circuit contains many more bits than those in the original message. As the message moves up through the layers at the opposite end, each layer strips off its corresponding header and uses the information contained in it to handle the message properly (see Fig. 35.4). The contents of the headers and trailers must be rigidly defined by the standards and protocols that control the functions of each layer.

MANUFACTURERS' ARCHITECTURES   The architectures for distributed processing from the various mainframe and minicomputer manufacturers contain all or part of the seven layers we have described. An example of this can be seen in Chapter 39. Layers 1, 2, and 3 are usually clearly distinguished in all manufacturers' architectures, but the functions of layers 4, 5, 6, and 7 may be intermixed and may not correspond exactly to the layers specified in the OSI model. Increasingly, as distributed processing technology and computer networking evolves, the clean separation of the layers will be necessary.

As the various architectures evolve, the compatibility between manufacturers' architectures and the OSI reference model is likely to increase. For example, the Digital Equipment Corporation has stated that DEC's long-term intention for its DECNET architecture is to come into complete conformance with the OSI model. And the protocols for IBM's Advanced Program-to-Program

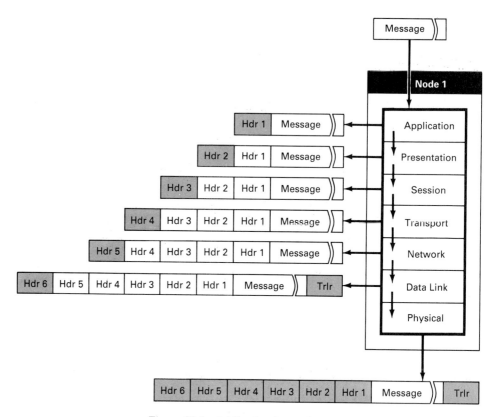

Figure 35.3   Adding headers and trailers

Communications (APPC) SNA functions have been accepted as an international standard for the high-level layers of the OSI model (see Chapter 39).

DIFFERENT
MACHINES

In a distributed processing network the layers may be spread across a variety of machines. Figure 35.5 shows several types of machines. A central processing unit may be designed to contain all seven layers, as with the computer on the left in Fig. 35.5, or probably better, some of the layers may be removed to a separate communications controller. A communications controller might handle the lower three layers, or it may handle layer 4 functions as well.

Terminals containing microprocessors may have enough power to handle all the layers, as the intelligent terminal in Fig. 35.5 does. This is less complex than the networking software at a computer site because the terminals support only one session at a time, use only one logical channel, and contain few management functions. In many cases the terminals are simpler machines con-

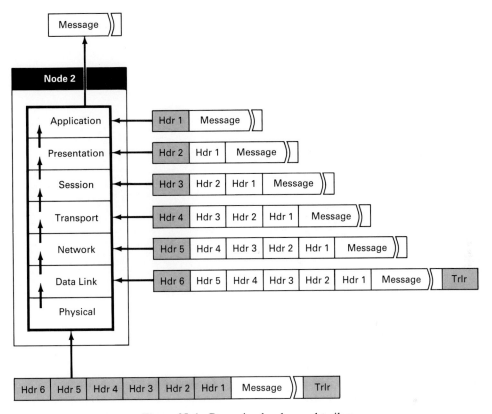

Figure 35.4   Removing headers and trailers

nected to a terminal cluster controller, and it is this controller that contains the networking software, as shown at the bottom of Fig. 35.5. The terminals may be in the immediate vicinity of the controller, or they may be far away, connected by telecommunications, in which case the controller may be regarded as a concentrator. A concentrator may contain only the lower three layers.

Figure 35.5 does not show mid-network nodes such as packet switching machines or concentrators. These may be part of the transport subsystem, with no layer 5, 6, 7, or even layer 4 functions.

SYMMETRY

In some cases the networking layers are symmetrical. In other words, when a certain level of software exists at opposite ends of a link, both ends carry out the same functions. In Fig. 35.2 the outermost machines execute all seven layers; the inner machines (drawn as circles) execute only transport subsystem functions; but the layering is symmetrical. In a horizontal computer network all machines may contain the

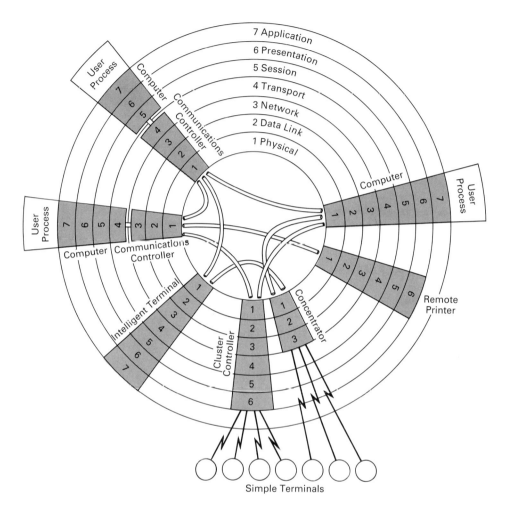

Figure 35.5 Allocation of functional layers

same networking software (with the exception of such functions as network monitoring and statistics gathering). On the other hand, vertical networks are often asymmetrical. For reasons of economy the machines lower in the hierarchy have simpler software or control mechanisms than do those at the top (at least at the higher-level layers).

In some networks the terms *primary* and *secondary* are used to describe asymmetrical relationships between machines. In some, the terms *master* and *slave* are used. In links between a computer and terminal controller, or a large computer and a minicomputer, a *primary/secondary* relationship is often employed. The management of the link is the responsibility of the *primary* machine. This machine takes most of the initiative. It sends messages, and the secondary machine responds. The primary machine is responsible for recovery when failures or problems occur.

Chapter 36 examines the public data networks and information utilities that are being built using some of the high-level standards and protocols we have been discussing in this chapter and Chapter 34.

36 PUBLIC DATA NETWORKS AND INFORMATION UTILITIES

During the mid-1970s furious debates ensued among the major common carriers of the world about whether they should build a public data network, what form it should take, and how much they should spend on it. The common carriers and telecommunications administrations desired to provide better service to the computer community. They also perceived that there was a revenue which would grow to tens of billions of dollars worldwide, which could go either to themselves or to the computer industry. This is the revenue from the switches, concentrators, multiplexors, polling equipment, line control equipment, and so on, used in the interconnection of machines. Common carriers operate the equipment for switching and routing telephone calls; it seemed natural that they should operate the new equipment for switching and routing data. As discussed in Chapter 28, there are two main types of switching that are commonly used in creating public computer networks: packet switching and fast-connect circuit switching.

PACKET SWITCHING

As we have seen, a packet switching network divides the data traffic into blocks, called packets. Each packet of user data travels in a data envelope that gives the destination address of the packet and a variety of control information. Each switching node reads the packet into its memory, examines the address, selects the next node to which it will transmit the packet, and sends it on its way. The packets eventually reach their destination, where their envelopes are stripped off. Then they may have to be reassembled to form the original user messages. A packet switching network operates somewhat like a postal service in which letters in envelopes are passed from one post office to another until they reach their destination. The typical delivery time on today's packet networks is about a tenth of a second. Most of today's public data networks use packet switching techniques. The technology that packet switching networks use is discussed in Chapter 37.

Many advanced nations now have one or more public packet switching networks. These are becoming interconnected into multinational networks so that packets can travel around the world or at least part of it. As we introduced in Chapter 15, the first major public packet switching network was Telenet. This derived its techniques (and its management) from Arpanet, the first private packet switching network. Telenet was bought in 1979 by General Telephone and Electronics.

Later in this chapter we discuss the major packet switching public data networks operating in the United States. Figure 36.1 shows examples of some of the national packet switching networks operating outside the United States. Figure 36.2 shows the overall structure of Euronet, a transnational network that carries packets between the national networks in Europe.

In Figs. 36.1 and 36.2, the packet switches and lines interconnecting them are shown in red. Most users are linked to the networks by telephone lines going directly to a switching node or else to a concentrator. Many subscribers are a long distance from a switch, so concentrators are used to bring the traffic of these distant users to and from the network. The concentrators may form a small star-structured network linked to a packet switch, connecting many users to the nearest packet switch. The use of telephone lines restricts their maximum data rate to that of a telephone line: 9600 bps. In some cases users have higher-speed digital links into their premises.

User machines connected to a packet switching network need to observe a rigorous set of rules for communicating via the network. It is desirable that networks in different countries should follow the same set of rules so that user machines around the world can employ the same software and control mechanisms and so that packets can pass easily from one network to another. There has been a high degree of international agreement on the rules, protocols, and message formats for public packet switching networks, centering around *CCITT Recommendation X.25*. The standards and protocols of CCITT Recommendation X.25 are also discussed in Chapter 37. Next we discuss the major packet switching public data networks operating in the United States.

TELENET

The *Telenet Public Data Network* was the first packet switching public data network to begin operation in the United States. It began operation in 1975 as the Telenet Public Data network. GTE acquired Telenet in 1979. In 1986, Telenet acquired the Uninet network, another major packet-switched data network that was formerly operated by the *United Telecommunications Company*. The Telenet network consists of high-speed digital transmission facilities interconnected by switching centers, called *Telenet central offices* (TCOs), located in major U.S. cities (see Fig. 36.3). The network is controlled by a network control center (NCC), which

1. Bell Canada's DATAPAC, the X.25 packet switching system of the Trans Canada Telephone System.

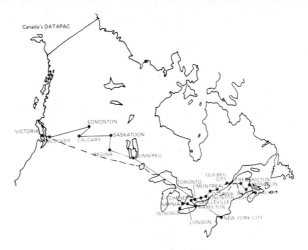

2. TRANSPAC, the public packet-switching network of France. Whereas Tymnet and Telenet are private corporations offering value-added service, the networks of European countries are operated by the government telecommunications organization like their telephone networks.

3. United Kingdom PSS network.

Figure 36.1 Public data networks outside of the United States

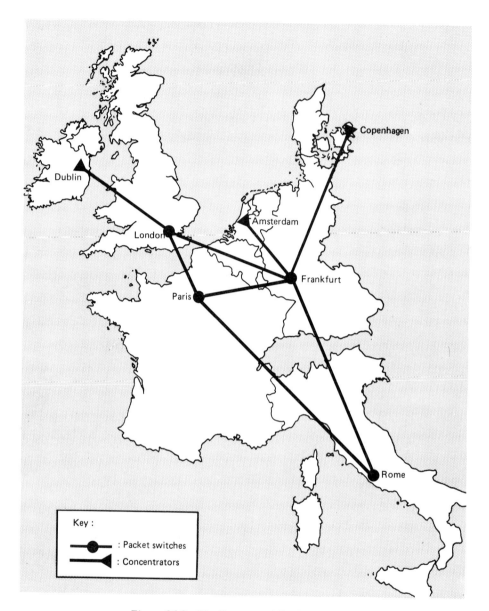

Figure 36.2 The Euronet public data network

work status and assists in correcting malfunctions. Network reliability is enhanced through the use of redundant switching equipment, parallel physical circuits, and standby power supplies.

Each Telenet central office implements one or more packet switches that are connected to the high-speed Telenet trunk lines. The packet switches support

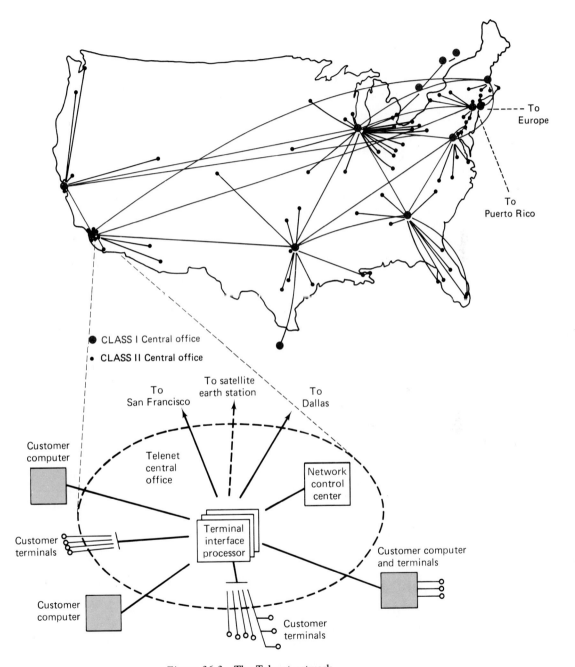

CLASS I Central office
CLASS II Central office

To
Europe

To
Puerto Rico

To
San Francisco

To satellite
earth station

To
Dallas

Telenet
central
office

Network
control
center

Customer
computer

Customer
terminals

Customer
computer

Terminal
interface
processor

Customer
terminals

Customer computer
and terminals

Figure 36.3   The Telenet network

the X.25 protocol and also implement a PAD facility for connecting non-X.25 devices to the network.

There are basically three ways that user equipment can interface with the Telenet network:

- **Public Dial-Up Lines.** Users of simple asynchronous terminals can use ordinary dial-up telephone facilities to access the nearest TCO.
- **Private Dial-Up Lines.** Users can also lease private dial-in or dial-out ports for a particular customer's exclusive use.
- **Dedicated Access Facility.** Users can lease private channels into the equipment at a TCO for dedicated access to the network.

User terminals can be individually connected to the equipment at the TCO over any of the types of connections listed above. Alternatively, equipment that performs concentration and protocol conversion can be purchased from GTE or other equipment vendors to allow multiple terminals to communicate with the Telenet network over a single channel.

Each TCO supports a number of protocols for attaching a variety of terminals and host computers to the network, including the following:

- Asynchronous
- 3270 binary synchronous
- 2780/3780 binary synchronous
- HDLC
- SDLC
- X.25

GTE also provides consulting services and markets equipment by which users can construct their own private packet switching networks. These networks can be installed and operated independently, or they can be connected to the Telenet network to provide a hybrid private and public switched network. This is shown in Fig. 36.4.

Telenet also offers additional services that use the Telenet network as a backbone. These optional services include:

- **Telemail.** Telemail is a computer-based message switching service that can be used for the purposes of electronic mail.
- **MICRO-FONE.** The Micro-Fone service combines a telephone with an inexpensive data terminal that can be used to implement simple transaction processing systems.
- **MINET.** Minet is a medical information system that is used to provide health care data to medical professionals.

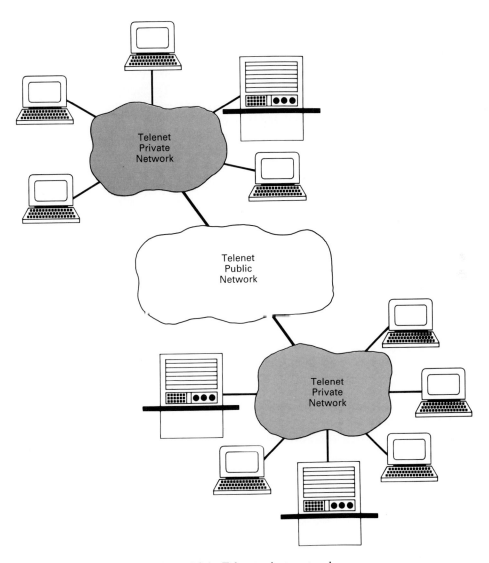

Figure 36.4   Telenet private networks

Information about Telenet can be obtained from Telenet Communications Corporation, 8229 Boone Boulevard, Vienna, VA 22180; telephone: (703) 442–1000.

TYMNET

The *Tymnet* network is operated by a wholly owned subsidiary of *McDonnell Douglas Automation*. The network that eventually became Tymnet began operation in 1971 to support the time-sharing services marketed by *Tymshare, Inc.* Tymnet began operation as a packet-switched public data network in 1977.

The backbone network consists of a number of regional switching centers that are connected by redundant, high-speed, dedicated digital circuits. A large number of nodes, each of which runs a specialized Tymnet processor, are connected to the backbone network via dedicated lines running at speeds that range from 4800 to 56,000 bps. User equipment is connected to the nearest network node via terminal interfaces, called Tymsats, and host interfaces, called Tymcoms (see Fig. 36.5). Some terminal and host interfaces are installed on Tymnet premises and are shared by multiple subscribers. Other terminal and host interfaces are installed on subscriber premises and are dedicated to the use of one customer.

Although the internal interfaces of the network conform to the X.25 protocols, there are a number of different ways that customer terminal equipment can be connected to the Tymnet network, including the following:

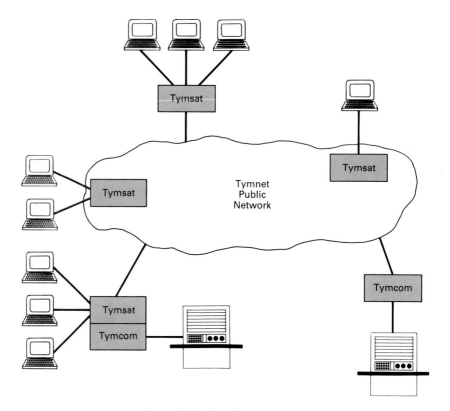

Figure 36.5   The Tymnet network

Protocol	Facility
Asynchronous	Public local dial-up connection
	Public WATS dial-up connection
	Dedicated dial-up connection
	Dedicated leased lines
	Dedicated Tymsat facility
	Dedicated customer-provided facility
3270 binary synchronous	Dedicated leased lines
X.25	Dedicated leased lines
	Dedicated synchronous dial-up ports
SDLC	Dedicated leased lines
RJE/HASP	Dedicated leased lines
	Dedicated synchronous dial-up ports

Customer host computers can be connected to the Tymnet network via similar options:

Protocol	Facility
Asynchronous	Dedicated asynchronous Tymcom facility
	Dedicated customer-provided facility
3270 binary synchronous	Dedicated leased lines
X.25	Dedicated leased lines
	Dedicated node at 56,000 bps
SDLC	Dedicated leased lines
RJE/HASP	Dedicated leased lines

Like Telenet, Tymnet will build and install a private network using its own equipment for a customer's own use. Tymnet also offers a message switching service called OnTyme-II that supports a wide variety of terminals, including many facsimile devices, and has evolved into a fully integrated data communications, electronic mail, and word processing system.

Information about Tymnet can be obtained from Tymnet, Inc., 2710 Orchard Parkway, San Jose, CA 95134; telephone: (408) 946–4900.

ADP AUTONET

The *ADP Autonet* network is operated by a subsidiary of *Automatic Data Processing, Inc.* (ADP). The ADP Autonet network evolved from a private network that ADP developed to service its own clients. Autonet supports ADP facilities that allow customer equipment to be attached to the network via asynchronous and X.25 connections. The backbone network consists of high-speed communication lines that link main switching centers called Autonet central offices. These main switching centers are linked to a large number of switching nodes distributed across the country.

There are four methods by which customer terminals can be attached to the network and two methods for connecting host computers. These are summarized in Fig. 36.6. Terminals can be attached using the following techniques:

- **Public Dial-Up Access.** An authorized user can attach an asynchronous terminal to the network by placing a toll-free call to the nearest switching node.

- **Private Dial-In Access.** A customer can lease a dial-in port that is dedicated to that user.

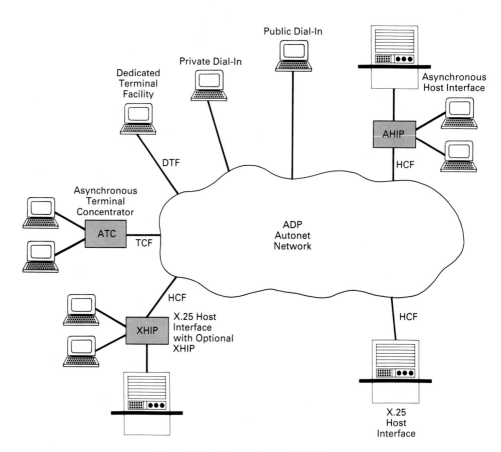

Figure 36.6   Connecting to ADP Autonet

- **Dedicated Terminal Facility (DTF).** A customer's terminal can be permanently connected to the network with a leased line between the terminal and the nearest switching node.

- **Asynchronous Terminal Concentrator (ATC).** An ATC is an intelligent terminal concentrator that is installed by Autonet at the customer's location. ATCs are available for as few as four and as many as 80 terminals. The ATC is then connected to the nearest switching node via a leased connection.

A customer can attach a host computer to the Autonet network using either of the following three methods:

- **Host Computer Facility (HCF).** An HCF consists of an access port, a leased communication line, and associated modems that are used to connect to the network a host computer that is capable of handling the X.25 protocols.

- **X.25 Host Interface Processor (XHIP).** An XHIP is an optional processor, installed at the location of the host computer, that allows the user to attach asynchronous terminals to the HCF as well as the host computer.

- **Asynchronous Host Interface Processor.** A host computer that does not support the X.25 protocols can be attached to an HCF via an AHIP, installed at the location of the host computer. The AHIP handles the X.25 protocols for the host computer.

Autonet also operates an electronic mail service that it calls Auto Mail. Information about ADP Autonet can be obtained from ADP Autonet, 175 Jackson Plaza, Ann Arbor, MI 48106; telephone: (313) 769–6800.

AT&T ACCUNET PACKET SERVICE

The *AT&T Accunet* Packet Service is the newest of the five major packet-switched public data networks described here. Unlike the other packet-switched services, AT&T's packet switching network does not allow simple terminals to be connected to the network that do not provide their own packet assembly and disassembly (PAD) facility. A terminal or computer must support the X.25 interface in order to operate on the network. Optionally, the subscriber can install a PAD facility to which it can connect any desired terminals or host computers.

Both virtual calls and virtual circuits are supported by the Accunet Packet Service. The subscriber can gain access to the packet-switched network over dedicated Dataphone Digital Service digital channels at speeds of 4800, 9600, or 56,000 bps or via conventional leased telephone channels at speeds of 4800 or 9600 bps. An interesting feature of the network is that logical channels are supported. Logical channels allow multiple simultaneous data calls to be made over a single leased connection.

Information about the Accunet Packet Service can be obtained from a local AT&T representative or from AT&T Communications, 295 North Maple Avenue, Basking Ridge, NJ 07920.

FAST-CONNECT CIRCUIT SWITCHING   A fast-connect circuit switching network establishes what is in effect, a physical circuit between communicating machines. The circuit is set up rapidly under computer control; it remains set up while the data passes, which might take a second or less, and is then automatically disconnected so that other users can employ the same facilities. The reader might think of a copper path, carrying electricity, which is set up for a second or so between the communicating machines and is then disconnected. In fact, the path is not a simple copper circuit because time-division switching is used in which many streams of bits flow through an electronic switch, all interleaved with one another. Circuit switching has been used for decades in telephone exchanges and in the worldwide telex network. The difference with computer networks is that the user circuit is set up and disconnected very quickly. The switched connection is often used only for the time it takes one message to pass, or for one message and an interactive response; sometimes it remains connected for the transmission of a batch of data. This form of switching has not been used as much as packet switching in setting up public data networks, although many fast-connect circuit switching networks are in operation.

The first public circuit-switched public data network was built by the Datran Corporation in the United States, and was subsequently taken over by Southern Pacific Communications. Southern Pacific no longer offers the Datran type of switching publicly. Whereas Datran built a digital microwave trunk specially for the purpose, other circuit-switched data networks use conventional wideband circuits between the switching nodes. Figure 36.7 shows the structure of the Nordic data network of Scandinavia. The switches are interconnected by trunks operating at 64,000 bps. Multiplexors and concentrators carry users' traffic to the nearest switching node. These also are connected to the network by 64-kbps trunks. There may be two or more trunks connecting two switches, or connecting a concentrator and a switch. More trunks are allocated to a data network as its traffic builds up. The network provides switched synchronous data circuits at various speeds. Asynchronous terminals can also be connected to the network.

A user of any circuit-switched network can encounter a network busy condition, just as there are busy signals from the telephone network when all circuits are in use. This is different from a packet-switched network, in which no busy conditions occur. When a packet-switched network is overloaded, packet delivery time simply gets longer. The designer of a circuit-switched network adds trunks and switching facilities until a sufficiently low proportion of the calls encounter a network busy condition. The probability that an attempted call

The structure and components of the Nordic data network

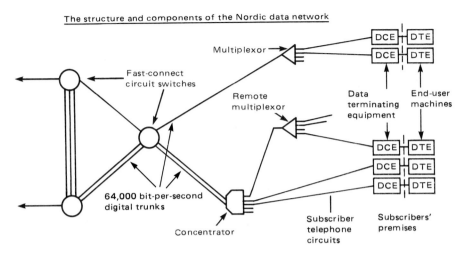

The geography of the Nordic data network. The first phase uses 88 concentrators and 84 multiplexors not shown here

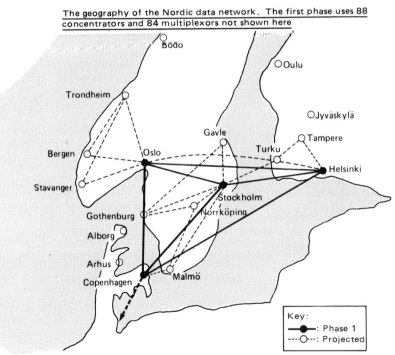

Figure 36.7 The Nordic switched-data network

will be unsuccessful is a basic design parameter of a circuit-switched network. The Nordic network is designed so that less than 0.5 percent of calls will fail to be connected due to network faults or congestion. This figure is determined by the numbers of trunks. Because the call setup time is fast and most calls are brief, the unit that controls the user connection to the network can retry an unsuccessful call quickly and have a high probability of succeeding on a second attempt.

DTEs AND DCEs   As we have seen, the term *DTE*, for *data terminal equipment,* is used to refer to an end-user machine, such as a terminal, computer, or controller. This machine must plug into a unit called a *DCE*, for *data circuit-terminating equipment,* which is the termination point of the communication circuit. This plug-in connection forms the interface between the user's equipment and the common carrier equipment.

For a leased telephone line the DCE is normally a modem. With a fast-connect circuit-switched network a different type of DCE is needed for establishing and disconnecting the calls automatically. A switched connection can be established either automatically or by hand. The DCE used to interface to packet switching networks is more complex. Packets with precise formats must be interchanged to set up a call and to control the flow of data. A DCE on a packet switching network usually conforms to the formats and protocols of *CCITT Recommendation X.25*.

CONNECTIONS   Sometimes it is desirable to employ more than one
BETWEEN   type of network to achieve a given connection. A
NETWORKS   dialed telephone call can be made to access the concentrator of a packet-switched network. A multinational call can be set up involving a packet-switched network in one country and a circuit-switched network in another. Not all packet networks have identical formats, and messages may need to pass from one network to another.

To deal with network connections, interface machines are needed. The connection between different data networks is called a *gateway*. A gateway is typically implemented in the form of a small computer that appears to each network as though it were a normal node of the network. It takes data in the format of one network and translates it into the format expected by the other. The use of a gateway is illustrated in Fig. 36.8. CCITT Recommendation X.75 describes the way a gateway could be implemented to interconnect different X.25 packet switching networks.

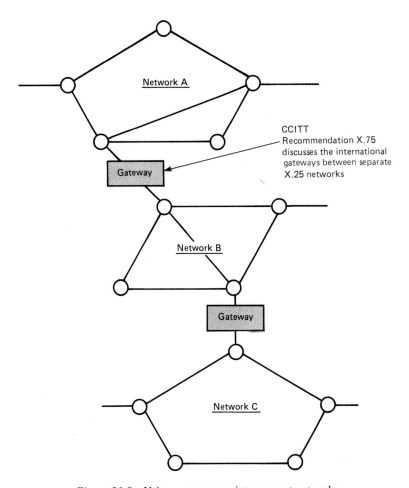

Figure 36.8   Using gateways to interconnect networks

The CCITT label reads: CCITT Recommendation X.75 discusses the international gateways between separate X.25 networks

EIGHT TYPES OF TARIFFS

The switched networks provide two types of connections between machines: first, a connection switched through the networks so that a machine can request a switched path to any other machine connected to the network; and second, a connection that is permanently established between two machines. In some cases the virtual path through a circuit-switched and a packet-switched network can be made to appear identical.

A "permanent" connection does not imply a permanent physical path. On a circuit-switched network it implies a continuous stream of bits or bytes derived by submultiplexing. On a packet-switched network it means that when one of the connected machines sends a packet, it is routed automatically to the other machine with no preliminary call setup. In the future, then, there could be eight main types of basic tariff associated with telephone and telegraph circuits and the two types of data networks, as shown in Table 36.1.

A few countries already have all eight of these types of tariffs. Some countries have a packet network but not yet a circuit-switched network. Some countries have a fast-connect circuit-switched network but not yet a packet network. Most countries with a circuit-switched data network are saying that they may also acquire public packet switching facilities. We could be working toward a time when advanced countries will have them all. The designer of corporate systems will then attempt to select that mix of communication facilities that meets the established objectives at minimum cost.

In addition to the foregoing forms of tariff, there will be tariffs for other services that are not pure communications, such as those associated with processing and storage in the nodes.

VALUE-ADDED NETWORKS   The concept of value-added common carriers was important in the development of computer networking.
A value-added carrier leases communication facilities from conventional common carriers and uses these in conjunction with computers to build a network that offers new types of communication services and tariffs. These are called value-added networks (VANs). The packet-switched data networks discussed earlier in this chapter are all examples of value-added networks. Box 36.1 describes the services that value-added networks typically provide in addition to basic communication services.

In 1971 the United States Office of Telecommunications Policy recommended a policy of first-tier and second-tier common carriers. The first-tier carriers construct and own telecommunication links and lease channels to their customers. They typically own 50 to 100 percent of the channel miles in service and lease the remainder from another carrier. The second-tier carriers are the

Table 36.1 Eight types of tariff

	Switched	Nonswitched
Telegraph	Telex, TWX	Leased subvoice-grade circuit
Telephone	Dialed telephone connection	Leased telephone circuit
Packet-switched data network	Virtual call	Permanent virtual circuit
Circuit-switched data network	Fast-connect circuit-switched path	Permanent submultiplexed bit stream

BOX 36.1   Value-added services

- **Conversion Services.** The conversion services offered by a value-added network fall into the categories of *protocol, code,* and *speed* conversions. For example, a simple terminal that uses the ASCII code and an asynchronous data link protocol might be connected to the network via a 1200-bps data link. A computer with which it communicates might use the EBCDIC code and a bit-oriented data link protocol to communicate over a 56,000-bps data link.

- **Routing Services.** The network performs the task of deciding by what physical route the data should traverse the various links that make up the network. When one physical link fails, another can usually be substituted to make the failure transparent to users.

- **Network Control and Management.** The network controls the physical resources that implement the network and frees the user from such concerns.

- **Error Detection and Correction.** The network provides the user with what appears to be an error-free virtual channel through the network. Error control procedures implemented by typical value-added networks typically provide error rates as low as one undetected error bit in 10^9 bits transmitted.

value-added carriers. They add equipment, including multiplexors and computers, to channels leased from first-tier carriers and sell services that they create in this way, including message-delivery services, computer networks, and possibly information retrieval and computer time-sharing services. It seems likely that secondary markets will develop in many telecommunications areas. The second-tier carrier may minimize investment in terminals by letting the customer provide these. Legislation in favor of second-tier carriers has increased the diversity and competitiveness of the telecommunications industry in those countries where it has been passed. In many countries, such legislation does not yet exist.

Telecommunications systems use computers in different ways. Some use them for switching, some for sorting messages that are transmitted, and some for processing the data transmitted. At one extreme the computer merely switches the circuits; at the other extreme the circuits are merely links into a data processing system. The term *computer utility* became used for describing public access to computer networks, and in 1966 the U.S. Federal Communications Commission (FCC) initiated a lengthy inquiry to determine whether public computing services should be regulated. The inquiry terminated in 1973 and defined the six categories of operation shown in Fig. 36.9 (FCC Docket No. 16979). Local and remote data processing services are not to be regulated, whereas communication systems are. There is a hybrid service between these two in which a subscriber sends data, which is processed and transmitted to another subscriber. If the data processing is the primary part of this operation, it is not regulated. On the other hand, if the operation is primarily one of communication between the parties, it is regulated. The former is referred to as hybrid data processing and the latter as hybrid communication. There is a gray area between the two about which lawyers will argue. It is difficult to say whether certain intelligent functions are "computing" or "communication" functions.

Hybrid communication services must be completely tariffed and regulated by the FCC. Common carriers may not offer data processing services (hybrid or otherwise) except through a separate corporation with separate facilities, officers, and accounting.

Most countries do not have these legislative problems because the state telecommunications authority rigorously enforces its absolute monopoly over all telecommunications, no matter how bad its service may be.

INFORMATION UTILITIES

We use the term *information utilities* to refer to services that provide customers with access to information rather than simply access to data communication services. These services operate one or more host computers that maintain information in which their customers are interested. For example, an information utility might provide online access to such information as airline schedules, stock listings, or bibliographic search services. An information utility might implement its own data network, possibly using packet switching, for connecting customer terminals to its host computers, or it might use one of the public data networks discussed earlier to provide basic communication facilities. Some information utilities offer both forms of access. Box 36.2 lists some of the more popular information utilities and describes the main services they offer.

STANDARDS AND CAPABILITY

For computer networks and information utilities to be as useful as possible, it is desirable that they should employ standard interfaces so that many different machines can connect to many different networks. Just as telephone devices can connect to telephone networks everywhere, so data devices should be able to connect to data networks everywhere, and the data networks themselves should be linked up worldwide.

The interface to a data network is likely to be more complicated than that to a telephone network because it cannot rely on any human intelligence as does the making of telephone calls. It must be completely automatic. However, if the

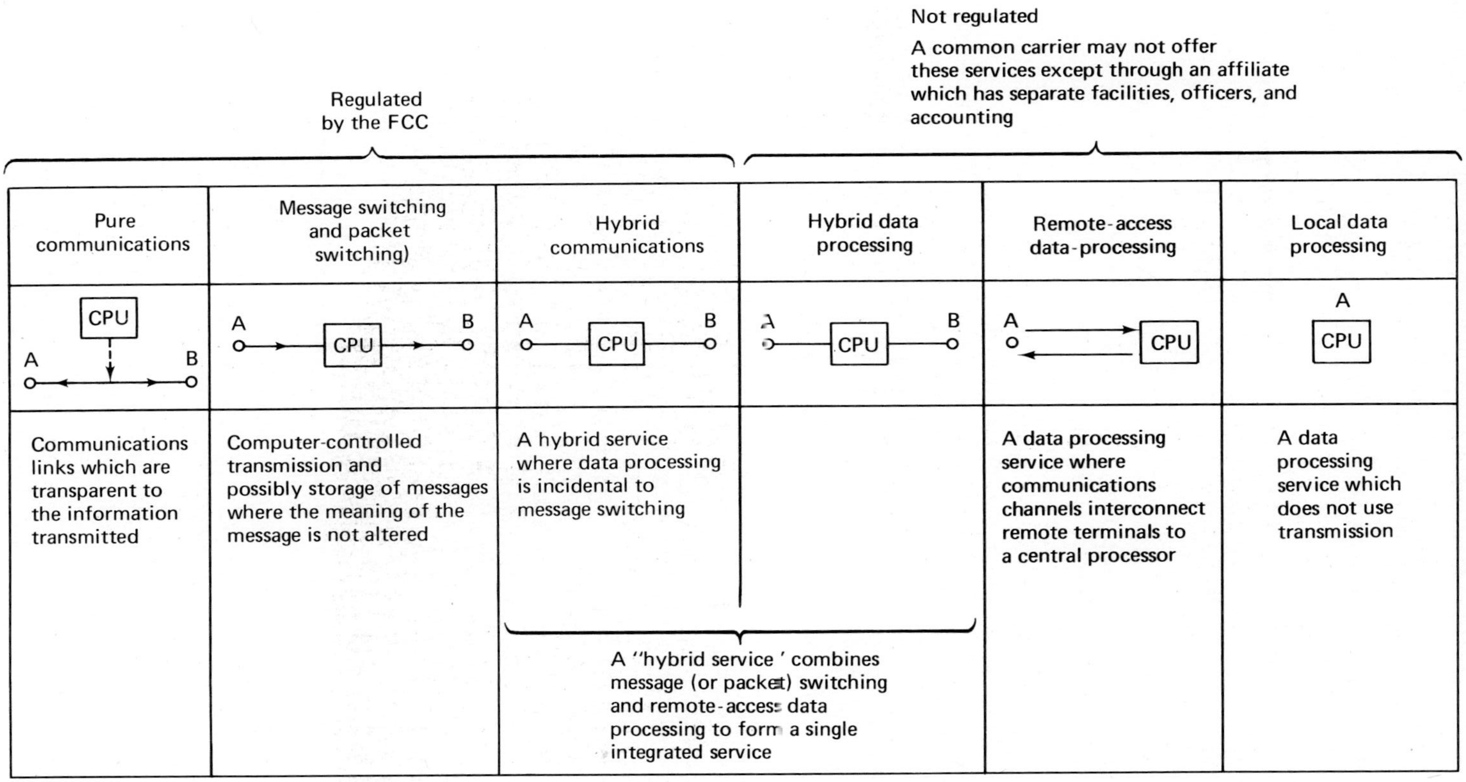

Regulated by the FCC

Not regulated

A common carrier may not offer these services except through an affiliate which has separate facilities, officers, and accounting

Pure communications	Message switching and packet switching)	Hybrid communications	Hybrid data processing	Remote-access data-processing	Local data processing
Communications links which are transparent to the information transmitted	Computer-controlled transmission and possibly storage of messages where the meaning of the message is not altered	A hybrid service where data processing is incidental to message switching		A data processing service where communications channels interconnect remote terminals to a central processor	A data processing service which does not use transmission

A "hybrid service" combines message (or packet) switching and remote-access data processing to form a single integrated service

Figure 36.9   Range of services defined by the FCC

BOX 36.2 Popular information utilities

- **Bibliographic Research Services (BRS).** BRS offers access to bibliographic data and many full-text databases on more than 70 topics, including finance, business and management, engineering, medicine, physics, computer science, education, books in print, and government documents. In addition to the standard databases, the user can create custom databases that can then be searched using BRS software. BRS can be contacted at 1200 Route 7, Latham, NY 12110.

- **Compuserve Information Service.** Compuserve is a consumer-oriented information utility that provides access to a wide range of services, including airline schedules, current and historical financial information, corporate profiles, and news retrieval from newspapers and wire services. Compuserve has many services that fall into the entertainment category, including theater, book, movie, and restaurant reviews; interactive games; and advice columns. Various types of personal computer user groups engage in constant dialogs using computer conferencing services. Compuserve also operates an electronic mail service that is used extensively for sending messages. Compuserve can be contacted at 5000 Arlington Center Blvd., Columbus, OH 43220.

- **Dialog.** Dialog is another bibliographic service that offers access to over 200 databases that summarize data from thousands of publications. Subjects are divided into several major categories, including agriculture and nutrition, bibliography, business/economics, chemistry, current affairs, directories, education, energy and environment, foundations and grants, law and government, material sciences, medicine and biosciences, multidisciplinary, patents and trademarks, science and technology, social sciences, and humanities. Dialog can be contacted at 3460 Hillview Ave., Palo Alto, CA 94304.

- **Dow Jones News Retrieval Service.** The Dow Jones Service is a general-interest information utility that provides a wide range of information services, including airline schedules, business and economic news stories, the entire text of the *Wall Street Journal,* current and historical securities prices, company profiles and 10K extracts, and the complete text of the *Academic American Encyclopedia.* Dow Jones can be contacted at P.O. Box 300, Princeton, NJ 08540.

- **Merlin Dial Data.** Merlin is an information utility that specializes in providing financial data covering the NYSE, AMEX, NASDAQ, and government issues exchanges, including current and historical information on the prices of stocks, bonds, rights, warrants, commodities, options, and indices. Merlin can be contacted at 1044 Northern Blvd., Roslyn, NY 11576.

- **The Source.** The Source is another consumer-oriented information utility that provides a broad range of information services, including airline schedules, financial information, entertainment services, travel services, news and sports, electronic games, and computer conferencing. The Source, like Compuserve, also offers an electronic mail service for sending and receiving messages.

interface is rigorously defined, it can be built into mass-producible VLSI machines, and quantity production will make the cost low. The interface software can reside in inexpensive terminals and in computers. One of the distributed logic elements employed by a computer can be the standard network interface unit.

Perceiving this, as we mentioned earlier, the common carriers and telephone administrations of the world used their international standards organization, CCITT, to agree upon an internationally recognized set of protocols for making calls on packet-switched data networks. This is referred to as *CCITT Recommendation X.25*. Most public data networks that use packet switching techniques now conform to *Recommendation X.25*.

Chapter 37 shows how *Recommendation X.25* defines the formats of packets of data that are used both for carrying information and for setting up and disconnecting calls on data networks, and for dealing with the errors and failures. Many countries of the world have already built X.25 data networks, and a wide variety of machines using the X.25 protocols are now being manufactured.

37 PACKET SWITCHING AND X.25

With digital channels proliferating and the use of computer terminals growing by leaps and bounds, a particularly important technology is the building of public data transmission networks. As we discussed in Chapter 9, packet switching is one way to build a public network capable of handling interactive computer traffic. In this chapter we discuss more details of packet switching networks. We begin with a general discussion of packet switching techniques. We continue by describing *CCITT Recommendation X.25*, which documents a set of standards and protocols that are widely used in implementing packet-switched data networks.

Box 37.1 shows commonly used formal definitions for the terms *packet* and *packet switching*. These definitions apply to all networks that use packet switching techniques, including the networks for which the terms were originally coined, such as the Arpanet network, the Telenet network, the Datapac service in Canada, and the British Post Office EPSS (Experimental Packet Switched Service).

RAILROAD TRAIN ANALOGY

We might compare the various types of data networks with a railroad network. With circuit switching there is an initial switch setting operation in which the switches are first set into the desired position. The switches then remain set and the entire train travels to its destination over the same route. With packet switching, each of the cars of the train is sent separately. When each car arrives at a switch, the decision is made where next to send it. If the network is lightly loaded, the cars will travel to their destination by a route that is close to the optimum. If the network is heavily loaded, the cars may bounce around or take lengthy or zigzag paths, possibly arriving in a different sequence to that in which they departed.

BOX 37.1   Packets and packet switching

- **Packet:** a group of binary digits, including data and call control signals, that is switched as a composite whole. The data, call control signals, and possibly error control information, are arranged in a specified format.
- **Packet Switching:** the transmission of data by means of addressed packets whereby a transmission channel is occupied for the duration of transmission of the packet only. The channel is then available for use by packets being transferred between different data terminal equipment. Note— The data may be formatted into a packet or divided and then formatted into a number of packets for transmission and multiplexing purposes.

A train with only a single car can head off into the network with no initial setup operation. However, if the train has many cars, it should not start its journey until it is sure that there is enough space for all of the cars at the destination. On some networks an engine has to be sent to the destination and return with a go-ahead message before the remaining cars of the train can set off.

PACKET SWITCHING AND MESSAGE SWITCHING

As we saw in Chapter 9, packet switching is a form of *store-and-forward* switching. Messages are stored at the switch nodes and then transmitted onward to their destination. Store-and-forward switching has existed for decades in telegraphy message switching systems. Conventional message switching is intended primarily for non-realtime people-to-people traffic; packet switching is intended primarily for realtime machine-to-machine traffic, including terminal-to-computer connections. These differences in purpose are such that there are major differences in operation between message switching and packet switching systems. Some of these differences are described in Box 37.2.

NETWORK STRUCTURE

A typical packet switching network is shown in Fig. 37.1. A number of network nodes, each of which consists of a specialized network computer, are linked together with point-to-point data links. The network computers each have three functions:

- Establishing a link between the network and the data processing equipment that uses the network

BOX 37.2   Message switching versus packet switching

- **Transmission Speed.** A packet switching network may be expected to deliver its packet in a fraction of a second, whereas a message switching system typically delivers its message in a much longer period, such as a fraction of a minute or even a fraction of an hour.

- **Storage Capacity.** Another important difference is that a message switching system typically files messages for possible retrieval at a future time. A packet switching system deletes each message from memory as soon as its correct receipt is acknowledged.

- **Network Structure.** Because a message switching system files messages, usually at one location, it tends to use a *centralized* star-structured or tree-structured network (although not in all cases). A packet switching network almost always has a *decentralized* mesh structure, with no particular location dominating the system.

- **Message Segmentation.** In many message switching systems long messages are sent in a single transmission. In packet switching systems long messages are chopped up into relatively small slices. This is because as messages get longer in a message switching system, delivery time gets longer also. Chopping up long messages helps the network to maintain an acceptably short delivery time for all users. At its destination the original message is reassembled from the slices.

- Carrying out switching operations by determining the route by which the data will be sent
- Transmitting data from one network node to another

There are a number of ways that a user device, such as a computer or a terminal, can be connected to a packet switching network. A very large user might have a network computer located at that user's own site, in which case the user's machine can be connected to the network computer via a simple hard-wired cable. This is shown in Fig. 37.2. In other cases, a terminal might be located in the same city as the network node, but remote from it. In this case, the user's computer or terminal might be connected to a network node via two high-speed modems and a leased wideband line, as shown in Fig. 37.3. In other cases, the user might establish a connection to the network computer using a dial-up voice-grade connection.

When one user machine sends data to another, it first breaks long messages into pieces, adds control information to each piece forming a packet, and passes the packets to the local network computer. Each packet contains the control

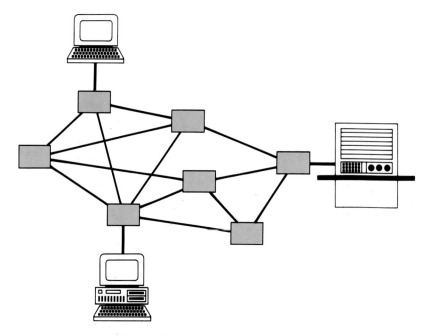

Figure 37.1　Packet switching network

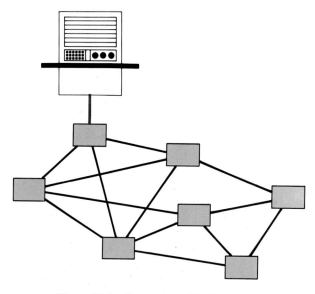

Figure 37.2　Connecting a local computer

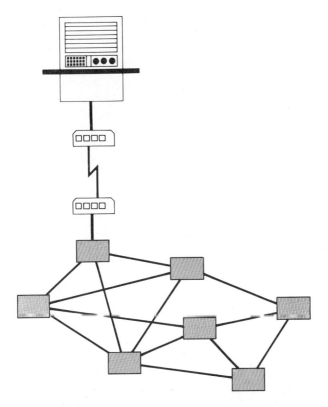

Figure 37.3 Connecting a remote computer

information needed to transmit the data correctly, and the packets are transmitted from one network computer to another until they reach their final destination. A network computer receiving a packet places it in a queue to await attention. When a message reaches the head of the queue, the computer examines its destination address, selects the next network computer on the route, and places the packet in an output queue for that destination. The final network computer passes the received packets to the destination user machine.

PACKETS

The packets might be thought of as envelopes into which data is placed. The envelope contains the destination address and various pieces of control information in the form of a header. The header contains such information as the destination address, the source address, packet number, and so on. The network computers do not interfere in any way with the data inside the envelopes.

PAD FUNCTION   Most packet switching networks can vary the routing of packets depending on network conditions. Because of this, it is possible that packets can arrive at their destinations out of sequence. Terminals that are attached directly to a public data network must have enough intelligence and storage to be able to break large messages into packets and to reassemble received packets into the proper sequence. A limited-function terminal that does not have the necessary intelligence to break up and reassemble messages can connect to and use the facilities of a packet switching network through the use of a *packet assembly and disassembly* (PAD) function, as shown in Fig. 37.4. The PAD facility can be supplied either by the user or by the operator of the packet switching network.

The use of the PAD function allows simple asynchronous terminals to establish connections to a distant host computer through a packet switching network. It is thus possible for the user with only a simple asynchronous display terminal to dial up a PAD facility operated by the network in order to gain

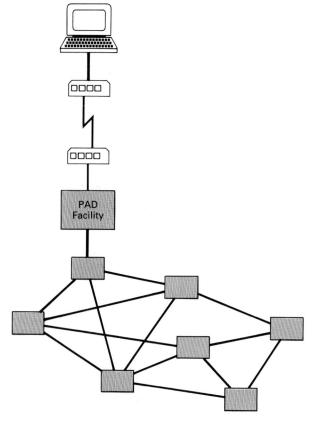

Figure 37.4   PAD facility

access to network facilities. This is the way the average terminal or personal computer user can dial the telephone number of a public data network and gain access to a host computer attached to the network.

CONTROL
FUNCTIONS
The transmission of the packets through the network requires three types of control procedures: error control, routing control, and flow control.

Error Control Procedures

Error control procedures are applied to each point-to-point link at the Data Link level, typically using a bit-oriented data link protocol, as discussed in Chapter 23. When a node receives a packet, it checks its accuracy using the error-detecting code bits. As discussed in Chapter 20, error-detecting codes can be made very powerful so that the probability of a transmission error being undetected is very low.

Routing Control Procedures

When a packet switching computer receives a packet addressed to another location, it must determine to which of the neighboring nodes of the network to send it. The computer will have a programmed procedure for routing the packet. A variety of different routing strategies are possible, including *predetermined routing, calculated routing, static directory routing, dynamic directory routing,* and *adaptive routing* (see Box 37.3). Most packet switching networks in operation today use adaptive routing.

Flow Control Procedures

Flow control helps avoid traffic jams by preventing too many packets from converging on certain parts of the network. The control messages that are passed between nodes to control the packet routing play a part in avoiding traffic jams. However, if too many packets enter the network heading for a given destination, routing control alone will not prevent a traffic jam. Traffic congestion can be harmful because packets bounce around from node to node occupying an excessive share of the transmission capacity. The network performance degenerates out of proportion to the increased load, like the roads out of a large city at rush hour.

The best way to prevent congestion is to control the *input* to the network. Control messages can warn all input nodes that congestion is beginning to build up. The most common cause of potential traffic jams is when one user machine suddenly sends a large volume of traffic to another. If the packets for this traffic

BOX 37.3   Routing alternatives

- **Predetermined Routing.** With predetermined routing, the route of a packet is determined before the packet starts on its journey. The packet then carries routing information that tells network computers where to send it. The determination of the route may be done by the originating location, or it may be done by a "master" station controlling the entire network. Only very simple packet switching networks use predetermined routing.

- **Calculated Routing.** With calculated routing, the addresses of the destination nodes in a network are chosen in such a way that it is possible for any interim node to determine which way to send a packet by performing a calculation on its address. If a node has received information about a failure in that direction, it may calculate a second-best routing. Calculated routing is simple but in general too inflexible and is not often used in practice.

- **Static Directory Routing.** With static directory routing, each node has a table telling it where next to send a packet that has a given destination. The table may give a first-choice and a second-choice path for a particular message. If the first-choice path is blocked or inoperative, a node will use the second-choice path. As a packet travels through the network, each node does a fast table look-up and sends it on its way to the next node, until the final destination is reached.

- **Dynamic Directory Routing.** With dynamic directory routing, routing tables are used that can be changed automatically as conditions on the network change. There are several possible criteria that could be used in selecting the entries for such routing tables. These include minimizing the number of nodes that must be traversed, spreading the traffic to avoid uneven loading, and minimizing the delay under current network conditions.

- **Adaptive Routing.** With adaptive routing, each node transmits a service message at specified time intervals, say every half-second. Based on the information obtained from the transmission and receipt of these service messages, routing algorithms are changed to reflect current conditions on the network. Adaptive routing sometimes results in oscillatory behavior, with the routing pattern oscillating rapidly backward and forward under peak-load conditions. Minor changes in the routing algorithm can affect the routing behavior under heavy loading in ways that are difficult to predict without simulation of the network.

follow each other at the speed of the input node, there may be a traffic jam on the route. The rate of input needs to be controlled rather than merely opening a sluice gate wide.

DATAGRAMS

Because of the extra processing associated with message reassembly, two types of packet switching have evolved. The first handles multipacket messages and so has to have protocols that permit error-free message *assembly* without causing traffic jams. The second handles only single-packet messages, and hence avoids complex protocols that increase the network overhead. Canadian common carriers coined the term *datagram* to relate to the second type of service. In a datagram service users can send messages up to but not exceeding the maximum capacity of one packet. This permits simple control procedures to be used, which results in low overhead and fast transit times. A datagram network is of value for many applications, including the vast future needs of electronic funds transfer. A datagram network could be designed to operate with very inexpensive terminals. A datagram service is also offered as a lower-cost option on some public data networks that also provide full message assembly and disassembly facilities for those users that require it.

NETWORK TRANSPARENCY

It is the intention of the designers of packet switching networks to make the communication techniques as unobtrusive as possible to the users. The network operation should be *independent* of the nature of the computing operations that employ the network. Many new types of computers and new types of operations could then employ it. The network should connect two computer processes, perhaps thousands of miles apart, as though they were directly interconnected via a precisely defined interface. This illusion of direct interconnection is referred to as *network transparency*. To make the network appear transparent, the transmission must be fast and the software must hide the complexity of its operations from the process that uses it. Many packet switching networks define a *network virtual terminal,* which has its own character set and control procedures. The network may then allow a wide variety of incompatible machines to be connected to the network by converting their codes and control procedures to those of the network virtual terminal. This enables customers to interact with a large variety of terminal types without special software having to be written for each.

CCITT RECOMMENDATION X.25

Of particular importance to the technology of packet switching is a recommendation of the CCITT called *Recommendation X.25.* CCITT Recommendation

X.25 defines a standard interface between a packet-switched data network and any user machine connected to that network. Many terminals, computers, and other data communications products have been designed to conform exactly to this interface. All of these devices can be attached successfully to a variety of networks in different countries that conform to CCITT Recommendation X.25.

Recommendation X.25 documents standards and protocols that conform to the specifications for the first three layers of the OSI model (physical, data link, and network layers) (see Fig. 37.5). X.25 defines the interface between a DTE and a DCE for a terminal operating in the *packet mode* on a public data network. The OSI network layer is concerned with getting a packet from its source to its final destination.

An X.25 network uses the packet switching techniques discussed earlier in this chapter in routing data through the network. The X.25 interface is located in various places, depending on how a user device is connected to the X.25 network. If the X.25 network node is located on the premises of a user machine and the user machine is connected to the network computer via a hard-wired cable, the X.25 interface resides at the connection between the user machine and the network computer (see Fig. 37.6). If the user machine is located remote from the network computer, the X.25 interface is located as shown in Fig. 37.7.

PAD-RELATED CCITT RECOMMENDATIONS

A limited-function terminal, or one that does not implement the X.25 interface, can connect to an X.25 network through the use of a PAD function,

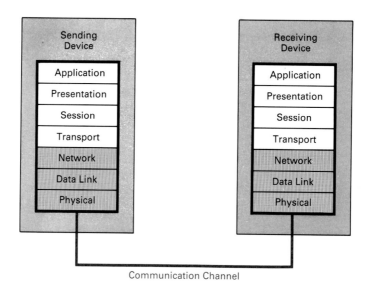

Figure 37.5   X.25 and the OSI model

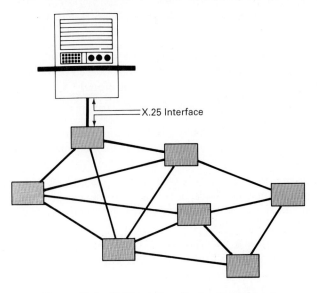

Figure 37.6   X.25 interface for local attachment

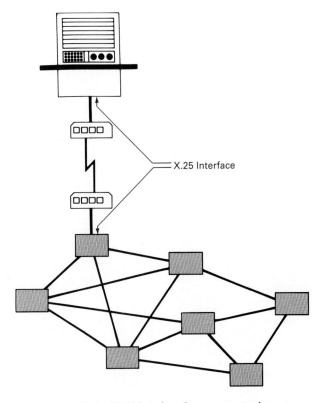

Figure 37.7   X.25 interface for remote attachment

as discussed earlier in this chapter. When a PAD function is used, the X.25 interface resides as shown in Fig. 37.8. The use of a PAD facility in conjunction with an X.25 network is described by three additional CCITT recommendations. These are illustrated in Fig. 37.9 and are described below.

- **Recommendation X.3.** This CCITT recommendation describes the functions that are performed by the PAD facility and defines the various parameters that can be used to specify its mode of operation.

- **Recommendation X.28.** This CCITT recommendation describes the interface between a non-packet-mode device and the device that implements the PAD function. X.28 describes the way an asynchronous terminal connects to and controls the PAD facility.

- **Recommendation X.29.** This CCITT recommendation describes the interface between an X.25 device and the device that implements the PAD function. X.29 describes the way an X.25 device communicates with an asynchronous terminal by way of the PAD facility.

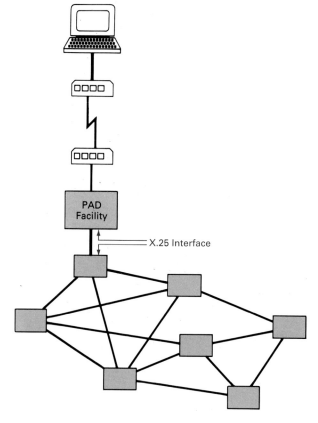

Figure 37.8   X.25 interface with PAD facility

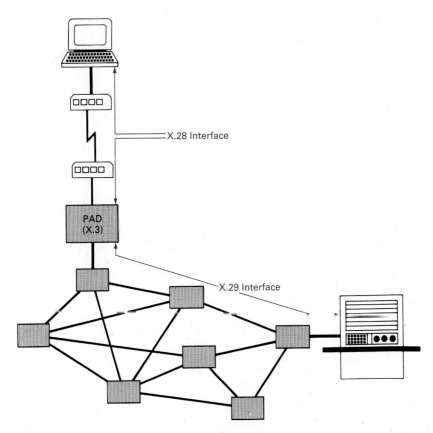

Figure 37.9   CCITT PAD-related recommendations

OTHER CCITT X-SERIES RECOMMENDATIONS

Recommendations X.3, X.25, X.28, and X.29 are part of a series of recommendations for data communication networks. All of the CCITT X-series recommendations are described in Volume VIII of the CCITT Red Book. The CCITT X-series recommendations that are of particular importance to public data networks are listed in Box 37.4.

X.25 SERVICES

An X.25 network provides a number of useful services for its users. Typical services that X.25 networks provide are *permanent virtual circuits* and *virtual calls*.

Permanent Virtual Circuits

A public data network user may wish to be connected permanently with another network user, in much the same way that two users are connected using a leased

BOX 37.4 CCITT X-series recommendations

Volume VIII—Fascicle VIII.2: Data Communication Networks—Services and Facilities.

- **Recommendation X.1:** international user classes of service in public data networks

- **Recommendation X.2:** international data transmission services and optional user facilities in public data networks

- **Recommendation X.3:** packet assembly/disassembly facility (PAD) in a public data network

- **Recommendation X.4:** general structure of signals of International Alphabet No. 5 code for data transmission over public data networks

- **Recommendation X.10:** categories of access for data terminal equipment (DTE) to public data transmission services provided by PDNs and/or ISDNs through terminal adapters

- **Recommendation X.15:** definitions of terms concerning public data networks

Volume VIII—Fascicle VIII.3: Data Communication Networks—Interfaces

- **Recommendation X.20:** interface between data terminal equipment (DTE) and data circuit-terminating equipment (DCE) for start-stop transmission on public data networks

- **Recommendation X.20 bis:** use on the public data networks of data terminal equipment (DTE) which is designed for interfacing to asynchronous duplex V-series modems

- **Recommendation X.21:** interface between data terminal equipment (DTE) and data circuit-terminating equipment (DCE) for synchronous operation on public data networks

- **Recommendation X.21 bis:** use on public data networks of data terminal equipment (DTE) which is designed for interfacing to synchronous V-series modems

- **Recommendation X.22:** multiplex DTE/DCE interface for user classes 3 to 6

- **Recommendation X.24:** list of definitions for interchange circuits between data terminal equipment (DTE) and data circuit-terminating equipment (DCE) on public data networks

BOX 37.4   *(Continued)*

- **Recommendation X.25:** interface between data terminal equipment (DTE) and data circuit-terminating equipment (DCE) for terminals operating in the packet mode and connected to public data networks by dedicated circuit

- **Recommendation X.26:** electrical characteristics for unbalanced double-current interchange circuits for general use with integrated-circuit equipment in the field of data communications

- **Recommendation X.27:** electrical characteristics for balanced double-current interchange circuits for general use with integrated-circuit equipment in the field of data communications

- **Recommendation X.28:** DTE/DCE interface for a start-stop mode data terminal equipment accessing the packet assembly/disassembly facility (PAD) in a public data network situated in the same country

- **Recommendation X.29:** procedures for the exchange of control information and user data between a packet assembly/disassembly (PAD) facility and a packet mode DTE or another PAD

telephone connection. A permanent virtual circuit, illustrated in Fig. 37.10, provides this facility. The users are connected permanently to their respective network computers. They use the actual communication facilities of the network only when they are actually transmitting data; however, they remain permanently connected as though a physical circuit always connected them. Typically, the user of a permanent virtual circuit pays a monthly connect charge plus a charge based on total data transmitted. Users of public data networks are not ordinarily charged based on distance. One of the advantages of using a public data network is that it costs no more to send a message between New York and Los Angeles than it does to send a message across town.

Virtual Calls

When making a virtual call, a user logs onto the network, establishes a virtual circuit with another user, exchanges messages for a time, and then breaks off the connection. Users that make virtual calls are generally charged based on connect time, quantity of data transmitted, or both. In making a virtual call or using a permanent virtual circuit, the user perceives no difference between using a public data network and using ordinary telephone facilities. All the complexities of packet assembly and disassembly and routing through the network are typically transparent to the user.

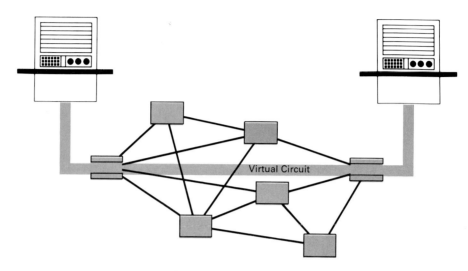

Figure 37.10   Permanent virtual circuit

X.25 PACKET FORMAT

As mentioned above, Recommendation X.25 defines the interface between a user device and a packet switching network. This interface consists of a precise definition of the format to which each information packet must conform and the specifications of the various command packets that user machines send and receive to control how the network is used. Figure 37.11 shows the format of an X.25 packet. All packets, both information packets and X.25 commands, follow the same basic format. Each packet begins with three bytes that contain the following information:

- **General Format Identifier.** This specifies general information about the format of the packet. For example, this field indicates whether modulo 8 or modulo 128 is used for message sequence numbers for flow control.

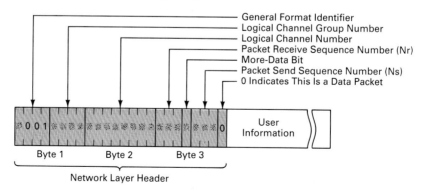

Figure 37.11   X.25 packet format

- **Logical Channel Group.** Each user machine attached to the X.25 network has one or more channel groups assigned to it. This field identifies which logical channel group is used to transmit this particular packet.

- **Logical Channel Number.** Each logical channel group is made up of up to 255 logical channels. This field identifies which logical channel is used to transmit this particular packet.

- **Packet Type Identifier.** This field identifies the packet's type. A *data packet* is used to contain part of the text of a message that is being transmitted through the network. Several types of *control packets* are used to transmit various types of network commands through the network.

The control information in the packet is used by the network nodes in determining which point-to-point links to use in routing the packet through the network. As a packet moves through the network, each node places the packet inside a transmission frame in order to transmit it from one network node to the next. Frame transmission at the data link level is handled by one of two bit-oriented data link protocols: *link access protocol* (LAP) or *link access protocol—balanced* (LAPB). These are effectively functional subsets of the HDLC protocol defined by ISO. As far as the data link protocol is concerned, the information field of the packet and the four control fields are all treated as data as the packet moves across a single point-to-point link. This is shown in Fig. 37.12.

X.25 COMMANDS   In addition to defining the packet format, X.25 also defines a number of control packets that can be transmitted through the network in order to control network functions. Box 37.5 contains brief descriptions of some of the control packets that are used.

THE FUTURE OF PACKET SWITCHING   Many organizations have announced an intention to build or experiment with packet switching networks. As public data networks grow, there will continue to be arguments about the relative merits of packet

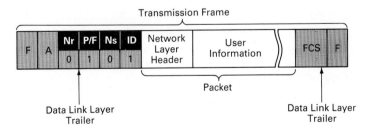

Figure 37.12   Transmission frame envelope

BOX 37.5   X.25 control packets

- **Call Request.** A sending machine sends a Call Request packet to request the establishment of a virtual call.

- **Incoming Call.** A network node converts the Call Request packet into an Incoming Call packet and sends it to the destination machine. This asks the destination machine if it can accept the call request.

- **Call Accepted.** The destination machine transmits a Call Accepted packet as a positive response to an Incoming Call packet.

- **Call Connected.** The originating machine converts the Call Accepted packet into a Call Connected packet as the final step in establishing a virtual call.

- **Clear Indication.** A Clear Indication packet is transmitted when a destination station is not able to accept an Incoming Call packet and gives the reason for refusing to accept the call.

- **Clear Request.** A Clear Request packet is transmitted when a station wants to disconnect a virtual call.

- **Clear Confirmation.** A Clear Confirmation packet is used as a positive acknowledgment to a Clear Request and is transmitted as a final step in disconnecting a virtual call.

switching and fast-connect circuit switching networks. It seems likely that the existing packet switching networks will grow steadily, acquiring more traffic and more nodes. When they become very large and ubiquitous, economies of scale may make some form of switched data network replace many of the private leased-line networks that corporations and government departments use today. There are several future directions in which packet switching networks will probably evolve if their traffic grows sufficiently. Some of these future directions are listed in Box 37.6.

We have characterized the years ahead as an *era of great invention* in telecommunications. In an era of great invention the users need to be protected from the proliferation of new mechanisms. Protection can come from appropriate standards and "virtual" techniques that make any form of network appear as though it used simple standard interfaces. Users ought to demand such protection, both nationally and internationally. Standards come into existence from government-supported organizations such as the CCITT. Manufacturers or designers, given appropriate standards and protocols, can then be free to invent all manner of ingenious new mechanisms using those standards and protocols.

The virtual call and virtual circuit recommendations of X.25 relate to

BOX 37.6 Future directions of packet switching

- The high-speed digital links used by the telephone companies, such as the T1 carrier, will probably become the links used by packet switching networks. Transmission rates of millions of bits per second will permit systems with very fast response times to be built.

- To fill such high-speed links the networks will have to attract a high traffic volume. Much of this traffic may come from relatively new uses of data links, such as electronic mail, electronic funds transfer, and other forms of message delivery.

- As networks grow very large it will be economical for them to become multilevel networks with a hierarchy of switching offices. Just as the telephone network has five classes of office, so data networks might acquire two, three, and eventually more levels.

- Several classes of traffic might be handled, perhaps differentiating between datagrams and long messages.

- Several classes of priority might be handled, including perhaps immediate delivery (a few milliseconds), 2-second delivery for interactive computing, delivery in minutes, and overnight delivery.

- Some message traffic might be *filed* as on a message switching system. Messages intended to be read on visual display units or spoken over the telephone might be filed until the recipient requests them. Distributed storage rather than centralized storage might be used, especially for bulky data, depending on the relative costs of storage and transmission. A hybrid between message switching and packet switching may thus emerge.

- Fast-connect circuit switching has advantages over packet switching for some types of traffic. The nodes of a large data network may be designed to select whether a circuit-switched or packet-switched path is used. A hybrid between circuit switching and packet switching may evolve. As discussed in Chapter 41, the emerging ISDN standards include provisions for both circuit switching and packet switching.

- The user-interface computer may become separate from the switching computers and have an entirely different set of functions. It may be designed to convert the transmission of all terminals to a standard format, code, and protocol so that completely incompatible machines can be interconnected.

- Elaborate security procedures may be used.

- The user-interface devices may be designed to receive from and transmit to conventional facsimile machines or other analog devices.

(Continued)

BOX 37.6   *(Continued)*

- The interface machines may be designed to compress messages before transmission, to increase the transmission efficiency. This is valuable with data, but especially valuable with facsimile messages.

- The interface machines may be designed to handle packet radio terminals or controllers. Portable data terminals may be linked to the system.

- One of the most cost-effective data transmission facilities will be the satellite, and packet switching networks will probably use them. To use future satellites in an optimal fashion will substantially change the topology and protocols of packet switching networks.

- Economies of scale and flexibility may require that telephone or continuous-channel traffic and burst traffic be intermixed. Networks, especially satellite networks, capable of handling both continuous-channel and packet-switched traffic may emerge.

- An interlinking of separate national networks will occur—the goal of ISDN technology. Satellites will interlink nodes in many countries, giving users of packet switching the capability to use computers around the world and to send messages worldwide.

- When vast numbers of computers are available on the networks, directory machines will be very important for enabling users to find the facilities they need.

packet switching over terrestrial telephone circuits. This may be a dominant technology for a period of time, but as we have seen, there are many other techniques and uses of telecommunications. If satellites, CATV, fast-connect circuit switching, packet radio, and other new technologies play a major role in some countries, then virtual operation, which makes links using these facilities appear to be the same as other types of links, is desirable. As the transmission of facsimile documents, voice messages, video signals, music, electronic mail, and so on, assume major importance, standards and forms of virtual circuits will also be needed for them.

Now that we have examined the characteristics of public data networks, in Chapter 38 we discuss the private networks that many organizations have built for data transmission.

38 PRIVATE NETWORKS

We can divide data networks into two broad classes: public networks and private networks. Public data networks, discussed in Chapter 36, are built by common carriers or government telecommunications administrations. Their transmission and switching facilities are shared by the computers and terminals of individuals, corporations, and other organizations. Any one machine using a public data network can send data to any other (if permitted by security and software constraints). Most industrialized nations have built, and are continuing to expand, data networks for this purpose and these have become a vital part of a nation's service infrastructure.

Private data networks, the subject of this chapter, are built within one corporation or government organization. The implementors lease circuits for private use, usually telephone circuits or digital transmission facilities, and construct networks that may or may not have their own switching facilities. The majority of corporate networks today use private leased lines rather than public switched data networks. One reason for this is that public data networks are still in their infancy. As they grow the incentive to use them will increase.

The argument has frequently been expressed that widespread use of public data networks rather than the installation of multiple private networks would be better for a nation. Public networks would carry greater traffic volumes and would benefit from economies of scale. Greater traffic volumes would lead to higher line utilizations and to the use of wideband trunks that would provide faster response times. Public networks can afford diversity of routing, which enables faulty trunks or equipment to be circumvented. On the other hand, the line utilization of many private networks is higher than the early multiple-user switched networks because they are tightly designed for a given relatively stable traffic pattern.

Corporations and government departments in many countries, including the United States, are generally free to choose whether to build their own private networks or use public networks. Their choice will depend on the relative cost and the general availability of the required services. The designer of a network uses techniques to adjust the network configuration and choice of circuits so as to achieve a given result at a minimum cost. Today, costs still often favor the use of leased circuits, and hence the widespread use of private networks. However, this is changing rapidly. In the future, lower tariffs and greater availability of public-switched data networks will increase their use—at least in some countries. To achieve economies of scale in public networks it might pay a telephone administration to adjust its prices so that users are encouraged to desert the private lines and use the public networks. This is being done in some countries. Another factor affecting the choice will be whether the software of a chosen manufacturer is compatible with the public network protocols.

**PRIVATE
NETWORK
STRUCTURES**

Most private networks are vertical in structure rather than horizontal. This was natural when data processing systems were highly centralized. Even with distributed processing systems there is usually a hierarchy of work activities. An organization tends to have many relatively simple repetitive jobs at its lower levels. Higher in the organization there tends to be a few complex jobs. The lower levels interchange data with the higher levels as shown in Fig. 38.1, but there is often little interchange among the lower-level units themselves. Sometimes the lower work units share common data that is maintained at a higher level.

Because of the vertical patterns of data flow, most private networks are star-structured or tree-structured. A growing proportion of private networks interconnect separate self-sufficient computer centers, and these are often themselves structured horizontally. Sometimes there are separate vertical networks with horizontal links between their tops, as shown in Fig. 38.2. The network mechanisms for hierarchical or star-structured networks are fundamentally simpler in certain respects than those for horizontal or mesh-structured networks. Some types of software have been designed for star-structured networks only, avoiding the complexities of mesh-structured networks, such as alternate routing, deadlocks, flow control, and distributed network management. There are various mechanisms used to implement hierarchical networks, including:

- Multipoint lines with polling
- Frequency-division multiplexors
- Time-division multiplexors
- Looped lines
- Concentrators
- Concentrators on multipoint lines

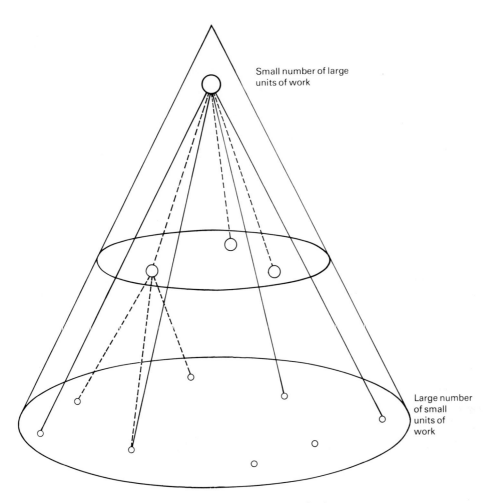

Figure 38.1 Vertical communication

  The techniques listed above have all been discussed in earlier chapters, and all of these techniques have been in common use prior to the era of computer networks.

  Many large corporations have a proliferation of leased-line networks. Separate networks have been implemented by different teams for different purposes, some for different divisions or subsidiaries of a corporation. Most governments have a much greater proliferation of separate networks. Boxes 38.1 through 38.9 illustrate typical private data networks. In these examples they have all grown up in the same corporation. (The systems described are fictional but are based on the systems of an existing corporation, simplified somewhat for reasons of clarity.)

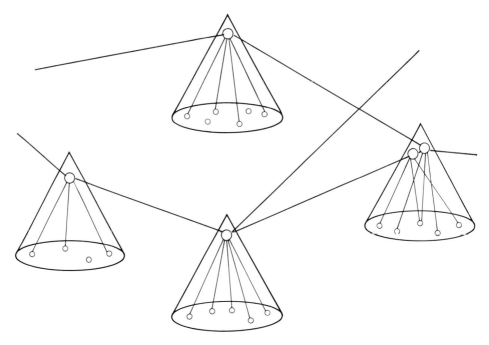

Figure 38.2   Horizontally linked vertical networks

The systems shown cover the information needs of the corporation from selling their products and maintaining them, to deciding what to manufacture, giving instructions to the plants, and controlling the manufacturing process. They handle accounting operations, provide networks for relaying administrative messages between most corporate locations and data between computer locations, and gather together, for management, many types of information, which they endeavor to make conveniently accessible. In addition, they provide terminal services for staff ranging from scientists to clerical workers and give remote access to large computers.

INTEGRATED NETWORKS   As the diversity of information resources grows in an organization, it becomes less predictable what remote computers are likely to be used at any given location. It therefore becomes more desirable to have a horizontal network spanning the major locations, rather than a collection of disjoint vertical networks as in Boxes 38.1 through 38.9. Also, with the growth of word processing and electronic mail, there is a need to transmit mail and documents between locations. An integrated network, such as the one shown in Box 38.10, acts as a switch that

BOX 38.1   Electronic mail

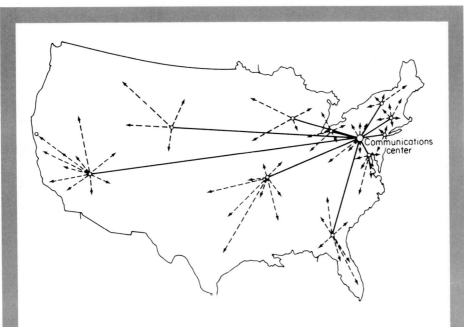

      The electronic mail network consists of voice-grade lines that link major corporate locations to a communication center. The communication center uses a message switching computer to forward messages to their destinations. In this network, up to eight 1200-bps channels are multiplexed onto 9600-bps leased voice lines, and many terminals are connected to each 1200-bps channel.

      This network was the first to be installed by the corporation and remains separate from those installed later. Its purpose is to relay administrative messages from any major location in the corporation to any other. Such locations have printers and display terminals that are used for receiving and transmitting messages. A message normally reaches its destination in a few seconds, and all messages are stored for future reference and can be broadcast to many locations.

interconnects all the various locations. In Boxes 38.1 and 38.2 the switch is in one place. In Box 38.10 it is distributed.

      Conversion from separate networks to an integrated network has in practice proved to be a difficult task. The message formats and protocols of the integrated network are often different from those used in the earlier networks.

BOX 38.2   High-speed batch transmission

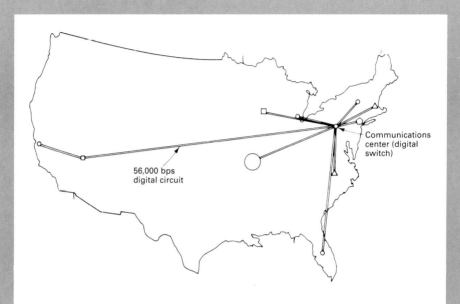

56,000 bps
digital circuit

Communications
center (digital
switch)

This network uses 56,000-bps digital circuits to transmit batches of data at high speed between the corporation's major computer centers. The digital circuits coming from the various computer centers are connected to a digital switch that is capable of handling the high bit rates. Connections can be established between any of the computer centers.

Whereas the network shown in Box 38.1 is for people sending messages to people, this network is for machines sending data to machines. The lines are not physically switched in the network in Box 38.1; here they are. Also, the electronic mail network, having been installed before the widespread availability of digital circuits, uses analog lines with modems and frequency-division multiplexing; this network uses digital technology. There is also a great difference in line speed: individual channels transmit at 1200 bps in Box 38.1; 56,000 bps here.

BOX 38.3   Engineering division system

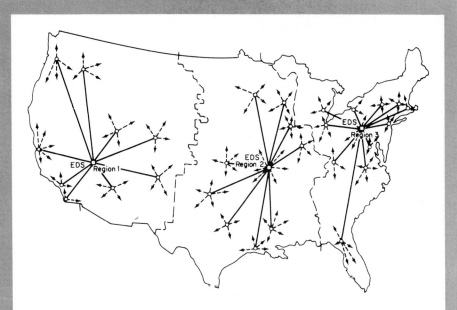

The engineering division of the same corporation is divided into three regions, each of which has a computer center. The *Engineering Division System* (EDS) network links interactive display terminals and slow-speed printers to a central computer for each region to give support to the field engineers. The field engineers can obtain a variety of services from their terminals. For example, they can make inquiries about technical information and, in some cases, receive lengthy instructions.

Engineers use the EDS network to order components that are needed and to obtain delivery-time estimates. They report full details of all failures. The EDS computers analyze the failure reports and the repair activity. They maintain inventory control of the spare parts kept at all locations in each region, with terminals being used for this purpose in all the warehouses where spare parts are kept.

The EDS network uses a combination of leased and dial-up voice lines using a system of multiplexors and modems of various speeds to provide a 2400-bps channel between each terminal and its associated computer center. The EDS network has been designed and optimized without consideration of the two networks in Boxes 38.1 and 38.2.

BOX 38.4 Sales administration system

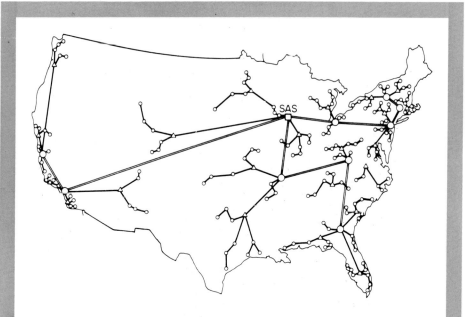

A separate Sales Administration System (SAS) network supports thousands of display screen terminals in the branch offices of the sales division. SAS terminals are used to enter details of all orders taken, of all customer payments, and of all customer requirements, such as training course bookings.

Because of the large quantity of information that flows in and out of the main SAS computer center, leased 56,000-bps digital circuits are used to connect concentrator computers in various parts of the country to the main computer center. A combination of 56,000-bps digital circuits, 9600-bps digital circuits, and voice-grade analog lines is used to connect the various branch offices to the closest concentrator. Digital service units, modems, and multiplexors are used as appropriate to provide each terminal with a connection having the required bit rate. The network is designed so that terminal users receive a response time of about 2 seconds to most of their terminal actions.

The sales division is organizationally separate from the other divisions of the corporation and designed the SAS network without reference to other existing networks.

BOX 38.5   Evening transmission on the SAS network

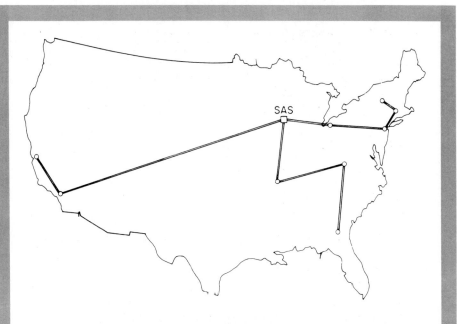

SAS

After the sales branch offices shut down for the evening, the main SAS computer center switches to offline work and handles routine data processing tasks. The leased digital connections that connect the concentrator computers to the main computer center are used for high-volume batch transmissions, such as data to be used for customer mailings. Large data files are also transmitted over the network to be used for backup and recovery operations. Invoices and other documents are composed, mailed, and controlled at the locations of the concentrator computers.

New software is needed and often, terminals have to be changed. This usually requires modification to application programs. Sometimes the use of a new terminal necessitates a new user interface structure, which causes major application program rewriting. Because of these difficulties, there are often arguments from groups who want to retain their old network. To make matters worse, sometimes the performance aspects of the new network are worse, due to longer software path lengths, more main memory needed, and longer response times.

The network in Box 38.10 can be described as an integrated network for data transmission. The typical organization today spends much more for telephone voice transmission than for data transmission. Many organizations have

BOX 38.6 Manufacturing central system

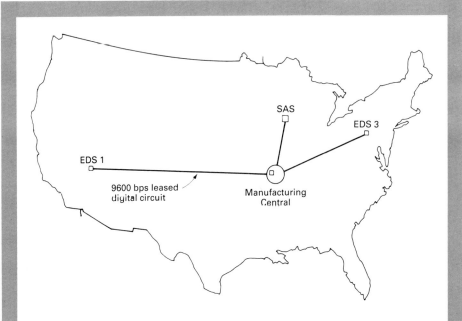

The corporation has several manufacturing plants. The planning of what should be manufactured takes place centrally at the location of the largest plant and is handled with the aid of the *Manufacturing Central System* (MCS) network.

The input for the decision of what to manufacture comes from market forecasts and from day-to-day knowledge of what orders have been taken and what spare parts are needed. The latter two are kept by the sales (SAS) and engineering (EDS) systems. These are transmitted, once daily, to the Manufacturing Central System. The MCS central computer then transmits details of the manufacturing status of orders and when they will be completed to the SAS and EDS central computers.

Leased digital circuits operating at 9600 bps are used for these transmissions. The transmissions are sufficiently long that leased digital circuits have a lower cost than the use of public telephone lines and high-speed modems. Also, the 9600-bps digital circuits have a higher speed and greater reliability than can be achieved using dial-up, long-distance voice circuits.

BOX 38.7 Plant information system

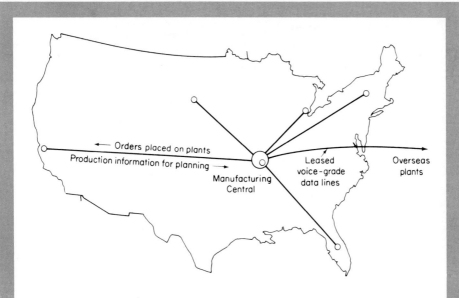

A two-way interchange takes place between the central MCS computer and the computer centers at the individual manufacturing plants. The MCS computer sends the plants orders of what to manufacture. The plants return to the MCS computer progress details, estimates of completion dates, and information about plant schedules that will aid the central planning process. The orders are then processed by the plant computers. Here breakdowns into individual components are fed into the production shop schedules. The plant computers maintain files giving order and stock status plus other files that can be interrogated by the staff at the location of the MCS central computer.

The information interchange between the plant computers and the MCS central computer was again designed to take place over leased voice lines. Leased voice lines were chosen because digital service was not available at some of the locations and also because leased voice lines were in this case the cheapest form of connection if done without consideration of other systems.

BOX 38.8 Corporate information system

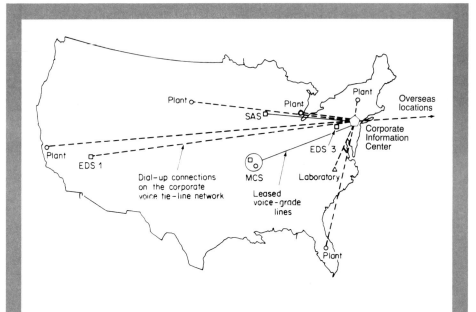

The Corporate Information System (CIS) network was designed to provide the information needed by functional and strategic management. A group of CIS specialists is familiar with all the sources designed to satisfy this need. Much of the information comes from the files maintained at the Corporate Information Center. However, for many queries it is necessary to go farther afield and inspect other files or question the staff of other information centers.

Each plant has an information center for its own management. At the location of the MCS central computer is a group of specialists who are able to interrogate MCS files. The SAS central computer center also has such a staff. The CIS staff call on these specialists when necessary, converse with them, and link their terminals into those systems.

In some cases, the staff of the SAS or MCS systems do the file interrogation with their own terminals and then switch the results to the CIS terminals. The staff here, in turn, display the information they have located on the screens or terminals used by management. Several mechanisms for doing so exist. The manager in question may have a compatible terminal, so the data is switched for display on it. Some of the managers in the corporate headquarters building, which

BOX 38.8 *(Continued)*

houses the Corporate Information Center, have closed-circuit television links to the information room. On these screens they can see the faces of the staff members who assist them, plus whatever printouts or displays they may generate. The boardroom and other meeting rooms are equipped with display terminals, printing terminals, and closed-circuit television.

The Corporate Information Center needs links to other systems to support its operations. Only the links to the SAS and MCS networks are used frequently enough to make a permanent leased line economical. The other locations are accessed by dial-up telephone connections, most often using the corporate tie-line network. All data links are implemented using 2400-bps modems.

a telephone tie-line network of leased private lines that are used for internal telephone calls. An integrated network designed to minimize communication costs should take into consideration telephone traffic and electronic mail as well as computer traffic. Groups of circuits can be leased and organized so that they can handle telephone, facsimile mail, and data traffic. As we will see in Chapter 41, it is the goal of the ISDN technology, toward which today's common carriers are evolving, to provide all types of communication over the same integrated digital network.

Communications satellite technology is rapidly evolving and is dropping in cost much faster than are land-based circuits. The leased T1 facilities shown in the network in Box 38.10 might actually be implemented in the form of satellite circuits, as shown in Fig. 38.3. Here, a small satellite earth station, with an antenna of 7 meters or less in diameter, is used at each location that requires a high-speed connection. The control equipment at each earth station permits that station to transmit to or receive from any other station. The station equipment may permit voice and data traffic to share the same facilities. This sharing helps to cost-justify the use of relatively expensive satellite earth stations. Some corporations are now installing satellite networks using the facilities of independent satellite communication companies.

Some countries have satellites for domestic use and others do not. Some satellite users have their own earth stations; others lease circuits from a satellite common carrier that routes them via its own earth stations. The use of satellites can result in substantially different network mechanisms, as discussed in Chapter 14.

BOX 38.9 Time sharing and information retrieval

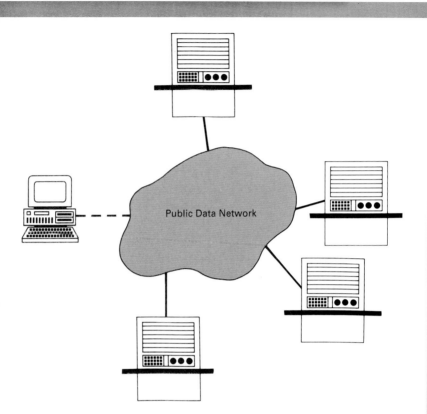

The corporation supports a growing set of services to which employees can gain access with various types of terminals and personal computers. These services include programmed tools of various types, the capability to search for and retrieve technical information, financial and accounting information, library services, statistical analysis packages, and so on. Some users also have their own programs available on the centrally located computers. Some maintain their own files at the computer center. Some scientists and clerical workers have terminals and personal computers at their desks, and in many locations there is a room with communally used terminals and personal computers.

Different large computers can be accessed from the terminals and personal computers, and each of the computers is connected to a public data network via leased lines. Users dial up the local access number of the public data network and gain access to the desired computer using a simple log-on sequence. The existence of the public data network made it possible for the corporation to avoid the creation of yet another extremely complex private network.

BOX 38.10   Integrated network

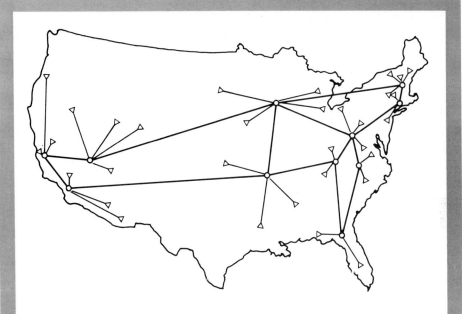

The proliferation shown in Boxes 38.1 through 38.9 involves wasteful duplication of routes. There is a desire in many such corporations today to replace the separate networks with a common network. The network shown above illustrates what this might be like. Leased T1 facilities are used to provide connections that operate at 1.544 million bits per second between major computer centers. Lower-capacity—56,000-, 9600-, and 2400-bps—digital circuits are used where such a high bit rate is not required. Leased voice-grade lines are used to connect those locations where digital facilities are not yet available or are too expensive.

This integrated network has a lower overall cost than that of the individual networks it replaces. An integrated network can also have better reliability because it can be designed to use alternative routes when failures occur. Further, it gives greater flexibility of interconnection. One terminal can reach many computers, and information can be interchanged between the separate computer systems.

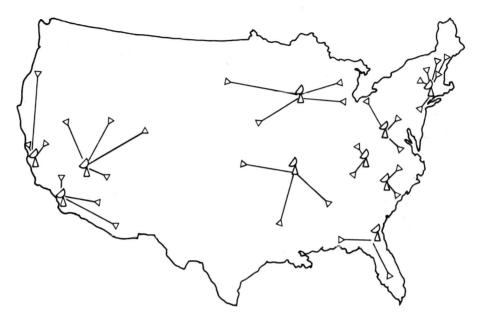

Figure 38.3   Integrated network with satellite channels

THE NETWORK RESOURCE

Once an integrated network exists it often becomes a valuable corporate resource. The economics of combining telephone, electronic mail, and data traffic make it possible to obtain wideband data circuits at what is effectively a low cost. Once such a network exists in an organization, it can have a major effect on the planning of computer resources. Different locations may specialize in different functions, giving economies of specialization. In a corporation, one computer center might specialize in scientific computing or operations research, both of which require a powerful processor. Another might do corporate-wide payroll. Yet another might handle mass-mailing operations. Different systems carrying out specific operations—such as inventory control, production scheduling, order processing, and so on—may pass data via the network to a separate system that stores summary data with indices appropriate for providing management information. Separate systems might transmit financial figures to a head office computer for cost accounting control. One location might have a system for providing patent and legal information to lawyers throughout a corporation.

Figure 38.4 illustrates a corporate network with specialized facilities at different locations. Networks in university and research environments, such as Arpanet in the United States and Cyclades in France, give access to a variety of general-purpose or specialized computers, to research data banks, to systems that permit the searching of technical abstracts, libraries, patents, legal documents, and so on.

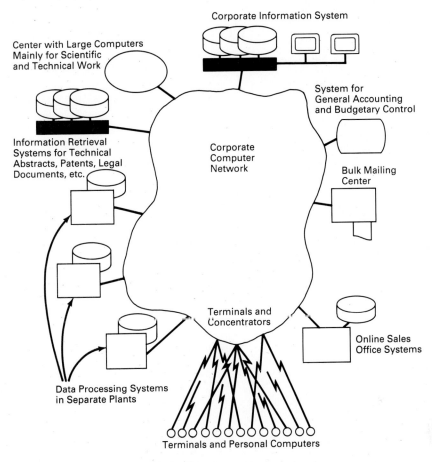

Figure 38.4   Corporate computer network

MULTICORPORATE NETWORKS

A few private networks link computer centers in multiple separate organizations. Two leading examples are the SITA network, which passes messages between airline computers around the world, and the SWIFT electronic funds transfer network, which passes financial transactions between banks.

To operate multiple corporate networks, a separate service corporation is sometimes set up to create and operate the network. SWIFT *(Society for Worldwide Interbank Financial Transactions)* is a nonprofit organization set up and wholly owned by banks that are connected to it. SWIFT implements and operates the network shown in Fig. 38.5, the purpose of which is to send money, messages, and bank statements at high speed between banks. The participating banks finance the system, and a tariff structure charges for its use. The banks range in size from very small to those with as many as 2000 branches.

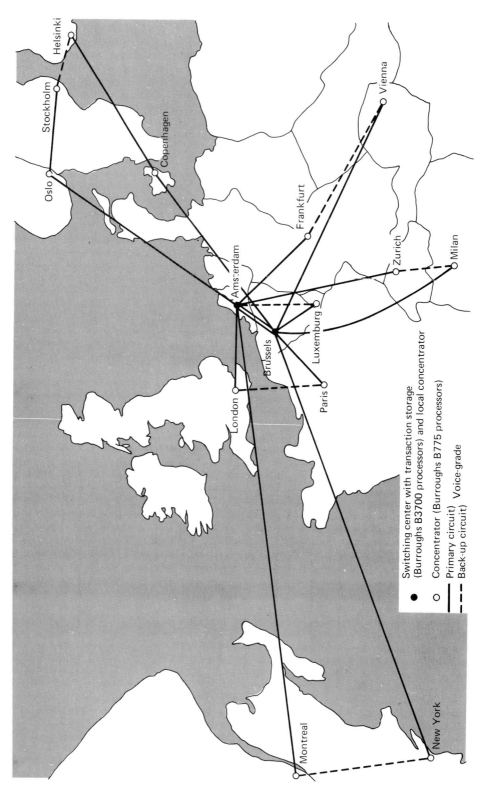

Switching center with transaction storage
(Burroughs B3700 processors) and local concentrator

○ Concentrator (Burroughs B775 processors)

Primary circuit) Voice-grade

Back-up circuit)

Figure 38.5 The SWIFT network

The SWIFT system is a message switching network that originally had two switching centers, as shown in Fig. 38.5. Hundreds of banks are connected to the system. It can expand without functional redesign to use more switching centers. It uses voice-grade circuits, and most traffic is delivered in less than 1 minute. All traffic is stored at the switching centers for 10 days after transmission and during that period can be retrieved if necessary. Transactions can be entered into the system regardless of whether or not the recipient bank's terminals are busy. The originator of an urgent message will automatically be informed by the system if there is a delay in delivering the message.

For multicorporate networks to be useful, it is necessary that the corporations using them agree on message formats and application procedures. There must be a set of corporate standards for network use over and above the standards for transmission. SWIFT imposes such standards on its users. These standards enable the banks to send and receive messages between countries in computer-readable form. Figure 38.6 shows typical SWIFT messages. There is much scope for other multicorporate networks.

Approximately 70 percent of all first-class mail in the United States is originated by computer. Most of this—invoices, orders, receipts, payments, and so on—is destined to be fed into another computer, often in another form. It should be transmitted directly using data communication facilities. Instead, it is usually printed, burst, stuffed into envelopes, sent to a mail room, stamped, sorted, delivered to a post office, sorted again, delivered to the destination post office, sorted again, delivered to a corporation, handled in the mailroom, opened, and laboriously rekeyed into a medium that the receiving computer can read. All this when a message sent on a public data network costs a small fraction of a cent.

A corporation, such as SWIFT or SITA, that provides the service of multicorporate networking is, in essence, a private common carrier. In countries where all mail and electronic transmission is handled by government postal and telecommunications administrations, such a corporation may not be allowed to operate. SWIFT has had severe political problems with the European telecommunications administrations. Its political problems have been far more difficult to solve than its technical ones.

Multicorporate data transmission in the future may employ public data networks, where these exist, rather than private networks. In those few countries where the laws allow freedom of choice on this issue, private multicorporate networks may still be built if this gives lower transmission costs than the public tariffs.

There is massive scope for the interconnection of computers in different organizations. In the United States there is a potential of several hundred million messages per day. The difficulty is in achieving agreement among organizations on message formats. Most computer sales personnel sell to *single* organizations, and systems designers work for *single* organizations, where *one* person is responsible—not to multiple organizations. Sooner or later, however, the ma-

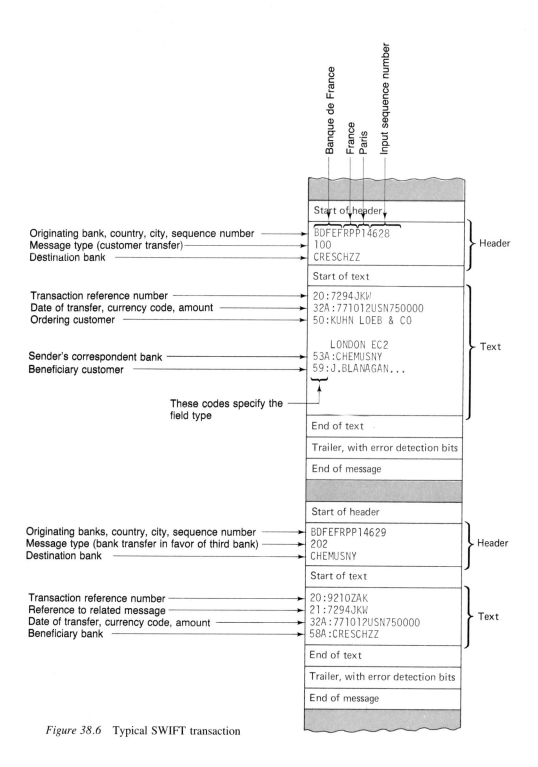

Banque de France
France
Paris
Input sequence number

Start of header

Originating bank, country, city, sequence number ——→ BDFEFRPP14628
Message type (customer transfer) ——————→ 100
Destination bank ————————————→ CRESCHZZ   } Header

Start of text

Transaction reference number ——————————→ 20:7294JKW
Date of transfer, currency code, amount ————→ 32A:771012USN750000
Ordering customer ————————————→ 50:KUHN LOEB & CO

                                                LONDON EC2
Sender's correspondent bank ——————————→ 53A:CHEMUSNY
Beneficiary customer ——————————————→ 59:J.BLANAGAN...   } Text

These codes specify the ———————————
field type

End of text

Trailer, with error detection bits

End of message

Start of header

Originating banks, country, city, sequence number ——→ BDFEFRPP14629
Message type (bank transfer in favor of third bank) ——→ 202
Destination bank ————————————————→ CHEMUSNY   } Header

Start of text

Transaction reference number ——————————→ 20:9210ZAK
Reference to related message ————————→ 21:7294JKW
Date of transfer, currency code, amount ————→ 32A:771012USN750000
Beneficiary bank ——————————————→ 58A:CRESCHZZ   } Text

End of text

Trailer, with error detection bits

End of message

Figure 38.6 Typical SWIFT transaction

596

chines in separate organizations will become linked and the world will be laced with networks over which corporate and government computers exchange information.

The developers of private networks are free to use whatever standards and protocols are appropriate in implementing their networks. The most widely used network architecture for the construction of private data communication networks is IBM's *Systems Network Architecture* (SNA), the subject of Chapter 39.

39 SYSTEMS NETWORK ARCHITECTURE

As we discussed in Chapter 38, private networks are being built at a rapidly increasing rate, and these networks are of increasing complexity and diversity. Intelligent terminals, minicomputers, desktop workstations, and programmable devices that control groups of terminals are spreading rapidly, and as the cost of microelectronic devices continues to drop, this spread will continue to gain momentum. This proliferation of devices, however, can cause substantial compatibility problems.

During the mid-1970s, several of the major computer manufacturers perceived that a large part of their future market was to come from distributed data processing. A wide range of machines would be hooked together into all manner of configurations. A user or application program at one machine would want to employ the facilities, data, or processing power of another, easily and inexpensively. For widely varying devices to be linked together, the hardware and software of those devices would have to be compatible; if compatibility was not achieved, complex interfaces would have to be built for meaningful communication to take place. To facilitate this compatibility, hardware manufacturers developed *network architectures* that allow complex networks to be built using a variety of equipment. We introduced the major purpose of network architectures in Chapters 4 and 34. As we mentioned there, the most widely used of these manufacturers' architectures is IBM's *Systems Network Architecture* (SNA).

SNA USERS

To understand SNA, it is necessary to have a clear idea of what IBM means by the term *SNA user*. An SNA user, or simply a *user,* is either a person or an application program that uses the SNA network to communicate with some other user. *People* use networks to send or receive information, and thus the person interacting with the network through a terminal is considered to be a user of the network. Often, however, a person does not interact directly with the network, but rather works through or with an *application program*. Application programs that use an SNA network are also considered users of the network. These application programs may be located at different points within the network; for example, they may be located in a terminal, in a terminal controller, or in a host computer. These application programs may, in turn, provide services either to people or to other application programs; but whenever they draw on the services of the SNA network, they are considered SNA users. Figure 39.1 illustrates this concept, with the dotted lines representing logical interconnections that are implemented by the network between various network users. It is important to realize that SNA users are not themselves known to the network; SNA users are defined outside the architectural definition of SNA itself.

LOGICAL UNITS   An important purpose of an SNA network is to implement a virtual or logical path between users so that they can communicate with one another easily. To establish a virtual or logical connection with another user, each user must gain access to the SNA network. SNA defines *logical units* (LUs) that provide points of access through

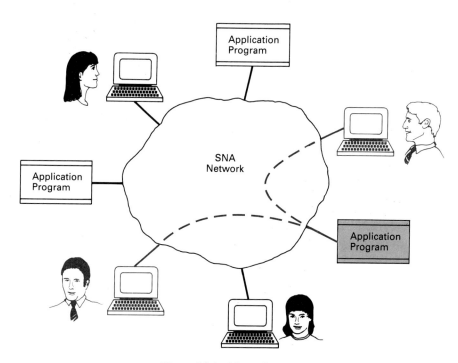

Figure 39.1   Network users

which users interact with the SNA network. A logical unit can be thought of as a *port* or *socket* into which a user plugs. An LU is not a *physical* port or plug, but a *logical* one. SNA defines several logical unit types; each provides *transmission capabilities* and a set of *services* that are related to a particular type of user.

Logical units are implemented in the form of software or microcode and reside in the various devices that make up an SNA network. Logical unit types are identified by a number. Currently, seven major LU types are supported; they are identified by the numbers 0 through 7. (There is currently no type 5 logical unit.) The type 2 logical unit, for example, is designated as LU type 2, or simply as LU 2. As the functions performed by the various logical units evolve, new versions of the supporting software are often released. For example, the capabilities of LU 6 has been enhanced over time, and its latest version is now known as LU 6.2. LU 6.2 is the logical unit type that currently has the most comprehensive set of defined capabilities. LU 6.2 is used to implement a set of functions collectively called *Advanced Program-to-Program Communication* (APPC). Figure 39.2 shows the relationship of network users to logical units. Logical units provide one user with the ability to communicate with another user without the two users having to know detailed information about each other's characteristics.

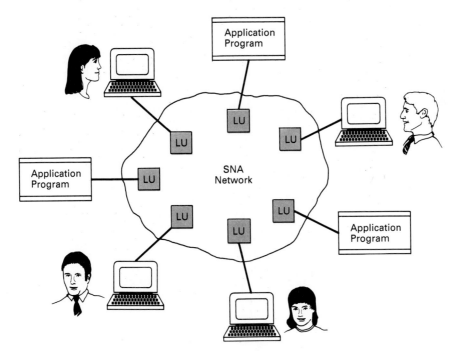

Figure 39.2   Logical units

PHYSICAL UNITS   An SNA network consists physically of various types of devices and the communication links that connect them. The devices that typically make up a network are computing systems, various types of controllers, and terminal devices. Just as SNA users (people or programs) that use the network are not part of the architectural definition of SNA, neither are the actual devices and communication links that are used to implement the network. Instead, SNA uses *physical units* (PUs) to *represent* actual devices to the SNA network. A physical unit provides the services needed to manage and use a particular type of device and to handle any physical resources, such as communications links, that may be associated with it. A physical unit is implemented with some combination of hardware, software, and microcode within the particular device that the physical unit represents.

SYSTEM SERVICE   In addition to logical units and physical units, an
CONTROL POINTS   SNA network also has entities called *system service control points* (SSCPs). A system service control point provides the services needed to *manage* an SNA network (or some portion of a complex network) and to establish and control the interconnections that are necessary to allow network users to communicate with one another. Thus an SSCP has a broader function than a logical unit, which represents a single user, or a physical unit, which represents a physical device and its associated resources.

SNA COMPONENTS   The components that make up an SNA network can be divided into two major categories, each of which consists of hardware, software, and microcode that are contained within the devices that make up the network. Figure 39.3 shows the relationships between these two major categories:

- **Network Addressable Units.** An NAU consists of all the logical units, physical units, and system service control points that reside in a single network device. NAUs provide the services necessary to move information through the

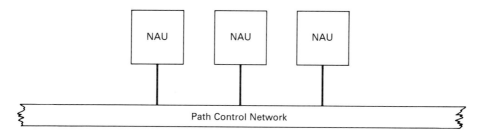

Figure 39.3   NAUs and the path control network

602

network from one user to another and to allow the network to be controlled and managed. Each network addressable unit has a *network address* that identifies it to the other NAUs in the network.

● **Path Control Network.** The path control network consists of lower-level components that control the routing and the flow of data through the network and handle the physical transmission of data from one device in the network to another.

SNA NODES

An *SNA node* is defined as a physical point in the SNA network that contains one or more network components. Each node contains both network addressable units and path control network components. An SNA node corresponds to a physical device and thus contains an SNA physical unit to represent that device to the network. If the node has application programs or terminal devices that offer users access to the network, then the node also contains one or more logical units that correspond to the capabilities of those programs or terminals. One or more SNA nodes in the network must contain an SSCP. If a node does not contain an SSCP, it contains a *physical unit control point* (PUCP). A PUCP implements a subset of SSCP functions that are needed to activate or deactivate that particular node. Each node also contains path control network components that provide the services needed to enable the node to link to and communicate with other nodes. Figure 39.4 shows the relationship between SNA nodes and the various SNA components.

Each terminal, controller, or computing system that conforms to SNA specifications and contains SNA components can be a node in an SNA network. These nodes, together with the transmission links that connect them and any peripheral devices attached to them, are the *physical building blocks* of SNA. They contain the network service and control capabilities required both to operate the network and to handle information exchange between network users.

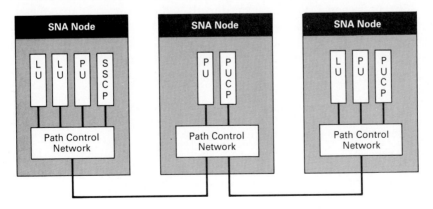

Figure 39.4   SNA nodes and components

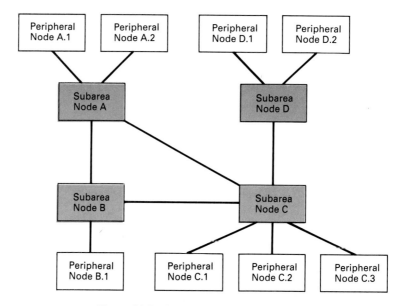

Figure 39.5   Subarea and peripheral nodes

An SNA network can contain several different types of nodes that can be divided into two major categories: *peripheral nodes* and *subarea nodes*. Figure 39.5 shows these two major node types.

Peripheral Nodes

A peripheral node communicates directly only with the subarea node to which it is attached. For example, the two peripheral nodes attached to subarea node A in Fig. 39.5 cannot communicate directly with one another or directly with other subarea or peripheral nodes in the network; they exchange data only with subarea node A. For a peripheral node to exchange data with other nodes in the network, it must do so through its subarea node. Peripheral nodes are often called *cluster controllers*. There are two types of peripheral nodes:

- **Type 2 Nodes.** Type 2 nodes have greater processing capabilities than type 1 nodes and in particular are typically user programmable. Most of IBM's newer terminal systems are implemented as type 2 nodes.

- **Type 1 Nodes.** Type 1 nodes have fewer capabilities than type 2 nodes and are typically not user programmable. Many of IBM's older and less powerful terminals and controllers are implemented as type 1 nodes.

Subarea Nodes

A subarea node is a node that can communicate with its own peripheral nodes and also with other subarea nodes in the network. For example, in Fig. 39.5, subarea node A can communicate directly with subarea node B and subarea node C. It can also communicate with subarea node D by going through subarea node C. Subarea nodes are also of two types:

- **Type 5 Nodes.** A type 5 node is a subarea node that contains an SSCP. A type 5 node is typically contained within a general-purpose computing system and is often called a *host node*.

- **Type 4 Nodes.** A type 4 node is a subarea node that does not contain an SSCP. A type 4 node is typically contained within a communications controller and is often called a *communications controller node*.

Physical Unit Type

An SNA node always contains one physical unit, which represents the device and its resources to the network. A physical unit is given the same *type designation* as its corresponding node type. Thus each physical unit in the network is one of four possible types:

- Physical unit type 5 (PU type 5 or PU 5)
- Physical unit type 4 (PU type 4 or PU 4)
- Physical unit type 2 (PU type 2 or PU 2)
- Physical unit type 1 (PU type 1 or PU 1)

The architectural definitions of the various physical unit types have been enhanced as SNA has evolved. The version of the type 2 physical unit that implements the most comprehensive set of functions is now known as PU type 2.1, or PU 2.1. This is the physical unit that is used in conjunction with LU 6.2 in implementing Advanced Program-to-Program Communication (APPC) facilities.

A SIMPLE SNA NETWORK   Figure 39.6 shows a configuration of nodes that makes up a simple SNA network. At the top of the figure is a host node (type 5) that manages the network. Connected to the host node is a communications controller node (type 4). There are three peripheral nodes (type 2) attached to the communications controller. Two of the peripheral nodes have various terminal devices attached to them; the other peripheral node has a terminal integrated within it. Each of the

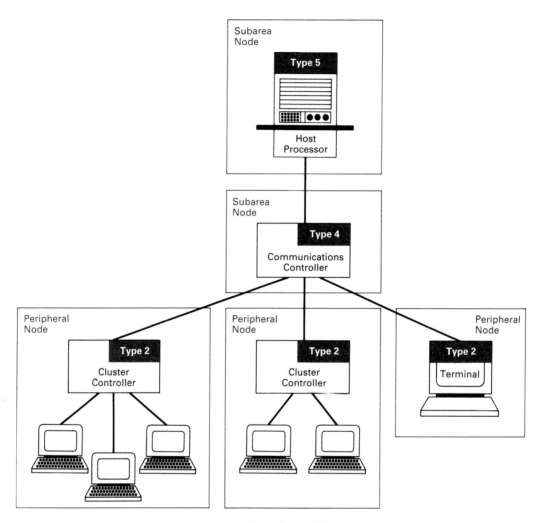

Figure 39.6   Simple SNA network

nodes in the network contains the hardware, software, and microcode necessary to perform its required functions within the SNA network.

Figure 39.7 shows the various NAUs that might be contained in the network from Fig. 39.6. The host node contains the SSCP, which provides network management and user interconnection functions. Each of the nodes contains a physical unit (PU), which represents the device and its resources to the network. Some of the nodes also contain logical units (LUs) that provide users with access to the network. Users of this network include the terminal users shown at the bottom of the diagram and the application program running in the host node.

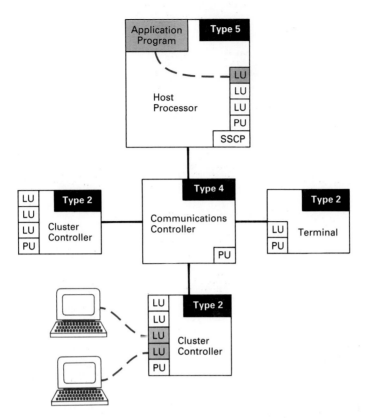

Figure 39.7   Simple network with NAUs

As indicated in the diagram, some nodes are capable of supporting multiple concurrent users, and thus will contain multiple logical units.

**DOMAINS AND
SUBAREAS**

Figure 39.8 shows the structure of a somewhat more complex SNA network. In this network there is a single host node, two communications controller nodes, and six peripheral nodes. All of the devices and nodes (with their resident NAUs) shown in Fig. 39.8 constitute a single *domain* that is managed by the system service control point (SSCP) in the host node. A domain is defined as *that set of SNA resources known to and managed by an SSCP*. This includes physical resources (the devices and the transmission links that tie them together) and software and microcode resources (operating systems, control programs, etc.) that are used to implement SNA components. A domain typically consists

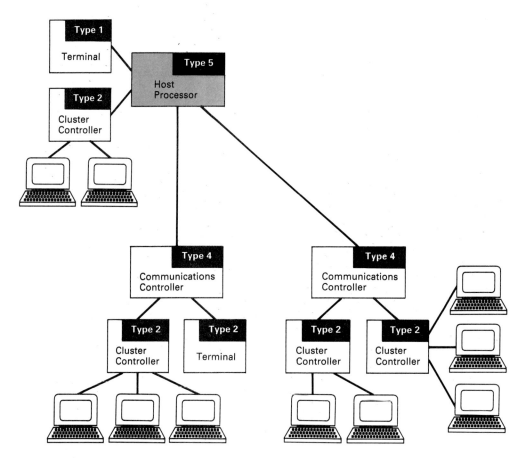

Figure 39.8   An SNA domain

of multiple *subareas*. A subarea is defined as one subarea node and all of the resources it controls, including the peripheral nodes attached to it. Figure 39.9 shows the three subareas that make up the domain from Fig. 39.8.

MULTIPLE-DOMAIN NETWORKS
The simplest SNA networks have only one domain and consequently only one host node with its SSCP. But this is not the case for all SNA networks; many SNA networks contain several domains. The network shown in Fig. 39.10, for example, has seven domains, each of which is managed by a type 5 host node having its own SSCP. Notice that domains C, D, E, and G do not have com-

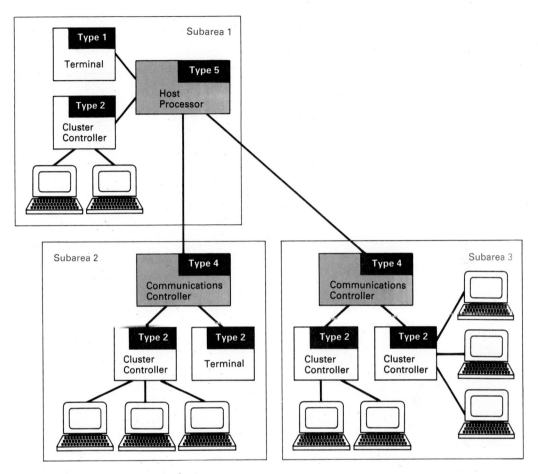

Figure 39.9   Three subareas

munications controllers, and domain C consists of a host node having no subordinate nodes.

When an SNA network consists of multiple domains, a terminal attached to one host processor is able to communicate with an application program running in some other host processor in the network. For example, a terminal in domain A could communicate with an application program running in the host processor in domain C. The host processor in domain A is involved only in establishing a connection between the terminal and the host node. Once the connection is established, the terminal is free to communicate with the program running in the host processor in domain C without further involvement of the host processor in domain A.

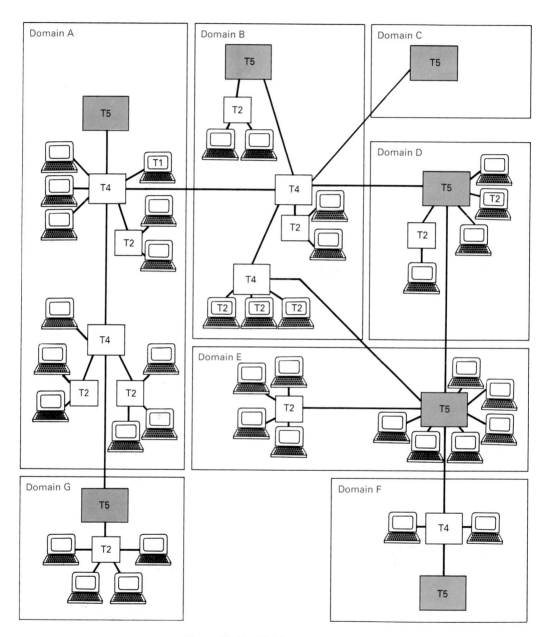

Figure 39.10   Multiple-domain SNA network

**NETWORK
ADDRESSES**
The SNA software uses a system of network addresses in establishing connections, or *paths,* between logical units and in transmitting messages across those paths. Each network addressable unit—physical unit, logical unit, or SSCP—has a *network address* that uniquely identifies it within the network. In addition, each network addressable unit has a *network name.* Typically, network users refer to NAUs by their network names rather than by their network addresses. The SSCP then translates each network name into its corresponding network address using a facility called the *network directory service.* The use of network names helps to shield users from changes that might occur in the physical or logical structure of the network. If the network is changed, and a logical unit is assigned a new network address, network directory services are updated to reflect the change. This allows network users to continue to use the same network name to refer to the logical unit and thus not be affected by the change.

**SNA
COMMUNICATION
LINKS**
As we have seen, messages are passed from one node to the next across a *communication link* that connects those two nodes. There are two types of communication links that can connect nodes. For nodes that are in close physical proximity (same room or same building), the link can be implemented by a cable that is connected to one of the computing system's I/O channels. SNA includes protocols that can be used to control data transmission over a standard channel. If the nodes are not close enough for a direct cable connection using an I/O channel, conventional data communication facilities are used to implement the link, such as a voice-grade line or other telecommunication facility. The data communication link can take the form of either a point-to-point or a multipoint connection, and it can be either switched or non-switched. Regardless of the form taken, transmission over any communication link that is not implemented by a standard I/O channel connection is controlled by the synchronous data link control (SDLC) protocols that are defined as part of SNA (see Chapter 23). Although SDLC is the standard SNA data link protocol, other protocols, such as the older binary-synchronous protocol, are supported in certain situations. Figure 39.11 illustrates the various types of communication links that might be implemented in an SNA network.

Parallel Links

In many cases, two subarea nodes will be connected by a single communication link. It is possible, however, to implement multiple SDLC links between the

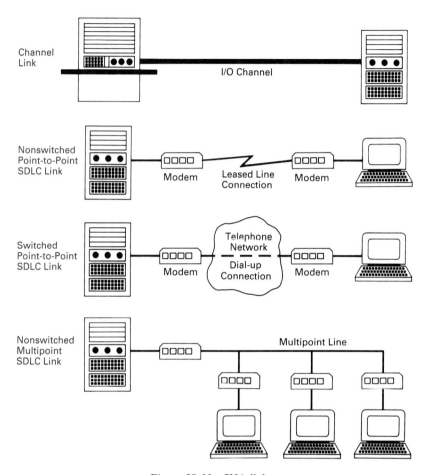

Figure 39.11   SNA links

same two subarea nodes. These links, which operate concurrently, are called *parallel links*. This is shown in Fig. 39.12. Data moving through the network is distributed among parallel links based on various routing considerations. Parallel links can be used to increase the efficiency of the network and also to increase its capacity.

Transmission Groups

When subarea nodes are connected by parallel links, each link belongs to a *transmission group* (see Fig. 39.13). A transmission group is a set of parallel SDLC links that have similar characteristics. They form a single *logical* link

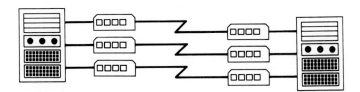

Figure 39.12　Parallel links

that has a higher capacity than each of the individual *physical* links in the group. In addition to providing higher capacity, a transmission group can also provide better availability. As long as any one of the links in the group is operating, the transmission group can be used. If one of the individual links fails, data flow will automatically be reassigned to the other links in the group; communication that is in progress between two network users is not disrupted by the failure.

SESSIONS

A fundamental concept of SNA is that no communication takes place between network addressable units until a *session* is established between them. A session is defined as follows: "A session is a logical state that exists between two network addressable units to support a succession of transmissions between them to achieve a given purpose."

Some types of sessions are permanent and are established automatically when the network is brought into operation; they remain established as long as the network is operational. Other types of sessions are dynamic; they are established as required and broken when they are no longer needed. At any given moment on an SNA network, it is likely that many concurrent sessions will be established. Many of these separate sessions may share the same physical devices and communications links. For example, a logical unit in a host processor or in a cluster controller might be involved in multiple sessions at one time. A logical unit located in a terminal device, on the other hand, normally participates in only one session at a time with another logical unit.

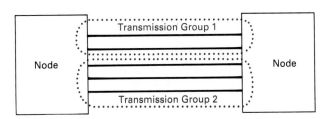

Figure 39.13　Transmission groups

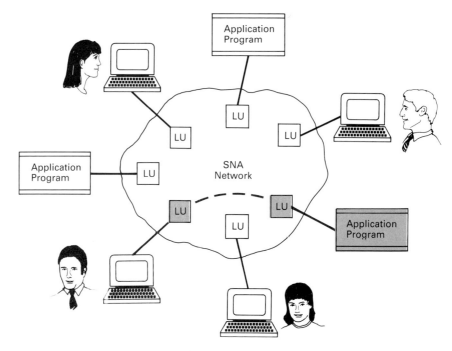

Figure 39.14   LU-to-LU session

The most fundamental type of session is that which is established between two logical units; this type of session allows the network users they represent to communicate with one another by means of the network. Figure 39.14 demonstrates this concept, with the dotted line representing the session that has been established between the terminal user and the application program. In addition to sessions between logical units, there are four other types of sessions that can be in operation in the network. Box 39.1 describes the five types of SNA sessions.

An LU-to-LU session is logically similar to a telephone phone call between two people. To set up a telephone call between myself and you, all I need to know is your telephone number. Assuming that we are both SNA users and have logical units that represent us in the network, all I need to know in order to set up an SNA session with you is the network name of your logical unit. In neither case do either of us have to know where the other party is physically located. Nor do we have to know how the communication is taking place. The user of an SNA network is no more aware of the complexities of the computer network than a telephone user is aware of the complexities of the

BOX 39.1   SNA session types

- **LU-to-LU Sessions.** This is the type of session that fulfills the primary purpose of the network. An LU-to-LU session allows users of the network to communicate with one another. LU-to-LU sessions are typically established dynamically as given pairs of users have the need to communicate.

- **SSCP-to-SSCP Sessions.** This type of session applies only to SNA networks that consist of multiple domains. All required SSCP-to-SSCP sessions are normally established automatically when the network is initialized and remain established as long as cross-domain communication between LUs is allowed. SSCP-to-SSCP sessions allow control information to be exchanged between the various SSCPs in the network.

- **SSCP-to-PU Sessions.** An SSCP must also be permanently in session with each of the LUs in its domain. An SSCP-to-LU session must be established before an LU can be accessed by a network user. In most cases, an SSCP-to-LU session is established for each LU when the network is initialized. As with PUs, the network administrator can make an LU temporarily inactive by terminating a particular SSCP-to-LU session.

- **SSCP-to-LU Sessions.** An SSCP must also be permanently in session with each of the LUs in its domain. An SSCP-to-LU session must be established before an LU can be accessed by a networker user. In most cases, an SSCP-to-LU session is established for each LU when the network is initialized. As with PUs, the network administrator can make an LU temporarily inactive by terminating a particular SSCP-to-LU session.

- **PU-to-PU Sessions.** No specific session types are defined for communication between PUs; however, adjacent PUs may need to exchange network control information. This may need to be done, for example, to transfer a control program from a host processor to a cluster controller, or to perform certain activation, deactivation, or testing functions.

telephone system; the network is transparent to the user. SNA provides all required management and control functions, and also achieves this transparency, by employing a system of functional layers of control.

SNA FUNCTIONAL LAYERS

As we have seen, a basic concept underlying all network architectures is the division of network functions into well-defined functional layers. As with the OSI model, the functions of SNA are broken into layers, with each layer pro-

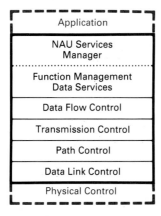

Figure 39.15   Physical control and application layers

viding a different group of services. In Box 39.2 we illustrate the five major SNA functional layers and briefly describe the functions of each.

Operating below SNA's lowest layer, as shown in Fig. 39.15, is a still-lower-level layer generally called the *physical control* layer. The physical control layer addresses the transmission of bit streams over a physical circuit. The SNA architecture itself does not define the functions that are performed in the physical control layer, and specific methods of transmitting bits are not defined by SNA. Various methods of physical transmission can be employed in an SNA network, including computer channels, telephone lines, satellite links, and microwave transmission.

We can think of a still-higher-level layer, generally called the *application* layer, operating above the function management layer of SNA. The application layer represents the users—the application programs and the people that interface with the SNA network. As with the physical control layer, the application layer is not defined by the SNA architecture. Although this layer, too, is important, it is defined outside the SNA architecture.

SNA LAYERS AND   Figure 39.16 shows how the SNA functional layers
NETWORK   relate to the two major SNA components: the net-
COMPONENTS   work addressable units (NAUs) and the path control
                            network. The NAUs are implemented in the top three
layers: function management, data flow control, and transmission control. The services of these layers are concerned primarily with enabling network users to send and receive data through the network and with assisting network operators with controlling and managing the network. The path control network component encompasses the bottom two layers: the path control layer and the data link control layer. These layers are concerned with controlling the routing and flow of data through the network and with the transmission of data from one node to another.

BOX 39.2   SNA functional layers

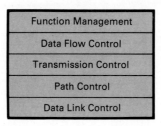

| Function Management |
| Data Flow Control |
| Transmission Control |
| Path Control |
| Data Link Control |

- **Data Link Control.** This layer is responsible for the transmission of data between two nodes over a particular physical link. A primary function of the data link control layer is to detect and recover from the transmission errors that inevitably occur.

- **Path Control.** This layer is concerned with routing data from one node in the network to the next in the path that a message takes through the network. In a complex network, this path often passes over many separate data links through several nodes and may cross multiple domains.

- **Transmission Control.** This layer keeps track of the status of sessions that are in progress, controls the pacing of data flow within a session, and sees that the units of data that make up a message are sent and received in the proper sequence.

- **Data Flow Control.** This layer is concerned with the overall integrity of the flow of data during a session between two network addressable units. This can involve determining the mode of sending and receiving, managing groups of related messages, and determining what type of response mode to use.

- **Function Management.** This layer performs services for the user of the SNA network and is divided into the following sublayers:

  —**Function Management Data Services.** The services performed by this sublayer include coordinating the interface between the network user and the network, presenting information to the user, and controlling the activities of the network as a whole.

  —**NAU Services Manager.** This sublayer provides services to the function management data services sublayer below it and also to the data flow control and transmission control layers below the function management layer.

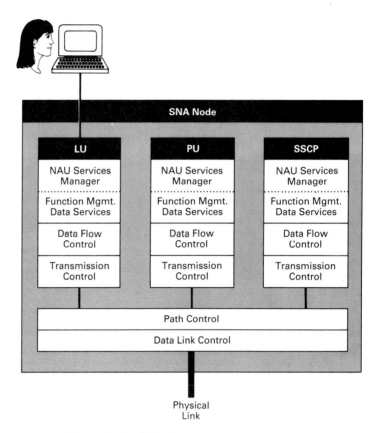

Figure 39.16   SNA layers and network components

SNA SOFTWARE PRODUCTS

Thus far we have examined SNA as an architecture, which defines formats and protocols that are independent of any particular product. Next we look at the key IBM software products used to implement SNA networks. The types of products we will look at fall into the following four categories:

- Telecommunications access methods
- Network control programs
- Application subsystems
- Network management programs

TELECOMMUNICATIONS ACCESS METHODS

As discussed in Chapter 31, telecommunications access method software resides in a host processor and provides an interface between the

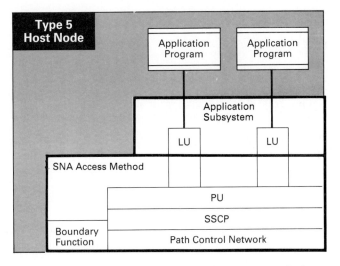

Figure 39.17   SNA telecommunications access method

host processor and other resources in the network. Figure 39.17 shows the relationship that exists between an SNA telecommunications access method and SNA components. If the host processor is a node that contains an SSCP, the SSCP is contained within the access method. Similarly, the physical unit, path control network components, and boundary function are all part of the access method. The logical units are implemented partially within the access method and partially within either an application subsystem (described later in this chapter) or an application program. There are three primary SNA telecommunications access methods:

- ACF/TCAM: Advanced Communications Function for the Telecommunications Access Method
- ACF/VTAM: Advanced Communications Function for the Virtual Telecommunications Access Method
- ACF/VTAME: Advanced Communications Function for the Virtual Telecommunications Access Method—Entry

The three access methods all perform similar functions. ACF/TCAM and ACF/VTAM are designed to be run on a host processor that runs a version of the MVS operating system; ACF/VTAME runs under the control of the VSE operating system and is the VSE counterpart of ACF/VTAM. ACF/TCAM supports a number of data queuing functions that are not provided by either ACF/

BOX 39.3   Telecommunications access method functions

- Identifying network resources by name, without knowledge of their locations or addresses
- Controlling allocation and sharing of network resources, such as terminals, communication links, or communications controllers
- Initiating, maintaining, and terminating sessions, for both logical units and non-SNA devices
- Transferring data as part of a session
- Queuing data and passing data directly to application subsystems (TCAM only)
- Allowing the network operator to monitor and modify network operations
- Allowing the network configuration to be modified while the network is in operation
- Detecting and correcting problems in the network

VTAM or ACF/VTAME. Some of the functions that are performed by all three telecommunications access methods are listed in Box 39.3.

NETWORK CONTROL PROGRAMS
Included in a second major category of SNA software that is used to implement an SNA network are the *network control programs* (NCPs) that run in communications controllers. The primary SNA network control program is called Advanced Communications Function for Network Control Program (ACF/NCP). ACF/NCP resides in the communications controller and interfaces with the SNA access method in the host processor to control communications across the network. It supports both single-domain and multiple-domain networks. Figure 39.18 shows how SNA components are incorporated in ACF/NCP. ACF/NCP contains path control network components, a PUCP, a physical unit, and boundary function elements.

ACF/NCP controls the physical operation of the links in a network and performs routine transmission functions. It also performs bit assembly and disassembly, code translation, polling, routing, error recovery, line tests, device tests, and other physical management functions.

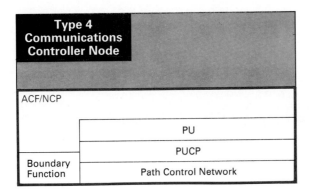

Figure 39.18   SNA network control program

APPLICATION SUBSYSTEMS

Application subsystems form another category of programs that may be involved in an SNA network.

Typical examples of application subsystems are transaction processing systems and interactive support systems. Typical transaction processing systems that implement SNA support include CICS/VS, IMS/VS, DPPX/DMS, and ACP/TPF. Typical SNA interactive support systems are TSO, VSPC, and VM/VCNA. These systems interface with other SNA products and contain part of the code that implements logical units. Application programs or end users are then able to use the services of the application subsystem; through those services they have access to the SNA network.

Figure 39.17 showed the relationships that exist between an application subsystem and an SNA access method in a host processor. Figure 39.19 shows the relationships that exist in a peripheral node. A peripheral node typically contains a control program that is implemented in hardware, in software, or in a combination of the two. The control program contains path control network components, a PUCP, a physical unit, and portions of the code that implements logical units. The application subsystem contains the remainder of the logical unit implementation code. The logical units are then accessed via the application subsystem by either application programs or end users.

NETWORK MANAGEMENT PROGRAMS

In addition to telecommunications access methods and network control programs, which support transmission of data throughout the network, there are also a number of application programs that provide network management functions.

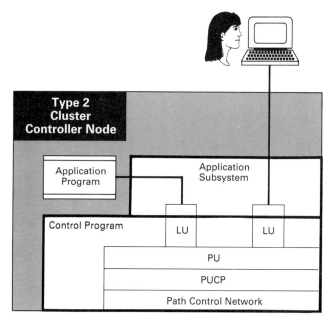

Figure 39.19   Peripheral node with application subsystem

- **Network Communication Control Facility (NCCF).** NCCF provides enhanced operator control for multiple-domain networks. With NCCF, a network operator can use a single terminal to issue commands to any host processor on the network. There may also be multiple, distributed operator terminals. NCCF also provides database and data communications facilities related to collecting, storing, and retrieving data about network errors.

- **Network Problem Determination Application (NPDA).** NPDA is designed to help with online problem determination. It does this by collecting, monitoring, and storing data that relate to network problems and then allowing network operators to display this data. NPDA can be used by an NCCF operator to request and display statistical maintenance data on nodes either in that operator's domain or in other domains throughout the network.

- **Network Logical Data Manager (NLDM).** NLDM collects information about sessions and routes, and allows a central operator to examine that information to help in identifying network problems. NLDM collects information for both single-domain and cross-domain sessions, and about the logical routes currently being used by active sessions. NLDM also collects response-time data. NLDM runs as an application under NCCF and uses system functions provided by NCCF.

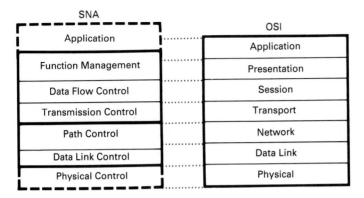

Figure 39.20   SNA and OSI layer correspondence

- **Netview.** Netview is a network management product that combines the capabilities of NCCF, NLDM, and NPDA, as well as providing a number of other functions. Netview is designed to make it easier to use these functions in an integrated manner and to provide network operators greater flexibility in configuring and managing networks. Through the use of the network status monitor facility, the operator can access data on a particular network segment or see an overview of all network resources. Netview helps detect hardware and software errors and problems with accessing a particular application. It also provides links to other sources of network diagnostic information.

OTHER PROGRAM PRODUCTS   The programs described in this chapter are those that play a key role in implementing SNA, and are those that are most directly involved with the transmission of data through the network. There are many other program products, however, that are used in SNA networks. There are general-purpose programs, such as operating systems, utilities, and language processors, that are part of the overall computing environment. There are also many other programs available that are specifically designed to provide network management or support functions.

SNA AND THE OSI MODEL   Both SNA and the OSI model use a layered approach to their architectures, and in large part their definitions include similar services. However, there are many differences in the services that are specified and in how the services are distributed among the various layers. Figure 39.20 shows a somewhat oversimplified view of the correlations between the SNA and OSI layers.

SNA Function Management	OSI Application Layer
	Application Management • Initiation and termination of applications • Deadlock detection and prevention • Security • Checkpoint and recovery
Configuration Services • Activation and deactivation of nodes and links • Program loading and dumping • Reconfiguration and restarting of the network • Maintenance of network names and addresses • Maintenance of NAU and link status	**System Management** • Activation and deactivation of network resources • Loading of programs • Reconfiguration and restart of network • Monitoring and reporting of network status
Maintenance and Management Services • Identification and analysis of failures • Collection of test results and error statistics	• Detection, diagnosis, and recovery from errors • Monitoring and reporting of network statistics
Network Operator Services • Communication with network operator	
Session Services • Activation and deactivation of sessions • Verification of LU authority • Conversion of network names to network addresses • Determination of protocols and rules • Determination of virtual route • Initiation of request queuing	**Application Services** • Determination of availability of internal partners • Establishment of authority • Identification of intended partners • Agreement on dialogue discipline, responsibility for error recovery, and procedures for control of data integrity • Determination of quality of service • Determination of adequacy of resources
Application-to-Application Services • Program-to-program communication • Synchronization	• Information transfer • Synchronization • Agreement on privacy mechanisms • Authentication of intended partners • Determination of cost allocation methodology • Identification of constraints on data syntax
	OSI Presentation Layer
Session Presentation Services • Formatting of data streams • Compression and compaction of data • Formatting of data display	• Data representation syntax • Transformation between syntaxes • Data formatting syntax

Figure 39.21   Function management versus application and presentation layers

SNA FUNCTION MANAGEMENT

SNA's function management layer corresponds to the combination of the application layer and the presentation layer in the OSI model (see Fig. 39.21). As part of the OSI application layer, a set of application management services is defined, which relates to the management of OSI application processes. In general, SNA defines no counterpart to these management services. In SNA, the management of applications is left to the applications that interface with SNA, and is not defined as part of the SNA architecture. However, both SNA and the

SNA Data Flow Control	OSI Session Layer
• Determination of send/receive mode • Grouping of messages into chains • Identification of logical units of work with brackets • Control of request/response processing • Interruption of data flow, on request	• Management of transmission interaction • Providing quarantine services • Brackets (candidate for extension) • Synchronization • Stop-and-go transmission (candidate for extension) • Expedited data flow • Exception reporting • Security (candidate for extension)
SNA Transmission Control	**OSI Transport Layer**
• Session level pacing • Sequence numbering • Request/response headers • Multiple sessions sharing virtual route • Encryption	• Flow control • Sequencing of data units • Error detection and recovery • Multiplexing and splitting of transport connections into network connections • Monitoring quality of service • Conversion of transport addresses into network addresses • Segmenting, blocking, and concatenation of data units

Figure 39.22   Data flow and transmission control versus session and transport layers

OSI model include definitions of services related to the overall management of network resources and to the monitoring of their status. In addition to management services, both the OSI model and SNA provide services that relate to the establishment and maintenance of sessions between network users for purposes of communication across the network. In the OSI model, these are application services. In SNA, these include session services and application-to-application services. As can be seen from Fig. 39.21, many of the functions performed at this level are common to both SNA and the OSI model. Finally, both the OSI model and SNA define services that are related to the formatting and presentation of data. For SNA, these are session presentation services; for the OSI model, these services are performed in the presentation layer.

SNA DATA FLOW CONTROL

The data flow control layer in SNA is analogous to the session layer in the OSI model. These layers are concerned primarily with the integrity of the overall data flow. Figure 39.22 lists the major services provided in each. Although the names used for a service in the two architectures may be different, their functions are often very similar. These services involve determining and managing the interactions involved in the transmission. These roughly comparable layers

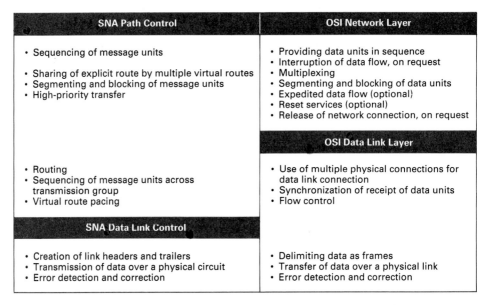

SNA Path Control	OSI Network Layer
• Sequencing of message units	• Providing data units in sequence
	• Interruption of data flow, on request
• Sharing of explicit route by multiple virtual routes	• Multiplexing
• Segmenting and blocking of message units	• Segmenting and blocking of data units
• High-priority transfer	• Expedited data flow (optional)
	• Reset services (optional)
	• Release of network connection, on request

	OSI Data Link Layer
• Routing	• Use of multiple physical connections for data link connection
• Sequencing of message units across transmission group	• Synchronization of receipt of data units
• Virtual route pacing	• Flow control

SNA Data Link Control	
• Creation of link headers and trailers	• Delimiting data as frames
• Transmission of data over a physical circuit	• Transfer of data over a physical link
• Error detection and correction	• Error detection and correction

Figure 39.23   Path and data link control versus network and data link layers

also demonstrate how SNA and the OSI model sometimes differ in the way in which services are assigned to layers. Two of the services included in the session layer—exception reporting and security—have their counterparts in the transmission control layer in SNA, not in the data flow control layer.

SNA TRANSMISSION CONTROL

Figure 39.22 also shows the correspondence between the SNA transmission control layer and the OSI transport layer. Here again there are a number of parallel services and also a few differences. Monitoring of the quality of service, which is part of the transport layer in the OSI model, finds its counterpart in virtual route control, which is part of SNA's path control layer.

SNA PATH CONTROL AND DATA LINK CONTROL

There is greater overlap between layers as we move down to the next two layers, as shown in Fig. 39.23. The services provided by the network layer of the OSI model find many matches in SNA's path control layer. These services provide transfer of data in a way that makes the physical network structure transparent to the higher layers. The path control layer in SNA also contains sequencing services that are involved in ensuring that data is properly reassembled. In the OSI model, these services are part of the data link layer. The OSI data link layer also provides the services involved in controlling the transmission of data over a specific physical link. The corresponding SNA services are provided by the data link control layer. A key standard that has been developed in support of the data link layer in the OSI model is high-level data link control (HDLC). The SNA counterpart to the HDLC protocol, as mentioned earlier, is synchronous data link control (SDLC), which is effectively a subset of ISO's HDLC.

THE PHYSICAL LAYER

The physical layer in the OSI model, which is responsible for the transmission of bits across a physical medium, does not have a counterpart in SNA. Rather than explicitly defining this layer, SNA assumes that this layer is defined outside the SNA architecture using various international standards.

SNA-OSI COEXISTENCE

Although we have seen that SNA and the OSI model are quite different, the two architectures need not be viewed as competitive. SNA is an architecture designed to allow IBM to develop a wide range of hardware and software products that can easily be interconnected to form complex networks. The OSI model defines an architecture that is best suited for interconnecting what might otherwise be incompatible systems. The OSI model and its associated standards can be used as a basis for developing individual networks; however, the OSI model can also be used as a basis for interconnecting dissimilar networks. For example, the OSI model might be used to define architectural guidelines for interconnecting an SNA network with other proprietary or nonproprietary networks. Moreover, IBM offers support of the CCITT X.21 and X.25 recommendations within the SNA product line. It is likely that the SNA and OSI architectures will become more complementary as the two architectures evolve. For example, about the time that this book was completed, the protocols used by SNA's Advanced Program-to-Program Communications (APPC) functions were adopted as one of the standards for the higher-level layers of the OSI model. The APPC protocols are those protocols used with SNA LU 6.2 and PU 2.1 that govern the way intelligent machines communicate in a network.

40 LOCAL AREA NETWORKS

Most of the technology we have discussed thus far in this book has been concerned with conventional data communication systems that most typically connect one or more general-purpose computing systems to large numbers of terminals. In these systems, individual data machines are connected to one another through the use of data links. The data machines and various point-to-point and multipoint data links can be combined to form complex networks. The following are typical characteristics of conventional data links:

- **Station Relationships.** One of the stations on the links is often designated as the primary station (typically, a computing system); all others are secondary stations (typically, terminals). Secondary stations cannot communicate with one another except through the primary station.

- **Message Exchange.** A single exchange of messages takes place at a time on the data link.

- **Transmission Speed.** Transmission speeds are generally low, typically 9600 bps or lower, although, as we have seen, some data communication systems use data links that operate at speeds of 56,000 or even 1.544 million bits per second (T1 carrier).

- **Distance.** Data communication can take place over any desired distance given the availability of the appropriate communication facilities.

- **Transmission Medium.** Public communication facilities, such as telephone circuits, are typically used for data communication.

LAN CHARACTERISTICS

In this chapter we discuss a relatively new class of protocols that support a fundamentally different type of data communication facility than those discussed thus far. These protocols are used to implement *local area networks* (LANs).

The following characteristics of local area networks distinguish them from conventional data communication networks:

- **Station Relationships.** With a typical LAN, all stations that access the common communication facility are peers on the network; there is generally no distinction made between primary stations and secondary stations.

- **Message Exchange.** A LAN is designed to give the appearance of supporting multiple message exchanges at any given time between various pairs of stations, although in actual practice only a single message can be transmitted at any given instant.

- **Transmission Speed.** Transmission speeds are very high, typically millions of bits per second.

- **Distance.** A LAN is designed to support communication over a limited geographical area: for example, within a building or a group of related buildings.

- **Transmission Medium.** A LAN typically uses private, user-installed wiring as the communication medium.

Figure 40.1 contrasts a conventional multipoint data link with a typical local area network configuration. With the multipoint data link, a central computer communicates with a number of relatively simple terminals. Communica-

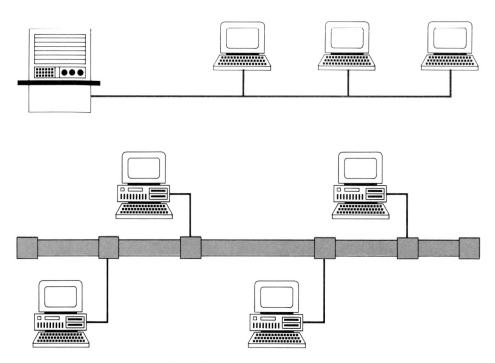

Figure 40.1   Data link versus local area network

tion is controlled by the central computing system and communication takes place at relatively slow speed only between the terminals and the central computer. With the LAN, each device attached to the communication medium is a relatively intelligent machine, and any device attached to the LAN can communicate with any other device at very high speed.

RESOURCE SHARING

A major purpose of a LAN is to allow flexible resource-sharing networks to be created. Figure 40.2 is a more detailed look at a typical LAN implementation. One of the stations attached to the LAN supports a high-capacity disk; another drives a high-speed printer. Other stations might be personal computers without disk or printer resources of their own. With appropriate networking software, each of the other stations on the LAN can have access to the high-capacity disk and the high-speed printer just as if it were directly attached to that station. The very high speed communication capability of the LAN allows data to be transmitted between stations in such a way that the communication medium itself appears transparent to the user of any station attached to the LAN.

CLASSIFYING LOCAL AREA NETWORKS

There are a great many hardware and software systems on the market today for implementing local area networks. All share the general characteristics discussed above, but all are implemented in different ways. The following is a discussion of the ways in which local area networks

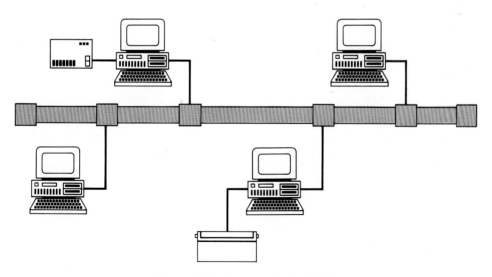

Figure 40.2   Resource-sharing LAN

can be classified. In general, local area networks can be classified according to the following criteria:

- Network topology
- Transmission medium
- Transmission technique
- Access protocol

Network Topology

The network topology relates to the logical way in which stations attached to the LAN are interconnected. The three major topologies are the *star,* the *ring,* and the *bus,* as illustrated in Fig. 40.3. Box 40.1 describes the three main topologies.

In many cases, a specific local area network implementation may use combinations of the above three topologies to create hybrid configurations. Figure 40.4 shows an example of a *star-wired logical ring.* Notice that the topology is

BOX 40.1   Network topologies

- **Star.** With the star topology, all stations are connected through a central control point. Typical examples of control points are the wiring closets used with some systems or a PABX (private automatic branch exchange) used with some systems that employ telephone-type equipment for interconnecting processors. The advantages of the star topology include ease of fault isolation and ease of bypassing and repairing faulty stations. A disadvantage is that to interconnect all stations, the star topology requires more cable than do most other topologies.

- **Ring.** With a *ring,* each station is connected to the next one to form a closed loop. Each station has a transmitter and a receiver, and data is transmitted in one direction around the ring. Advantages of the ring include decreased distance sensitivity, since each station regenerates the signal, and ease of implementing distributed control and checking facilities. The disadvantages include sensitivity to station failures (a failed station might break the ring) and difficulty of adding and changing stations.

- **Bus.** With a *bus,* all stations are attached to a single length of cable. The advantages of the bus topology include low cable lengths and low sensitivity to station failures. Disadvantages include high sensitivity to distance and difficulties of prewiring for future expandability.

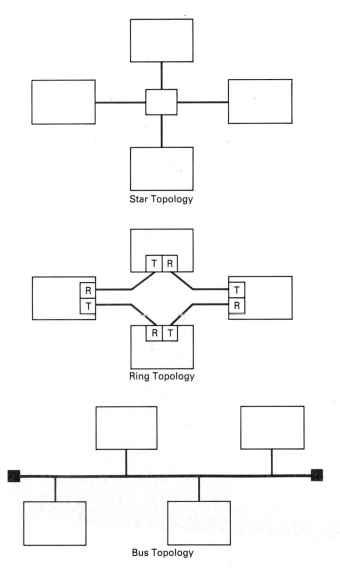

Star Topology

Ring Topology

Bus Topology

Figure 40.3   Network topologies

really that of a ring, but the wiring is installed in such a way that the topology physically resembles a star. Such a network might be constructed when cabling is installed using wiring closets, as is done when the IBM cabling system is used to wire a building. Figure 40.5 shows a *multiple-star* configuration. A number of individual star networks are interconnected with point-to-point links.

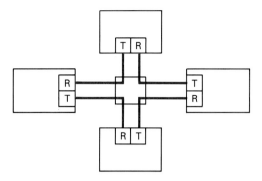

Figure 40.4   Star-wired logical ring topology

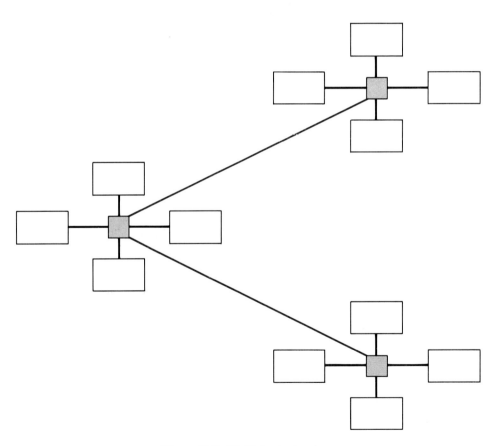

Figure 40.5   Multiple-star topology

Transmission Medium

The second criterion by which local area networks can be classified is by the type of medium that is used to interconnect processors. Most local area networks use some form of cable to connect the various devices on the network, although LANs that employ radio transmission are in use. Box 40.2 describes a few of the types of media that are used in present-day local area networks.

Transmission Technique

The third criterion for classifying local area networks is according to the method that is used for transmitting signals over the cable. There are basically two methods used: *baseband* and *broadband*. Box 40.3 describes these two transmission techniques.

BOX 40.2   LAN transmission media

- **Unshielded Twisted Pair.** This is the ordinary twisted pair typified by conventional telephone wiring. Its major advantages include low cost and the fact that this type of medium is already installed throughout many existing facilities. Its major disadvantage is that it is typically limited to relatively low transmission speeds (a few megabits per second).

- **Shielded Multiple Twisted Pair.** With this medium a number of individual twisted pairs are enclosed in a single cable with shielding. The individual twisted pairs are better isolated from noise and other disturbances, but each twisted pair is still limited to relatively low transmission speeds.

- **Coaxial Cable.** With a coaxial cable, a single central conductor is surrounded by an outer tubular conductor. An example of coaxial cable is the cable used to implement cable television systems. For data communication systems, coaxial cable is reasonable in cost and can support very high transmission speeds.

- **Twinaxial Cable.** This is similar to coaxial cable, but instead of a single central conductor, two central conductors are surrounded by an outer tubular conductor.

- **Fiber Optics.** A fiber optic cable transmits a light beam rather than an electrical signal. Fiber optic links provide an almost unlimited bandwidth that can support extremely high transmission speeds. However, fiber optic links are relatively high in cost.

BOX 40.3   LAN transmission techniques

- **Baseband.** When a baseband technique is used for transmitting signals, the entire cable is used to propagate a single digital signal. Depending on the transmission medium used, very high transmission speeds can be achieved, and channel sharing is generally accomplished using conventional time-division-multiplexing (TDM) techniques. An example of a baseband local area network is Ethernet, in which stations communicate using a bus-structured network at approximately 10 million bits per second. The main advantage of the baseband technique is that interface units are simple and inexpensive; the main disadvantage is that the entire cable is allocated to a single channel.

- **Broadband.** When broadband techniques are used, information is transmitted over the cable in the form of radio-frequency signals. The bandwidth is normally divided into a number of individual channels, each capable of carrying different types of information. An example of a broadband local area network is IBM's PCNET. With PCNET, the various channels can be allocated to computer data and video signals. The disadvantages of the broadband technique are that relatively expensive radio-frequency modems must be incorporated into the interface units, and, depending on the distance, the broadband cable may be difficult to install and to tune properly.

Access Protocol

The fourth and final way in which local area networks are classified is according to the protocol that governs the way individual stations access the transmission medium. Any number of access protocols can be devised, but the following three major protocols, described in Box 40.4, dominate the LAN marketplace:

- Carrier-sense multiaccess with collision detection (CSMA/CD)
- Carrier-sense multiaccess with collision avoidance (CSMA/CA)
- Token passing

The CSMA/CD protocol is the protocol used by Xerox in its Ethernet LAN, and token passing is used in many of the LAN products offered by IBM. The CSMA/CA protocol is used less often than the other two.

The CSMA/CD protocol is well suited for use with bus-structured networks. It works well because of the typically very high transmission speed of the LAN and because a very small percentage of the total transmission capacity is used. When traffic on the LAN increases, collisions begin to occur for an

BOX 40.4   LAN access protocols

- **CSMA/CD.** With the CSMA/CD protocol, all stations attached to the network monitor the transmission medium at all times. When a station needs to transmit data, it waits until the line is quiet and then transmits. If two or more stations transmit at the same instant, a *collision* occurs. Each station detects the collision and then waits for a variable amount of time before testing the medium again and retransmitting. Since each station waits for a different amount of time, the probability is low that the collision will occur the second time.

- **CSMA/CA.** The CSMA/CA protocol is similar to CSMA/CD except that all stations implement an algorithm that helps to avoid collisions rather than simply to detect when they occur and then retransmit.

- **TOKEN PASSING.** With the token-passing scheme, typically used on ring-structured networks, a special message called the *token* is passed from one station to the next around the ring. When a station receives the token it either transmits a message, if it has a message to send, or it passes the unused token to the next station on the ring. Each station receives one chance to transmit during the time that it takes for the token to circulate around the ring.

unacceptably large number of messages and performance of the LAN degrades. However, many analyses have been done on typical Ethernet LAN implementations. These analyses have found that typical channel utilization even at peak times generally falls in the 10 percent or less category, and more than 99 percent of all transmissions take place without collisions.

With the token-passing protocol, the protocol favored by IBM in many of its LAN products, a higher percentage of the total capacity of the medium can be used effectively before the performance of the LAN degrades. However, each station must wait its turn before transmitting, and thus token passing may be less efficient than the CSMA/CD protocol on networks that use a very low percentage of the total transmission capacity. (It should be noted that most LANs use a very low percentage of the total capacity.)

INTERNATIONAL LAN STANDARDS   An important set of standards for local area networks has been documented by the *Institute of Electrical and Electronics Engineers* (IEEE) (see Chapter 4). The IEEE has published a comprehensive standards document that describe several recommended ways for implementing LANs. The IEEE LAN standards describe an implementation of layers 1 and 2 of the OSI reference model discussed in Chapter 35. The IEEE LAN model divides the OSI data link layer into two sublayers, as shown in Fig. 40.6. The *medium access control* sublayer performs the access function for the particular access control method employed by the network. Typical access control methods are the CSMA/CD and token-passing methods discussed earlier. The logical link control sublayer performs functions comparable to the other data link protocols examined in Part IV. These functions include framing, addressing, and error control. The following IEEE standards are important in the local area network marketplace:

- **IEEE Standard 802.2.** This standard describes the functions of the logical link control sublayer of the IEEE LAN architectures.

- **IEEE Standard 802.3.** This standard describes the medium access control sub-layer and physical layer functions for a bus-structured network that uses CSMA/CD as an access protocol.

- **IEEE Standard 802.4.** This standard describes the medium access control sub-layer and physical layer functions for a bus-structured network that uses the token-passing access protocol.

- **IEEE Standard 802.5.** This standard describes the medium access control sub-layer and physical layer functions for a ring-structured LAN that uses token passing as an access protocol.

IEEE Standard 802.3 was developed in cooperation with Xerox and describes the techniques used in implementing Ethernet LAN products. Ethernet is one of the most widely used types of local area network, and Ethernet-compatible products are marketed by Xerox as well as by a great many other

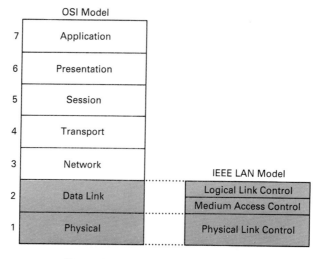

Figure 40.6 IEEE LAN standard layers

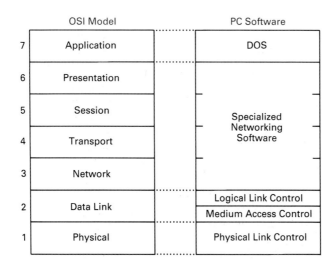

Figure 40.7   Personal computer LAN implementation

LAN vendors. Many of the token-passing ring LAN products that are marketed by IBM conform to IEEE Standard 802.5.

Figure 40.7 shows how a typical IBM personal computer implementation of a local area network fits into the OSI model. IEEE Standard 802.5 describes the functions that take place at layers 1 and 2, special networking software performs the functions of layers 3 through 6, and the personal computer's operating system runs at layer 7.

In the final chapter in this book we describe the goal toward which standards organizations, common carriers, and telecommunications administrations are striving in attempting to create a worldwide *integrated services digital network* (ISDN).

41 INTEGRATED SERVICES DIGITAL NETWORK

As we saw in Chapter 13, the world's analog telecommunications plant is rapidly being replaced by more efficient and cost-effective digital facilities. It is important to realize that the installation of digital telecommunications facilities involves two complementary technologies: digital *transmission* and digital *switching*. Both of these technologies are well established. The first T-carrier transmission system was introduced by AT&T in 1962, and the first large-scale digital switch to use time-division multiplexing was the Western Electric 4ESS switch, first used in 1976. Although either digital transmission or digital switching is powerful by itself, these two technologies are revolutionary when used together.

CONVENTIONAL ANALOG NETWORK

Figure 41.1 shows the conceptual structure of a conventional analog telecommunications network. Typically, this type of network is designed and managed by two separate organizations. The transmission facilities have traditionally been referred to by the common carrier as *outside plant,* while the switching facilities are typically called *inside plant*. The wideband signal that is transmitted from one switching office to another must be demultiplexed before it is switched, and then must be remultiplexed before a new wideband signal can be sent on to the next switching office.

INTEGRATED DIGITAL NETWORK

Contrast the conventional analog network configuration with the network shown in Fig. 41.2, which uses both digital transmission and digital switching. In such a network, voice signals that enter the network at one end are digitized by equipment in the switching office. The signal can then be sent in this digital form through any number of intermediate switching offices without having to

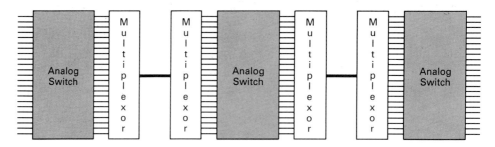

Figure 41.1   Analog transmission and switching

decode them. Only when the signal arrives at its destination is it converted back into its original analog form. While digital transmission and switching are advantageous even for voice communication, digital technologies provide even greater benefit for data communications. This is because the digital data signals do not have to be converted from their original digital form into analog signals for transmission or for switching, and because very high bit rates can be sent economically over digital transmission facilities.

The conversion of the world's telecommunications facilities into an *integrated digital network* (IDN) is well under way, and most observers agree that a worldwide integrated digital network will eventually become a reality. The economies inherent in digital technologies make this inevitable. It is important to realize, however, that the creation of an integrated digital network is of the most benefit to the common carrier. The end user most often is given an ordinary analog channel that happens to be converted into digital form once it reaches a common carrier's switching office. The end user benefits indirectly, of course, by sharing in the cost savings that digital facilities provide.

INTEGRATED SERVICES DIGITAL NETWORK

The next step in the evolution of common carrier facilities from an analog environment to a completely digital environment lies in the creation of an *inte-*

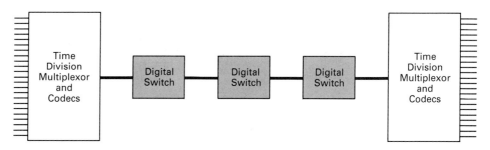

Figure 41.2   Digital transmission and switching

grated services digital network (ISDN) on top of the IDN. With the ISDN, a digital channel is provided directly to the end user. In such a network, equipment on the user's premises performs any necessary signal conversion that might be necessary to create a digital signal. The digital signal is then transmitted directly to the common carrier's switching office over local loops that are engineered to carry signals in digital form. One definition of ISDN is as follows: "An Integrated Services Digital Network (ISDN) is a network evolved from the telephony Integrated Digital Network (IDN) that provides end-to-end digital connectivity to support a wide range of services, including voice and nonvoice services, to which users have access by a limited set of standard multipurpose user-network interfaces."

Because all signals handled by the ISDN will be digital, the user can connect any desired equipment to the network, as long as that equipment is capable of generating a digital bit stream that conforms to ISDN standards. It is the stated goal of ISDN technology to allow any type of equipment to be connected to the network, permitting it to communicate with a complementary piece of equipment at the other end. The ISDN will be able to detect the nature of the terminals that are connected to it and will automatically be able to supply the type of service that is required by the user. For example, one user of the ISDN might plug a digital telephone into the wall socket and dial up another digital telephone connected to the network. The ISDN would automatically supply the type of channel required to support the connection and would allow the two users to conduct a conversation in the same manner as two users of today's public telephone network.

The only difference between the use of the ISDN and the use of today's public network for ordinary voice telephony would be in the equipment that would be required by the two users. Each user's telephone would require the circuitry needed to convert the analog voice signal to and from the digital form necessary for transmission and switching within the network. As we saw in Chapter 13, this signal conversion is performed by a device called a *codec*. Since codecs have already been implemented on a single silicon chip, the cost of the codec should not significantly increase the cost of the telephone instrument.

The individual telephone user might not perceive a great deal of difference between the ISDN and a conventional analog network, although the ISDN will allow additional services to be offered that are not offered today. On the other hand, the *data* user will derive enormous benefits. The user of a data terminal could dial up another data terminal user, and the two could exchange messages at very high bit rates over the same channel that is used for voice. As we will see, the basic channel provided by the ISDN will support a bit rate of 64 kbps rather than the very limited bit rates that can be achieved over an analog telephone channel. The ISDN will also provide much higher bit rates than 64 kbps for users that need them.

ISDN STANDARDS The creation of a worldwide ISDN is not a problem of technology—the technology already exists; the challenge lies in creating the necessary standards and getting all countries to agree to them. The main coordinating body for ISDN standards development is the CCITT. The study groups that are currently involved with ISDN standards development are listed in Box 41.1. The CCITT describes the ISDN in terms of the following six attributes that are governing the development of ISDN standards and of the worldwide ISDN itself:

- The ISDN must evolve from the existing telephone networks that are already in operation throughout the world. The existing networks are themselves in the process of evolving from analog networks into IDNs.
- New services that are to be offered in the ISDN environment must be compatible with the basic 64-kbps switched digital channel.
- A worldwide ISDN will probably not be fully operational until the end of the 1990s and possibly later, although some ISDN services are already available in some areas.
- During the transition period, the ISDN will rely heavily on interconnections between national ISDNs and existing non-ISDN public data networks.
- The ISDN will implement intelligence in order to perform such functions as maintenance, system control, and network management.
- The ISDN will use a set of layered protocols that conform to the OSI reference model (see Chapter 35).

ISDN CHANNELS The main building block of the ISDN is a 64-kbps channel known as the *B* channel. Many channels in the United States are already capable of carrying a 64-kbps bit rate. However, U.S. common carriers typically use a portion of the 64-kbps bit stream for control and signaling purposes and provide only 56 kbps to the user. An ISDN B channel is a *clear channel* that provides a full 64 kbps to the user. With the ISDN, signaling is handled in a separate *D channel*. D channels are typically packet switched and provide a bit rate of either 16 or 64 kbps, depending on the level of service that is desired. Other types of channel are also being considered. The incompatibility between the 64-kbps B channel and the 56-kbps channel provided in the United States is a major stumbling block to rapid deployment of a worldwide ISDN, and this issue is currently under study by the CCITT.

ISDN LEVELS OF SERVICE Although many levels of service are under study by the CCITT, one of two alternative levels of service is likely to be used by the majority of ISDN customers. These two levels of service are the *basic access interface* and the *primary access interface*.

BOX 41.1   CCITT ISDN standards development

Study Group II

- Network management
- Human factors
- Nontelephone use
- Network failures
- Traffic and operations requirements

Study Group IV

- General maintenance organization
- Measuring instruments
- Network quality
- New system maintenance

Study Group VII

- Call setup and cleardown time
- Grade of service
- DTE/DCE interface
- Maintenance of public data networks
- Digital data switching
- Internetworking of packet-switched networks
- Multiplex structure of international links
- Integration of satellite systems

Study Group IX

- Signaling systems
- Switch design
- Digital transfer exchanges
- High-level languages

(Continued)

BOX 41.1   *(Continued)*

Study Group XVIII

- General network aspects
- Customer/network interface
- Synchronization
- ISDN signaling
- ISDN switching
- Network performance
- Network availability
- Network maintenance
- Internetworking
- Digital network interfaces
- Multiplexing
- Non-PCM encoding methods
- Digital speech interpolation

Basic Access Interface

The basic access interface level of service defines a bit rate of 144 kbps, which is divided into two 64-kbps B channels and one 16-kbps D channel. This is the level of service that an individual residential or small-business subscriber would probably use for voice and data applications. The basic access interface would allow a typical user to conduct a voice telephone call and a data call simultaneously over the same telephone line. The basic access interface might be employed to connect an individual subscriber directly to the central switching office. A typical existing unloaded local loop can often be made to carry the 144-kbps bit rate of the basic access interface if the local loop is not too long. Longer local loops can sometimes be reengineered through the installation of additional equipment to carry the 144-kbps bit rate.

Primary Access Interface

The primary access interface level of service defines a bit rate of 1.536 Mbps, which is divided into twenty-three 64-kbps B channels and one 64-kbps D channel. This is the level of service that might be used by a larger company to connect a digital PBX to the central switching office. The primary access inter-

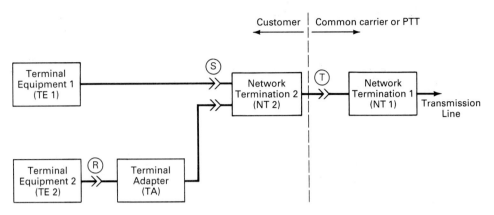

Figure 41.3   ISDN reference model

face might also be used to connect a high-speed data machine directly to the ISDN. The ubiquitous T1 carrier can be made to carry the primary access interface bit stream.

ISDN USER INTERFACE

To make it easy to connect all manner of different devices to the ISDN, it is important that a limited number of connection points be defined for the network and that these connection points be well standardized. Figure 41.3 shows the interface points that have been defined for the ISDN. The boxes in the diagram represent the groupings of functions that have been identified for the equipment that will be used to connect to the network. These functional groupings are as follows:

- **Network Termination 1 (NT1).** The NT1 functional grouping will be implemented in a device that will probably be owned by the common carrier. It will be installed at the end of the local loop that provides ISDN service to an individual customer. The NT1 grouping performs the functions that are associated with layer 1 (the physical layer) of the OSI reference model.

- **Network Termination 2 (NT2).** The NT2 functional grouping will be implemented in a device that will probably be owned by the ISDN customer, not by the common carrier. It will allow a number of ISDN terminals to be connected to a single ISDN connection. The NT2 grouping performs the functions associated with layers 1, 2, and 3 (the physical, data link, and network layers) of the OSI reference model.

- **Network Termination 12 (NT12).** This functional grouping will typically be used in regulatory environments that are different from those that exist in the United States. The NT12 grouping combines the functions of NT1 and NT2. The NT12 functional grouping is likely to be used by most European telecom-

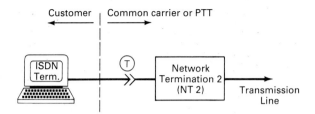

Figure 41.4   Connecting a terminal at point T

munications administrations, where more of the telecommunications equipment is under the control of the telecommunications administration rather than the end user.

● **Terminal Adapter (TA).** This functional grouping will be implemented in a device that allows a non-ISDN terminal to be attached to the ISDN.

● **Terminal Equipment 1 (TE1).** A TE1 is a terminal that conforms to ISDN standards. Examples of TE1s are digital telephones, ISDN-compatible data terminals, and ISDN-compatible facsimile machines.

● **Terminal Equipment 2 (TE2).** A TE2 is a terminal that is not compatible with the ISDN, such as one that implements the X.21 or RS-232-C interface.

The simplest way for a customer to connect a device to the ISDN is to plug an ISDN terminal (TE1) into the ISDN at point T. This is shown in Fig. 41.4. In this case the NT2 grouping is implemented by a set of wires directly connecting a terminal to the ISDN at interface point T. In a regulatory environment such as the one that exists in the United States, point T will probably define the dividing line between the equipment that is supplied by the common

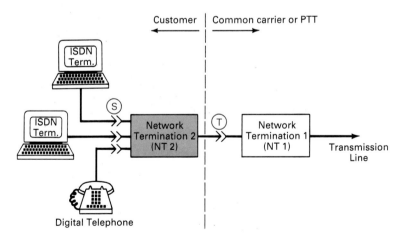

Figure 41.5   Connecting terminals at point S

carrier and the equipment that is supplied by the user. However, this issue is still under discussion.

Figure 41.5 shows a more complex arrangement in which the user plugs an NT2 type of device into the ISDN at point T. Each terminal is then connected to the NT2 device at interface point S. The NT2 device might provide any number of S-type connection points into which users can plug ISDN-compatible terminals. The NT2 device might take the form physically of a digital PBX, a terminal controller, or even a local area network. As shown in Fig. 41.6, a non-ISDN terminal might also be connected to the NT2 via a terminal adapter that connects to the NT2 device at point S. The non-ISDN terminal is connected to the TA device at interface point R.

Note that the same physical connector will be used for both interface point S and interface point T. For the ISDN basic access interface, the S and T interfaces will probably take the form of a small plastic plug similar to the modular plug that is used today to connect a device to the telephone network. It will probably contain eight wires rather than the four typically used for analog telephony. The connector may be different for the higher-speed primary access interface.

The initial ISDN recommendations also allow for an analog terminal, such as an ordinary telephone, to be connected to the NT1 device, as shown in Fig. 41.7. Compatibility with conventional analog channels will be important for the interim period as the world evolves to the ISDN. The way in which all types of analog channels are to be supported by the ISDN, such as voice channels and channels used for television transmission, are currently being studied by the CCITT.

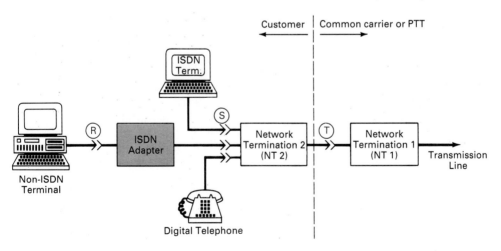

Figure 41.6   Connecting a non-ISDN terminal

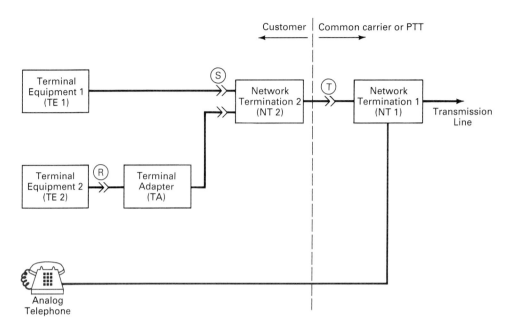

Figure 41.7   Analog channels

ISDN SERVICES

In addition to providing telephone services in a more economical fashion and providing better facilities for data communication, it is envisioned that the ISDN will make possible a number of additional services that are either not available today or are available on only a limited basis. Box 41.2 lists a number of services that could be offered in conjunction with the ISDN. Most ISDN services could be provided using the 64-kbps B channel, although some services would require the use of higher-speed facilities. Some services that common carriers offer today might require even higher bit rates than would be provided by the ISDN primary access interface. In some cases, these services might be provided by higher-speed channels that operate outside the ISDN, such as the services involved with the long-distance transmission of television signals. However, it is possible that these services would be controlled by the ISDN and might even share some of the same transmission links that are used to implement the ISDN.

EVOLUTION TOWARD ISDN

Conversion to the ISDN will be an expensive, time-consuming process. It will necessarily be done a piece at a time, with ISDN facilities first being made available to those that have a specific need for ISDN services and are willing to

BOX 41.2 Potential ISDN services

- Local voice telephone service
- National long-distance services
- International long-distance services
- Malicious call blocking
- Automatic call transferring
- Abbreviated dialing
- Prerecorded messages
- Conference calls
- Camp on busy
- Restricting outgoing toll calls
- Hot lines
- Detailed billing information
- Automatic wake-up or reminder calls
- Leased voice circuits
- Information retrieval using speech recognition
- Music transmission
- Packet-switched data services
- Circuit-switched data services
- Leased channels
- One-way telemetry services
- Electronic funds transfer
- Information retrieval
- Electronic mail
- Alarm services
- High-speed computer communications
- Automatic call dialing
- Automatic call answering
- Closed user groups
- Calling-line identification
- Called-line identification
- Automatic call transferring
- Teletex services
- Videotex services
- Facsimile services

pay for them. In the United States, the evolution toward an ISDN environment is likely to take place in four stages:

1. New transition services will first be introduced that offer services that are similar to those that will be provided by a true ISDN. These new services will allow the common carriers to test the marketplace in a cost-effective manner.
2. As ISDN-like services become more widely used, existing equipment will begin to be replaced with equipment that conforms to the emerging ISDN standards.
3. True ISDN services will then be provided in selected market areas, which have the highest concentration of users that are likely to need ISDN facilities. ISDN facilities will be made available to those customers outside the areas that initially have access to the ISDN through various types of remote-access arrangements.
4. Finally, ISDN services will be provided universally to all customers of a common carrier.

At the time of this writing, there is no common agreement about how long it will take to implement a worldwide ISDN; in fact, some observers are doubtful that it will ever happen. However, most experts agree that worldwide deployment of the ISDN is only a matter of time, and the end of the 1990s is the time frame most often mentioned for its completion. At this time it is impossible to determine exactly what form the ISDN will take and what types of services will be offered, but the ISDN will be market driven, not technology driven, and common carriers will offer those types of services that they feel users will be willing to pay for. Many new services will be offered, and some of these will fail when common carriers discover that customers do not use them. Only time will tell when the ISDN will become a reality and what services it will provide.

GLOSSARY

ACCUNET. Trademark of AT&T that refers to a collection of digital data transmission services offered in the U.S.

ACOUSTICAL COUPLER. A particular type of modem that contains a microphone and speaker and interfaces with a communication channel using audio tones and a standard telephone handset.

ADCCP. (*See* **Advanced Data Communication Control Procedure**.)

ADDRESS. A coded representation of the destination of data, or of its originating location. Multiple devices on one communication line, for example, must have unique addresses. There is a distinction between a station's data link address, which must be unique on a single data link, and a station's network address, which must be unique within an entire network.

ADVANCED DATA COMMUNICATION CONTROL PROCEDURE (ADCCP). A bit-oriented data link protocol standardized by the American National Standards Association (ANSI) and documented in ANSI Standard X3.66 and in Federal Standard 1003. ADCCP is similar to HDLC. (*See also* **High-level Data Link Control**.)

ALPHABET. A table of correspondence between an agreed set of characters and the signals that represent them. Often called a *data code* or *character set*.

ALTERNATE ROUTING. (*See* **Routing, alternate**.)

AMERICAN STANDARD CODE FOR INFORMATION INTERCHANGE (ASCII). Usually pronounced "ask'-ee". A 7-bit code for data transfer adopted by the American National Standards Association to achieve compatibility between data devices. ASCII is a variation of the CCITT International Alphabet No. 5.

AMPLIFIER. An electronic circuit, used on an analog transmission facility, that detects a weak signal and makes it stronger. An amplifier often amplifies the noise on the channel as well as the original signal.

AMPLITUDE MODULATION. One method of modifying a sine wave signal in order to make it "carry" information. The sine wave, or carrier, has its amplitude modified in accordance with the information to be transmitted.

ANALOG DATA. Data in the form of continuously variable physical quantities. Compare with **Digital data**.

ANALOG TRANSMISSION. Transmission of a continuously variable signal as opposed to a discretely variable signal. Physical quantities, such as temperature, are continuously variable and so are described as "analog." Data characters, on the other hand, are coded in discrete, separate pulses or signal levels, and are referred to as "digital."

ARCHITECTURE. An overall scheme or plan that may not necessarily be fully implemented. An architecture represents the goal toward which its implementors strive. The term *architecture* is often used to describe database management systems, operating systems, data communication systems, and other highly complex software/hardware mechanisms. A good architecture relates primarily to the needs of the end users rather than to enthusiasms for particular techniques.

ARQ (AUTOMATIC REQUEST FOR REPETITION). A system employing an error-detecting code and so conceived that any false signal initiates a repetition of the transmission of the character incorrectly received.

ASCII. (*See* **American Standard Code for Information Interchange**.)

ASYNCHRONOUS TRANSMISSION. Data transmission in which each group of code elements corresponding to an alphabetic signal is preceded by a start signal that serves to prepare the receiving mechanism for the reception and registration of a character, and is followed by a stop signal that serves to bring the receiving mechanism to rest in preparation for the reception of the next character. Contrast with **Synchronous transmission**. Asynchronous transmission is also called *start-stop* transmission.

ATTENDED OPERATION. In modem applications, individuals are required at both stations to establish the connection and transfer the modems from voice to data mode. Contrast with **Unattended Operations**.

ATTENUATION. Decrease in the magnitude of current, voltage, or power of a signal in transmission between two points. Can be expressed in decibels.

ATTENUATION EQUALIZER. (*See* **Equalizer**.)

AUDIO FREQUENCIES. Frequencies that can be heard by the human ear (typically 30 to 20,000 hertz).

BANDWIDTH. The range of frequencies available for signaling. The difference expressed in hertz (cycles per second) between the highest and lowest frequencies of a frequency band.

BASEBAND SIGNALING. Transmission of a signal at its original frequencies, i.e., a signal not changed by modulation.

BAUD. Unit of signaling speed. The speed in baud is the number of discrete conditions, or signal events, per second. If a signal event represents only one bit condition, the line speed in baud is the same as the bit rate in bits per second. When each signal event represents other than one bit, baud does not equal bits per second.

BAUDOT CODE. A code for the transmission of data in which 5 equal-length bits represent one character. This code is used with some teletype machines.

BCC. (*See* **Block check character**.)

BEL. Ten decibels. (*See* **Decibel**.)

BIAS DISTORTION. In teletypewriter applications, the uniform shifting of all marking pulses from their proper positions in relation to the beginning of the start pulse.

BIAS DISTORTION, ASYMMETRICAL DISTORTION. Distortion affecting a two-condition (or binary) modulation (or restitution) in which all the significant conditions have longer or shorter duration than the corresponding theoretical durations.

BINARY-SYNCHRONOUS PROTOCOL. A data link protocol, defined by IBM, that uses synchronous transmission to transmit frames of arbitrary length. The binary-synchronous protocol is a character-oriented protocol that uses either the ASCII or EBCDIC character set to define control functions. A character-stuffing procedure can optionally be used to make it possible to carry any desired character in the data portion of the transmission frame.

BIT. Contraction of "binary digit," the smallest unit of information in a binary system.

BIT-ORIENTED PROTOCOL. A class of data link protocols that are independent of any given code set. Protocol control functions are specified in particular positions of the transmission frame, thus allowing any desired bit stream to be carried in the data portion of the frame. A flag bit configuration (0111 1110) identifies the beginning and ending of each frame and a zero-bit insertion procedure ensures that six consecutive one bits never appear in the frame itself.

BIT RATE. The speed at which bits are transmitted, usually expressed in bits per second. Compare with **Baud**.

BIT REPEATER. (*See* **Repeater, regenerative**.)

BITS PER SECOND. Measure of the bit rate (data carrying speed) of a data transmission channel. Compare with **Baud**.

BIT STUFFING. (*See* **Zero-bit insertion**.)

BLOCK CHECK CHARACTER. A set of bits (usually 16), carried at the end of a binary-synchronous transmission frame, that is used in error detection. The sending station puts each character of the data portion of the frame through an arithmetic algorithm to develop the BCC character value. The receiver puts each character of the received frame through the same algorithm and compares the calculated BCC value with the received BCC value. If the values are different, the receiving station transmits a negative acknowledgment, thus requesting that the frame be retransmitted.

BROADBAND. (*See* **Wideband**.)

BROADCAST ADDRESS. A data link or network address that indicates that all stations on the data link or network are to receive a transmission.

BUFFER. A storage device used to compensate for a difference in rate of data flow, or time of occurrence of events, when transmitting data from one device to another.

CABLE. An assembly of one or more conductors within an enveloping protective sheath, so constructed as to permit the conductors to be used separately or in groups.

CARRIER. A continuous frequency capable of being modulated or impressed with a second (information-carrying) signal.

CARRIER, COMMUNICATIONS COMMON. A company that furnishes communication services to the general public and that is regulated by appropriate local, state, or federal agencies.

CARRIER SYSTEM. A means of obtaining a number of channels over a single path by modulating each channel on a different carrier frequency and demodulating at the receiving point to restore the signals to their original form.

CCITT. (*See* **International Telegraph and Telephone Consultative Committee**.)

CENTRAL OFFICE. The place where communications common carriers terminate customer lines and locate the switching equipment that interconnects those lines. Also referred to as an *exchange, end office,* or *local central office.*

CENTRONICS INTERFACE. A data link protocol originally developed by the Centronics Corporation for parallel transmission of data over a direct cable connection. The Centronics interface generally employs a 36-pin connector and is often used for connecting a printer to a computer.

CHANNEL. A path for electrical transmission between two or more points. Also called a *circuit, line, link, path,* or *facility.*

CHANNEL, ANALOG. A channel on which the information transmitted can take any value between the minimum and maximum limits defined by the channel.

CHANNEL, VOICE-GRADE. A channel suitable for transmission of speech, digital, or analog data, or facsimile, generally with a frequency range of about 300 to 3100 cycles per second.

CHANNEL GROUP. The assembly of 12 telephone channels, in a carrier system, occupying adjacent bands in the spectrum, for the purposes of simultaneous modulation or demodulation.

CHARACTER. Letter, figure, number, punctuation, or other sign contained in a message. Besides such characters, there may be characters for special symbols and control functions.

CHARACTERISTIC DISTORTION. Distortion caused by transients which, as a result of the modulation, are present in the transmission channel and depend on its transmission qualities.

CHARACTER STUFFING. A technique used by the binary-synchronous data link protocol for allowing any desired character (including control characters) to be carried in the data portion of a transmission frame.

CIRCUIT. A means of communication between two points. (*See also* **Channel**.)

CIRCUIT, FOUR-WIRE. A metallic circuit in which four wires (two for each direction of transmission) are presented to the station equipment. (*See also* **Duplex Transmission.**)

CIRCUIT, TWO-WIRE. A metallic circuit formed by two conductors insulated from each other. It is possible to use the two conductors as either a simplex transmission path, a half-duplex path, or a full-duplex path.

CIRCUIT SWITCHING. Switching in which a physical path is set up between the incoming and outgoing lines. Contrast with message switching in which no physical path is established. With circuit switching, an actual physical circuit is established between the sender and the receiver for the duration of a transmission.

CLUSTER CONTROLLER. A device, often a stored-program computer, that is used to control the functions of a group of terminals generally located in close physical proximity.

CODEC. Contraction of "coder/decoder". A codec is a device that is used to convert a telephone voice signal into a digital bit stream. A codec generally uses pulse code modulation (PCM) to perform the conversion. (*See also* **Pulse code modulation.**)

CODER/DECODER. (*See* **Codec.**)

COMITÉ CONSULTATIF INTERNATIONAL TÉLÉGRAPHIQUE ET TÉLÉPHONIQUE (CCITT). (*See* **International Telegraph and Telephone Consultative Committee.**)

COMMON CARRIER. (*See* **Carrier, communications common.**)

COMMUNICATIONS CONTROLLER. A device, generally a stored-program computer, that attaches to a host computer and controls data communication functions.

COMMUNICATIONS NETWORK ARCHITECTURE. (*See* **Network architecture.**)

COMMUNICATIONS SATELLITE. A device, generally in geosynchronous orbit, that is essentially a microwave relay in the sky. In the satellite, devices called *transponders* receive microwave signals from a sending earth station and retransmit the signals to other receiving earth stations. (*See also* **Earth station** and **Transponder.**)

COMPANDOR. A compandor is a combination of a compressor at one point in a communication path for reducing the volume *range* of signals, followed by an expandor at another point for restoring the original volume range. Usually its purpose is to improve the ratio of the signal to the interference in the path between the compressor and expandor.

COMPRESSOR. Electronic device that compresses the volume range of a signal, used in a compandor. An "expandor" restores the original volume range after transmission.

CONDITIONING. The addition of equipment to a leased voice-grade channel to provide minimum values of line characteristics required for data transmission.

CONTENTION. A method of line control in which the terminals request to transmit. If the channel in question is free, transmission goes ahead; if it is not free, the terminal waits until the channel becomes free.

CONTROL CHARACTER. A character whose occurrence in a particular context initiates, modifies, or stops a control operation—e.g., a character to control carriage return.

CONTROL MODE. The state that all terminals on a line must be in to allow line control actions or terminal selection to occur. When all terminals on a line are in the control mode, characters on the line are viewed as control characters performing line discipline, that is, polling or addressing.

CONTROL STATION. (*See* **Primary station**.)

CROSSTALK. The unwanted transfer of energy from one circuit, called the *disturbing circuit,* to another circuit, called the *disturbed circuit.*

CROSSTALK, FAR-END. Crosstalk that travels along the disturbed circuit in the same direction as the signals in that circuit. To determine the far-end crosstalk between two pairs, 1 and 2, signals are transmitted on pair 1 at station A, and the level of crosstalk is measured on pair 2 at station B.

CROSSTALK, NEAR-END. Crosstalk that is propagated in a disturbed channel in the direction opposite to the direction of the propagation of the current in the disturbing channel. Ordinarily, the terminal of the disturbed channel at which the near-end crosstalk is present is near or coincides with the energized terminal of the disturbing channel.

CYCLICAL REDUNDANCY CHECK. Use of a particular type of arithmetic algorithm for generating error detection bits in a data link protocol.

DATA CIRCUIT-TERMINATING EQUIPMENT (DCE). Class of device that interfaces between a device of the class *data terminal equipment* (DTE) and a data transmission facility. A DCE normally performs some type of signal conversion between the terminal device and the transmission facility.

DATA COMMUNICATION. The electronic transmission of data, including information generated by computers and other forms of data, including telegraph and telemetry signals.

DATAGRAM. A message sent over a packet-switched network that consists of a single packet only. (*See also* **Packet** and **Packet switching**.)

DATA LINK. A communications facility and related line termination equipment that allows data to be transmitted over the facility.

DATA LINK PROTOCOL. A standard that governs the way in which communicating machines interact at the data link level. A set of rules that all devices on the data link follow in controlling transmission over the link.

DATAPHONE. Both a service mark and a trademark of AT&T. As a service mark it indicates the transmission of data over the telephone network. As a trademark it identifies the communication equipment furnished by AT&T for data communication services.

DATAPHONE DIGITAL SERVICE (DDS). A data communication service offered by AT&T that provides digital channels of various bit rates to its users.

DATA SET. A device that performs the modulation/demodulation and control functions necessary to provide compatibility between business machines and communication facilities. (*See also* **Modem**.)

DATA TERMINAL EQUIPMENT (DTE). That portion of a data processing machine that is capable of transmitting digital data over a communication circuit. A DTE is generally attached to a DCE (data circuit-terminating equipment) in order to send and receive data over a communication facility. (*See also* **Data circuit-terminating equipment**.)

DATA TRANSMISSION. (*See* **Data communication**.)

DCE. (*See* **Data circuit-terminating equipment**.)

DDS. (*See* **Dataphone Digital Service**.)

DECIBEL (db). A tenth of a bel. A unit for measuring relative strength of a signal parameter, such as power, voltage, etc. The number of decibels is ten times the logarithm (base 10) of the ratio of the measured quantity to the reference level. The reference level must always be indicated, such as 1 milliwatt for power ratio.

DELAY DISTORTION. Distortion occurring when the envelope delay of a circuit or system is not constant over the frequency range required for transmission.

DELAY EQUALIZER. A corrective network designed to make the phase delay or envelope delay of a circuit or system substantially constant over a desired frequency range. (*See also* **Equalizer**.)

DEMODULATION. The process of retrieving intelligence (data) from a modulated carrier wave; the reverse of modulation.

DIAL PULSE. A current interruption in the DC loop of a calling telephone. It is produced by an electronic circuit, or by the breaking and making of the dial pulse contacts, in a calling telephone when a digit is dialed or a pushbutton pressed. The loop current is interrupted once for each unit of value of the digit.

DIALUP. The use of a dial or pushbutton telephone to initiate a station-to-station telephone call.

DIBIT. A group of two bits. In four-phase modulation, each possible dibit is encoded as one of four unique carrier phase shifts. The four possible states of a dibit are 00, 01, 10, 11.

DIFFERENTIAL MODULATION. A type of modulation in which the choice of the significant condition for any signal element is dependent on the choice for the previous signal element.

DIGITAL DATA. Information represented by a code consisting of a sequence of discrete elements. Compare with **Analog data**.

DIGITAL SIGNAL. A discrete or discontinuous signal; one whose various states are discrete intervals apart. Compare with **Analog transmission**.

DIGITAL SPEECH INTERPOLATION (DSI). A form of dynamic channel assignment for increasing the utilization of a digital voice channel in which channel capacity is assigned to a user only when that user is actually speaking. (*See also* **Dynamic channel allocation** and **Time assignment speech interpolation**.)

DISCONNECT SIGNAL. A signal transmitted from one end of a subscriber line or trunk to indicate at the other end that the established connection should be disconnected.

DISTORTION. The unwanted change in waveform that occurs between two points in a transmission system.

DOUBLE-CURRENT TRANSMISSION, POLAR DIRECT-CURRENT SYSTEM. A form of binary telegraph transmission in which positive and negative direct currents denote the significant conditions.

DSI. (*See* **Digital speech interpolation**.)

DTE. (*See* **Data terminal equipment**.)

DUPLEXING. The use of duplicate computers, files, or circuitry, so that in the event of one component failing an alternative one can enable the system to carry on its work.

DUPLEX TRANSMISSION. Simultaneous two-way independent transmission in both directions. Compare with **Half-duplex transmission**. Also called **Full-duplex transmission**.

DYNAMIC CHANNEL ALLOCATION. A technique in which channel capacity is assigned to a user only when the user actually requires it.

EARTH STATION. That part of a communications satellite transmission system that resides on the ground. A sending earth station transmits a signal up to a communications satellite in earth orbit; a receiving earth station receives a signal that is retransmitted by the satellite.

EBCDIC. (*See* **Extended Binary-Coded Decimal Interchange Code**.)

ECHO. An echo is a wave that has been reflected or otherwise returned with sufficient magnitude and delay for it to be perceptible in some manner as a wave distinct from that directly transmitted.

ECHO CHECK. A method of checking data transmission accuracy whereby the received data is returned to the sending end for comparison with the original data.

ECHO SUPPRESSOR. A line device used to prevent energy from being reflected back (echoed) to the transmitter. It attenuates the transmission path in one direction while signals are being passed in the other direction.

EIA. (*See* **Electronics Industry Association**.)

ELECTRONICS INDUSTRY ASSOCIATION (EIA). An organization whose members are electronics companies. An important standard published by the EIA is RS-232-C, which describes the way a terminal is connected to a modem.

END DISTORTION. End distortion of start-stop signals is the shifting of the end of all marking pulses from their proper positions in relation to the beginning of the start pulse.

END OFFICE. (*See* **Central office**.)

EQUALIZATION. Compensation for the attenuation (signal loss) increase with frequency. Its purpose is to produce a flat frequency response while the temperature remains constant.

EQUALIZER. Any combination (usually adjustable) of coils, capacitors, and/or resistors inserted in a transmission line or amplifier circuit to improve its frequency response.

EQUIVALENT FOUR-WIRE SYSTEM. A transmission system using frequency division to obtain full-duplex operation over a single pair of wires.

ERROR-CORRECTING CODE. An error-detecting code incorporating sufficient additional signaling elements to enable the nature of some or all of the errors to be indicated and corrected entirely at the receiving end.

ERROR-DETECTING CODE. A code in which each signal conforms to specific rules of construction, so that the departures from this construction in the received signals can be detected automatically. Such codes necessarily require more signaling elements than are required to convey the basic information.

ESCAPE MECHANISM. A mechanism in a data code that permits a control character (the escape character) to signify that one or more following characters is to be given an alternative interpretation.

EVEN PARITY CHECK. (*See* **Parity check.**)

EXCHANGE. A unit established by a communications common carrier for the administration of communication service in a specified area, usually embracing a city, town, or village and its environs. It consists of one or more central offices together with the associated equipment used in furnishing communication service. (This term is often used as a synonym for **Central office.**)

EXCHANGE, PRIVATE AUTOMATIC (PAX). A dial telephone exchange that provides private telephone service to an organization and does not allow calls to be transmitted to or from the public telephone network.

EXCHANGE, PRIVATE AUTOMATIC BRANCH (PABX). An automatic exchange connected to the public telephone network on the user's premises.

EXCHANGE, PRIVATE BRANCH (PBX). A manual or automatic exchange connected to the public telephone network on the user's premises.

EXCHANGE, TRUNK. An exchange devoted primarily to interconnecting trunks.

EXCHANGE SERVICE. A service permitting interconnection of any two customers' stations through the use of the exchange system.

EXPANDOR. A transducer which for a given amplitude range or input voltages produces a larger range of output voltages. One important type of expandor employs the information from the envelope of speech signals to expand their volume range. Compare with **Compandor**.

EXTENDED BINARY-CODED DECIMAL INTERCHANGE CODE (EBCDIC). An 8-bit data code that is used on much IBM equipment both internally and sometimes for data communication purposes.

FACSIMILE (FAX). A system for the transmission of images. The image is scanned at the transmitter, reconstructed at the receiving station, and duplicated on paper.

FAST-CONNECT CIRCUIT SWITCHING. A form of circuit switching, well suited to use on computer networks, in which connections are established in milliseconds.

FCC. (*See* **Federal Communications Commission**.)

FD OR FDX. Full duplex. (*See* **Duplex transmission**.)

FDM. (*See* **Frequency-division multiplexing**.)

FEDERAL COMMUNICATIONS COMMISSION (FCC). A board of seven commissioners appointed by the President under the Communications Act of 1934, having the power to regulate all interstate and foreign electrical communication systems originating in the United States.

FIBER OPTICS. A generic term for the technology that allows data to be transmitted over a thin strand of glass using a modulated light beam.

FIGURES SHIFT. A physical shift in a teletypewriter which enables the printing of numbers, symbols, upper-case characters, etc. Compare with **Letters shift**.

FILTER. A network designed to transmit currents of frequencies within one or more frequency bands and to attenuate currents of other frequencies.

FLOW CONTROL. A mechanism in a data communication system for regulating the flow of data over a network. (*See also* **Pacing**.)

FOREIGN EXCHANGE SERVICE. A service that connects a customer's telephone to a telephone company central office not normally serving the customer's location.

FORTUITOUS DISTORTION. Distortion resulting from causes generally subject to random laws (accidental irregularities in the operation of the apparatus and of the moving parts, disturbances affecting the transmission channel, etc.).

FORWARD ERROR CORRECTION. A form of error handling in which sufficient redundancy is built into each message so that the receiving station can both detect and automatically correct errors that occur during transmission.

FOUR-WIRE CIRCUIT. A circuit using two pairs of conductors, one pair for the "go" channel and the other pair for the "return" channel.

FOUR-WIRE EQUIVALENT CIRCUIT. A circuit using the same pair of conductors to give "go" and "return" channels by means of different carrier frequencies for the two channels.

FOUR-WIRE TERMINATING SET. Hybrid arrangement by which four-wire circuits are terminated on a two-wire basis for interconnection with two-wire circuits.

FRAME. The unit of data that is handled by the data link level layer of software in a data communication system.

FREQUENCY-DERIVED CHANNEL. Any of the channels obtained from multiplexing a channel by frequency division.

FREQUENCY-DIVISION MULTIPLEXING. A multiplexing system in which the available transmission frequency range is divided into narrower bands, each used for a separate channel.

FREQUENCY MODULATION. One method of modifying a sine wave signal to make it "carry" information. The sine wave or "carrier" has its frequency modified in accordance with the information to be transmitted. The frequency function of the modulated wave may be continuous or discontinuous. In the latter case, two or more particular frequencies may correspond each to one significant condition.

FREQUENCY-SHIFT SIGNALING, FREQUENCY-SHIFT KEYING (FSK). Frequency modulation method in which the frequency is made to vary at the significant instants. 1. By smooth transitions; the modulated wave and the change in frequency are continuous at the significant instants. 2. By abrupt transitions; The modulated wave is continuous but the frequency is discontinuous at the significant instants.

FSK. (*See* **Frequency-shift keying**.)

FULL-DUPLEX TRANSMISSION. (*See* **Duplex transmission**.)

GATEWAY. A device that serves as a bridge between two different networks.

GEOSYNCHRONOUS ORBIT. An earth orbit 22,282 miles high at which point a satellite above the equator travels around the earth in exactly the time it takes for the earth to rotate on its axis. A satellite in geosynchronous orbit appears to hang stationary over a particular point on the earth.

GRADE OF SERVICE. The probability of receiving a network busy signal on a communication network.

GROUP. (*See* **Channel group.**)

GROUP ADDRESS. A data link or network address that specifies a collection of stations on the data link or network.

GUARD BAND. Range of frequencies that separate one subchannel from another when frequency-division multiplexing is used.

HALF-DUPLEX CIRCUIT. A circuit designed for transmission in either direction but not both directions simultaneously.

HALF-DUPLEX TRANSMISSION. (*See* **Half-duplex circuit**.)

HANDSHAKING. Exchange of predetermined signals for purposes of control when a connection is established over a data link.

HARMONIC DISTORTION. The resultant presence of harmonic frequencies (due to nonlinear characteristics of a transmission line) in the response when a sinusoidal stimulus is applied.

HD OR HDX. (*See* **Half-duplex circuit**.)

HDLC. (*See* **High-level Data Link Control**.)

HERTZ (Hz). A measure of frequency or bandwidth. The same as cycles per second.

HIGH-LEVEL DATA LINK CONTROL (HDLC). A bit-oriented data link protocol standardized by the International Standards Organization (ISO) and documented in ISO standards 3309 and 4435.

HOME LOOP. An operation involving only those input and output units associated with the local terminal.

HUB POLLING. A form of polling in which the polling signal is sent from one terminal to the next on the data link.

IDN. (*See* **Integrated digital network**.)

IEEE. (*See* **Institute of Electrical and Electronics Engineers**.)

INFORMATION UTILITY. A company that is in the business of providing information to its customers typically via computer terminals connected to a public data network.

IN-HOUSE. (*See* **In-plant system**.)

IN-PLANT SYSTEM. A system whose parts, including remote terminals, are all situated in one building or localized area. The term is also used for communication systems spanning several buildings and sometimes covering a large distance, but in which no common carrier facilities are used.

INSTITUTE OF ELECTRICAL AND ELECTRONICS ENGINEERS (IEEE). An organization that, among other activities, produces data communication standards. Particularly important are the IEEE 802 group of standards for various types of local area networks.

INTEGRATED DIGITAL NETWORK (IDN). A communication network that combines the technologies of digital switching and digital transmission of information. (*See also* **Integrated services digital network**.)

INTEGRATED SERVICES DIGITAL NETWORK (ISDN). A communication network that uses an integrated digital network (IDN) to carry all forms of traffic, such as voice, computer data, and facsimile. (*See also* **Integrated digital network**.)

INTERNATIONAL ALPHABET NO. 2. Five-bit character code, standardized by the CCITT, widely used in telegraphy.

INTERNATIONAL ALPHABET NO. 5. Seven-bit character code widely used in data transmission. ASCII is a dialect of International Alphabet No. 5.

INTERNATIONAL STANDARDS ORGANIZATION (ISO). An international organization for standardization. ISO publishes many standards that are important for data communication. The OSI reference model is being developed by the ISO. (*See also* **Reference Model for Open Systems Interconnection**.)

INTERNATIONAL TELECOMMUNICATION UNION (ITU). The telecommunications agency of the United Nations, established to provide standardized communication procedures and practices including frequency allocation and radio regulations on a world-wide basis. The CCITT is part of the ITU. (*See also* **International Telegraph and Telephone Consultative Committee**.)

INTERNATIONAL TELEGRAPH AND TELEPHONE CONSULTATIVE COMMITTEE (CCITT). An organization in the International Telecommunications Union that publishes recommendations of importance to data communication. *Recommendation X.25* is published by the CCITT.

INTEROFFICE TRUNK. A trunk between toll offices in different telephone exchanges.

IRMA BOARD. Circuit board for personal computers that permits 3270 terminal emulation.

ISDN. (*See* **Integrated services digital network**.)

ISO. (*See* **International Standards Organization**.)

ITU. (*See* **International Telecommunication Union**.)

JUMBOGROUP. The assembly of six mastergroups (3,600 telephone channels) in a carrier system, occupying adjacent bands in the spectrum, for the purposes of simultaneous modulation or demodulation. (*See also* **Mastergroup**.)

JUMBOGROUP MULTIPLEX. The assembly of three jumbogroups (10,800 telephone channels) in a carrier system, occupying adjacent bands in the spectrum, for the purposes of simultaneous modulation or demodulation. (*See also* **Jumbogroup**.)

KEYBOARD SEND/RECEIVE (KSR). A combination teletypewriter transmitter and receiver with transmission capability from keyboard only.

KSR. (*See* **Keyboard send/receive**.)

LAP AND LAPB. (*See* **Link Access Protocol**.)

LEASED FACILITY. A facility reserved for sole use of a single leasing customer. (*See also* **Private line**.)

LETTERS SHIFT (LTRS). A physical shift in a teletypewriter that enables the printing of alphabetic characters. Also, the name of the character that causes this shift. Compare with **Figures shift**.

LINE CONDITIONING. (*See* **Conditioning**.)

LINE SWITCHING. (*See* **Circuit switching**.)

LINE TERMINATION DEVICE. A device, such as a modem or service unit, used to attach a data machine to a transmission facility. (*See also* **Data circuit-terminating equipment**.)

LINK ACCESS PROTOCOL (LAP) AND LINK ACCESS PROTOCOL—BALANCED (LAPB). Bit-oriented data link protocols standardized by the CCITT that specify the functions of the data link level of CCITT Recommendation X.25. LAP and LAPB are compatible subsets of HDLC. (*See also* **High-level Data Link Control**.)

LOADING. Adding inductance (load coils) to a transmission line to minimize amplitude distortion.

LOCAL AREA NETWORK (LAN). A data communication network, usually operating at high speeds (typically hundreds of thousands or millions of bits per second), operating over a limited geographical area (typically within a building or group of buildings), using privately-installed communication media.

LOCAL EXCHANGE, LOCAL CENTRAL OFFICE. An exchange in which subscribers' lines terminate. Also referred to as an *end office*.

LOCAL LOOP. A channel connecting the subscriber's equipment to the line terminating equipment in the central office exchange. Usually a two-wire or four-wire twisted pair circuit.

LONGITUDINAL REDUNDANCY CHECK (LRC). A system of error control based on the formation of a block check following preset rules. The check formation rule is applied in the same manner to each character.

LOOP CHECKING, MESSAGE FEEDBACK, INFORMATION FEEDBACK. A method of checking the accuracy of transmission of data in which the received data is returned to the sending end for comparison with the original data, which is stored there for this purpose.

LOOP CONFIGURATION. Data link configuration in which the stations are arranged in a ring.

LRC. (*See* **Longitudinal redundancy check**.)

LTRS. (*See* **Letters shift**.)

MARK. Presence of signal. In telegraph communication a mark represents the closed condition or current flowing. A mark impulse is equivalent to binary 1.

MARK-HOLD. The normal no-traffic line condition whereby a steady mark is transmitted. This may be a customer selectable option. Compare with **Space-hold**.

MARK-TO-SPACE TRANSITION. The transition, or switching from a marking impulse to a spacing impulse.

MASTERGROUP. The assembly of 10 supergroups (600 telephone channels) in a carrier system, occupying adjacent bands in the spectrum, for the purposes of simultaneous modulation or demodulation. (*See also* **Supergroup**.)

MASTERGROUP MULTIPLEX. The assembly of 3 mastergroups (1,800 telephone channels) in a carrier system, occupying adjacent bands in the spectrum, for the purposes of simultaneous modulation or demodulation. (*See also* **Mastergroup**.)

MASTER STATION. (*See* **Primary station**.)

MEAN TIME TO FAILURE. The average length of time for which a system, or a component of a system, works without fault.

MEAN TIME TO REPAIR. When a system, or a component of a system, develops a fault, this is the average time taken to correct the fault.

MEASURED-USE SERVICE. A data communication service for which a common carrier or PTT charges only for time the service is used by the customer. Placing a call on the public telephone system is an example of employing a measured-use-communication service.

MESSAGE SWITCHING. The technique of receiving a message, storing it until the proper outgoing line is available, and then retransmitting. No direct connection between the incoming and outgoing lines is set up as is done in line switching.

MICROWAVE. Any electromagnetic wave in the radio-frequency spectrum above 890 Megahertz.

MODEM. Contraction of "modulator-demodulator." The term may be used when the modulator and the demodulator are associated in the same signal-conversion equipment. (*See also* **Modulation**.)

MODULATION. The process by which some characteristic of one wave is varied in accordance with another wave or signal. This technique is used in modems to make data machine signals compatible with communication facilities.

MODULATION WITH A FIXED REFERENCE. A type of modulation in which the choice of the significant condition for any signal element is based on a fixed reference.

MODULATOR/DEMODULATOR. (*See* **Modem**.)

MULTIDROP LINE. (*See* **Multipoint line**.)

MULTIPLEXING. Use of a common channel in order to make two or more channels, either by splitting of the frequency band transmitted by the common channel into narrower bands, each of which is used to constitute a distinct channel (frequency-division multiplexing), or by allotting this common channel to several different information channels, one at a time (time-division multiplexing).

MULTIPLEXOR. A device that uses several communication channels at the same time, and transmits and receives messages and controls the communication lines.

MULTIPOINT LINE. Line or circuit interconnecting several stations. Also called a **Multidrop line**.

NETWORK ARCHITECTURE. An overall plan that governs the design of hardware and software components that make up a data communication system.

NEUTRAL TRANSMISSION. Method of transmitting teletypewriter signals, whereby a mark is represented by current on the line and a space is represented by the absence of current. By extension to tone signaling, neutral transmission is a method of signaling employing two signaling states, one of the states representing both a space condition and the absence of any signaling. Also called *unipolar*. Compare with **Polar transmission**.

NOISE. Random electrical signals, introduced by circuit components or natural disturbances, which tend to degrade the performance of a communications channel.

NULL MODEM. RS-232-C cable with the appropriate circuits crossed allowing a DTE to be attached to a DTE or a DCE to be attached to a DCE.

ODD PARITY CHECK. (*See* **Parity check**.)

OFF HOOK. Activated (in regard to a telephone set). By extension, a modem automatically answering on a public switched system is said to go "off hook." Compare with **On hook**.

ON HOOK. Deactivated (in regard to a telephone set). A telephone (or modem) not in use is "on hook."

ONLINE. An online system can be defined as one in which the input data enters the computer directly from its point of origin and/or output data is transmitted directly to where it is used. The intermediate stages, such as writing magnetic tapes or diskettes or offline printing, are largely avoided.

OPEN SYSTEMS INTERCONNECT REFERENCE MODEL. (*See* **Reference Model for Open Systems Interconnection**.)

OPEN WIRE. A conductor separately supported above the surface of the ground, i.e., supported on insulators.

OPEN-WIRE LINE. A pole line whose conductors are principally in the form of open wire.

OPTICAL FIBER. A thin strand of glass over which data can be transmitted using a modulated light beam.

OSI REFERENCE MODEL. (*See* **Reference Model for Open Systems Interconnection**.)

PABX. Private automatic branch exchange. (*See* **Exchange, private automatic branch**.)

PACING. A mechanism on a data communication system for regulating the timing of message flow through the network. (*See also* **Flow control**.)

PACKET. The unit of data, of some fixed maximum size, that is transmitted over a packet switching data network. A packet carries a header containing control information such as a packet sequence number, the network address of the station that originated the packet, and the network address of the packet's destination. (*See also* **Packet switching**.)

PACKET ASSEMBLY AND DISASSEMBLY (PAD). The process of dividing up a message into packets for transmission over a packet-switching network and then reassembling the packets into the original message. The term *PAD* also refers to a device that performs the packet assembly and disassembly function. (*See also* **Packet** and **Packet switching**.)

PACKET SWITCH. A device that accepts an incoming packet and determines, from information contained in the packet's header, the next node in a packet-switching network to which the packet should be transmitted.

PACKET SWITCHING. The technique of transmitting units of data (called packets) of some fixed maximum size, through a mesh-structured network, from an originating station to a destination station. In packet switching, a physical path is not set up between the originating and destination station. Instead, the packet is relayed from one node of the network to the next until it finally reaches its destination. Contrast with **Circuit switching**. (*See also* **Packet** and **Packet switch**.)

PAD. (*See* **Packet assembly and disassembly**.)

PAM. (*See* **Pulse-amplitude modulation**.)

PARALLEL TRANSMISSION. Simultaneous transmission of the bits making up a character or byte, either over separate channels or on different carrier frequencies on the channel. The simultaneous transmission of a certain number of signal elements constituting the same telegraph or data signal. For example, use of a code according to which each signal is characterized by a combination of 3 out of 12 frequencies simultaneously transmitted over the channel.

PARITY CHECK. Addition of noninformation bits to data, making the number of ones in a grouping of bits either always even or always odd. This permits detection of bit groupings that contain single errors. It may be applied to characters, blocks, or any convenient bit grouping.

PARITY CHECK, HORIZONTAL. A parity check applied to the group of certain bits from every character in a block. (*See also* **Longitudinal redundancy check**.)

PARITY CHECK, VERTICAL. A parity check applied to the group which is all bits in one character. Also called **Vertical redundancy check**.

PAX. Private automatic exchange. (*See also* **Exchange, private automatic**.)

PBX. Private branch exchange. (*See also* **Exchange, private branch**.)

PCM. (*See* **Pulse-code modulation**.)

PDM. (*See* **Pulse-duration modulation**.)

PHASE DISTORTION. (*See* **Delay distortion**.)

PHASE EQUALIZER, DELAY EQUALIZER. A corrective network designed to make the phase delay or envelope delay of a circuit or system substantially constant over a desired frequency range.

PHASE-INVERSION MODULATION. A method of modulation in which the two significant conditions differ in phase by radians.

PHASE MODULATION. One method of modifying a sine wave signal to make it "carry" information. The sine wave or "carrier," has its phase changed in accordance with the information to be transmitted.

POINT-TO-POINT CONFIGURATION. A network configuration in which two communicating stations are connected by a single communication channel that is not shared by any other stations.

POLAR TRANSMISSION. A method for transmitting teletypewriter signals, whereby the marking signal is represented by direct current flowing in one direction and the spacing signal is represented by an equal current flowing in the opposite direction. By extension to tone signaling, polar transmission is a method of transmission employing three distinct states, two to represent a mark and a space and one to represent the absence of a signal. Also called a *bipolar*. Compare with **Neutral transmission**.

POLLING. This is a means of controlling communication lines. The communication control device sends signals to a terminal saying, "Terminal A. Have you anything to send?" if not, "Terminal B. Have you anything to send?" and so on. Polling is an alternative to contention. It makes sure that no terminal is kept waiting for a long time.

POLLING LIST. The polling signal will usually be sent under program control. The program maintains a list for each channel that tells the sequence in which the terminals are to be polled.

PPM. (*See* **Pulse-position modulation**.)

PRIMARY CENTER. A control center connecting toll centers; a class 3 office. It can also serve as a toll center for its local end offices.

PRIMARY STATION. The station on a data link that is responsible for controlling transmission on the data link. Contrast with **Secondary station**. Also called a **Master station** or **Control station**.

PRIVATE AUTOMATIC BRANCH EXCHANGE. (*See* **Exchange, private automatic branch**.)

PRIVATE AUTOMATIC EXCHANGE. (*See* **Exchange, private automatic**.)

PRIVATE BRANCH EXCHANGE (PBX). (*See* **Exchange, private branch**.)

PRIVATE LINE. Denotes the channel and channel equipment furnished to a customer as a unit for that customer's exclusive use, without interexchange switching arrangements.

PROPAGATION DELAY. The time necessary for a signal to travel from one point on a circuit to another.

PROTOCOL. Rules that govern communication at a given layer in a network architecture.

PROTOCOL CONVERTER. A network device that attaches devices that use one data link protocol to a communication facility that uses some other data link protocol. A protocol converter typically combines the individual transmissions from multiple, simple asynchronous terminals for transmission over a communication facility using a more efficient synchronous data link protocol.

PUBLIC. Provided by a common carrier for use by many customers.

PUBLIC DATA NETWORK. A communication network, designed specifically for the transmission of computer data, that is used by many individual subscribers. Most public data networks use the technique of packet switching rather than circuit switching. (*See also* **Packet switching**.)

PUBLIC SWITCHED NETWORK. Any switching system that provides circuit switching to many customers.

PULSE-AMPLITUDE MODULATION (PAM). A modulation technique in which an analog signal, such as speech, is converted into pulses whose amplitudes are proportional to the amplitude of the signal at the sampling instant.

PULSE-CODE MODULATION (PCM). A modulation technique in which a pulse train is created in accordance with a code. With PCM, the input signal is first quantized, and the signal amplitude at a particular instant in time is represented by a binary number that can be transmitted over a digital communication channel as a series of pulses of some fixed amplitude. PCM is used to convert an analog signal, such as telephone voice, into a digital bit stream. (*See also* **Codec.**)

PULSE-DURATION MODULATION (PDM) (PULSE-WIDTH MODULATION) (PULSE-LENGTH MODULATION). A form of pulse modulation in which the durations of pulses are varied.

PULSE MODULATION. Transmission of information by modulation of a pulsed or intermittent carrier. Pulse width, count, position, phase, and/or amplitude can be the varied characteristic.

PULSE-POSITION MODULATION (PPM). A form of pulse modulation in which the positions in time of pulses are varied, without modifying their duration.

PUSHBUTTON DIALING. The use of keys or pushbuttons instead of a rotary dial to generate a sequence of digits to establish a circuit connection. The signal form is usually multiple tones. Also called **Tone dialing, Touch-tone, Touch-call**.

REALTIME. A realtime computer system can be defined as one that controls an environment by receiving data, processing it, and returning the results sufficiently quickly to affect the functioning of the environment at that time.

REASONABLENESS CHECKS. Tests made on information reaching a realtime system or being transmitted from it to ensure that the data in question lies within a given range. It is one of the means of protecting a system from data transmission errors.

RECOMMENDATION X.25. (*See* **X.25**.)

REDUNDANCY CHECK. An automatic or programmed check based on the systematic insertion of components or characters used especially for checking purposes.

REDUNDANT CODE. A code using more signal elements than necessary to represent the intrinsic information.

REFERENCE MODEL FOR OPEN SYSTEMS INTERCONNECTION (OSI MODEL). A network architecture being developed by the International Standards Organization (ISO) that provides a common basis for the coordination of standards development for the purpose of the interconnection of information processing systems. The term *Open Systems Interconnection (OSI)* qualifies standards for the exchange of information among systems that are ''open'' to one another for this purpose by virtue of their mutual use of applicable standards.

REGENERATIVE REPEATER. (*See* **Repeater, regenerative**.)

REGIONAL CENTER. A control center (class 1 office) connecting sectional centers of the telephone system together. Every pair of regional centers in the United States has a direct circuit group running from one center to the other.

REPEATER. 1. A device whereby currents received over one circuit are automatically repeated in another circuit or circuits, generally in an amplified and/or reshaped form. 2. A device used to restore signals, distorted because of attenuation, to their original shape and transmission level.

REPEATER, REGENERATIVE. A repeater whose function is to retime and retransmit the received signal impulses restored to their original strength. Also called a **Bit repeater**.

REPEATER, TELEGRAPH. A device that receives telegraph signals and automatically retransmits corresponding signals.

RESIDUAL ERROR RATE; UNDETECTED ERROR RATE. The ratio of the number of bits, unit elements, characters, or blocks incorrectly received but undetected or uncorrected by the error-control equipment, to the total number of bits, unit elements, characters or blocks sent.

RESPONSE TIME. This is the time a system takes to react to a given input. If a message is keyed into a terminal by an operator and the reply from a computer, when it comes, is displayed at the same terminal, response time can be defined as the time interval between the operator pressing the last key of the input and the terminal displaying the first character of the reply.

ROLL CALL POLLING. A polling technique in which the primary station on a multipoint communication facility consults a polling list in determining the order in which to send polling signals to each of the secondary stations attached to the communication facility.

ROUTING. The assignment of the communication path by which a message will reach its destination.

ROUTING, ALTERNATE. Assignment of a secondary communication path to a destination when the primary path is unavailable.

RS-232-C. A physical level standard, developed by the Electronics Industry Association (EIA), that defines 25 circuits that can be used to connect two communicating stations and describes the electrical characteristics of the signals carried over those circuits. The RS-232-C interface allows for serial transmission at speeds up to about 20,000 bits per second at a distance of typically 50 feet or less.

SDLC. (*See* **Synchronous Data Link Control**.)

SECONDARY STATION. A station on a data link that cannot initiate a transmission. A secondary station transmits data only when given permission by the station in control of the data link. Also called a *tributary* or *slave* station. Contrast with **Primary station**.

SELECTION. Addressing a terminal and/or a component on a selective calling circuit.

SELECTIVE CALLING. The ability of the transmitting station to specify which of several stations on the same line is to receive a message.

SELF-CHECKING NUMBERS. Numbers that contain redundant information so that an error in them, caused by noise on a transmission line, for example, can be detected.

SERIAL PORT. A circuit installed in a computer that allows the computer to be attached to a line termination device such as a modem or line driver for the purpose of data communication.

SERIAL TRANSMISSION. Used to identify a system wherein the bits of a character occur serially in time. Implies only a single transmission channel. Also called *serial by bit*.

SHANNON'S LAW. Mathematical formula for determining the theoretical maximum signaling rate of a given communication channel.

SIDEBAND. The frequency band on either the upper or lower side of the carrier frequency within which fall the frequencies produced by the process of modulation.

SIGNAL-TO-NOISE RATIO (S/N). Relative power of the signal to the noise in a channel.

SIMPLEX CIRCUIT. A circuit permitting transmission in one specific direction only.

SIMPLEX MODE. Operation of a communication channel in one direction only, with no capacity for reversing.

SLAVE STATION. (*See* **Secondary station**.)

SLOW-SCAN TRANSMISSION. Type of transmission that allows a signal to be transmitted over a communication channel of lower bandwidth than the original signal.

SNA. (*See* **Systems Network Architecture**.)

SPACE. 1. An impulse that, in a neutral circuit, causes the loop to open or causes absence of signal, while in a polar circuit causes the loop current to flow in a direction opposite to that for a mark impulse. A space is equivalent to a binary 0. 2. In some codes, a character that causes a printer or display screen to leave a character width with no printed symbol.

SPACE-HOLD. The normal no-traffic condition whereby a steady space is transmitted. Compare with **Mark-hold**.

SPACE-TO-MARK TRANSITION. The transition, or switching, from a spacing impulse to a marking impulse.

SPACING BIAS. (*See* **Bias distortion**.)

SPECTRUM. 1. A continuous range of frequencies, usually wide in extent, within which waves have some specific common characteristics. 2. A graphical representation of the distribution of the amplitude (and sometimes the phase) of the components of a wave as a function of frequency. A spectrum can be continuous or, on the contrary, contains only points corresponding to certain discrete values.

START BIT. The first bit of a character in asynchronous (start-stop) transmission, used to permit synchronization.

START ELEMENT. (*See* **Start bit**.)

START-STOP TRANSMISSION. (*See* **Asynchronous transmission**.)

STATE PUBLIC UTILITIES COMMISSIONS. State agencies that are responsible for regulating telecommunications within a given state in the U.S..

STATION. One of the input or output points of a communication system, e.g., the telephone set in a telephone system or a terminal or computer in a data communication system.

STATISTICAL MULTIPLEXOR. A multiplexor that uses intelligence and buffer storage to combine several signals or bit streams into a combined signal or bit stream of lower bandwidth or bit rate than the total of the combined bandwidth or bit rate of the individual signals or bit streams.

STOP BIT. The last bit of a character in asynchronous (start-stop) transmission, used to ensure recognition of the next start bit.

STOP ELEMENT. (*See* **Stop bit**.)

STORE AND FORWARD. The interruption of data flow from the originating terminal to the designated receiver by storing the information enroute and forwarding it at a later time. (*See* **Message switching**.)

SUBSCRIBERS LINE. (*See* **Local loop**.)

SUBVOICE-GRADE CHANNEL. A channel of bandwidth narrower than that of voice-grade channels. Such channels are usually subchannels of a voice-grade line.

SUPERGROUP. The assembly of five 12-channel groups, occupying adjacent bands in the spectrum. (*See also* **Channel group**.)

SUPERVISORY SIGNALS. Signals used to indicate the various operating states of circuit combinations.

SUPPRESSED CARRIER TRANSMISSION. That method of communication in which the carrier frequency is suppressed either partially or to the maximum degree possible. One or both of the sidebands may be transmitted.

SWITCH HOOK. A switch on a telephone set, associated with the structure supporting the receiver or handset. It is operated by the removal or replacement of the receiver or handset on the support. (*See also* **Off hook** *and* **On hook**.)

SWITCHING CENTER. A location that terminates multiple circuits and is capable of interconnecting circuits.

SWITCHOVER. When a failure occurs in the equipment, a switch can occur to an alternate component. This can be, for example, an alternative file unit, an alternative communication line, or an alternative computer. The switchover can be automatic under program control or it can be manual.

SYNCHRONOUS. Having a constant time interval between successive bits, characters, or events. The term implies that all equipment is in step.

SYNCHRONOUS DATA LINK CONTROL (SDLC). A bit-oriented data link protocol standardized by IBM as part of IBM's Systems Network Architecture (SNA). SDLC is a compatible subset of HDLC. (*See also* **High-level data link control**.)

SYNCHRONOUS TRANSMISSION. Data transmission in which the sending and receiving instruments are operating continuously at substantially the same frequency and are maintained, by means of correction if necessary, in a desired phase relationship. Compare with **Start-stop transmission**.

SYSTEMS NETWORK ARCHITECTURE (SNA). Network architecture that defines the formats and protocols used by IBM computing system equipment in performing data communication functions.

T1 CARRIER. Digital data transmission carrier that supports a bit rate of 1.544 million bits per second. T1 carriers are used by common carriers in providing long-distance telephone service and by individual subscribers for voice and data communication.

TANDEM OFFICE. An office that is used to interconnect the local end offices over tandem trunks in a densely settled exchange area where it is uneconomical for a telephone company to provide direct interconnection between all end offices. The tandem office completes all calls between the end offices but is not directly connected to subscribers.

TANDEM OFFICE, TANDEM CENTRAL OFFICE. A central office used primarily as a switching point for traffic between other central offices.

TARIFF. The published rate for a specific unit of equipment, facility, or type of service provided by a communications common carrier. Also the vehicle by which the regulating agencies approve or disapprove such facilities of services.

TASI. (*See* **Time assignment speech interpolation**.)

TELECOMMUNICATIONS. The electronic transmission of any kind of electronic information, including telephone calls, television signals, data communication of all forms, electronic mail, facsimile transmission, telemetry from spacecraft, and so on.

TELECOMMUNICATIONS ACCESS METHOD. Software subsystem that supplements conventional operating system services by providing low-level programming support for data communication functions.

TELEPROCESSING. A form of information handling in which a data processing system uses communication facilities. (Originally, but no longer, an IBM trademark.)

TELEPROCESSING MONITOR. Software subsystem that uses the services of a telecommunications access method to provide high-level programming support for data communication functions.

TELETYPE. Trademark of Teletype Corporation, usually referring to a series of different types of teleprinter equipment, such as tape punches, reperforators, page printers, etc., used for communication systems.

TELETYPEWRITER EXCHANGE SERVICE (TWX). An AT&T public, switched teletypewriter service in which suitably arranged teletypewriter stations are provided with lines to a central office to other stations throughout North America.

TELEX SERVICE. A dial-up telegraph service enabling its subscribers to communicate directly and temporarily among themselves by means of start-stop apparatus and of circuits of the public telegraph network. The service operates worldwide. Computers can be connected to the Telex network.

TERMINAL. Any device capable of sending and/or receiving information over a communication channel. The means by which data is entered into a computer system and by which the decisions of the system are communicated to the environment it affects.

TIE LINE. A private-line communication channel of the type provided by communications common carriers for linking two or more points together.

TIME ASSIGNMENT SPEECH INTERPOLATION (TASI). A particular form of dynamic channel assignment for increasing the utilization of an analog voice channel in which channel capacity is assigned to a user only when that user is actually speaking. (*See also* **Dynamic channel allocation** and **Digital speech interpolation**.)

TIME-DERIVED CHANNEL. Any of the channels obtained by dividing up a channel using time-division multiplexing.

TIME-DIVISION MULTIPLEXING. A system in which a channel is established by connecting intermittently, generally at regular intervals and by means of an automatic distribution, its terminal equipment to a common channel. At times when these connections are not established, the section of the common channel between distributors can be used in order to establish other channels, in turn.

TIMEOUT. A predefined period of time that elapses before the initiation of an expected event.

TOLL CENTER. Basic toll switching entity; a central office where channels and toll message circuits terminate. While this is usually one particular central office in a city, larger cities may have several central offices where toll message circuits terminate.

TOLL CIRCUIT (AMERICAN). (*See* **Trunk circuit**.)

TOLL SWITCHING TRUNK. (**AMERICAN**). (*See* **Trunk junction**.)

TONE DIALING. (*See* **Pushbutton dialing**.)

TOUCH-TONE. AT&T term for pushbutton dialing.

TRANSCEIVER. A terminal that can transmit and receive traffic. On some local area networks, the device that attaches to the transmission medium for transmitting and receiving data.

TRANSLATOR. A device that converts information from one system of representation into equivalent information in another system of representation. In telephone equipment, it is the device that converts dialed digits into call-routing information.

TRANSPARENT. A facility, device, or function is transparent if it appears not to exist but in fact does.

TRANSPARENT TEXT MODE. Mode of a data link protocol that allows the message text to contain all possible bit configurations. Bit-oriented data link protocols always operate in transparent text mode. Some character-oriented data link protocols support transparent text mode as an option.

TRANSPONDER. Device in a communications satellite that receives a signal from a sending earth station and retransmits the signal to one or more receiving earth stations.

TRIBIT. A group of three bits. The eight possible states of a dibit are 000, 001, 010, 011, 100, 101, 110, and 111.

TRIBUTARY STATION. (*See* **Secondary station**.)

TRUNK CIRCUIT (BRITISH), TOLL CIRCUIT (AMERICAN). A circuit connecting two exchanges in different localities. *Note:* in Great Britain, a trunk circuit is approximately 15 miles long or more. A circuit connecting two exchanges less than 15 miles apart is called a *junction circuit.*

TRUNK EXCHANGE (BRITISH), TOLL OFFICE (AMERICAN). An exchange with the function of controlling the switching of trunk (British), or toll (American) traffic.

TRUNK GROUP. Those trunks between two points both of which are switching centers and/or individual message distribution points, and which employ the same multiplex terminal equipment.

TRUNK JUNCTION (BRITISH), TOLL SWITCHING TRUNK (AMERICAN). A line connecting a trunk exchange to a local exchange and permitting a trunk operator to call a subscriber to establish a trunk call.

TWX. (*See* **Teletypewriter exchange service**.)

UNATTENDED OPERATIONS. The automatic features of a station's operation permitting the transmission and reception of messages on an unattended basis.

VERTICAL PARITY (REDUNDANCY) CHECK. (*See* **Parity check, vertical**.)

VIRTUAL. A virtual device, facility, or function is one that appears to exist but in fact does not.

VIRTUAL CHANNEL. A channel that appears to be a simple, direct connection but in fact is implemented in a more complex manner.

VOGAD (VOICE-OPERATED GAIN-ADJUSTING DEVICE). A device somewhat similar to a compandor and used on some radio systems; a voice-operated device that removes fluctuations from input speech and sends it out at a constant level. No restoring device is needed at the receiving end.

VOICE-FREQUENCY, TELEPHONE-FREQUENCY. Any frequency within that part of the audio-frequency range essential for the transmission of speech of commercial quality, i.e., 300-3100 hertz.

VOICE-FREQUENCY CARRIER TELEGRAPHY. That form of carrier telegraphy in which the carrier currents have frequencies such that the modulated currents can be transmitted over a voice-frequency telephone channel.

VOICE-FREQUENCY MULTICHANNEL TELEGRAPHY. Telegraphy using two or more carrier currents the frequencies of which are within the voice-frequency range. Voice frequency telegraph systems permit the transmission of up to 24 channels over a single circuit by the use of frequency-division multiplexing.

VOICE-GRADE CHANNEL. (*See* **Channel, voice-grade**.)

VOICE-OPERATED DEVICE. A device used on a telephone circuit to permit the presence of telephone currents to effect a desired control. Such a device is used in most echo suppressors.

VRC. Vertical redundancy check. (*See also* **Parity check**.)

WATS (WIDE AREA TELEPHONE SERVICE). A service provided by telephone companies in the United States that permits a customer by use of an access line to make calls to telephones in a specific zone on a dial basis for a flat monthly charge. Monthly charges are based on the size of the area in which calls are placed, not on the number or length of calls.

WIDEBAND. Communication channel having a bandwidth greater than a voice-grade channel, and therefore capable of higher-speed data transmission. Sometimes called **Broadband**.

X.25. A recommendation of the CCITT specifying the protocols and message formats that define the interface between a terminal operating in the packet mode and a packet switching network. (*See also* **Packet** and **Packet switching**.)

XMODEM PROTOCOL. A data link protocol employed with asynchronous transmission for the purposes of transferring data files from one computer to another.

ZERO-BIT INSERTION. The technique employed with bit-oriented protocols to ensure that 6 consecutive one bits never appear between the two flags that define the beginning and the ending of a transmission frame. When 5 consecutive one bits occurs in any part of the frame other than the beginning and ending flag, the sending station inserts an extra zero bit. When the receiving station detects 5 one bits followed by a zero bit, it removes the extra zero bit, thus restoring the bit stream to its original value.

INDEX

THE JAMES MARTIN BOOKS

Quantity	Title	Title Code	Price	Total $
_____	Action Diagrams: Clearly Structured Program Design	00330–1	$38.50	_____
_____	Application Development Without Programmers	03894–3	$54.95	_____
	A Breakthrough In Making Computers Friendly:			
_____	The Macintosh Computer (paper)	08157–0	$25.00	_____
_____	(case)	08158–8	$31.95	_____
_____	Communications Satellite Systems	15316–3	$59.95	_____
_____	Computer Data-Base Organization, 2nd Edition	16542–3	$54.95	_____
_____	The Computerized Society	16597–7	$26.95	_____
_____	Computer Networks and Distributed Processing:	16525–8	$54.95	_____
	Software, Techniques and Architecture			
_____	Data Communication Technology	19664–2	$36.75	_____
_____	Design and Strategy of Distributed Data Processing	20165–7	$57.95	_____
_____	Design of Man-Computer Dialogues	20125–1	$54.95	_____
_____	Design of Real-Time Computer Systems	20140–0	$54.95	_____
_____	Diagramming Techniques for Analysts and Programmers	20879–3	$49.95	_____
_____	An End User's Guide to Data Base	27712–9	$42.95	_____
_____	Fourth-Generation Languages, Vol. I: Principles	32967–2	$42.95	_____
_____	Fourth-Generation Languages, Vol. II: Representative 4GLs	32974–8	$42.95	_____
_____	Fourth-Generation Languages, Vol. III: 4GLs from IBM	32976–3	$42.95	_____
_____	Future Developments in Telecommunications, 2nd Edition	34585–0	$56.95	_____
_____	An Information Systems Manifesto	46476–8	$49.95	_____
_____	Introduction to Teleprocessing	49981–4	$44.95	_____
_____	Managing the Data-Base Environment	55058–2	$57.95	_____
_____	Principles of Data-Base Management	70891–7	$44.95	_____
_____	Principles of Data Communication	70989–9	$44.00	_____
_____	Programming Real-Time Computer Systems	73050–7	$46.95	_____
_____	Recommended Diagramming Standards for Analysts and Programmers	76737–6	$45.00	_____
_____	Security, Accuracy, and Privacy in Computer Systems	79899–1	$57.95	_____
_____	SNA: IBM's Networking Solution	81514–2	$44.95	_____
_____	Software Maintenance: The Problem and Its Solutions	82236–1	$49.95	_____
_____	Strategic Data Planning Methodologies	85111–3	$43.95	_____
_____	Structured Techniques: The Basis for CASE, Revised Edition	85493–5	$52.00	_____
_____	Systems Analysis for Data Transmission	88130–0	$60.00	_____
_____	System Design from Provably Correct Constructs	88148–2	$49.95	_____
_____	Technology's Crucible (paper)	90202–3	$15.95	_____
_____	Telecommunications and the Computer, 2nd Edition	90249–4	$54.95	_____

(over)

——— Telematic Society: A Challenge for Tomorrow	90246–0	$31.95 ———
——— Teleprocessing Network Organization	90245–2	$34.95 ———
——— Viewdata and the Information Society	94190–6	$41.95 ———
——— VSAM: Access Method Services and Programming Techniques	94417–3	$44.95 ———

Total: ———
-discount (if appropriate) ———
New Total: ———

AND TAKE ADVANTAGE OF THESE SPECIAL OFFERS!

When ordering 3 or 4 copies (of the same or different titles) take 10% off the total list price.

When ordering 5 to 20 (of the same or different titles) take 15% off the total list price.

To receive a greater discount when ordering more than 20 copies, call or write:

Special Sales Department
College Marketing
Prentice Hall
Englewood Cliffs, NJ 07632
(201)592–2046

SAVE!

If payment accompanies order, plus your state's sales tax where applicable, Prentice Hall pays postage and handling charges. Same return privilege refund guarantee. Please do not mail cash.

☐ **PAYMENT ENCLOSED**—shipping and handling to be paid by publisher (please include your state's tax where applicable).

☐ **SEND BOOKS ON 15-DAY TRIAL BASIS** and bill me (with small charge for shipping and handling).

Name ————————————————————————————

Address ——————————————————————————

City ———————————————— State ———————— Zip ————

I prefer to charge my ☐ Visa ☐ MasterCard

Card Number ———————————— Expiration Date ————————

Signature ——————————————

All prices listed are subject to change without notice.
This offer not valid outside U.S.

Mail your order to: Prentice Hall Book Distribution Center
Route 59 at Brook Hill Drive
West Nyack, NY 10994

Dept. 1: D-JMAR-NK(4)

Announcing . . .

TECHNOLOGY'S
CRUCIBLE

by James Martin

Order Your Copy Using This Form and Receive a *SPECIAL 50% DISCOUNT!*

- How will today's high technology and human nature impact tomorrow's quality of life?
- Through a television series set in the year 2019, a narrator asks the question, "Would the course of history have been different if the public in the 1980s had understood the journey on which they had embarked?"
- In *Technology's Crucible,* James Martin, a renowned computer-industry consultant, world-wide lecturer, and best-selling author of over 30 computer text and reference books, describes the forces that are shaping the environment of tomorrow. This book does not forecast the future; it provides a vehicle for helping people think constructively about the future.

QUANTITY	TITLE/AUTHOR	TITLE CODE	PRICE	TOTAL
_____	*Technology's Crucible* (Martin)	90202-3	$15.95	$_____
			−50%	$_____
			New Total	$_____

SAVE! If payment accompanies order, plus your state's sales tax where applicable, Prentice Hall pays postage and handling charges. Same return privilege refund guaranteed. Please do not mail cash.

☐ PAYMENT ENCLOSED—shipping and handling to be paid by publisher (please include your state's tax where applicable).

☐ SEND BOOKS ON 15-DAY TRIAL BASIS and bill me (with a small charge for shipping and handling).

Name_____

Address_____

City_____ State_____ Zip_____
I prefer to charge my   ☐ Visa   ☐ MasterCard

Card Number_____ Expiration Date_____

Signature_____

All prices listed are subject to change without notice.
Prices and offer not valid outside the U.S.
For quantity orders and special discounts call either (201)592-2046 or (201) 592-2498

Mail your order to: Prentice Hall Book Distribution Center
Route 59 at Brook Hill Drive
West Nyack, NY 10994

Dept. 1: D-CAJB-YM(4)

AN INFORMAT

Suitable for End Users

Books On Society	Books On Information Systems Management And Strategy	Books On Programming	Books On Analysis And Design
THE COMPUTERIZED SOCIETY	INFORMATION ENGINEERING (Volume I: Introduction and Strategy)	APPLICATION DEVELOPMENT WITHOUT PROGRAMMERS	DIAGRAMMING TECHNIQUES ANALYSTS AND PROGRAMME
TELEMATIC SOCIETY: A CHALLENGE FOR TOMORROW		ACTION DIAGRAMS: CLEARLY STRUCTURED PROGRAM DESIGN	
TECHNOLOGY'S CRUCIBLE			

More Detailed Books

Books On Society	Books On Information Systems Management And Strategy	Books On Programming	Books On Analysis And Design
SECURITY, ACCURACY, AND PRIVACY IN COMPUTER SYSTEMS	INFORMATION ENGINEERING (Volume II: Analysis, Design, and Construction)	PROGRAMMING REAL-TIME COMPUTER SYSTEMS	RECOMMENDED DIAGRAMM STANDARDS FOR ANALYSTS AND PROGRAMM
	STRATEGIC DATA-PLANNING METHODOLOGIES (second edition)	FOURTH-GENERATION LANGUAGES (Volume I: Principles)	STRUCTURED TECHNIQUE A BASIS FOR CASE
	SOFTWARE MAINTENANCE: THE PROBLEM AND ITS SOLUTIONS	FOURTH-GENERATION LANGUAGES (Volume II: Representative 4GLs)	ACTION DIAGRAMS: CLEARLY STRUCTURED PROGRAM DESIGN
	DESIGN AND STRATEGY FOR DISTRIBUTED DATA PROCESSING	FOURTH-GENERATION LANGUAGES (Volume III: 4GLs from IBM)	DATABASE ANALYSIS AND DESIGN
	CORPORATE COMMUNICATIONS NETWORKS		DATA COMMUNICATION DESIGN TECHNIQUES
			SOFTWARE MAINTENANCE: PROBLEM AND ITS SOLUTIO
			SYSTEM DESIGN FROM PROVABLY CORRECT CONSTRUCTS
			EXPERT SYSTEMS: DESIG AND CONSTRUCTION

Books On Society

Books On Information Systems Management And Strategy

Books On Programming

Books On Analysis And Design